CW00651755

THE TAME AND THE WILD

The Tame and the Wild

PEOPLE AND ANIMALS AFTER 1492

MARCY NORTON

Harvard University Press

CAMBRIDGE, MASSACHUSETTS · LONDON, ENGLAND 2024

Printed in the United States of America
First printing
Library of Congress Cataloging-in-Publication Data
Names: Norton, Marcy, author.
Title: The tame and the wild : people and animals after 1492 / Marcy
    Norton.
Description: Cambridge, Massachusetts ; London, England : Harvard
    University Press, 2024. | Includes bibliographical references and index.
Identifiers: LCCN 2023008306 | ISBN 9780674737525 (cloth)
Subjects: LCSH: Human-animal relationships—America—History. |
    Human-animal relationships—Europe—History. | Animals and
    civilization—America—History. | Animals and
    civilization—Europe—History. | Indians—First contact with other
    peoples. | Europeans—First contact with other peoples. | Human
    ecology—Europe—History. | Human ecology—America—History. |
    Indians—Colonization. | America—Colonization.
Classification: LCC QL85 .N68 2023 | DDC 591.5094—dc23/eng/20230412
LC record available at https://lccn.loc.gov/2023008306

To those who practice caring for all beings

Contents

THE TAME AND THE WILD

Introduction

*a*n ancient account of creation tells of a god who created the elements of the cosmos—night and day, sky and earth, plants and creatures—over a series of days. Some creatures were to live in the skies, others in the seas, and others on the surface of the earth. Finally, this god made a special kind of being, declaring, "Let us make man in our image, after our likeness: and let them have dominion over the fish of the sea, and over the fowl of the air, and over the cattle, and over all the earth, and over every creeping thing that creepeth upon the earth."[1] This powerful story continued to hold sway in Europe centuries after it was first written (fig. I.1).

Across the Atlantic Ocean, people also told stories about the origins of the earth and its inhabitants. In a Nahua account, creation began when two deities transformed themselves into gigantic snakes and ripped an enormous amphibian in half. The sundered reptilian body became the earth itself, a fertile and blood-thirsty organism who catalyzed the detritus of death into the matter of life. Sometimes, in pictorial sources, she appears only as a gaping, feeding maw (fig. I.2).

A European, attempting to understand these beliefs, explained that "the earth was considered to be a goddess, and they painted it like a fearsome frog with mouths in all of the joints full of blood, saying that it ate and drank and swallowed everything."[2] On the Caribbean island of "Aitii," the *jobo* trees (*Spondias lutea*) that bore savory, bright yellow fruit were descendants of cave-dwelling ancestors who had gazed too long at the sun.[3] Birds known for their plaintive morning song descended from ancestors who had stayed out fishing until dawn. Frogs whose cries sounded like those of babies had once been human infants, hungry to nurse, who were abandoned by their mothers near a brook. Plants, animals, and even mineral formations descended from people.

These divergent creation stories reflect radically different ideas about humans' relationships to other kinds of animals. In Genesis, the force behind

1

Figure I.1   Jan Brueghel the Younger, *Adam's Creation in Paradise,* oil on copper, 69.9 × 87.5 cm, seventeenth century. Hampel Fine Art Auctions.

creation was a singular, anthropomorphic Creator, whereas in the Indigenous stories, the forces tended to be multiple and zoomorphic. Genesis makes a clear-cut divide between people and other kinds of beings—with each class of being created separately—but Indigenous accounts depict creation as, fundamentally, a process of transformation, one that emphasized the permeability and interconnectedness of all beings. Genesis presents the singularity of people—unique because they alone were made in the image of this God—whereas Indigenous creation stories show all kinds of beings possessing subjectivity or personhood. Genesis insists on humans' superiority, given their proximity to God and preordained "dominion," while Indigenous creation stories that tell of animals' and plants' human ancestry highlight kinship across species. In this system, animals and plants were relations, not resources.

Undergirding these creation stories are "modes of interactions"—my phrase for the structures that organize how people relate to and think about

Figure I.2   A skeletal coyote (death) decapitates and feeds a quail to the sun and earth, Codex Borgia, plate 71, detail, pre-1500. Borg.mess.1.f.pl 71r, photo © Biblioteca Apostolica Vaticana. Reproduced by permission of Biblioteca Apostolica Vaticana, all rights reserved.

other animals. Developed over millennia, modes of interaction include the entrenched customs, patterns of behavior, institutions, and, above all, quotidian technologies that people used to observe, listen to, capture, nurture, kill, eat, tan, breed, herd, train, communicate with, feed, or heal other beings.[4] This book is about such modes of interaction, how they help explain the ontological divide between European and Indigenous cultures, and how these differing modes' post-1492 entanglement led to transformations—both destructive and generative—on both sides of the Atlantic. Although these creation stories have largely been supplanted by the Big Bang and evolutionary theory, the modes of interaction that underlay these ancient accounts are still part of the fabric of modern life. Many of the horrors of the present day—colonial dispossession, environmental catastrophe, and the abject conditions endured by animals classified as livestock—are rooted in them. Likewise, many pleasures of the present day—kinship across the species divide, wonder at the faculties of nonhuman animals, and consumption of animal flesh—originate with them.

~

HUNTING AND HUSBANDRY were the most significant modes of interaction organizing human-animal relationships in Europe and the Mediterranean in the early modern age. Ecologically informed and socially created over the *longue durée,* they were differentially linked to other structures of power. Elite hunting, *caza* or *montería* in Spanish, was integrally associated with dynastic warfare and crucial to the tactics and ideology of the aristocratic ruling class and upwardly mobile, wealthy commoners. Animal husbandry, or *ganadería* in Spanish, organized the labor and activities of the plebeian majority and provided income and products for the Church, nobility, and wealthy commoners. It was a building block of subsistence and market economies and a defining structure of European and Mediterranean societies for millennia. However, hunting and husbandry created different kinds of relationships between humans and other animals. The hunt fostered the recognition of (certain) animals as subjects, whereas livestock husbandry produced human subjects and (mostly) animal objects. Hunting created a privileged class of vassal animals; horses, hawks, and hounds were engaged as essential collaborators and noble beings, invested with individuality, material resources, and symbolic value that elevated them among many human contemporaries. Prey, too, were understood as intelligent, cunning, and often dangerous adversaries. In contrast, husbandry made livestock into objects whose *beingness* was largely negated, even while alive. In addition to many other uses, livestock became food (their muscles and fat became flavor and protein), clothing (sheep's coats became wool, cow skins became leather), lighting (the fat of cows became tallow), and medicine (cow, pig, and chicken fat became ingredients in recipe books). These animals, along with plants and minerals, belonged to the domain of "nature," and were thus viewed above all as resources necessary to keep the human body alive and comfortable. They were most often constituted as things—bodies denied living spirit—and objects of passive management rather than active engagement.

Across the Atlantic, in Greater Amazonia (a term I will use to refer to Indigenous regions in both the Caribbean and lowland South America) and Mesoamerica, the primordial modes of interaction were "predation" and "familiarization." In part, I use these outsider ("etic") concepts to reflect my engagement with an extensive anthropological literature concerning Amazonian cultures.[5] However, I also employ these terms because they align with ideas and concepts articulated in early modern sources that reveal Indigenous perspectives. These sources emphasize all beings' dependence on nourishment and uphold distinctions between the categories wild and tame rather than those of "human" and "animal." Predation, above all, produced food. Human and nonhuman hunters alike obtained prey for nourishment. Humans cooked meat to supplement diets centered on cultivated manioc, maize, or both. Humans also valued the nonputrefying parts of animals, above all, feathers, pelts, and bones, which were also assimilated into the body. They were affixed directly to the skin or refashioned into potent ritual objects, such as headdresses, necklaces, or flutes. These objects allowed the wearer to appropriate some of the beauty and power of the prey, perhaps even take on what Eduardo Viveiros de Castro famously called the "enemy's"—or rather the prey's—"point of view."[6] Indigenous predation emphasized how hunting transformed both predator and prey by way of mimesis during both the hunt and the consumption following it. It was integrally related to human warfare, as is expressed in the vocabulary of Indigenous languages in both regions that employed the same word for hunting and for warfare.[7] While Europeans insisted that *hunting was like warfare*, people in Greater Amazonia and Mesoamerica, by and large, spoke of *warfare as hunting*. One of the reasons I choose to use the term *predation* to refer to Indigenous practices related to the pursuit and acquisition of animals for various kinds of consumption is to distinguish it from European hunting. Another way that hunting and predation differ is that while dogs assisted in hunts in other parts of the Americas (including highland regions in South America), they did not play this role in the regions explored in this book, at least in the time period prior to 1492.[8] Without the mediation of vassal animals, Indigenous hunters had a more direct relationship with prey.

While predation in Greater Amazonia and Mesoamerica shared many attributes, it also differed in some fundamental respects. These differences relate to social organization: Like those in Europe, Mesoamerican communities were intensively stratified in comparison to the relatively egalitarian social structure that generally characterized Greater Amazonia. Perhaps even more than the European nobility who prized their status as hunters, Mesoamerican elites invested in their predatorial identities. In addition to pursuing hunting as a pastime, these elites also monopolized meat and coveted

Figure I.3   An Indigenous hunter returning with a dead bird and a live bird, Histoire Naturelle des Indes, illustrated manuscript, ca. 1586, Morgan Library, bequest of Clara S. Peck, 1983, MA 3900, fols. 113v–114r. Morgan Library and Museum, New York.

skins and feathers, restricting commoners' access to these items. In contrast, in Greater Amazonia, as a rule, any man could hunt or fish, and doing so was an important aspect of masculinity (fig. I.3).

Whereas hunting and husbandry existed in uneasy tension in Europe, predation and familiarization were complementary modes of interaction in Greater Amazonia and Mesoamerica. If predation centered on making others into food, familiarization centered on providing food to others. In Greater Amazonia, some wild animals were captured live (or sometimes they came of their own accord), and tamed: they were made into kin. Parrots, monkeys, deer, tapirs, sloths, capybara, manatees, and even humans, were among the many species that became familiarized. In contrast to domesticated creatures, these animals were born in the wild, and their reproduction was not controlled. Familiarization was customarily the work of women in charge of creating new members of the community. It encompassed the care given to a newborn baby, a stranger from another land, or an animal captured in the wild. The essence of making kin is feeding, as pithily articulated by the seventeenth-century missionary who defined the Kalinago word and concept *iegue* as "an animal whom one feeds."[9] Once a fellow being was fed and accepted food, they were *iegue*, and once *iegue*, they were to be cherished, not consumed as food. From this perspective, the essence of European livestock husbandry—feeding animals to make them into food—makes no sense at all. Both the interdependence of and differentiation between familiarization and predation in Greater Amazonia are evocatively depicted in a late sixteenth-century painting made by a presumed outsider (the illustrator is unknown): a hunter returns with two birds, one to be eaten and one to be fed (fig. I.3).

Like predation, Mesoamerican familiarization is both similar to and different from its South American counterpart. A concept similar to *iegue* appears in Mesoamerican vocabularies. In Nahuatl the term is *tlatlacacihuitilli*. The familiarization practices that accompanied this concept—above all those related to the sacred calendar and the participation of nonhuman animals in religious ceremonies known in Spanish as *veintena*—have been even less visible than those related to *iegue* in Greater Amazonia. This is the case even though familiarization of this sort underpinned the famed menageries of Tenochtitlan and other city-states in Mesoamerica. Part of the reason for such practices' invisibility to outsiders may be related to a fixation on practices that both European colonizers and today's scholars misleadingly labeled as "sacrifice." While it was anathema to kill a being who was fed in

Greater Amazonia, in Mesoamerica some captive, formerly wild animals were killed, among them humans.[10] The practice of killing animals who have been fed is the most significant distinction between familiarization as practiced in the two regions.

That "sacrifice" was a form of familiarization from an insider ("emic") perspective can be seen by looking at imagery in the Codex Borgia, an *amoxtli* (pictorial "book") crafted in the Central Highlands prior to the invasions. A prominent panel depicts one of the most common and important rituals: the killing and feeding of a decapitated quail to deities (fig. I.2). The figure occupying the position of the killer and feeder is depicted as a super predator; part coyote (carnivore) and part skeleton (death). This scene shows the moment immediately after the coyote-skeleton twisted off the quail's head, when he holds the bird's body in one hand, and the head in another. It also shows what happens next: at the same instant, the bird's blood spurts out of the body and up into the mouth of the solar deity, rendered as a personified reddish orb, and the head drops into the open maw of a reptilian monster, identified with the earth. The image demonstrates the intertwining of killing and feeding, and shows that the powerful beings most responsible for creating food—sun and soil—must themselves be fed. As this illustration suggests, the notion of reciprocity was fundamental to Mesoamerican predation and familiarization.

As suggested by European and Indigenous origin stories alike, modes of interaction are powerful structures for creating subjectivities. They condition how people experience *being* in their worlds (ontology) and what they *know* (epistemology). The ways that people relate to other animals—whether following a hunting dog, mimicking a monkey's call, caressing a pig, defanging a rattlesnake, dancing in a quetzal feather headdress, buying cow flesh at a butcher, collecting fruit for a macaw, hand-feeding a deer, apologizing to a horse—are generative of how people understand themselves and others. How people categorize, think about, and learn from other animals stems from the contexts in which they interact with them. An investigation of modes of interaction reveals the conditions that allow for the recognition or the denial of another's subjectivity. The interactions generated by animal husbandry were an important "cause" of Europeans' sense of separateness from other kinds of animals and their sense of a self divided between mind and body. In contrast, predation and familiarization in Indigenous America revealed commonalities across the species divide and recognition of the materiality, permeability, and contingency of the self.

~

THE TAME AND *the Wild* challenges the enduring and insidious myth that livestock husbandry is a necessary and inevitable part of human progress.[11] This idea has ancient roots—the biblical story of Jacob and Esau can be read as the triumph of the farmer over the hunter—but the notion of animal domestication as a boundary between "civilized" peoples and primitive "barbarians" took hold as Europeans began to invade the Americas and justify their brutal military campaigns and dispossession of Indigenous land, labor, and life. In 1513, one of the jurists King Ferdinand tasked with finding a legal rationale for Spanish conquest focused on how *indios* in the Antilles interacted with animals: they eat "fish but not meat, other than little animals similar to hares," and "they love like children their domestic birds and animals and do not eat them because that would be like eating their progeny." Such behavior was among the evidence he marshaled to show that *indios* lacked "reason" and "in this they are no different from the animal."[12] Juan Ginés de Sepúlveda, one of the most famous proponents of the idea that Indigenous people were "natural slaves," argued in 1544 that just as the body is subject to the soul, "the appetite to reason, and brute animals to man," so should "barbarians, uncultivated and inhuman," be subjected to the *imperio* of those who are "more prudent, powerful, and perfect." While he acknowledged that the justifiable war waged against "barbarians" would cause great "harms and losses," it was outweighed by "greater goods" they would receive in the form of salvation, iron tools, and domesticated animals—the "horses, mules, asses, oxen, sheep, goats, pigs."[13] This idea was further entrenched in the progressivist narratives of seminal Enlightenment thinkers and nineteenth-century scholars who claimed that domestication "perhaps more than to any other cause we must attribute the civilizable and the civilized state of mind."[14]

This assumption that animal husbandry is a necessary milestone and marker of advanced civilization continues to shape both modern scholarship and popular perceptions in the present. Scholars who would reject any overt notion of intrinsic European cultural superiority still take for granted the idea that the Eurasian style of animal domestication is a natural and inevitable component of progress. Alfred Crosby wrote in his groundbreaking *Columbian Exchange* that "when Columbus arrived, even the most advanced Indians were barely out of the Stone Age. . . . They had few domesticated animals, and those were not very impressive."[15] Jared Diamond built on this notion when he wrote, "Did all those peoples of Africa, the Americas, and

Australia, despite their enormous diversity, nonetheless share some *cultural obstacles* to domestication not shared with Eurasian peoples?"[16] He seemingly settles on a less Eurocentric conclusion by rejecting the notion of a cultural "obstacle" to domestication and instead argues that the native species of Africa, Australia, and the Americas were not suitable "candidates" for domestication.

The assumption that only obstacles would explain non-Eurasians' failure to fully embrace domesticated animals reinforces the ancient belief that human progress depends on animal domestication. The idea that domestication is a mark of advanced culture is even evident in scholarship about Indigenous America. The cultures of Mexico and Peru, because of their cities, states, writing systems, priesthoods—and their domestication of turkeys and llamas—have been judged more advanced than the "primitive" lowland cultures of Amazonia that lacked domesticated animals. Even more subtly, the naturalization of livestock has shaped historical scholarship by normalizing the objectification of animals and neglecting practices that emphasize non-human subjectivity. This perspective can be seen in the long tradition of scholarship that assumes an instrumental approach toward animals is more natural than one characterized by care and appreciation.

~

HOW IS HISTORICAL perception, understanding, or scholarship transformed if livestock husbandry is no longer assumed to be more advanced, natural, or inevitable than other modes of interaction? What happens when livestock husbandry is denaturalized and "provincialized"?[17] In other words, what happens when livestock husbandry is no longer viewed as the most natural and self-evident way for people to interact with other animals and is instead considered as a particular arrangement that developed in particular times and places?

The Tame and the Wild reassesses the transformations wrought by colonization on both sides of the Atlantic and suggests a reevaluation of many of our dominant narratives about the history of the environment, religion, science, and subjectivity. *The Tame and the Wild* demonstrates how European and Indigenous ontologies and epistemologies—rather than occurring in separate historical silos—have been entangled since 1492.[18] It is a corrective to the histories of early modern Europe that still pay inadequate attention to the transformative effects of Europeans' entanglement with Indigenous cultures. Likewise, anthropological studies of contemporary Indigenous communities often ignore the degree to which current-day cultures, *both* European and Indigenous, have been transformed by more than five hundred years of entanglement.[19] American modes of interaction not only conditioned how Indigenous people—as well as free and enslaved people of African descent—responded to colonialism. They also affected colonizers and contributed to changes within European societies.[20]

Rather than approaching these questions within a framework of "Columbian Exchange," *The Tame and the Wild* connects the histories of nonhuman animals to histories of dispossession and extractivism.[21] Although conquistadores believed that their nonhuman vassals were their most powerful weapons in wars against Native communities, the most important instrument in the process of dispossession was livestock husbandry. Colonizers not only imported but transformed animal husbandry. Beginning in the fifteenth-century Caribbean, European colonizers reinvented animal husbandry as an extractivist industry that became the basis of settler colonial fortunes.[22] Livestock husbandry became the linchpin connecting the dispossession of Indigenous labor, land, and life and contributing to the compounding conditions that led to the stratospheric death toll among Native peoples. As such, this book contributes to the deep history of modern meat. Global consumption of meat is the second largest source of climate change; it poisons soil and waterways, destroys wildlife habitats, and confines and kills billions of chickens, pigs, and cows. Some historians see the roots of modern meat in the deep hominid history of hunting, animal domestication, and development of patriarchy, whereas others understand it primarily as a product of early or late capitalism.[23] *The Tame and the Wild* focuses on developments occurring in between, thereby illuminating the deep origins of livestock husbandry's ethos that constructs and separates human subjects from animal objects. In alignment with those who see the emergence of the "Anthropocene" as an effect of European colonization, this study also reveals the degree to which the contemporary ecological catastrophe originated with the earliest colonization of the Americas.[24]

For all of its destructive power, however, extractivist livestock husbandry did not extinguish Indigenous modes of interaction. Native peoples responded to the arrival of European modes of interaction and livestock animals in ways consistent with extant modes of predation and familiarization. In some cases, they adopted European warfare and hunting practices organized around vassal animals, riding horses in battle and using dogs to hunt.

They did so not only for pragmatic ends but also because these practices aligned with their existing modes of interaction that recognized the subjectivity of nonhuman animals. Nevertheless, when free to choose, Indigenous people in Greater Amazonia generally rejected animal husbandry, abhorring the practice of killing animals whom they fed. However, the rejection of animal husbandry did not preclude the embrace of European domesticated animals. Indigenous peoples accustomed to familiarization found creative and often ingenious ways to incorporate European-originating animals into their modes of interaction.

These material and ecological histories are inseparable from the entangled histories of epistemology, religion, and science that also unfold in these pages. Given the different practices and ideas about human and nonhuman subjectivity generated by different modes of interaction, it is unsurprising that these entanglements had epistemological and even ontological consequences. In revisiting demonological discourses, I suggest that European anxieties about witches and Hell reflect suppressed and repressed anxieties about the subjectivity of nonhuman animals. In turn, the ethos produced by livestock husbandry hindered missionaries' ability to comprehend the species boundary-crossing beliefs and practices produced by Indigenous modes of interaction. As a result, they projected demonological discourses onto Indigenous practices and beliefs, bringing, one could say, enchantment to the Americas.

No less consequential than the colonizers' epistemological exports were their epistemological imports. Native hunters and animal tamers—those engaged most directly in predation and familiarization—learned about the behaviors, habits, and appearances of animals, as well as their relationships to broader ecological networks. Moreover, the *amoxtli* (fig. I.2) reveal that this knowledge, at least in Mesoamerica, related to abstract ideas sharing elements with modern ecological concepts. Some of this Indigenous knowledge was used by colonizers and filled the pages of influential works on natural history, such as those by the conquistador Gonzalo Fernández de Oviedo. However, the consequences for the history of science go beyond European incorporation into natural histories of Indigenous knowledge generated by hunters and tamers. Colonizers' appropriation of Indigenous knowledge produced by predation and familiarization also bore epistemological effects. Crucially important was the work of the Nahua scholars who coauthored a natural history—what became Book 11 of the Florentine Codex—that integrated European genres and Mesoamerican ecological concepts.[25] In turn, the Spanish naturalist Francisco Hernández appropriated, disavowed, and transformed this knowledge into a form that inspired new forms of zoological inquiry in seventeenth- and eighteenth-century Europe—epistemological changes that form part of the so-called Scientific Revolution.[26]

Finally, these entanglements reveal the myriad ways that people on both sides of the Atlantic cherished affective relationships with nonhuman animals long before the emergence of the modern pet. They show the joy and pleasure that such relationships afforded and the care work that they required. Aristocratic hunters cherished their raptors, horses, and dogs, while shepherds developed intense attachments to their dogs and to a select few sheep or goats classified as *mansos* (tame ones) and were horrified at the thought of killing them. Nevertheless, the vast majority of domesticated animals in Europe—those classified as livestock—were not eligible for such relationships. The pleasure that Europeans found in their bonds with nonhuman animals was generally a by-product of collaborative relationships, such as those required by hunting or herding, while in many parts of Indigenous America, the joy of nonhuman companionship could be an end in itself. This is suggested by the name that a sixteenth-century Tupinamba woman gave to her macaw (*Cherimbaue*, or "thing that I love"), a tamed manatee who provided "joy to the whole Island" of Hispaniola, and three pigs whose Indigenous companion called them "my friends and good company." Colonizers themselves became enmeshed in relationships mediated by familiarization. This process began when Columbus accepted a gift of tame parrots upon making landfall in the Bahamas. It continued when tamed animals themselves, nurtured by Indigenous women, arrived in Europe.

~

THE TAME AND *the Wild* suggests a new approach to the history of subjectivity and human-animal relationships. In recent years, scholars from a variety of disciplines have challenged human exceptionalism and anthropocentrism. Ethologists and animal behaviorists observe that capacities and aptitudes such as cognition, language, aesthetics, and empathy—among other traits once thought uniquely human—are, in fact, shared with other species.[27] Philosophers contest the "Kantian subject" organized around reason and instead show, as Cary Wolfe writes, "how our shared embodiment, mortality, and finitude makes us . . . 'fellow creatures' in ways that subsume the more traditional markers of ethical consideration, such as the capacity for reason, the ability to enter into contractual agreement or reciprocal behaviors, and so on."[28] Theorists such as Donna Haraway, Bruno Latour, and Jane Bennett emphasize the co-constitution of beings and objects and seek to dismantle the nature-culture divide.[29] Historians have also sought to approach animals as historical actors, moving beyond treating animals as "objects of human analysis" and instead writing histories where they figure, writes Erica Fudge, "as beings in the world who may themselves create change."[30] Scholars of Latin America, including Martha Few, Zeb Tortorici, and Abel Alves, among others, have been at the forefront of developing methods for these kinds of histories.[31]

In this book I do not rely on Western science or philosophy in order to conceptualize nonhuman agency. Nonhuman subjectivity and agency were not "discovered" by Europeans or their descendants. The recognition that nonhuman animals share ancestry and faculties with people long predates Darwin and Derrida.[32] Indigenous people—today and centuries ago—have recognized and celebrated both the subjectivity of nonhuman beings and kinship across the species divide.[33] Thus, I come to the question of both human and nonhuman subjectivity from a different angle. I start with this inquiry: How do interactions create subjectivities? This approach is partly inspired by scholars, like Michel Foucault, who reject the idea of a universal, trans-historical "self," arguing instead that the "self has to be considered as the correlate of technologies built and developed throughout our history."[34] It is also inspired by philosopher Cora Diamond's observation that "the difference between human beings and animals is not to be discovered by studies of Washoe [the much-studied chimp taught American Sign Language] or the activities of dolphins." Instead, she points out that our understanding about other animals is created by quotidian interactions more than abstract studies: "We learn what a human being is in—among other ways—sitting at a table where WE eat THEM. We are around the table and they are on it."[35] Haraway, too, emphasizes "ongoing becoming with" in humans' relationships with other animals.[36] In other words, our embodied experiences with other beings are generative of how we experience our own and others' subjectivities.[37] Subjectivity is the way self is experienced—its defining traits, its locations in or outside the body, its contours, its malleability, its permeability—and this experience happens in relationship with other things and beings.

~

HISTORIANS, LIKE SCIENTISTS, filmmakers, and other storytellers, need to decide where to begin and end and what to include. Although I have chosen to use a wide lens in terms of both space and time, I do not believe that the *longue durée* is an inherently superior time scale. Rather, as a filmmaker might choose a close-up to convey personality and a wide lens to show landscape, or one scientist might employ satellite imaging and another an electron microscope, I intentionally use scale to reveal certain features of the historical past while acknowledging that this scale will mean that other features remain occluded or even invisible. My choices about scale are informed by my desire to approach Europe and Indigenous America coevally.[38]

However, as scholars who work on the early modern Atlantic world well know, the sources themselves are products of highly asymmetrical power relations. To write a history that puts European and Indigenous communities on equal footing requires a variety of approaches that are tailored to the diversity of sources. For Greater Amazonia and Mesoamerica, many of the richest sources for the early modern era cannot be divorced from the colonial context in which they were created. Nevertheless, because of differences between Indigenous societies before European arrival and the strategies of European colonists in these areas, the abundance and types of sources vary significantly. Brazilian anthropologist Aparecida Vilaça has observed that "although comprising the main topic of interest for native peoples themselves, everyday life in the heart of the family and domestic nuclei appeared to be far too chaotic and commonplace to be a research topic" for the (mostly male) anthropologists who "were fascinated by the study of the exotic rather than the mundane."[39] In this regard, modern anthropology reproduced the biases of conquistadores and missionaries who preceded them. It is not that traces of the care work required by familiarization are absent in the colonial archive; rather, a full portrait of this phenomenon is possible only when these fragments are brought together in a single frame. As a result, I take fragmentary traces from a large swath of communities to observe patterns that characterized the diverse communities in South America. Then, where the evidence is available, I zoom in to capture some of the texture and diversity of individuals and communities.

The people who presented tame parrots to Columbus and his entourage on October 12, 1492 were among the easternmost residents of a cultural area that some scholars designate as Greater Amazonia. It stretched westward to the Amazon basin in what is today Colombia and Peru, northward to Costa Rica, and southward into the tropical savannahs of Paraguay and northern

Argentina. This vast region encompassed a multiplicity of Indigenous ethnicities, tremendous linguistic diversity, and separate political units. Nevertheless, outsiders, including early modern European observers and contemporary scholars alike, have recognized common elements in belief systems, ritual practice, and material culture—the result of migration and trading patterns that developed over millennia.[40] After 1492, the region also included many Black people, some enslaved and some free. They were enmeshed in—and influenced—European and Indigenous modes of interaction. Many of the first herders in the Americas were free or enslaved Blacks, often having first gained experience in Iberia. In other cases, Black people fleeing enslavement and finding their freedom in maroon communities lived, sometimes permanently, in Native communities; there they became embedded in societies marked by predation and familiarization.

The timeline of colonialism across the Caribbean and lowland South America is staggered. Some communities, such as those in the Greater Antilles, suffered near complete "ethnocide" within decades of the arrival of European colonizers.[41] Others have been able to maintain autonomous polities for centuries. These different Indigenous groups, although separated by time, place, and often language, were connected in the early modern period by the fact that they often wielded considerable power in their relationships with Europeans.[42] The relative autonomy of some of these Indigenous communities does not mean they were unscathed by the devastating effects of European colonialism. This reality is illustrated by the answer that a French missionary received when he asked one of his Kalinago hosts on Dominica "why there were so few" Indigenous people still living in the Lesser Antilles. His interlocutor responded "that the Christians were the cause," that twice the Spanish had massacred all the savages on Saint Christopher (St. Kitts) and one time on Guadeloupe, "where no one escaped except a woman and her children who saved themselves in the mountains," and that they had wanted to do the same on his island and had succeeded in "massacring at least half." Then there was the *variola* (smallpox), of which many died, and "finally it's that the whole world enslaves or kill them—Flemish, English, Spanish and the Arawaks who are their enemies."[43] Even when Indigenous communities retained autonomy in their practices and beliefs, they were nonetheless deeply affected by the expansion of settler colonial communities and their attendant violence (massacres, slave raids, rape), proselytization, and disease, as well as ethnogenesis (the creation of new ethnic identities as a result of the mergers of different communities after slave raids, massacres, or disease outbreaks).

Because of the variable timelines of colonialism, the Caribbean and low-land South American sources I use in *The Tame and the Wild* focus on the sixteenth, seventeenth, and eighteenth centuries, but span the more than five hundred years that European and settler colonialism has been a force in the Americas. These sources are far from neutral accounts or transparent windows: These authors' strategic interests informed their portrayals of themselves and Indigenous people. Their own assumptions about culture sometimes made it difficult for them to understand what was going on. However, their objectives also made them careful observers and led them to achieve varying degrees of proficiency in Indigenous languages. The acuity of these authors' observations was also a function of their vulnerability. In many cases, outsiders were allowed to live or visit among Indigenous settlements only because they were seen as actual or potential allies or trading partners. This very vulnerability motivated outsiders to pay careful attention to the customs of their hosts. If they were to achieve their goals or even to survive, they needed to understand, if not conform to, local practices.

In 1517, having ravaged Native communities and established settlements in the Greater Antilles and along the northern coasts of South America, Europeans began their sustained entanglement with another cultural region in the Western Hemisphere. "Mesoamerica" is a name given to the societies that developed in the expanse that stretched from what is today Nicaragua to northern Mexico. In 1519, Europeans arrived at Tenochtitlan, the capital of the Mexica (Aztec) people, and were awestruck by its orderliness, grand temples, opulent palaces, and intricate rituals. By the end of the postclassic period (ca. 1300–1521), the Aztec Empire was politically ascendant. The intense social stratification found in the societies of what is today central and southern Mexico, Guatemala, Honduras, Belize, and parts of Nicaragua was attractive to the Spanish colonizers, as they could use Indigenous elites to assist in colonization. The nature of postclassic and colonial Mesoamerican sources led me to maintain a relatively tight geographic lens, focusing on the region that had been part of or proximate to the Aztec Empire before it fell in 1521. I focus in particular on the Nahua communities of the Central Highlands in the valleys of Mexico and Tlaxcala and those Mixtec and Zapotec polities to the south and east. I chose this focus, in part, because of a rich, nuanced scholarship that demonstrates the ways that the year 1521 did not mark the "conquest" of Indigenous people in Mesoamerica but rather the beginning of new era in which they lived under (an often brutal) colonial regime.[44] Another reason for the tight focus on Central Mexico relates to the survival of some pre-Hispanic *amoxtli*. These sacred artifacts (fig. 1.2) are singular in their ability to illuminate practices and ideas about humans' relationships to other kinds of beings before the transformative effects of colonialism. Unlike sources produced in the colonial era, they are not mediated by European perspectives or technologies.

In comparison to the methodological challenges posed by Indigenous history, reconstructing the history of human-animal relationships in early modern Europe might seem a straightforward task. But this is not the case. There are also difficulties related to the problem of overwhelming familiarity. Approaching the technologies and ideologies of livestock husbandry coevally with those of predation and familiarization requires treating the former as no more natural or inevitable than the modes of interaction that developed in Indigenous America. This task is made difficult by the fact that livestock husbandry—being the dominant mode of interaction organizing land use, commodity chains, and diets in the world today—shapes many prevalent attitudes about animals and ecologies. As a result, the challenge is not to mistake the abundance of sources from the early modern period—including agricultural manuals, lawsuits, and inventories that presume animals are first and foremost resources and property—for proof of its inevitability. Moreover, many of the conventions informing historiographies of nonhuman animals internalize rather than question their premises (e.g., economic and social histories treat livestock as commodities rather than as beings vulnerable to objectification). As a historian of Indigenous America, I sought to piece together a picture from fragments and read against the grain to excavate perspectives hidden or silenced in European sources. As a historian of Europe and settler colonies, I sought ways to examine this system as an outsider, to undertake close readings in order to find cracks in a seemingly smooth surface, and to learn from Indigenous perspectives. Thus I attempted to estrange myself from European and settler-colonial modes of interaction.

~

TODAY, HUMANS' RELATIONSHIPS with other animals are extremely paradoxical. In certain respects, the divide between humans and animals is narrower than ever. For many people, dogs and cats and other animals are beloved, akin to human family members. In other respects, the divide is wider than ever: people eat, wear, and otherwise consume more animals than at any other point in history, and more creatures live in torturous conditions of confinement before their short lives end in slaughter. In addition, many wild animals are on the verge of extinction because human lifestyles degrade habitats. No satisfactory solution to this paradox and the ethical and environmental chaos that it creates is possible without understanding the historical conditions that made it possible. The early modern Atlantic world was the site of a seminal and singular stage of globalization—the crucible that catalyzed the modern paradox of simultaneous closeness and distance between people and other animals.

PART I

Subject and Object

1

Hunting Subjects

he boar, sent by the offended and vengeful goddess Diana, had ravaged the kingdom of Calydon. The king dispatched his son, Meleager, to slay the beast. The prince assembled a group of brave huntsmen with their horses and dogs and went in pursuit. The powerful beast, depicted with an imposing mane and large tusks in Peter Paul Ruben's *The Calydonian Boar Hunt* (fig. 1.1), would not be easily vanquished.

The boar killed Meleager's friend and accomplice Ancaeus and several of the hounds, their bodies lifeless beneath the boar's hooves. Ultimately, the prince prevailed and speared the animal. Next to him is his beloved (and fellow hunter) Atalanta, whom he will soon reward with the boar's head. The painting depicts the prince and the boar as near equals and puts the human, equine, and canine huntsmen on the same level, all of them noble vassals and essential to the success of the hunt. This tale circulated, along with many other classical stories about hunters and their travails and triumphs, in the ancient Mediterranean and sixteenth- and seventeenth-century Europe in text and image.[1] Although mythological, it encapsulated the central ethos that aristocratic hunters believed to be the essence of the hunt. It not only showcased their bravery and greatness but also celebrated nonhuman vassals and prey.

It would be difficult to exaggerate the importance of hunting for the nobility in medieval and early modern Europe. Huge amounts of social, economic, and political capital were invested in its pursuit—specifically, in time devoted, resources expended, artworks created, palaces built, laws promulgated, and grounds patrolled.[2] The series of events that composed the hunt required both adherence to a script and improvisation. The hunt operated inside both a hierarchy organized by social convention and a meritocracy based on strength and intelligence. It was at once ritual, performance, and "deep play," as defined by Clifford Geertz, that brings into being "central preoccupations" by "assembling actors and arranging scenery."[3] The hunt

Figure 1.1   Peter Paul Rubens (Flemish, 1577–1640), *The Calydonian Boar Hunt,* ca. 1611–12, oil on panel, 59.2 × 89.7 cm, Getty Museum, 2006.4. Digital image courtesy of the Getty's Open Content Program.

rewarded individuals for valorous feats and punished them for poor choices and bad luck. It also engendered moments when collective action subsumed individual subjectivities. All of these elements, and others, produced strong somatic states that anchored social and cultural meaning in the body.

In her study of medieval hunting treatises, Susan Crane argues that the noble hunt "affirm[ed] the rightness of a single social and natural order headed by the aristocracy."[4] In other words, it constructed a chivalric ethos that legitimated oligarchy. The hunt also fostered interspecies relationships. Hunting—in which a primary objective was to kill an animal—appears at first glance to exemplify "anthropocentrism," the notion that there are, in the words of Keith Thomas, "rigid barriers between humanity and other forms of life," that "in drawing a firm line between man and beast, the main purpose of early modern theorists was to justify hunting, domestication, meat-eating, vivisection . . . and the wholesale extermination of vermin and predators."[5] However, if one considers the particular techniques and practices produced by the aristocratic hunt, another perspective emerges. Hunting required human participants to recognize canine, equine, and avian vassals and prey (above all, boar and deer) as fellow subjects with desires, emotions, and even reason.[6] This mode of interaction is fundamental if one is to understand why people in early modern Europe understood animals as fellow subjects even as they also often insisted that they lacked reason or souls. As Karen Raber has written, glossing the work of Erica Fudge, "before the Cartesian scheme and the invention of the beast-machine, explanations of the divide between human and animal were beset by troubling inconsistencies."[7] It may appear paradoxical, but a major reason that people recognized the subjectivity of other animals was because they hunted them.

~

JUAN MATEOS COMMEMORATED a number of aristocratic hunts in his 1634 *Origen y dignidad de la caça* (Origin and Dignity of the Hunt). He personally participated in some of them in his capacity as "chief huntsman" for Philip III and Philip IV, and he learned about others from his father, Gonzalo Mateos, who served as a huntsman for the Marquis of Villanueva del Fresno, and, subsequently, for King Philip III. While living in the Marquis's titular town in Badazjoz (Extremadura), Gonzalo heard rumors of an enormous and unusually fierce boar. The boar left distinctive tracks because part of one of his left hooves was missing. He liked to graze in the wheat fields near the town (Villanueva del Fresno), and he had killed dogs belonging to some local rabbit hunters. The Marquis asked his nephew (the future Count of Montijo), who was in charge of the grandee's hounds, to organize a hunt. Waiting for the sweltering heat of summer to dissipate, which would impede the dogs, they set out on a rainy day in October. The hunt ended with disappointment and carnage: the boar not only escaped but also slaughtered more than fifteen of the hounds and injured the rest, and then escaped.

Four years passed before there was news of this boar again.[8] The tracks revealed that the "Boar of the Partial Left Hoof" (as he became known) was now roaming with another male boar—a rare but not unheard-of practice, as male boars usually preferred to live alone. The huntsmen concluded that the Boar of the Partial Left Hoof was dominant and the other one, although larger, was the subordinate "squire" because of behaviors revealed by their tracks. Partial Left Hoof led "in those parts where one walks easily," so that the squire could cover his scent with his own. But where there were difficult traverses, "the squire led," so he could carefully select a path leading his dominant companion to safety. A widespread belief among huntsmen was that a squire boar was willing to sacrifice himself (or was forced to sacrifice himself) for the survival of his liege lord.

Hearing this news, the Marquis was anxious to have a hunt as soon as possible, but he had to wait for a day without winds that were too strong (which would reveal the presence of the hunters) and that was not too wet (which would mask the boars' scent from the hounds). The chosen day was still less than ideal from the point of view of his huntsmen. The reconnaissance of Mendo Alfonso, a man singularly accomplished in the techniques of the *concierto* (the process by which prey were stalked in utter stealth by a huntsman and his hounds), indicated that the boars were sharing their bed with several deer ("don't be shocked by this because I have seen others do this, although it is true they didn't come with a squire"). He worried that the deer would distract the dogs and lead them away from pursuing the boar. Nonetheless, the Marquis was resolved, and thus his three chief huntsmen—Alfonso, Gonzalo Mateos, and another nicknamed "Gago"—made the necessary preparations.

A call from the hunters' *bozinas* (horns of ox bone that the huntsmen were required to carry) announced act 1 of the hunt: the assembly of humans, horses, and dogs. The gathering took place outside the Marquis's lodge, known as "Majada Verde," its halls likely hung with paintings celebrating actual and mythological hunts and portraits of the family with favorite dogs. Those gathered included the Marquis and several noble guests, including a "gentleman named Villarubia," renowned for killing many boars with his lance. The party also included at least twelve other huntsmen, about thirty dogs, and the horses of the noblemen and the chief huntsmen.

In act 2, the chief huntsman reviewed the location of the quarry and the strategy of pursuit with the highest-ranking nobleman. The huntsmen proposed an *armada*, in which a pack of dogs would raise the boar from his lair and chase him toward stations (*paradas*) where several huntsmen and more dogs awaited. Memories were still fresh of a previous hunt that had ended in the prey's slaughter of numerous dogs. Four years earlier, the chief huntsman—an intemperate man named Cristóbal—had vetoed an *armada*, declaring that "in the forty years I have worked in the *Montería* [the hunt], I have never organized an *armada* because *armadas* are only for inept hunters" and that for the chase "organized by my Lord this is not needed." A "very young" huntsman, Gonzalo Mateos, retorted, "The inept hunters are those who don't use *armadas* because though it is true that there are those who have hunted 40 or 50 years without using them, it's because in losing sight of the game, they don't know where to go or the reasons for doing it . . . and for this reason they don't use *armadas* and you must be one of those." Gonzalo was castigated for his impudence, and the nobles deferred to the view of the senior huntsman. Now, with the earlier canine massacre in mind, the Marquis consented to the *armada.*

Meanwhile, a few huntsmen and their dogs crossed into the "wilderness," a rolling landscape of open plains broken by rocky outgrowths and hilly pockets of dense brush and thickets of oak trees. Their task was, again, the *concierto.* Specialist hounds known as *can de trailla* (lymers or tracking hounds) worked on leash. They were trained to keep silent and indicate the presence of game by raising their snouts and licking their chops.[9] When the dogs discovered the boar on a hilltop, their huntsmen then made smoke signals to beckon the rest of the party to assume their posts. Hunters were stationed along two paths, downwind and out of earshot from the lair. At each post there was a mounted hunter, accompanied by a greyhound and an alaunt (*alano*). The greyhound was the pinnacle of the canine hierarchy—a dog renowned for ferocity as well as speed, described by a huntsman as having a "thin body, big eyes, large and narrow head, and of great swiftness."[10] The alaunt was "much stockier than the greyhound, of wide and prominent forehead, sunken and blood-thirsty eyes, and the fearsome gaze."[11] The alaunt was remarkably aggressive, even when confronting a dangerous boar. Each mounted hunter was also also accompanied by three or four smallish, speedy dogs (harriers known as *conejeros* or *podencos*) and at least three unmounted huntsmen, who handled the dogs. Other dogs were held in reserve for the chase.[12]

While the dogs, horses, and people waited in silence, specialist hounds known as *ventores* (running hounds) and their masters sought to "raise" the boar from their lair. Unlike the *can de trailla* of the *concierto,* the *ventores* worked unleashed, out in front of their humans. They were trained to keep very quiet ("if a dog barks while en route, remove it from the hunt, or kill it" advised Mateos). Upon finding the boar, the *ventores* communicated to the rest with "two barks."[13] In response, the huntsman signaled on his horn that it was time to unleash six or so hounds and two alaunts to give chase and so initiate act 3, the pursuit of the boar.

These chases could go on for hours, or even days, but this one was much briefer. As feared, the dogs of the *montería* pursued the deer rather than the boars. Still, the two fleeing boars ran in the direction of the Marquis's station. Seeing their approach, the Marquis ordered his huntsmen to let loose the greyhound and the alaunt. Partial Left Hoof escaped, but the dogs pursued and cornered the squire. The Marquis, "who was very dexterous and a great horseman," followed. He speared his foe felling "one of the largest Boars ever killed in that region, being thirteen palms length from the snout to the claws on its foot."

Partial Left Hoof remained at large until he neared Villarubia's position. Seeing the boar approach, the hunter set free his *conejeros*. These smallish, "very swift," "cunning and keen" dogs were renowned as fierce biters and possessed "a sharp snout and wide head, ears wolf-like sticking straight up, [and a] tightly coiled tail."[14] Villarubia followed on his horse. As he prepared to spear the boar, his horse spooked, and the boar charged and gored the horse, slicing his leg and belly. Villarubia cast his lance into the boar's flank, but that did not stop Partial Left Hoof. The man and wounded horse pursued the boar for 200 feet until the horse collapsed, spilling his innards in the thick brush. Three of the dogs suffered the same fate, leaving only the dog Bezerro to keep after the boar. (With gallows humor, Villarubia lamented later, "the other three dogs stopped their flight in order to keep company my horse.") The huntsmen accompanying Villarubia sounded on their horns to request backup, and the chief dog handler ("Perrero mayor") released the tethered dogs. They ran toward the sounds, "became excited" by scent of blood, and raced faster until they reached the boar.

Act 4 began when the Marquis and some others arrived at a horrifying scene under darkening skies. Inside a forest dense with trees and underbrush, they found dogs ripped apart, and intestines hanging off shrubs—"it appeared they were in hell." They waited for the Marquis's greyhounds to arrive. The dogs lunged and gripped the boar, grasping his ears. The boar gored. The Marquis dismounted and entered the enclosure with a few of his huntsmen. The boar, still fighting, was exhausted and outnumbered. Gripped by the surviving dogs and speared by Villarubia, the boar collapsed, his vital organs ravaged by the sharp metal lance tip and canine incisors. Many others died too: "He left dead eight *Conejeros,* not counting those of Villarubia or the greyhounds, and almost the entirety of the *Montería* injured." Villarubia exclaimed, "I have battled against that demon, that pig. I killed the boar—he slaughtered my dogs and my horse but could not destroy me." The Marquis, too, "grieved greatly the death of one of his greyhounds who he loved a lot."[15] "It was," wrote Mateos decades later, "the Marquis's most celebrated day." The hunters marveled not only at the impressive size of both boars but also at the singular tenacity and ferocity of the Boar of the Partial Left Hoof, "dying as he did."

~

IN CERTAIN RESPECTS, this hunt—like all hunts—was singular. No two hunts ever unfolded identically, as the techniques, terrain, and season would affect the experience. In addition, no human, horse, dog, or boar would behave identically in the same situation; not even the same individual would behave the same way on different days. The diversity of hunts was even greater when one considers that boar was not the only desirable quarry. Deer and bear were included in the prestigious triumvirate of big game, while wolves, foxes, and hares were also deemed worthy prey. Moreover, *caza de montería* or "venery"—the pursuit of prey with dogs and horses—was one of the two major categories of medieval and early modern hunting. The other category was falconry, tracking birds and small mammals in collaboration with raptors, often with the assistance of dogs as well.

Despite the diversity of hunting techniques, vassal animals, and prey animals, there were striking similarities and continuities among aristocratic hunting technologies across Europe and throughout the Middle Ages, the early modern period, and even to the present.[16] The cosmopolitan nature of aristocratic culture ensured shared approaches and attitudes toward hunting across Western Europe and beyond. The circulation of hunting treatises, vassal animals, and human hunters themselves across political and religious boundaries reinforced common pratices and mores.[17] Hunters sought the best dogs, birds, and horses from abroad, making such animals essential currency in diplomatic exchanges. Mateos described the different techniques used by visiting delegations from England, France, and Flanders and took the opportunity to make invidious comparisons of the abilities of hunting parties and the fierceness of prey of other kingdoms compared with those of Iberia ("it is thus well proven the proposition that the game of Spain is more brave and daring than of the other kingdoms"). Nevertheless, these comments display the shared culture of noble hunters.[18] While the stag may have been the premier quarry in England and France, and the boar was preferred in Iberia and German lands, tactics and values were widely shared.[19]

~

A CHIVALRIC ETHOS was common to medieval and early modern hunts. Hunting was a way to celebrate and realize this ethos, for it scripted a performance in which a "lord" accumulated and maintained power by vanquishing enemies with the assistance of vassals who owed him obedience and allegiance. As central to the hunt as the relationship of hunter-prey (synonymous with warrior-enemy) was the relationship of lord and vassal animal, built around hierarchy and reciprocal allegiance: the lord dispensed rewards (animal parts and honor) for military service and obedience.

The ideology of aristocratic rule was tied to the tradition of seeing the "second estate"—the nobility—as a warrior class by virtue of descent and deed. For this reason, the hunt was paramount. Put bluntly in the *Libro de la Montería* (Book of Hunting), a fourteenth-century hunting treatise published in the sixteenth century: "Of all the orders that God created the highest is that of knights (*cavallería*). . . . The knight must always use everything that pertains to weapons and chivalry. And when he cannot use them in war, he must always use them in things which are similar to it. And it is certain that there is nothing closer to war than hunting."[20] According to the *Siete Partidas*, the enduring law code first promulgated during the reign of Alfonso X (1252–1284), "hunting is the art and knowledge of waging war and conquest, of which Kings must be very knowledgeable."[21] Given that the defining trait of the nobility was their identity as warriors, it is no surprise that hunting was perceived as both preparation (developing courage, equestrian skills, and physical resilience) and practice for war.

Aristocratic hunters and their apologists took pains to explain that theirs was a noble leisure pursuit, not to be confused with the hunting conducted by commoners, pursued for ignoble purposes such as obtaining food and other life necessities (noble hunters would eat their prey, but that was not the *reason* that they hunted). A 1543 treatise, *Auiso de caçadores y de caça* (Counsel on Hunters and Hunting), written at the behest of a powerful aristocrat, firmly distinguished between elite and plebeian hunting. For "kings and great lords and gentlemen," the purpose of hunting was not to procure food in order to "survive" but rather "to push away cares and thoughts . . . to bring happiness to the soul by subjugating fierce animals."[22] Hunting was so ennobling that non-noble hunters employed in royal hunts in Castile were given the privileges of *hidalgos* (gentry), including exemption from commoners' tax burdens.[23] In this, it mirrored the expansionistic wars of the Middle Ages, in which "the dream of every foot soldier" was to find himself on horseback, "to make the magical transition from the dusty *pedites* to the galloping *equites.*"[24]

THE NONHUMAN ANIMALS of the hunt were perceived and understood in the context of this chivalric ethos. The vassal animals were horses, dogs, and birds, carefully bred in the case of the first two categories, and selected from particular species of raptors (born in the wild) in the third (fig. 1.2).[25] Privileged vassal animals—horses, dogs, and birds of prey of the hunt—were conceded a status superior to many humans. It is hard to overemphasize the prestige and value of service animals who assisted in the hunt. Put most pithily by Michel de Montaigne, "The men that serve us do so more cheaply, and for a

Figure 1.2   A hunting scene in Cantigas de Santa María de Alfonso X, the Wise, thirteenth century. Real biblioteca del Monasterio de San Lorenzo de El Escorial, fol. 64-r. Patrimonio Nacional.

treatment less careful and favorable than the one we give our birds, horses, and dogs. To what care do we not stoop for the comfort of these? It does not seem to me that the most abject servants do willingly for their masters what princes take honor in doing for these animals."[26]

The animals' material comforts were one index of this high status. French huntsman Jacques du Fouilloux, author of a manual first published in the mid-sixteenth century, advised that the doghouse of the kennel should have three chambers, one with a chimney and another where the horns and other equipment would be lodged. It should have glass windows. It should have a courtyard sufficiently expansive for the hounds to "have greater pleasure to play themselves and to skimmer through the middest of it," and that it is desirable "to have a little chanell of good fountayne water." Apparently, this blueprint was considered somewhat modest compared with the "sumptuous chambers which Princes cause to be made for their hounds, wherein there be closets, stoves, and other magnificences."[27] A Spanish aficionado of falconry cautioned that if you procured your bird from a "rustic," you should be sure to have the raptor delivered the same day and not allow him to spend the night in the cottage of the said "rustic," for if the bird ate the customary provisions of peasants, the bird's health might be compromised. This advice suggests that hawks in captivity consumed a more expensive, nourishing diet than human peasants.[28] In the *Libro de la Montería*, misbehaving or disappointing human huntsmen were subject to harsher disciplinary action (having a hunting horn broken on their head) than the dogs undergoing training.[29] Prescribed veterinary care for sick dogs and birds included expensive imported medicines such as mastic and galbanum—medical treatment of better quality than many of their human contemporaries received.[30]

Prey (*caza* or *venado*) was the other category of participant in the hunt. Prey animals were conceived as "enemies," as in war—destined for death but respected for their clever stratagems. Alonso Martínez de Espinar, author of *Arte de ballestería, y montería* (Art of Archery and Hunting) and a huntsman to Philip IV, wrote, "The Good soldier in order to vanquish his enemies uses, among other strategies, ambushes to take them unaware. The same is attempted by the Hunter with prey utilizing tricks sometimes to conquer her."[31] A seventeenth-century English treatise defined hunting as "a curious search or conquest of one beast over another, pursued by a naturall instinct of enmity, and accomplished by the diversities and distinction of smels onely, wherein Nature equally dividing her cunning giveth both to the offerend and offended, strange knowledge both of offence & safety."[32] Prey—the enemy—were targeted for killing, but before, during, and after the hunt, they were closely observed, respected, and admired.

An impressive quantity of human labor was mobilized to care for and train these vassals and to scout and stalk the prey.[33] In his 1582 "Discourse" appended to the medieval "Libro de la Montería," the Andalusian aristocrat Gonzalo Argote de Molina, described the permanent staff of the Castilian royal hunt and named all of those employed. In charge was the *sotomontero* (lieutenant hunter), followed by a chaplain and the "bailiff of the nets." There were three categories of huntsmen: the *monteros de trailla*, of whom four were on horseback and eight were on foot, who worked with the tracking hounds; the *monteros de lebrels*, who oversaw the greyhounds; and the *monteros de ventores*, who supervised the running hounds. In addition, there was a kennel master in charge of the *perros de Montería*, the less elite, smaller dogs trained to chase hares and foxes but also often employed in hunts of larger game. There were also *criadores de perros*, or dog breeders, whose ranks included an assistant *criador* bearing the apt surname *Cachorro* (Puppy).[34] In the seventeenth century the late medieval position of the *montero mayor* or "chief huntsman"—an honorary position bestowed on a high-ranking nobleman—was revived, although the *sotomontero* managed day-to-day operations. Several royal personnel lists of the "huntsmen and personnel of the *Montería*" survive from the 1630s and indicate that the practice of the royal hunt closely matched that described by Argote de Molina. They show that the permanent hunting staff hovered above fifty.[35] One Eugenio Montiño— a huntsman in charge of greyhounds—had a tendency to dress inappropriately and often had to be sent back to change; others failed to bring the requisite *bozinas* (horns). Even more people were involved when one considers the trainers and breeders, among many others involved in finding, raising, and training vassal animals.

~

HUNTERS RELATED TO their equine, canine, and avian collaborators, and to the targeted prey, through what I will call "deep observation" and careful investigation. Understanding the uniqueness of each vassal animal was imperative if training were to succeed and if the horse, dog, or raptor were to "perform very well at their trade." In addition to highly refined tracking skills, hunting dogs were taught to have the "forbearance to stay quiet and without movement even if they see the beasts six feet away" and to attack and kill—but not eat—the game.[36] Martínez de Espinar emphasized that training had to match the disposition of the dog: "If he is proud, correct him in that which is necessary to diminish it" but "for the one that has little willfulness, and is mild, it is necessary to treat him by petting and praising, because those who treat them with force are going against their nature."[37] In other words, the good trainer worked with the dog's "nature," not against it, and understanding that nature required careful observation.

No less than contemporary dog trainers, hunters understood that observational practices were at the root of knowing how to train a vassal animal. They stressed the individuality of each particular animal. Martínez de Espinar wrote that "as concerns the instruction of hounds, it is obvious that neither men nor animals are all of the same disposition [and] accords to the nature they have. [T]here are some choleric ones and other phlegmatic ones, and according to which of these two qualities he has, the dog will be more inclined to follow one prey than another [prey]."[38] Huntsmen were well aware of the differing abilities of their dogs and believed that the dogs possessed similar discernment. According to Mateos, if two hounds disagreed about the location of prey, the rest of the hounds would "follow the best dog of the foursome because they themselves are aware and know best who is the best, even better than the very Hunters, and so govern themselves by [that dog]. And we see here in Castile that if we let loose the Hounds in a hunt, and one who is no good, and is a liar, calls by lifting his head, and in knowing that, [the others] will ignore him and continue to hunt, and if a 'perro de opinion' [a dog of good repute] calls, then all will follow him."[39]

From the pages of hunting and falconry manuals, vassal animals emerge as distinct personalities, some more able and others more foolish. Horses were considered to have astrological signs.[40] Some dogs were known to be better at following a scent and others prone to be fooled by the tricks and stratagems of a cunning boar, a wily stag, or crafty hares.[41] The recognition of each vassal's uniqueness was rooted in training efficacy but also became part of the commemorative practices of the hunt. These esteemed dogs came equipped with genealogies, not dissimilar to their noble masters and mistresses. Almost one hundred years after the conquest of Granada, a hunting treatise praised a dog named Mahoma for his service as "a brave warrior against the Moors." Argote de Molina named and celebrated individual hunting dogs in the kennels of Philip II. The Master of the Order of Santiago, Lorenzo Juárez de Figueroa, commissioned an alabaster sculpture of his beloved dog Amadis to adorn his own grave.[42] Horses who distinguished themselves in hunts were similarly commemorated, such as Philip IV's horse Guijarillo, who was declared "more clever than strong."[43] The Castilian grandee Pedro López de Ayala, author of a fifteenth-century falconry treatise, memorialized a falcon named Botafuego ("Fireboot"), who, despite his small size, could kill cranes.[44]

Deep observation and investigation engendered more interactive ways of relating. In the case of vassals, this interaction was collaboration. In a hunt, whatever the type, be it "*par force de chiens*" ("by force of dogs," a tightly organized hunt with multiple dog breeds), falconry, or fowling, vassal animals were recognized as partners, offering valuable and skilled labor as transporters, trackers, and killers. Martínez de Espinar expressed bluntly the hunters' dependence on the hound: "Without him the Hunter cannot practice hunting, not being able to know where to find the prey, nor where to confront it in order to kill it, and the hound makes this possible . . . because [the hound] knows the terrain in the same way that the prey does, there is no hole or ravine, however hidden it may be, that [he] has not stepped on."[45] Sometimes hunters guided dogs (when finding tracks or evidence of lairs), and sometimes dogs guided hunters—for example, once they were on the correct scent or, in the case of gazehounds, caught sight of a faraway deer.[46]

Perhaps the dimension of the hunter-vassal animal relationship that most underscores the importance of intersubjectivity was the insistence on mutual affection as the foundation for collaboration. The horse-riding manuals speak of the importance of "cherishing" one's horse, including the recommendation to "weare sweete gloves, wiping his face, and chieflie his nostrhils with perfumes & sweet handkerchiefs: for neatness & sweetness, be two things wherein a horse dooth singularlie take pleasure."[47] Jean du Fouilloux stated simply that a successful kennel master or valet must love dogs. The emotional attachments to horses, dogs, and raptors led proud owners to have them depicted in portraits and to mourn their deaths.[48] In falconry manuals, above all other genres of hunting treatises, the language of love is most pronounced. An English manual suggested that the falconer approach his hawk with "a continual carrying of them upon your fist, and by a most familiar stroaking and playing with them, with the Wing of a dead Foule or such like, and often by gazing and looking of them in the face, with a loving and gentle Countenance, and so making him acquainted with the man."[49]

Communication between people and their vassal animals was critical. For instance, Mateos described how the hounds told hunters about the severity of a boar's injuries. If the creature's wounds are serious, the hound will bark "very quickly, and, if not, [bark] *poco a poco.*" The hunters respond to the dog by "howling like a Wolf, so the dog knows his master is there."[50] For Nicholas Cox, the writer of an English manual, dogs' ability to follow human commands was proof of their "understanding . . . For as right Huntsman knows the Language of his Hounds, so they know his, and the meaning of their kind, as perfectly as we can distinguish the voices of our friends and acquaintances from such as are strangers."[51] Two-way communication was also central to raptor training. Simon Latham explained that a successfully trained hawk will "always and inwardly in her mind [be] attending and listening for your voice, and some other pleasing reward from you."[52]

The intensity of the collaboration between hunters and vassals was such that their attunement could lead to a temporary sense of porous boundaries and a merger of subjectivities similar to what humans might experience during collective rites, sexual intimacy, and meditation.[53] Some neuroscientists speak of "blending bodies" when investigating how negotiating shared spaces is the task of certain parts of the brain. They propose that the brain experiences "peripersonal space"—the immediate space around the body—as part of the body, that "through a special mapping procedure, your brain annexes this space to your limbs and body."[54] Several centuries earlier, equestrian experts likewise described riding as a perfect communion of horse and rider. John Astley wrote in *The Art of Riding* (1584) that "in everie act that you shall doo, [the horse] will accompanie you, and you shall accompanie him in time and measure, so as to the beholders it shall appeare, that he and you be one bodie, of one mind, and of one will."[55] More pithy yet, the author of another equestrian treatise wrote, "These two several bodies may seeme in all their actions and motions to be as it were but one only body."[56]

This "blending" of bodily space was also an essential aspect in the falconers' relationship with their birds. The process of taming a wild raptor depended on constant physical contact and touch, as well as food rewards and soothing vocals. Falconer Edmund Bert strongly believed that in the first day of "reclaiming," as taming was known, a hawk should always be on the fist of a trainer—"she should sit and walke all that day," "either upon my fist or upon some man's else"—and warned that even momentarily setting her "downe upon a pearch but whilest I should change my Glove, she would be more impaired thereby then she would profit in tenne days travaile." He writes that throughout the taming period, "for the most part my fist is her perch," even when eating and taking care not "to hasten to bed for love of my Hawke." The end result was to "make her love me as her perch."[57] The gendered language here is purposeful: though raptors could be of any sex, Bert defaults to a male human and female bird to intimate a heterosexual erotic bond that calls attention to the intense intimacy of the relationship between falconer and bird.

The collaboration at the heart of *par force* hunting was scripted into the closing ceremony of the hunt. After the prey was killed, the entire hunting party—including the hounds—congregated for a ritualized division of the spoils. Known in English as the "breaking up," in this ceremony included huntsmen distributing the "brains reeking hot" to the dogs. It honored the hound who cornered the stag by giving him the first bite, paralleling the way that human huntmen who first sighted or shot the game was honored with the best cuts.[58] Argote de Molina described how huntsmen made a special dish by toasting together the intestines, blood, and bread. Then they blew on their horns to summon the dogs, and a huntsman showed the dogs their rewards by holding a piece up high on the end of the stick, leading the dogs to "jump" with excitement. He explained that this had the effect of making the dogs "greedy for the hunt" but also made clear its ceremonial purpose: while such feedings usually took place "in the country," there were "many other tines when it is done in the Palace, in the presence of His Majesty, when they bring to the Palace the [game] Animals in their entirety."[59]

~

DEEP OBSERVATION AND the consequential recognition of individuality were no less important in how hunters related to their wild prey. Huntsmen such as Mateos and Martínez de Espinar devoted mornings, afternoons, evenings, and nights to watching and listening to boar and examining their tracks, lairs, beaten down grass, and tree scrapings. The hunters sought the mud holes where the boar wallowed, the place in the brush where she entered and exited, the clay he tracked on the forest floor. Sometimes hunters crawled on all fours, and they went barefoot so as to not make a sound; they sat for hours without moving.[60]

As a result, they had an intimate knowledge of boar and deer within an ecological context. They knew that in the fall, boar dined on acorns, and in the winter, they searched out the acorns stashed away by rodents ("they make big holes to get them out and if there is a big crag they can't topple, you will feel it from far away because of the big snorts they give for not being able to reach the acorns"). When they depleted these stolen reserves, they dug out roots ("working later and getting up earlier because this food is less nutritious and it obliges them to work more to sustain themselves"). In the spring, they grazed on grasses called *pampillos, cerrajas,* and *pico de cigueña* (stork's beak) that grew where cattle had been left to pasture.[61] Mateos saw that "during the great freezes," the boars, particularly the *machos,* "wallow more often because the mud that sticks to them serves as a coat" and "go to mud holes to cure themselves of wounds." He knew that except "when they are very large and close to giving birth," the females banded together in groups with their young, until the newborns began to mature; otherwise, the sows would cannibalize each others' offspring. When the sows "leave the company," they search for a new-growth forest, not the "old and thick forests." They make birthing beds out of branches they have cut and carried in their mouths and have it "covered and protected for all sides" and "exposed to the sun to keep the children warm and protected from the overgrown woods." The sows stay close to "their children until they are weaned and they nurse with great order, giving each little one his own teat, and each knows his teat, and doesn't nurse from another's."[62]

The stalking could become a form of mimesis. Martínez de Espinar advised that the hunter harmonize his movements with his prey: "If the beast begins to eat, move when she moves, because with movement she loses her attention to listening; and when she stops, do the same."[63] The stalking hunter, then, possessed more than a passive awareness of his prey; he felt in his body the movements of the other animal. It is also telling that Mateos favored the verb "to sense" (*sentir*) when describing watching or listening to a boar he was stalking. Sensing implies a bodily knowing that surpasses mere visual or auditory perception.[64] Descriptions of these activities are resonant with what today's neuroscientists posit happens with "mirror neurons." "Perceiving the other's behavior," writes neuroscientist Vittorio Gallese and his colleagues, "automatically activates in the observer the same motor program that underlies the behavior being observed." As a result, "embodied simulation . . . constitutes a fundamental basis for an automatic, unconscious, and noninferential understanding of another's actions, intentions, emotions, sensations," and "such body-related experiential knowledge enables a direct grasping of the sense of the actions performed by others, and of the emotions and sensations they experience."[65] The techniques of the hunter described by Mateos and others fostered an "intentional attunement" that created "a peculiar quality of familiarity with other individuals."[66]

This deep observation or intentional attunement was integral to the stalking phase of the hunt. The consequent appreciation for each animal's personality was also part of the formal articulation of the hunt. A key preparatory stage was the selection of an *individual animal* to be chased. This initial phase entailed several huntsmen and their hounds dividing up the forest amongst themselves and surveying the population of boar or deer; the huntsman sought to identify the oldest and largest male stag or fiercest boar. They reported their discoveries to the chief hunter or hunt warden, who in turn advised the lord or prince, if a royal chase. From these reports, the "best" boar or "hart" (a male deer) was chosen, and signposts, known as "blemishes," were put near his tracks so the hunting party could track the chosen quarry the following day. Manuals devoted ample attention to the process by which an individual was to be selected—how one could determine a deer's sex or age by studying the marks left by scraping horns on a tree, his excrement, his tracks, and the places in a covert where he entered and exited.[67] When the actual hunt was initiated, it was paramount to keep on the track of the selected boar or deer and not be waylaid by another. If dogs or hunters began to follow a deer other than the identified quarry, they were in error, and part of hunting ritual included punishments for dogs and huntsmen alike who "hallow[ed] a wrong Deer."[68] The individuality of distinctive prey was even commemorated. Argote de Molina evinced a certain admiration for a boar "who was so fierce that when he ran across the gardens, farmers in that region would not go to their farms from fear," thus making Phillip II a hero for slaying him (even though the king did so from the safety of a carriage due to his gout).[69] Mateos recalled the *machorra* (a term typically designating masculine-presenting women but here applied to an intrepid sow) was so "bothered" by lusty male boars that she decided "to leave the forests in order to be left alone."[70]

If vassal animals were engaged as subjects through collaboration, prey animals were so engaged through competition. Hunters were dazzled by the ingenuity of their escape tactics, and, in the case of bear and boar, ferocious resistance. Mateos referred repeatedly to the "cleverness" of deer and boar alike.[71] He marveled at "the industry and sagacity of this brute [boar] who knows how to conceal his body and hide himself in impossible ravines." "I say," wrote Mateos, "there are traitor Boars" who "fool the Hunters by departing from their usual habits of eating and frustrate their efforts to track them."[72] Cox described the hart or stag as a "wild deceitful and subtile Beast," one that "by windings and turnings does often deceive its Hunter."[73] As with the boar, "the crafty great beast" might attempt to save himself by tricking a younger, less experienced buck to become the bait, sending "forth his little Squire to be sacrificed to the Dogs and Huntsmen, instead of himself; lying close in the meantime."[74] Alternatively, the "wise Hart, who, to avoid all his

Enemies, runneth into the greatest Herds and so bringeth a Cloud of errour on the Dogs, to keep them from further prosecution; sometimes also beating some of the Herd into his Footings, that he may the more easily escape, and procure a Labrythnth to the Dogs." And the "wise hart" would not just attempt to confound his pursuers with other deer; Cox claimed that some deer ran into herds of "Cows, sheep [et cetera] leaping on an Ox or Cow, laying the foreparts of his body thereon, that so touching the Earth only with his hinder feet, to leave a very small or no scent at all behind the Hounds to discern."[75]

The hunting treatises reluctantly admire the prey-enemies who triumphed and eluded detection, escaped the pack, or repulsed their human and canine stalkers. Mateos recounted two hunts in which he participated while serving the Marquis of Villanueva del Fresno as exemplary of boar intelligence and tactical skill. A week in advance of a hunt that he and his father were preparing for the Marquis, Mateos set up a lure. He knew the boar were hungry during the "August sterility," when acorns were ripening on the oak trees but not yet falling to the ground. The huntsman, astride his horse, raked the trees with a stick, maybe a dozen times, so they would drop their fruit. He then went a step further to ensure the success of his lord; Mateos decided to remove two dry brambles so they would "not interfere with his [Lord's] mark." The day of the hunt, he perched himself in a lookout spot to see what the boars were doing and know at what hour they came to eat. He recalled that at about a half hour before dawn:

> I saw a Boar approach, go underneath one of the oaks that was raked, and there he ate a little, and then moved to the others. . . . And when he arrived at the oak, where I had removed the brambles, he stopped very still, just as do bird dogs, and he noted something missing, beneath the oak. Seeing that, he fled running, as if he had been shot with a gun . . . and then we saw another approach, who came acorning from oak to oak, until he arrived at the oak we have said, and what the first one did, so did the second, and that evening came five Boar, each one doing what did the first.[76]

He concluded from this "that every day game teaches he who must know most about the Art of hunting."

A singularly savvy sow won Mateos's admiration for her capacity to elude crossbows and firearms and canine incisors, not only for herself but for the herd of adult sows and their young that she led.[77] In Estoçones, a mountainous wilderness of dense forest with slices of grassy pasture, lived a herd of about fifteen or twenty *Javalinas* (female boars) and their thirty or so young. Because of the ingenuity and leadership of their *guía* (leader), the boars endured many months, even years, without a single loss to hunters. They maintained their safety by ensuring that dogs could not catch their scent, moving "with the wind in their face, without taking a step or path unless the wind was against them." The leader also protected the others while they wallowed by circling around the mud hole and keeping guard. The sows "made a fool" of Mateos on many occasions by eluding detection and diverting him.

Eventually, Mateos and his hound were able to vanquish their formidable foe. One morning, Mateos's hound succeeded in leading him to a spot where he could stake himself, and that night, "his legs and arms trembling from desire in the bright moonlight," he shot the powerful sow. After she was shot, "the others not having a leader," were directionless in that dense forest, waiting for the arrival of their leader. When Mateos examined the sow's "fat and large" corpse, he discovered her ear had been perforated by two bullets long ago, leading him to conclude that "this was the reason that she lived with so much caution." Being so impressed with her "cunning and trickery," the huntsman noted that whenever "we found traces of some cunning Boar we said that he must have been raised by that herd of Boars in Estoçones." Mateos's sustained contact with the sow, whose tactics and acumen he celebrated, led him to conclude that the she had possessed "reason and understanding" because "she did things that shocked all of us, against nature." Throughout his treatise, Mateos marveled at stratagems employed by boar and deer: "The things they do to defend their lives that cannot be believed and cannot be told without suspicion, as in the *monte* there are no witnesses who can verify these things."[78] In other words, the skillful hunter is singularly equipped to understand and appreciate the subjectivity of prey.

~

TO ASSERT THAT the hunt required humans to recognize the subjectivity of prey animals may seem counterintuitive or even perverse, given that its apotheosis was the killing of the prey. This apparent tension is due to a commonly asserted truism that if we see an "other" as a subject (as opposed to an object), then we will seek consensual interactions and eschew using violence and depriving this being of its life. It is indeed true that certain kinds of killing—such as that which takes place in the slaughterhouse—is predicated on objectification. It does not follow that objectification is a precondition to killing.

The kill phase of the hunt itself revealed the intersubjectivity of participants because it dramatically revealed the interchangeability of the roles of prey and predator. Textual and visual representations alike underscored the possibility—and actuality—of the hunters becoming the hunted, a reality reflected not only in the numerous canine and equine deaths but also in human fatalities. Argote de Molina made mention of hunts in which the prey became predators, such as the "two princes of Spain" who "died at the hands of Bears."[79] Mateos also devoted several pages to his own near-misses and the escape "tricks" (jumping side to side, leaping over the boar) he perfected when confronting a charging boar and with which "God has seen fit to rescue" him "a few times." He warned that "there is no Lion who is more of a *carnizero* [butcher] than a Boar when he is injured or accosted by dogs" and told of instances in which boars "have killed and injured many Hunters."[80] Similarly, painters of hunting scenes consistently depicted men, as well as dogs and horses, being killed by boar and bear.

Because of its insistence on animal subjectivity, hunting contained the seeds of its own destruction. Although confessing that "the chase is a violent pleasure . . . for myself," Montaigne wrote in his essay, "Of Cruelty," that "I have not even been able without distress to see pursued and killed an innocent animal which is defenceless and which does us no harm. And as it commonly happens that the stag, feeling himself out of breath and strength, having no other remedy left, throws himself back and surrenders to ourselves who are pursuing him, asking for our mercy by his tears . . . and that has always seemed to me a very unpleasant spectacle."[81]

This passage is often considered to be one of the most precocious criticisms of hunting in the early modern period.[82] However, Montaigne's empathy is made possible because of hunting, not in spite of it. The precondition for Montaigne finding the killing of a stag repugnant was identifying with him as a fellow subject—something made possible by the hunt itself.

And yet for all of the admiration, empathy, and appreciation that nonhuman vassals and prey elicited, philosophers and other cultural authorities upheld the human-animal divide. For instance, the sixteenth-century natural philosopher Gómez Pereira argued that humans were unique in their possession of a rational soul, while nonhuman animals were guided only by "natural instinct."[83] At the root of this insistence on human exceptionalism was the ontologically generative force of livestock husbandry.

Objectifying Livestock

*I*n medieval and early modern Europe, animalistic creatures populated Hell. The demons in Fra Angelico's fifteenth-century *Last Judgment* have reptilian scales, mammalian fur, canid ears, sharp incisors, cloven hooves, webbed claws, or bat wings (fig. 2.1). Many have visible tails. The Devil himself is hairy, horned, and fanged. The demons use poles to herd condemned humans into Hell. Once there, people with pale, naked bodies boil in a big cauldron. The Devil devours humans, their sundered bodies spurting blood. Hell is a livestock operation. The artist made real, and vivid, its torments—except that people were corralled, cooked, and eaten, rather than cows, sheep, or pigs. In their fantasies of Hell, the Devil, and his minions, Europeans grappled with the objectification at the core of livestock husbandry.

~

LIVESTOCK HUSBANDRY WAS the dominant mode of interaction structuring humans' ways of relating to animals in premodern Europe. It included all activities that employed animals for the products that their bodies delivered when alive (wool, milk, eggs) or dead (meat, tallow, hides), the labor they offered (plowing, transportation, shepherding), and the wild animals (wolves, foxes, hawks) killed for the threat they posed to domesticated animals. Husbandry, as a mode of interaction, linked cart mules, plow oxen, herding dogs, barnyard chickens, sheep flocks, and butcher-ready cattle. It connected herders, muleteers, butchers, and tanners, as well as the consumers who ate and wore the bodies of animals—all of whose lives were shaped by a common set of beliefs and practices. Social and economic historians have long recognized the paramount place of livestock husbandry in medieval and early modern Europe.[1] Its importance, however, transcends its role in political economy.

Figure 2.1   Fra Angelico (1387–1455), *Last Judgment*. Painted 1432–35 for the church of S. Maria degli Angeli, Florence, tempera on wood, 105 × 210 cm, detail. Museo di S. Marco, Florence.
Alfredo Dagli Orti / Art Resource, NY.

Animal husbandry created temporal and spatial distance between those who owned and managed living animals and those who taxed and consumed their corpses. This alienation—and the objectification that followed—separated consumers from the animals whose bodies they ate and wore and was one of the most powerful effects of livestock husbandry. Nevertheless, alienation and objectification could never be total. As suggested by the way people imagined the Devil, even the powerful technologies of livestock husbandry—above all, the herd and the butcher—could not fully suppress the subjectivity of nonhuman animals.

Following the terminology and concepts found in medieval and early modern sources, I will use "livestock husbandry" as a synonym for *ganadería*. This Spanish word is derived from the medieval period when Christian warriors referred to the animals that they plundered from Muslim communities as their winnings (*ganado*). This etymological history reflects how Christian conquerors inherited and appropriated many aspects of livestock operations from Muslim communities. The term also points to the animals' object status expressed by the English term "livestock." The specific origins of these terms reveal the problems associated with the commonplace treatment of pastoralism as a universal category that can be applied interchangeably to any society that manages herd animals. Differences in "pastoral" regimes can be more important than commonalities. Although scholars also employ the term "husbandry" generically to describe ways of relating to animals that encompass everything from interacting with wild herds of reindeer to very controlled management of domesticated cows, I will use this term to refer to the specific sets of practices that surrounded livestock in medieval and early modern Europe.

Livestock or *ganado* were and are those animals bred, raised, managed, and, very often, killed so as to turn their body parts into consumer goods, and the vast majority of domestic animals employed in husbandry were livestock. Objectification was produced through multiple technologies and institutions that had developed over millennia. In particular, the interrelated complexes of herding and the butcher-slaughterhouse were crucial to construing creatures as vessels of disenchanted *things*. The asymmetrical intersubjectivity of husbandry was articulated in manuals published throughout Europe. Gabriel Alonso de Herrera, the author of *Libro de agricultura* (Book of agriculture), first published in 1513, wrote of sheep "that without them people could not live, or we would have to wander naked and savage, because from them wool dresses kings, nobles, people of middle estates and even lowly shepherds."[2] Cattle, likewise, were "necessary and beneficial for people" for "the sustenance they provide" and "the labor they offer."[3] The logic of objectification was pithily articulated in a little poem, "Praise of Sheep," that Englishman Leonard Mascall included in his treatise *Government of Cattell*. He wrote that "these cattle (sheep) among the rest, is counted for the man one of the best. . . . His fleece of wool doth cloath us all. . . . His flesh doth feed both young and old; his tallow makes the candles white. . . . His skin doth pleasure divers ways, to write, to eat. . . . His guts, thereof we make wheel-strings; They use his bones for other things. . . . His dung is chief I understand, to help and dung the Plowmans land."[4] Even when still breathing, an animal categorized as livestock was envisioned as a carcass ready to be transformed into useful things for people's consumption. The aristocratic hunt was organized around the principle of engagement, whether through collaboration or competition, and rendered visible the animals' subjectivity. Conversely, in husbandry livestock were considered objects to be managed. Livestock's beingness was suppressed to emphasize their thingness. Cow bodies contained beef, candles, and leather; sheep bodies provided fleece, mutton, milk, and cheese.

Although it is important not to universalize pastoralism or husbandry, it is also true that this type of husbandry, which turned domesticated animals into food and other objects, has very deep roots, omnipresent in Europe and the Mediterranean for centuries, if not millennia.[5] Archaeological evidence demonstrates that many of the technologies and even some of the institutions of animal husbandry in medieval and early modern Iberia date back to the prehistoric Mediterranean and the Near East.[6] Continuities are also suggested by the fact that classical treatises on husbandry, such as the first-century treatise, "De rustica," were published and cited throughout the early modern period. Likewise, Herrera's *Libro de agricultura* appeared in multiple editions in the sixteenth through eighteenth centuries, indicating the durability and relative fixity of this mode of interaction in the early modern period.[7] Nonetheless, the particular geography and social organization that underlay animal husbandry in the late Middle Ages and early modern periods were also related to more recent developments in political, social, and religious history, particularly those related to Muslim rule and Christian "reconquest."[8]

~

THE HERDING COMPLEX was both an institution supported by law and custom and a macrotechnology that aggregated many other technologies. It was fundamental to the transformation of an animal into fungible property and consumable goods. Many of its most important features were rooted in the deep past. Archaeological evidence indicates that "fully formed agro-pastoral" colonies, some of which had an abundance of sheep, appeared along the Mediterranean coasts by 5,700–5,600 BCE and were followed several centuries later by agro-pastoral settlers along the Atlantic coast of Portugal. Then came the "subsequent spread of agricultural economies into the interior" through processes likely both voluntary and compulsory.[9] In many respects the Romans established regional livestock patterns that lasted at least until the eighteenth century. The arrival of Arab and Berber rule in the eighth century did not fundamentally transform these patterns, although the new conquerors brought from North Africa the practice of long-distance sheep *transhumance*—the practice of moving herds of sheep hundreds of miles over the course of the year to take advantage of seasonal pastures. They also introduced merino sheep, prized for the quality of their fleece. Later Christian conquerors appropriated extensively from technological and aesthetic forms of the Muslim Mediterranean, including various strains of sheep—above all, the merino.[10] And Arabic terms such as *rabadán* (herder) and *zagal* (herding assistant) persisted.[11] The Christian conquerors adopted and intensified transhumance—driving great herds of sheep from the northern mountains and plateaus in winter to pastures in the more southern regions of Extremadura, La Mancha, and Andalusia, covering distances between 250 and 750 kilometers per year. By the thirteenth century, these herd owners formed an organization, the Mesta, which received special privileges from the crown and remained powerful throughout the early modern period.[12]

In the medieval period, the majority of domesticated quadrupeds living amid human society in Europe fell into the category of livestock. Most numerous were ovine and bovine animals, with much smaller numbers of pigs, goats, and equines. In 1519, the number of sheep owned collectively by the Mesta peaked, likely surpassing 3 million. However, locally grazed sheep almost always outnumbered transhumant sheep in any region.[13] In the regions around Jaén and Córdoba, sheep alone numbered more than 400,000 in 1512.[14] The proportions of different kinds of livestock varied according to locality. Although sheep were the most numerous, some regions focused on other types of livestock, often in alignment with local ecology.[15] In Seville, in the early sixteenth century, bovines constituted about 78 percent of the livestock.[16] In the villages in the Condado of Belalcázar, "the raising of pigs" was indicated as the "principal trade and livelihood" in 1587, whereas in 1634, "the principle *granjería*" was "bovine livestock."[17] Herds consisted mostly of a single species of animal, although sometimes sheep and goats mingled. In fact, some ordinances did not allow shepherds to own any of the sheep in a herd that they tended, but they were permitted to graze a few of their own goats along with the sheep. Herding structured the experience of the majority of domesticated animals while they were alive and enabled the production of goods that depended on their aliveness—above all, wool and cheese. The herd was the common denominator for cows, sheep, goats, and pigs. It was an assemblage of livestock and implements such as herding poles, netting, huts, and shears. It was managed by a small number of human and canine overseers. When a herd exchanged hands, it was often sold as an entire assemblage without distinction between the animals and equipment.[18]

The labor and knowledge that transformed animal beings into necessary objects for the sustenance and enjoyment of primarily human subjects belonged largely to the herders, who supervised the lives and often the deaths of the majority of domesticated animals in Europe and the Mediterranean. The humans in charge had specialized knowledge and technologies specific to the animals in their herds, as is indicated by their titles. The ordinances mandating the salary of herders for those in the jurisdiction of Madrid in the thirteenth century referred to a cow herdsman as a *vaquerizo*, the sheep and goat shepherd as a *pastor,* the herder of equines as a *yeguerizo*, and the swineherd as a *porquerizo* or *porquero.* For larger flocks, the human laborers included several herders working within a hierarchal structure, with the second-in-command known as the *rabadán* and the assistant (often teenagers or even children) as the *zagal.*[19] Boys were apprenticed to shepherds—often their fathers—at a young age, learning the craft by watching and participating.[20]

A key feature of the medieval and early modern pastoral regime was the high ratio of livestock to herders. In her study of animal husbandry in late medieval Andalusia, Carmen Argente del Castillo found that sheep herds ranged in size between 40 and 650 individuals.[21] Minimum herd sizes were mandated by law. According to the thirteenth-century royal charter for Madrid, the nobleman who owned a herd of cattle ranging from forty to one hundred "heads" could have no more than one cowboy (*vaquerizo*); if his herd was larger, he could also employ a *rabadán.* For sheep and goats, the ratio was one herder per hundred, and the code specified that if the herd exceeded one thousand, there could be several assistant herders. For herds of one hundred pigs, the owner "was to use one swineherd and no more."[22] The municipal ordinances of Jaén legislated that herds of sheep, goats, or pigs should contain "thirty animals and above." In Murcia, the municipal council recommended fifty sheep for each shepherd. In practice, herd size varied considerably according to extant inventories, account books, and lawsuits. Sheep and goat herds tended to range between forty and several hundred, although some were smaller. A 1542 document from Belalcázar declared that a single shepherd could be in charge of a herd of "up to 650 heads," although ones of that size likely included assistants.[23] Cattle herds ranged between ten and four hundred adults, in addition to calves, although there are abundant instances of herds smaller and much larger. Pig herds also tended to be somewhat smaller, with examples of herd sizes of forty-six and thirty-six being sold in Ubeda in the mid-sixteenth century and others that ranged between four hundred and six hundred.[24]

Although the unit of the herd was a core feature of livestock husbandry in Spain (and elsewhere in Europe and the Mediterranean), this does not mean the owners resembled each other. A wealthy magnate might own hundreds of thousands of animals, grouped into hundreds of herds, and huge swaths of land. At the other end of the spectrum, poor commoners might own only a few animals. Although the outlook of the owners may have differed vastly, the experiences of the herder and the animals, whether or not they were owned by a peasant or a magnate, were likely very similar. Very large flocks of wealthy owners were subdivided into smaller herds, each overseen by an individual shepherd assisted by a *rabadán*, a *zagal*, or both.[25] In the eighteenth century, the flocks of the Mesta were divided into herds of 1,000–1,500 sheep or 800 rams, which were managed by five shepherds and five dogs: a ratio of one shepherd per 200 sheep.[26] When individuals owned only a small number of animals, they arranged to have their cattle and sheep pasture together, and, according to Karl Butzer, smaller owners had "to pool their cattle to reach the minimum count of 400 head to send out on seasonal drives."[27]

Records pertaining to the sheep herds of the Count of Oropesa in the sixteenth and seventeenth centuries underscore how livestock within the pastoral regime were regarded as anonymous and generic. For instance, in 1559, the estate administrator Diego Gonzalo created a document that indicated salaries paid to individual shepherds. A typical list indicated that "Juan Corregidor" was "the shepherd of the flock of the black ones," that Miguel Conde was "shepherd of the rams," and that Juan Tordesillas was "shepherd of other flock of rams." The list also indicated, but did not name, the *zagal* for "the herd of the white ones" and "herd of the black ones."[28]

Although shepherds and their dogs were referenced in the singular, sheep were almost always discussed in the plural.[29] In the *Government of Cattell*,

Leonard Mascall advised that "among a herd of many pigs, ye must have divers and sundry marks, to know which is which. For else it will trouble his wits to know one from another."[30] Rather than being given names, individual animals were rendered as units of the broader collective through the practices of ear clipping and branding. It was common for municipal and Mesta ordinances to require branding.[31] In Carmona, for instance, it was mandated that "if someone buys some livestock, they must heat the iron and brand and mark [their animals] within 9 days" (allowing for delays during summer heat waves) and likewise that the "*rabadán* or the person knowledgeable about cows is required to mark calves with the brand of their owner within 9 days after being born."[32]

Recovering early modern insiders' understanding of herding operations is challenging for historians because herders transmitted their knowledge, technologies, and expertise between generations orally and so did not leave texts for historians. However, eighteenth-century accounts from those working directly with sheep have survived. For example, Enlightenment author Antonio Ponz recorded his observations about sheep husbandry near Segovia from a 1781 trip across Spain. Ponz also summarized the 1762 account of Alonso Cano, a friar and the son of a herder for the large flocks of the Marquis of Iturbieta.[33] Additionally, Manuel del Río, a shepherd with the Mesta, wrote his *Vida pastoril* (The shepherd's life) in 1825 after roaming for over 50 years with his flocks across pastures and mountains in Soria, Cuenca, Segovia, and León.[34] Analyzed together with more fragmentary sources (charters and municipal ordinances, legal depositions, and husbandry treatises) from earlier periods, these documents suggest the stability of the herding complex over centuries and illustrate the objectification process at the heart of the herding enterprise.

Charged with the task of creating the most abundant and desirable wool, shepherds of transhumant merino sheep carefully controlled the process of living and dying in the herd. The shepherds placed the rams chosen to sire (known as *morouecos*, or *sementales*) in herds of females at the end of June, allowing them to mingle in the herd for a month "for generation, regulating them for 6 males for every 100 females."[35] The shepherds selected sires for certain traits. The list made by the shepherd Del Río is over a page. The traits of the ideal ram included a "fine, velvety ear, not scrunched or wrinkly," "a thick neck accompanied by some very fine and small wrinkles but without hairs that overflow," "many ribs low to the ground," and a "jaunty gait, not clumsy or heavy."[36]

Breeding was as much about death as it was about reproduction. A new-born lamb had close to a 50 percent chance of being slaughtered within twenty-four hours of birth. The shepherd classified the infants into three groups—those who had all of the desired characteristics, those who had clear defects and would be killed immediately, and an in-between "reserve" group that would be kept if there were too many deaths among the desirable newborns and slaughtered if there were not. Del Río described the ideal newborn lamb as one with long and fine hairs covering the shoulders, flank, and nape, although not reaching the hooves or throat, for this "is the best stock (*res*); the wool will have growth and elasticity."[37] "The lambs who are born with black patches," wrote del Río, "should have their throats slit immediately, because their wool is not valuable for shearing." Short fuzz suggested a lack of desirable springiness, while too much thin hair meant the "animal would not be able to tolerate storms." Coarse and stiff hair on a newborn indicated wool that was "poor, defective, and thin," resulting in something "ordinary and not deserving of the name merino."[38] Females were favored over males because of their reproductive capacity, but castrated males comprised about a quarter of the flocks. Shepherds also culled a significant percentage of newborns to maintain the approximate flock size and ensure that the living sheep could subsist and flourish on the available pasturage.[39]

A large number of transhumant sheep babies were also killed to provide surviving offspring with two mothers, the biological ewe and an adoptive one.[40] This was because four- or five-month-old sheep needed milk from two ewes in order to be sufficiently strong and sturdy for the long-distance trek to southern pastures. Manuel del Río believed that this extra supply of milk also ensured the quality of the "offspring and the wool." He devoted a considerable portion of his treatise to this practice known as "doubling" (*doblar*), in which mothers who lost their newborns to slaughter or natural causes were compelled to suckle another's surviving offspring.[41] His insistence on doubling's benefits suggests that some shepherds were reluctant to go through the painstaking process of coercing grieving sheep to become what the shepherds called "stepmothers." In the reserve corral enclosing new mothers and their infants, the shepherd needed to identify "the bad offspring who had to have their throats slit and those who should be removed to be doubled." For this reason, del Río advised that it was best for shepherds to kill the "bad offspring" on the day of their birth, although some shepherds "delayed the operation for their interest in the rennet [enzymes produced in the stomachs of ruminants used in the production of cheese]." The pelts of the slaughtered lambs "were put in front of their mothers," and then the shepherd covered the newborn with the skin of the deceased lamb and "took her to the stepmother, [putting her] in front of her muzzle, who believing it was her child, pacified it."[42] Cano explained that the shepherd "put the pelt of the dead lamb, open at the neck, in such a way that it covered everything." Then the shepherd spread some salt on the pelt to entice the would-be adoptive mother to investigate. Once she started licking the salt, she smelled her deceased lamb, and then "the mother of the dead one recognizing it, she licked [the lamb] as they tend to do, she becomes engrossed and takes affection" for her adoptive lamb.[43] If this ruse failed, the lamb-deprived mother was tied up so as to force her to nurse until she accepted. Del Río also noted that the bereaved mothers were kept apart so that their distress would not upset the other ewes.[44]

Shearing was one of the primary ways that sheep bodies became objects. It generally took place in late spring or early summer. Shepherds hired day laborers, often local farmers, to help with the process—in the eighteenth century, as many as three hundred shearers could work together in a shearing hall to process thousands of sheep at a time. The night before shearing, adult merino sheep spent a night in a sweating hall to soften the crust that the body's thick yellow lanolin formed on the fleece. The next morning, laborers tied together the female sheep's feet with esparto grass and carried them to the shearers. Sometimes the workers pushed too hard, dislocating the animal's limbs, rendering the sheep useless in their view, and thus subject to slaughter. Rams, however, did not receive this treatment. It was thought that a ram would resist so much that he would hurt himself, potentially to the point of suffocation. At the very least, resistance would make shearing impossible. According to an English observer, there were strategies to "beguile him out of his fleece." He was laid down carefully and his belly petted, so that he would allow the shearers to do their work. Using shears with foot-long blades, the men attempted to cut the fleece as close to the skin as possible. It was easy to accidentally pierce the skin or even wound the sheep so badly that the animal experienced shock or infection. When shearers competed with each other to work the fastest, these accidents were even more likely. Local boys were hired to move around the shearing station carrying charcoal to stanch cuts. After the shearing, the animals were inspected, and those who were aged were sent to slaughter. Those chosen to live were watched carefully to make sure they stayed warm and didn't experience lethal shock. Nevertheless, some always died from the ordeal. The shepherd's adage "better hungry than dead" referred to the practice of keeping sheep enclosed rather than letting them eat pasture if the weather was cold or wet. From the sheep's perspective, shearing was a trauma: at best, it left them restrained, cold, and hungry; at worst, it resulted in lethal wounds or was a prelude to slaughter.[45]

The shepherd's core task was to suppress or manipulate the desires of some animals (ovine) to align with the objective of creating things to satisfy the desires of other animals (human). If the desire of the animal was to avoid the discomfort of having their fleece sheared or the pain of having their tails or horns amputated, it was the shepherd's job to oversee the use of human bodily force, restraints, and sharp tools. If it was the desire of a grieving mother to nurse her slaughtered lamb, it was the shepherd's job to motivate her to suckle another ewe's offspring. The shepherd's desire for easily manageable and identifiable bodies meant that the sheep endured great pain when her skin was burned with hot iron, when his horns were severed, when her tail was broken, and when his testicles were twisted. The desire for abundant, soft, elastic wool meant that sheep endured forcible restraint of their bodies, dislocation of their skeletal structure, wounds cut by errant blades, shock induced by exposure to cold and rain, and hunger when their access to pasture was restricted. It was the shepherd's job to manipulate the animals' desires in order to optimize their utility as objects.

The fact that the shepherd had to manage the herd in such a way as to optimize the quantity and quality of wool and meat did not mean that he failed to recognize the shared animal nature of humans and ovines. The shepherd fully recognized that the ovine body suffered in ways similar to the human body. He understood that humans and ovines were more similar than not in their desire for food, sex, comfort, attachment, and life. It is visible when shepherds used restraints during shearing because they understood that it was a fearsome, uncomfortable, and often painful procedure. It is visible when they sequestered grieving ewes so that their plaintive cries would not upset the other sheep. Nevertheless, because the operations of the shepherd were designed to deny the interests and appetites of the sheep in order to fulfill those of people, the shepherd's relationship to the livestock could not be intersubjective.

~

THE PROFOUND WAYS that husbandry structured the experience of both people and other animals can be seen at the end of the livestock's life in the butcher-slaughterhouse complex, as well as in the beginning of life in the care of the shepherd. Since at least the early medieval period, the *carnicería* (butcher) was the site where specialized artisans killed animals; cleaned, skinned, and cut their carcasses; and sold meat, organs, fat, and skin directly to consumers or other tradespeople. Although the butcher probably did not have origins as ancient as the herding complex, its development spanned at least centuries; it is telling that the men who weighed animal carcasses used .Roman scale technology and thus were called *romaneros*.

As suggested by the very name—*carnicería* literally means "meat-ery" or "flesh-ery"—the paramount function of the butcher was to turn a living animal into flesh ready for cooking. The rights and obligations of the *carnicerías* were based above all on the idea that the public was entitled to an ample, healthy, and affordable supply of meat. This sentiment was articulated in ordinances across kingdoms, such as the one in Cuenca asserting that it be "well provisioned with meat for the contentment and good public of the said city." A lawsuit involving the butchers of Palencia decided that the "city should be well provisioned with good meat and food so that there are no frauds or deceptions," and guaranteed consumers the right to "eat good meat" that was to be "served cleanly with speed and according to their estate."[46] Municipalities contracted with *carniceros*, defined as those "obligated to provide meat to the city," and set prices.[47] In 1500, a royal official (*corregidor*) in Málaga castigated the city's councilors for trying to sell meat at 5 maravedis per pound when he deemed the fair price to be 4.5 maravedis per pound.[48] Butchers presented the meat to consumers on *tablas* (tables) or *tajos* (blocks)—generally one was reserved for mutton and, depending on the season, the other for beef or pork. Butchers could be sued or otherwise penalized if they were found to cheat customers by selling the wrong kind of animal, by using weights and measures deceptively, or by raising prices to take advantage of a situation, such as the visit of a princess in Valladolid in the late fifteenth century.[49] In some towns, like San Sebastián, butchers were forbidden from sitting on the town council in 1492 because it was thought that this would lead to a conflict of interest and would unduly elevate prices.[50]

All of the public was entitled to take part in eating the animals killed by municipally contracted butchers and regulated slaughterhouses, but this did not mean they were entitled in equal ways. As in all other aspects of early modern European life, one's rank was crucial for determining the specifics of meat consumption. Miguel de Cervantes noted that the poor gentry have a pot "with more beef than mutton."[51] The importance of meat and its relationship to social class is dramatized by a 1534 conflict in Plasencia (Extremadura) in 1534 regarding the conduct of a nobleman seeking to buy meat at "the *carnicería* of this city that was called the *tajo* of the clergy"—in other words, the butcher dedicated to selling meat exclusively to members of the first estate (clergy).[52] One day, while the butcher was serving the domestic servants of the clergy, the nobleman, who served on the city council, insisted that the butcher "stop what he was doing and give him a cow udder." The butcher told the town official "to let him finish serving those servants (*despenseros*) in conformity with the obligation of oath that he had made." This infuriated the councilor, causing him to "respond to the aforementioned *cortador* with much anger." The case wasn't resolved until it was heard by an appellate court in 1567.

The expectation that everyone was entitled to and should have regular access to meat extended to the poorest and sickest people and was not confined to the upper echelons of society. It was customary to provide poor people with the animals' innards—that is, the less prized parts.[53] Even though butchers were not supposed to operate during Lent and on other Church-mandated meat-free days, special provision permitted the sick to purchase and consume meat at those times.[54] In the medieval period, adherents of each religion were served by butchers of their own faiths and followed different meat diets, as Jews and Muslims did not eat pigs.[55] However, medieval monarchs did not question their subjects'—of whatever faith—entitlement to acquire affordable and plentiful animal flesh.[56] This came to an end with the expulsion of Jews (1492) and Muslims (1499–1525) from Spain.

The laws and regulations that developed around the *carnicería* were designed to ensure that people had things to put not only in their bodies but also on their bodies. It was common to require butchers to sell the skins of slaughtered animals to tanners, cobblers, and other artisans within the city limits to ensure an affordable supply of shoes and other leather goods to the public.[57] In these regulations, it is made clear that only one kind of animal—the human subject who, in aggregate, composed a public—was entitled to provisions and protection. Excluded from this public were the animals whose lives ended in the *carnicerías*. They were not recognized as having interests, despite their resistance (some tried to escape) or their protests (many bellowed or brayed or oinked in distress).

The interest of the people who composed the public went beyond their roles as consumers and tradespeople. Law and tradition recognized their entitlement to live in clean and healthy neighborhoods. This right was a significant impetus for one of the most important developments for people's ways of being with other animals in the modern world: the separation of the two central tasks of the butcher—the killing of animals and the selling of their body parts to consumers or other tradespeople. Complaints addressed to municipal and royal officials in the late fifteenth century revealed increasing discomfort with the killing of animals in proximity to homes and holy spaces. In 1480, San Bartolomé's abbot, monks, and neighbors complained that the owner of the buildings in front of the monastery's chapel "of the Very Holy Crucifix" had been rented to royal butchers who were using them to slaughter livestock.[58] The petition emphasized that the chapel attracted "many people every day continually" from the town and elsewhere "because of the great miracles it delivers." The monks were unhappy because "the filth that the said buildings emit are pernicious" and upset "because of the killing (*matanza*) of the said cows and sheep in the said buildings there comes a great noise to the said monastery before the said crucifix and for this and for the bellows of the said cows in the said buildings where they are killed," leading to "the devotion being disturbed and lost." If anyone thought that the cries of a distressed sheep about to be slaughtered might actually have been a fitting accompaniment to the veneration of Christ, not infrequently identified with a sacrificial lamb, that sentiment does not survive in the documentation.

At the end of the fifteenth century, King Ferdinand and Queen Isabella responded to increasing numbers of complaints from townspeople about butchers within city and town limits. The Salamanca neighbors of Antonio de Medina complained in 1493 about the beheading of bovine livestock in their neighborhood, from which "they received manifest grievance and injury because of the bad smell of the blood that results from the said livestock (*reses*) that greatly harms the health of the people." In addition, "boys and girls cannot enter into their own homes because of the presence of the livestock that are in the streets and for the danger and fear of walking among them," even leading some neighbors to "leave their houses depopulated."[59] In 1495 Palencia (northwest Spain), residents complained when a *matadero of carnes* ("butcher of meat") decided to operate in "an empty building that had been a synagogue." They objected not because what had been a sacred space for their exiled neighbors was desecrated but because they "received much harm because of the bad smells that emitted from there and from the reses that were killed there." They claimed it had caused the "three surrounding streets to become depopulated because they say 'there is no one who can suffer that bad smell.'"The city leaders refused to make the butcher move his operation, but Ferdinand and Isabella overruled that decision through their royal official.[60] While the sounds and presence of scared and angry animals and the smell and feel of streets made muddy by blood were becoming increasingly unacceptable to the public, their desire for meat was unabated.

At least partly as a result of such sentiments, in many towns and cities across Spain, laws started to mandate that the killing of cows and sheep take place in a separate facility at the edge of or outside city limits. Such centralization also served the fiscal interest of authorities, as it facilitated the collection of taxes.[61] Edicts requiring the construction of slaughterhouses (*mataderos*) appeared in a number of cities at the end of the fifteenth century, including Seville (1489) and Madrid (1495), as well as León, Guadalajara, Jaén, Málaga, and Córdoba.[62] In 1585, municipal records revealed that 100,324 sheep and 5,522 cows were killed in Madrid slaughterhouses.[63] The *mataderos* and tanneries were to be located beyond the town walls, or at least out of its center.[64] However, the selling of meat was still to take at the *carnicerías* in the city center; the term came to denote places where animal flesh was sold but not where animals were killed. The separation of the slaughterhouse from the butcher was partly a response to increasing urbanization and the growing populations of towns and cities.[65] Nevertheless, making the killing of animals less visible and increasing the number of steps and specialists that separated the living animal from the commodified parts of their corpse was also a logical extension of the objectifying processes that had already been developing for centuries, if not millennia.

The emergence of the slaughterhouse as a separate institution constituted less a transformation of butchers' deeply entrenched technologies and institutions than an intensification of them. The Seville slaughterhouse and its related operations—like those in Madrid, Granada, and other cities— resembled the butchers that preceded them in important ways and operated in parallel in smaller towns. The preamble of the *Ordinances of the Slaughter-house of the Very Noble and Very Loyal City of Seville* (first issued in 1601 and slightly revised in 1686) was similar to the medieval laws that preceded it: "One of the things that is most fitting is for the Republic of this City" was to ensure that "the citizens of it be provisioned and sustained as they used to be with an abundance of meat and fish."[66] A comparison of detailed inspectors' reports from butchers in central Castile with the ordinances of the seventeenth-century Sevillan slaughterhouse reveals that most of the essential technologies—the corrals, their locks, the killing and storage rooms—were identical. The challenges, like thieving cats, were also strikingly similar.[67]

The experiences of a cow, a sheep, or a pig who ended their lives in a medieval butcher or an early modern slaughterhouse were probably similar. The *Ordinances* from Seville, read alongside other sources, allow a rough reconstruction of a cow's transition from living being to fungible commodity. A cow who ended her life in the city's slaughterhouse likely began her life in one of the herds owned by the wealthy cattlemen among the Sevillian elite.[68] Her life would have revolved around her fellow herd members and the pasture on which they grazed. One of her earliest experiences would have been the sensation of burning iron searing her skin—the branding that would denote to humans that she was property of a particular owner. Early in life she would also become familiar with the cowboys with their long poles (*garrocha*) and their equine assistants, in charge of moving her herd to the pasture.

Her life would be coming near its end when she was moved to a new pasture; bovines were usually slaughtered in spring, summer, and early fall months. Her owner decided the most profitable time for her to be killed— the time when she had reached her full body weight and her flesh would taste best. Just outside the city limits of Seville, her new pasture was either Tablada and Tabladilla, literally, the "Table" and the "Little Table"—a reference, perhaps, to the *tablas* where the animals would be sold as processed flesh.[69] These pastures were under the control of the *conocedor* ("the knower"), who was required to "live in the said pasture in a house that the City has appointed" and whose primary duty was to prevent fraud or smuggling. As soon as the cow arrived, the *conocedor* and the slaughterhouse bookkeepers (*fieles*) would list the cow in "a large, big book" that was divided into sections "for each kind of livestock that is registered," along with their prices. These records would be consulted to ensure accurate accounting of all the cattle leaving for the slaughterhouse. They would identify the cow by her brand and sex and make sure that she matched the number with that brand and sex in the book. Assisting the *conocedor* was the *veedor* (overseer), a cowboy who was required to "have a mare and a *garrocha*" and live in the nearby neighborhood of San Bernardo. The *Ordinances* regulated access to "the said Pastures," prohibiting entrance to anyone who was employed by the slaughterhouse and to all "mares, horses or other livestock that is not registered."[70]

On the day before the cow's slaughter, the *veedor*, and his assistants rounded up our cow along with others in the herd (called a "rodeo").[71] If the ordained protocol was followed, the cow arrived in the slaughterhouse corral between 3 p.m. and 5 p.m. to be ready for the nighttime killing. Once in the corral, the *conocedor* and the *fieles* again ensured that all registered livestock were accounted for. In the corral, the cowboys sometimes entertained themselves—and soon others—by mocking and assaulting the animals, especially the fierce bulls—a practice perhaps related to the stress of having to guide the resistant animals to the place of their demise. This practice prompted municipal authorities in 1546 to decry the fact that "the bullfighting (*torearse*) of the cattle in the slaughterhouse" led "a great number of children and teens [to] climb onto rooftops" and to order "an absolute prohibition against fighting (*lidiar*) the livestock."[72] As was so often the case, the prohibitions had little effect, and by the late sixteenth century, municipal authorities decided to coopt rather than resist. By the second half of the century, rather than trying to ban the activities of the cowboys, city officials in Seville were ordering the construction of viewing stands so that they and other members of the elite might enjoy the performance in the comfort and grandeur they considered their due. The origins of various early modern and contemporary spectacles involving bulls were integrally related to practices of the butcher and the slaughterhouse.

When the cow arrived in the slaughterhouse corral, she entered a heavily regulated space. The counterpart to the *conocedor* of the pastures was the "*alcalde*" (sheriff) of the slaughterhouse, assisted by the "*soto-alcalde,*" his second in command. Required to live in the building, the *alcalde* was obligated to make sure that the only humans who entered the space were its employees and the only animals were those destined to be killed. He was authorized to "seize and jail and report to the justices" any thief. The *Ordinances* specified that the men in charge of the weighing (*romaneros*) were also required to live in the slaughterhouse and to keep the corral locked until the animals "were delivered to those charged with their killing." The *Ordinances* further specified that only designated professionals were allowed entrance to its premises: only those charged with the killing (*colgaderos*), the weighing (*romaneros*), and the recording (*fieles*) and these officials' supervisors. They emphasized that "no butcher (*cortador*), nor tripe-maker (*menudero*), nor any person of whatever kind or station they may be is permitted to take out or cut the livestock that is killed in the said slaughterhouse."[73] In other words, anyone who might be tempted to steal or smuggle animals or their corpses was to be kept out. Potential thieves included cats and dogs in search of some tasty meat or entrails.[74] The locks and surveillance required by law were also intended to prevent unwanted exits—that is, to prevent the cow from escaping—as the men in charge of weighing the carcasses would be held responsible for any missing livestock, including "one who exited out of the door."[75]

After midnight, our cow was led from the corral to the slaughterhouse. Killing took place between the hours of midnight and the morning prayers to ensure a ready supply of meat for the public at daybreak. In the dark, candle-lit space, several *colgaderos* inverted her and hoisted her onto a large upright beam and attached heavy ropes to her four limbs to restrain her.[76] The strength required for this task is reflected in the name *colgadero*, which literally means "hangers"; eight were employed by the slaughterhouse, according to the *Ordinances*.[77] One of them took a knife to her neck and forced the blade through her skin, muscles, nerves, veins, and arteries. She died before her head fell to the ground, before her blood drained out from the cavity. This arduous labor of killing in this way might have tempted butchers to seek easier methods; in the fifteenth century, municipal authorities in Madrid mandated that butchers not clobber cows to death.[78] In his short story about two conversing dogs (Berganza and Scipio), Cervantes suggested that their killing wasn't necessarily containable, observing that "these slaughterers (*jiferos*) will kill as easily as they kill a cow. . . . They put a knife in a man's stomach as readily as [if] they were killing a bull. It's a rare thing for a day to pass without quarrels and wounds, and sometimes deaths."[79]

Only when she was dead did the cow fulfill her purpose—at least from the perspective of the people who bred her, raised her, sold her, killed her, weighed her, taxed her, skinned her, cut her, and ate and wore her. After slaughter, the animal's carcass began its long, multistep transformation into different kinds of goods. The first step was to expulse the one part of her body that was not saleable and potentially an environmental nuisance—her blood. Then her body was weighed by the *romanero*, and her weight and value were recorded by the *fiel*. The latter was required by the *Ordinances* to "wake up at midnight in order for the weighing of the said livestock" and to "record the livestock that was registered" and, in "another big book," record the "value of the livestock that had been weighed." During this process, the head of the slaughterhouse, as well as the *soto-alcalde*, were supposed to be present to prevent theft or fraud, like claiming a "lamb where there had been a mutton" or a "piglet for a pig" and to ensure that no animal had *viruelas*.[80] After exsanguinating and weighing the animal, the *colgaderos* skinned her, gutted her, and split her carcass into eighths (if she had been a sheep it would have been quarters).

No longer a carcass, the cow provided varying quantities of four kinds of commodities: skin, internal organs, fat, and flesh. In the case of cows, the most profit was generated by the edible parts of the body. The historian José Ubaldo Bernardos Sanz estimates that in Madrid in 1551, the value of the flesh and organ meat was 81.7 percent of the total, skins were 16 percent, and fat was 2.3 percent, whereas in 1623, the edible parts were valued at 90.1 percent, the skins at 8.6 percent, and tallow at 1.3 percent. The proportions might have changed related to the influx of hides from the Americas.[81] Her flesh might be hauled to the *Carnicería mayor*, where members of the third estate bought their meat, or to *Tabllillas de las Dignidades* (Butcherblocks of the Dignitaries), where the servants of tax-exempt members of the first and second estates bought theirs. Her organs went to the *tablas de los menudos* (organ-meat tables), and her skins and fat were returned to the owners, who took charge of their resale.[82]

The experiences of the cow in seventeenth-century Seville were similar to those of other cows in earlier centuries, but the slaughterhouse changed the experience of people—laborers and consumers alike—in crucial ways. The objectifying logic of livestock husbandry was amplified by this separation between killing animals and selling meat. What had been the work of a single butcher in the medieval period was now split among at least four different kinds of workers. In addition, the emergence of the slaughterhouse meant that consumers no longer bought their meat where the animal had been killed. The emergence of the modern slaughterhouse intensified the preexisting process of "alienation." Karl Marx used this term to describe the estrangement that capitalist relationships created between workers, their labor, and the goods they produced.[83] William Cronon, in his seminal history of capitalism and nineteenth-century Chicago, extended the concept to describe how the "growing distance between the meat market and animals whose flesh it dealt . . . betokened a much deeper and subtler separation— the word 'alienation' is not too strong—from the act of killing and from nature itself."[84] But alienation long preceded both capitalism even industrial agriculture, for it was an effect, perhaps even a purpose, of livestock husbandry, as seen in the technologies of the herd and the slaughterhouse. As organized in early modern Iberia, husbandry created both temporal and spatial distance between those who owned and managed living animals and those who consumed their corpses. This distance ensured that consumers did not experience an intersubjective relationship with the animals whose bodies they ate and wore.

~

NOT ALL DOMESTIC animals who became meat or otherwise had their bodies consumed spent their lives in a herd or died at the hands of a professional butcher or *colgadero*. There were, above all, chickens and pigs who resided just beyond the house or even within it. They dwelled outside the herd and the slaughterhouse, but their paramount role as food producers led to their objectification. Like other livestock, poultry became objects through the processes of collectivizing, managing, and alienating.[85] Unlike the hawk deployed in falconry, chickens, geese, ducks, and other domesticated fowl were regarded in the plural. Herrera used *gallina* generically to refer to all female hens, whether they were chickens, ducks, or geese. Whereas falconry treatises referred to particular avian individuals and insisted on their unique personalities, hens rarely emerged as individuals in the pages of the husbandry manuals.[86] The recommended management of poultry in *Libro de agricultura* and other manuals, designed to produce the best meat and eggs, was part of the process of alienation. Feeding and fattening instructions promised to deliver the best flesh or the best egg-layers.[87]

Although some pigs lived in herds and died in the slaughterhouse,[88] many swine were raised in the household. If men were in charge of animals of the pasture, women (commoners) were primarily tasked with raising pigs and chickens in the household.[89] In the words of a seventeenth-century Catalan husbandry treatise, the "mother of the country house . . . must take governance of the Pigs."[90] The primary consideration that dictated the choices in rearing pigs was optimizing the flavor of their flesh, although their skins sometimes became leather and their fat was used not only for cooking but also for medical treatments and to grease cart wheels.[91] Herrera advised castrating pigs between the ages of one and three because, later than that, "the flesh" had a "bad, hard taste."[92] Much attention was paid to the procedures of "fattening" (*engordar*) to ensure the tastiest meat: "These are animals that fatten marvelously, so much so that it happens that many times they cannot get up onto their feet, even to pee," wrote Herrera. "Bread, whatever kind, fattens them much and make the best meat." He admonished those who "blind pigs destroying their eyes, thinking that will fatten them more," explaining that "those do this who feed them in their homes, which in addition to being a cruelty, the majority of the pigs die losing an eye, and even more if they lose both of them."[93] Another reason pigs were raised in homes was to help them better endure weather extremes. According to Herrera, if pigs were "to grow and fatten," it was "most necessary" to keep them "in a warm and dry place." But such proximity also brought dangers, such as the swine's tendency to "undo the buildings." They even endangered children: "many times it has happened" pigs "eat babies in their cradles," or in "taking the bread from the hand they eat the hand and, after that, the body." Proximity did not breed affection when the object of feeding was itself intended to become food.

The changing sensibilities that led to the separation of the slaughterhouse from the butcher also affected attitudes toward pigs and chickens. In the late fifteenth century, it became less acceptable to have pigs and chickens roaming around larger cities, particularly when nobility and others of high rank resided in these towns. In 1492, an edict from Ferdinand and Isabella decreed that no one "raise or kill nor raise any pigs, whether large or small, inside or outside of their homes in Valladolid." They explained that they were responding to municipal leaders' petition that "gave us a report of the bad and dangerous custom" of "raising pigs in the town and bringing them freely through the streets," from which "follow many harms and problems not only in the way of buildings of homes but also in the many sicknesses and infections which follow from the streets and alleys always being dirty." In order to enforce the edict, there were bounties for free-roaming pigs. The person who captured one of these pigs received half of the value "of the product" while the other half would go toward "the repair of the walls and streets and public buildings of this town."[94] Records of efforts to enforce this code survive from Valladolid. In November 1591, officials fined those in violation of these ordinances against keeping pigs and chickens in urban domestic spaces. Ana Vidal, whose business was located on the Plaza Rinconada, was fined four *reales* for having "piglets inside her inn" (the official noted that she "threw them outside" when he arrived). Nearby, Francisco Alvárez "declared that he has *cochinos* but has them outside of the house," and Alonso Hernández "declared that his wife has two piglets." Damiana Fernández, who said she was not the owner of the inn just outside the "Puerta del Campo" (Gate to the Country), was nonetheless fined for having a piglet, a "poorly cared for manger," and a "tub filled with cooked leftovers for the piglet."[95] Similar laws were passed in Madrid, which became the permanent site of the Royal Court in 1561 and whose population thereafter grew quickly.[96] In 1588 and again in 1609, municipal authorities outlawed pigs running freely in the city's streets, adding the provision that "whoever encountered them could kill them and benefit from them." Similar decrees were passed throughout the early seventeenth century.[97]

The pastoral and butcher complexes of medieval and early modern Europe and the Mediterranean created layers of separation between those who worked intensively with animals and those who owned them, and between those who processed their bodies and body parts and those who consumed them. A person who ate a stew, nibbled on a piece of cheese, donned a leather shoe, and lit a candle had no relationship—not even a fleeting one—with the particular animal whose flesh, skin, or innards they consumed and used. Where hunting animals were appreciated for their individuality, livestock creatures were viewed as units of a collective. In contrast to the individuation that occurred in the noble hunt, when a single prey animal would be targeted, the individuality of singular animals was (and is) effaced in husbandry. If the optimal condition for intersubjectivity is a one-on-one relationship—where close observation and empathic response are possible—the corollary is that it becomes much easier to relate to beings as objects when they are viewed collectively. Where hunting animals were seen as subjects with whom collaboration or competition was taken for granted, *ganado* were objects to be managed—the passive recipients of often physically and emotionally excruciating practices seen as necessary for their breeding, feeding, shearing, and slaughtering. While living, livestock were conceived as existing in a transitional state that would culminate in their death or the dispossession of their body parts. Where hunters identified with vassal and prey animals, the people who owned, managed, and consumed livestock were alienated from them.

~

NOT ALL ANIMALS involved in husbandry were livestock. Pastoral technologies also produced the category of "predators": *animales carniceros* (literally, "meat-eating animals") and *savandijas* (vermin). Those wanting to protect their livestock killed vermin through trapping, netting, and shooting. Although the desire to exterminate "predators" and "vermin" might, at first glance, appear similar to hunting, from an intersubjective perspective, this form of killing wild animals was seen as distinct by early modern Europeans. It had a functional purpose designed to eliminate threats to husbandry, and as the connotations that continue to inflect the word suggest, vermin were despised rather than respected in the manner of prey animals of the hunt. Vermin included birds who pillaged fields and grabbed fish from ponds and raptors who feasted on chickens.[98] They were also wolves and foxes, who feasted on sheep and goats, and sometimes even dogs with the wrong attitude.[99] It was common for owners of livestock to award bounties to locals who killed wolves, particularly litters of pups. An account ledger for the supervisor of a noble family's shepherds shows a payment of "three cheeses which were given to the men who brought some wolves plus the three cheeses which were given to the 3 men who brought 3 litters of wolves."[100]

Livestock husbandry also produced the category of servant animals.[101] Like human servants, the animals who fell into this category were indispensable for making the earth yield its resources. They included, among others, the ox or plow horse who tilled the soil, the mule who carted goods from country to city, and the dogs who guarded sheep, protected property, and guided bulls.[102] Of oxen, Herrera wrote, "Of the four parts of toil and work, the three quarters are theirs and of these they relieve us: how they work to open the earth, to sow, to harvest, to thresh [wheat], to bring it home, on the road, to bring firewood and stone, and so many labors and burdens that we want. How certain it is they are our companions and ever steadfast and great helpers of people."[103] Servant animals assisted in the slaughterhouse as well as the wheat field. This transit of cows and bulls required not only human but also bovine and canine assistance. Tamed, castrated steers known as *cabestros,* or "those who are heads," had the job, as their name suggests, of leading bovines on their walk to the butcher or slaughterhouse.[104] Dogs, too, assisted in this process.[105] Cervantes famously depicted and ventriloquized one such canine, Berganza, who reminisced at how his master, a slaughterhouse worker named Nicolás, "taught me and other puppies to run at bulls in company with old dogs and catch them by the ears. With great ease I became an eagle among my fellows in this respect."[106] Servant animals were needed for their "brute force" (hence, the term), in contrast to livestock valued for their consumable parts. These categories could, however, become blurred in husbandry, as in the case of oxen, who were often eaten when they could no longer labor.

Among servant animals, canine shepherds enjoyed perhaps the most prestige. That they belonged to a different order from livestock is made clear by Herrera in the *Libro de Agricultura.* He praised their "excellencies." "What animal who so loves his master? . . . Who guards so loyally? Who accompanies so continuously? Who keeps watch without sleep? What friend without duplicity or deceit?" Their intimacy with humankind was suggested in the advice to choose one's dog "with a face that seems like a man's" and the aside that "although these are animals without reason"—a necessary concession to avoid charges of heresy—"nor do they entirely lack it."[107] Del Río, too, emphasized that every flock should have three dogs "in order to defend it from the attack of *animales carniceros*," elaborating that "each shepherd should have one or two well accustomed to his voice, so that in this way they stay vigilant and obedient to his command." Del Río further argued that when dogs performed their work well, "it is fitting to praise them a lot in order to demonstrate that they have done a good action and have them disposed to execute it another time, because in general dogs appreciate an infinity of praise from man."[108]

That a working relationship between human masters and canine servants could produce intense, even dangerous, affection and loyalty is borne out by a 1677 lawsuit filed by the owner of a flock of goats in the village of Caleruela, near Toledo.[109] Sebastián Bravo alleged that a shepherd named Juan Garro had a dog who massacred his goats (thirty adults and twelve juveniles), killing some and biting others "in such a way that they could be of no use." The dog in question, never named, was a russet *mastín* (Spanish mastiff), a very large breed. Herrera wrote that ideal *mastín* "should have a big head so that it seems to be a third of the animal's body and that looks like the face of a man's," eyes that are "shiny and alive like sparkling stars," and "a great and terrifying bark."[110] The plaintiff wanted Garro to "pay him for the damage that his dog had done" and to "kill [the dog] so that he could [not] continue to cause so much damage to him and others who have livestock." Garro compensated Bravo (somewhat more than 1,500 *reales*), but he refused to put down his dog. According to Bravo, Garro said that "he didn't want to kill the dog because he had paid him for the damages that his dog had done." Garro's lawyer mounted a defense that Bravo was at fault for "pasturing his goat livestock (*ganado cabrio*) without a shepherd or a dog without guard, at their liberty." Moreover, Garro alleged that Bravo's goats had caused "very pernicious damages" to nearby vineyards and olive groves, and that Bravo himself did not take good care of his goats. The justices decided to obtain witness statements from villagers to get further background on both men and their animals. Among the questions was one about Garro's *mastín*, whether he was "by nature fierce or ravenous, accustomed to killing and mistreating goats (*ganado cabrio*) and other kinds of animals." The testimony revealed that the russet *mastín* had quite a record of carnage: Garro's own cousin testified that the dog had killed a ram belonging to the parish priest, and another witness declared that the canine had mauled to death a number of local sheep and had so injured a pregnant pig that she miscarried. This case suggests a very strong attachment: although Garro quickly paid the damages, he did not want to part with his beloved dog, even though this companion animal was clearly a liability.

Another kind of servant animal was the sheep, known as *mansos* (tame ones), a role that the goat sometimes occupied as well.[111] According to del Río, shepherds took great care in choosing the sheep for their *mansos*, a role limited to males. Once selected, the shepherd castrated and trained the *manso* to respond to commands. A French observer in the eighteenth century described these sheep admiringly. When the shepherds wanted the herd to begin moving, they "gave the sign to the *mansos*, who instantly, began to walk, and were followed by other sheep. The sound of the large bells that the sheep wore around their necks warned the lazy ones or the ones grazing at a distance." They were treated differently than the sheep of the nameless herd. "The shepherds tame them," he wrote, "and make them accustomed to their voice while petting them, and feed them with grass, leaves and bread."[112] Unlike the majority of sheep in the herd that the shepherd was charged with managing, shearing, and killing, the *mansos* were beloved. Del Río, with his insider's perspective, offered a glimpse of the strong feelings of affection that the shepherd developed for his ovine servant, "whose destiny was to guide." He wrote that "when a shepherd has an extraordinary *manso* he would rather keep him then allow him to die." Del Río wrote disapprovingly of shepherds' unwillingness to allow the aged sheep to be sold for slaughter after their ability to serve well as *mansos* came to an end, complaining that it "deprived an owner of the [sheep's] value" and was "a mode of thinking that is reprehensible." Nevertheless, he also resignedly acknowledged that the shepherds "kept [their *mansos*] until they were old and had no use." Del Río's comment suggests that shepherds were inclined to preserve the *mansos* even when this practice was not in the interests of their employers.

Servant animals needed to work closely with humans to do their work. This situation created the intersubjective conditions required of training— cultivating an individual relationship organized around touch, sound, and nurturing. In certain respects, the master-servant relationship in husbandry was structurally similar to that of the lord-vassal relationship in hunting. In both modes of interaction, servants and vassals were engaged with and appreciated as individuals and collaborators and understood as reasoning subjects, not unlike people. However, whereas hunters were literally ennobled by their relationships with vassal animals, dominant opinion considered those who worked most closely with animals in husbandry—shepherds, goat herders, and muleteers—as degraded by the relationship. On the one hand, pastoral discourse in Christian scripture, Golden Age religious paintings that depicted John the Baptist as a shepherd, and plays that glamorized shepherdesses made the figure of the shepherd into an appealing, benevolent figure, at odds with the actual violence of his work.[113] On the other hand, one of the central jokes in Cervantes's *Don Quixote* (1612) relies on the recognition that there was a fundamental similarity in the relationship that a hunter might have with his equine vassal and one that a lowly commoner might have with his draft horse. In mocking the powerful identification and intense admiration Don Quixote feels for Rocinante (whom he compares to the mount of the medieval hero of the Reconquista, El Cid), Cervantes did not deride the genuine aristocrat's attachment to his horse but rather upheld the firm boundaries between creatures that belong to the noble hunt and those that belong to plebeian husbandry.[114] Quixote's confusion of one for the other is proof of utter madness, and his squire Sancho's insistence on riding an ass rather than a horse reinforces the point. Fundamental to the difference between elite hunting and animal husbandry was the practices' relationship to social structure. Whereas ownership skewed toward the first two estates, the labor of husbandry belonged to the realm of commoners. Nobility and wealthy commoners who hoped to gain nobility disdained and eschewed hands-on involvement in husbandry. Those humans most in contact with such animals were considered degraded by these relationships.

~

THE TECHNOLOGIES OF husbandry could not and do not completely conceal the subjectivity of livestock. The incomplete suppression was due to the visibility of servant, vassal, and prey animals, whose subjectivity was fully recognized and often admired. The contradictions produced by different modes of interaction in Europe generated various kinds of cultural productions, perhaps most familiarly and vividly, the bull fight.[115] But we can also see how people in the medieval and early modern period grappled with the insistent subjectivity of nonhuman animals and the objectifying practices of livestock husbandry in their thinking about the Devil, his kingdom (Hell), and his minions (witches). The histories of demonology and witchcraft beliefs and of livestock husbandry are usually kept in separate silos, but they are intimately connected: the everyday work of peasants engaged in livestock became targets for clerics immersed in demonological theory that emphasized the animality of demons and the Devil. Conversely, depictions—in words and images—of Satan, demons, Hell, and witches revealed the pain inflicted on livestock animals. That the abject horror of livestock husbandry was addressed in inverted fantasies about Hell shows the power of this mode of interaction in limiting empathy for the suffering of nonhuman animals. The fact of such fantasies also suggests that husbandry was not able to fully efface the subjectivity of nonhuman animals.

European demonology changed in important ways during the premodern period. But one of the most significant continuities was the commitment to the zoomorphic qualities of demons, the Devil, and witches alike.[116] In his 1646 treatise on painting, the Sevillian artist and theorist Francisco Pacheco insisted that demons should be represented in the form of a snake, dragon, or vulture and added they could also appear in human form if they were "naked, ugly and dark with long ears, horns, the claws of eagles, and tails of snakes, as Michelangelo did in his celebrated [Last] Judgment."[117] One of the shifts in learned demonology was the relative demotion of multiple demons and simultaneous elevation of a singular Satan (a shift that took place in tandem with the demotion of angels and elevation of God).[118] The power of these images was such that they appeared in the dreams, visions, and hallucinations of people, as evidenced by the testimony of those questioned by inquisitors.[119]

The demonic was connected not just to animals but specifically to livestock husbandry, an aspect of demonology that has gone unnoticed but deserves particular emphasis. In Fra Angelico's "Last Judgment" (fig. 2.1), painted in a Florentine Church in the early fifteenth century, Hell becomes a place where people are subject to the same procedures they inflicted on animals during their lives. Similar visualizations are found in other paintings in the late medieval and early modern period, including the Cathedral in Salamanca. The notion of Hell as a livestock operation is even more explicit in Pieter Bruegel the Elder's *Triumph of Death* (1562–63) (fig. 2.2). People take the place of sheep; they are corralled with the same kinds of nets and ropes used by herders.[120] In another scene in the painting, Death is personified as a cowboy mounted on an emaciated nag, herding people into a slaughterhouse.

The scope of the Devil—and the role of the diabolical as a site for anxieties about livestock husbandry—expanded with the diabolization of

Figure 2.2   Pieter Bruegel the Elder (ca. 1525–69), *Triumph of Death,* ca. 1562, oil on panel, 117 × 162 cm., Museo del Prado, Madrid, P001393. Erich Lessing/Art Resource, NY.

witchcraft. Throughout the Middle Ages, there was a widespread belief that some people were skilled in magical arts and that some practiced those arts for good and others for bad. Among the bad were female peasants who thought they had magical capacities but were fooled by dream- or drug-induced states of fantasy that the Devil manipulated—both Augustine and Thomas Aquinas believed this to be true. In the fourteenth century, some clergymen—particularly the inquisitors combatting "heresy" in southern France—began to opine that witches received supernatural powers by pledging themselves in a "diabolical pact" with Satan. In conjunction with the growing power attributed to the Devil, these witches were credited with more power than they had been previously. Whereas earlier authorities believed that witches' ability to move through the air or turn themselves into animals was the result of drug-induced hallucinations (the "illusionist" position), a growing number of clerics and their lay followers began to believe that witches could actually accomplish such feats (the "realist" position).[121] One of the most influential texts espousing the hardline view was the *Malleus maleficarum* (The Witches Hammer), published in 1486 by the German-speaking Dominican inquisitors Heinrich Kraemer (Institor) and Jakob Sprenger.

Belief in this kind of witchcraft was inextricably entangled with the view that the Devil sought to have his own diabolical Church—one in which the most sacred rites of Christianity were imitated, inverted, and profaned.[122] Instead of priests administering the sacraments of the Holy Church, witches acted as Satan's disciples. In works such as Dominican Johannes Nider's *Formicarius* (1435–37) and the *Malleus maleficarum,* as well as those by lesser known inquisitors, ideas found in classical and biblical texts commingled with the beliefs and practices of local communities in which livestock husbandry was ubiquitous. In this context, the tropes of the witches' sabbath took their most comprehensive form. In the influential texts of the fifteenth century, the animality of witchcraft, like the Devil himself, was omnipresent. Under cover of night, witches, following the goddess Diana, rode on animals to worship the Devil, who usually assumed the form of a "black animal," such as a bear or ram, but most often as a "he-goat, sometimes as a dog or monkey, never in human form," to quote an inquisitor describing crimes of sorcerers in Arras.[123] They pledged allegiance to the Devil, often kissing his anus and "submitting to his pleasure" or that of his demons (who could take the form of attractive men and women as well as animals). Sometimes they traveled incognito, taking on the shape of animals, or turned others into animals. Kraemer and Sprenger's *Malleus maleficarum* included chapters entitled, "Whether sorceresses work on humans by turning them into the shapes of beasts through the art of conjuring," and another, "The methods by which [sorceresses] change humans into the shapes of wild beasts."[124] They recounted that in antiquity, Circe "turned the companions of Ulysses into wild beasts" and "that certain tavern girls turned their customers into beasts of burden."[125] They befriended animals and had special powers over them. Consequently, for these clerics, witches were similar to animals (in their enjoyment of sex and ability to fly), knowledgeable about animals (in their ability to supernaturally harm or help animals), proximate to animals (in their proclivity engaging in bestiality and their tendency to befriend them), and sometimes even became animals. And, like the Devil, they inverted the logic of livestock husbandry by engaging in cannibalism. They kidnapped children and ate them or dug up bodies at cemeteries to remove their hearts for use in their brews. Nider explained that the Swiss witches boiled children in cauldrons, using the solid parts for ointments and filling vessels with their liquids.

Church authorities in Iberia hewed to the illusionist position longer than many of their peers to the north. However, in the 1520s, there was a seismic shift. There were reports of an outbreak of witchcraft in the valleys around Roncal and Salazar (or Roncal-Erronkari), a Basque region in Navarre. The Basque country had long been seen as a site of heretical activity because of the linguistic difference, because Christianity had arrived later there than in other parts of the Iberian Peninsula, because of its remoteness, and because it had only recently been incorporated into the Habsburg-Spanish polity. Officials of the Navarrese Inquisition, based in Calahorra, began to investigate at the end of 1524. And in 1525, an itinerant magistrate spent eight months investigating and arresting witches, resulting in the execution (burning at the stake) of approximately forty.[126]

As is so often the case with persecuted groups in the early modern period, it is difficult to know what people themselves thought and believed in this region because the surviving sources were produced by outsiders.[127] As in earlier (and later) witch hunts, the surviving documents make it difficult to distinguish those elements that were part of the local "popular belief" and those that were the projections of devil-obsessed judges and inquisitors. Moreover, by the late fifteenth and early sixteenth centuries, popular belief and inquisitorial discourse had already become somewhat commingled after decades of preaching, confession, and interrogation by demonologically oriented clerics.[128] With that in mind, some hazy outlines of local beliefs and practices are suggested: Witches were powerful, athletic women who could jump out of high windows "that would kill a cat."[129] Many were forthright in their sexuality, such as the "respectable and married woman" who told her confessor about her frequent dreams of riding with other women through the air on mules until they arrived to the coast where a "man joined with her and she felt an intense pleasure in the act."[130] It was believed that some were able to ride through the air with Diana "and that they transformed into other beings." It may be that some men and women gathered with each other at parties that commenced at midnight on Fridays, where they drank wine and ate bread; engaged in sexual activity, perhaps even orgies; and interacted with a large goat, or perhaps someone dressed in goat skins.[131] In explaining why witches were more likely to be women than men, an investigating cleric wrote that "old women fulfilled their appetites" with the Devil "when men no longer paid them any attention" and that this was the case even more with younger women who "were inclined and given towards the vice of the flesh."[132] Some of them were known as *xorguino* or *sorguina*, which a cleric explained "comes from the word *sortilego* (sorcerer)." They were sometimes blamed by their neighbors for the inexplicable deaths of children and live-stock and for intensely destructive hailstorms.[133] There were men and women who were famous for their power to heal both people and animals. They sometimes healed the latter by sprinkling them with or permitting them to drink holy water from baptismal fonts.[134] (This practice "is not bad," one of the investigating clerics remarked, recalling that St. Francis cured his ani-mals "with great devotion.") There were those who used "certain words to control or enchant wolves or foxes" to keep them from harming their do-mestic animals, and those who excommunicated locusts who were ravaging crops.[135] It was also believed that some made lethal potions from the bodies of toads and the hearts of babies to kill people and domestic animals.[136]

The witch hunts inspired a number of publications, including Martín de Castañega's 1529 *Tratado de las supersticiones y hechizerias y vanos conjuros y abusiones y otras cosas* (Treatise on superstitions and sorceries and vain con-jurations and abuses and other things).[137] Along with Pedro de Ciruelo's treatise on "superstitions" and "sorcery," published the same year, it marks a shift in Iberia toward the "diabolization" of witchcraft.[138] Castañega, a member of the Franciscan order, drew from his experiences investigating the Basque communities under suspicion ("I knew and saw some [witches] burn").[139] Among his close colleagues and fellow witch hunters were the Franciscan friars Juan de Zummárraga and Andrés de Olmos who would later lead "idolatry" extirpation campaigns in central Mexico in the 1530s.[140] Castañega's treatise analgamates the observations produced by the investi-gations into Basque localities with tropes of clerical discourse that had developed over the preceding centuries. Specifically, its rendition of dia-bolical witchcraft highlights the animality of witches and the abject horror of livestock husbandry. Like the fifteenth-century authors who influenced him, Castañega asserted that the fundamental modus operandi of the Devil was to imitate and pervert the Church by inverting its rituals, ex-plaining that there were "two churches in the world, one that is Catholic and the other that is diabolical," and that "just as there are sacraments in the catholic church, there are *execramentos* in the diabolical church."[141] Many of those inversions involved suspicious interactions with animals. Whereas church sacraments used things related to "life and human conservation," such as water, bread, and wine, diabolical *execramentos* used "unguents and powders made of rare things from animals and birds that are found with great difficulty."[142]

Witches' sexual behavior emphasized their animality; "the venereal acts and flesh works" were "used by the devil to deceive," and "the carnal acts" afforded the Devil greater power.[143] In addition to behaving like animals, witches had special relationships with them, and were thought to share some of their qualities. Castañega wrote that the Devil could make "his minsters" in the "form that he wants without taking or removing anything from the true substance, quantity or shape that the person has," offering the fox, goat, and bird as likely alter egos.[144] Finally, the Devil's witches emulated him in his diet, it was alleged, seeking to suck the blood of babies and children. The cleric wrote that in antiquity, "much human blood was spilled in the temple as if in that [the Devil] delighted." "Now his ministers do the same," wrote Castañega of his own day, singling out "the idolaters of New Spain" and those Devil's "ministers," the witches in the Basque country who "who suck human blood as a delicacy."[145]

Immanent in Castañega's text—and in the previous works of Nider, Kraemer, and Sprenger—was the view that certain kinds of cross-species relationships were not just suspicious but indicative of diabolism. In particular, evidence of animal subjectivity—the very thing suppressed by the technologies of livestock husbandry—provoked concern. What was implicit in the work of Castañega and Ciruelo became explicit in an influential work of Martín del Río, a learned Jesuit, who wrote on magic and witchcraft in the late sixteenth century. He suggested that obvious evidence of animal subjectivity might be indicative of diabolical interference. Like the authors who preceded him, he sought to explain the various ways that the Devil could transform people into animals. "Sometimes (and this is a fact derived from a number of people's confessions)," wrote the cleric, "he wraps actual people very tightly in genuine animal skins, and in this case he gives them a wolf pelt which they are supposed to keep hidden in the hollow of a tree," while at other times the Devil "manufactures from air the likeness of an animal, surrounding the magicians with it, and builds the copy round each part of their body, fitting head to head, mouth to mouth, belly to belly, foot to foot, and arm to arm." Del Río proceeded, logically, to chapters that addressed the questions of whether magic practitioners can "make animals speak . . . and understand what animals are saying" and whether an "evil spirit" can "bestow upon animals the ability to reason." Although del Río did not see all indications of animal subjectivity (e.g., desire, communication, and reason) to be necessarily indicative of demonic agency, he clearly thought they were anomalies that required explanation.[146] The diabolization of animal subjectivity reveals both the attempt to suppress livestock's personhood and the impossibility of totally suppressing this personhood. An animal who manifested intelligence, consciousness, and other qualities was actually a person impersonating an animal or the Devil endowing an animal with rational faculties. If an animal seemed to display too many traits that resembled human traits, then demonology explained that it was a human in animal form, something made possible by the diabolically enhanced powers of a witch or the illusion of such.[147]

Fears about demons, witches, and Hell suggest that the alienating effects of livestock husbandry were not totalizing. The common denominator between the troublemaking snake in Eden, the slaughterhouse corral inside the gates of Hell, and the people imprisoned within the bodies of animals is the violation of the boundaries that were supposed to demarcate humans from other kinds of animals. The snake of Genesis and formerly human animals are characterized by an excess of personhood and subjectivity. Likewise, by depicting Hell as a slaughterhouse operation whose victims are humans, artists illustrated that nonhuman animals experiencing these torments might also be subjects. The devil, his Hell, and his minions made visible the subjectivity of animals whose existence the technologies of husbandry rendered almost, but not quite, invisible. There were spaces and moments when livestock animals' subjectivity expressed itself in ways that humans could not help but notice.

3

Conquering Animals

*A*s soon as he made landfall in the Caribbean on October 12, 1492, Christopher Columbus had animals on his mind. He scanned the new landscape and found "no animal of any kind . . . except parrots." Four days later, while still in the Bahamas, he took stock of beautiful fish, a whale, lizards, a snake, and more parrots, but the absence of livestock animals was worthy of note: "I saw neither sheep nor goats nor any other beast."[1] By December, when Columbus and his crew had begun to explore the island they named Hispaniola, this absence had become an imagined conquering presence: "oxen would be able to plow" the biggest mountain, and "livestock of all kinds" could graze the valleys.[2] As Columbus populated the landscape in his mind's eye, contemplation led to action. On his second voyage to the Americas in autumn 1493, the Admiral of the Ocean Sea brought a veritable ark. The passengers on the seventeen ships included horses, dogs, cows, goats, sheep, pigs, and chickens, as well as approximately 1,200 humans.[3]

As Columbus's observations and actions demonstrate, European colonizers understood that nonhuman animals were at the center of their colonial enterprise. Since Alfred Crosby published *The Columbian Exchange* in 1972, scholars have used his framework to investigate the way that horses, sheep, and cattle, and other domesticated animals, helped make colonial America.[4] Although the model of "Columbian Exchange" has dominated environmental histories of colonial America, it has outlived its usefulness and has even contributed to confusion about the relationship between interspecies interactions and settler colonialism. One problem built into Crosby's "Columbian Exchange" is the colonialist and progressivist conception of a hierarchy of civilizations. Specifically, the model assumes that Native Americans remained in the "Stone Age" because they had only domesticated a "few" species and these "were not very impressive."[5] Another shortcoming with the "Columbian Exchange" framework is its tendency to collapse separate phenomena into a singular "biotic" exchange. If we instead pay attention to modes of interaction, the different kinds of roles played by vassal animals and livestock come into greater focus: we see the former deployed in campaigns of terror, and the latter as essential for the "slow violence" of on-going wealth extraction.[6] Moreover, it becomes clear that it wasn't that domesticated animals didn't enable Europeans to "conquer" Native America.[7] Proliferating numbers of pigs, cows, sheep, and even chickens were so harmful to Indigenous communities not because these animals "invaded." Their harm instead derived from colonizers' establishment of livestock husbandry as a mode of interaction. Indeed, Indigenous people who encountered domesticated animals outside of settler-colonial spaces had no difficulty managing these hungry and fertile newcomers in beneficial ways. Indigenous people were not harmed by trampling hooves and munching mouths. Instead, human colonizers who mobilized livestock husbandry deprived Indigenous people of their labor, their land, and, not infrequently, their lives.

Extractivism can replace the "Columbian Exchange" as a framework to make sense of the colossally destructive and enduring changes colonizers wrought in their use of domestic animals, and of the inseparability of settler-colonialism and ecological transformation. The word evokes the "extraction" of nonrenewable mineral wealth, above all mining for silver and gold in the colonial context. But it has also been theorized in a more expansive way. I find Maristella Svampa's definition of "neo-extractivism" generative: "the phenomena of recolonization of nature and of dispossession, visible in the process of land grabbing, the destruction of territories, and the displacement of populations." In addition, the work of Vera Candiani (water), Molly Warsh (pearls), Gabriel de Avilez Rocha (fisheries), Daviken Studnicki-Gizbert (mining), and Anne Berg (waste) have helped me to think about extractivism in a capacious way.[8] While some might find it odd to discuss settler colonists' use of animals in terms of extractivism, livestock husbandry proved to be the most wide-ranging and enduring of all extractive industries. Livestock husbandry was a connective tissue for diverse colonial institutions that contributed to the dispossession of Indigenous labor, land, and, often, life. These included slavery, *encomienda* (the system that entitled conquistadores to tribute and labor from Indigenous subjects), and *estancias* (Crown-authorized ranches).

~

THE CORE FEATURES of equine and canine deployment that emerged within the first decade of European colonization set the course for centuries.[9] The island of Hispaniola—with a preconquest population of at least 100,000—was under Spanish control within ten years after Columbus first made landfall, despite a comparatively miniscule number of human invaders. When Europeans returned in autumn 1493 and discovered that all thirty-nine soldiers left at a hastily built fort at La Navidad were dead, they mobilized horses for violent assaults. The conquistadores began to terrorize Native inhabitants in the countryside surrounding their second settlement, Isabela, on Hispaniola—particularly those in Cibao, where gold had been found—to force them to provide food, labor, and sex. When the depredations led to counterattacks from the island's inhabitants, these reprisals became the rationale for Columbus's decision to authorize all-out war in March 1495 in the Vega Real, the inaugural large-scale campaign against an Indigenous polity in the Americas. Aware that Native Taino inhabitants of Hispaniola were unwilling to tolerate the escalating attacks by individuals and groups of colonists, Columbus decided that it was necessary to lay waste and "subjugate by the force of arms." "For this effect," wrote Bartolomé de Las Casas, Columbus "selected 200 Spaniards, the healthiest ones (because many were sick and weak), footsoldiers and twenty on horseback, with many crossbows, muskets, lances and swords, and the other most terrible and frightful weapon for the Indians, after the horses, and this was twenty greyhound catch-dogs (*lebreles de presa*), whom after being set loose or told 'sic him') in one hour each one tore 100 Indians into pieces."[10] The outcome of the battle was a horrendous defeat for the Taino: "Those on horseback fell a great multitude of people, and the rest were torn to pieces by dogs and swords." Five hundred of the survivors "were condemned as slaves." This marked the beginning of the systematization of New World slavery.[11]

Horses and dogs were essential not only for military campaigns but also for maintaining control of the conquered population and forcing them to labor under brutally oppressive conditions—processes that imperial officials and colonists referred to as "subjugation" and "pacification." The animals were necessary to "keep the island and its people subjugated" in Columbus's words. Writing to the Crown, he elaborated that he could maintain control on Hispaniola with only 300 men, as "having 20 or 30 on horseback is enough to tear everyone into pieces . . . because with one dog that a Spaniard brought with him, he went as securely as if he were with 50 or 100 Christians."[12] The "success" of the conquest, according to Columbus, lay largely with the assistance provided by nonhuman conquerors: "Look what the horses, on the one hand, and the *lebreles* (dogs), on the other, gave," he was said to have remarked, "all of them, tracking and killing, wrought such ravages, that in little time God was served to give us this victory, with so many now dead and others captured and destroyed."[13] As a consequence of this kind of warfare and terror, during those first ten years, the cost to Native life and culture on Hispaniola was incomprehensibly enormous. Thousands were massacred or enslaved. Rape and torture were wanton. Many died because of forced relocation and destruction of agriculture. Even as the conditions of warfare changed over the succeeding centuries, horses and dogs remained important. These strategies would soon be adopted and developed by Spain's and Portugal's rival colonial powers—above all, by British, French, and later US settlers in the maintenance of slave regimes.[14]

Although conquistadores disagreed about many things, one thing that they—and Indigenous combatants—agreed on was the paramount importance of equestrian technology in warfare. Bartolomé de Las Casas, who participated in warfare against Taino people on Hispaniola in the early sixteenth century before dedicating himself to criticizing conquistadores, wrote at length about its potency: "For people who have never seen them and imagine that horse and man are one animal . . . It is certain that only 10 on horseback, at least in this island (and in all the other parts of the Indies, if they are not high mountains), it is sufficient to wreck and sink them."[15] He wrote of the dismay of Native leaders who saw their "subjects and vassals" suffering from "such outrageous affronts and injustices" and that it was "the horses which was the thing that made them afraid."[16] Galeotto Cei, a Florentine-born conquistador who participated (and, by his own account, pillaged, raped, enslaved, and massacred Native peoples) in the settlement of Tocuyo (Venezuela) and various campaigns in Tierra Firme (the coasts of Colombia and Venezuela) and New Granada from 1544 to 1553, was unequivocal that equestrian warfare was the Europeans' most important military technology. "The fear which all of the Indians have for horses one cannot believe, nor even understand," he explained, "even our Indians of service (i.e., victims of the Indigenous slave trade), who brush them and care for them, they make tremble." "Without horses," he wrote, "it would not have ever been possible to conquer this land."[17]

Europeans in the fifteenth and sixteenth centuries believed in the particular efficacy of their horses partly because they faced combatants who did not have them. Cavalry attacks were based on techniques and technologies perfected in Eurasia over millennia and deployed in the centuries of armed conflict between and among Christians and Muslims in Iberia. Iberian Christians considered themselves to belong to the lesser equestrian culture— Christian soldiers envied the horses of their Muslim opponents, seeking to acquire them whenever possible, and admired to the point of imitation the riding and training techniques of Muslim equestrians.[18]

European conquistadores tried to leverage the asymmetry to the utmost. Cortés, sharing the conviction of Spanish soldiers in the Caribbean that horses terrified Indigenous Americans, was quick to try to augment what he saw as a significant tactical advantage. In spring 1519, Cortés combined a show of intimidation and generosity in his effort to secure food and military assistance in a meeting with Chontal Maya leaders. He told a group of his soldiers including Bernal Díaz del Castillo, who is responsible for the recollection, "Do you know, gentlemen, I believe it is the horses that the Indians are most frightened of. They probably think that it is just they and the canon that they have been fighting, and I've thought of a way of confirming their belief."[19] He outlined a plan whereby one of the mares, who had recently given birth, would be placed nearby the stallion of "Ortiz the musician"; the stallion "is very randy, and we can let him get a sniff of her." Accordingly, the horses were placed in such a way that when the "horse began to paw at the ground and neigh and create an uproar, looking all the time towards the Indians and the place from which the scent of the mare came," it had the effect of making the visiting leaders think "that he was roaring at them and were terrified once more." And "when Cortés observed their terror he rose from his seat, went over to the horse, and told two orderlies to lead him away. He then informed the Indians that he had told the beast not to be angry, since they were friendly and had come to make peace."[20] The charade had the desired result, for the next day the visiting dignitaries brought them beautiful objects of precious metals, textiles, and, critically, enslaved women, among whom figured Malintzin (known to the Spanish as Doña Marina) who would prove important as a translator and negotiator as Cortés and his forces moved through the Aztec Empire. Pleased with these outcomes, Cortés and other conquistadores orchestrated similar theatrical displays in Mesoamerica, and beyond, that featured equine power and, no less importantly, their human masters' ability to deploy and constrain it.[21]

Leaders of military expeditions from Columbus onward routinely requested the importation of horses and cavalry, indicating that horses were considered to be among their most important weapons.[22] Díaz del Castillo wrote that some of the men who responded to Cortés's invitation to accompany him on a military campaign in 1519 to the newly discovered lands north of Cuba "sold their farms to buy arms and horses." At the time, horses and Black slaves were "worth their weight in gold," and the reason "why we had had no more horses"—there were only fifteen or sixteen in the initial enterprise—"was that there were none to be bought."[23] Diego de Almagro, who led a campaign to Chile in 1535, paid between 1,500 and 1,400 *castellanos* for a horse when an enslaved human cost 2,000. Cortés offered the pithy aside in one of his letters to Charles V that "stallions and mares gave us our lives"—a sentiment that he also manifested in his constant efforts to procure more of them.[24]

Horses and equestrian technologies helped Spanish warriors massacre people and win battles *before* epidemic diseases decimated Indigenous communities.[25] Moreover, these early dramatic military victories disrupted food supply and rent the social and political fabric, thereby making communities susceptible to disease. Likewise, the advantages of equestrian warfare were among the factors that made it possible for Europeans to recruit Native allies. When Cortés arrived with Cempolan allies in the town of Zautla (Puebla), the local rulers inquired of the latter about their unusual and intimidating accessories: guns, dogs, and horses. The Cempolans—eager to intimidate those in Zautla because of regional rivalries—boasted that their new allies' "horses ran like deer and could catch anyone we told them to chase."[26]

The fact that horses were seen as enabling military victories did not mean that soldiers and colonists—or those avoiding them—were blind to their weaknesses, as Las Casas was also quick to note.[27] If the advantages of horses for the military and colonial enterprises in the Americas were immediately clear, so too were their limitations. The ability of horses to assist in battle was largely dependent on attacks taking place on optimal terrain: open, dry, level ground. The Europeans' ability to exploit the gold in the Cibao region was hindered because of the rough ground, making it "very difficult to walk, especially for the horses . . . because they couldn't handle the height and harshness of the mountains."[28] Realizing this, when the Taino decided that the best strategy was to avoid rather than ally or fight with European intruders, they moved to regions they knew to be inaccessible to horses. Similar strategies were pursued on the mainland. Las Casas, writing several decades after these events, generalized that not only in Hispaniola but also "in all the other parts of the Indies," horses were effective only "if there are not high mountains" or other topographical conditions that challenged horses' ability to move quickly.[29]

The corollary to the notion that horses were fundamental to European military success was that in regions where horses could not be used effectively, Indigenous people had the advantage. The Italian conquistador Cei wrote that, without horses, "the Indians have little respect for the Christians," and "in the countries where horses cannot be used . . . they resist valiantly and cannot be conquered."[30] He described the way that horses were a major factor—if not *the* major factor—in determining resettlement patterns of Indigenous groups avoiding conquest in the wake of European incursions: "In all of those regions in which one can ride horses, the Indians flee more than a mile, without imagining or considering the distance between them, even when there are forests, cliffs, rivers and brush in the middle to cross." "These *llanos* are very depopulated," he wrote of the savannahs around Tocuyo, explaining that because of "malignancy and necessity the Christians had destroyed everything, taking the youngest Indians, male and female, leaving the old ones to die"; the survivors "retreated to the mountains, where they cannot be easily captured by horses, as in the *llanos*." Even allied groups modified their living patterns with horses in mind. Europeans were dependent on Caquetio allies in their efforts to settle Tierra Firme, but it was a strained relationship given the colonists' tendency to pillage, rape, and massacre even those whom they favored. Cei noted that even though they were "friends of the Christians," it was still considered wise to "be among them in groups of ten or twelve, armed and mounted on horses." In turn the Caquetio "for fear of us they had retreated to the mountains for their lodging," although they continued to sow crops in the *llanos*.[31] Accounts of military campaigns are replete with references to terrain that horses could not access, including not only steep, mountainous areas but also swamps, thickly wooded landscapes, and savannahs where grasses were too high. Further study is needed of how horses' limitations became a major factor in patterns of Indigenous diaspora after 1492. At the same time, the tactical advantages afforded by horses also diminished as Indigenous warriors devised strategies—ranging from the use of elaborate traps to the much-feared arrows laced with lethal poison—to counter them, strategies as novel to the Europeans as their horses were to Native peoples.[32] Before too long, Europeans faced Indigenous combatants who were themselves equestrians.[33]

The significant limitations of equestrian warfare were important in restricting the expansion of Europeans into Indigenous America. Based on their experiences with dramatic losses of human and equine life in many failed campaigns, and their own sense of vulnerability when they could not use horses, Spanish conquistadors and caudillos often avoided areas where their horses trod with difficulty. Accordingly, although Spanish invaders had subjugated a significant number of communities by the end of the sixteenth century, many more communities remained free of European rule, in part because they were located in places where horses fared poorly.

Because of these limitations, some historians believe that contemporaries have overestimated the importance of horses in the colonizers' military victories.[34] However, such reassessments might have swung the pendulum too far in the other direction. It is true that horses did not make European conquistadores invincible or guarantee them victory, and other factors such as Indigenous alliances and Old World diseases, as well as the limitations of equestrian military tactics, were extremely important. But horses themselves were a factor in enabling Europeans to make military alliances and to terrorize populations to a degree that made them vulnerable to the shocks of epidemic disease.

~

ALTHOUGH CONQUISTADORES AND chroniclers celebrated dogs and horses equally, the roles of these nonhuman conquerors and colonizers differed significantly. Dogs were weaponized in the Americas as they were not in European warfare. Canines were employed as sentries and guard dogs in Europe but were not mobilized to systematically attack people. The use of dogs to fight in battles and terrorize civilian populations was, Las Casas wrote, "a diabolical invention" inaugurated by European settler-colonists in the Western Hemisphere.

It may be that Columbus already imagined this repurposing of hunting dogs before he arranged his second voyage, but what seems undeniable is that dogs were among those who boarded the fleet for the Americas in 1493 to perform the same duties as they would back in Europe. Some were brought to herd and guard the livestock imported to the colonies, but above all, dogs were collaborators in hunts—and hunt they did.[35] When Bartolomé Columbus, the acting governor in his brother's absence, ordered a group of conquistadores to keep watch over a failing gold mine in circumstances of extreme food scarcity, he left ten men and "an excellent hunting dog for chasing the game."[36] The rabbit-like *hutia* and the *cori* (guinea pig) were hunted much in the manner that Europeans tracked and killed rabbits and hares "with the greyhounds and *galgos* and bloodhounds and even the *gozques* and *podencos* that were brought from Spain," wrote the conquistador Gonzalo Fernández de Oviedo.[37] Writing in the 1530s and 1540s, Oviedo mentioned seven different kinds of hunting dogs—*lebrel, sabueso, galgo, gozque, podenco, ventor, mastín*—various specialists in tracking, harassing, and killing different kinds of prey.[38] The first recorded incident of dogs attacking Indigenous people took place in Jamaica in May 1494.[39] The following year, twenty dogs were deployed in the battle at Vega Real, an occurrence celebrated in the frontispiece of Antonio de Herrera y Tordesilla's chronicle of conquest (1601).[40]

The use of dogs in conquering and exploiting Indigenous communities soon became systematized, and defenders and critics alike attested to their value in warfare and terror campaigns. Bartolomé de las Casas wrote that on Hispaniola "a Spaniard doesn't go anywhere without bringing a dog—the fierce dogs [who are] well indoctrinated in eviscerating and tearing to pieces the Indians."[41] Such was their value that the war dogs were treated like human soldiers. Oviedo described how the practice of rewarding soldiers a certain "portion" of gold for their service had been extended to dogs, or rather their masters. Leoncico or Leoncillo (Little Lion), with a reddish coat, black snout, and many scars, was the progeny of another famous war dog (Becerrilo) and the lead dog in Vasco Núñez de Balboa's campaigns on the South Sea (Pacific) of Panama in 1513. He earned a lot of gold as a result. "As an eyewitness," wrote Oviedo, "I know that he deserved, at times, more than 500 *castellanos* that he won, in the parts that were given in the campaigns."[42]

The pervasiveness of hunting as an activity might help explain the origins of the mobilization of "war dogs" in the subjugation campaigns waged against the Indigenous humans of the Americas. The notion that dogs trained to hunt nonhuman animals were repurposed to pursue and kill Indigenous peoples is suggested in some of the earliest accounts of the practice. Apropos of a military campaign on the continent in the early sixteenth century, the chronicler Pietro Martire d'Anghiera, or Peter Martyr, wrote that the "dogs that they had brought with them for hunting as watch-dogs" had become "of great use to them in fighting with the Indians," describing how "these animals throw themselves with fury on the armed natives as if they were timid deer."[43] Sources are vague about the types of breeds used for lethal warfare; some scholars propose they were of the *mastín* type used to protect livestock from wolves, while others think they must have been the *alanos* and *lebreles* (greyhounds) that collaborated in hunts.[44]

These canine vassals were used in many ways. In his *De orbe novo* (Of the new world), based on letters and conversations with a number of veteran conquistadores, Martyr explained to a European audience the power of canine assaults. "Astonishing things are said of these dogs the Spaniards take into battle," he wrote, so "it often happens that there is no need of swords or javelins to rout the enemy. A command is given to these dogs who form the vanguard, and the natives at the mere sight of these formidable Molossonians; and the unaccustomed sound of their baying, break their ranks and flee as [though] horrified and stupefied by some unheard of prodigy." Martyr noted, however, that they were less effective against Carib peoples, "who are braver and understand more about war" and, with poisoned arrows, shot "with the rapidity of lightning . . . [and] kill the dogs in great numbers."[45]

Not only did dogs kill, intimidate, and disperse Indigenous combatants in offensive assaults, they were also required to terrorize and pacify noncombatants. In "pacification" campaigns, dogs assisted Europeans in their effort either to enslave Native populations or to make them into subjects who would provision or labor for them in extractive industries such as mining and pearl harvesting. That dogs were key tools in efforts to force civilian populations to cooperate with onerous colonial demands involving labor and tribute is demonstrated by the fact that many recorded incidents of *aperreamiento* ("dogging" or a lethal canine mauling) involved allied rather than enemy Indigenous groups. In 1518, the royal official Alonso de Zuazo wrote to Charles V about a notorious *aperreamiento* that took place in the context of gold mining. A captain serving under Vasco Núñez de Balboa on Tierra Firme, having been generously treated by a cacique with "roasted venison made on their barbeques, and many cooked and roasted turkeys, and fish grill," took the cacique hostage. He threatened "that he would *aperrerar* him, which means thrown to the dogs and torn into pieces." So the cacique brought him gold, but the captain thought it was too little and demanded more, and so more was brought but still not enough. Even though the cacique insisted that "he had no more and if he had he would give it to him," the captain killed him with molten iron "and dogged (*aperreo*) the others with great cruelty." He inflicted the same treatment on neighboring caciques, so that they were "robbed and dogged and burned and [others] chained and enslaved."[46]

Las Casas and others' efforts to end the practice of *aperreamiento* had some effect. The Crown issued edicts repeatedly demanding that conquistadores curtail—although not end—the practice. In 1541, for instance, a royal edict commanded that Franciso Pizarro, then governor of Peru, address the "matter of *perros carniceros* (butchering dogs) that the Spanish feed with Indians, who the dogs attack and injure where they find them" and ordered that "the dogs of this type are to be killed" but then added "once [the dogs] are no longer necessary."[47] The final part of the decree indicates that this was a royal sanction as much as it was a ban on the practice. A few years later, the Crown began promulgating royal edicts that outlawed the use of "perros bravos."[48] The repetition of these edicts in different locations in Spanish settlements attests to both the pervasiveness of the practice and the limitations of royal power to reform it.

European chroniclers' assessment that dogs were among the most feared invaders is corroborated by Indigenous perspectives on the conquest. Dogs occupied a central place in Nahuas's memories of conquest. Describing what Moctezuma's spies reported to their ruler about the recent arrivals in Veracruz, they gave considerable attention to their weapons in these recollections. They began with a description of guns, then discussed "all [the] iron [that] was their war array," and concluded with a description of their canines: "Their dogs were very large. They had ears folded over: great dragging jowls. They had fiery eyes—blazing eyes: they had yellow eyes—fiery yellow eyes. They had thin flanks—flanks with ribs showing. They had gaunt stomachs. They were very tall. They were nervous; they went about panting, with tongues hanging. They were spotted like jaguars; they were varicolored. And when Moctezuma so heard, he was much terrified. It as if he had fainted away."[49] A Nahua-made manuscript (c. 1560) depicted an Indigenous ruler in Cholula being punished by *aperreamiento* (fig. 3.1).[50]

Examining the role of vassal animals in the pacification of Indigenous Americans illuminates the historical conditions that made conquest possible and helps transcend generalizations about "dehumanization" of the "other." Oviedo's treatment of canine combatants reveals the mindset of early sixteenth-century conquistador communities. Tellingly, in his 1535 *Historia general*, his celebration of these dogs does not appear in the section on "terrestrial animals" or even in his chapter devoted to "domesticated mongrel dogs" of the Taíno.[51] Instead, they are set apart and referred to in the same way as human warriors—either en masse, in reference to certain campaigns, or individually commemorated. In so doing, Oviedo elevated dogs, along with horses, above other animals, including many humans. In a chapter in which he recalled the most notable conquistadores, he introduced his hagiographic treatment of dogs:

Figure 3.1   Manuscrito del aperreamiento, Bibliothèque nationale de France, Département des Manuscrits, Mexicain 374. Bibliothèque nationale de France.

For not only should men be praised and rewarded according to their virtues and merits, but also (as those who have written well have taught us) brute animals . . . because brute animals distinguish themselves and demonstrate virtues through their actions, and even surpass men in their good acts and deeds.[52]

The elevated status of war dogs reflected the European hunting tradition that ennobled dogs, horses, and raptors who participated in the hunt as vassal animals. Just as European hunting dogs were rewarded with part of the "share" of the prey, so were war dogs compensated with some of the plunder.

If the exportation of hunting and warfare to the Americas augmented the subject status of dogs and horses, it also contributed to an intersubjective framework of proto-racial categories that desubjectified Indigenous people and those of African descent. The *Aviso de caçadores y de caça* (Counsel for Hunting and Hunters) explained that hunting was "the subjection of birds and wild beasts in the way of war."[53] But this formula was reversed in the Americas: rather than approaching prey animals as enemies, the human enemies—the Indigenous inhabitants and, subsequently, rebellious Black slaves—were approached as prey. It became commonplace to refer to *montería de indios* (the hunt of Indians).

~

FOR ALL OF the grotesque violence inflicted by weaponized vassal animals, livestock husbandry played an even more important role in the conquest and subjugation of Indigenous Americans over the long term. From the earliest days of European settlement on Hispaniola, colonizers actively used livestock husbandry as a tool to impose a colonial regime predicated on the forceful alienation of bodies, lands, and resources of people of Indigenous and African descent.[54] This continued throughout the colonial period and long after it, into the present, as today's Indigenous peoples struggle to protect their lands and lives from extractivist regimes. If the Americas were transformed by the imposition of European modes of interaction, the reverse was also true: husbandry, as with hunting, was changed as a result of its transplantation to the Americas. Livestock husbandry became the linchpin for the dispossession of non-European labor and life.

Since the publication of Crosby's *Columbian Exchange,* the story of the explosion of European livestock has largely been told as the unintended consequence of Old World animals encountering "virgin" pastures. Contemporaries took note of this as well. They were amazed by how European animals flourished in American habitats. Martyr wrote of the impressive size of animals in Darien (Panama), with oxen resembling elephants and pigs the size of mules. In 1511, he recorded that "horses, pigs, and oxen grow rapidly and become larger than their sizes" in Europe.[55] Settlers in Hispaniola reported that the meat tasted different: because the "grass grows as high as the crops . . . the cattle become extraordinarily fat, but their flesh loses its flavor; their muscles become flabby," whereas for "pigs it is just the contrary; for they are healthy and of an agreeable flavor. This is due doubtless to certain of the island's fruits they greedily devour." And the livestock grew in number. In 1518, an official wrote that Hispaniola was "a land where livestock abounds in marvelous multiplication." With some exaggeration, he elaborated: "The calf still nursing gets pregnant; the cows commonly give birth to two and to three many times and everything grows, nothing dies."[56] Colonists were impressed not only with the population increase but also with the size of the animals themselves.[57] By the middle of the sixteenth century, millions of quadrupeds descended from cows, sheep, pigs, goats, and horses domesticated in Europe over millennia roamed the Americas. They were concentrated in the plains of the Antilles, on the coasts and highland plateaus in South America, and in Central America and Mexico. Oviedo wrote in the mid-sixteenth century that the population of cows had come "to now be innumerable," leading men to own herds of sizes rarely seen in Europe, reaching 10,000, or even that "of the widow Diego Solano who has 18,000 or 20,000" on Hispaniola, or that of the Bishop of Venezuela "who has 25,000 or more."[58] The cattle on Cortés's two ranches on the Tehuantepec Isthmus numbered more than twelve thousand in the mid-sixteenth century.[59] It is estimated that in the Valle de Mezquital (60 kilometers north of Mexico City) that the sheep population quadrupled in the late 1550s to 2 million in 1565.[60] A French visitor to the Central Highlands in the late sixteenth century was amazed by the "great, level plains stretching endlessly and everywhere covered with an infinite number of cattle," with individual owners possessing herds of ten thousand or more.[61] When Jesuit missionaries arrived in Brazil in 1549, seventeen years after the colony of Rio had been founded, cows, sheep, pigs, goats, and chickens were rapidly proliferating. By the late sixteenth century, herds of one thousand heads were not uncommon.[62]

The spike in new animal populations had ripple effects in local ecology. Feral dogs contributed to the decimation of the rodent population in the Greater Antilles; by the 1520s, several species were extinct on Hispaniola.[63] Some native animals welcomed the new arrivals—European livestock were tasty treats for jaguars, coyotes, and possum, among other predators. Oviedo marveled at the latter's ravenousness and propensity for beheading and sucking out the blood of chickens: "One of these *churchas* beheaded 14 chickens of mine in one night in Darien, and the truth is even I would not wish so many birds for my pleasure in one day."[64] Colonial authorities in late sixteenth-century Caracas wrote of "dangerous" jaguars that "attack all kind of large and small livestock and tend to kill Indians, going to look for them in their houses."[65] There were increasing numbers of attacks on people by jaguars as a consequence of their frequent proximity to livestock.[66] The presence of the new animals also influenced vegetative change. Trees appeared where savannahs once were. The enormous population of pigs on Hispaniola who delighted in the *jobo* tree created new forests where there were once savannahs by spreading the tree's seeds across the islands in their feces. Cows also contributed to a new arboreal landscape of guava trees.[67]

But the framework of Columbian Exchange, with its emphasis on the autonomous impact of new "biota," has shortcomings. At its most extreme, some scholars seem to suggest that "conservationist" colonists improved an ecology that had suffered at the hands of Indigenous people whose agriculture had "disrupt[ed] vegetation cover" and "test[ed] environmental thresholds." They argue that by the time the Spanish arrived, "high population densities were already testing environmental thresholds, with native agriculture periodically disrupting vegetation cover and causing the erosion of soil from hillside fields. As Indigenous populations declined in a series of sixteenth-century epidemics, vegetation invaded abandoned fields and restabilized slopes. Only then did the Spanish flocks and herds expand; through the use of conservationist management practices . . . overgrazing rarely occurred. Livestock, from that perspective remains innocent of any immediate, widespread degradational effect on the environment."[68] But even the more measured work of Crosby himself has a problem: It views the growth in ungulates and the contraction of Native human population as independent variables, two different and separate aspects of the Columbian Exchange. Moreover, Crosby and many of the historians who have adopted his framework view ecological changes as a universal phenomenon, rather than recognizing their divergent impact on different social groups. It is an error to see the transformations in American ecosystems—including the spread of exogenous species and extinction of native species—as an inevitable result of biology. It is necessary to put the role of proliferating European livestock within a framework of extractivism.

The role of livestock husbandry in the colonial development of the island of Hispaniola, the first region that saw European settlements, was paradigmatic. The much-desired extraction of precious metals from the Americas could not have happened without livestock, and because mines were quickly exhausted in many places, livestock often replaced mining as an extractivist enterprise and fueled others, such as slave-trading and cash crops such as sugar.

The successful adaptation of livestock husbandry in the "Indias occidentales" did not seem inevitable in the fifteenth century. Initially, scarcity reigned. Transporting quadrupeds across the Atlantic was no easy feat: the body of water between Andalusia and the Canary islands became known as the "gulf of yeguas" because of the numbers of mares who died en route and were thrown overboard. It has been estimated that only half of the cows who boarded ships on the eastern side of the Atlantic arrived alive in the Caribbean and that the mortality rate for sheep making the transatlantic voyage was even worse, ranging between 50 and 75 percent.[69] Once in the Caribbean, it was initially difficult to acclimatize sheep and cows to the tropics, despite the efforts of early colonizers, with Columbus's son prominent among them. As one report noted, "In all of the land the grass is so high that from this the dew kills" the sheep.[70] The first arrivals of cattle hardly did better.[71] Nevertheless, by 1498, observers on Hispaniola said the porcine population was "without number," although their populations also suffered huge losses periodically due to the depredations of increasing numbers of feral dogs as well as hurricanes.[72] By the time the new governor Nicólas de Ovando arrived in 1502 (along with 2,500 human settlers, including then-conquistador Bartolomé de Las Casas, and a number of cows and horses from Andalusia and pigs and goats from the Canary Islands), he found an embryonic colonial society that primarily featured the symbiotic relationship between mining and livestock husbandry. Settlers on the north and south coasts were engaging in commercial pig and chicken husbandry to support the mining projects in the center of the islands. The success story began with pigs and chickens, given their capacity to flourish in a variety of environments and their rapid reproductive rates.[73] In the first decade of the sixteenth century, the majority of settlers who did not live in mining regions specialized in raising pigs.[74] Ovando himself invested: by the end of his term in 1509 (recalled for his treatment of Indigenous people), he owned six pig ranches throughout the island.[75]

A new phase began when livestock changed from being auxiliary to mining to being the focus of extractivist commodification itself. Rather than supporting the extractive industry of mining, livestock supported the extractive industry of plunder, slaving, and expeditions. This shift took place on Hispaniola at the end of the first decade of the sixteenth century, after gold deposits were exhausted and the Indigenous population declined catastrophically, which compelled settlers to leave the island in search of new lands to plunder. By the second decade, livestock was the chief commodity of Hispaniola. Bovine and equine ranching and even some sheep raising in the southeast part of the island had started to become profitable. Hispaniola transitioned from an importer to an exporter of livestock. Even horses were being imported into Spain, and the Antilles supplied pigs for the Spanish campaigns on the mainland.[76] Between 1511 and 1520, the ranchers of Hispaniola found new markets in incipient colonies.[77] They traded pigs, pork, and horses for enslaved Indigenous people and mineral treasure captured in neighboring islands and the mainland—first in the Greater Antilles, followed by those in New Spain and Central America, then Tierra Firme, and finally those in the interior of Peru and Colombia. Just the act of assembling an expedition for conquest was enough to raise the price of livestock, "simply because of the expectation of obtaining the means of exchange—bullion and slaves—with which the advance guard paid for [them]," writes historian Justo Lucas del Río Moreno.[78]

The 1530s began a new phase of livestock extractivism on Hispaniola. Cattle themselves—or rather their hides, exported to Spain—were the chief commodity of the island. Pork and livestock exports remained important through the mid-sixteenth century, but hides were the primary export through the late sixteenth century in Hispaniola. By the middle of the 1550s, the island was exporting more than thirty thousand hides annually.[79] As in Europe, the largest herds were concentrated in the hands of a relatively small number of owners. The most prosperous and powerful colonizers were heavily invested in ranching, which is unsurprising given the power and influence of sheep and cattle herd owners in Castile. In Hispaniola, one of the first large-scale ranchers was Christopher Columbus's son, Diego. In 1526, before leaving for the conquest of Santa Marta (Colombia), Rodrigo de Bastidas had at least nine herds of cattle, amounting to more than eight thousand heads, and several sheep herds.[80] Over the long term, ranching was a better bet than mining; with the perspective of hindsight, Las Casas observed about the early settlers in Hispaniola that it was "those who invested in ranching, rather than mining gold, who became rich"—a viewpoint supported by modern historians.[81] A symbiotic relationship soon developed between cattle ranching and sugar plantations, as profits from hides were used to capitalize the expensive machinery for sugar, and animals themselves provided much of the necessary energy to run it.

Interregional exports for Hispaniola ended, predictably, when livestock were sufficiently established in these other regions—by the early 1520s for the Greater Antilles, mid-1530s for New Spain and Central America, and 1540s for Tierra Firme and, because of the protracted wars of conquest, not until the 1560s for the interior of Peru and Colombia.[82] Different timelines and ecological diversity, however, did not preclude commonalities; broad patterns unite the development of livestock husbandry across far-flung regions in the Americas. In successive decades and centuries throughout the Americas, each new generation of conquistador-settlers refined their strategies based on previous experiences and structures that underlay surging profits and the proliferation of animals in Hispaniola.

Based on the early experience with scarcity, it became not only customary but often mandatory for conquistadores to bring chickens, pigs, and sometimes cows and sheep on their initial campaigns. Because of pigs' adaptability to diet and environment, they were the most important in the early stages of settlement. It was standard for every military expedition in the sixteenth century to include pigs.[83] Cei described in vivid detail the role played by livestock in the base camps for military expeditions. He participated in a 1545 campaign that resulted in the foundation of Tocuyo; the humans included about ninety Europeans and more than one thousand enslaved Indigenous people. Their entourage included more than two hundred horses and some hunting dogs, along with two hundred sheep, eighty cows, fifty goats, and "some donkeys and pigs." Cei and other conquistadores raised pigs, cows, sheep, and chickens in base camp, both because they couldn't imagine an existence without regular consumption of their flesh, as well as cheese and eggs, and because they could sell them at handsome profits to other settlers, given their scarcity; the capital was used to fund subsequent expeditions. He reflected on the discordance between his elite upbringing and his engagement in livestock labor. Despite his initial disgust at treating the open sores of his animals, "I learned to medicate them and care for them" for "there is no better teacher than necessity."[84] This was no easy task—the animals suffered open sores and were beset by worms, and not a few were eaten by jaguars or drowned in unsuccessful river crossings by canoe.[85]

Three decades of experience in the Caribbean and Tierra Firme influenced how conquistadores established subsequent settlements. Despite local diversity, "the influence of livestock culture affected all of colonial society," writes Río Moreno, "and in many regions came to be more important and enduring than mining itself."[86] Conquistadores sometimes established ranches even before military conquests were completed and full political control established. Cattle predominated as the lucrative livestock in tropical regions; sheep dominated in the cooler, high-altitude zones; and goats and pigs prevailed on the dry plains of Peru.[87] In Brazil, cattle from Cape Verde arrived alongside the sugar plantations established under Alfonso de Sousa in 1532.[88] Likewise, conquistadores exported to successive settlements in the Americas the extractivist regime organized around mining and, later, monocultural export crops such as sugar that depended on livestock. The mines established in Peru and New Spain depended entirely on livestock. Equipment relied on tallow, finished sheepskins held mercury, enslaved laborers were fed pig flesh and clothed with coarse wool fabrics, equines transported the ore, and equine saddles were made out of cattle hides. There was no mining without extensive livestock operations.

As José Miranda noted many years ago, "with the exception of mining no other industry exercised greater attraction for the Spaniards than livestock husbandry" in New Spain.[89] The conquistador Gregorio Villalobos brought the first cattle to New Spain in 1521.[90] Cortés immediately seized for himself vast amounts of land for his "Marquesado." He chose the areas that would become his *encomienda* largely based on their suitability for ranching operations and appropriated for himself the power to grant ranching permissions to other conquistadores, before it was taken over by the *cabildo* (city council) in Mexico City. In 1536, the Viceroyalty took charge of the system that had been developed in the Caribbean for issuing the *mercedes* (favors, or grants) for *estancias* (ranches), although they were often merely confirming the land grabs of Spanish conquistadores. In the 1540s, wrote François Chevalier, "cattle spread like waves of a rising tide over the northern plains and prairies of the warm zones along the coasts."[91] In Toluca Valley, by 1555, there were sixty *estancias* and more than 150,000 cows and horses belonging, in the words of a royal official, to the "right and might, as well as few of His Majesty's officials," some of whom owned herds numbering in the tens of thousands. The biggest phase of livestock expansion came in the late sixteenth and early seventeenth centuries, when the mining boom fed the demand for meat (pigs and cows), tallow (cows), and textiles (sheep). It has been estimated that by 1620, cattle grants in New Spain authorized settlers to land covering 1,770 square leagues for their cows and 991 square leagues for their sheep and goats.[92]

The European export of livestock husbandry had been on the minds of the conquistadores from the moment their imaginations converted "empty" savannahs into pasture. This vision emerged out of how livestock husbandry had developed over thousands of years in Eurasia, but its export to colonial America transformed husbandry into an extractivist industry. Its extractivist character can be seen in its necropolitical waste of animal and vegetative life and in the interrelated dispossession of Indigenous labor, land, and life. Nowhere can this be seen more clearly than in the place of meat in the diet of subjugated populations and colonists themselves. Newcomers from Europe were shocked by the low price of meat afforded by the exponential increase of herd animals and that it had become the staple for both enslaved and slave-owning people. The production of gold that took place in the central districts of Cibao and San Cristobal depended on the labor of Indigenous laborers who were fed pig flesh.[93] This was also the case of the Taino laborers forced to work in the Spanish *encomienda* system: it was estimated that a town of three hundred Taino might consume a minimum of five hundred pigs annually during this decade; if we conservatively estimate that the average weight of the pig was two hundred pounds, the annual per capita consumption of pork exceeded three hundred pounds a year.

Cattle ranching also exemplifies the transformation of livestock husbandry into an extractivist regime. Because their skins brought great profits in Europe, and the population was too small to consume the meat, many cattle (especially those who were feral) were killed in pasture rather than in a slaughterhouse. The novel tool used to kill bovines in the Americas epitomizes the extractivist, necropolitical logic of the colonial cattle industry. The *desjarretadera* was a long pole with a crescent-shaped blade on the end that allowed cowboys to *desjarretar* (hamstring)—that is, to slice the muscle of a cow's or bull's back leg—without dismounting. The cowboy could then kill the crumpled animal in place, skin and collect the hide, and leave the flesh to rot or for vultures to eat. The tool was banned, although largely ineffectively, from at least 1528 on Hispaniola and 1574 in New Spain because it was blamed for the decimation of herds and allowed cowboys to traffic illegally in hides.[94] The wanton destruction of cows afforded by this tool shocked newcomers from Europe as much as the profligate consumption of meat. It marked a significant divergence from the European regime, where husbandry was built around the making of meat and the careful use of all parts of the animal's body.

If one side of extractivist livestock husbandry was profligate killing of nonhuman animals, the other side was dispossession of Indigenous and Black labor, land, and, in many cases, life.[95] In the European settlements of America, and in major contrast to medieval and early modern Europe, livestock husbandry was entangled with colonial institutions of slavery and *encomienda*. Implemented simultaneously, the two mechanisms of coercive labor turned Indigenous people into pig-eating miners in the sixteenth century. A significant proportion of the humans—herders, ranch workers, and, later, textile laborers—who turned quadrupeds into fungible commodities or who harnessed their labor power to turn other matter into fungible commodities were either enslaved or were required to give their labor as part of an *encomienda* system.

The twin coercive labor regimes of slavery and *encomienda* were mechanisms for extracting the Indigenous labor of livestock husbandry in New Spain, as they had been in the Caribbean and South America. In the early days, livestock animals were mostly tended by enslaved and free Black herders and field hands, but enslaved Indigenous people also labored in ranches, as they had in the Caribbean.[96] When describing a sale of an *estancia* in 1541, the notary described its contents as including 1,500 sheep, 300 pigs, and "three Indian slave women," named as Isabel, Catalina, and Francisca, and an enslaved boy, Juanillo.[97] Despite Crown edicts prohibiting Indigenous slavery, some were still sold along with property in the seventeenth century. For instance, the bill of sale for a small hacienda in Tepeaca included not only mares and plows but also nineteen Indigenous laborers.[98]

The reinvented institution of *encomienda* (originally developed over centuries as part of the process of "Reconquista" in mainland Iberia) was another mechanism of dispossession in which livestock were central. Although, in principle, the people who were *encomendado* (entrusted) to the conquistadores were supposed to be able to keep enough of their own labor to maintain their agrarian system, in reality they were forced to move to mining regions to the detriment of their crops. In turn, these enslaved laborers (whether in *encomienda* or slavery) were also forced to labor in livestock operations: the subjugated Indigenous populations were not just eating pigs; they were also forced to care for them. Although the chief swineherds were of European or African descent, they were assisted by many laborers. Las Casas claimed that two of the richest *encomenderos* of the island required the fifty thousand people whose labor they claimed to raise pigs. While that number is doubtless an exaggeration, the notion that many people were required to dedicate themselves to pig husbandry was not.[99]

As they had done in the Caribbean, colonizers in New Spain forced Indigenous subjects to participate in animal husbandry through the labor required by *encomienda*.[100] Laws on the books prohibited this practice, but they were not enforced. In these milieus, the *encomienda* laborers worked alongside enslaved laborers, both of Indigenous and African descent, as well as free blacks, as revealed in the account books from Hernán Cortés's extensive ranching operations in the Tehuantepec Isthmus.[101] According to a midcentury report, twenty-two communities under the control of *encomenderos* were required to provide ranching assistance.[102] In Tepeque (Oaxaca), for instance, subjects were forced to "guard some cows and mares of the said Pedro Nieto."[103]

Livestock husbandry also facilitated dispossession through tribute. Secular and clerical institutions alike required Native populations to give them goods produced by or for livestock husbandry, in the case of *encomienda*, or from their proceeds, in the case of tithes as well as *encomienda*. In New Spain, conquistadores were thrilled that it had been customary for commoners to give elites turkeys and quail as tribute—the former raised at home and the latter caught in the wild and kept in pens. In some respects, the demands that Indigenous subjects give the *encomenderos* and Crown officials a certain number of turkeys and sometimes quail could be understood as an extension of the pre-Hispanic system. However, litigation from the late 1520s and 1530s shows that the demands were much more onerous than what had been customary. The community of Huexotzinco, part of Cortés's *encomienda,* sued royal officials for demanding too much tribute. The pictorial document they submitted to the Crown showed that they were required to give 340 turkeys and 8,000 quail daily to royal officials.[104] As a result, witnesses were asked whether the officials demanded "more than ten thousand fanegas of maize and thirty thousand fowl and forty thousand quail and three hundred thousand eggs," along with slaves, chile, cotton textiles, and featherworks. Although witnesses did not corroborate that number—one of the Indigenous leaders, a man named as Baltasar, said that the community gave the officials six turkeys and six quail a day—the quantity involved was still clearly viewed as more than what was customary.[105] *Encomenderos* and royal officials soon demanded chickens in addition to native turkeys and quail as part of tribute.[106] When colonial officials reported on tribute given by communities in 1548–1550 in New Spain, they reported that 275 of the 908 communities surveyed were obligated to provision turkeys, quail, chickens, or some combination of these (this amount is almost certainly an undercount because some responses do not specify all forms of tribute and make mention of additional unspecified tributes).[107] Maize was often also levied for the purposes of fattening livestock.[108] The forty-person community of Calpan (Panuco), for instance, provided "no tribute except to sow a field and with the maize raise some pigs."[109]

Extraction of labor continued even after Indigenous slavery was curtailed and the *encomienda* reformed by the 1542 "New Laws." The *repartamiento* system required communities to donate a certain number of labor hours to individual Spaniards and to public work projects, and this labor included ranch work.[110] Even "free" Indigenous laborers were often working under conditions of such coercion that they approximated captivity.[111]

A new kind of institution, organized around dispossession of labor and livestock industry, emerged in New Spain. The *obrajes,* the weaving mills associated with flocks of sheep, depended on involuntary labor (fig. 3.2).[112] The bulk of the inexpensive coarse textiles in these mills were destined for clothing and hats intended for Indigenous people working in the mines. By 1571, there were more than eighty *obrajes* in New Spain.[113] The mechanisms for dispossession took on new forms in the *obraje.* They included the commissary store (later extended to the hacienda) whereby, in the words of the

Figure 3.2   A wool *obraje*, Codex Osuna, fol. 38v, ca. 1565. Biblioteca Nacional de España, MSS. FACS/999. Image from the collections of the Biblioteca Nacional de España.

viceroy in 1590, men and women purchased with credit, "shoes, hats, stockings and other objects at exorbitant prices; as a result, they never get out of debt and die like prisoners after spending 20 years or more in one weaving mill." Despite some half-hearted efforts by the Crown to curb these practices, officials soon saw that their interests as tax collectors were aligned with those of the hacienda and *obraje* owners. In the mid-seventeenth century, viceroys ruled in favor of the practice of detaining workers for four months who were unable to pay tribute.[114]

The Church was as invested in the development of husbandry as the *encomendero* class. On founding monasteries, the regular clergy—Franciscans and Dominicans—required members of the local Indigenous community to provide them with poultry (first turkeys, and soon chickens) and to help with their flocks of pigs, sheep, and goats. The enormous ranching enterprises founded by Jesuits and other orders in New Spain, the *llanos* of northern South America, and the savannahs of Gran Chaco, among other regions, required the local population and Black slaves to labor. Because tithes funded the secular clergy, these clerics advocated on behalf of ranchers.[115] Moreover, some religious orders became significant ranch owners in their own right. The Dominican Order brought sheep husbandry to the Mixteca Alta, and the sheep population of the Jesuits' enormous Hacienda St. Lucia numbered at least sixty thousand by 1602. By the midcentury, Indigenous subjects also had to pay tithes. Because certain goods—such as game and products of the forests—remained exempt from tithes, clergy had an incentive to encourage Indigenous communities to adopt European livestock, which were quintessentially tithable. They also took a portion of the share of the tribute that went to the *encomenderos.*

In Mesoamerica, the relationship between livestock husbandry and dispossession of land became particularly important. In contrast to those regions where inhabitants were labeled as *caribes* or cannibals, the Crown recognized Indigenous subjects' rights to property and self-governance in New Spain. Because outright theft of land was less permissible, settler colonists found loopholes to exploit. These enormous loopholes accommodated millions of pigs, cows, sheep, and even chickens, and facilitated the dispossession of Indigenous labor, life, and land. Spanish official Alonso de Zorita described in the mid-sixteenth century the effects of the expansion of settlers' ranching operations in Central Mexico:

> There is no ranch (*estancia*) nor land that has been given to Spaniards that is not in detriment to the *indios,* because of both the injuries that they receive as for having taken their lands and stretching their boundaries and made them work continually to protect their cultivated fields and even with that the livestock eat and destroy them. . . . In some towns that are very close to the fields of the Spanish, there isn't any [land] left for the Natives [*naturales*] where they can cultivate, and in other areas that are so close to ranches of *ganado mayor,* the harms they receive are so great that what little they sow is eaten and destroyed because the livestock roams without a guard, and it is not worth it to the natives to be working and losing night and day guarding the fields for which reason they suffer great necessity and hunger all of the year.[116]

Spanish, as well as Indigenous, observers understood that dispossession of Indigenous labor, land, and life was inseparable from the expansion of

European livestock and that colonialism, ecology, and demography were inextricable.

Already in 1520, Indigenous subjects of the Central Highlands and those living within Cortés's Marquesado were complaining to the Crown about the destructiveness of herd animals.[117] Across New Spain, Native communities used the legal system in an attempt to stop livestock from destroying their fields.[118] In Tlaxcala, local leaders were able to secure in 1535 a royal guarantee that their lands would be free of Spaniards and their animals. But after vigorous pushback from powerful settler ranching interests, a compromise was finally brokered in 1553: Cattle *estancias* were forbidden, and to be moved; laws requiring *estancias* to be a certain distance from agricultural lands were decreed; but nine ranches were allowed populations upwards of 51,000 sheep. As this initial guarantee suggests, Crown and royal officials tried to mitigate the effects of livestock on Indigenous agriculture; this policy aligned with their desire to prevent the *encomendero*-rancher class from becoming too powerful and to continue receiving tributes from Indigenous communities. Consequently, cattle ranching was banned from the Valley of Mexico and other densely populated regions in New Spain (cattle were more destructive than sheep because of their size), and sometimes Indigenous supplicants won legal battles against individual ranchers. And in 1560, the viceroy authorized subjects in New Spain to kill animals they encountered in their fields.[119] Nevertheless, royal officials ultimately could not resist the combined forces of wealthy ranchers and Mexico City ecclesiastics who benefited from tithes.[120] The overwhelming presence of these animals was powerfully depicted by the Indigenous artist who made the map to accompany the "Relación geográfica" for Hueytlalpan, in a cattle-intensive region (fig. 3.3). The accompanying text explained that "many livestock—sheep, goats, cows, and pigs—graze," and "it was "once very populated with great numbers of Indians" but "now there are very few."[121]

Faced with the invasions and destruction, Indigenous people in New Spain fought back in myriad, creative ways. Some fled into the mountains and stopped sowing, causing the price of maize to increase eightfold.[122] Others adapted their traditional methods of deterring wild animals from eating or trampling their fields to livestock.[123] A few responded by trying to eradicate the culpable, killing animals and even burning down ranches.[124] Residents of San Gregorio Acapulco, in the Xochimilco area, recalled in a late sixteenth-century Nahuatl chronicle how they reacted when a Spaniard set up a ranch, bringing his "goats, his sheep, his horses," and soon after "let

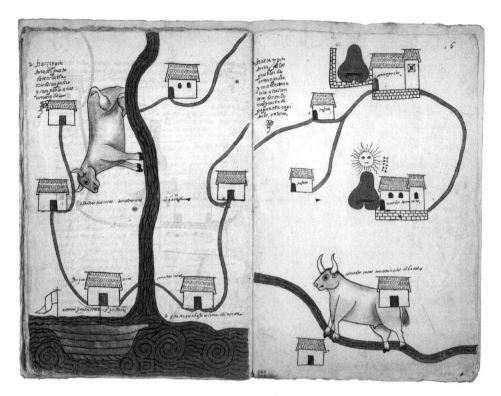

Figure 3.3   Maps of Tecolutla and Papantla de Olarte (Veracruz) in Relación Geográfica of Gueytlalpa (Hueytlalpan), 1581. Benson Latin American Collection, LLILAS Benson Latin American Studies and Collections, University of Texas at Austin.

his animals at liberty and so made suffer" their orchards, their nopal cactus, "ruining everything, causing damage." When they confronted the rancher, he "became enraged," and so they asked the friar Juan Luzano for permission to go to Mexico to file a lawsuit. But the friar said it would be better to return to the rancher and tell him to leave. This only further enraged the rancher. And so, according to their account, the friar told them "go make war . . . go and burn down his house . . . and we did." Guided by the friar, with a trumpet, "we all of the citizens of the town went to burn his *rancho*. We burned everything. Nothing was left, not even a *xicara* (gourd for drinking)." When another would-be rancher appeared with "his laborers and cattle" and promises that his fences would ensure "the animals won't cause damage," the friar warned him that "the same will happen to you"—and it did.[125] The numerous acts of sabotage and destruction, as indicated by the repeated laws increasing the punishment for sheep, cattle, and horse rustling, were other forms of violent resistance.[126]

It was not only that herd animals immediately jeopardized Indigenous peoples' ability to feed themselves by damaging or destroying their agriculture. They also led the way to "legal" land transfer. The trampling quadrupeds—cows and sheep, especially—inadvertently assisted with dispossession by converting *milpas* (fields of maize and other subsistence crops) into *baldíos* (commons). Fundamental to this process was the repurposing of the legal and agricultural concept of the *baldío*. In Spain, *baldíos* were spaces that were not owned by any individual but could be used by community members to find firewood, forage plants, and graze animals. In New Spain, Spanish ranchers laid claim to *baldíos* if they could show that they were lands not under cultivation and converted them into private property for their cattle and sheep. In practice, the sequence was often reversed: cows and sheep first occupied Indigenous lands, destroying fields, and thereafter colonists could claim that these lands were "vacant" and then lay claim to them. Those vacant lands were, by Spanish law, available for *estancias* (ranches) if one submitted a request for a land grant. In the words of Elinor Melville, "Spanish pastoralists treated the Central Highlands as an open commons, as they had in Spain. . . . The Spaniards viewed the introduction of domestic livestock into the agricultural lands of the population as a perfectly legal use of an unexploited resource, but they had to use force in order to establish their operations, and to gain and maintain access to pasture."[127] Charles Gibson estimated that in the Valley of Mexico, "considerably more than half of the agricultural and pastoral area of the Valley was officially transferred from Indian to Spanish hands during the first century after the conquest," also recognizing that "it was a universal tendency among Spaniards to encroach beyond the limits of the grants." In some places it reached even more extreme levels: "By the early 1560s Spanish intrusions in Tacuba had reached the point at which it could be said that Indians were barely able to settle around their church."[128]

The ultimate form of dispossession—death—is intimately related to these other forms of livestock-driven (and livestock-driving) dispossession. Colonizers reduced Indigenous peoples' abilities to grow their food by appropriating their labor, damaging their crops, and taking their land, and this damage to agriculture contributed substantially to the death of Indigenous populations. This disruption of food supply caused some to die outright in

famine and weakened the population as a whole such that epidemic outbreaks became much more lethal. The harms included not only the immediate effects of livestock that destroyed crops but also the coercive labor regimes that required a significant portion for Indigenous communities to
spend a significant portion of their time raising chickens, feeding pigs, and
tending sheep rather than tending their own crops. If we know well from our
own time that the lethality of disease outbreaks depends heavily on preexisting social conditions, then this vulnerability was even more extreme in the
case of Indigenous subjects, whose lives were structured by the institutions
of slavery, *encomienda*, missions, and *repartamiento*, among others. In well-
studied New Spain, current estimates suggest a death rate of 10 percent
during the wars of conquest in the 1520s, from the combined effects of epidemic disease and warfare. Although such death rates were calamitous, they
were less so than those that ravaged New Spain during outbreaks of epidemic disease in 1544–1545 and 1575–1576. Revising the so-called "virgin soil"
framework of epidemic disease, scholars such as Massimo Livi-Bacci have
argued that the role of new diseases in the "depopulation" of America has
been exaggerated and that the "demise of the Indians" was caused "not only
by the blind determination of germs but also [by] no less deadly human
forces."[129] Chief among these human forces was the extractivism that compounded the "blind determination" of disease. The catastrophic effects of the
epidemics that raged across New Spain in 1544–1545 and 1575–1576 have to be
considered within a context in which the food security of the Indigenous
population had been severely compromised by the social context that allowed for devastation by livestock. Together, dispossession of labor and land
compounded and contributed to the lethal effects of epidemic disease.

These effects were mutually reinforcing. Mortality made it easier for colonizers to seize land. Ranchers instrumentalized the damaged lands and lost
lives to usurp Indigenous lands under Spanish law by claiming "vacant"
fields as *baldíos*. Colonists also took possession of Indigenous lands through
sales. There are numerous examples of violent intimidation and more subtle
forms of fraud behind such sales. Moreover, those sales must be placed in the
context provided by Zorita—that the effort to maintain fields safe from livestock exhausted the ability of the diminished population, so that "selling"
land was often the most sensible route in these desperate circumstances. Entangled were the mass casualties of disease, damage from European livestock, and colonizers' usurpation of lands. This loss of life and, in turn, the
creation of *baldíos* became the basis on which Europeans were able to claim

ownership of Indigenous properties or induce members of communities in desperate straits to sell their lands

~

LIVESTOCK HUSBANDRY DEVELOPED over the course of millennia in Eurasia but was transformed radically in the context of American settler-colonialism. Livestock became an object of profligate consumption in its own right, leading to staggering numbers of dead pigs and cows, and had an essential role in other extractive industries—slave-trading, mining, and sugar production, above all. No less importantly, livestock was an instrument of dispossession in a variety of colonial institutions, ranging from slavery to *encomienda* to tithes. The theft of their labor and land, in turn, compounded the effects of epidemic disease and contributed to unfathomable numbers of Indigenous deaths. An emphasis on "biology" that is separate from society and culture has done a disservice to our understanding of colonialism in the Americas. Husbandry in the Americas became an extractivist mode of interaction that not only objectified nonhuman animals but also led to a casual attitude toward their killing and relied on dispossession of labor, land, and life of Indigenous and Black people.

PART II

Tame and Wild

4

Absorbing Prey

ince the fifteenth century, Europeans have been fascinated by stories of inter-species transformation told to them by Indigenous people in the Americas. In 1494, Christopher Columbus assigned a Catalan missionary, Ramón Pané, to investigate the "ceremonies and antiquities" of the inhabitants of the island of "Aiti."[1] Pané learned about cave-dwelling ancestors who, because they gazed at the sun, turned into *jobo* trees, known for their savory, bright yellow fruit. Another forebear became a bird when he stayed out fishing too long, and his morning song now plaintively announces his transformation. Still others, infants left by their mothers near a brook and asking to nurse, cried *toa, toa*—that is, "mama, mama"—and so turned into the frogs who "speak with that voice in springtime." In the early seventeenth century, another missionary learned from Kalinago on Dominica that "a fish of monstrous size that they called Akaiouman [who] is today still full of life in their river" was the ancestor who had founded the colony many years ago: "the nephews of his nephews" attempted to murder him out of "their extreme cruelty," but their poisoning resulted instead in his aquatic metamorphosis.[2] A Spanish Jesuit noted in the eighteenth century that the Saliva people in the Orinoco region understood themselves to be "children of the earth" because "in ancient times the earth sprouted men and women, in the way that it now sprouts thorns and thistles." Another wrote that the Achagua "believed themselves to be the children of either trees or rivers."[3]

These are highly mediated, imperfect renditions of stories that, in their original contexts, were often performed with song, dance, and costume or narrated by charismatic raconteurs skilled in pantomime.[4] Even in their decontextualized form, they reveal widespread, enduring sets of beliefs: Personhood or subjectivity is far from an exclusive property of humans but rather is characteristic of the animal, vegetable, and mineral world—indeed, of all phenomena. There is no anthropocentric distinction separating humans from other entities; instead, there are common capacities for desire, communication, and transformation, among other traits, that humans share with other organisms. Likewise, the stories show the mutability of phenomena—change rather than fixity is an essential attribute. The power of the sun apprehended through the gaze turns men into trees who bear yellow fruit. The plaintive cry of an exiled man is that of a bird who sings at dawn. The cries of a hungry baby who wants her mother are made by frogs. Seemingly disparate phenomena are related through shared materiality of movements, sounds, intentions, textures, and forms.

These stories cannot be separated from hunting and fishing practices—or rather, predation—that constituted a fundamental mode of interaction in South America and the Caribbean before and after 1492. Hunters, primarily men, killed fish, birds, and quadrupeds whose flesh supplemented diets that revolved around dishes made from manioc or maize (primarily tended by women), along with a plethora of other cultivated and foraged plants. Prey were not exclusively valued as food. Their pelts, feathers, teeth, and bones were turned into artifacts—feather headdresses and ornaments, teeth necklaces, bone flutes, among other things—that were cherished as potent vectors of the animals' essential attributes. The common denominator that united otherwise diverse kinds of hunting and fishing practices was the intersubjective relationships fostered between humans and other kinds of beings. Many techniques of predation led the hunter to take on attributes of the prey or auxiliary entities.

Like the European aristocratic hunt, predation required careful attention to the prey—a kind of attention that led to the recognition that human predator and nonhuman prey shared essential aspects of their subjectivity. Nevertheless, Indigenous predation and European hunting also diverged because people in the Caribbean and lowland South America developed techniques to pursue and kill prey without the assistance of dogs, raptors, or horses. Partly as a result of this less mediated form of hunting, the field of intersubjectivity in predation was more expansive. The hunter understood himself to be in relationship not only with animals but also with other agents, such as the plants used to make poisons and other weaponry to catch, immobilize, or kill prey.

I adopt the terminology of predation from anthropologists of the Amazon and especially their insight that it could lead to the "appropriation of the victim's capacities and incorporeal constituents" and that "predation in Amazonia is of necessity a social relation between subjects."[5] Whereas this anthropological tradition has taken warfare—particularly cannibalistic warfare—to be paradigmatic, the way that people related to nonhuman animals is, I suspect, even more important given that cannibalism was a much more restricted activity, and difficult, perhaps impossible, to disentangle from colonizers' efforts to legitimate their own brutal methods. By focusing on relationships of predation between humans and other kinds of animals, I explore in this chapter how Indigenous forms of hunting and fishing produced concepts of subjectivity. I connect the material practices of predation—observing, stalking, killing, eating, wearing, remembering—to Brazilian ethnographer Aparecida Vilaça's observation that for many Indigenous people in the Amazon "humanity is conceived of as a position, essentially transitory, which is continuously produced out of a wide universe of subjectivities that includes animals."[6]

Soldiers and missionaries who visited and lived among Indigenous communities in the early modern period left detailed descriptions of Indigenous predation.[7] This is hardly surprising given that these observers came from societies invested in hunting and, perhaps more important, were themselves dependent on the fish and game traded or stolen from Indigenous people, so they had an immediate, material interest in understanding the methods used to obtain them.[8] These outsiders lived among communities in the Greater and Lesser Antilles, on the coasts of mainland South America, along the tributaries of the Orinoco and Amazon rivers, and in the Gran Chaco region. To varying degrees, they learned Indigenous languages, including Arawak, Carib, and Tupi-Guarani, and Pano dialects. Although the sources span centuries, the outsiders' arrival was a common event in the histories of these diverse Indigenous peoples. On the one hand, these communities maintained considerable autonomy, ranging from those who possessed dominion in their lands to those who resided in Christian missions but who lived much as they had before, even practicing traditional spiritual activities, much to the missionaries' chagrin. On the other hand, the very presence of soldiers and priests meant that the communities were contending with the consequences of Europeans' colonial ambitions. Those consequences included new alliances and access to European trade goods, conversations with missionaries about the nature of divinity, incursions of livestock and epidemic diseases, and kidnappings, rapes, and massacres. For some groups, this liminal period came in the fifteenth century and lasted a few brief years—such was the case for the Taino in the Greater Antilles. For others, such as the Maiypure in the Orinoco Basin, it arrived in the eighteenth century and lasted decades. And for still others, it came even later.[9]

~

DESPITE PROFOUND COMMONALITIES in predation across Caribbean and South American communities, there was also considerable variety in the kinds of animals hunted and fished and the techniques used to track and kill them, reflecting both ecological diversity and cultural proclivities. In the Lesser Antilles, most prey were marine life, including manatees, sea turtles, and crabs.[10] A missionary noted in the seventeenth century that the Kalinago of Dominica had names for fifty-seven different fish, at least four varieties of turtles, and several different kinds of shellfish. In addition, he observed that they hunted birds and iguana and "chase Agouti [a guinea pig–like rodent] with the same avidity as the French do the hare."[11] On the mainland, some groups focused their predatorial pursuits on freshwater fish, finding their prey in "pools, streams, and swampy areas"; they used arrows, or "they take the lives of fish with roots of fruits that they scatter in the water." Other groups were "more pleased by the meat of terrestrial animals, deer, pigs [e.g., peccary], tapir, etc."[12] In the eighteenth century a missionary in the Orinoco region remarked that "every Nation of Indians likes one species of monkeys and abhors the others: the Achaguas lose themselves for the yellow monkeys they call Arbata. . . . The Tunevo Indians like very much the black monkeys. . . . The Jiraras, Ayricos, Betoyes, and other Nations abhor these two said species of Monkeys, and pursue and like the white monkeys."[13] Whereas the Guamo found caiman a pleasing dish, "this serpent . . . is greatly abhorred by the other Indians."[14]

In general, Indigenous men were expected to hunt, fish, or both; notions of masculinity and predation were intertwined. This was a significant difference from early modern Europe, where hunting was often the exclusive pursuit of the nobility and therefore not practiced by a majority of men. The association between masculinity and predation was reinforced throughout a male's lifetime. Jean de Léry, the French Protestant missionary who lived among the Brazilian Tupinamba in the mid-sixteenth century, wrote of customs around birth, noting that "if the child is a male, the father makes him a little wooden sword, a little bow, and little arrows feathered with parrot plumes" and "then, placing it all beside the infant, and kissing him, he will say to him, his face beaming, 'My son, when you come of age, be skilled in arms, strong, valiant, and warlike, so that you take vengeance on your enemies.'"[15] Antoine Biet, who lived in the French settlement of Cayenne in the mid-seventeenth century, marveled at the hunting skill of the Galibi Caribs, writing that "they are so adept at shooting with a bow that they never miss any animal, however little they are. I saw a child of 10 years hit a humming-bird from thirty feet, without missing."[16] Felipe Gilij, an Italian Jesuit, spent eighteen years in the Orinoco watershed, living for extended periods of time among Tamanaco and Maipure people who resided in his order's missions. He observed that little boys became "infatuated" with their fathers' arrows, and the fathers, "following their [son's] wish, make them small ones so they can become accustomed over time to the hunt. In this way they happily pass the days, killing little birds in the scrub and the forest."[17] The unknown French artist and writer—probably a soldier—who painted scenes of Indig-enous life throughout the Circum-Caribbean wrote of the imperative that a young man prove his prowess in hunting to find a spouse. The man showed "his reverence to the father and the daughter" by taking his "bow and arrows to hunt in the wood and having found his prey, takes it to the house" and "giving it to his beloved or sweetheart to please her and make her cook it."[18]

At death, men were buried with bows and arrows. "It's almost universal among those Nations of the Orinoco," wrote Jesuit priest José Gumilla, "to bury the deceased with his arms and jewelry or to burn them." He described how Saliva people eulogized deceased relatives or friends by exclaiming, "Oh, what an excellent fisherman we have lost!" or "Oh, an admirable archer has died! He never erred in his strike."[19] However, women also participated in hunting expeditions. Sometimes they accompanied men on long-distance hunting expeditions—as they did on war raids—to prepare meals and to take care of husbands and sons by painting them with *roucou* (or *bija*), the red ointment made of the *bixa orellano* fruit, that afforded protection against insects, sun, and malign spirits. In some instances, they participated directly in hunts, as in a husband-and-wife canoe endeavor to track and kill a man-atee, with "the wife serving as pilot," or on collective pig or peccary hunts.[20]

~

THE CONQUISTADOR GONZALO Fernández de Oviedo described how Taino men in Cuba and Jamaica hunted geese in their traditional manner.[21] The geese, with glistening black feathers, white on the chest and stomach, and bumps that "look like very true and fine corals" ringing their eyes, choose the lakes in Hispaniola as their temporary residence during yearly migrations, Oviedo explained. The hunters began by placing some "large, round and empty gourds" in the water. At first, the strange bobbing objects frightened the geese, causing them to fly away or stare at the gourds uneasily, "but when they see that they do them no harm, little by little they lose fear, and day by day, they are tamed by these gourds," and eventually they became "so unworried" that they "dare to climb on top of them, and so move from one part to another, according to the breeze that moves them." The hunters wait until they know "by their appearance and their movement and their use of the gourds" that the birds are "very confident and tame." Then one enters the lake, places one of the gourds over his head and submerges his body; watching the birds through a peephole, he gradually moves closer. When one of the birds decides to perch on top of the gourd encasing his head, the man begins to swim "without being heard or felt by the one who is on top of him or any other, because you have to understand," wrote the conquistador, "that the Indians have the greatest facility in swimming that you could imagine." The man moved away from the other birds when "it seems to him the right time," and then seized the bird's legs and plunged the animal beneath the water until they drowned. The hunters repeated the technique with other birds, explained Oviedo, because the others "do not leave nor get frightened" because they think that others "have dove under in order to catch some fish." The goose hunt as described by Oviedo is a guide to predation as an intersubjective practice. His account illuminates how the hunt was a process of transformation comprising observation, attraction, attack, and, finally, assimilation. All of these elements can be glimpsed in other accounts and, in aggregate, show not only how these processes worked in the hunt but also pervaded social relations more broadly.

In his account of the goose hunt, Oviedo showed the intensive multisensory attunement that predation required. This sensory awareness is what allowed the hunter to profoundly understand the habits (migration patterns), preoccupations (unfamiliar objects), and desires (comfortable perching spots) of these geese. The hunter also apprehended the environment intimately, noting the way the wind moved the water and how the breeze and waves moved the gourds. Other outsiders, likewise, were in awe of the multisensory attunement that allowed Indigenous hunters to find their way in the deep forest and to understand and track their prey. Matías Ruiz Blanco, who established missions among the Arawak-speaking Cumangoto in the early seventeenth century, remarked that they and neighboring groups in Píritu (Venezuela) "generally have very keen sight and great knack; even though they are enveloped in those forests, they never get lost."[22] Gilij, one of the Jesuits who lived among different Orinoco groups in the eighteenth century, remarked on Indigenous people's attentiveness to their surroundings, "very curious to observe every new animal that they encounter, noting minutely their color, their size, and their limbs in particular." He recalled, "'Look over there on that tree,' says one, 'there is a monkey,' and all dropping for a moment the oar, if they are traveling by the river, they became alert and without thinking, watch it." Gilij marveled at their ability to navigate terrain and remember the landscape with precise detail, referring to his own experiences being guided through forest and field and river:

> I want to talk of all their ways that they employ with great care to distinguish one part from another in the region, they know where they are, although it may be many years, without confusing anything. Take them with you where you want to go, on long rides, whether it is through dense brush, fields well covered with vegetation, high mountains. At the end of the day, they will know how to tell without fail, pointing with a hand directly where one has to return, 'from this way we came' and it can be said certainly (so great is their knowledge) that it is that one.

He also attempted to explain their methods: "They note very carefully the high mountains, and lacking those, big trees, and climbing these they observe with curious and attentive eyes all the country that for whatever side can be seen."[23]

That Indigenous people cultivated their capacity to attend to surroundings, along with the patience required to sit in silence and stillness, appears fleetingly but suggestively in the outsiders' accounts. Jean-Baptiste du Tertre, a French Dominican who lived among the Kalinago, recounted how they might "spend an entire half-day seated on the point of a boulder by a bank, their eyes fixed on the land or the sea, without sound or a single word," and tellingly noted that locals found it strange that the Europeans were always walking from one place to another, finding it difficult to remain still.[24] He also commented on ceremonies among people that began with shared silence, as well as its necessity when hunting manatee: "All keep a profound silence, because this animal has such subtle hearing, that a single word or the smallest lap of water against the canoe is enough to make it thwart the aspirations of the fishers."[25] This kind of deep, still observation was also an important technique in warfare. The Kalinago sent "their spies in the lands of their enemies, who carefully observe their behaviors and the times in which it is easiest to surprise them," according to one missionary.[26]

The outsiders also wrote about techniques and technologies used to lure prey. Oviedo's account depicts the Taino hunter manipulating the environment in such a way as to lure the prey to him—he knew how to transform the gourds from something frightening to something useful and even playful to the birds. Oviedo revealed how the techniques of attraction were full-body practices requiring the hunter to tread in water with imperceptible movement, to place the gourd in such a way as to not evoke the suspicions of nearby birds, and to manipulate gourds so as to make them an attractive landing pad for the migrating geese. Another technique of attraction much remarked on was the use of lures.[27] Cumangoto hunters in the seventeenth century carried some shells filled "with particular roots and herbs in order to have success in fishing" and others that look like "small black deer horns produced by a beetle that they bring to be successful in the hunt."[28] José Gumilla, a Jesuit who helped to establish missions along the Middle Orinoco River and its tributaries for more than thirty years before his death in 1750, described a "rare resin" called *mara,* employed by Guyaba, Tunebo, and Chiricoa hunters, that "doesn't have bad smell, although it is singular and intense." Upon seeing a deer, the hunters would "apply to their chest and parts of their arms with Mara; they observe the direction in which the wind blows, and putting themselves there, each one takes a branch to cover his face, carrying his bows and arrows: when the Deer perceive the smell of the Mara, they go in search, their heads held very high and entranced," allowing "the Indians to shoot them from safety." Gilij understood that there was a connection between these techniques and those used for seducing fellow humans. He complained about the Christian converts who persisted in using fragrant plants to mend relationships, unhappy that "they attribute to certain small fragrant roots, when wearing them, the power of conciliar the affection of the people they fear might be contrary to them," and disapproving of the men who used "special love roots that they believe capable of overtaking all hearts" that they wear "attached to a little bag or around their wrists." The missionary knew "a Guaiquire youth, who said he was Christian and was born among the Christians" who nonetheless "wore a necklace of these roots graciously strung." Confronting the young man and chastising him for wearing these roots instead of a rosary, the man replied immediately that they are used "in order to kill deer."[29] When applied to the body, fragrant resins turned the hunter—or lover—into a seductive lure for his prey. These connections were made explicit, too, in stories recorded in later periods that likened the relationship between hunter and prey to that of courtship.[30]

Oviedo was far from the only outsider to take note of Indigenous hunters' ability to "imitate animals with great exactness."[31] Mimetic practice based on knowing how prey communicated or moved and a hunter's ability to adopt attributes of his prey was another form of attraction. Achagua hunters along the Orinoco knew when and where tapirs left the river to eat young grass and so they "placed themselves in that same grass and they know how to imitate well the sound of a tapir." Gumilla described a hunter who intervened in a conversation between two tapirs, succeeding in luring—and killing—them both through his mimicry.[32] The missionary also described how hunters in the area hunted wild turkeys, remarking that the "Indians imitate their song with such exactness that [the birds] go running from all parts" and arriving to his "hiding spot," behind branches, the hunter is able to shoot them with his arrows, and "even when one hen falls, others come, having heard again the mimicry."[33] Francisco Figueroa, a Jesuit who resided in the western Amazon in the late eighteenth century, described a certain kind of snake who was expert in imitating the sounds of "some bearded reddish monkeys." He added that the "Indians use this call in order to attract to these and other species of monkeys and birds in order to hunt them, and to a kind of toad that they eat and even to tigers in order to fool them."[34]

These methods of mimesis required the hunter to transform himself, to take on the attributes of the animal he was hunting, learning how to move, speak, and even smell in ways that made the hunter alluring. Alternatively— or often simultaneously—the hunter might immerse himself in its environment, as did the goose trappers in the Antilles or the deer hunters described above. Kalinago children simulated pleasing sounds to attract a red-throated, swallow-like bird. They moved long, pliable branches "with all of their force, to the right and to the left . . . and these animals listening to the sound these branches made blowing the air," arrived, "flying freely, and so they [the children] could kill them."[35] The traps used on the mainland to capture peccary, deer, armadillo, and other mammals can be understood as based on a similar logic, as were the fishnets used extensively across the region.[36] The hunters needed to be extremely knowledgeable about the animals' feeding and movement habits to situate traps. They also knew how to build the devices so that they blended seamlessly with the environment.

As with hunting and human seduction techniques, mimesis was an intersubjective practice that transcended the species divide. Gilij commented on the pleasure that Orinocans took in mimicking others, noting that an Indigenous man "would never forget the appearance" of a person, even if they only met once, and could, much later, "return dressed or painted in whatever strange manner, and immediately, without vacillating [the observer] would say 'this is the one that I met as a child. I recognize his eyes, his nose, his way of walking and his voice.'" The Italian Jesuit described how they had fun mimicking the speech of the missionaries, so well "that you would believe that he was him himself." The observational-mimetic capacity infused interactions in the realms of humans and nonhumans alike. Mimicking another person— effectively imitating their sounds, gestures, and styles—could be considered an expression of affection and friendship. It was also relevant to warfare— the strategy of infiltrating the habitat of prey extended to human enemies. European colonizers across the centuries were quick to invidiously compare the stealthy warfare tactics of Indigenous warriors to the battlefield style of European warfare, contrasting putative cowardice and bravery. However, the effectiveness of the "ambushes, false withdrawals, nocturnal assaults" was evident in the great fear they inspired in these same observers.[37] Tertre directly linked the Kalinago's observational and espionage tactics described to practices of infiltration and ambush during warfare, writing that "having arrived at the enemies' land, they will not attack directly . . . but they will hide along a river or some deserted islands, where the other Savages their enemies tend not to go."[38]

Oviedo's account of goose predation also illustrated how Indigenous hunters entered into a relationship not only with animal prey but also with other elements in the surroundings. The hunter's merger with the gourds illustrates a broader phenomenon of the hunters' approach toward vegetative elements within predation. This can be seen through the outsiders' discussion of hunting weaponry in which wooden spears, for instance, were understood as having their own agency.[39] These conceptions of vegetative agency also filter into the descriptions of the plant-based poisons that colonists admired and feared.[40] Hunters applied the compound to arrows and spears to kill birds and mammals, a practice that notoriously extended to humans in warfare in some regions. Fish in ponds or enclosed pools in rivers could be killed or stunned so they could be easily speared or grasped.[41] The ingredients varied by region, but many included potent varieties of the *Styrchos* plant family.

Gumilla devoted an entire chapter to the potent *curare,* expanding on the observations of earlier chroniclers.[42] He described how in the Orinoco Basin, only the Caverres community "retains the secret, and manufacture" of the *curare* and traded it to "other Nations" directly or by third parties, "selling it in little pots or bottles of clay . . . holding no more than four ounces of that venom."[43] He explained that the most potent ingredient came from a certain brown-colored root, known as either *curare* or *bejuco,* that was difficult to find: "It always is hidden, we could say, afraid to show its occult malignity, and so that it could hide itself even more, the Author of Nature appointed it not in the common earth of the rest of plants, but rather in the corrupt and rotten seat of those lakes that don't have any outlet." The root was washed, cut into pieces, pounded, put in large pots, and cooked over a low flame.

The poison was not understood as inert matter but rather as an active participant in the process. When Gumilla imbued the poison with a certain "animacy," such as the notion that *curare* root might "hide itself" and "its malignant secrets," he may have been inadvertently reflecting notions of animacy. Indigenous attributions of animacy to weapons are manifest in stories that explain the origins of arrows, poison, and other weapons. In the nineteenth century the English missionary William Brett learned how the *haiarri* root came to be, and many ethnographers that followed recorded similar stories about the origins of the poison.[44] There was an old man who often caught fish in the river. He brought his son with him, and wherever the boy swam, the fish would die. But after they cooked the fish, they could eat the fish without harm. The fish, tired of losing their friends and relatives, decided to kill the boy. They waited until he was sunning on a log and then he was attacked by a group of spiny fish, the deadly stingray inflicting the fatal wound. The father carried his dying son through the forest. As the boy's blood seeped into the ground, the boy told his father to look for the plants that would grow in those places. Those plants became the *haiarri* root, which "washed after bruising, in pools and small streams, makes the fishes our prey."

By the seventeenth century, certain groups, such as Caribs who allied with Dutch settlers, were making systematic use of guns in warfare. Some Indigenous people started to use European firearms to kill nonhuman prey as well.[45] Yet other Indigenous hunters explicitly viewed firearms as inferior to *curare* in hunting. The Enlightenment naturalist Alexander von Humboldt, guided by missionaries during his tour of the Orinoco basin, described an exchange he had with an Indigenous man renowned for making potent *curare*. Humboldt wrote: "'I know,' said [the man] 'that the whites have the secret of making soap and manufacturing that black powder which has the defect of making a noise when used in killing animals. The curare, which we prepare from father to son, is superior to anything you can make. . . . It is the juice of an herb that kills silently, without any one knowing when the stroke comes.'"[46] Even through Humboldt's patronizing lens—the German complained that his informant spoke with a "tone of pedantry," suggesting that Humboldt was uncomfortable being treated as an equal, or an inferior, by someone who wasn't White—the hunter's view still comes across that the silent, undetectable curare was vastly superior to noisy guns when interacting with prey.

Key aspects of predation are further illuminated when this mode of interaction is considered alongside shamanic practice. The ritual specialists variously known as *behique* (Taino), *caraibe* (Tupinamba), *boyé* (Kalinago), and *piache* and *mojan* (mainland Arawak and Carib groups) alarmed the missionaries who, correctly, viewed them as obstacles to their evangelical ambitions. Furthermore, they struggled to understand the roles of these ritual specialists since they did easily fit into European categories.[47] But despite their misapprehensions, the missionaries understood that a fundamental skill of these shamans was their ability to access special forms of knowledge with the help of botanical agents such as tobacco, *anadenanthera peregrina* (known as *cohoba* or *yopa*), and datura. This knowledge revealed the root cause of sickness, the likelihood of warfare, or imminent famine, among other matters important to individuals, families, and entire communities.

One of the most extensive early descriptions of shamanic practice appears in the text written by Ramón Pané, the friar assigned by Columbus to collect information about the customs of Taino on Hispaniola. After inhaling hallucinogenic *cohoba*, the *behique*—which "means physician"—"is able to speak with *cemis* who tells him the source of sickness." Sometimes community leaders could take on a shamanic role, as "when they want to find out if they will achieve victory over their enemies." A cacique might be the one who "relates the vision he has had, inebriated from the *cohoba* that he has inhaled through his nose" after he "has spoken with the *zemi* [*cemi*]" and has learned if "they will achieve victory, or their enemies will flee, or there will be a great loss of life, or wars or hunger or other such things."[48] These *cemi* were made from stones, trees, or logs. Although the missionary referred to them as "idols," they are better understood as natural entities that decided to enter into relationships with people and that required care (offerings of food, drink, and lodging) and, in return, nurtured plants, encouraged rainfall, and healed ailments, and offered vital information. Pané explained that a *cemi* that belonged to a principal cacique and originated when some men "were hunting" and "they happened upon a certain animal." They pursued it until it fled into a hole, and then "saw a log that seemed to be a living thing." Or a man "walking along" sees "a tree that is moving its roots" and so "fearfully stops and asks it who it is." The tree commands the man to summon a *behique* "and he will tell you who I am." The *behique* then sits next to the tree and prepares *cohoba* and then asks the tree, "Tell me who you are and what you are doing here, and what you wish from and why you have summoned me. Tell me if you want to be cut down or if you want to come with me, and how you want to be carried, for I will build you a house with land." Another time, a *behique* who had been severely beaten by relatives of a former patient entered a *cohoba* trance. In that state, he was visited by snakes "of various kinds, white, black, and green, and of many other colors," who healed his injuries by licking his flesh.[49] Common to these descriptions of shamanic practice is the notion that a powerful botanical agent, such as tobacco or *anadenanthera peregrina*, is what allowed humans to enter an altered state of consciousness and into dialogue with nonhuman entities who possessed superior knowledge.[50]

Predation and shamanism both linked sensory awareness to the acquisition of knowledge. For the hunter, this multisensory attunement led to a deep understanding of prey and their surroundings that allowed him to merge with the environment or take on the traits of his prey. For the shaman, tobacco or *cohoba* or *yopa* altered his consciousness so that he became capable of communicating with beings who might otherwise seem inert and inanimate, such as stones or logs or the gourd rattles known as maracas. This botanically induced state might allow a shaman to see visits from snakes or fly to the moon, as a missionary learned from his conversations with Kalinago *boyé*.[51] In both predation and shamanism, important connections were forged between plants and animals. Both the hunter and the shaman enter into relationships with powerful botanical agents to enhance their abilities to communicate with plants, stones, and nonhuman animals. The plant resins attract prey and lovers, the *curare* assists as a silent killer, and the *cohoba* allows the *behique* to interact with trees and snakes in ways not possible in normal states of consciousness.

~

OVIEDO'S ACCOUNT OF the goose hunt concluded with the killing of the birds. However, the process of predation did not end with the death of the prey. Other outsiders' accounts make clear that the assimilation of prey bodies into or onto the hunter, his kin, and his community was the climax of this mode of interaction. One outcome was the transformation of prey into food. Claude Lévi-Strauss famously suggested that cooking transformed the raw subject into a cooked object. "Eating and sharing food in order to produce kinship must be kept distinct from eating as a way of identifying with what is eaten," points out anthropologist Carlos Fausto, "but this requires work: the game animal needs to be produced as food, since it is not 'naturally' an object. . . . An animal subject needs to be reduced to the condition of an inert object."[52]

Cooking, however, was not always a completely effective mechanism for removing the subjectivity of prey. The consumer was still vulnerable to involuntarily taking on the properties of the one being eaten, as revealed by the myriad and complex array of food proscriptions that groups throughout lowland South America upheld. André Thevet wrote of the Tupinamba, "They are so superstitious that they will not eat any beast, be it terrestrial or aquatic, that is slow to walk . . . because they are of the opinion that their flesh will render them too heavy, which will be troublesome when they find themselves assailed by their enemies."[53] Biet wrote of the mainland Galibi, "They do not want to eat certain big fish, like the manatee, believing that the soul of some of their relatives had entered it, and that they would eat it."[54]

There was no greater period of vulnerability for the transfer of subjectivity than during the gestation and infancy of a child. Vilaça writes that at birth the body is particularly prone to "permutability," and what enables this "is precisely the equivalence of spirits"—including those of animals—"all are equally human, equally subjects."[55] Among the Kalinago, new fathers abstained from birds and fish for the first six months of their baby's life, believing that, otherwise, their children "would share in the natural defects of the animals. . . . If the father ate a turtle, the child would be deaf, and would have hardly any brain like this animal, and if it was manatee, he would have little small eyes like the manatee, and so on of the others."[56] Gilij related how he learned about these concerns among people in the Orinoco: After the construction of a fort to house soldiers guarding the mission, the Spaniard in charge rewarded the laborers ("still *gentiles*") with "a good meal to please them," but "a certain Marcayuri finished the work without eating, not even taking a bite." The "surprised" Spaniard asked the other laborers, "'What? Doesn't he have an appetite?': 'He certainly has [an appetite]' his companions told him, 'but now that his wife has given birth, he cannot eat these foods, because the baby would die.'" The missionary learned that "not only can the fathers not eat but they cannot kill fish or any other animal during those days, or that would also be dangerous for their children." Wanting to investigate further, Gilij sought out Tomás Keveicoto, a Tamanaco man and "one of the most rational savages." After talking to Keveicoto he "realized that there was supposed to be almost an identity between father and son."[57] It was always work to ensure that prey did not transfer its properties to the host.

The same porousness of the self that sometimes resulted in unwanted transfer of a prey's subjectivity also allowed for purposeful appropriation of the prey's "point of view."[58] A Kalinago rite exemplifies consumption in which the objective was to assimilate the "animistic capacities" of another.[59] It was described by Raymond Breton, a French missionary who lived on Dominica between 1642 and 1654, during which time he was often the only European on the island, himself a guest of Halannena, or, as he was known to the French, "Captain Baron."[60] Halannena was feared and respected by French and English who were augmenting their efforts at colonization and attacks on Spanish hegemony in those years. He was one of the charismatic leaders who strategized to maintain Kalinago independence, taking advantage of Dominica's high mountains and lack of ship-friendly harbors.[61] Halannena allowed the missionary to reside in his community, likely because he was a source of European trade goods and the French had shown themselves to be useful—although not entirely dependable—allies in Kalinago wars against European and Native enemies alike. Consequently, Breton learned their language (Arawak, but with a Carib-based dialect used exclusively by men that reflected alliances and migration from mainland Caribs) and wrote dictionaries dense with ethnographic observations—uniquely rich sources for practices and beliefs of the Kalinago.

This Kalinago rite—Breton described it as "one of their most solemn"—centered around raptors, one of them a *mansphoenix* (likely a kind of kite) that ate land prey and another that subsisted on fish.[62] Preparations began several months in advance, when men and boys kidnapped birds from their nests ("little ones for the little ones, and for the married men, big and heavy ones"). The boys had to ensure a steady supply of fresh fish or prey birds to feed the raptors, and, according to Breton, honed their hunting skills in this way.[63] On the day of the rites, the boy initiates had their flesh incised with a knife made with agouti teeth and, quite likely, a handle made of the bone of an enemy, so this device itself was a trophy, affording the transfer of some vitality of the deceased warrior. Then it was time to kill and incorporate the birds. The chief warrior began, killing his bird by smashing it against his head, letting the blood trickle down and leaving it there for the duration of the ceremony. Soon after, those who "have had a child or killed an Arawak" followed and crushed their birds with red chili. The men then smeared the bloodied, chili-covered carcasses on the boy initiates. At the end of the ceremony, the birds' hearts received special treatment. The hardiest ate the heart of "his bird," followed by a vomit-inducing tobacco infusion,[64] while others preserved the heart through a smoking treatment and wore it around their neck. By letting the raptor's blood trickle on his skin, seeping into cuts, and eating or wearing its heart, each boy and man was imbued with the raptor's essence, giving him the virile vigor necessary for fatherhood and predation in war and hunt. Similar ceremonies were practiced elsewhere in lowland South America.[65]

In addition, Breton mentioned several times in his dictionaries the practice of wearing a gourd filled with the flesh of the mansphoenix "that they wear around their neck like a relic in order to become strong and valiant." They often wore the "little gourds" containing "the fur of jaguars, claws of raptors and other similar things" at their feasts. He speculated, "I don't know whether this is out of superstition, or to maintain strength, keep away evil, or instill bravery, but probably it is for all of these reasons and especially for the two last ones."[66] The jaguar teeth and fur were likely obtained through trade with their Galibi (Carib) contacts on the continent, in the same way they procured the much-coveted snails out of which they made gleaming white *karakoulis*.[67] Missionaries who spent time on the mainland similarly commented on hunters' and warriors' practice of wearing the teeth, claws, and bones of predators. Cumangoto men in mainland South America used "claws of the Tiger [e.g., jaguar] as chokers as a trophy and they also make them of the teeth of whatever beast, and of other animals that they kill."[68] Guamo men had a predilection for wearing necklaces of caiman teeth "as a sign of their valor," draping them on "the necks of their children, no less than their own."[69] The seep of blood through the skin or the mouth, the transfer of breath through a bone flute, or the touch of feathers, teeth, and pelts on the body transformed the being of the human predator through his absorption of his prey.[70]

Human bodies were viewed similarly to those of other animals. The idea that the essence of a subject could be found in their less perishable remains can be seen in mortuary rituals. The Kalinago communicated with their dead by taking the bone or hair of their dead and putting it in a gourd vessel that they plugged with cotton, allowing "devils to speak through the bone or hair and they say that this is the soul of the deceased."[71] For this reason, Kalinago and Galibi fighters were careful to make sure that they collected the remains of their comrades who died in battle.[72]

Conversely, warriors made use of bodily remains of enemies to capitalize on their ferocity, much as they used teeth and bones of other apex predators. In the words of Fernando Santos-Granero, "The appropriation of enemy body parts, substances and essences" were to be "either consumed or kept as life-giving trophies." Skulls, bones, teeth, and hair were transformed into ritual objects that could be worn on or near the body.[73] Gumilla observed that the Caberres and Carib peoples of the Middle Orinoco region "use in their celebrations many necklaces of teeth and molars of people to make clear that they are very brave, that the remains that they there display are of their enemies, that they kill."[74] The missionary indicated that another way of appropriating enemy vitality was to transform their bones into flutes. Breton likewise noted that the Kalinago "wear around their necks whistles that they often make out of the bones of their enemies."[75] Figueroa described how men in the western Amazon prepared for warfare by wearing necklaces made of the "teeth of tigers and other animals and of men whom on other occasions they had killed."[76] Achuar-speaking "Jivaros" developed a technique of taking the corpses of vanquished warriors to make the shrunken-head *tsantas* that they would wear in warfare and related rites, a process described by Figueroa and ethnographers in the twentieth century.[77] In some cases, warfare cannibalism seems to have served the same purpose—it was a way to take "the potentialities of life from the enemy."[78] What appears to be common across the region is the understanding that the location of a human or other kind of animal's vital spirit was in their skin, feathers, hair, or bones—a concept remote from the invisible soul of Christianity.

It was not only predators whose qualities were appropriated through strategic consumption. The importance of feathers of parrot species and other brightly colored tropical birds was immediately clear to European observers (fig. 4.1). They noted the appearance of feathers in headdresses and on maracas, shields, swords, hangings, "and other exquisite things."[79] Columbus remarked on the Ciguayo men he encountered on the Samaná Peninsula of Hispaniola in January 1493 who wore on their heads "plumes of parrot feathers and of other birds."[80] Breton described a plethora of practices related to feathers in his dictionaries: the Kalinago attached the long tail feathers of macaws to their hair, applied resin to paste downy feathers to their bodies (the word *namálinkienli* means "I affix feathers all over his body" or "I re-dress him with little feathers"), and "the wings of diverse birds which they dangle onto their backs and stomachs." A hugely important moment in a baby's life occurred when their ears were pierced with feathers.[81] A crest of a particular hummingbird was used by "women . . . during their festivals." The missionary lavished the most attention on a headdress that he described as a "crown," the *ioumáliti*, ornamented on top with the tail feathers of parrots and macaws and "on the base, they put other [feathers] in the form of a band." It was "the most honorable one because of its beautiful plumage."[82] In addition to the plumage of parrot and

Figure 4.1   Men dancing with feather ornaments in the presence of a tame macaw and monkey, Jean de Léry, *Histoire d'un voyage fait en la terre de Brésil,* (Geneva, 1580), p. 246. Reproduction courtesy of John Carter Brown Library, Brown University.

hummingbird species, Indigenous communities valued feathers from many other beautiful birds, such as the helmeted curassow and the toucan.[83] Jean de Léry illuminated the animistic qualities attributed to feathers in his description of Tupinamba maracas, the gourds filled with seeds used in dances and healing rites. Sometimes their shamans (caraibes) "go from one village to another and have each family adorn three or four of these big rattles that they call maracas, using the finest plumes they can find." "When the maracas are thus decked out," the missionary wrote, "they stick the long end of the rod that runs through them into the earth, and arrange them along the sides of the houses; they then demand that the maracas be given food and drink." The missionary added, "They have a strange belief concerning these maracas (which they almost always have in hand)." Not only did they attribute a "certain sanctity to them," but "they say that whenever they make them sound, a spirit speaks."[84] While nervous about their possibly diabolical associations, some colonizers found Tupinamba featherworks so alluring that they took mantles back to Europe and today they are found in collections of European museums.[85]

If the fur, feathers, and bones of predators could be mobilized to augment fierceness, bravery, and aggression, what was transmitted by the gorgeous glint and glimmer of feathers from nonraptorial birds? Tupinamba activist and artist Glicéria Jesus da Silva explains that these featherworks are not only objects but also "our ancestors," and "it is time to listen to them."[86] Early modern outsiders faintly understood the idea that the feathered things were vessels of knowledge related to the lived experiences of birds. Outsiders frequently observed the attention Indigenous people paid to birdsong in order to acquire otherwise unobtainable knowledge. In entries for birds, Breton included notes about their ability to forecast weather—one who "by its song presages good weather" and another who "presages the rain."[87] Gilij noted that in the Orinoco region, "the inhabitants are of the opinion" that when a certain bird (uacavá) "sees strangers, it announces their arrival, whether on water or on land, to their communities," adding that "in reality" the birds "do often announce" the movements of outsiders. He also wrote that Tamanacos believe "the song of birds is truly speech" and that "the song of the birds is a kind of instruction given from above high to people. From this comes their fear or alternatively their happiness when they listen to singing in the forests."[88] Likewise, Figueroa wrote that the Jivaro "say that birds talk and forecast their misfortunes and events, although they don't understand their language. They are persuaded that they speak among each other, each casta has a different language and speech, as it is in the nations of men, and the same is true for terrestrial animals."[89]

The notion that birds, particularly, were notable because they both possessed knowledge and transmitted it to people was also conveyed by a story that Breton included in the entry for a tiny hummingbird ("no bigger than a finger") called *ierétté*. These birds were known for their gorgeous plumage and for making nests out of strands of cotton on the trunks of a certain tree or sometimes even on the wooden pegs that jut out of lodgings. The missionary explained how the Kalinago believed that the moon—"that they took for a man"—once upon a time saw a girl while dreaming. He "embraced" her, and as a result, "a child was born of this girl." The child, named Hiali, became one of the "first founders of the Caribe [Kalinago] nation." So, "they chose the little bird in question to take the child to his father, which he did with great fidelity, and he received in recompense a beautiful crest on his head and diverse colors on his plumage, which has made him a marvel of nature and the object of our admiration."[90] This Kalinago foundation story is similar to others recorded by modern ethnographers that explain the origin of extraordinary plumage of various kinds of birds—for instance, linking the red plumage of macaws to the blood of ancestors or burning flames.[91] This story not only explains how the hummingbirds came by gorgeous plumage but also reveals that the tiny hummingbird, through flight, moves between people's restricted terrestrial reality and the oracular realm of sky beings. The story connects this avian ability to their beautiful plumage. To adorn a human body with a feather, then, is a way to augment beauty and knowledge, taken to be inseparable.

Feathered artifacts were displayed in both quotidian and ceremonial occasions.[92] Above all, feathers were inextricably associated with dances and songs performed during feasts.[93] Breton included an expression that translated as "those who are all covered in feathers and dance."[94] Gumilla witnessed dancers moving with feathers as part of bereavement rites in a Saliva village and tried to convey the effect to his European readership. After feasting on turtle, fish, and alcoholic *chicha*, a series of dances began inside a lodge that had three pairs of columns: one pair featured feathered headdresses, another "two birds very well imitated," and the third "masks" representing "the gestures of weeping ones, with the hands over the eyes." The dancers were organized into groups of twelve and befeathered "to the greatest degree," each wearing "a singular adornment of feathers and long plumage of macaw" and carrying "in his right hand a staff, all covered with a variety of feathers. The point of the said staffs were attached on the top with a crown, covered in feathers, and the weight of this made the 12 staffs fold towards the bottom, each one forming a semi-circle and all together forming a dome, or a gorgeous half-orange in whose center was hanging the crown." Gumilla sought to convey the "notable variety of postures, turns, and circles" of the dancers, who moved "without ever wrecking or disturbing the said half orange." The music was expressed in the "tone of the dancers because with their head, feet, and all of the body they made extraordinary courtesies and ceremonies." He continued, "Each circle of people, seen from afar, represented a variety of florid garden. In particular they had painted their faces with such strange figures and colors, that except for these words, no one would know." He struggled to find words to convey the power of the "spectacle" of "sound, feathers, and movement" that matched anything in a "Court in Europe."[95]

Dances could be an occasion to integrate all elements of predation. Ruíz Blanco wrote that the "principal worship" of the Cumangoto is "in their dances and drunken parties. . . . They have them at the time they harvest their fruits or after fishing."[96] He noted that "in their celebrations they tend to dance for eight days continually, and he who paints himself most monstrously is considered the most beautiful. In the dances they imitate the animals of the land as well as fish, and dance in a circle, holding hands, some singing, accompanied by the drum and some thick pipes."[97] In one particular dance, they "bring figures of fish made of wood in their hand," and he notes elsewhere that they "fashion animals with complete exactness."[98] Gilij lamented that Maipure men, even after becoming a "Christian population," were "determined" to continue practicing the dance called *cueti,* which, he explained, "signifies animal." The dance was designed to attract snakes, who, it was believed, "come from time to time to their villages, bringing with them drinks and that they enjoy dancing together with the men."[99]

Outsiders in the nineteenth and twentieth centuries offer more extensive commentary on dances "named after animals whose antics or noises they sought to imitate." Richard Schomburgk, visiting a Warrau settlement along the Aruka River, was told about dances centered around a monkey, a sloth, and a bird, respectively, all three involving "dissolute rowdy dancers" who "banished sleep from the camp."[100] The German anthropologist Theodor Koch-Grünberg, who visited Guiana and Brazil in 1911–1913, wrote "all of the dances and dance songs of these tribes have an intimate relationship with their myths and legends. The songs are in certain manner poetic accounts of the myths that are passed from father to son."[101] His Taulipág associate, Mayulaipu, told him the origins of the "kikuyikog" dance, which tells the story of how a baby girl and her mother were transformed into the falcon "Kukui" and the falcon "Inakin."[102] Rafael Karsten likewise learned about connection between song-dance and origin stories during his visits among Jivaro in the early twentieth century. A dance that featured vocal mimesis of animals connected to another story about "ancient times, it is told to us, there another kind of people existed. All jaguars [were] like Jibaros, all sloths like Jibaros, all black monkeys, all howling monkeys, all brown monkeys, all capuchin monkeys like Jibaros," likewise all birds, fish, crabs, and even snails.[103] Dances were the fulcrum of the intersubjective practices of predation transposed from the realm of the quotidian into ritual. Here the observational and mimetic practices that allowed men to stalk and kill other animals were self-consciously reproduced as transformational practices that strengthened the origin stories being told. Dances were occasions to tell song-stories about human ancestors who transformed into other kinds of beings or other kinds of beings who were the parents of human ancestors.

Traces of these stories register in the accounts of outsiders since the fifteenth century, decontextualized from the transformative practices of costume and dance. The stories recorded by Ramón Pané, André Thevet, Raymond Breton, José Gumilla—among many others—are not only origin accounts but also reflections on the nature of subjectivity or, we might say, personhood. These stories have been bewitching to Europeans and their settler descendants for more than five hundred years not only because of their contrast with Genesis but also because they diverge so strikingly from Western ideas about subjectivity. They posit that a subject's temperamental tendencies, affective aptitudes, physical abilities, and psychological experiences—traits encompassing ferocity, expressiveness, attentiveness, grief, and desire, among others—are inseparable from what the outsiders might call "exterior" attributes.[104] As a result, the nature of subjects is that they are permeable to others' subjectivity. Perhaps the most distinct attribute of human subjectivity in these stories is a singular tendency toward change and porousness (in stark contrast to the Western tradition that accounts for human singularity because of "reason"). And, finally, this porousness means that personhood is by definition a relational, intersubjective thing. Humans' relationships with all kinds of beings—plants as well as other animals—are what make them persons. Such a conception of personhood was produced as much as it was reflected in the intersubjective practices of predation (it is no accident that the Taino ancestors who became *jobo* trees were out fishing). The multisensory attunement, mimetic practice, and corporeal transformation that were essential to South American predation are inseparable from beliefs that recognize the subjectivities of other beings and the permeability of one's own.

These fragmentary stories of transformation and predation that pervade the outsiders' accounts are vestiges of the practices and beliefs of Indigenous communities. In addition, the texts used in this and the next chapter to reconstruct Indigenous predation and familiarization are also traces of epistemological transformation occurring in Europe. The natural histories penned by colonizers depended on Indigenous knowledge, albeit attenuated and mediated by the process of translation.[105] Among the most influential was Oviedo: the 1526 *Sumario* circulated widely in translation and later authors of natural histories reproduced many of his entries on flora and fauna.[106] While Oviedo presented himself as the designated "authority" in his writings, many of his observations were mediated by the knowledge and practices of Indigenous experts.[107] In fact, Oviedo himself acknowledged his dependence on Indigenous knowledge in the prologue to his 1535 work, by way of apology: "if some strange and barbarous vocabulary is found here, the cause is the novelty of what is being treated," and justifying the frequent use of foreign "names or words . . . in order to make understood the things that the Indians want to signify."[108] And, indeed, the great number of Indigenous signifiers for animals—hutia, iguana, manatee, *cocuyo* (firefly), among many others—are lexical traces of Oviedo's dependence on Indigenous knowledge.[109] Moreover, his and other colonizers' adoption of Native hunting technologies—aspects of predation—for obtaining skunks, peccary, rabbits, hares, armadillo, partridges, foxes, and pigeons, among others, represents another way that Indigenous practice affected European epistemology. The insight so central to Indigenous predation—that predators are transformed by predation as much as their prey—also applies to colonizers. The colonizers who described a soldier's torment as he died from a curare-tipped arrow, explained the flavor of iguana meat, and revealed how Taino hunters concealed themselves under gourds to catch geese were also writing about their own transformation.

5

Taming Strangers

One of the soldiers most celebrated by Gonzalo Fernández de Oviedo was a dog. "Brought from this island of Espanola to San Juan [Puerto Rico]," Becerrillo was "of reddish color, and a black snout, with forward eyes; of medium size and not beautiful, but of great understanding and valor," and Oviedo so esteemed the dog's qualities and abilities that he considered him three times as valuable as any human soldier.[1] "Like a man," Oviedo wrote, Becerrillo "had understanding and could distinguish the tame Indians [*indios mansos*] and did not do them harm. And among many tame Indians, he could identify the one *bravo* (fierce or enemy) Indian." Oviedo also described an occasion when Becerrillo disobeyed his master. The episode took place after the Spanish had suppressed a revolt by an important cacique on the island. In the aftermath, the Spanish captain decided that one of the war captives, an elderly woman, should be put to death since she had no value as a slave. So he chose to kill her in a particularly cruel manner, gratuitously violent even by conquistador standards. He gave the woman a letter and said to her, according to Oviedo, "Go on, get you, take this letter to the governor," Juan Ponce de León. And so the woman "went very happily, because she thought that for bringing the letter that they would liberate her." But then he released Becerrillo to go after her and kill her by *apperreamiento*. Oviedo described what happened shortly after the captain released the dog:

> When the woman saw [Becerrillo] going aggressively for her, she sat on the ground and in her language started to speak and said to him, "Dog, Sir Dog, I am going to bring this letter to the Lord governor" and she showed him the letter or the paper she was carrying and said to him, "Do not do me any harm, Sir Dog." And indeed the dog stopped as if he had heard her speaking, and arrived very tamely to her and picked up a leg and peed on her, as dogs tend to in the corner when they want to urinate, without doing any harm.[2]

Oviedo recounted the amazement of the Spaniards, who found Becerrillo's behavior to be "a very mysterious thing," given the dog's renowned fierceness. The captain rethought his plan, upon "seeing the clemency that the dog had shown" to the woman, and so ordered that Becerrillo be tied up. When Ponce de León arrived, he "did not want to be less pious with the Indian woman than had been the dog and ordered that she be let free." While notable, the gratuitous cruelty of the captain and his change of heart upon seeing the dog's behavior is not what is most remarkable about this episode. What most stands out is the bravery of the unnamed woman, her sophisticated animal training technologies, and the profound skill with which she deployed them. We can only view this incident through Oviedo's perspective—and it is a perspective that includes predictable derision and mockery at the woman's naiveté in thinking she was freed and that the dog could read. Nonetheless, Oviedo shows us that this woman was able to persuade a dog renowned for his intelligence and obedience, who was trained to kill on command, not to listen to his master and to listen to her instead and spare her life. She knew how to tame the wild.

Although this episode may have been unusual—I have not read of any other war dogs defying their masters to spare a life—the mode of interaction that underlay it was not. I will refer to this mode as *familiarization*, a word and concept used by Philippe Erikson and other anthropologists who have studied Indigenous practices of animal taming in the Amazon.[3] Familiarization differs from domestication in that familiarized animals were not bred in captivity—at least before encounters with Europeans—but rather animals found or captured in the wild. My understanding of familiarization is also informed by the way that Indigenous people in the Caribbean and lowland South America conceptualized these practices themselves. Based on his extensive experiences living among the Kalinago of Dominica in the seventeenth century, the missionary Raymond Breton wrote that *iegue* denoted "an animal that one feeds" in the *Dictionaire caraibe-françois* (1665). In the companion volume *Dictionaire françois-caraibe* (1666), the missionary defined *iegue* as "*my* animal."[4] These pithy definitions underscore a bond between tamer and tamed, organized most fundamentally around a nurturing relationship of the feeder and the fed. Breton further noted that "animals that come tame before them, they believe to belong to their Gods, and that they dare not kill [them]."[5] Breton understood that *iegue* differed fundamentally from European livestock because while the latter were fed in order to be eaten, the former could not be eaten *because* they were fed. Familiarization is the flip side of predation. If predation is the process by which one pursues and consumes another being, familiarization—or feeding and therefore taming—is how one turns a wild being into kin.[6] *Iegue* was the Kalinago term for familiarized animals and the one I will use hereafter, for there is no English word that fully captures this concept.[7]

Ethnographers have observed and written extensively about taming practices in Indigenous communities for approximately 150 years.[8] Yet, until recently, there has been very little attention to their deep history.[9] However, it is not difficult to find historical evidence of *iegue* in the Caribbean and South America, for it is ubiquitous (map 1).[10] Why, then, were *iegue* hiding in plain sight? This neglect among historians is partly rooted in the biases of early modern sources. While many noted taming practices in passing, European colonizers did not view them as particularly important, as it was hard for them to understand the practices given their perception was conditioned by the categories created by hunting and livestock husbandry. Furthermore, the early and late-modern visitors were predominantly male and much of the work of familiarization was gendered female; male outsiders had minimal exposure or access to these practices. (It is no accident that female anthropologists predominate in the early ethnographies that consider taming practices.) The scattered and fragmentary nature of the sources touching on early modern taming practices is a primary reason why this study employs capacious geographic and temporal parameters. The lack of attention paid to the history of familiarization is also rooted in the fact that scholars—among them Jared Diamond—have misleadingly interpreted taming practices through the teleological lens of domestication. In other words, they have assumed taming wild animals was a "stepping stone" to "full" domestication.[11] By aggregating fragmentary traces and avoiding a teleological view of domestication, the importance and complexity of familiarization as a mode of interaction can come into view.

~

THE EARLIEST WRITTEN appearance of a word related to familiarization appears in the Italian conquistador Galeotto Cei's account of his time in a colonizing expedition in Castilla del Oro (Colombia) between 1539 and 1553. He wrote that the Arawak-speaking groups with whom he interacted called the monkeys who they raised "*damoteies*" adding that the word means "companions."[12] Breton's somewhat longer gloss—"those animals who come tame before

Map 1   Familiarization in South America, 1492–2010. © Marcy Norton.

them they dare not kill"—suggests the centrality of the wild-tame dichotomy as an organizing concept for familiarization. Examples from other South American languages support this idea. The Jesuit missionary Filippo Salvatore Gilij, who learned Tamanaco (Carib) and Mapure (Arawak) languages, noted that "although there are no domestic animals among the Orinocoans there are nevertheless ones who are domesticated to whom the savage nation gives a particular name in order to distinguish between those that are wild and tamed [*amansadas*]."[13] According to a dictionary compiled at the end of the eighteenth century, the Conibo (a Panoan language in the Peruvian Amazon) word *rágue áqui* means "to tame" or "to domesticate." Its root words are *rag*, meaning "friend," and *ácqui*, meaning to "cause someone to be a friend."[14] Among the Araweté (who speak a Tupi language), writes Eduardo Viveiros de Castro, there is a linguistic prefix that "designates the untamed, that which one eats, as opposed to that which one raises and cares for."[15] This linguistic evidence shows how familiarization was fundamentally the process by which something wild became tame, or kin was made.

~

ALTHOUGH ONLY A few early modern observers recognized that familiarization was a phenomenon unto itself, many offer fragmentary glimpses of Indigenous people's predilection to tame wild animals. They are visible in Peter Martyr's (also known as Pietro Martire d'Anghiera) 1516 *De orbe novo*, which is based on the accounts of the first Europeans to visit the Caribbean islands and the coasts of northern South America, known as "Tierra Firme."[16] Unsurprisingly, parrots appear as one of the animals most frequently chosen for familiarization. As a result, during his first voyage along the coasts of Cuba and Hispaniola, Christopher Columbus was able to acquire "as many parrots" as he asked for, no less than forty.[17]

One of the earliest extensive descriptions of familiarization practices centers around parrots. André Thevet, the French Franciscan missionary who lived for more than two months in a settlement among the Tupinamba in what is present-day Rio de Janeiro, wrote, "The savages of this land hold [these parrots] very dear." He proceeded to outline key features of familiarization. He noted that "women in particular nourish them," and that "they hold them very dear, to the point of calling them in their language 'their friends.'" He emphasized the importance of communication: "our Americans teach these birds to speak in their language how to ask for the flour that they make or roots" and "very often teach" the parrots to exhort them to wage war against their enemies and "capture them so as to eat them." The missionary noticed, too, that the Tupinamba "keep these birds in their lodgings," but, very significantly, the parrots were free to come and go, and so the Tupinamba did not have "to enclose them, as we do here." In addition to affection and care, the birds also provided beautiful feathers: "three or four times a year they pluck their feathers to make hats, decorate shields, wooden swords, tapestries, and other exquisite things."[18] Jean de Léry, too, connected featherworks to tamed animals, for the illustration in his work showing Tupinamba dance and featherworks included a tamed macaw as well as a monkey (fig. 4.1). He also wrote of a woman who cherished her parrot so much that she would not consider any amount of money to part with the bird. (He also described the ire he evoked when he killed a man's cherished duck, mistaking it for a wild one rather than a beloved companion.)[19]

Although birds, particularly parrots and macaws, were the familiarized animals most visible to outsiders, they were far from alone. Martyr described a tamed manatee who lived in the Baiona province of Hispaniola in the first decade of the sixteenth century.[20] Indigenous people and invading Spaniards alike prized manatee meat for its succulence. Oviedo wrote that manatee is "one of the best fish in the world and that which most resembles meat"— Europeans knew this mammal as a fish despite tasting like "beef or veal."[21] One day, however, when a cacique caught a young manatee in his nets, he decided to feed rather than eat him. Martyr recounted that the cacique named him Matu, "meaning generous or noble" and fed the youngster "for several days with yucca, bread [cassava], millet, and the roots the natives eat." The manatee was then brought to "a lake near to his house." And so for twenty-five years Matu "lived at liberty in the waters of the lake" and "grew to an extraordinary size." The manatee had a particular bond with one of the cacique's "attendants": when the man called him from the bank, Matu, "remembering favors received, raised its head and came towards the shore to eat from the man's hand." The manatee also liked "to play upon the bank with the servants of the cacique, and especially with the cacique's young son who was in the habit of feeding it."[22] Matu's fondness for humans did not extend to the European colonists: "it had once been beaten by a peevish young Christian, who threw a sharp dart at this amiable and domesticated fish." While the manatee's thick skin protected him from injury, "the fish never forgot the attack, and from that day forth every time it heard its name called, it first looked carefully about to see if it beheld anybody dressed like the

Christians." "A joy to the whole island," according to Martyr, the manatee "was more amusing than a monkey," and locals and invaders alike "daily visited this animal."

Both Martyr and Oviedo described another kind of familiarized aquatic being—remora (suckerfish) or *guaicano* in Taino Arawak.[23] The Spanish called them "backwards fish" (*pescado reverso*) because they appeared to swim upside down. Oviedo wrote that they were captured and "trained," and though "ugly to look," they possessed the greatest (*grandíssima*) "bravery and intelligence." He wrote that "when the Indians want to keep and raise some of these," they keep them "in saltwater, and there feed them, and when they want to fish with them they bring them to the sea in their canoe or boat." They attach a thin, strong cord to the fish and wait until they see a large fish, a turtle or even a manatee." As with other *iegue*, the remora were viewed as persons who required a familiarizing process grounded not only in capture and feeding but also in physical affection and communication. When it was time for the fish to go after the prey, "the Indian takes in one hand this *pescado reverso* and strokes it with his other hand, saying *manicato* to it in his language, which means to be brave and of good heart and to be diligent, and [the man utters] other words of encouragement so that the fish aspires to be brave and to hook the large and best fish that it can find and when it seems right, [the fisherman] frees it and throws it where there are fish about."[24] Once in the water, the remora quickly located and attached themselves to prey. When the fish grew "tired," the fisherman reeled in the remora along with the "prisoner" under guard. Soon other fishermen drew the catch ashore, spearing the manatee or overturning the turtles, sometimes so large that they required as many as six men to do so. As they detached the sucker fish from the remora, the "Indians utter[ed] sweet words" and gave "it many thanks for what it has done and achieved."[25] Seizing on the cooperative relationship between the fish and human, Martyr likened this method of fishing to the Europeans' way of hunting prey with dogs.[26] Martyr and subsequent chroniclers made clear that the Taíno viewed their relationship with remora as based in affection and reciprocity.

Reptiles, too, could be *iegue*. Breton observed that sometimes lizards who started sitting on the tops of Kalinago homes "became tame." These lizards were said to "belon[g] to their gods," he reiterated, and wrote that the Kalinago feared that if they killed these lizards, then their "gods" would kill them.[27] Such practices even endured in places where European settlement was advanced: the English naturalist Hans Sloane, when living in Jamaica in the seventeenth century, encountered a snake "tam'd by an Indian, whom it would follow as a Dog would his Master."[28]

Missionaries in later centuries likewise noted familiarizing practices throughout South America. In French Guiana, it was observed in the seventeenth century that young parrots were "taken home to feed."[29] José Gumilla, one of the Jesuits who founded missions in the Middle Orinoco and its tributaries (Venezuela) in the early to mid-eighteenth century wrote succinctly of the animals "whom [Indigenous people] raise with care."[30] Gilij, who spent eighteen years in the region, went a step further, pondering the phenomenon in more detail. "Among the Indians" in the Orinoco region, he wrote, "there are always those animals converted into domesticates; they seize them in the forests as toys for their children or in order to trade with other nations. . . . These animals, tamed by the Indians, are incredible in how tame and manageable they become."[31] He described birds, rodents, peccaries, tapir, and deer, especially marveling at the affectionate nature of the latter.[32] Of monkeys he wrote that they are "more fierce than other tamed animals and they are never tamed to the point that if they freed from their tether that they won't return quickly to the forest. But if they are close to their masters, they are very tame, especially the *micos* who seem to even understand one's very thoughts."[33] He was astounded by the "incredible ability of the Indians to tame the wild beasts," asking rhetorically, "Will [it] be believed by those who have never been to the Orinoco?"[34]

Visitors to the western Amazon also noted such practices. An early seventeenth-century report about the "discovery and pacification of the provinces of the Maynas, Cocamas, and Gibaros Indians" noted that a diverse assortment of birds—including pauxis, parrot, and macaw species—were "caught when little and raised domestically in homes."[35] In the nineteenth century, Manuel María Albis, who worked as priest in the Caquetá region (present-day Colombia), wrote, "It is incomparable the patience that Indian women possess in order to raise animals"—those "baby birds the Indian men take from their nests or the monkeys shot by their arrows."[36] The naturalist Henry Walter Bates recorded "twenty-two species of quadrupeds that he has found tame in their encampments of the tribes" he visited in the Amazon, including the tapir, agouti, guinea pig, and peccary, in addition to many kinds of birds.[37]

The Jesuits who founded missions in the Gran Chaco region in the eighteenth century also commented on these familiarization practices. Martin Dobrizhoffer, an Austrian Jesuit who lived among Guaraní and Abipon people for eighteen years, admired their ability to tame guanaco, monkeys, caiman, and various species of birds. He was impressed by these peoples' ability to make crows "wonderfully tame," while observing that the birds "sometimes suffer[ed] themselves to be enticed away by flocks of crows which they meet on the road." He described how emus, when "taken young . . . are easily tamed and walk up and down the streets or yards, like dogs and hens, suffer children to play with them without fear, and never run away, though the plain be close by and in sight." According to Dobrizhoffer, there was "scarcely any Indian town in which you do not see tame emus of this kind."[38] José Sánchez Labrador, who lived in Guaraní communities, described tame birds who asked for dinner and a shaman who had a companion jaguar.[39]

Although a pervasive practice, the process of taming wild beings was a complex, lengthy, and labor-intensive. The descriptions above reveal the most important characteristics of familiarized animals: *iegue* shared domestic space with their humans, but they possessed "liberty" rather than being enclosed; they were fed and named; they communicated with their human companions. The labor of taming was gendered female. And even though these beings sometimes provided functional services—for instance, parrots providing feathers—they were held "very dear," called "friends," and "loved." In other words, they were kin.

~

THE FAMILIARIZATION PROCESS began with the capture of a being from the wild. The anonymous author and illustrator of the sixteenth-century "Histoire Naturelle des Indes" devoted significant space to the procurement process, choosing scenes of parrot capture to represent the "Indians of Trinidad" and "Indians of Nicaragua" alike. The author wrote that in Trinidad, hunters "make a trap with a string attached to it. In this trap they put a parrot with his feet tied and next to him a small animal called *catille* which plucks him. When the parrot cries and the other parrots, hearing his voice, come to his rescue, freely joining him in the trap, the Indian seeing this pulls the string and the parrots are instantly trapped." The "Indians of Nicaragua," however "use an arrow with a cotton pad at the end and when the bird is struck, it does not die, but only falls, being dazed"[40] (fig. 5.1).

Another image captured the interconnectedness of predation and familiarization by showing a hunter returning from a hunt, carrying a pole that

Figure 5.1 A hunter capturing live parrots, Histoire Naturelle des Indes, illustrated manuscript, ca. 1586, Morgan Library, bequest of Clara S. Peck, 1983, MA 3900, fols. 87v–88r. Morgan Library and Museum, New York.

has a dead bird, hanging upside down, on one end and on the other a bird who is sitting contentedly, very much alive (fig. I.3). In the Maynas (western Amazon) region, a boy "had climbed a tree to get a monkey who was stunned because of the herb."[41] Gilij described how people in the Orinoco captured baby monkeys. Seeing a mother with her baby or babies clinging to her back is the "opportune moment for the hunter. He directs a spray of poisoned arrows at the mother and she falls to the ground with the children still clinging strongly to her back, as when she was alive. They are still quite fierce onwards but not so much to be afraid of taking them back in order to raise them."[42] Anticipating their featured role as animal-tamers, women participated in at least some of these expeditions, Gilij offering the aside that during peccary hunts, "the women take part in order to bring back piglets."[43]

Once captured, a wild being needed to be tamed. The process of animal familiarization shared many elements with the practice of rearing human infants and welcoming strangers. Colonial sources and more recent anthropological ethnographies of Amazonian groups alike confirm that it was women's work to tame and raise nonhuman, as well as human, babies.[44] In the context of discussing child-rearing practices, Matías Ruiz Blanco, the seventeenth-century Franciscan who evangelized among Carib-speaking groups (Cumangoto, Palenque) along the South American littoral, noted Indigenous women's "gift for raising the little animals (*animalejos*) that they capture."[45] Similarly Albis observed that after the capture, an "Indian woman takes charge of the little animal," displaying "sincere amiability," while taking "better care of them than [they do] their own children." He added that their husbands were forbidden to come near during the taming process. Albis painted an illustrative scene he titled "the Indian woman cares for birds" (fig. 5.2). In the scene of domestic contentment, a large red macaw perches on the woman's hand, and while the macaw and woman gaze at each other, a spider monkey clasps her neck and a green parrot and two other birds look toward her.[46] In her 1973 study, ethnographer Ellen Basso wrote that in the Kalapalo community (Brazil) where she lived, taming animals was equated with mothering. Likewise, ethnographer Catherine Howard, who lived in a Waiwai community in northern Brazil in the 1980s, observed that it was women who converted the birds into either "food or humanized pets."[47]

Common elements are found in the hospitality rites offered to strangers, the care given to newborns, and the methods used to tame nonhumans; all are forms of familiarization. Feeding is one of familiarization's most central processes, whether applied to humans or other animals. Breton's discussion

Figure 5.2 "La india cuida a los pájaros" (An Indian woman cares for her birds). From Manuel María Albis, Cusiositá della foresta d'amazzonia e arte di curar senza medico, Biblioteca Nazionale Universitariadi Torino segnatura ms. S.III.2, cc. 39 e 63, fol. 38r; Edición, traducción y notas Alberto Guaraldo, Torino: Il Segnalibro, 1991. Ministero per i Beni e le Attività Culturali e per il Turismo, Biblioteca Nazionale Universitaria di Torino.

of the term *iegue* itself captured the inextricability of taming and feeding when he translated *iegue* as "an animal that one feeds." (He included a related term for "I don't have an animal," which he translated as "I don't make any food.") Similarly, ethnographers Carlos Fausto and Luiz Costa write that "commensality for the Kanamari is part of a continual process of making kin. It is what happens to the feeding bond between a woman and her pet who, in time, come to 'love' (*wu*) each other and who thus see their relation of feeding veer towards commensality."[48] Naming also appears to be an important aspect of nurturing subjectivity to a being in formation.[49]

Before human babies were given solid food, they were breastfed, and this could also be the case with nonhumans. The Franciscan Ruiz Blanco noted that if baby animals "do not eat, [mothers] give them their breasts."[50] While describing unsuccessful efforts to convert an Arawak chief named Sabaiko in early nineteenth-century British Guiana, the missionary-ethnographer William Henry Brett provided additional evidence of this practice. At one point, Brett reports, Sabaiko's "wife made her appearance with what seemed at a distance to be a singular head-dress." This proved, in fact, "to be a young 'baboon' or red monkey" that she carried on her shoulders, "its grinning visage resting on its fore-paws upon her forehead." This prompted Brett to observe that "the Indian women take great care of various young animals, even suckling them as if they were their children."[51] Young animals were also frequently given premasticated food, a common practice for introducing human babies to solid food. This practice was observed by Everard Im Thurn, a missionary turned anthropologist, and the first outsider to systematically write about familiarization. Im Thurn, like other outsiders, noted that tamed animals were "fed with cassava bread chewed by the women."[52] In such anecdotes, we see evidence supporting ethnographer Howard's contention that nursing and premasticating food constitute the "social birth" of adoption.[53]

The process of turning wild animals into tame *iegue* could sometimes include the application of a paste made from the fruit of the *bixa orellano* shrub. Covering the body with bixa, also known as *roucou*, and *achiote* was, significantly, part of what constituted care for people as well. Gumilla described how mothers applied it to themselves and then "also grease all of their little ones, even those who are nursing, at least twice a day, in the morning and in the evening, and then anoint their husbands with great prolongation."[54] The substance was appreciated for numerous qualities: its aesthetic effect of smoothing and reddening skin, as well as the protection it afforded from the sun, insects, and invisible malignant forces. In fact, its application was a prerequisite for full personhood. Early modern European visitors grasped this, noting that *achiote* and the black dye *gengiap* were essential elements of identity for Indigenous people throughout the Caribbean and Greater Amazon. Without body paint, people across the Caribbean and South America felt bare and unfit for public presentation. In this vein, Breton characterized *roucou* as a "chemise blanche," an essential garment that adorned and also protected from sun, ocean water, and insects.[55] This concept was also applied to nonhuman animals. Breton described seeing his Kalinago hosts tame a raptor who, when he was a fledgling "his plumage was reddened (*rougi*)." When the bird grew bigger "he went to the sea," yet even "when this bird became big he returned without fail every evening to his accustomed place."[56] Without being explicit, Breton grasped that the application of *roucou* is part of what made the bird so tame as to return to his human family.

Parrots also received a similar treatment. A process, known as *tapirage* and observed among Amazonian and Orinoco Indigenous people since the early colonial period, involved plucking the feathers of green parrots, and applying bixa and other ointments to the follicles.[57] As a result, parrots produced yellow, rather than green, feathers. Most accounts of *tapirage* consider that its purpose was to produce the beautiful yellow feathers later incorporated into ritual headdresses and objects. However, as it was essentially the identical treatment—removing feather or hair, applying *achiote*—used on other human and nonhuman animals, it seems likely that it was also an element of familiarization, as tameness was associated with hair removal and the application of red dye. The application of bixa extended beyond birds: Im Thurn reported that a newly captured animal was "picked up, its face is rubbed with faroa—the red pigment used by the Indians for their own bodies—in order to show the poor victim that its captors are 'good people and kind.'"[58]

Taming also entailed communication, a fact evoked most dramatically when the Indigenous woman beseeched the fierce dog Becerrillo to spare her life. Similarly, the conquistador Cei, reported that he knew Caquetio people who would ask jaguars to refrain from attacking people.[59] And, of course, the process of taming many parrot species included teaching the birds to speak. Early European observers unfailingly remarked on the facility for speech displayed by parrots tamed by South Americans. In his entries for at least seven varieties of parrots, Breton noted which ones were particularly adept at speaking. Antoine Biet, a French missionary in mid-seventeenth-century Cayenne, wrote of seven or eight different parrot species "which we see flying like pigeons in France. . . . They all learn to talk and become so tame they wander in the courtyard like chickens."[60] Lionel Wafer wrote of the parrots tamed by Cuna of Panama that "they will exactly imitate the Indians' Voices, and their way of Singing."[61] Conversely, humans could also speak in the language of the animal, as in the case of whistling to birds. Finally, a sense of understanding was sometimes present in the absence of language, as with the *mico* (monkeys) with whom Gilij was acquainted "who seem to even understand one's very thoughts."[62]

What was the purpose of all this taming? First and foremost, it provided pleasure, as Martyr noted, particularly the pleasure afforded by love.[63] Léry noted that the previously mentioned Tupinamba woman named her parrot "thing that I love."[64] Protestant missionary Charles de Rochefort observed that the Kalinago of the Lesser Antilles were "great Lovers of divertisements and recreation" and "to that purpose they take pleasure in keeping and teaching a great number of Parrots and Paraquitos."[65] Among the Taruma of the Essequibo River region (British Guiana), there were several origin stories underscoring the primordial importance of affectionate relationships between humans and other kinds of animals. John Ogilvie was a Scotsman who served as a government Indian agent in southern British Guiana, residing there between 1899 and 1921.[66] While working near the headwaters of the Essequibo River—he learned from a Taruma elder—"who spoke Wapichan and Waiwai equally well as also his own language"—"over [a] flickering fire" stories about the origins of the world. The elder told of a primordial time of happiness for humans in which "people did no work" and "they played with the children or the animals." In those early times people shared "a common language with all the beasts, the birds and other forms of life, such as a few privileged people today still have." Outsiders also could perceive and appreciate the affective bonds between *iegue* and their nurturers. Im Thurn wrote of the trumpet birds, who liked to have their heads stroked and "follow[ed] their masters . . . like dogs," even "some distance from home."[67] The missionary's description evokes the casual physical intimacy and sense of play that likewise were counted among the affective pleasures of parenthood.

Various kinds of sources suggest the importance of having *iegue* in the domestic, familial space. Early images depicting domestic space among the Tupinamba included parrots or monkeys sitting on the rafters, just as Albis's painting of a woman cherishing her birds and monkeys locates the scene inside of a dwelling.[68] Antonio Caulín, a missionary among Carib and Cumangoto groups in Venezuela in the early eighteenth century, observed that tamed birds "eat at the table and clean [people's teeth] with their beaks, and remove dandruff, and do a thousand other cute things."[69] Another animal prone to groom its masters was the *cusicusi* (perhaps a bushy-tailed olingo), a species related to the raccoon, and known for nocturnal habits and a long tongue, used for investigating small crevices. According to Gumilla the *cusicusi* would climb "on the bed of his master," then use his tongue to clean his master's "nostrils and if he finds his mouth open, that too."[70] Anthropologist Ellen Basso noted that tamed animals "are ideally supposed to be fed, reared, and kept within the confines of the house."[71]

Intrinsic to the notion of *iegue* was the notion of volition and agency on the part of the tamed being. Accordingly, once tame, the animals were allowed freedom of movement, much to the surprise of European observers. The latter were impressed with the liberty granted to the adopted animals, such as the manatee who swam freely in Hispaniola and the tamed raptors who returned to their Kalinago companions. In the seventeenth century, Wafer wrote of Panamanian Cuna and their macaws: "The Indians keep these Birds tame, as we do Parrots, or Mag-Pies: But after they have kept them close some time, and taught them to speak some Words in their Language, they suffer them to go abroad in the Day-time into the Woods, among the wild ones; from whence they will on their own accord return in the Evening to the Indian's Houses or Plantations."[72] Similarly, Gilij said of tamed animals in Orinoco communities, "Even though they always have their ancestral forests before them they never . . . abandon their love for their masters."[73] Bates offered similar observations when marveling at the taming techniques of the "old woman" who familiarized his parrot in the Amazon: "the chief reason why almost all animals become so wonderfully tame in the houses of the natives is . . . their being treated with uniform gentleness, and allowed to run at large about the rooms."[74] Im Thurn was comparably impressed by the freedoms enjoyed by tamed monkeys, noting "they, too, are generally loose, and often follow the women like dogs when they go through the forest to their distant fields, or elsewhere."[75]

Iegue provided pleasure and diversion, but they sometimes contributed in other ways as well. As previously noted, Breton, Thevet, and many others observed that plumage used in featherworks could be obtained from tamed birds.[76] As experienced by Columbus, another service provided by familiarized animals was their role in various forms of exchange. As Gilij succinctly stated, the Indigenous peoples in the Orinoco basin tamed animals "for their children or in order to trade with other nations."[77] That Europeans were the recipients of tamed animals in gift and trade exchanges from the beginning of their arrival in the Americas (including Columbus's parrots) attests to preexisting, well-developed networks to trade familiarized animals.[78] A Portuguese military official described the importance of monkeys in a 1786 peacemaking meeting that took place in the settlement of Borba, a garrison and colonial town on the Madeira River (Amazonas Brazil), between several delegations of different groups that totaled 140 men and women. The official wrote in his report, "The said principals bring with them some from the Torá Nation, who have here a principal named Jozé, and various women of that same nation; and these [Torá visitors], as soon as they arrived, went into the house [of the women], and brought their tame monkeys (*macacos de mimo*)."[79] Historian Heather Roller has suggested that the "sharing" of these monkeys was "a way of affirming kin relationships" in which "women played a key role in building (or rebuilding) these social connections."[80] Howard observed that the primary reason her Waiwai hosts exchanged familiarized animals was to create "social ties" between families and villages.[81]

In this way, nonhuman animal exchanges functioned similarly to marriage and traditional forms of captivity in Greater Amazonia. Neil Whitehead argues that "forms of warfare and marriage . . . are usually seen in active thought as analogous mechanisms for the exchange and flow of persons between groups." According to Whitehead, "To make the prestation of a woman in marriage created a debt on the part of those receiving wives such that this, a fundamental social fact, became an idiom through which many forms of imperial tribute systems and their associated labor regime were understood."[82] In fact, Howard noted that in negotiating the exchange of familiarized animals, her hosts made use of a formal kind of discourse, "the same that is used in marriage negotiations, sorcery charges, and work recruitment." Likewise, "mothers would grieve over the loss of their pets in the same standardized vocabulary as they mourned the departure of their married children, who likewise left behind memories, nostalgia, and palpable absences (silence, an empty hammock space, ungrated manioc, uncaught game.)"[83]

The exchanged animals were not commodities in the European sense. Fernando Santos-Granero and Whitehead contrast the Indigenous trade in human captives with early modern European systems of commodified, market-oriented servitude. Whereas for the latter, the labor of the captive was "alienable for monetary gain," in the former, "that labor remained invested in the social person, because the servility of labor was enforced by kinship or ritual obligation, not the institution of law."[84] The same was true of nonhuman *iegue*—their exchange was foremost about creating social ties between groups. From initial capture to familiarization to exchange, the life cycle of nonhuman and human *iegue* were similar. As suggested by these parallels in captive taking of human and nonhuman animals and in linguistic terms, the concepts of the wild and the tame bridged the human and non-human binary: on the one side, the "wild" encompassed newborn infants, human strangers and wild animals, and on the other side, the "tame" encompassed human and nonhuman kin. Strangers might submit to familiarization voluntarily, a foreigner might seek a friendship or join a community as a spouse, or one could be captured against their will during warfare and adopted as new kin. Likewise, a nonhuman animal might be captured during a hunting expedition, or choose to reside on top of a human's dwelling, becoming one of the tame animals that the Kalinago of Dominica "dare not kill."

Because of Europeans' interest—and anxiety—about modes of warfare, early modern sources are quite revealing about the involuntary familiarization of people that occurred as a result of warfare. The missionary Breton succinctly described the two possible outcomes of captive warfare among the Kalinago. Breton explained that "they kill their [adult male] prisoners with a hit of *bouttou*" but "if they are women, they give them as wives and slaves to old men; if they are children, they keep them as slaves."[85] A geographically varied body of sources from the colonial and later periods features practices similar to those Breton described for the Kalinago. Ethnographer Patrick Menget documented the meanings of *egu* [a variant of *iegue*] during visits to the Txicao, another Carib-speaking group along the Xingu River, in the twentieth century. They included a "familiar animal who lives in one's lodging"—such as the various parrots, monkeys, and capybara who had been tamed—children kidnapped in war raids to replace deceased relatives, and "trophies taken from enemy cadavers, in particular flutes made of tibia and human teeth mounted into necklaces."[86] If one object of South American warfare was to capture "vital capital" that is "contained in war trophies [and] bodily substances," writes Santos-Granero, this concept "also comprises the capabilities of actual men and women—namely, the reproductive power of female captives, the warring abilities of captive boys brought up as members of their masters' societies, and the labor force of slaves, servants, and tributaries who contribute services or goods."[87]

These two outcomes are also described by Europeans who themselves became enmeshed in modes of familiarization. Sometimes they submitted voluntarily, as with Columbus and others seeking to trade and form alliances, and sometimes involuntarily, as when they became war captives as a result of their or other Europeans' depredations. This involuntary taming was experienced by Spanish settlers on Puerto Rico, who, in response to Spanish attacks and enslavement campaigns that began in the late fifteenth century, were subjected to predatory familiarization by the Kalinago. A Spanish woman who had escaped from captivity among the Kalinago testified that on the "said island of Dominica that there are two women and a man who are already as much *caribes* as the rest of them," and who "no longer remember God."[88]

~

THE INHABITANTS OF Europe and lowland South America alike were accustomed to and comfortable with the idea of eating animals. However, they developed different solutions to reconcile this fact with their awareness that they could and did form affective relationships with some of these beings. The European solution was to prohibit eating certain beings and to objectify most of those beings whose consumption was licit. The South American solution was to classify beings according to the contingent condition of their wildness and tameness. While livestock husbandry was most fundamentally about killing and eating animals who were fed, familiarization was predicated on the belief and practice that those who were fed were kin and, therefore, not to be killed and eaten. The essential difference between livestock and *iegue* is in the relationship to food. Livestock are fed in order to become food, whereas *iegue* are fed and thus prohibited as food. One apparent exception to this rule was the aforementioned coming-of-age rite recounted by Breton in which boys captured and cared for raptors for a period of time before killing them in a ceremony (see Chap. 4). But this was no casual eating of livestock: rather, it was parallel to the treatment of prisoners of war who were kept for a period of time before being killed.[89] This was an intentional and extraordinary modification of existing practice to permit the act that otherwise was prohibited. The latter is made particularly clear by the revulsion that Indigenous people across South America and the Caribbean evinced to the idea of eating livestock, a revulsion that Breton summarized by declaring that the Kalinago "would rather die" than eat a chicken "or even an egg."[90]

As hunting and husbandry created subjectivities in early modern Europe, so did predation and familiarization in South America and the Caribbean.

The mimetic practices of Indigenous predation, as well as ritualized ways of assimilating flesh and skins of nonhuman animals, facilitated awareness of the self's porousness and erased boundaries between species. These practices sit in stark contrast to the operations of livestock husbandry that generated notions of human distinctiveness by alienating animal bodies from their personhood. In complement to predation, familiarization actualized the reality of interspecies kinship. There are commonalities in the way that Europeans related to their vassals (and servant animals), and the way Indigenous people related to *iegue*: like familiarization, hunting and husbandry required people to recognize their vassals and animal servants' subjectivity in order cultivate relationships with them. Yet the love and care that connected people to their vassal and servant animals were understood as a by-product of these relationships whose purpose was to produce ennoblement and generate wealth, respectively. In contrast, services and labor might too be offered by one's *iegue*, but the reasons for entering into relationship with *iegue* were bestowing care and experiencing love.

6

Hunting Ecologies

ahuas in the *altiplano* (central highlands) of what is today Mexico knew themselves to be the descendants of nomadic hunter foragers. These ancestors, known as Chichimec, lived far to the north in an arid high desert where barrel cactus, agave, deer, and jaguar abounded. One day, two of these progenitors—brothers named Xiuhnel and Mimich—decided to go hunting. Their prey, two deer with two heads each, had descended from the sky. The brothers spent many hours in chase, trying to shoot the animals with their arrows. They continued throughout the night. When they became exhausted, they made a shelter with branches and leaves, and they rested. The deer then transformed themselves into women and beckoned the men to visit, beseeching, "Come here, come eat, come drink," with invitations for sex as well as sustenance. The brothers knew to be suspicious and told each other to ignore the entreaties. But Xiuhnel could not resist. When one of the women, named Itzpapalotl, offered him blood to drink, he accepted, and while they were having sex, she got on top of him, ripped open his chest, and ate him. Mimich, seeing what had happened to his brother, decided to stay the course and ignore the other deer-woman's offer of food. She persisted: She pursued him all night and even into the next day. He was only saved when a thorny barrel cactus fell from the sky and struck the deer-woman. Then he returned, "parting and tying up his hair, painting his face and weeping for his elder brother who had been eaten." Afterward, fire divinities incinerated the bones of Itzpapalotl, reducing them to five colored flints. Another Chichimec, Mixcoatl, selected and bundled a sacred white flint, and put it on his back and went "off to make conquests" with the assistance of the spirit power of Itzpaplotl's crematory remains.[1] Xiuhnel, Mimich, and Itzpapolotl were remembered throughout Central Mexico in songs sung at feasts, in pictures carved into stone, and, after the colonizers introduced alphabetic writing, in texts recorded in Spanish and Nahuatl alike (map 2).[2]

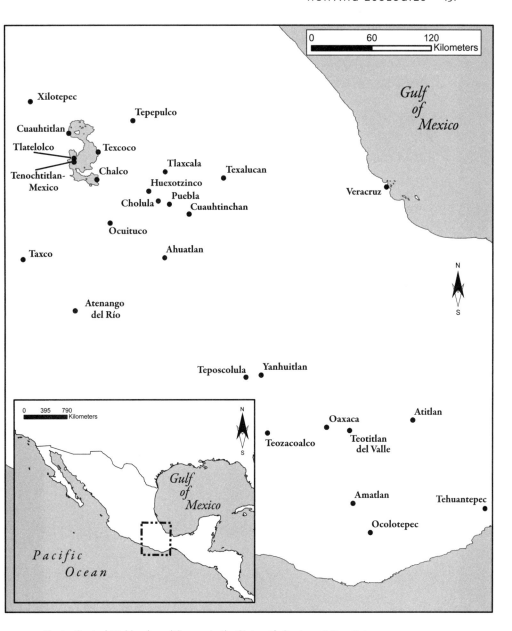

Map 2   Central Highlands and Oaxaca in the Sixteenth Century. © Marcy Norton.

A Nahua author composed this version on European paper in alphabetic Nahuatl in the mid-sixteenth century.[3] He mobilized European technologies—paper and alphabetic writing—to uphold the values of Indigenous modes of interaction. In recounting the experiences of Xiuhnel, Mimich, and the deer-women, the Nahua author encapsulated fundamental beliefs generated by predation and familiarization in Central Mexico and elsewhere in Meso-america. Attraction and violence define the relationship between prey and predator, a relationship unstable and susceptible to reversal. It emphasizes reciprocity—one hunter felled his prey, and another hunter became the prey. It underscores the inextricability of life and death; the line between living to eat and dying to become food is inevitably breached. It describes the gen-dered organization of the hunt—men kill prey, and women turn prey into food. It illustrates that a being is made of perishable parts that become food, and its enduring parts (exemplified by Itzpapalotl's bones) allow for the transfer of essential qualities. It shows that the essence of being is muta-bility: deer become women who become deer, one of whom becomes a pow-erful flint. It reveals the interrelatedness of hunting and war. It highlights distributive agency: the success of the hunter is never due to his own skill alone; the cactus is a proxy for all the different elements that are essential for a hunt to succeed. And hunting is understood as a process that intertwines predation and familiarization, insisting on the inseparability of feeding and dying and of hunting, sex, and generation.[4]

These notions about predation and familiarization were not only trans-mitted in stories but also through ritual. Hunting practices before and after the invasions were occasions to embody the values described in these stories. Moreover, in order to fully understand the fundamental importance of pre-dation and familiarization in Central Mexico, it is imperative to consider pre-Hispanic "books" (*amoxtli*)—particularly those made of animal skins—as well as colonial-era sources. The subset of *amoxtli* known as *tonalamatl* contain abstract ecological diagrams that conceptualize predation in ways that align with contemporary ideas about food webs. These diagrams—cosmograms—demonstrate that the processes of killing and eating unite all forms of life.[5] They diagram not only the interdependence of living and dying but also the universality of subjectivity and personhood. The ontolog-ical and epistemological power of predation and familiarization—before and after the Spanish invasions—can best be understood when cherished stories about ancestral hunters, the embodied experiences of hunting, and these animal-hide *amoxtli* are considered together.

~

AS IN EUROPE and South America, the importance of hunting was ontological and epistemological, as well as social and political.[6] The beliefs about predation and familiarization articulated in origin stories such as those about Xiuhnel and Mimich were even more powerful because of rites that anchored these ideas in the body. A missionary described, for example, how Nahua celebrants "not only prayed and honored and praised their gods with songs in the mouth but also with the heart and all of the senses of the body . . . with all parts of the body they sought to call and serve their gods."[7] These sensory performances were central to the celebrations of hunting that took place during the rites of Quecholli, one of the 20-day intervals (called *veintenas* by the Spanish) that composed the Mesoamerican solar calendar. (The calendar comprised eighteen "months" of twenty days, along with five days at the end of the year.) Quecholli fell at the beginning of the dry season, likely in late October and early November.[8] The performances and rites that occurred during this *veintena* honored the hunters—and their technologies—who supplied communities with delicious game and beautiful, potent pelts and feathers. They also celebrated the ecology of the high desert and the Chichimec ancestors such as Xiuhnel and Mimich who learned how to flourish there.[9]

The most extensive sources for the rites of Quecholli are colonial-era recollections of Nahua elders, especially those recorded in what eventually became book 2 of the Florentine Codex or, as it was titled at the time, *Historia universal de las cosas de Nueva España* (Universal history of the things of New Spain).[10] The latter originated in the project supervised by the Franciscan friar Bernardino de Sahagún.[11] The missionary arrived in New Spain in 1529, when he was about thirty years old, and learned from his fellow Franciscan Andrés de Olmos (previously met in his capacity as a Basque witch hunter) that if the friars were ignorant of how "these people" were "in the time of their idolatry," they would fail to recognize the "many idolatrous things in our presence without our understanding."[12] To reconstruct putative idolatrous practices in order to better eradicate them, Sahagún relied heavily on Nahua collaborators, his former students at the Real Colegio de Santa Cruz Tlatelolco, described by a missionary as a "college for the Indian nobility" to train "the principal lords of the larger towns and provinces of this New Spain."[13] Sahagún greatly admired these scholars, his former students, whom he referred to collectively as the *gramáticos* (grammarians) and *colegiales* (collegians), and praised them as "experts in three languages, Latin, Spanish and

Indian." They included Antonio Valeriano, Alonso Vegerano, Martín Jaco-
bita, and Pedro de San Buenaventura (who may have also been responsible
for this version of the story of Xiuhnel and Mimich). Sahagún himself recognized the determinative role of his collaborators' labor, noting, for instance, that when they prepared the penultimate Nahuatl draft in 1569, "the
Mexicans added and corrected many things in the twelve books while they
were being put into smooth copy."[14] As a result, many scholars now see these
Nahua intellectuals as coauthors, and the project's scope goes well beyond
the early mandate to help with idolatry extirpation.[15] Accordingly, I will
refer to the authors of the Florentine Codex and its earlier drafts collectively
as "the Tlatelolco scholars" unless it is possible to discern a particular author
or set of authors (as is the case with the Spanish prologues written by
Sahagún).

The Tlatelolco scholars carried out interviews in two phases. The first took
place in 1558–1560 in Tepepulco, sixty miles northeast of Tenochtitlan and
under the cultural sway of Texcoco. A draft with images and text, now known
as the "Primeros memoriales," survives from this period. A second phase of
interviews began in 1561 in Tlatelolco, where the Nahua *gobernador* made
available "as many as eight or ten leaders" who were "very capable in their
language and in their ancient customs." Sahagún explained that during the
meetings, "everything which we discussed was given to me by means of pictures, which was the writing they had used of old."[16] There was a complete
draft in 1569, but the final version—now known as the Florentine Codex,
which includes a Spanish translation and a new set of images—was mostly
written in 1575–1576. Detailed descriptions of Quecholli also appear in the
work of the Dominican friar Diego Durán, a resident of Mexico since early
childhood and fluent in Nahuatl.[17] His work, written primarily in the 1570s,
was based not only on direct interviews with elders but also on a now-lost
Nahuatl chronicle that he amply paraphrased, as well as pictorial manuscripts (*amoxtli*) similar to those used by the Tlatelolco scholars.[18]

Just as the cactus that ensnared Itzpapalotl represented the different elements essential for a successful hunt, the rites of Quecholli did the same. The
elders of Tlatelolco recalled that the ceremonies began with the ritualized
honoring and making of weapons—fashioned from reed shafts, wooden
points, maguey fiber, and pine resin—for the hunt. On the first day, the "sea-
soned warriors" made offerings of reeds to deities. On the second day, they
straightened them over fire. On the third day, the warriors, accompanied by
"youths, young men of marriageable age" and even small boys, marched in

procession with the reeds, blowing shell trumpets and cutting their flesh to make offerings of blood. After the arrows were honored, they made spears from wood, "spears were being born." They were now ready to complete the manufacture: the reeds were cut, fitted with bolts, the ends tied with maguey, the points set and affixed with glue, and the arrows bound together in groups of twenty. On the fourth day, "everyone used arrows, each one at his home, only to amuse themselves with them. Yet there were continual trials of skill with them. They would put up a maguey leaf at a distance. . . . There appeared some who could knock it down, those who were dexterous." On the fifth day, the dead were honored with offerings of small arrows. These were burned, along with the "costly banners, and the shields, and the capes, and the breechclouts of those slain in battle." These were placed on a dry maize stalk and affixed with red cotton thread, a dead hummingbird, and four hundred white feathers from herons—birds associated with Chichimec ancestors.[19] When celebrated in Huexotzinco, according to Durán, one of the presiding priests dressed in the garb of Camaxtle (another name for Mixcoatl, the Chichimec god of the hunt), arrayed in a rabbit pelt and headdress of eagle and quetzal plumes, and carrying a bow, arrow, and hunting net.[20]

Durán's account also reveals how the inaugural ceremonies of Quecholli brought attention to the interdependent nature of the hunt. He recounted that during this period, priests taught the hunters the way to "sacrifice to fire" and the "general invocation to all the things of the woods, together with a promise of offering sacrifice to the fire by roasting the fat of the game which was captured." The hunters "invoked the clouds, the winds, the earth, the water, the skies, the sun, the moon, the stars, the trees, the plants, the shrubs, the forests, the cliffs, the hills, the plains, the snakes, the lizards, the tigers [jaguars], the [mountain] lions, and all the kinds of wild beasts, all brought together in that hunt."[21] Among the causes and conditions that allowed for a hunt were the trees and plants that provided the materials for weapons, the earth that nourished these plants and the game animals, the ancestors who passed down the technologies and taught young boys how to use them. This animist sensibility was also conveyed by a song with lyrics the Tlatelolco scholars recorded, recounting a hunt from the perspective of a personified arrow. The arrow tells of his origins in the "house of spears," of being "grasped," and intones, "I am sent, I am sent, I am sent unto his duck."[22] Such animism also permeates the painted deerskins, on which all manner of game animals are shown pierced and killed by arrowheads anthropomorphized with eyes and mouths (see fig. 6.1). Nahuas fully recognized what theorist Jane Bennett calls "distributive agency"[23]: the success (or failure) of the hunter is never due to his own intentions and capacities alone but rather results from a myriad of causes and conditions.

A collective hunt marked the dramatic midpoint of Quecholli. On the tenth day, hunters from Tlatelolco and Tenochtitlan went to Zacatepec, a mountainous semi-desert terrain abundant with game.[24] The hunters slept in shelters made of grass (such as the one where Xiuhnel and Mimich rested after they became too weary to continue hunting), made fires for warmth, and woke at dawn. They formed a cordon "like a rope they stretched; nowhere was it cut." They "encircled all the deer, coyotes, rabbits, jack rabbits. Cautiously they closed in upon them."[25] Durán described how the Huexotzinco men set for the hills garbed like hunting deities, wearing only "beautifully adorned breechcloths," their faces painted with black circles around their mouths and eyes, their limbs and torsos with white stripes, evoking the deity Mixcoatl (see fig. 6.3), their heads adorned with red feathers and red leather ties, and bundles of eagle feathers trailed down their backs. They went "with such cries and shrieks it seems that the mountain might collapse," in "such good order, so close to one another, that a mouse would have found it impossible to escape." In this disciplined form, they finally arrived at the shrine on the crest of a hill. The animals, "seeing themselves surrounded, struggled to escape," and "the killing, the shooting with arrows took place now together with the catching of deer, hares, rabbits, pumas, mountain lions, and other beasts, squirrels, weasels and snakes."[26] After the killing ended, the hunters returned but brought only heads of game—they "carried them each with them in their hands . . . dripping blood"—and hung these heads prominently. The elders of Tlatelolco noted pointedly that the ruler rewarded those who succeeded in killing large game, "those who yet caught a deer or a coyote, those Moctezuma gave gifts of capes whose edges were striped with feathers,"[27] showing how the ruler (*tlatoani*) of the Mexica (Aztec) Empire could deploy these local traditions in a larger festival to bolster his own legitimacy.

The rites of Quecholli also echoed the idea of reciprocity and the tenuous, unstable relationship between prey and predator articulated in Xiuhnel and Mimich's hunt. In the days prior to the collective chase, hunters made offerings of their own blood, cutting their earlobes, thighs, and perhaps genitals. As recalled by the Tlatelolco elders, "They anoint themselves with blood because of the deer" and then they "fasted for the deer, so that [the deer] would be hunted."[28] An even greater offering was made at the end of the rites, when war captives were slain. The elders described how the captives were carried like deer, with their feet and hands bound, their heads "bobbing up and down" and "hanging toward the ground." Priests killed them by cutting out their hearts and then "it was said: 'Thus they slay them as deer; they serve as the deer, who thus die.'"[29] Notably, Durán's account diverged on this point. His informants pointedly remarked that no people were "sacrificed" during the rites of Quecholli, and the missionary wrote that "game, not men, were sacrificed on this day."[30] It seems that, at least, in some communities, Quecholli served in part to commemorate an earlier historical epoch, associated with more egalitarian hunting societies, in which people killed only nonhuman animals and not each other. In Nahua cosmogonies, the solar deity invented warfare because hunting did not generate enough prey to nourish it. Once the sun started consuming human prey, it generated stronger radiant heat (*tonalli*) that, in turn, made maize agriculture possible.[31] While many today associate a diet based on domesticated plant life as less violent than one based on hunted game, the inhabitants of postclassic Central Mexico understood their maize-based lifeways to be historically linked with structural warfare.

~

IN MANY RESPECTS, the arrival of the Spanish did little to alter the place of hunting in Nahua and other Indigenous communities in New Spain. Because most Spanish missionaries and secular officials considered the technologies and techniques of the hunt in a neutral or even positive light—as opposed to other kinds of activities deemed idolatry—hunting itself became a pathway for ensuring that predation and familiarization remained ontologically generative, even as other aspects of ritual life were destroyed or transformed.

European invaders were quick to notice and appreciate hunting's centrality to Indigenous society. Hernán Cortés, in his 1519 letter to Charles V, remarked on the blowpipes gifted to him by Moctezuma II. Used by Moctezuma and other Nahuas of the highest rank to shoot pellets at birds and other small animals, their "perfection" was such that the conquistador could not find adequate words to describe it "to Your Highness." They were "painted in the finest paints and perfect colors" and depicted "all manner of small birds and animals and trees and flowers." Cortés also remarked on the great marketplace in Tlatelolco where there was a "street where they sell game and

birds of every species found in this land," including deer, hares, rabbits, turkeys, partridges, quail, ducks, parrots, eagles, owls, falcons, and hawks, and
"they sell the skin of some of these birds of prey with their feathers heads
and claws" and "deerskins with and without the hair, and some are dyed
white or in various colors."[32]

Conquistadores and secular colonial authorities saw no reason, then, to
interfere with the hunting practices of Indigenous subjects. As a result, traditional hunting practices thrived in the colonial period.[33] In the mid-sixteenth
century, a colonial official noted that the Indigenous residents of Teopantlan
(Puebla) made their livelihood, in part, "from game that they take and sell it
in the markets."[34] In particular, the *Relaciones geográficas* (the responses to a
questionnaire that the Crown administered in the late 1570s and early 1580s)
reveal continuity in hunting practices. In the Zapotec community of Oce-
lotepec (Ozolotepec), the "foods that they used then are those that [they] use
now, which are maize and chile and beans and some deer, which they always
hunt."[35] Similarly, the official writing for the town of Tonameca (Oaxaca)
wrote that "the foods that they ate are the same ones as they now eat which
are tortillas and tamales and fish and iguana which is a little animal like a
lizard and chile and salt and flesh of deer when they hunt it."[36] The Nahua
gobernador of Ayutla (Guerrero), Don Andrés Obrejón, recalled that the
tribute due to the Mexica included fish and deer hides. When asked "what
kinds of food they ate in the past," Obrejón responded "the same as now, that
is maize and poultry, honey, and venison and fish," adding that "with this" his
community "lived very contentedly" but in his own time many people die
from overwork.[37] Significantly, a number of the *Relaciones* suggested that access to game expanded in the colonial period, as prior to Spanish rule, eating
meat had been mostly the prerogative of the elite in Mesoamerica.[38]

While most colonizers viewed Indigenous hunting with neutrality or enthusiasm, a few missionaries worried that hunting was a vector for "idolatry."
Some came to understand that it was an important bridge to the pre-
Hispanic past. Consequently, they revealed the continuity and entanglement
of Indigenous hunting technologies and religious beliefs in sometimes exacting detail, as well as how such continuity could easily coexist with Indigenous forms of Christianity.[39] Durán was one of these. After describing the
rites of Quecholli, he added that "these incantations circulate today in writing,"
and "I have them in my power and I could put them down here if it was a
thing that mattered but in addition to it being a thing that is not necessary
in our Spanish language, they are absurdities because all of them conclude

with invocations to hills, waters, trees, clouds and sun, moon, and stars and all the many idols that they adore and all the kinds of creatures of the woods. . . . I can affirm that today they are still in use, together with a thousand other incantations . . . all of them founded in idolatry and ancient rites." The cleric fully apprehended that these "miserable Indians" understood themselves to be Christians while practicing these rites: "With both hands they believe in god and simultaneously adore their idols and use superstitions and ancient rites mixing the one with the other."[40] In this revealing passage, Durán showed how Christianity was not perceived by Nahuas as an obstacle to continuing pre-Hispanic hunting traditions and that some colonial technologies, such as alphabetic writing, could actually help preserve them.[41]

Rites similar to those performed during Quecholli persisted into the colonial period and beyond. This was much to the dismay of the cleric Hernando Ruiz de Alarcón (b. 1574). Raised in the Taxco mining region and fluent in Nahuatl, he entered the clergy and served as one of the first parish priests in San Juan Atenango del Río at the beginning of the seventeenth century.[42] Without permission from his superiors, he sought to identify and extirpate what he considered heretical behavior, disciplining offenders with floggings and other harsh punishments. The priest used all manner of strategies to get information—sometimes an incantation on paper was found and brought to him by a parishioner sympathetic to his pursuits or vengeful toward the suspected idolater.

The zealous cleric recorded "conjurations" concerning hunting and related activities, such as fishing, collecting honey, and warding off marauding pigs, in his 1629 treatise.[43] At the most basic level, these conjurations describe the reality that the speaker (hunter, fisher, healer, among others) wished to affect. This reality was one of multiple, complex scenarios evoking layered sets of relationships among various kinds of entities—sky, water, animals, plants, people, implements, and others—who are often deified. The vigilante priest explained that in these rites "they speak . . . to the fire, to the earth, to the ropes, to the forests and grassy places, to those whom they believe to be forest gods, even to the deer themselves."[44] The language of the conjurations was a poetic, metaphorical Nahuatl, whose full meanings often eluded Ruiz de Alarcón and continues to inspire divergent translations by modern scholars.[45] They share some features with hunting "songs" that were recorded by Sahagún and his Indigenous collaborators in the 1550s.

One of the longest conjurations recorded, translated, and explained by Ruiz de Alarcón was a "spell and an incantation that they use for hunting deer with snares." The hunter made sure to address all of the elements that played a role in the hunt, in the same way that the rites of Quecholli and the story of Xiuhnel and Mimich emphasized distributive agency. He addressed the earth, the rope and the wood stakes used in the snares, the fire that would cook the meat, and, of course, the deer themselves. Each one was beseeched in highly specific ways and envisioned in scenarios that put them in relationships to each another. The earth was "My mother, Tlaltecuin," and the hunter suggests that she should be angry because the deer "make you live as [a] miserable hole-scarred one [i.e., the ground after being trampled by hooves]." The hunter called out to "my older sister, one-grass"—the rope used in the snare—and asked, tauntingly, does the deer "make raveled-out threads hang from you?" The fire—"Four Reed, He-is-scintillating . . . Yellow comet"—was beseeched and promised that he will be rewarded before the hunter: "First you will be happy. First you will see the warm blood, the fragrant blood, his heart, his head."[46]

The hunter was now ready to "depart immediately for the forest and rough terrain" and find a "swept place" where he could set up his snare with a "round rock" and four ropes. All of the entities invoked earlier—the earth, the snares, the deer, the fire—were again the objects of entreaties, but now so were the mountains, named as "you who are priests, you who are Tlalocs, you who are lying there toward the four directions . . . you who lie gripping the sky."[47] Even his own hands—named as "Five-tonals-owners, beloved goddesses"—were invoked, for they were the agents that would throw the woven net over the deer caught in his trap. At this point, the hunter shouted "toward the four winds energetically," and called the deer, "imitating a wild beast." He addressed the deer directly, saying, "It is already over with you. You have been dispatched. . . . A game of fortune has been played. Ha ha! People have captured things. It is already over with." Yet he also lamented the deer's impending death. The role of the Tlaloc mountains, it seems, was to bear witness and grieve the inevitable: "Let your hearts which are within you be sad, you Tlalocs. . . . For him since yesterday and even the day before, my older sister Xochiquetzal, has been crying, because of him she has been sad. For him since yesterday and even the day before I have been crying, because of him I have been sad." And then the hunter spoke of the deer themselves as children and grandchildren: "Already at this instant I have come to seize them, I have come to call them. Already I have created, have brought to life the wall-doorway, the wood-doorway [the snare] . . . from where they will go come out, for I am their mother, I am their father, I am their grandmother, I am their grandfather."[48]

These rituals show how belief and practice were bound together inextricably. In performing these rites, hunters declared that different entities were connected in familial relationships: they were variously siblings, children, uncles and aunts, and parents to each other. The empowered hunter tried to influence the outcome by identifying the convergence of interests as well as fissures, so that the earth should be angry at the deer for being "wounded" by antlers and hooves; the fire will anticipate sharing in the quarry; and the rope, stakes, and branches "hug" each other in an alliance to make the snare work. This conjuration illustrates most aspects of predation and familiarization described earlier: the hunter beseeched all the entities that might be involved—not just deer, but fire, ropes, and snares. He used metaphors of feeding, for instance, to promise the grass and ground the first fruits of the dead deer's flesh. The complex affective stance taken by the hunter and his wife toward their prey, viewed at once as enemy and kin, is the same one that warriors had toward their captives on the battlefield.

The deer-trapping incantation recorded by the priest was one of the ten "incantations" and "invocations" documented by Ruiz de Alarcón that Nahua men used for hunting deer and other game, trapping birds, fishing with nets and hooks in rivers, and gathering honey and wax from beehives.[49] The priest noted that there were many more because they "use different incantations for each different kind of bird and animal that they attempt to hunt." He explained that there was no need to discuss all of them, as "they differ only in the names of the animals or birds." As with the incantation for trapping deer, implements and physical features of the environment were likewise personified in the dramatizations: the hunter's bow, the reed arrow shaft, the flint arrowhead, the stakes that held up bird nets in the river (visualized as the "throat, the belly, the armpits" of the water), the cane used to make a weir ("green air-spirit"), the fishhook, the earthworm, other fish used as bait ("a food as delicious as fruit"), and the sandals ("earth-face-slapper") of the honey and wax collector.[50] The entanglement of the material and ritual in these practices is fundamental for understanding how such hunting incantations and their attendant technologies and beliefs remained robust throughout the colonial period and beyond.

Mesoamericans, who did not recognize the boundaries that often demarcated religious and quotidian practice in Europe, approached material and symbolic realms as an integrated whole. Among the most important vehicles for the persistence of traditional Indigenous beliefs and practices in the colonial period and beyond were hunting practices that the colonizers, with the exception of a few knowledgeable clerics, not only tolerated but also, in many instances, encouraged.

~

THE RITUAL PERFORMANCES of Quecholli, the stories about ancestral hunters Xiuhnel and Mimich, and the incantations of colonial hunters alike reveal an understanding of predation as a generative process. The conceptual power and reach of predation, however, is perhaps most clearly evident in the objects outsiders have called "books," "codices," or, more specifically, "divinatory almanacs." Although these objects share some properties with codices and books, they also have properties and capacities not captured by these European terms.[51] For that reason I will follow the practice of referring to the general class of screenfold "books" as *amoxtli*, and those belonging to the Borgia subgroup as *tonalamatl*, a term composed of *tonalli* and *amatl*. The word *tonalli* signifies the radiant heat emitted by the sun—and the vital energy thought to reside in blood, iridescent feathers, and pigments applied to deerskins.[52] *Amatl* denoted an outer layer of the ficus tree used to make paper for some of the codices and for other ritual uses. Ana Díaz has suggestively connected the concept of *amatl* to the animal skins that formed the substrate of the *tonalamatl* and to the representations of the earth's surface within the *tonalamatl* as a reptilian skin (see fig. 6.3).[53] The very materiality of the *tonalamatl* suggests a microcosm of creation itself: *amatl* was connected to female earth and *tonalli* to male sun. The person who made a *tonalamatl* was known a *tlacuilo* and the expert who interpreted it was a *tlamatini*. A colonial-era source described *tlamatinime* (plural) as "those who noisily turn the pages," "who have possession of the black and red ink and of that which is pictured; they lead us, they guide us, they tell us the way."[54] Among its central uses the *tonalamatl* was a guide to *tonalpohualli*, as the 260-day sacred calendar comprising twenty 13-day periods was known. These objects stored knowledge about the past, present, and future, guided ritual activity, and, I believe, diagrammed ontological concepts.

Scholars have named the five extant *tonalamatl* created prior to the European invasions the "Borgia group." Its longest and most elaborate member is the eponymous "Codex Borgia," named after one of its owners, Cardinal Stefano Borgia, and now housed in the Vatican Apostolic Library. Much remains unknown about this *tonalamatl*, though new methods of material analysis, developed by Davide Domenici and Élodie Dupey García, among others, have offered new clues.[55] There is no exact date for its creation; most likely it was made in the fifteenth or early sixteenth century, before the European invasions. Nor is the exact provenance known, much less the identity of its maker, but many scholars coincide in thinking that it came from the Valley of Puebla, perhaps near Cholula or Tlaxcala.[56] Like the other extant pre-Hispanic *tonalamatl*, it was fabricated from bands of animal hide (presumably deer) and folded in accordion fashion. It measures 10.5 meters long and 27 centimeters high, and by way of folding, it has seventy-six pages (front and back). The creator(s) applied gypsum to the surface to make a smooth white background, and painted red bands (produced by cochineal dye) to create cells within the pages. The artist used black charcoal to outline the elaborate imagery, then colored them in with yellow, orange, blue, and green pigments.[57] It shares "vocabulary" with the other four main members of the eponymous Borgia group.[58]

There is on-going debate on how to best interpret a *tonalamatl*.[59] Early twentieth-century German scholar Eduard Seler's belief that the "codices" represented "myths" remains influential, while his view that they corresponded to astronomical events has largely (but not completely) fallen out of favor.[60] Rejecting both the mythological and astronomical traditions, Seler's student Karl Nowotny emphasized that interpretations should reflect the codices' divinatory character—that their primary purpose was to guide ritual specialists' understanding of which days are auspicious and which ones are unfortunate in order to help people organize their lives.[61] Nowotny's interpretive framework has been extended and greatly enriched by the studies of Ferdinand Anders, Maarten Jansen, Luis Reyes García, Sebastián van Doesburg and Michel Oudijk, in large part by their collaborative work with Indigenous communities (the scholar and activist Reyes García (1932–2004) was himself Nahua).[62] While also emphasizing the divinatory purpose of these "books," Elizabeth Boone has convincingly shown that there is correspondence in at least one section of the Borgia *tonalamatl* to cosmogonies described in colonial-era texts.[63] Guided by Boone's method, my interpretations, in part, emerge from reading the *tonalamatl* alongside colonial-era texts that I believe originated with interpretations offered by *tlamatinime*. I also read the "cosmogram" section (explained below) of the Borgia *tonalamatl* through what might be called an ecological semiotic lens, one inspired by the work of Robin Kimmerer. An ecologist who is also a member of the Citizen Potawatomi Nation, she has written about notable convergences in academic ecology and traditional Indigenous beliefs.[64] I read the cosmogram as depicting concepts that have striking resonances with ideas that are central to contemporary ecology.[65]

Imagery within the Codex Borgia reveals the centrality of predation in the conceptualization of the *tonalamatl*.[66] A paired set of images—similar ones are found in other members of the Borgia group—depict two deer: on the left an anthropomorphized arrowhead spears a deer; on the right the deer is now deceased (indicated by his closed eyes), white, bejeweled, and befeathered (fig. 6.1).[67] Below the deer images are day-signs associated with different *trecenas*: the white deer is associated with those related to the "East" (generation) and the brown deer with those related to the "North" (predation).[68] The images also, I believe, show the transformation of a living deer into the animate *tonalamatl* itself. The deer's whiteness alludes to the gypsum-covered surface of the *tonalamatl*. The deer's precious accouterments—a headdress with quetzal and other iridescent feathers, a necklace and earrings comprised of gleaming gemstones, and flowers—all contain *tonalli* and indicate the way that the colorful pigments quite literally enlivened the deerskin. The deer died when he lost his *tonalli*-rich blood, but his skin became reanimated through the process of painting. The dead deer became a living repository of knowledge, one that can speak, as suggested by the transformation of his tongue into an oversized speech scroll.

The generative qualities of predation are conceptualized with even more exquisite detail in the dense five-page section in the Borgia *tonalamatl* sometimes referred to in scholarly literature as a "cosmogram."[69] In Alfredo López Austin's conceptualization, the cosmogram is organized around an "axis mundi"—paradigmatically via the "cosmic tree"—that connected heavenly strata of gods to the terrestrial land of mortals to a subterranean realm of death.[70] Similar series and imagery can be found in the other codices as well as their colonial-era copies.[71] Most famously, the Codex Fejérváry-Mayer (part of the Borgia group) depicts a cosmogram on its first page centered around four "cosmic trees" that emerge from the center square in a cross formation.[72] Common to the cosmograms is a quadripartite division that corresponds to segments of time (paradigmatically the 13-day intervals of the ritual calendar) and space (designated by the cardinal directions of East, North, West, and South). Each direction corresponds to a cell containing a bird perched atop a so-called "cosmic tree" (the vegetation is not necessarily arboreal). In the Borgia cosmogram a fifth cell features another plant-bird dyad and represents a synthesis of the preceding panels. I find it productive to think about this 5-panel section as a cosmogram, but I understand its

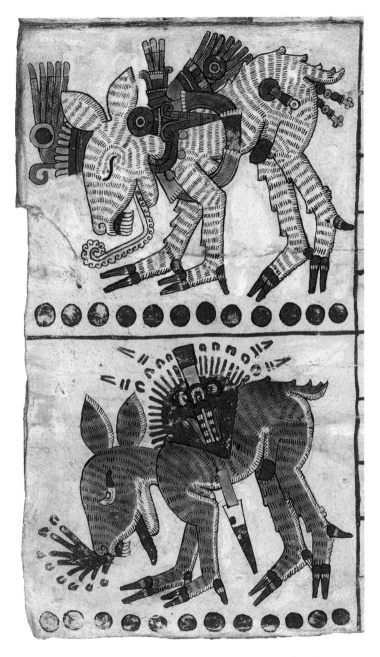

Figure 6.1   Deer becoming a *tonalamatl*, Codex Borgia, plate 22, detail, pre-1500.

meaning differently than López Austin. Similarly indebted to the iconographic analysis of Seler, Anders, Jansen, Reyes García, and Boone, my reading also diverges from theirs.[73] Different interpretations, however, are not necessarily contradictory: the density of the imagery and the malleability of the accordion construction, as well as the active role of the *tlamatini*, suggest that these objects were designed to generate multiple readings.

I propose that the cosmogram, rather than depicting an enchanted cosmos that shows relationships between people and gods, diagrams relationships within and between the atmosphere, hydrosphere, and lithosphere. Or, put another way, predation is the catalyst for the transfer of energy and nutrients from sun, water, and soil to the biosphere, and then from plant to animal life, and finally the destruction and transformation of organic matter to its primordial elements. While depicting this universal process, the cosmogram also vividly portrays the particularities of different kinds of species and habitats, or what we today call ecosystems. As such, the cosmogram represents predation as a generative process in ways that loosely align with concepts fundamental to modern ecology. An ecosystem, according to ecologist Brian Fath, "comprises an ecological community and its energetic and material interactions with the nonliving atmosphere, hydrosphere, and lithosphere"; while different ecosystems are marked by particular flora, fauna, soil and climatic conditions, and so on, they universally depend on these energetic and material transfers. Likewise, the Borgia cosmogram diagrams both the particularity of various ecological communities and the universality of processes that govern "energetic and material interactions" between these biotic entities and sun, water, and soil.[74]

The cosmogram is a powerful device for representing the interplay of the universal and the particular. Universality is expressed through repetition: each of the four directional panels of the Borgia cosmogram has an identical layout. It includes an upper register with two cells featuring deities; the much larger lower register is composed of nine vignettes or scenes arranged in loose circular form, of which the most prominent (largest and centered) is the tree-bird dyad. Identical actions are featured in each scene across the directional panels. While repetition conveys universality, difference reflects particularity: while the actions are the same, the actors—the plants, the animals, the deities, the costumes, the colors, and so on—vary across the panels.

A close reading of the first panel (East) illustrates how the commonalities across the four directional pages show the universality of predation, or the

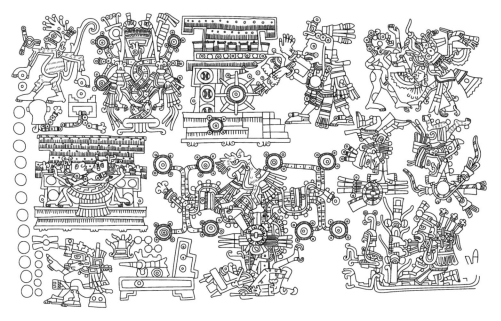

Figure 6.2   Panel associated with the East, arboreal level, and the first sun in cosmogram, drawn after Codex Borgia, plate 49. Drawing by Ardeth Anderson. © Marcy Norton.

transformation of the fed into food (fig. 6.2). The scene in the upper right corner is paradigmatic: it shows a lethal interaction between two predators, a monstrous bat and a skeletal being, the latter the personified representation of death itself. (In the imagery of the *tonalamatl*, death was viewed as the quintessential predator—the entity who "eats" the flesh and blood of the dead.) The bat, holding a decapitated head, extracts the heart and drinks the blood of the skeletal being.[75] The *tlacuilo* underscored killing as a primordial act of generative destruction by emphasizing the release of the *tonalli*, indicated by spurting blood. The animal attack scene also recalls the Nahua cosmogony that ascribed the origins of the sky and earth to the evisceration of a giant reptile by two deified serpents.[76] This primordial act sets into motion the processes that sustain various forms of life. This killing of a predator highlights the reciprocal nature of predation and familiarization by showing the way that the fed become food, much in the same way as the interactions among Xiuhnel, Mimich, and the deer-women.

Adjacent to this act of primordial predation are a cluster of three scenes that personify and deify the elemental forces of sun, water, and earth, or what ecologists today call the atmosphere, hydrosphere, and lithosphere. In each case the entities appear as beings dependent on violent predation in order to access vital nourishment. At the center top, the second most prominent scene shows the sun in the act of receiving nourishment: a figure attired in the garb of a solar deity (Tonatiuh) feeds the glowing orb with a human heart folded into a stream of blood, suggestive of the words recorded in a colonial text explaining that "in order to light the earth," the sun "ate hearts and drank blood, and for this they made war."[77] Directly below the bat-skeletal struggle, the hydrosphere is personified by two figures who descend from the sky with the implements of war. The male figure on the left holds flint-tipped arrows, a shield, and the white flag that denoted war captives; the female figure on the right holds the cotton cords that bound the captives.[78] The male is identified with combat, and the female with the result, the captive. Human captives were the quintessential source of blood and hearts fed to deities.[79]

If the atmosphere is represented by a hungry sun, and the hydrosphere by blood-seeking warriors, then the lithosphere appears as a fierce serpent. In a vignette on the bottom right, the *tlacuilo* depicted the earth's predatorial ferocity by showing the fangs inside the gaping hungry mouth and its fleshy embodiment, indicating the layers of blood and muscle that lie beneath the skin with bands of red and yellow. Atop the earth-serpent a figure creates fire with a feather-covered drill that penetrates the earth-serpent, flames emanating from her mouth.[80] Across Mesoamerica, the fire that cooked food, lit torches, and heated hearths was celebrated in dramatic ceremonies of fire drilling.[81] Fire-drilling, too, connected to the idea of geothermal heat, that in order "to give life to the earth," divine forces "took light from the sticks."[82] The imagery in the cosmogram reflects this idea, showing the earth receiving its heating vitality, its *tonalli*, by way of the drilling stick; it simultaneously evoked an impregnating phallus, the ceremonial drinking tube used for ingesting pulque, and an arrow used in warfare. The seminal act of fire drilling tied acts of killing, feeding, and insemination, mirroring the actions in the vignettes that corresponded to the atmosphere and hydrosphere.

After being fed and impregnated, the elemental forces of solar energy, water, and soil become food to nourish vegetative life. The adjacent cosmic tree, the focal point of the panel, is a flowering tree on whose canopy perches a quetzal bird.[83] The trunk is formed by a double helix of blue and green bands and bears four branches bearing large, round blossoms. This helix-trunk, or *malinalli*, was associated with complementary oppositional forces, such as fire from the sun and water from the earth.[84] The tree appears as an apex predator, consuming solar energy, liquid water, and soil nutrients. The quetzal bird is, in part, a solar proxy, who is "feeding" the tree by irradiating *tonalli*—the life energy emitted by sun and iridescent feathers alike.[85] The vignette aligns closely with the idea that "energy flow in ecosystems begins with the capture of solar radiation by photosynthetic processes" in plants.[86] Water also nourishes: the aquatic element is indicated by a flowering, jeweled stream that encircles the branches and twinned trunk; in the center of the trunk is the same shield-arrow-banner assemblage that is held by the adjacent descending warrior figures discussed above. And the tree absorbs nutrients from the soil: its roots pierce the belly of a supine, clawed, skull-headed earth deity Cihuacoatl. In this conceptualization, trees are the ultimate predators, uniquely capable of transforming the radiant energy of the sun, water from the environment, and nutrients from the soil into food.

Plant life, in turn, enables animal life. Plants are "primary producers" because they turn the energy of the sun into material that animal "consumers" can eat.[87] The vignettes on the left side of the cell center the animal life made possible by this vegetation. The human couple, adjacent to the flowering tree, are the quintessential animal consumers. The woman and man lie under a cover in an enclosure, their arms around each other, their naked legs visible—a depiction of reproductive sexual activity. Their dependence on plant life is signified not only by the arboreal vegetation to their right but also by the flowers that jut up from the roof of the structure in which they embrace. Their biological and social existence, in turn, enables political life. Below the copulating couple, in front of a throne-like chair over which hovers a year-sign ("4 House"), a man points to the day sign ("4 Movement") and sits on a seat covered with a jaguar skin. Both the jaguar skin seat and "throne" are symbols of political authority, literal seats of power in postclassic central Mexico.

The final scenes of the cell concern transformative destruction and the inevitable death of all living things, including ecosystems and societies, as well as individual beings. There is a second arboreal scene on the top row, to the left of the sun, in which the direction of predation is reversed once again. It is now the sun—depicted as a carnivorous eagle—who devours plant and animal life: it receives blood flowing out of the bodies of two decapitated quetzal birds. The tree is no longer depicted as an impaling predator; it is now rendered as food, or prey, as indicated by its bleeding uprootedness. This diagram corresponds with the idea that all organic matter—all life—will eventually be reabsorbed into the atmosphere, hydrosphere, and lithosphere. It will become, again, raw energy and material. The final vignette—the monkey running, poised to leave the cell—also corresponds to destructive generation. Beneath him are symbols of social upheaval—overturned crockery out of which flows blood, indicated by flowers signifying preciousness and blood. These markers of social collapse correlate with the environmental destruction suggested by the decapitated birds and amputated tree to his right. This is apocalyptic predation that will lead to mass death of humankind but also to the generation of a new species, monkeys, as will be discussed in more detail below.[88]

The actions depicted in each of these nine scenes are replicated in the other three directional cells and show the universality of these processes of energy transfer to and within the biosphere. Each cell has identical compositions in terms of the *actions* represented, thereby indicating what might be called fundamental laws of nature. So, for instance, in the second, "North" panel, we see that the identities of the predatorial animals, sun, tree, and bird have all changed (fig. 6.3). The "tree" is now a flowering prickly pear cactus on which perches an eagle with flinted feathers. The primordial predator at the top right is now a human hunter (his body paint of red and white stripes connects him to the hunting deity Mixcoatl) spearing a jaguar who has eaten a hunter. The "sun" inside the temple is now a lunar dark orb; the figure feeding it is attired in the garb of Itztlacoliuhqui, a deity identified with frost and death. The descending male warrior carries an ax, spiked club, and bleeding obsidian ball, while his female counterpart holds nourishing water, a cognate to blood, produced as a result of killing. In the second solar-arboreal vignette, on the upper row next to the temple platform, the lunar sun reappears and drinks the blood spurting upwards from decapitated turkey (right) and jaguar (left). The overturned crockery that indicates the eradication of people now contains dismembered body parts (an arm, a heart, an eye). Some of the people have become turkeys, suggested by the bird exiting to the left. The common elements among the four directional panels show that no matter the place or the time, the cosmos is governed by the same process of generative predation: energy and vital nutrients move from the atmosphere, hydrosphere, and lithosphere into the biosphere; within the biosphere plant life enables animal life; and finally, all of this life will once again "feed" the primordial elements.

If the commonalities *across* the five panels point to the universality of generative predation, the specificity of the flora, fauna, costumes, structures, and

Figure 6.3   Panel associated with North, terrestrial level, and second sun in cosmogram, Codex Borgia, plate 50, pre-1500. Borg.mess.1, f.pl 50, photo © Biblioteca Apostolica Vaticana. Reproduced by permission of Biblioteca Apostolica Vaticana, all rights reserved.

objects reflect particularity. More precisely, the differences evoke temporal and ecological diversity. The tree and bird dyads represent the symbiotic plant and animal communities of different regions and so indicate the diversity of ecosystems and biomes. The outer, eastern and southern panels suggest the tropical biome that lay to the East and South of the Valley of Puebla (the regions that the Spanish labeled *tierras calientes* or "hot lands"). The large blossoms of the eastern tree and the gleaming iridescent feathers of the quetzal symbolized, in the words of Eduard Seler, "precious, fructifying moisture," or, we might say, a high-altitude tropical forest.[89] The fourth "southern" cell (fig. 6.4) features a red, spiky flowering tree upon which perches another heat-loving bird, the red macaw, perhaps indicative of lower lying tropics. In contrast, the "inner" North (fig. 6.3) and West (fig. 6.4) panels represent the cooler biome of the semi-desert, high altitude plateau. The thorny cactus and fierce eagle clearly suggest the high-altitude desert. The bird of the West is also some kind of raptor, perhaps a hawk, though in

other cosmograms the characteristic bird is a hummingbird, both endogenous to the high desert.[90]

If the differences among flora and fauna in the four quadrants indicate diversity of biomes—tropical forestland and high desert—on a horizontal plane, they also point to diversity in ecosystems on a vertical plane. The four panels, from right to left, or rather from top to bottom, signify four habitats: the upper level is arboreal (fig. 6.2); the second level is terrestrial (fig. 6.3), the third level is aquatic; and the lowest level is subterranean (fig. 6.4). In the first scene of each directional panel—the "animal attack"—the predator triumphs over a representative of the preceding panel, or the level proximate to it, in a circular manner. So, in the first (East) panel, corresponding to the arboreal canopy, a bat kills a skeleton, the being of the last (South) panel, corresponding to the subterranean realm. There are also canopy-dwellers in the other vignettes of the arboreal (eastern) panel (fig. 6.2): on the left side the sun devours quetzal birds, and humans become monkeys. The second

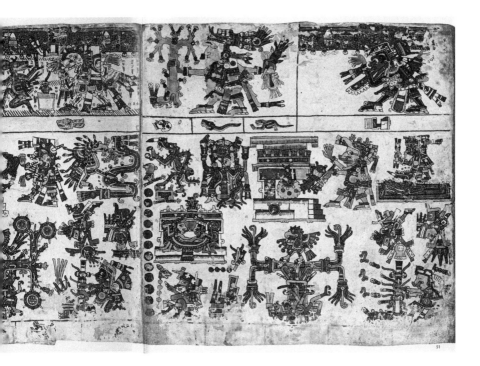

quadrant corresponds to the terrestrial plane as well as the North (fig. 6.3). The victorious predator is a human—a land-dwelling animal—who kills a jaguar, now a representative of the tree canopy since these big cats were known for their fondness for resting or stalking in trees.[91] The decapitated animals are a human and a turkey, the latter of which reappears in the final scene as the species into which people are transformed. Turkeys, like people, spend most of their time on the ground, and so are associated with terrestrial habitats, as is indicated by the colonial texts discussed below. The third "western" panel also indicates riparian and marine environments (fig. 6.4): now a caiman amputates the leg of a humanoid land-dweller; a fish and caiman are decapitated, and a lizard flees in the final scene. The fourth, South panel is also the domain of the subterranean, exemplified by the animated skeleton (similarly depicted by the being vanquished by the bat in the first vignette of the first panel) in the upper left corner. It is more difficult to show how the predatorial vignette—an eagle eviscerates a snake with his sharp talons—relates to the subterranean. However, the flints that emanate from the raptor's feathers are suggestive of death itself since flints were the paradigmatic instrument for killing (used to extract the hearts of enemy captives), and so perhaps the scene diagramed the concept of death, the catalyst for decomposition and regeneration that takes place in the soil.

The differences among the panels mark temporal variety as well as spatial diversity. Most explicitly, each panel was associated with a different grouping of the thirteen-day interval of the 260-day ritual calendar (*tonalpohualli*). The day symbols border the bottom register, only faintly visible because of deterioration of the pigments, each of them marking the first day of the thirteen-day interval.[92] The cells were connected to other kinds of cyclical time as well. They indicated diurnal cycles: the glowing orb of the eastern cell signified the sun's morning hours, while the gourd containing *tonalli*-rich *picietl* (tobacco) of the western cell corresponded to the afternoon sun.[93] The "sun" of the North was actually a nighttime moon, and that of the South was a fierce nocturnal owl drinking the blood of a decapitated person, suggestive of the dark hours before dawn.

If the first four panels show the universality of generative predation and the particularity of spatial zones and temporal cycles, the fifth panel—sometimes referred to as the "center"—represents a kind of synthesis of the preceding cells (fig. 6.4). Here the plant is not a tree but rather a giant maize bearing fearsome, anthropomorphized ears of corn at its base and on its stalks. The maize appears as an exemplary predator. The *tlacuilo* indicated the maize's fierce hunger—and the predatory nature of plants—by painting large eyes and bared teeth on the enfaced corncobs. The solar entity—represented here by its proxy, the quetzal bird, with its glimmering iridescent feathers—feeds the plant by irradiating *tonalli*. Paralleling the descending warrior figures in the previous four panels are the deities, identified as Quetzalcoatl and Macuiltonaleque, who pierce their penises in order to release the blood-water the maize needs to grow; the nourishing water is indicated by the undulating blue and black circles that surround the plant. The stalk impales and feeds on the skeletal earth deity, who lies prone on the reptilian skin of the earth. The fifth, last panel is suggestive of the collective unity of all quadrants. Spatially, it is the center, for the "tree" is a maize plant of the West on which is perched a quetzal of the East.

The five scenes of this cosmogram make clear that it is not only people who need to be fed; everything that provides food needs food, including the sun, water, and soil, as well as plants and animals. The depicted enmeshment of predation and familiarization—the way that animals and plants alike are both food and fed—and the emphasis on the inextricability of processes of living and dying has parallels to concepts used in contemporary ecology. The cosmograms' interpretation aligns closely with the contemporary ecological notion that certain universal processes characterize all biological systems.

Modern ecologists and the creators and interpreters of the cosmogram alike describe "food cycles" in which plants receive nourishment from the sun, water, and soil. They are both interested in how plants feed animals, and how the bodies of all of these entities feed the earth through their decomposition. Contemporary ecologists, like the creators and readers of the folded deer-skins who preceded them by centuries, employ alimentary metaphors to describe interdependent relationships of predation among beings, as suggested by phrases such as "food webs" and "nutrient recycling."[94]

~

MISSIONARIES AND COLONIAL officials sought to destroy the *tonalamatl* tradition. They understood these "books" to be central to the idolatrous and diabolical practices they were determined to eradicate. But sometimes they were not destroyed. Some were sent as curiosities back to Europe; the Borgia *tonalamatl* may have been transported to Italy in 1532–1533 by a Dominican friar.[95] Others were copied and annotated so that the missionaries could understand better the idolatry they wanted to extinguish.[96] The clerics who sought to understand "idolatrous" beliefs and practices also met with Indigenous experts and asked them to explain their "books." A missionary responsible for one of the resulting texts stated that his account came from "elders who were their priests" who "gathered before me and brought their books and paintings which appear to be old."[97] The *tonalamatl* tradition also survived, albeit in a transformed way, when Nahua intellectuals adapted new technologies introduced by the colonizers—above all alphabetic writing—to reflect upon and transmit the concepts embedded within the cosmogram. One way that colonial-era Spanish, Nahuatl, and pictorial works preserved—and transformed—the *tonalamatl* and its conceptualization of predation as a generative, ecological process is in an account scholars refer to as the "Legend of the Suns." One of the earliest textual versions is found in the "Histoyre du Mechique" a French translation of a lost Spanish text, the latter probably composed by Olmos when he was residing among the Mexica.[98] The missionary explained that Nahuas' "wizards" told them of an earlier world "that was destroyed." In the "first creation," he wrote, "the gods had created four suns under four figures, according to what is shown in their books." The first sun they called Chachuich tonajo [Chalchiuhtlicue tonatiuh], "who is like the god of precious stones"—is an aquatic deity. "Those who lived under this sun," he explained, "were sustained by a river grass [*acicintli*]." This world "was destroyed by water" and so the people drowned, "but some turned into fish." In the second eon, there was a new sun. The people who lived in that time ate a maize-like plant described as "*centecupi*"—perhaps a corruption of *cintli* or maize cobs[99]—until they "were burned by fire from the sky." Some of these people transformed into "hens [turkeys], the others into butterflies, and the others into dogs." The third sun was "the dark sun or the night," and those who lived during its reign were giants, and they "ate mir and pine resin of which there is a great abundance in this country" until they died "from earthquakes." The fourth sun was that of the "air," and the people "ate a fruit which comes from a tree named *mizquitl* and there are a great number in this New Spain and is much esteemed by the Indians for breads that keep a long time," and "those died in windstorms and were transformed into monkeys."

These earlier ages and their suns were followed by the current age. The missionary author explained that under the "fifth and current sun" Nahuas believed in the co-creation of a new population of humans and their staple plant maize. The creator deities Tezcatlipoca and Ehecatl (a wind divinity associated with Quetzalcoatl) "descended to hell to demand that Mictlan-teuctli give the ashes of the dead to make new people."[100] The newly created people "were nourished by a god named Xolotl," or perhaps a divinity who took the form of a turkey, "who fed them with ground corn rather than milk."[101] The first people emerged from the ground through a cavern—the geological version of a vagina in the Mesoamerican imaginary. In a mid-century Nahuatl version, Quetzalcoatl recovered bones that were ground by the earth deity Cihuacoatl in the fashion that women grind corn. The bones turned into human life when "all of the gods sacrificed from their tongues."[102]

None of the versions of the "Five Suns" are identical: the variations may reflect different local traditions (although most appear to have a Mexica slant), different interpreters, or confusion among those listening and recording.[103] Nevertheless, they converge in the notion that there were previous epochs in which different suns sustained earlier populations of people until cataclysms led to their destruction. Most variants tie together the creation of humanity and maize, paralleling the earlier ages in which each population had a staple plant food associated with the animals into whom they transformed after the apocalypse. In these accounts, the traces of the four previous eons live on in the present in the multiplicity of plant and animal species.

It has not been previously recognized that there is a close correspondence between the "Legend of the Suns" texts and the five-panel cosmogram in the Borgia *tonalamatl*. While the textual accounts originate from the Valley of Mexico and the Borgia *tonalamatl* is likely a product of the neighboring

Valley of Puebla, the commonalities are striking enough to suggest a common tradition. In the Borgia, the four directional panels correspond to the four ages that preceded the current one. Like the ages described in the colonial texts, each panel or eon features a different "sun" (Tonatiuh, Itztlacoliuhqui, Xochipilli, Mictlanteuctli). Each shows a different human population, as reflected by the copulating couples. Each shows different staple plants (as suggested by the central tree and/or the vegetation sprouting on top of the couples' enclosures). Each shows a different sun devouring the blood of different decapitated animals, symbolizing the destruction of each successive age. And each shows a different animal—monkey, turkey, caiman, and skeleton—exiting stage left; the transformed humans.

The fifth panel of the Codex Borgia cosmogram (fig. 6.4) corresponds to the present age of the fifth sun. The skeleton who emerges at the end of the fourth panel—or the fourth age—provides the raw material of bones that will allow for the creation of new people. In the upper register of the fifth panel, a man, naked save for a garment around his waist, emerges from an inverted cave; the surface of the earth is depicted as scaly skin, below which are the layers of blood and muscle that compose the fecund soil.[104] Below him is the gigantic maize plant, a cosmic "tree" larger than those of all of the preceding panels—the plant that will become the defining food of this population of humans of the fifth sun. The "Legend of the Suns"—in the Borgia *tonalamatl* and the colonial texts alike—offers an evolutionary account of the diversity of plants and animals "evolved" in ways to adapt to the apocalyptic transformations of the earlier ages. But where modern scientific accounts explain that humans are descendants of other kinds of animals, in the "Five Suns" tradition, humans are the progenitors of other creatures. Yet, as with modern evolutionary theory, these stories demonstrate ancestral kinship between people and nonhuman animals.

If the cosmogram offered a history of deep time, it also connected to the history of people *during* the fifth sun. Another dimension of the cosmogram tradition—and the conceptual importance of predation—can be seen in its adaptation by the Mexica. The glyph for their city Tenochtitlan is itself a compressed cosmogram: a nopal cactus is the cosmic tree that grows from a heart (an image that lives on in the modern Mexican flag).[105] The cosmogram appears too in a postclassic stone carving of a cactus impaling a prone Chalchiuhtlicue, the water/earth deity, and offering a perch to an eagle holding in his beak the water-fire (*atl-tlachinolli*) glyph for war.[106] This cosmogram is not only present but an organizing idea in the histories of the Mexica, and other Nahua communities written in the colonial period (and

Figure 6.5 Mexica cosmogram in Diego Durán, Historia de las Indias de Nueva España e islas de la Tierra Firme, fol. 226r, ca. 1570–1579. Image from the collection of the Biblioteca Nacional de España.

beyond). These include a "History" of the Mexica that Durán composed alongside his treatise on "Rites." Durán acknowledged that he adapted the history from a Nahuatl source; this now-lost text also appears to be the source for at least two other colonial works, one in Spanish written about 1585 by the Jesuit missionary Juan de Tovar, and another in Nahuatl, the "Crónica Mexicáyotl," composed (or copied) in the seventeenth century by a Nahua scholar, Hernando Alvarado Tezozómoc.[107] Both Durán and Tovar's manuscripts include iconographically similar—though stylistically different— illustrations painted by Indigenous artists.

The cosmogram appears in a full-page spread that precedes the text in the second part of the manuscript (fig. 6.5).[108] The nopal cactus with its red fruit emerges from the sediment of a human heart that lies below the brackish lake water. The eagle perching on its branches is beginning to eat a smaller bird whom he grips with his talons. Flanking the cactus and birds are two men wearing cotton cloaks who sit on reed mats associated with rulership. Marshland rushes sprout in the foreground, and mountains rise in the background. Above the eagle is a shield and arrows, a symbol for warfare. This image is similar to the center panel of the Borgia cosmogram (fig. 6.4) in that it shows the cactus as an apex predator receiving nourishment from soil/heart below and bird/sun above. And like the "center" cosmic tree of the Borgia cosmogram, it merges elements from the different cardinal directions into one scene. While the cactus and eagle are quintessentially the flora-avian pair associated with the North, the lacustrine environment suggests the West, while the bird being consumed is a precious one of the South and East. While the "Crónica Mexicáyotl" is solely an alphabetic text, it nonetheless vividly summons this image in its very first lines, in its promise to tell the history of Tenochtitlan, "The signal and famous place" was "where grows the prickly pear cactus in the middle of the water, where the eagle rests and shrieks, where he extends his wings and eats, where the snake hisses, where the fish swims, where the blue and yellow waters merge and burn . . . among the rushes and the reeds."[109]

In part, the image is a *mise en scène* of the 1325 foundation of Tenochtitlan, the dramatic midpoint of the history elaborated in all three texts. Huitzilopochtli, a tutelary deity of the Mexica and the deified solar complex, told the ancestors of the Mexica to "go among the marshes of reeds, rushes, and cattails" to look for a "prickly pear cactus standing upon a rock." "You will find the eagle at all times on this prickly pear cactus that sprouted from the heart of my nephew Copil," Huitzilopochtli's mortal enemy, "and all around it you will see the innumerable green, blue, red, yellow, and white feathers from the splendid birds on which the eagle feeds."[110] Durán wrote that when the Mexica's ancestors found the cactus, they saw the "eagle with his wings stretched out towards the rays of the sun, basking in their warmth and the freshness of the morning. In his talons he held a bird with very fine feathers, precious and shining," and "when the people saw the eagle, they humbled themselves, making reverences as if the bird were a divine thing. The eagle, seeing them, also humbled himself, bowing his head low in their direction.[111] The Nahuatl author of the "Crónica Mexicáyotl" put more emphasis on the violence of the predation: the eagle was "eating, tearing apart his food," his nest "covered with all kinds of precious feathers, that of the cotinga, the spoonbill, the quetzal, and they saw, too, spread on the ground the heads, the feet, and bones of precious birds."[112]

In both image and text, these colonial sources depict the foundation of Tenochtitlan as a synthesis of different ecosystems—those reflected as well in the four panels of the Borgia cosmogram—and the cultural traditions that evolved in tandem with them. Like other Nahua groups of the Central Highlands, the Mexica understood themselves to be heirs of both migrating, nomadic hunting Chichimec ancestors and the settled agriculturalists whom they conquered.[113] Where evolutionary time began with the East, historical time began with the North. The first milieu of the ancestors was Chico-moztoc. It was "a terrifying place" with "countless fierce animals, such as wolves, jaguars, mountain lions, snakes." The Crónica Mexicáyotl details the vegetative life, mentioning not only the exemplary barrel cactus but also ma-gueys and grasses growing amid the rocky terrain. The ancestral Chichimec learned how to flourish in this challenging terrain, "with their arrows they shot deer, rabbits, fierce animals, snakes and birds" and "ate them as they went and wore their skins as capes" and knew how to make use of wild plants.[114] Not coincidentally this is the same kind of environment evoked by the imagery of the northern cell in the Borgia *tonalamatl*. In other words, we can see that the eagle-cactus dyad of the *tonalamatl* could be read as a synec-doche for the different animals and plants who collectively comprised the high desert ecosystem. These Mexica histories also describe another kind of settlement that preceded their foundation in Tenochtitlan, a place of clear springs and whiteness: white cypress and willow trees, white reeds and rushes, and white frogs, fish and snakes "swimming in the water."[115] This marshy wetland teemed with life. It may be that in the Fejérváry-Mayer *tonalamatl*, the avian-arboreal dyad of the western cell is a white cedar and blue heron, a synecdoche, perhaps, for this type of marshland ecology.[116]

Tenochtitlan marked a midpoint in the histories. If the past was described in terms of ancestral homelands of Chicomoztoc of the North and a wetland paradise of the West, then the future was connected to the region of Anahuac (South and East) that the Mexica were destined to conquer. This region was connected to the bird consumed by the eagle, who was a stand-in for "all kinds" of the birds "of precious feathers," in other words, "the cotinga, the spoonbill, the quetzal . . . the precious birds."[117] If this bird prefigured the Mexica con-quests in the South and East, so did the promises made by Huitzilopochtli. He promised the Mexica a future in which they become "lords" over other peoples. "You will have beneath you," promised the deity to the Mexica, "innumerable commoners, who will give you in tribute an abundance of jade, gold, quetzal feathers, . . . they will give you various and precious feathers of cotinga (*xiuh-tototl*), spoonbill (*tlauhquechol*), trogon (*tzinitzcan*). You will have cacao of

[many] colors and cotton of [many] colors."[118] In these speeches the histories not only evoked the birds of the eastern and southern cells, but also their vegetation, the trees of cotton and cacao, the latter, indeed, pictured in the Fejérváry-Mayer *tonalamatl* as the cosmic tree of the South. The East and South were associated with Anahuac, where the sensory delights of cacao and iridescent feathers originated, and that motivated the Mexica empire-building that unfolded after 1325 from their base in Tenochtitlan.

In these textual interpretations of the cosmogram, predation was the transformative process for history just as it was for ecology. In identifying themselves with an eagle that fed on the bird of "precious feathers," the Mexica glossed a more general history in which northern and western Uto-Aztecan migrants moved south, and whose final stage—in the Mexica version—led to the Aztec Empire's expansion to the East. European settlers interpreted these origin stories through a hierarchical framework of civilized and barbarian societies. Thus, they understood the Chichimec—hunters clad in animal skins—to be culturally inferior to the cotton-clad horticulturalists, and some Indigenous and Mestizo writers in the later colonial period also took this view.[119] Moreover, the colonizing Spanish, as well as their Indigenous auxiliaries, labeled the Chichimeca as "savage," not only because of their nomadism and egalitarianism but also because many of their communities successfully resisted Spanish occupation throughout the sixteenth century and beyond. Nevertheless, in the postclassic period, Nahuas did not view their hunting ancestors as inferior to the farmers whom they conquered; rather, they were grateful for and fascinated by both of their inheritances. Nahua communities throughout the Central Highlands admired and wanted to sustain the ascetic, tough, and bellicose characteristics of the Chichimeca—as well as their hunting prowess. Their transformation into horticulturalists, in fact, depended on the martial prowess that derived from their past as hunters.

While the "historical" interpretation of the cosmogram dominates in the Spanish texts, the ecological meanings persist clearly in the images. These cosmograms evoke the lacustrine ecosystem of the Mexica homeland. And like the center panel of the Borgia cosmogram, they show the cactus as an apex predator receiving nourishment from soil/heart below and bird/sun above. But there are traces of the ecological reading in the texts as well, above all in the Nahuatl "Crónica Mexicáyotl." When the priest transmitted the message from Huitzilopochtli to his people, he commanded that they "look for a nopal, on top of which you will see an eagle who eats and warms himself in the sun, know that this is the heart of Copil . . . from the heart of

Copil sprouted this nopal."[120] The text makes explicit the connection between the sun and eagle, and articulates the idea of the nopal as the apex predator who takes nourishment the heart/soil and eagle/sun. In image and in words the Mexica cosmogram conveyed the universal ecological relationships organized around predation and the particularity of the ecosystems whose bounty the Mexica enjoyed.

~

THE ECOLOGICAL MEANINGS of the cosmogram also appeared in an emerging genre: the modern natural history. In addition to "books" concerning Nahua beliefs and ritual, the Tlatelolco scholars wrote a text entitled, "Yn ixquich tlalticpacyotl" ("Things pertaining to the earth," or more concisely "Earthly Things").[121] In a reorganized, expanded form, it became book II of the Florentine Codex. The first draft was composed in the early 1560s, when the scholars were working in Tlatelolco.[122] They devoted 327 entries to different animals, along with entries for plants, minerals, and colors.[123]

Scholars have assumed that Sahagún and the Tlatelolco scholars used the same research process that was employed for the earlier books on religious ceremonies. In other words, they infer that the research team interviewed Nahua elders according to a questionnaire created by Sahagún during their stay in Tlatelolco in the early 1560s, proposing that the informants were long-distance traders, former attendants in the royal menagerie, hunters, and featherworkers.[124] However, I think an alternative, or at least additional, scenario is equally viable: It may be that the Nahua scholars largely wrote the text without use of direct informants, other than the interviews they had had previously conducted to write the other books. As members of the Nahua elite, they likely enjoyed hunting and could draw directly on those experiences, as well as those of others in their milieu. An examination of this manuscript itself suggests that the Nahua intellectuals were the primary authors. The majority of the Nahuatl text is in the clear hand of one person, although given the scribal practice described by Sahagún, it is entirely possible that there were multiple Nahua authors whose preliminary drafts were copied by a single scribe. The friar added, in his shaky hand, "paragraph" titles—for example, "las aves de rapiña" (birds of prey)[125]—when he was working on revisions in Mexico City between 1565 and 1569.[126] He also wrote marginalia next to many of the entries, indicating, for instance, an animal's "notable property" or writing "fable" next to a story about the dove.[127] He sometimes added Spanish translations in the margins, such as bear for the *cuitlachtli* and "lion" for the *miztli* (mountain lion).[128] The traces left behind by Sahagún show him to be a *reader* and an *editor* rather than the primary author.

In some respects, "Earthly Things" was the most European of the "books" of the "Historia universal." As Andrew Laird has demonstrated, the Mediterranean classical traditions profoundly influenced the Nahua scholars due to the education they received from Sahagún and others.[129] "Earthly Things" was particularly shaped by the entwined natural history and encyclopedic traditions that flourished in late medieval and early modern Europe. More precisely, the fifteenth-century encyclopedia *Hortus sanitatis* and Pliny's "Natural History" provided significant inspiration for "Historia universal," as Pablo Escalante Gonzalbo and others have shown.[130] The *Hortus* (garden) was invoked in the Spanish title given to book II, "Forest, Garden, and Orchard of the Mexican Language," which is among the titles found in the inventory of books owned by the Colegio.[131] The entries in "Earthly Things," like those in the *Hortus,* usually began with an explanation of the signifier and then provided a description of the animal's attributes (appearance and sounds), behavior, its uses for people, and its "notable properties." These European antecedents powerfully shaped perceptions, as is evident above all in the work's taxonomic organization. As was the case with Pliny's "Natural History" and the *Hortus,* in "Earthly Things," nature was divided into vegetable, animal, and mineral elements. Likewise, animals were subdivided according to environment; for Pliny, this entailed a fourfold division of creatures of land, water, and air, as well as a separate "book" for insects; in the *Hortus,* insects were subsumed under terrestrial animals, so there were only three treatises.[132] The work's adoption of schema shows profoundly the articulation and influence of the classical Mediterranean and European medieval understanding of nature. This impulse toward separation into discrete entities is at odds with the ecological cosmograms that were designed to show the relationships among earth, plants, and animals, rather than their differences.

The structuring power of the European encyclopedic tradition, however, did not extinguish the knowledge or ethos generated by Indigenous modes of interaction.[133] The primacy of predation is pervasive and can be seen clearly in the entries themselves. Many entries detail hunting, trapping, and fishing techniques.[134] Even when the mode of capture is not made explicit, it is clear that many animals were prey, valued for their flesh, feathers, or hides, to be used as food, medicine, or textiles. Rabbits are "good-tasting, savory, healthful, the best," and deer are "good to the taste, savory, edible."[135] Possum tail is recommended to accelerate childbirth or remedy constipation.[136] Some animals appear as predators instead of, or as well as, prey. Fearsome jaguars and rattlesnakes recognize people as prey, as does the *aueyactli* snake ("very big, thick, like a beam") who "bites one, it strikes one; it completely envelops things, it swallows them whole. It awaits one on the road . . . And if there is flight if there is departure from its presence, it pursues one, it flies at one."[137]

The entries in "Earthly Things" reflect not only the continuity of traditional hunting practices but also the ethos of intersubjectivity and reciprocity generated by Indigenous predation. As in the story of Xiuhnel and Mimich, the authors focused on the subjectivity of the prey, conveying the experience of the hunt from the animals' perspectives. Upon being trapped, the possum "cries, it squeals; true tears come forth, especially when it is taken with its young. Much does it weep for them; true tears come forth."[138] Likewise, the entry on the jaguar (*ocelotl*)—presented as both prey and predator—describes the hunt from the perspective of both man and feline:

> When [the jaguar] sees one, when it meets, when it comes upon a huntsman, a hunter, it does not run, it does not flee. It just settles down to face him. It places itself well; it hides itself not at all, this *ocelotl.* Then it begins to hiss so that by its breath it may make faint, may terrify the hunter. And then the hunter begins to shoot arrows at it. The forest reed, the arrow, which he shoots, the *ocelotl* just catches with its paws. It shatters it with its teeth. It seats itself upon it growling, snarling, rumbling in its throat. . . . And the hunters have their reckoning (as well as their custom) that they shoot only four times. If he shoots four [arrows], the hunter is [as good as] dead. Thereupon the *ocelotl* prepares itself; it stretches, it yawns, it stirs, it shakes itself; it cleans itself. It licks itself. Then indeed it crouches, springs, flies through the air. Whether the hunter stands ten spans—even fifteen spans—away there it goes to seize him. Only does it leap—fly—swish bristlingly, its hair ruffled. There dies the hunter; there he is eaten.[139]

Nor did the taxonomic ideas of the European classical tradition preclude the shaping power of Mesoamerican ecological geography. Whereas the *Hortus* and Pliny begin with terrestrial animals, the 1560s draft of "Earthly Things" loosely orders animals according to the vertical logic of the cosmogram. The first group is birds—creatures of the arboreal canopy—followed by groups that correspond, respectively, to dwellers of the terrestrial, aquatic, and subterranean realms.[140] Notably, the entries concerned with terrestrial birds, such as quail and turkeys, follow the birds who dwell in the arboreal canopy. By putting the land-dwelling birds last the Nahua authors could place them more closely to the four-legged land-dwellers and thereby find a compromise reconciling the European and Mesoamerican taxonomies. The biomic taxonomy of the cosmogram is also evident within the avian section: the groupings correspond, approximately, to birds of the East, South, West, and North, followed by other birds that don't fit the schema. The *quetzaltotol,* the iridescent green, most prized bird of "precious feathers" that sits atop the tree of the East in the cosmograms, is, fittingly, the first entry among the birds.[141] Then the Nahua authors describe other birds of precious feathers, such as various parrot species, all associated with the South, the flowery environs of the tropics.[142] These are followed by varieties of hummingbirds and waterfowl, all birds of the West.[143] Finally, there are the raptors, exemplary birds of the North.[144] Nahua taxonomy is also visible in the treatment of snakes. In Pliny and the medieval encyclopedias, "serpents" are included in the category of terrestrial dwellers. In "Earthly Things," snakes are split between the entries on aquatic and subterranean creatures and are given primacy in both sections, reflecting their status as among the most generative creatures in Mesoamerican cosmology.[145]

One need not choose whether the Nahua authors of the Colegio de Tlatelolco were more inspired by the European or Mesoamerican traditions. "Earthly Things" cannot be divorced from the colonial and Indigenous contexts that generated it and therefore owes an enormous debt both to European and Indigenous epistemologies. The schematic organization that endeavors to separate the world into divisible, discrete, and separate entities of animal, vegetable, and mineral is quintessentially a millennia-old European and Mediterranean tradition that is antithetical to the holistic vision of interdependence conveyed by the cosmograms and the solar festivals celebrated throughout postclassic Mexico. And yet this schematic organization far from occluded the Indigenous ideas of animistic interdependence or nonhuman subjectivity, among other values sustained, if not produced, by predation and familiarization. At the level of taxonomy, entry, and even syntax, the Nahua authors found ways to align European tradition with Indigenous categories and concepts. The medieval encyclopedia transformed Mesoamerican categories, and conversely, Mesoamerican "content" transformed European genres and notions of natural history. The Nahua authors selectively read European natural history and encyclopedic traditions in ways that resonated with Indigenous ecological concepts.

7

Nourishing Bodies

*T*he Mexica city of Tenochtitlan, the seat of an expanding empire, dazzled the Spaniards who arrived there in 1519. Hernán Cortés marveled at the gleaming whiteness of its masonry, the orderliness of its urban planning, the horrific grandeur of its temples, the luxuriousness of its palaces, and the splendor of its courtly rituals. But even among all these impressive sights, its animals occupied a special place. Cortés wrote at length to Emperor Charles V about a dizzying array of formerly wild animals who lived in captivity in the palace compound. One building exclusively housed carnivores. It had "certain large rooms, low, all filled with large cages" containing "lions [pumas], tigers [jaguars], wolves, foxes and different kinds of cats, many of each." Birds of prey—"from the sparrow hawk to the eagle, including all kinds found in Spain and many more kinds which have ever been seen there"—resided in other quarters, constructed to provide the birds with shelter from rain as well as a place where "they could sun and air themselves." Another building held "ten tanks of water where he had the breeds of water birds which are found in these parts, which are many and diverse, all tame, and for the birds bred to the sea there were tanks of salt water and for those of the river, ponds of fresh water." The conquistador noted the care taken in tending to these animals. Upward of five hundred people were employed to look after them. The big cats and raptors were fed "as many hens as they needed," and "each type of bird was given the sustenance proper to its nature," so that "some were fed with fish and other worms, or maize, or other seeds."[1]

For Cortés and the other conquistadores who watched the brilliant flutter of myriad birds and heard the fearsome roar of big cats, these animal compounds were evidence that the Mexica had developed a court culture rivaling that of Europe. If Cortés was awed by the resources and ingenuity invested in feeding these captive animals, another kind of feeding produced a very different kind of awe—that of horror. Like other conquistadores, Cortés wrote with revulsion about the human "sacrifices" that had been part of ritual life in Tenochtitlan. He proudly reported to Charles V, that on assuming control of the city, he cleaned those "chapels full of the blood of the human victims who they sacrificed" and "prohibited them from killing any creatures for the idols, as they were accustomed for" and claimed that "in all the time I stayed in that city I did not see a living creature killed or sacrificed."[2] Cortés—and the missionaries who wrote extensively about these practices— could not see that both the compound holding captive animals and the "sacrifices" of people and other animals were all aspects of familiarization in its Mesoamerican iteration. Their misunderstandings had enduring repercussions for how and what aspects of these practices and beliefs survived under colonial rule. These misapprehensions have also influenced modern scholarship by rendering familiarization invisible. Feeding—the defining act of familiarization—has been obscured by the Judeo-Christian and modern social theoretical conceptualization of sacrifice. A focus on familiarization in Mesoamerica reveals the limitations of assuming that domestication and sacrifice can be used as universal categories across time and space.

~

AS IN SOUTH America and the Caribbean, colonial-era vocabularies indicate the conceptual importance of familiarization practices across Mesoamerica. In his 1555 and 1571 Nahuatl-Spanish dictionaries the cleric and scholar Alonso de Molina revealed an extensive terminology related to taming. Such terms included *tlacacihuitia* ("to tame animals" or "to tame something"), *tlacaciuiltia* ("to tame another"), *tlatlacacihuitilli* ("tamed animal" and "something tamed this way"), *tlatlacacihuitiliztli* ("taming in this manner"), *tlatlacacihuitiani* ("the one who tames the wild").[3] The Nahuatl root word is the verb *tlacaciui* (to be tamed), a word that incorporates the noun *tlaca* or "person." The Jesuit scholar Antonio de Rincón discussed this terminology in his 1595 work on the Nahuatl language (*Arte mexicana*): "there are some verbs that end in *ciui* which signify to behave in the manner that the noun signifies." He then translated *tlacaciui* to mean "to become human" (*humanarse*) and "to become tame" (*amansarse*)."[4] It is notable that Rincón's explanation shows semantic overlap between behaving and becoming, and taming and humanizing. It suggests remarkable convergence in the concepts of *iegue* (as discussed in Chapter 5) and *tlacaciui*: in other words, the property of being a human is the property of being tame, suggesting that "human" in this concept is more akin to the idea of being a socially formed subject rather than being a biologically born *homo sapien*. Colonial Zapotec and Mixtec dictionaries likewise suggest the importance of taming. The 1578 Spanish-Zapotec dictionary of the Dominican friar Juan de Córdova contains the following entries: "to tame the wild" (*amansar lo fiero*) / *tocóchelachia*, "to tame wild animals" (*amansar animales zahareños*) / *tococitéea*, and "person who tames" (*amansador*) / *huecoçálaclahi*.[5] Michel Oudijk explains that the root in the Zapotec words is *lachi* which means "the source of emotions." Accordingly, the Zapotec vocabulary for taming contains the idea of lessening of strong emotions.[6] While the Zapotec terms have a different linguistic logic than those in Nahuatl, they share the idea that the taming process is one that augments a being's capacity to be in relationships with others.

The chapters on animals in "Earthly Things" drafted by the Tlatelolco scholars further illuminate how Nahuas conceptualized familiarization. Variants of *tlacaciui* appear in several avian entries, such as the "young yellow-headed parrot (*toznene*)" who "is captured [to be] tamed" and the scarlet macaw who is "tameable."[7] Some of the entries include additional details emphasizing communication and diet. For instance, in the entry for *cuitlaco-chin*, a bird distinguished by its long legs, curved bill, and ash coloring, the authors connect its "capacity for being tamed" and for being "teachable" to its talkativeness; it received its name for its vocalizations of "cuitlacoch, cuitla-coch, tarati, tarat, tatatati, titiriti, tiriti."[8] The authors also described the "white-fronted parrot" (*cocho*) as "a singer, a constant singer, a talker, a speaker, a mimic, an answerer, an imitator, a word-repeater."[9] Of a finch named *mo-lotl*, they wrote, "They tame it. I tame it; I teach it. It sings, it sings constantly." The Nahua scholars also connected familiarization to feeding. One fed "ground maize treated with lime" to a *nochtototl*, a finch so named because its "chili-red" head and rump recalled the red flower of the nochtli cactus.[10] The talkative *cuitlacochin* was also fed ground maize. Even snakes could become familiarized: "All serpents are stupefied by fine tobacco."[11]

The most detailed attention to familiarization in "Earthly Things" appears in the entry on the *ozomatli* (monkey).[12] Significantly, this entry is another instance that reveals how the Tlatelolco scholars found ways to align the European encyclopedia with Nahua traditions.[13] The first part of the monkey (*simia*) entry in the *Hortus sanitatis* (1491) considers the ways in which monkeys are and are not similar to humans.[14] It asserts that the monkey's "exterior" makes it the most similar to the human body, but that on the inside monkeys share little with men. Collating the work of previous authors, the *Hortus* author also explores how people captured and tamed monkeys. Citing Bartholomeus Anglicus's *De proprietatibus rerum*, the encyclopedia author described monkeys who played games, entertained little children, or lost their "ferocity," while cautioning that these simians hold grudges against those who harmed them. The entry concludes with a description of the way that hunters captured monkeys in the wild. Having located their whereabouts in trees or on rocks, the hunters conspicuously removed their shoes and made them heavy with weights. The monkeys, fascinated by these strange contraptions, imitated the humans and put them on their own feet. The monkeys became immobilized when they wouldn't quickly remove the leaden shoes. And so the hunters swooped in and captured the monkeys. The accompanying woodcut block depicts one monkey still in the branches of a tree, and the others are on the ground, vulnerable to human predation (fig. 7.1).

The structure of the entry for the *ozomatli* in "Earthly Things" generally follows that of the *simia* in the *Hortus*. The Tlatelolco authors emphasized the similarity of the primates' appearance and behaviors. The monkeys have "human hands, human feet, nails, real nails—long nails" and they "have a face which is a little human." However, they also discussed the differences, acknowledging their shaggy coats, rounded backs, and long, curled tails. In discussing monkeys' "actions," the authors focus on those that are relational and human-like. Monkeys communicate with sounds—shouting and whistling—and gestures. When angry, monkeys hurl stones or sticks at humans. Also, like humans, they tend to produce only one offspring per pregnancy. And, finally, they eat many of the same foods, enjoying maize, fruit, and even meat; i.e., they "eat like a human."[15]

After reflecting on the monkey's human-like traits, the Nahua scholars discussed the process for capturing and taming monkeys. Just as the *Hortus* author devoted substantial attention to particular methods of capture, so, too, did the Tlatelolco scholars:

> And to capture them, a large fire is built; ears or kernels of maize are put around the edge, and in the blaze is buried a very large [stone called] *cacalotetl*. And the trappers, the hunters, take cover. And when [the fire] smokes, these monkeys, wherever they are, smell the fire, the smoke. Then they come; they carry their young on their backs; they seat themselves; the ears of maize begin to roast [and] they eat roasted maize. They walk about as

Tractatus

Capitulum .cxxxiiii.

Irula. Spuens. z Syrena. Er li. de
na. rez. Sirula serpes est pu̅ z mali
ciosus. q̃ boiez siti interficit. hic tanta
varietate refulget: vt intu̅etes pulcritudine re
tardet. z que̅ natura dedit reptado pigriore mi
raculo stupetes detinet q̃s asseq̃ no̅ valet. Est
a̅tanti feruozis vt i bieme pelle deponat. hui⁹
mozsu q̃ tagit igneo cozrept⁹ ardoz succendit
¶Actoz. Situla gen⁹ est aspidis. q̃ grece dz
dypsa. De q̃ pleni⁹ dicit est s̃. ca. li. ¶Auicena
Spuens dz q̃da serpe̅s. q̃ sputo suo interficit
illud sup q̃ cadit. q̃. s. sputu pijciu̅t detes ei⁹
ostricti sup alios. Odoz etia̅ sputi ipsi⁹ interfi
cit. logitudo ei⁹ est vsq̃ ad duos cubitos. z cos
loz ei⁹ cinericeus ad citrinitate declinas. z illu̅
que̅ mozdet interficit anteq̃ redeat. Quez em
mozdet sine sensu remanet z sine motu q̃rus.
z pfunde dozmie̅s post saltos ptinuos z clau
sione oclo̅z z tozsione colli. z spasmu z pulsu in
ozdinatu. z no̅ sentit doloze intestino̅z. z intro
mittit digitos in guttur sui⁹ vt euomat. ¶ysio.
Syrene su̅t in arabia serpetes cu̅ alis q̃ plus
curru̅t q̃ eq̃. sz etia̅ volare dicit⁹. Quaz tn̅ v̅t⁹
est vt mozsu̅ ante mozs insequat q̃ dolo̅z.

Capitulum .cxxxv.

ymia. Er li. de na. re. Symia e̅ bestia
pdesa villo. i exteriozibz me̅bris super
oia aialia silat boi cozpis dispositio
ne: interi⁹at nulla cu̅ boie dispositione habes
co̅mune aut o̅mibz aialibz minoze. ergo o̅mes
fere bestie ma̅nillas bn̅t in posterioz i ő renes

vt eas in seri⁹positas fetus attingere possint. z
pmptas hie cu̅ velint. Homo tō z symia bn̅t
eas in pectoze. q̃ natura dedit eis manus abi
les ad omnem actu̅. q̃bz eleuare possi̅t fetus a
terra z aptare illos ad vbera. B at illi deest bu
mani cozpis. q̃ caret vmbilico. tga q̃z masku
li est vt tga canis. Calcaneum bz in pedibz. et
ppter b erigit vt bo̅ stat. z currit q̃nq̃. sed b io
pt nisi modice. q̃ natura bestia bac odidit n
faciem esse pstrata. Nam solus bo̅ naturali z
erecta bz statura. Dec bestia gestu in qeta t.
mozsu feroz. cauda caret. z pre ceteris aial o
gustu viget. Fluces z poma libe̅ter comedit. sz
cu̅ in eis amaru̅ coztice reperit totu̅ pijcit. sic⁹
q̃ ppter amaru̅ dulce respuit. In India dicit
Pli. esse symias toto cozpe cadidas. ¶Alexan
der. Symia domestica d̃m suu̅ agnoscit post
multa reuertente annoz curricula. ¶Et li. s
na. re. Symia ad oez ludu̅ docibilis est. et ad
ferocitat; oblinione. nu̅q̃ tn̅ sic est mansueta
vt no̅ sit rabida. libe̅ter cu̅ pueris ludit. z si co
pia data fuerit eos aliqn̅ stragulat. Si q̃s ea̅
leserit diu ö eu̅ ra̅coze custodit. Ingenio pol
lent. z emulat q̃cq̃d videt. vn̅ facil⁹ incidit in
man⁹venatoz. habitat at in arbozibz vel rupi
bus. At vbi eas habitare venatozes viderint
accepti; calciame̅t; boim vadu̅t z sedet in loc̃
vbi ab illis videri pn̅t: indunt̃q̃ calciame̅ta illa
pedibz suis ac diligeti⁹ligat. z post b expone̅te̅
ea sub arboze relinqu̅t z pcul abeu̅t. sic sy
mie desce̅dentes: q̃ eos facere videru̅t imitat.
sic q̃z calciate capiu̅tur. ¶ysio. Symie nomen
gre. est. i. pressis naribz. vn̅ symias dicim⁹ eo q̃
suppressis naribz sint z facie feda z z.

Figure 7.1   Monkey (*simia*), *Ortus sanitatis* ([Strasbourg], ca. 1497), leaf F3 verso (fol. 37v). Call no. INC H417 copy 1 Massey. Used by permission of the Folger Shakespeare Library.

they warm themselves; they change their children about as they warm and heat them. And when the *cacalotetl* stone has been heated (for it can no way endure fire) it then cracks, bursts open, explodes, blows up just like the firing of a gun. And the embers, the ashes, scatter all over; the embers spread all over these monkeys; the ashes get into their eyes. So they run, they flee, as if someone pursued them. They quickly abandon, throw aside, their young; although they still hunt for them, they can no longer see them. So there the hunters quickly seize them with their hands; there quickly are taken the young monkeys. Later they are raised, tamed.[16]

The Indigenous artist who made an image to accompany the text in the Florentine Codex depicted the process of capture: the hunters are popping corn on the hot rock; above them are monkeys becoming curious about the hot flames. This image suggests that the artist, too, was familiar with the *Hortus*: the illustration depicts one monkey finding safety in the trees, while the others are on the ground, vulnerable to capture (fig. 7.2).

After detailing the process of capture, the Tlatelolco authors explained that monkeys were then "raised" and "could be tamed" (*tlacacihuitilo*). They then offer a portrait of the "tame animal" (*tlacaciuhqui*). He is one "who sits like a person" and "who teases the young women." Perhaps reminiscing about relationships they observed in their own households, the Nahua authors describe a monkey who speaks by whistling, who "begs from [the young women], extends the hand, continually offers their hand in their presence." Both descriptions—of the capture and of the results of the taming process—emphasize the personhood of their simian subjects. Like people, monkeys enjoy eating roasted maize kernels and the comforting warmth of the fire; they experience maternal devotion to beloved offspring; they feel visceral fear and disorientation caused by alarming explosions and temporary blindness. Once tame, the monkey wants to be in the presence of others, wants to speak, to tease, and to receive nourishment.

While the Tlatelolco scholars' choice to use the *Hortus* entry on the *simia* as a model for the *ozomatli* suggests the influence of European encyclopedia tradition, it is also informed by Indigenous concepts connecting personhood to familiarization. More precisely, I believe the Tlatelolco scholars gravitated toward the entry in the *Hortus because* it aligned with Nahua traditions centering humans' kinship with other kinds of animals. It is helpful to recall that the Borgia *tonalamatl*, as well as the Spanish and Nahuatl textual explications of the cosmogram in the "Legend of the Suns," explained the affinities

Figure 7.2   Monkey (*ozomatli*), Florentine Codex, bk. 11, fol. 15v, ca. 1575–1577, Biblioteca Medicea Laurenziana, Florence, Med. Palat. 220, c. 169v. Reproduction used by permission of the Ministry for Heritage and Cultural Archives. All rights reserved.

between people and monkeys in evolutionary terms: an earlier population of humans turned into monkeys when predatorial winds swept the earth (as discussed in Chapter 6). The discussion of affinities between people and monkeys in "Earthly Things" not only suggests familiarity with the *Hortus*. It also suggests that the Tlatelolco authors were thinking through this origins account. The relevance of the cosmogram is also indicated by the way the Nahua scholars located monkeys in the space. They described the monkey as a "forest-dweller in Anahuac, toward the east." This was an allusion to the ecological geography of the cosmogram: it situated monkeys horizontally in the East, as denizens of "Anahuac," and vertically in the arboreal canopy. The Nahua authors read about the *simia* in a bestiary which centered primate commonalities, captive taking, and the arboreal habitat, through the lens of familiarization, the cosmogram, and evolutionary explanations for common- alities across species.

Another colonial-era source that illuminates Indigenous familiarization practices is Francisco Hernández's "Historiae animalium" (Histories of ani- mals). Appointed by King Philip II to write about medically useful plants in New Spain, Hernández decided to also write about animals. With enormous help from Indigenous interpreters, guides, artists, and probably, some of the Tlatelolco scholars themselves, Hernández mounted a three-year-long re- search trip in 1571, and, while based in Mexico City, continued to conduct research until 1576.[17] Hernández's five treatises on animals—quadrupeds, birds, aquatic animals, reptiles, and insects—reveal both the diversity of crea- tures subject to familiarization and the affective power of the relationships that they produced.[18] Among the tamed species of quadrupeds were the rac- coon, possum, porcupine, coati, monkey, and squirrels.[19] He found particu- larly endearing raccoons, known in Nahuatl as *mapach*, or the "animal who holds everything with his hands" (see fig. 11.1). Perhaps these creatures' win- someness led him to place them first in the treatise. When "domesticated"— or rather tamed—and "fed at home," raccoons "always shows affection to the household members." His description suggested personal experience, when he noted that the animals "follow [their people] with great affection, climbing on them and rolling around happily on the floor" and "play and frolic in a thousand ways." The Spaniard commented that "they are easily tamed and eat everything that they are offered," thereby inadvertently un- derscoring the connection between feeding and taming.[20] Likewise, the pec- cary (*coyametl*)—an animal whose tameability was also much appreciated by Indigenous groups throughout Greater Amazonia—"is easily domesticated [*sic*]" and "eats all the food that it is offered." He described the peccary as "a peaceful animal" who "plays in a thousand ways," though he cautioned they can "attack strangers."[21] As seen in these examples, Hernández not only described the behavior of familiarized animals, but also revealed how his own emotional state was affected by his interactions with these creatures. His palpable delight at the raccoon's affectionateness and the peccary's playfulness are themselves traces of the affective power of taming practices.

Birds—the subject of Hernández's second treatise—were also well represented. Many of the familiarized animals were songbirds.[22] These included the "tozcacoztli" (perhaps a yellow-throated warbler), who is "the size of our goldfinch" and has white legs with red markings, yellow and black plumage, and a short beak. The bird feeds on mosquitos and "is kept in cages and whose song, although weak, is most agreeable."[23] Another bird kept in cages was the *xiuhtototl*, "slightly larger than our sparrow though painted of so many and such beautiful colors," who "warbles agreeably."[24] He also noted a woodpecker ("quauhtotopotli") who "is tamed and raised in homes."[25] Hernández had a particular fondness for the *tepetototl* (likely a great curassow or *Crax rubra*), a bird the size of a duck, with brilliant black plumage and some white feathers near the tail and on the wingtips. This bird was "tame and a friend to man," who made a habit of "asking for food from those of the house by pulling on clothing" and "knocking on closed doors with its beak when he wants to enter into some place." The *tepetototl* "follows his master when he is loose, and when [the master] arrives home, [the bird] greets him with happy celebration."[26] The importance of familiarization is apparent even in the fifth treatise on insects: the aquatic larvae *axaxayacatl* was appreciated as a delicious food (Hernández conceded that when eaten cooked with maize, it was "a good aliment, abundant and not disagreeable") and was also "fed to innumerable varieties of the domestic birds, who in cages, delight with their song those who hear them."[27]

Reptiles were also candidates for familiarization. Hernández explained how people "feed and raise" rattlesnakes (*teuhtlacotzauhqui*) "in their homes" (see fig. 11.3).[28] Initially, the snakes were captured: "Indians grab them by the tail with impunity and hold them suspended," despite the rattling and twisting and desire to "take revenge on their hunter." After the venom is removed from the snakes' fangs, continued Hernández, many people "tame them and have them in their homes for pleasure." Taming also featured prominently in the chapter on *tapayaxin* (mountain horned lizard), who "seems to belong to a species of lizard, although its body is almost circular, flat and similar to that called a ray, but much smaller since it doesn't reach four thumbs in length nor width."[29] "Encountered in many parts," these lizards "like to be picked up and carried in the hands and touched, staying so immobile in tranquil calm, for which reason they were known as 'friend of man.'" And then there were "certain green snakes" who "Indians raise in their houses for enjoyment." They were brought from the wilderness, explained Hernández, "when they are the size of a finger and grow until the thickness of leg." They are kept in a *tinaja* (large ceramic vessel) padded with straw, where they rest and live for most of the time until "the meal hour." At that time the lizard "leaves his nest and climbs amicably on to the shoulders of its master, who benevolently tolerates the embrace of such a horrendous animal" or "in the middle of the patio" the reptile "curls into a big wheel" and "eats peacefully what is fed and then rests."[30] As was the case with European observers in South America, Hernández understood—although he found it disconcerting—that a primary reason for taming animals was the pleasure of their companionship.

In "Historiae animalium," Hernández generally avoided discussing anything that hinted at what colonizers would consider idolatry or "childish beliefs," but other sources suggest that the relationships people created with formerly wild animals were connected to traditional spiritual practice. Missionary accounts of Nahuas' celebration of Christian holy days suggests that nonhuman animals may have been appreciated actors in *veintena* performances, as I will discuss in Chapter 8. Colonial and pre-Hispanic sources from Oaxaca indicate that spiritual guides directed children to cultivate deep attunement with nonhuman animals as part of a devotional practice. Francisco de Burgoa, a Dominican friar fluent in both Mixtec and Zapotec languages, wrote extensively about his and other missionaries' experiences in the seventeenth century and shed light on these practices.[31] He explained that parents brought their infant—"boy or girl"—to a spiritual guide, who Burgoa characterized as a "sacrilegious Priest" or "minister of Satan."[32] This person, an expert in the sacred calendar—"knowing from memory all of the names of all the days of the year which come from animals or plants according to their count"—would name the child according to the day sign.[33] The calendar expert then pierced a vein "on the ear or beneath the tongue with a bone flint or with a fingernail," offered the blood "to the Devil" (or rather a traditional deity), and then indicated "the wild animal, a beast or bird who is going to accompany the child as a guardian Angel." But the child did not immediately enter into a relationship with the designated animal. Only upon reaching "the age of free will" was the child instructed "in innumerable errors." The guide taught "that God gave life," indicated "the day in which he was born," and found him "a friend and guardian in that animal." The guide and the youth went together then to make an unspecified "sacrifice," perhaps another bloodletting. And then "the Devil brought him an animal of that kind," one "so tame and subservient that although it was a Lion or Snake, it shows itself to be docile" and "the youth was compelled to caress it and talk to it as if it was a familiar." Burgoa described this practice as "taking up company with a brute." The cleric further explained that the Devil made it so these "children" who were "blind" to true faith would experience any "blow or injury that the animal friend (*amigo*) and *Nahual* (animal double) received." Burgoa revealed a source for his information: "It came to pass that I was questioning an Indian boy about this belief," and the boy "confess[ed] that he had an animal." When the friar reprimanded him, the boy replied, "Father this fortune was given to me when I was born, [it was] not one I sought." The boy went on: "Since I was very little, I saw this animal very close to me and I was used to eating what he ate and to feel in myself whatever injuries that he received." The child's experience was far from exceptional according to Burgoa, who insisted that such cases were "innumerable."[34]

Burgoa's account is shaped by his understanding of demonic agency and colonial ideas about *nahuals*, influenced by European ideas about animal "familiars."[35] He viewed the Indigenous guide as a Satanic priest and considered the boy's actions as the making of a demonic "pact." Clearly, Burgoa also assumed that an extraordinarily tame animal evidenced diabolical interference, and that only the Devil could make it possible for a human to experience the pain felt by an animal "friend." But there is a different interpretation possible, particularly if we pay close attention to the boy's words, look beyond Burgoa's diabolical discourse, and consider other explanations for taming practices. Then another story comes to light. We see parents who are told that their child will have a companion animal. They talk to their young one about this animal; others in their community learn of this connection. The family and their friends look for the animal on their walks in the forest, on their hunting expeditions, and on their journeys. They teach their child the animal's nesting habits, how to listen for movements and vocalizations, and how to identify tracks. Then, one day a young animal is brought home. Despite his fixation on the diabolical, Burgoa's account allows us to see that this relationship was comprehended as mutual and reciprocal. The child was not sent to hunt down and trap a wild animal. Instead, he was taught to cultivate his ability to watch and listen to his surroundings and wait until an appearance of an animal whose "tameness" suggested it consented to a companionate bond. The child and the animal share food and touch, spend hours in each other's company, and develop profound empathic attunement. The animal wanders freely but still chooses to sleep in the domicile or frequently returns for visits. The child not only enjoys friendship with this animal, but comes to perceive the world through the animal, expands their sense of the world through their closeness with another way of being in the world. This deep empathic alignment gives the child some idea, or rather a felt experience, of what it might feel like to be a monkey, or rattlesnake or ocelot, or parrot, or eagle or some other kind of being. If the animal is hurt, the pain is felt by the child. The relationship is personal, but also sacralized by the community. Because the relationship is integrated into spiritual practice (the blood offerings, the visit to the altar) and wisdom teachings, the affective and intellectual experiences that arise from this relationship are intensified. There is no reason to think that every newborn was directed to cultivate a relationship with an animal, but rather this was one possibility, based on the guide's reading of the calendar and his perception of the baby and the family.

Burgoa also wrote about familiarization at another point in the life cycle. He recounted the experience of a fellow missionary, Alfonso de Espinosa, who was known for his knowledge about the "rites, ceremonies and superstitions of the Indians" in valleys and highlands of Zapotec Oaxaca and his fluency in the Zapotec language.[36] One day, a Zapotec man—"among the most *ladino* (e.g., fluent in Spanish and likely acculturated to Spanish ways)" had come to report on the idolatrous activities of his father-in-law.[37] The suspect was an "old Indian man of this town," who "many years ago had retreated from interaction with others into thickets and solitude in a wilderness of this jurisdiction." There, "he made a life that is so singular that it is not imitable" because "what he loved most was a macaw . . . those big birds in the shape of a parrot that breed in these hot regions." The embittered son-in-law explained that the man "adores" the bird "like a God." In order "to keep this animal content," the man labored continuously, "sowing, harvesting and looking for fruits to feed it." The man showed the bird "so much devotion" offering "Sacrifices of blood that he takes from his tongue, his face, his ears, his arms, and other parts that he hardly remained in the form of a man." He offered "incense in intolerable ceremonies that he exercised without tiring."[38]

Eventually, Espinosa saw the man and the bird himself. One day the son-in-law told the friar, "if you want to see it and catch him in his miserable state, I will bring you with such secretiveness that no one will know." The "good friar" and the son-in-law hatched a plan. The priest made a visit to the local *Principales* with "gifts and tokens of love" and "proposed that they go to the thickets of that wilderness where there was an abundance of deer and other wild animals, where they were accustomed to go hunting for their festivals." Descended from a family of royal huntsmen in Castile, Espinosa sought to ingratiate himself by telling them of his "esteem" for their fondness of the "chase and hunt of wild beasts," telling them "I would be grateful if you take me to this mountain to see how you hunt." A few days later, they left early in the morning. The hunting expedition gave the treacherous "denouncer" an opportunity to lead the party to "a little hut of straw in the middle of that solitude." There they encountered "the old idolater on his knees with his arms crossed and the head bowed like a penitent, before a little altar of wood and flowers and in the middle standing was the Macaw, [where] the devil and [the macaw] were receiving the worship and adoration of this sacrilege and scandalous Ministry." When the macaw "saw the Cleric before him so noisy were the cries" that "its voice resounded throughout those rough lands as if high winds raged." Thus Espinosa, upset by the "clamor and riot," killed the macaw.

Despite the many levels of mediation—Burgoa's interpretation of Espinosa's account of a series of events—and the framework of diabolical idolatry, this text illuminates how familiarization could be a spiritual practice that pivoted around reverential care. In Burgoa's telling the son-in-law believed that the man "adored" the bird "like a God." And after killing the macaw, Espinosa turned his attentions to the Indigenous entourage—no doubt shocked at this act of violence toward their elder's beloved bird—and pronounced, "Look now, my children, what a dastardly [*ruin*] trickster is the devil, so that a rational man to whom God gave all the other animals to serve him has been subjected to serve [at the bird's] feet, as if he was his Master." But if, instead of the interpretations offered by Espinosa and Burgoa, we focus on the actions described along with clues from other sources, it does not seem that the man worshipped the bird as a "God." Instead, the practices of the elder resemble those prescribed to children when they came of age and were assigned a guardian animal: they linked offerings of blood to deities to cultivating attunement with nonhuman animals. The man dedicated himself to feeding the bird—the "sowing, harvesting and looking for fruits"—and feeding "gods" by offering blood drawn from his own body. The parallels between these two kinds of feeding suggest that the particular form of care that the man cultivated with his bird was a way of expressing a more general devotion to the community of beings on whom humanity depends for their existence. The deceitful behavior of the son-in-law is also revealing. The fact that he needed a subterfuge to bring the friar to the elderly man suggests that the rest of his family did not want to interfere with their elder's way of life, that they respected and honored the man's relationship with the macaw. Although the intensity of the man's devotion to this bird was perhaps exceptional, the family's tolerance for their relative's way of life suggests that the man's reverential bond with his macaw fell within the bounds of normative behavior.

These colonial-era sources suggest that we consider some of the imagery in painted hide screenfolds made in the Mixtec communities of Oaxaca before and after the Spanish invasions. Known as *tacu* (painting) and *ñee ñuhu* (sacred skin) in Mixtec, they were linked to ruling families in the communities of Teozacoalco and Tilantongo.[39] The three considered here—now known as the Codex Zouche-Nuttall (or Tonindeye Codex), the Codex Vienna (or Codex Yuta Tnoho), and the Codex Bodley (Codex Nuu Tnoo-Ndisi Nuu)—depict the rise to power of a hero-ancestor, known as Lord 8 Deer, and show his interactions with wives, siblings, and descendants, as well as enemies.[40] It was the convention to indicate these historical figures by their calendar name and a more poetic moniker. Accordingly "8 Deer" refers to the hero-ancestor's calendar name and scholars have designated his personal name as "Jaguar Claw" as one of these often appears next to him, though at other times he is garbed with a jaguar head and pelt (see fig. 7.5). A number of people in these screenfolds appear to have such personal names linked to the birds and quadrupeds situated next to or beneath them. For instance, Lord 4 Dog (one of Lord 8 Deer's sons) appears to be either capturing or caressing a coyote (scholars thus refer to his personal name as "Tame Coyote"). A seemingly young eagle sits to the left of Lord 9 Snake, while a fuzzy headed baby macaw is next to Lord 10 Death. A youthful raccoon appears by Lord 10 Jaguar, a baby puma is next to Lord 10 Reed, and a monkey sits on a disembodied knee next to Lord 12 Death (fig. 7.3).[41] Maarten Jansen and Gabina Aurora Pérez Jiménez have suggested that underlying the representations of creatures such as these is the concept of "nahual," or the idea that people in dreams "experience taking another identity and becoming one or more animals or other beings."[42] However, in light of Burgoa's account, I think it may be the case that some or all of these animals were tamed companion animals rather than (or in addition to) being "alter

Figure 7.3 Top (left to right): Drawings of Lord 4 Dog and coyote in Codex Zouche-Nuttall and Codex Bodley. Middle: Lord 9 Snake and young eagle, Lord 10 Death and young macaw in Codex Zouche-Nuttall. Bottom: Lord 10 Dog and raccoon, Lord 10 Reed and young puma, Lord 12 Death and seated monkey in Codex Zouche-Nuttall. Drawing by Ardeth Anderson. © Marcy Norton.

egos." That a number of these animals are babies or juveniles seems to support such an interpretation, given that younger creatures are easier to tame. Moreover, Lord 4 Dog's actions of either capturing or caressing both reflect practices related to familiarization. Similarly, the monkey's position on a knee suggests the close, tactile bond that forms between people and animal companions.

Another elder who cherished and was cherished by a companion bird was Marta de Carrillo, a resident of Pinula (Guatemala). The woman and her duck appear fleetingly in the account of Englishman Thomas Gage, a Dominican friar until he renounced Catholicism and embraced Protestantism. The ex-friar resided in Pinula, a multi-ethnic community that had a Maya majority (both Pok'omam and Kaqchikel speakers) and a minority of Nahuas, in the early 1630s.[43] According to Gage, Carrillo was "wont whithersoever she went about the town to go with a duck following her, and when she came to the church, the duck would sit at the door till she came out again, and then would return home with her."[44] However, a key difference between Marta and the Zapotec man was that while the latter had the support of his family and community, Carrillo was spurned by her neighbors. According to Gage, many residents "affirmed that certainly this Marta was a notorious witch." They blamed her for illnesses and envied her relative prosperity despite her "being a poor widow without any sons to help her." Gage reported that they took her companion as further proof of her diabolical dabbling: "This duck they imagined was her beloved devil and familiar spirit, because they had often set dogs at her and they would not meddle with her, but rather run away from her." Gage was initially sympathetic toward Carrillo, in part, per-haps, because she was enthusiastic about taking communion and brought him gifts of money and food. Gage soured on her after one of the gifts of food turned out to have bad fish ("full of maggots and stinking"), bad honey ("full of worms"), bad eggs ("some rotten and some with dead chickens within"). So, suspecting that she had cast a "spell," the Dominican sided with influential members of the community and decided to "rid the town of such a limb of Satan" and imprison Carrillo, who died just two months later.[45] Reading between the lines, I think it likely that the Indigenous woman, vul-nerable because she was an elderly widow without a supportive kin network, was mainly disliked for reasons unrelated to her duck. The townspeople hoped they could recruit the friar to their cause if they called attention to her close relationship with the bird and tap into missionary qualms about dia-bolical interference. This episode is not only a trace of familiarization but also of the way, once again, that missionaries—in this case abetted by Indige-nous people with their own agenda—viewed familiarization through a lens of diabolical sorcery.

Familiarization also suggests that we revisit the Tenochtitlan palace com-pound populated with formerly wild animals, described by Cortés, among others. Moctezuma was far from the only ruler in postclassic Mexico who possessed awe-inspiring menageries. In a scene of subjugation in the Codex Zouche-Nuttall, conquered subjects present their new overlord, Lord 8 Deer, with a baby jaguar and a baby eagle (fig. 7.4).[46] A descendant of a pre-Hispanic

Figure 7.4   Baby jaguar and eagle offered as tribute (*right column*), Codex Zouche-Nuttall, p. 47, ca. 1200–1521. British Museum Am1902,0308.1. Reproduction © The Trustees of the British Museum / Art Resource, NY.

ruler of Texcoco wrote of a compound where the "king had all of the kinds and diversity there existed of birds, animals, serpents, and snakes brought from diverse regions of this New Spain." There were tanks containing fish "that inhabit the sea as well as in rivers and lakes," and a bird house enclosed with more than "two thousand cypress trees." He emphasized that his ancestor did not lack any "bird, fish or animal of the land that wasn't either alive or sculpted in gold or gems."[47] It seems that this tradition continued—perhaps in a more limited fashion—well into the late sixteenth century, for a number of Hernández's observations about tame birds derive from the time he spent in a "palace" in Texcoco.[48]

The maintenance of the royal captive animals was an integral part of the Aztec imperial system itself. For example, the Mexica rulers required tribute of live birds. The Nahuatl account translated by Durán noted that these included jaguars and birds "of the finest plumage. Some were green, some red, others blue; parrots, large and small; other splendid and handsomely colored birds such as eagles, buzzards, hawks, sparrow hawks, ravens, herons and wild geese."[49] Annotated colonial-era copies (ca. 1522–1530) of Mexica imperial records indicate live birds were expected from some tributaries, such as Xilotepec, which had to deliver ten eagles every year.[50] Even farther north, Oxitipan also was levied "one live eagle at each tribute, other times they gave two, sometimes three, other times more or less, according to what they captured."[51] The respondent to the *Relaciones geográficas* (the questionnaire responses) for Icxitlan wrote that in the pre-Hispanic period, the community was obligated to send "live snakes in order to feed the birds of the aviary" and the "many kinds of the precious birds that they have [there]"; the respondent for Tlacotalpan (Veracruz) recalled they were required to supply parrots as part of their tribute to Moctezuma.[52]

As in so many other respects, the Mexica rulers of Tenochtitlan and other postclassic elites were the heirs to centuries-old, if not millennia-old, traditions. Archaeological evidence from sites throughout Mesoamerica attests to the longevity and geographic breadth of practices related to maintaining wild animals in captivity.[53] Scholars have emphasized that menageries such as these allowed ruling elites to display power, maintain prestige, and intimidate potential enemies.[54] While this was undoubtedly the case, there is good reason to think that they also reflected the upscaling of the tradition of capturing and taming wild animals—familiarization as it had developed in Mesoamerica. Moctezuma and other rulers expected to procure a wide range of wild animals from communities they conquered. Animals held captive in urban spaces reflect local traditions of capturing and taming wild animals practiced at greatly expanded scale.

~

WHEN THE RULING elite in Mesoamerica maintained captive animals they not only extended local practices around familiarization but also transformed them. One of the ways that this form of familiarization diverged from those described by Burgoa and Hernández was that at least some of these captive animals were killed. Leonardo López Luján, Ximena Chávez Balderas, and other archaeologists have concluded that "many living animals were confined alive to await ceremonies in which they were offered to the gods in the sacred precinct" of the Templo Mayor.[55] Among the many different animal remains uncovered were those belonging to two adult eagles. Both, one female and one male, were buried with metal bangles, and the female also had a "mother of pearl, ring-shaped pectoral over the sternum." The "robust" condition of the bones suggest they were "kept in captivity" and "cared for by expert hands."[56] This analysis also points to an important way that familiarization, at least occasionally, diverged significantly from that of Greater Amazonia: whereas in the latter region, it would have been repellent to eat a being you had fed, in Mesoamerica, there were contexts in which beings were both fed and eaten.

To better understand how and why captive animals were sometimes killed, it is helpful to look at a particular class of animals: humans. They too appear among the offerings in Templo Mayor and other sacred sites in the Central Highlands and elsewhere in Mesoamerica. Some scholars remain skeptical of the focus on human so-called sacrifice in colonial-era documents and modern scholarship alike. They are—rightly—suspicious that these early documents served colonists looking to justify their savage and legally dubious conquests and that modern scholars fixate on "othering" Nahua culture.[57] Nevertheless, the archaeological record and depictions of ritual killing in pre-Hispanic screenfolds, among other sources, leave no doubt that the killing of people was indeed an important part of ritual life.[58] The problem with colonial-era discourse about Indigenous sacrifice is not so much that it exaggerated the importance of ritual killing but that it superimposed Judeo-Christian concepts that distort the actual meanings attached to ritual killing in pre-Hispanic Mexico. In turn, this missionary discourse has directly and indirectly influenced modern scholarship: sacrifice has been reified as a universal category in social theory, and this, too, has flattened Mesoamerican concepts and practices.[59]

One of the problems with the term *sacrifice* is that it obscures the centrality of offering nourishment in many varieties of ritual killing. The notion that people and other animals were killed in order to feed the sun, water, and earth is articulated in the origin stories recorded in Spanish and Nahuatl and embedded in the *tonalamatl*. A starting point for understanding from the inside what outsiders have called "sacrifice" is the Nahuatl word *tlama*. Molina defined it "to hunt or capture something" or, one might say, to predate. Significantly, as Guilhem Olivier points out, it "reveals the equivalence between hunting and war" and so does not distinguish between people and other kinds of animals.[60] It is related to the word *tlamaca* which Molina translated as "to serve the table or administer food and delicacies." A third, related word is *tlamacazqui*. It is usually translated as "priest" by missionaries and modern scholars alike, but, as Michel Graulich explains, a more literal translation is "the one who makes offerings," noting that it also means "[the one] who serves food."[61] In aggregate, the terms contain and collapse the concepts of both predation (killing) and familiarization (feeding). The elders in Tepepulco, were explicit that it was the task of the *tlamacazqui* to present the still-beating heart to the sun.[62] They described the process as "feeding." It required the attending priests "to collect the blood in a bowl" and then "they smeared the blood, all the blood" of the captive on the "devil," or rather, the divinities.[63] The Nahuatl prayers recorded by the Tlatelolco scholars likewise emphasize the feeding aspect of ritual killings: "The sun receives, is gladdened, is content; it takes great pleasure in the sipping of blood."[64] The Nahuatl terminology emphasized the transformation of the soft, mushy, liquid innards—flesh, heart, and blood—into food and drink for elemental forces.

The entanglement of predation and familiarization was made potent through its embodiment in the rites of the *veintena* of Tlacaxipehualiztli, the "feast of the flayed one," celebrated in early or mid-March.[65] These rites celebrated the fecundity of harvests and the structural warfare associated with settled agrarian lifeways, as scholars such as Johanna Broda and David Carrasco have shown.[66] They were conceptual performances that emphasized that everything is both food and fed, in turn—the core principle of predation and familiarization.

The rites began by emphasizing the contingent status of captor and captive. The elders of Tlatelolco recalled that the warrior who had taken a captive was reminded by his family that it was not yet his turn to feed the sun—the captor "would yet go to die" and "would go to pay the debt" later. In this way, the victorious warriors, and their anxious family members, remembered that it could just as easily have been them in place of their captives and that eventually all who were fed would become food. The connection between captor and captive was also embodied: both were painted in stripes with white chalk that marked the hunting deity Mixcoatl and those destined to be killed as food alike (fig. 6.3).[67] On the next day, the captors and their

Figure 7.5   Lord 8 Deer ("Jaguar Claw") captures and kills warrior (*right columns*) and priests sacrifice quail (*left column*). Codex Zouche-Nuttall, pgs. 83–84, ca. 1200–1521. British Museum Am1902,0308.1. Reproduction © The Trustees of the British Museum / Art Resource, NY.

captives (maybe as many as sixty) arrived at the temple associated with solar power and war—in Tlatelolco, that of Huitzilopochtli, and in Tepepulco, that of Yopitli.[68] (Isotopic studies of the bones of victims confirm that some of them originated from outside of the region and so were "warriors captured during warfare who were brought to the Basin of Mexico and sacrificed soon thereafter.")[69] The elders of Tlatelolco recalled that "the entire city was present at this spectacle," including foreign dignitaries secretly summoned by Moctezuma. The captors led their captives to the top of the pyramid. Sometimes the "captive lost his strength, faint," resisting by "continually throwing himself on the ground, they just dragged him." But the elders made clear it was appreciated when a captive who "made an effort," when he

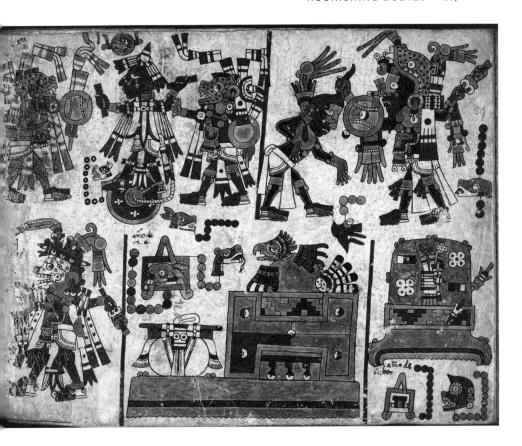

"went strong of heart," when he "went shouting," when he "did not go downcast" or "spiritless."[70]

Once on top of the temple, the captive was fed: he was made to drink pulque (*octli*), sucking it from the cup out of a long, hollow cane. Then a priest "beheaded a quail for the captive, the striped one," and then "raised the captive's shield [to the sun], and he cast away the quail behind him." The captive, having inhabited the role of one who receives drink and food, now became the source of drink and food. The captive was set on top of a round stone *temalacatl,* affixed by a woven cord, and armed with a war club that had feathers rather than "obsidian blades."[71] Such a rite is depicted on the penultimate panel of the Codex Zouche-Nuttall—with Lord 8 Deer, cloaked in a jaguar pelt, fighting the captive warrior tied to the round stone platform (fig. 7.5). The captive faced four warriors, the captors. Two were garbed in jaguar skins and two in eagle headdresses. They embodied the grace and power of the animals whose skins they were wearing: They "came dancing; they each went turning about . . . they went looking from side to side; they each went leaping upwards; they each went fighting." Despite the imbalance in weapons and numbers, sometimes a "captive was valiant, courageous." But there came a point when the captive "no longer did anything, no longer used his arms, no longer defended himself." Then "he faltered, he fainted, he fell on the surface, he threw himself down as if dead." When the captor had been defeated, "went faltering, only went on all fours, went fainting," or had surrendered, wishing that "breath might end . . . that he might cast off the burden of death," then came the moment when they "quickly grabbed him, quickly seized him, held him thrown down, held him stretched him out on the edge of the round stone." The captors had finished their work as predators and turned over their prey to the officiating priest.[72]

If the role of the warrior was "to capture" (*tlama*) the game, it was the role of the priest—*tlamacazqui* or the "one who offers"—to feed the game to the deified sun and earth. The presiding priest wore the pelt of an apex carnivore; in the recollections of the elders of Tepepulco, he "was the one called 'Old Bear.' It was as if he were the uncle of the striped one [e.g., the captive]." Durán wrote that he was cloaked in the skin of a wolf or perhaps a mountain lion. "Thereupon came forth, arrived, were ranged in order," recalled the elders, "the impersonators, the proxies of all the divine ones." They referred to the priests who were wearing the garb of the deities of war, sun, and generation. The priest in Totec's costume was first. He "gashed the breast, seized his heart, and raised it as an offering to the sun."[73] The interdependent relationship between killing, feeding, and eating—the entanglement of predation and familiarization—provided the climax of the rites of the "flayed one."

This dramatic moment of killing was followed by a celebration of feeding, an enactment of the solar feeding depicted in the Borgia *tonalamatl* (figs. 6.2, 6.4). The elders remembered that the priests offered the heart to the sun and "nourished him with it." A priest took a hollow eagle cane and put it in the breast cavity, "where the heart had been, stained it with blood, indeed submerged it in the blood," in a way not dissimilar to how the captive himself had drunk from a cane a short time before. The elders remembered that "it was said: 'Thus he giveth [the sun] to drink.'" As they described the process, they emphasized the feeding aspect precisely. They recalled how the captor "placed the blood of his captive" on "the lips of the stone images" so they could "taste" the blood with "the hollow cane."[74] The priests who oversaw offerings attended carefully to effective delivery of the corporeal food and drink, for this was the essence of the ritual. The earth was also fed: The bodies of the warrior-captives, those who were now known as "eagle men," were pushed off the edge of the temple top, like the quail whose bodies had been cast down after their beheading. The elders recalled that "they rolled them over; they bounced them down. . . . Thus they reached the terrace at the base of the pyramid." Then the body was "taken to his house, there they cut it up, that it might be eaten and shared, to bestow as a favor to others," with a first offering made to Moctezuma and then to others in the extended family of the captor-warrior. The connection between feeding the sun and the re-sulting agrarian fecundity was made explicit as the priests next danced with beautiful foodstuffs made of maize and amaranth: "clusters of ears of maize, coyote heads made of a paste of amaranth seeds, S-shaped tortillas, thick rolls covered with a dough of amaranth seeds which they covered on top with toasted maize, and red amaranth, and maize stalks with ears of green or tender maize."[75] Humans and deified forces alike benefited from the killing of the captive and the fruits of his body.

It needs to be emphasized that in Mesoamerica, unlike Europe, the fact that everyone and everything could potentially and—indeed—inevitably be-come food was not at odds with their subjectivity. The emphasis on the vul-nerability of and identification with those who were going to become food is a prominent feature of the rites. Immediately after the heart extraction, the priests performed a dance: "All severally took the head of a captive, of a striped one; with them they dance. It was said, 'They dance with the severed heads.'" Then they mourned the deaths of the captives: The priest known as "Old Bear man," was called the "uncle" of the captive and dedicated the rope that had tied the slain warrior to the four directions. The elders recalled, "He went weeping, he went howling like one bereaved; he wept for those who had suffered, who had died," much as hunters persecuted by Ruiz de Alarcón en-visioned the mountains mourning the death of the deer.[76] The elders point-edly remarked that "the captor might not eat the flesh of his captive" and "yet he might eat of someone else's captive."[77] The relationship between captor and captive was understood as one of kin, much like the relationship between hunter and prey imagined in the conjurations recorded by Ruiz de Alarcón. Moreover, family members of the captors were brought to tears, knowing full well that they could just as easily have been the ones whose heart and blood were fed to the eagle sun. The ritual words and rites emphasized the inter-changeability of captors and captives; because they were essentially the same, warriors could feed other warriors to the sun in their stead.

The role of the quail in these rites deserves special attention. The reconstructions of the *veintena* in the Florentine Codex and other colonial accounts probably understate the importance of the quail for they are paramount in the postclassic sources. They appear more frequently than any other kind of animal in the *ñee ñuhu* and *tonalamatl*.[78] In the Mixtec manuscripts, quail are depicted as one of the most important ritual offerings, along with copal, tobacco, and fragrant fire. It is no accident that quail offerings appear on the first page associated with creation and on the last page that commemorates the historical triumphs of Lord 8 Deer (fig. 7.3). Women and men, priests, and lords alike made offerings of quail.[79] Quail abound in the colonial-era pictorial and textual accounts based on postclassic histories and oral accounts of rituals.[80] The Tlatelolco scholars wrote that "each day when the sun arose, quail were slain and incense was offered."[81] The histories often memorialize specific quail offerings made by important personages in the past. Moctezuma's predecessor, Ahuizotl, showed gratitude for his military successes by his offerings that included "many quail killed by his own hand."[82] Quail also appear in the bioarcheological record. One of the eagles uncovered in the Templo Mayor cache "contained on its sternum a concentration of highly fragmentary Montezuma quail bones," suggesting that "the eagle, before being buried, had lived in captivity and was fed only quails."[83]

One of the most important panels in the Borgia *tonalamatl* depicts the feeding of a quail. At the center of the panel, the role of the *tlamacazqui* (the "offering one") is occupied by a skeletal coyote (fig. I.2, Codex Borgia plate 71). He decapitates a quail, the blood spurting upward from the bird's body into the mouth of the solar deity. The head has been cast down into the gaping maw of the scaly, reptilian earth deity. The scene mirrors the one recalled by the elders in which an apex-predator-clad priest "cast" the decapitated quail head to the sun and left its body "fluttering" on the ground.[84] The illustrator took great care to show the offerings as food and drink, depicting the stream of blood or other vital emanations touching the lips of deities.[85] The priest-coyote is giving the sun the blood that it requires to make plants grow and the flesh that the earth monster needs to provide nutrients to the soils. Even though the sun and the earth are powerful deified forces, they are also depicted here as dependent on feeding—or familiarization—by others. This role of the quail—as the exemplary animal food for sun and earth—also explains why quail were almost always embedded within the costumes of sun, fire, and earth deities in the *tonalamatl* (see fig. 7.6).[86]

One of the earliest textual descriptions of ritual quail killing is provided by the Franciscan Motolinia. In Cuauhtitlan, the missionary learned how the "fire god" (Xiuhtecuhtli) had been celebrated. Wearing the skins of enslaved women who had been killed for that purpose, two priests put on paper sewn into the shape of wings and tied to their lips "a quail already sacrificed and beheaded" and then danced. In preparation for the festival, many more quail—the number "surpassed 8000," according to the friar—were gathered with "much effort." On noon of that day, temple priests distributed the quail and, as the priests danced in their skin and bird vestments, "many people sacrificed and offered great numbers of quail . . . there were so many that they covered the ground."[87] Quail killing took place at the household level, where they were decapitated and offered to solar deities before the hearth fire, as well as in grand ceremonies such as those described by elders in the *veintena* cycle.[88]

It was important to make offerings of meek, vegetarian, unthreatening little quail to the deified sun and earth for two fundamental and connected reasons: their tastiness to people and other flesh-eating animals and their role in the vertical food web that made them a crucial link between maize and apex predators.[89] The Tlatelolco authors emphasized that the quail's diet was corn, their "food is dried grains of maize." In turn, quail were "edible, savory, good-tasting, exceedingly good-tasting."[90] They were tasty not only for people but also for other apex predators of the sky, earth, and water. These apex predators—warriors, eagles, and jaguars—fed the sun and earth, who in turn fed the maize plants that provided the nourishment for quail and other vegetarian beings, who in turn became the food for predators. But quail, too, were predators. In the "Legend of Suns," their hunger almost prevented Quetzalcoatl from creating the human population anew. When the deity went to retrieve bones from the subterranean realm, he was almost thwarted by a covey of quail who started to eat the bones, here associated with their preferred grain of maize.[91] Quail were the quintessential vegetarian animal, the beings that converted plant food into animal food. They exemplified the node in the food web that connected the plant life that feasted on the earth, sun, and water—plant life that, in turn, became the food for predators, who in turn became food for soil, solar, and aquatic deities. Ritual killing of people was overlaid on much older and more fundamental offerings of other kinds of beings, above all quail.

~

ANIMALS WERE NOT only killed because they provided nourishment. As in the Caribbean and South America, they were also valued for their nonperishable parts—their pelts, skin, bones, and, especially, feathers.[92] Even a cursory glance at the *tonalamatl,* as well as murals and monumental sculpture created in the postclassic period, speaks to their power. Bernardino de Sahagún recorded a Nahuatl saying concerning "the precious feathers of the lord," and likewise, Durán remarked that "they called [feathers] 'shadow of the gods.'"[93] To understand the meanings attributed to these materials, it is necessary to call attention to the revisionist understanding of Mesoamerican "gods." As was the case with "book" and "sacrifice," the first Europeans who arrived in Mesoamerica imposed concepts from the Judeo-Christian tradition onto Mesoamerican deities, and until fairly recently, modern scholars have followed their precedent. Nevertheless, groundbreaking work initiated by Arild Hvidtfeldt has led scholars to rethink their understanding of deities.[94] Molly Bassett explains that the literal meaning of *teixiptla* is "something characterized by a flayed surface" and so relates to a concept wherein people and things become deities "by taking on the physical appearance and comport" of something divine. Or, as Elizabeth Boone writes, "Aztec deity names are simply cultic terms denoting the persons and objects central to the ritual activities," and "the physical form, costume, and accouterments that comprise the *teixiptla* define the deity and even create it."[95]

Descriptions of the *teixiptla* in book 2 of the *Florentine Codex* elaborate how different elements of "costume" instantiated their defining qualities.[96] A rain deity wore "her paper cap with quetzal feathers in the form of a tassel of maize. It was of many quetzal feathers, full of quetzal feathers, so that it was covered with green, streaming down, glistening like precious green feathers."[97] On her calf, "she had bound jaguar skin on which were bells," and "when she walked much did she rattle, clink, jingle, and tinkle." Her sandals were made of loose cotton yarn "with flecks of raw cotton woven in." Her shield had feathers of eagle, quetzal, troupial, and yellow parrots, the latter formed into tassels that looked like locust heads. She also carried a reed staff "hung with paper spattered like rubber" and also "flowers, incense, and more feathers." As this description suggests, the *teixiptla* of deities associated with the East quadrant often bore abundant quantities of quetzal feathers, flowers, and reeds. The vestments of the fire deity included "a ball of yellow parrot feathers" on his head and a headdress with eagle and red macaw feathers that, "when he put it on, it appeared in truth to flare up" and a "cape made of only red macaw feathers." He wore a mask of shell mosaic and the

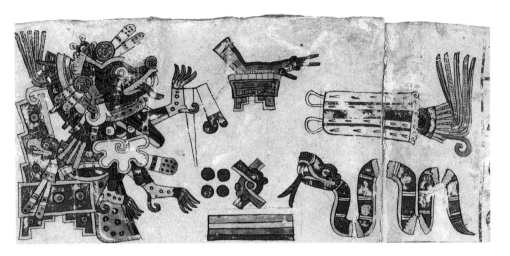

Figure 7.6   *Trecena* governed by Xolotl, Codex Borgia, plate 65, upper register, pre-1500. Borg. mess.1, f.pl 65r, photo: © Biblioteca Apostolica Vaticana Reproduced by permission of Biblioteca Apostolica Vaticana, all rights reserved.

lower part of his face blackened with black *teotetl* stones and black obsidian stones.[98] These descriptions evoke the way *teixiptla* sensorialized and personified divinity. Likewise, a *tonalamatl* attends to the feathers, jewelry, cloaks, staffs, footwear—in other words, the *teixiptla*—of deities with exacting precision. For instance, Xolotl—the deity with a dog head associated with the creation of humanity in the fifth age—is depicted with materials associated with both predation and generation (fig. 7.6). He wears an elaborate headdress with at least three kinds of feathers, including the long gleaming quetzal tail feathers. He wears gem spool earrings and a stone pectoral. A jaguar pelt covers his throne and also encases his feet and neck. He holds a broken bone knife, and a quail head is attached to his back. This notion of the divine was very different from the anthropomorphic gods of the West, for these deities may have taken a humanoid shape, but they were primarily constituted by materials associated with generative and destructive forces of the world.

It should come as no surprise that powerful human mortals, too, would want to appropriate the transformative power of a donned skin.[99] The elders of Tepepulco recounted that skins were among the most essential items owned by rulers.[100] The Mixtec pictorial histories memorialize ancestors such as Lord "Jaguar Claw" 8 Deer wearing not only elaborate feather headdresses with quetzal and other tropical plumage, but also costumes made of carcasses of jaguars, eagles, coyotes, and other flesh-eaters, thereby channeling the fierceness and bravery of apex predators (fig. 7.5). The transforming capacity of a pelt or skin can also be seen in the ubiquitous "thrones" made of jaguar skins (figs. 6.2, 6.3, and 6.4). It is less that military prowess, priestly prestige, or monarchical power is indicated by donned pelts and throne seats and more that beings *derived* power by wearing and sitting on the skins of potent animals and plants. The immense ritual importance of animals, and their feathers and pelts, made them indispensable as tribute and trade items. The *amanteca*, as the artists who made feathered objects were known, were among the most prestigious groups in the Mexica Empire (fig. 8.1).[101]

The importance of *teixiptla* helps explain the stunning language used to describe many of the animals in "Earthly Things." Mesoamerican epistemology and aesthetics inflected word choice and syntax, as well as the organizational schema of the text.[102] The authors describe the coveted, long quetzal tail feathers as "green, herb-green, very green, fresh green, turquoise colored. They are like slender reeds: the ones which glisten, which bend. They become green, they become turquoise. They bend, they constantly bend; they glisten." The language used to describe the quetzal evokes—and borrows from—the way that *teixiptla* were described in sections of the Florentine Codex concerned with deities and their rites. Both the quetzal entry and the descriptions of deities' *teixiptla* use repetition and synonyms characteristic of Nahuatl song and poetry. Stringing together color adjectives "green, herb-green, very green, fresh green, turquoise colored," evokes resplendence and iridescence and simulates the subtle shifts in hue as iridescent surfaces move.[103] The quetzal entry offers an exquisite description of the morphology and coloring of this bird that is inseparable from the essence of *teixiptla* itself in its intertwining of materiality, affect, and ritual.

~

ALTHOUGH IT APPEARS that any kind of animal was eligible to be both fed and eaten, in Mesoamerica, this was the norm for one particular subset: dogs and turkeys. The centrality of these two animals to the elite Mesoamerican diet is suggested by archaeological evidence, postclassic iconography, and sources from the early colonial period alike.[104] Moreover, while raising turkeys was a fairly widespread practice in which women specialized, dog breeding was a more specialized economic activity. According to Mackenzie Cooley, "breeding dogs led to elite social status."[105] Unlike the quail captured in the wild, "home-dwelling" dogs and turkeys depended on their owners for provisions. Turkey and dog "domestication" emerged from a distinctly Mesoamerican form of familiarization, and close analysis of it reveals the limits of domestication as a universal category.[106]

Part of what made livestock palatable for Europeans was objectification. In Europe, much work went into ensuring that livestock—the animals eligible for eating—were not recognized as subjects, as discussed in Chap 2. In contrast, Indigenous people throughout postclassic Mexico saw dogs and turkeys fully as subjects. Rather than being objectified, as livestock was in Europe, they figured among the divine. Tezcatlipoca and Xolotl, both deities who exemplified generative processes, sometimes took the forms of turkeys and dogs, respectively (fig. 7.6).[107] Moreover, turkeys and dogs were seen as animals with particular affinities to people. The "Legend of the Suns" offers an explanation for this. Many surviving variants, including the Borgia cosmogram, reveal that the earlier population of humans who transformed into turkeys or dogs were land-dwellers, like modern humans (fig. 6.3).[108] As a result, turkeys and dogs of the "Fifth Sun" share with humans their habitat on the Earth's surface, unlike other groups of transformed humans, such as monkeys and birds, who live in the arboreal canopy, or fish and reptiles, who live in aquatic environments. Moreover, in a number of the versions, the earlier humans who became turkeys or dogs had a diet organized around a plant that appears to be a precursor to maize, foreshadowing the fact that these animals share not only habitats but also diets with humans. Linguistic evidence also supports the notion that dogs and turkeys were thought to have a particularly close relationship with humans because of their common affinity for land-based living. The Tlatelolco scholars characterized dog and turkey alike as *techan* (house) *nemini* (dweller), referring to the way that these domesticated animals share space with people. The Tlatelolco scholars further stressed that a turkey "can be raised in one's home," and "lives near and by one."[109]

Attention to dwelling and feeding reveal that dogs and turkeys were, above all, associated with a particular subset of human: those who enslaved. Slavery for humans and domestication for animals were fundamentally united by the notion of dependence on others for maize. Rather than a hereditary state or one organized around ethnic and racial categories, enslavement in Mesoamerica was a contingent condition. It could result from warfare or tribute, but perhaps the most fundamental cause of enslavement was the inability to feed oneself and food insecurity in its various manifestations.[110] Missionaries who wrote about the codes governing the operation of the marketplace in Central Mexico revealed the close relationship between slavery and food dependence.[111] The most severe crime was the theft of unripened maize, which held the potential for harvests, and this crime was punishable by death. The still serious but lesser crimes of stealing fundamental foodstuffs—maize especially but also other vital foods such as maguey plants and turkeys—were punished by slavery. Another related and common mechanism—and perhaps the one most relevant for understanding fowl and dog raising—was hunger or famine. During dire times, parents would sell their children into slavery as a way of getting them fed. Enslavement was not necessarily a permanent condition, and especially those who gave up children to slavery seemed to hope that they could buy them back when times improved.[112] Nevertheless, sometimes these children were killed. Bioarcheologists who study the skeletal remains of children who were ritually killed have concluded that the victims "were likely slaves from within the Basin of Mexico region or Mexica individuals from low socio-economic households whose parents sold them into slavery or directly as sacrifices for specific Mexica ritual ceremonies."[113]

Further evidence suggests that Nahua slave-holders treated and categorized human slaves, turkeys, and dogs in a similar fashion. Colonial-era ethnographic texts told of funerary rituals for members of the elite that involved killing both slaves and dogs so that they could accompany and serve them in the underworld. Motolinia wrote that when "[Indigenous] lords of New Spain" were being cremated, so too were "sacrificed with him . . . 100 or 200 slaves, depending on whether the deceased was a major or minor lord." Some were his own slaves and others offered by his friends, some of them the "women, and also the dwarves and hunchbacks and deformed people that the lord had in his house," dressed in "new cloaks" so that they could serve "their master there in hell." The friar wrote that dogs, too, were interred with the lord, so that "he could guide the deceased . . . and they said that the dog would guide him and take him through all the difficult terrain" and lead "his soul" where it had to go.[114] The missionary's account is also revealing because it shows that despite being consumed as food, dogs also could be valued as loyal companions, as was also possible for enslaved people—some slaves became food offerings for deities and others became spouses. However, perhaps the best evidence for the associations between enslavement and home-dwelling turkeys and dogs comes from a phrase in the Florentine Codex that describes servitude (*tlacoyotl*) as being "someone else's dogs, someone else's turkeys."[115] The condition of servitude—such as being provisioned with maize by others—made one vulnerable to being killed and transformed into food.

Access also distinguished the eating of domesticated dog and turkey in postclassic Mexico from the eating of domesticated livestock in Europe. Turkey and dog primarily figured in sumptuous meals of the elite of Central Mexico. When the elders of Tepepulco recalled the "kinds of food and drink of the rulers and esteemed noblewomen," turkey appeared even before the list of chocolate beverages. Their flesh appeared in dishes such as "broken up tortillas with a sauce of turkey hen and yellow chilis," "fruit tamales with stewed turkey hens," and "yucca tortillas covered with a sauce of chili and turkey rump."[116] The Tlatelolco elders spoke of an array of dishes in which turkey and dog were cooked together and related "many manners of fowl roasted and stewed; some of them in dough, containing a complete fowl, another kind with pieces of fowl in dough, which they call fowl in dough, or cock, with yellow chile."[117] Prosperous merchants held feasts so large that up to 40 dogs and 100 turkeys were served.[118] The Tlatelolco scholars wrote that turkey was the best tasting of all the meats: "It is edible. It leads the meats; it is the master. It is tasty, fat, savory."[119] In contrast, "the commoner" ate such things as "bits of tortillas, dingy tortillas with tomato sauce and old nopal cactus."[120] Archaeological evidence from San Bartolo, Guatemala "suggests that the ancient Maya elite differentiated themselves from the lower classes by maintaining preferential control" over animals such as turkeys.[121]

Commoners did raise dogs and turkeys, but it seems they were required to offer the animals as tribute to local elites.[122] According to the *Relaciones geográficas*, before the arrival of the Spanish, "the ordinary people" in Iscateupa (Guerrero) "could not eat poultry or game" and "if they killed one [of these animals] they had to give it to the governor and cacique and to the *principales* (lords)."[123] Similarly, the respondent for the Mixtec town of Texupa wrote that the elite ate turkeys, deer, human flesh, and dogs during their feasts.[124] The respondent for Huazolotitlan, a predominantly Zapotec community in Oaxaca, wrote that the cacique and *principales* "sometimes ate turkey, hare, and rabbits and common people lacked this for not having the means to buy it" and instead ate vegetables, beans "and cactus that they call *nopales*, and tortillas of maize that they always had."[125] In another Zapotec town people only killed "a hen or a cock or a dog" once a year during the harvest.[126] By eating dog and turkey, as well as wild prey, the elite defined themselves as carnivores, similar to the animals, paradigmatically jaguars, categorized as *tecuani* ("those who eat people"). By eating animal flesh (including other humans), they embodied their supremacy over largely vegetarian commoners.

Eating meat was related to wearing the feathers of eagles and the pelts of large felines and canids. By digesting flesh and draping themselves in the skins of flesh-eaters, the elite embodied predators. It is not just that diet and clothing displayed status. Rather, in postclassic Mexico, as in South America, these practices revealed the singularity of humans. The defining characteristic of humans was their capacity for transformation, as suggested by the origin stories about humans who became animals and plants. Human skin was a bare surface that could easily be painted or cloaked in pelts, feathers, cotton threads, or maguey fiber. Likewise, the human body could subsist on plants or animals. The nakedness of their skin and their omnivorous diet distinguished humans from other creatures. Human exceptionalism was not the result of a special kind of interior soul or reason, as it was in Europe, but rather came from the potential for transformation.

~

THE INDIGENOUS INHABITANTS of Mesoamerica, like those of Amazonia and the Caribbean, were heavily invested in practices designed to turn wild animals into tame ones; however, they took a different path than the peoples in lowland South America. They reared dogs and turkeys who would be eaten as food and categorized them much as they did people who had lost their freedom and had become enslaved due to their inability to provide themselves with maize and thus had become dependent on others. Mesoamericans shared with South Americans and Europeans the practice of eating animals, but they reconciled this practice with their capacity to form affective relationships with some of these beings in their own way. The European solution was to classify certain beings as "off limits" and to objectify most beings who were to be eaten, and the Amazonian solution was to forbid eating those who were fed, whereas the Mesoamerican solution was to underscore the contingency of reciprocity. The misleadingly labeled practices of "sacrifice" were integrally related to those labeled as "domestication." This killing was not predicated on objectification, as it was in Europe. Instead, the subjectivity of captive and killed beings was celebrated. What made such killing tenable was the principle of reciprocity and a fundamental truth of the cosmos: everything is, in turn, both food and fed.

The conquistadores and missionaries could not help but filter these practices through the cultural frameworks that organized their perception, particularly those produced by European modes of interaction. For them, domestication and sacrifice were practices that shared little in common—the former was to be lauded and encouraged, and the latter was to be condemned and eradicated. They did not and could not see that both were aspects of familiarization in its Mesoamerican iteration. Their misunderstandings had enduring repercussions for how and what aspects of these practices and beliefs survived under colonial rule.

PART III

Entanglements

8

Transforming Animals

hristianity was not inherently incompatible with Indigenous modes of interaction. Christianity was (and is) a capacious tradition and Native converts found ways to
adapt the ceremonies and stories of their new religion in ways that aligned
with the values and ethos produced by predation and familiarization. Celebrations of holy days such as Easter and Corpus Christi became opportunities to incorporate elements of the *veintena* (20-day) cycle, feature tamed
animals, and animate the landscapes of the cosmogram. Yet the missionary
obsession with eradicating idolatry did pose challenges to Indigenous modes
of interaction, though sometimes in paradoxical ways. On the one hand, the
new colonial order brought an end to "human sacrifice." On the other hand,
ritual killing of birds—particularly European-originating chickens—flourished
and so helped maintain the practices and conceptions of reciprocity so central to Mesoamerican familiarization.

The impact of the evangelical project on predation and familiarization was
not only a product of the intentional actions of missionaries and Indigenous
Christians. It also related to the ontological chasm related to animals. The
clerics struggled to make sense of Mesoamericans' enthusiasm for tran-
scending species divides. They listened to origin stories in which animals
descended from human ancestors; they viewed "idols" with zoomorphic features; they confiscated ceremonial costumes made of the pelts of fierce predators and the feathers of myriad birds; they saw a dazzling variety of tamed,
formerly wild animals. They also arrived with an understanding that diabolically empowered witches and sorcerers could transform into animals, and
that uncommonly personable nonhumans indicated diabolical intervention.
Indeed, Juan de Zumárraga and Andrés de Olmos—among the most influential missionaries—had been deeply involved in the persecution of alleged
witches in the Basque country. Their inability to fully comprehend a culture
that did not uphold a species divide and their predisposition to see idolators

as shape-shifting sorcerers had consequential effects. The emergence of the colonial *nahual*—the animal double—was only partly connected to the Indigenous *nahualli* (knowledge manipulator) but above all reflected the entanglement of European diabolical discourse with Indigenous familiarization and predation practices.

~

SOME MISSIONARY PROJECTS assisted Nahuas and other people in Mesoamerica align Christianity to their existing beliefs and practices. Friars such as Bernardino de Sahagún believed that incorporating traditional Indigenous cultural forms into Christianity would strengthen their conversion efforts. For instance, Sahagún mobilized imagery associated with the eastern realm of the cosmogram—the lush tropical vegetation and brilliant plumaged birds— to evoke the Christian divine.[1] In the Nahuatl *Psalmodia christiana* (1583), Sahagún wrote of Paradise: "our lord's flowery world lies visible, lies giving off warmth, lies dawning. . . . The roses, dark red ones, pale ones, the red feather flowers, the golden flowers . . . waving like precious bracelets, lie bending with quetzal feather dew."[2] As suggested by this language, Christianity was not an obstacle but rather a new medium for the quetzal's continued association with sacred brilliance. The continuity was material as well as discursive. Indigenous people made and used featherworks in Christian ceremonies.[3] Friars lavished praise on the handsome feathered cloaks that Indigenous nobility wore during Christian holy days and the eucharistic containers, ciriales, and gorgeous crucifixes covered in gold and quetzal feathers.[4] The skilled *amanteca* (feather artists) depicted figures of saints and Christians (fig. 8.1).[5] Surviving wills and testaments reveal that elite Christian Nahuas continued to use and pass down featherworks made of quetzal feathers.[6] For Indigenous neophytes and some of their descendants, this material continuity could make Christianity more accessible and appealing, but it could also make Christianity into an instrument to maintain the pre-Hispanic material traditions that sustained the potency of "precious feathers."

Indigenous converts conformed their new religion to preexisting traditions, among other ways, through the celebration of Christian holy days. The Franciscan Motolinia (Toribio de Benavente) lavished praise on the Tlaxcalans' celebration of Corpus Christi in 1538, calling it "a thing very much worth seeing" that "deserves to be recorded." He admired the banners made of feathers and gold depicting Christian saints, the profusion and variety of

Figure 8.1   *Amanteca* making featherworks,
Florentine Codex, bk. 9, fol. 65r, ca. 1575–1577,
Biblioteca Medicea Laurenziana, Florence,
Med. Palat. 219, c. 373r. Reproduction used by
permission of the Ministry for Heritage and Cultural Archives.
All rights reserved.

flowers adorning triumphal arches and strewn during the procession, and the "many kinds of dances."[7] But what seemed to most impress him were the simulated landscape and its human and animal inhabitants—an animated cosmogram.[8] The Tlaxcalans fabricated a large track that turned around "four corners," suggesting a quadrangular shape. In each corner, like a cardinal point, there was constructed a different landscape, each organized around a mountain topped by a craggy peak and, below the mountains, meadows "with shrubs and flowers and all that can be found in the countryside," even "mushrooms and fungi." The flora and fauna were "so lifelike" that they "seemed to be placed there by nature." Motolinia emphasized that the landscapes were a study in contrasts. One featured an abundance of trees, some cultivated with fruit and others wild, and many flowers. Another landscape was "sparse" with moss-covered rocks and "old battered trees." There was a plethora of "small and large" birds and animals who thrive in the high-altitude desert; the trees hosted falcons and crows, and on the ground, "there was much game, including deer, hare, rabbits, jackals and a large multitude of snakes." The "wild and poisonous" reptiles had been made "sleepy and numb" with the use of tobacco, and Tlaxcalan performers took them "into their hands as if they were birds." Motolinia continued, "Because there was nothing missing in order to simulate nature, there were on the mounds some hunters well disguised with their bows and arrows." They were so well concealed by moss and branches that "one had to look very closely" to see them, and so "the prey would come up to their feet." The hunters "made a thousand gestures (*ademanes*) before shooting the unwary [game]." He noted they spoke not Nahuatl but "another tongue," and "because they live near the mountains they are great hunters." The hunters, likely Otomi, were an ethnic group that Nahuas associated with their own primordial Chichimec ancestors. In this Corpus Christi celebration, Tlaxcalan Christians created a living cosmogram and compressed the *veintena* cycle into a single holiday. The four simulated landscapes suggest the different biomes indicated by the cosmograms. The ecologies of the tropics and of the arid high plateau had fostered two different but equally valued cultural traditions and inheritances of hunting and horticulture.[9] The hunters enacted rites similar to those performed during Quecholli. These rites demonstrated the essential principles of predation: they displayed their attunement with the environment in their ability to blend into the landscape and to lure wild animals to their feet.

The celebration of Corpus Christi is notable not only because of its resonances with the *veintena* cycle but also because of the central roles enacted by tamed animals, such as the snakes who were held "as if they were birds." Familiarized animals likewise made striking appearances during another Corpus Christi celebration that, once again, featured realistic "counterfeit mountains."[10] It included a dramatic interlude in which Saint Francis interacted with a panoply of animals. The actor playing Francis "preached to the birds, telling them all of the reasons that they were obligated to praise and bless God, who adorned them with beautiful and varied feathers, without them needing to sew or weave them, and for the place they gave them, which is the air, where they go and fly." The birds then "approached the saint and seemed to ask him for his blessing." After the conversation with the birds, Francis left the mountain and a "wild beast"—perhaps a coyote, jaguar, or mountain lion—crossed his path. "It was so fierce that those who saw it jumped because of their fear," wrote the friar in attendance. However, Francis's special connections to animals enabled him to approach with ease. Making the sign of the cross, Francis went to the animal, and "gently reprimanded him" for being "a beast who destroys the livestock of that land." Next the saint led the fierce creature to "where the lords and *principales* of the town were seated." Then "the beast made a sign that he would obey him" and "never do damage again in that land," and "with that the vermin left." Francis then turned to the assembled people and preached to them: "if that wild animal can obey the word of God, then those who have reason have an even greater obligation to keep God's commandments." This performance and others were opportunities to display well-honed familiarizing techniques as well as to demonstrate knowledge of, and passion for, Christian stories and concepts. Moreover, the talkative parrots, sleepy snakes, and formerly fierce predator who so caught the attention of the friars throw into relief aspects of the postclassic *veintenas*. Specifically, such performances indicate that nonhuman animals may have played a more important role in *veintena* ceremonies than is suggested by the reconstructions in the Florentine Codex and missionary sources. In other words, they suggest that we attend to fleeting mentions of animal appearances, like the birds attached to poles carried by youths during the *veintena* of Etzalli that celebrated Tlaloc.[11] Additionally, these performances also allow us to see another aspect of the "Indigenization" of Christianity.[12] By focusing on St. Francis, the Christian saint most associated with interspecies harmony, and by portraying him as an expert in taming wild animals, the Indigenous performers showed both their interest in revering the saint and their desire to celebrate interspecies attunement.

Tamed animals were also protagonists in the Easter festivities that the Tlaxcalans celebrated in 1539. The focal point of this celebration was a dramatic reenactment of Adam and Eve's expulsion from Eden. Motolinia transcribed the account of another friar who witnessed the mesmerizing spectacle "performed by Indians in their own language."[13] He lavished descriptive detail on the "paradise on earth" where Adam and Eve lived. Surrounded by three "large peaks," the paradise even had four "rivers or springs," labeled Tigris, Euphrates, Pishon, and Geon—the biblical rivers that emanated from the Garden of Eden. This paradisical landscape featured varied and beautiful trees abounding in fruits and flowers, "some of them natural and others made of feathers and gold," and included "all the particular things that can be found there in April and May because these Indians have a singular grace for simulating natural things." In the middle were two trees, one "the tree of life" and the other that of "knowledge of good and bad with many and very beautiful fruits made of gold and feathers." In the trees were perched a "great diversity of birds, ranging from owls and other raptors to tiny little birds." Above all there were parrots—he "counted in a single tree fourteen large and small parrots"—and "so much talking and crying that at times it disrupted the performance." Interspersed among the live birds were those "counterfeit with gold and feathers, which was a great thing to see." On the ground were wild turkeys, which are "certainly the most beautiful birds I have ever seen anywhere," and numerous rabbits and hares "and other little animals which I had never before seen." Perhaps most enchanting were two young felines "*ocotochles* [ocelots] . . . neither cats not panthers"—who were known for being "very wild." But when Eve neared one of them, "he, well trained, turned in a circle for her." This was before the Fall, remarked the friar, for if it had been after, she would not "have been able to approach" the creature. The friar admired the nonhuman actors in the tableau vivant of Paradise. As was the case with the birds, some animals in the performance were actors wearing costumes, "walking about as if domesticated . . . and playing and joking with Adam and Eve." Another boy, "dressed like a mountain lion," played his part so authentically that "he was tearing apart and devouring a deer he killed." The deer, "lying in a crag between two rocks," was real.

The performance "lasted a long time" due to the extended conversations between the serpent, Adam, and Eve. First, the snake tried to convince Adam "three or four times" to eat the forbidden fruit, "Adam always resisting." Finally, the "indignant" snake went to Eve, beseeching her, saying "it seems that she had little love for him and that [the snake] loved her more than she loved him." Finally Eve acquiesced and accompanied the serpent to the forbidden tree, and ate an unnamed fruit and, inevitably, Adam "ate it too." God then appeared "with great majesty and accompanied by many angels." Adam tried to blame Eve, and Eve blamed the snake, and "God, cursing them, gave each their punishment." The angels dressed Adam and Eve in "two vestments" that were "well made of animal skins" and weeping they left, each "accompanied by three angels." The Franciscan took great pains to describe not only the luxuriousness of paradise but also what he perceived as the arid barrenness of a postlapsarian realm: "Once they were exiled, they were in a land different from the one they had left behind full of thistles and spines and many snakes, and also with hares and rabbits. And there they arrived as recent dwellers of the world, the angels showing Adam how to work and cultivate the earth and giving to Eve spindles in order to weave clothing for her husband and children."

From the missionaries' point of view, the gorgeous spectacle and heart-rending performance ("there was no one who saw it who did not cry") was evidence of evangelical triumph: the Tlaxcalan neophytes had so fully embraced their conversion that they had made a Christian passion play that rivaled anything that could be seen in Spain. But other interpretations were available to the Tlaxcalans. Likely they did not understand the contrast between green rainy Eden and the arid desert world in a dualist, hierarchical framework of the missionaries. Rather, they may have seen distinctive, yet equally valuable and necessary, ecosystems and their accompanying cultural traditions (Chichimec and Toltec), aligning with concepts celebrated in the cosmogram tradition. Similarly, *teixiptla* practices pervade the ceremonies. While in the Christian tradition, the animal skins that clothed Adam and Eve signified their expulsion, in the Nahua (and Mesoamerican) tradition, the act of cloaking with animal skins was a powerful mode of transformation. It was fundamental to *teixiptla*, the process of divine embodiment that centered around the strategic use of feathers and animal skins as discussed in Chapter 7. The boy who became a mountain lion—so thoroughly that he ate a deer raw—was wearing the predator's pelt. The trees were covered in "counterfeit" birds made of feathers interspersed with living birds.

Most significant, perhaps, was the snake. The friar did not elaborate on the appearance of the snake, but the descriptions of the *veintenas* suggest a large repertoire of possibilities. Sometimes snakes were made "of wood or of the roots of trees and they fashioned them with a head like that of a snake," or there were fire serpents "looking like a blazing pine firebrand" featuring a tail made of paper "two or three fathoms long" and a tongue "made of red macaw feathers" that "like that of a real serpent," darted "in and out." Sometimes a person was "representing a serpent" with "paper vestments daubed with liquid rubber."[14] Snakes were central protagonists in rituals centered around primordial ecological phenomena—mountains and fire. In parallel, cosmogonies that associate snakes with the power of Quetzalcoatl, the "feathered serpent," whose simultaneously destructive and generative energy contributed to the formation of the Earth and heavens. It is clear that the serpent's role in the play was not quite what Motolinia had expected, and his interactions with Adam and Eve perhaps dragged on a bit too long for the Franciscan's taste. The friar may have sensed that the outsized role given to the serpent was resonant with pre-Hispanic Mesoamerican belief and ritual.

These performances foregrounded notions of ecology and intersubjectivity profoundly different from those prevalent in sixteenth-century Europe. We see again how Nahua playwrights, set designers, and actors could interpret biblical and Christian hagiographic traditions in ways that aligned with their priorities—among them, the values related to familiarization and predation. These performances afforded an opportunity to display the dazzling taming abilities of certain members of the community. The Tlaxcalans chose to emphasize Christian traditions that featured prominent nonhuman animal protagonists. These enacted stories also dramatized the interdependence of humans and other animals and centered the subjectivity of nonhumans. We can see these ceremonies only through the missionary gaze, so it is difficult to know what Indigenous organizers, participants, and spectators had in mind. Nevertheless, it seems clear that the Tlaxcalans found a way to integrate aspects of the *veintena* cycle into their celebrations of Corpus Christi and Easter. The Nahuas were not "secretly" resisting Christianity but rather finding the Christian festival cycle compatible with the *veintena* repertoire, much in the way that the Tlatelolco scholars found aspects of the encyclopedia tradition compatible with that of the cosmogram.

~

WHILE THE FRIARS found certain Indigenous traditions unobjectionable when integrated into Christian devotional practice, others were deemed worrisome.[15] The practice that elicited the most concern was "sacrifice." Motolinia believed that before the arrival of Christians, "every day and every hour in all of the towns and provinces" of New Spain, the Native people "offered devils human blood."[16] The prevalence of sacrifice—human and animal—was considered potent proof of diabolical presence within Indigenous culture,[17] as evidenced by Motolinia's observation, "The devil our adversary was much served by the greatest idolatries and most cruel homicides that ever existed."

Nevertheless, the colonists' efforts to end sacrifice had paradoxical effects on Mesoamerican traditions of familiarization. On the one hand, feeding humans to the deified sun, earth, and water quickly became rare. On the other hand, the even older practice of feeding birds to deified elemental forces flourished in the colonial period. Church authorities' aggressive efforts to uproot idolatry in Central Mexico during the 1530s and 1540s left a documentary trail illuminating these rites of familiarization's persistence in the colonial period. Juan de Zumárraga, experienced in investigating witchcraft in the Basque country, initiated and oversaw the first idolatry extirpation campaign. He arrived to New Spain in 1528, became bishop in 1533, and, empowered as "Apostolic Inquisitor" in 1536, began to investigate accusations of idolatry against Indigenous Christians.[18] Many of the idolatry trials included accusations of blood "sacrifices" on altars in hidden rooms and caves. The blood sometimes came from the participants' own bodies as a result of bloodletting rites, and sometimes from the ritual killing of animals, especially quail, turkeys, and dogs.[19]

There were also allegations of human offerings. One of the latter occurred in the 1540s when the Dominicans in charge of evangelization in the Mixteca Alta prosecuted a case in Yanhuitlan. A populous and prosperous town known for textiles and ceramics, Yanhuitlan was ruled by the traditional hereditary lords, Don Domingo (*cacique*), Don Francisco (*gobernador*), and Don Juan. Outraged clerics, Indigenous rivals in neighboring towns, and relatives of those killed during such rites charged that throughout the 1530s and the beginning of the next decade, these ruling lords persisted in idolatry, sacrificing to their "devils" in secret domestic quarters and on remote hilltops.[20] The Indigenous *gobernador* of neighboring Etlatongo testified that Don Francisco and Don Domingo "arrange sacrifices in all of the feasts of the year of the devil, when there is sickness and when there is a lack of water, [when] they harvest in their fields" and that "all three in the current day have their devils and altars in their own houses, where they live, where they sacrifice and worship." When he and local authorities entered, they "found in a dark room boxes with sacrifices and idols, feathers and straw, and boughs bloodied from sacrifice," adding that it was "well known" that they sacrifice "doves, pigeons, quail and other things, and that they kill and sacrifice when the wife or some principals die."[21] Another witness, one of the Mixtec lords of Teposcolula, testified on October 20, 1544 that just two months earlier, Don Domingo and Don Francisco had "made a great feast" and consulted with priests where they had "killed many quail and birds," getting drunk and burning much copal to honor the devil.[22] Such offerings were made during illness, droughts, harvests, mortuary rites, and other events according to the ritual calendar.[23] In addition to those purchased in the market, some of these birds were procured through tributes that Mixteca's Indigenous nobles continued to impose upon commoners.[24]

In this case, the testimony about human sacrifices is very credible. A bereaved relative, an enslaved woman from the region, said through an interpreter that "priests" went to "the house of the said don Francisco" and "took a sister of the said witness who was named Xaxa who would have been 7 years old and took her with them and killed her and sacrificed her to the devil on a hilltop that is called Yncuymayo." The woman further testified that a few days later, when "don Francisco was feeling a little indisposed they [the priests] sacrificed an Indian slave that they had bought a few days before at the *tianguis* [market]."[25] Others concurred that the priests had sacrificed a number of enslaved people and even some low-status commoners when concerned about droughts, sickness, or other worrisome conditions.[26] The trial records from Yanhuitlan offer vivid descriptions of hereditary nobles doing their utmost to maintain rites despite the Dominicans' efforts. In addition, they help illuminate a central reason why animal killings supplanted human killings as the colonial period progressed. It was difficult to conceal the ritual killing of people because they often left behind distraught family who did not hesitate to denounce the killers to authorities.

Such was not the case with nonhuman animals, of course, and because the colonizers had routinized the slaughter of livestock, the ritual killing of nonhuman animals flourished in the colonial period and beyond. The devotional practices of Cristóbal and Catalina, the married Nahua lords of Ocuituco (a village south of Mexico City and near Xochimilco), illustrate the persistence of ritual animal killing in the colonial period. Francisco Coatl, an enslaved Nahua who worked for the couple brought a case against them, one likely motivated by his desire for freedom and escape from their harsh treatment.[27] Coatl and other enslaved members of the household testified through interpreters that the couple engaged in clandestine rites centered around the "sacrifice" of a hen (*gallina*)—probably a chicken, but possibly a turkey—and praying to stars at midnight.[28] Every twenty days, testified Francisco, as "during their festivals and offerings to the demons in their gentility, upon waking up the said Cristóbal, with his own hands, took a *gallina* and went with it to the fire, and there with a knife cut off the head of the said *gallina* and scattered all the blood that flowed out of the said *gallina* into the said fire . . . and left the said *gallina* in front of the fire with her head cut off in one part and [her body] in the other."[29] Then he and the other enslaved witnesses testified that Cristóbal required them to pluck and cook the bird, and the women made tamales. Afterward, "in a certain secret room," Cristóbal presented the tamales, along with chocolate, incense, tobacco pipes, and flowers, on an altar with a woven mat *petate* and a cloak devoted to two "idols"—Tezcatlipoca, Tlaloc, or Chicomecoatl (the identities varied according to the witness). After two or three days, Cristóbal and Catalina ate the food, sometimes sharing it with their slaves and "other times eating it the two of them alone."[30] During her interrogation, Catalina confessed that she and her husband "many times offered copal to the devils as they did in their heathendom" and that for each deity who oversaw a twenty-day month, they sacrificed a hen. She explained that her brother-in-law Martin Ticoc was a "counter of the sun and of the holidays of the devils"—in other words an expert in the 260-day *tonalpohualli*—who, when her husband was absent, told Catalina "'you know today is the day of such-and-such devil.'"[31]

These rites closely resemble those of the quail offerings made before the Spanish arrived.[32] However, this testimony also suggests some ways that traditional rites were changed by the invaders' missionary project. First, in this case, no people were killed. Whereas the lords of Yanhuitlan saw enslaved Indigenous people as viable prospects for human offerings, Catalina and Cristóbal tried to make them accomplices. Second, the birds were *gallinas,* a term that could refer either to chickens (*gallinas de Castilla*) or turkeys (*gallinas de la tierra*). Notably, they were not quail. The perception that quail were associated with idolatry in ways that the European-originated chickens were not is displayed in another trial, this one targeting a witness against Cristóbal and Catalina. Diego Díaz, the vicar and sometimes interpreter, was accused of planting false evidence to further incriminate Cristóbal, who was also in trouble for mocking Christian doctrine during mass. According to a witness, Díaz not only tried to plant fake idols in Cristóbal's house but also hired someone to go to the "*tianguis* [marketplace] . . . to trade for some quail . . . in order to put it in front of the said idol to make the thing more grave and make the said Cristóbal more guilty."[33] Perhaps

Catalina and Cristóbal had substituted chickens for quail because killing quail suggested idolatry to authorities, who tolerated and even encouraged raising chickens.[34]

The rites practiced by Catalina and Cristóbal closely resemble descriptions provided by friars intent on extirpating idolatry in subsequent decades and by current-day ethnographers.[35] Pedro Ponce de León, a priest fluent in Nahuatl, described similar "sacrifices" in Indigenous households in Zumpahuacán in the late sixteenth and early seventeenth centuries.[36] The villagers "cut off the heads of the *gallinas* before the fire, which is the God Xiuhteuctli." They offered hens, along with pulque, chocolate, tobacco, and flowers, to celebrate births, harvests, and the construction of a new house, as well as to heal sickness. Ponce explained that under these circumstances, chickens were to be beheaded and offered to Xiuhtecuhtli, the fire-solar complex. Some offerings were made in secrecy to shield children from the rites, presumably because they would be more likely than adults to divulge them to religious authorities, as had famously happened in the early sixteenth century and led to the persecution of several elders. Yet the villagers also took offerings to the church,[37] demonstrating that they had assimilated elements of older rites into Christian practice.

The pervasiveness of poultry "sacrifice" in colonial Mexico was likewise of great concern to Diego Villavicencio, a parish priest for the town of Quechula in the province of Tepeaca. In 1692, he observed that chickens and turkeys were sacrificed for many reasons: to increase the number and health of livestock, to sow fields, to plant new maguey, to reap first harvests, to make pulque, to begin construction of houses, to bring rain, to ensure health, to celebrate ancestors and new births, and even "when they have business or lawsuits in Mexico."[38] A confessant told Father Diego of an occasion when "more than thirty of those Native Idolaters convoked their ministers or sacrificers" and went to "those mountains and thickets bringing their poultry of the land and of Castile" to perform "sacrifices that they had to make for their Idols." The priest explained that they beheaded the birds "in front of their Idols" and afterwards, they ate "the birds in their homes." They all left the place of the offerings at separate times "so it would not be noticed in the village." Other sacrifices took place inside homes. The priest described how, in cases of illness, a ritual specialist would "pull off the head of the sacrificant" and then apply its blood to an idol and to specially cut out papers, "a kind of brown paper cut in the shape of a hand, with fingers or branches, and many of them resemble the devil."

Figure 8.2   Woman caressing a turkey, Florentine Codex, bk. 11, fol. 199r, ca. 1575–1577, Biblioteca Medicea Laurenziana, Florence, Med. Palat. 220, c. 351r. Reproduction used by permission of the Ministry for Heritage and Cultural Archives. All rights reserved.

The affective regime shaping the relationship between people and animals who would be turned into food also appears to have persisted in the colonial period. In his instructions to priests hearing confession from Nahua Christians, Juan Bautista described the persistence of a variety of "superstitions" related to poultry,[39] finding them odd and divergent from European husbandry practices. He reported that those who raised poultry, for instance, had their "boys or girls . . . wash the tips of the cloaks that they wear, and they give this water to the cocks or hens that are in the house to drink, so that they do not die." He explained that children also performed the feeding: "They order the girls or the boys to feed to cocks or hens from their hands so that they do not die." Although not qualifying as idolatrous practices, Bautista clearly thought something was amiss. The idea that children—and, therefore, their skins and clothing—had a particular connection to house-dwelling birds suggested that both were viewed as tender beings requiring care and concern. This tenderness toward birds who would eventually become food is also evident in the Florentine Codex, in which an illustration accompanying the entry about an herb used to fatten turkeys depicted a woman affectionately caressing her birds (fig. 8.2).

It may be that dogs, like quail, were used less frequently in ritual killings because this practice would arouse much suspicion. The Tlaxcalan Mestizo chronicler Diego Muñoz Camargo recalled that in the 1550s, "there was a slaughter of a great many dogs, sacrificed and their hearts extracted on the left side in the way of sacrifice." He noted, however, that the authorities "ordered that they stop, and then this error was uprooted." Contrary to Camargo's assurance, canine offerings did persist. Durán claimed to have seen "more than four hundred large and small dogs tied up in crates, some already sold, other still for sale." When he asked what they were wanted for, he was told "for fiestas, weddings and baptisms."[40] In the 1650s, Gonzalo de Balsalobre conducted a number of idolatry investigations in the Zapotec communities of Oaxaca. He found that, in addition to the killing of "chickens and of hens of the land [turkeys]," people continued to "practice horrendous idolatries and sacrifices of little dogs to the Devil." He discovered, for example, that on a hilltop near San Juan, "the Indians of the said town light candles, burn copal, behead dogs, chickens and hens of the land and offer it to the Gods of their Pagan days." On the occasion of a loved one's death, turkeys and dogs would be offered to the "God of Hell," and "being that [turkeys] are large it was customary to take it to the home of the deceased for it to be prepared and eaten by the previously fasting mourners."[41] In 1671, when Matheo Pérez became *gobernador* of the Oaxacan town of Atitlan, he proceeded to ritually kill "little dogs" and "chicks" among other animals on a nearby peak. He explained to the Inquisition officials investigating his actions that he made these offerings because his ancestors "originated from the said hill." Pérez further explained, "we do what our grandparents and parents and our ancestors did, and also my father, and we cannot lose this custom."[42]

Raising poultry became a vehicle for the survival and transformation of Mesoamerican ritual and belief. There are striking continuities with the pre-Hispanic period, such as the enduring importance of beheading as a means of killing and the invocation of traditional Mesoamerican deities, especially those associated with fire and sun. There were also significant differences. For one, these rituals were sometimes incorporated into Christian worship. Another change involved abandoning the ritual use of quail altogether. In the colonial period chickens frequently supplanted quail, and earlier, nuanced distinctions between the ritual killing of different animals—quail, parrots, turkeys—receded. In other ways, the colonial period's increased emphasis on the ritual killing of animals—rather than humans—may have constituted a return to much earlier Mesoamerican practices. Nahua cosmogonies explained that the practice of ritually killing and feeding the blood and flesh of birds to the sun and earth predated feeding them people. Though killing humans in order to feed the earth illustrated the reciprocity of feeding and eating, it was not the only way. Ritual killing of birds survived and flourished in the colonial period and sustained ancient beliefs about familiarization.[43]

~

IF NAHUAS AND other Mesoamericans Indigenized Christianity by, among other things, incorporating taming, offering, and *teixiptla* practices into it, the process also operated in reverse: missionaries used European categories to make sense of Indigenous concepts, as we have already seen with "sacrifice," among others.[44] Nowhere is this more important than in the way that missionaries came to understand and reinterpret the *nahualli*.[45] The colonial *nahual* resulted from the entanglement of the European ideas about *hechicería* (sorcerery) and *brujería* (witchcraft) with the Nahua ritual specialist *nahualli* (knowledge manipulator)—as well as practices related to predation and familiarization. This entanglement comes into view, in part, following Marie Musgrave-Portilla's recognition that "the sixteenth-century Mendicant friars" who wrote "our most valuable sources" for the *nahualli* were "brothers of the Dominican witch-hunters in Europe."[46] More precisely, the first sources were composed by Franciscan witch hunters themselves. The entangled properties of the *nahualli* also become visible by attending to Indigenous modes of interaction and Europeans' difficulty in comprehending the modes and the ontology they produced.[47]

In order to understand the *nahualli* prior to its entanglement with missionary ideas, it is helpful to consider the early drafts of the Florentine Codex. There is an extensive discussion of the *nahualli* in the "Primeros memoriales" (the draft of the "Historia universal" completed circa 1560, after the seminarians' investigations in Tepepulco).[48] The *nahualli* was powerful.[49] The Tlatelolco authors wrote that the *nahualli* "was a knower of the land of the dead, a knower of the heavens. He knew when it would rain or would not rain. He gave courage to the noblemen, to the rulers, and to the commoners." He determined the most propitious times to make offerings to deities, and he could change the weather: "If he hated a city or a ruler, if he wished that a city be destroyed," then "he ordered that there be a frost or that it should hail." The *nahualli* was also celibate: "No one was his wife. He stayed only in the temple; he lived in it."[50] It appears the *nahualli* was a general term encompassing a variety of ritual specialists. The special powers of these practitioners ranged considerably; some were known for inducing people to give away their possessions, others for preparing corpses for cremation, and others for performing magic tricks in the palace.[51] The authors indicate that *nanahualtin* (plural) could direct their talents for good or bad ends, that the *nahualli* could be beneficent or malevolent. This was made even more explicit in the revised version that appeared in the Florentine Codex: The "good" *nahualli* was a "wise man, a counselor, a person of trust, careful, helpful," whereas the "bad" one is "an enchanter . . . he deranges, deludes people, he casts spells over them . . . he causes them to be possessed."[52] Though the authors discuss the *nahualli* as male, the word does not indicate gender and there is evidence that women, too, could be *nanahualtin*.[53]

Some, though not all, *nanahualtin* appear to have powers related to inter-species interactions, according to these texts. The "Primeros memoriales" described a *nahualli* who practiced a kind of animal taming, a person "who made a serpent come alive in order to soothsay." This person would be hired when someone was missing or suspected neighbors or a family member of theft. The *nahualli* would appear before an assembly of the victim, relatives, and neighbors, and begin by asking that the guilty person come forward and "give [the possessions] to him calmly" of his own accord. But if "no one spoke, followed his conscience, then [the *nahualli*] uncovered a vessel" from which "a serpent came alive." Emerging from a dormant state, the enlivened snake then "stretched itself on the rim of the vessel. It looked in all directions" and "slithered off . . . when it saw the one who had committed the theft, it climbed up him, it stretched itself out upon him." But if no one present was guilty, then the snake "looked at no one, it just returned . . . to lie down in the vessel. It did not confirm the [accuser's word]."[54]

Perhaps (some?) *nahualli* were particularly skilled in accessing the powers of other animals through their skins. Such an idea is suggested by a passage in the jaguar entry in "Earthly Things," composed by the Tlatelolco scholars in the early 1560s. The Nahua authors wrote that *nahualli* "went about carrying the [jaguar] hide—the hide of its forehead and of its chest, and its tail, its nose, and its claws, and its heart, and its fangs, and its snout. It is said that they went about their tasks with them—that with them they did daring deeds, that because of them they were feared."[55] And, indeed, from a linguistic perspective, there does seem to be a strong connection between the figure of the *nahualli* and the practice of cloaking. Katarzyna Mikulska Dabrowska writes that "the root nahual" means "to transform, convert, transfigure, disguise, reclothe, mask oneself, conceal, camouflage, and finally to trick."[56] Depictions of cloaking appear throughout the Mixtec animal hide screenfolds.[57] For instance, Lord 8 Deer is depicted wearing the hide and head of a jaguar in the Codex Zouche-Nuttall (fig. 7.5) and Lord 4 Dog and Lord 10 Reed wear the hides of a coyote and mountain lion, respectively (fig. 7.4). In aggregate, it seems that *nanahualtin* were known for their abilities in relationship to other species—taming and cloaking—but that they also performed many other services, and that many others engaged in these practices. In other words, the *nahualli* encompassed much more than taming and cloaking, and taming and cloaking went well beyond the *nahualli*.

To understand the shifting meaning of the *nahualli* it is imperative to look at the role of the powerful missionaries, Juan de Zumárraga and Andrés de Olmos, in orchestrating trials and writing about the phenomenon. Both participated in the Basque witch hunts, traveled together in New Spain in 1528, and worked together during the idolatry trials of the 1530s.[58] It is no coincidence that the Church authorities most involved in persecuting the first Indigenous "idolaters" accused of transforming themselves into animals had prior experience writing about—and persecuting—men and women accused of diabolical witchcraft in Iberia.

A key event in the entanglement of the *nahualli* with missionary diabolical discourse was the very first idolatry trial overseen by Zumárraga. The accused were two brothers, identified in the proceedings as Tacatetl and Tanixtetl, rulers in the Otomi town Tanacopan near Tula.[59] The *encomendero* Lorenzo Suárez, a Portuguese conquistador who participated in the conquest of Tenochtitlan, initiated the June 1546 proceeding by making a denunciation.[60] It appears that Suárez wanted the brothers removed from town so he could collect all of the town's tribute for himself, rather than give the traditional lords their share in accordance with the law. Suárez testified that while visiting the community in the company of a local *corregidor* (royal official), he discovered that many of the residents were "missing from the village." Diego Xiutl informed the officials that the villagers "are now preparing for the celebrations of tomorrow . . . every twenty days they sacrifice to their gods and now it is time to fulfill the obligation of the said twenty days."[61] It is necessary to clarify Xiutl's somewhat perplexing role in the events that unfolded. Although identified as a resident of Mexico City, he was, according to Suárez's testimony, the informant who enabled the discovery of the hidden altar and secret rites in Otomi. Xiutl's knowledge of the Otomi leaders' activities might have been acquired from one of their children. Xiutl's testimony included the claim that one of Tanixtetl's sons had been educated in Otomi's Franciscan monastery, and had "argued with [his father] not to make sacrifices." This son had also destroyed some of his father's idols and altars, leading the Otomi rulers to "mistreat him in a way that [Xiutl] had never seen before."[62] This detail suggests that Xiutl may have been a friend of Tanixtetl's son, who, like a number of other children of the Indigenous nobility, was raised from boyhood by Franciscans.

Suárez demanded that Xiutl lead them to the idolaters, and after threats of violence, he agreed. Thus in the middle of the night, he led Suárez, the *corregidor*, and some of their Indigenous slaves to a secret shrine. Most participants—some other Indigenous religious leaders as well as Tacatetl and Tanixtetl—fled the scene, but they left behind the incriminating evidence: an "altar" with "idols" and offerings including marigold flowers, copal, chocolate, pulque, food, and "and much spilled blood on the said altar."[63] Also remaining were two frightened boys, weakened and immobilized because of ritual bloodletting. The next day, Suárez, with the assistance of an interpreter named Andrés, interrogated the terrified boys. They told the adults that "they were being taught to be priests and they didn't want to," and they were forced, with aggressive questioning and perhaps physical threats, to take Suárez and his entourage into "the mountains where there was a cave where there they had many idols," its "walls bloody from many sacrifices." Suárez closed his denunciation by reporting that the boys "heard from many people that Tacatetl was a sacrificer and idolater and priest of sacrifices and that he turns into a jaguar (*tigre*)."

This elliptical and highly mediated mention of shape-shifting—a scribe recording Suárez's recollection of a translator's interrogation of two frightened children—was elaborated in depositions taken later that summer in Mexico City, after the arrest of Tacatetl and Tanixtetl. On August 16, Zumárraga personally interrogated Xiutl. The latter testified that Tacatetl "is a sorcerer who turns into a jaguar (*tigre*) and witch (*brujo*) and all manners of animals that he wants and that is known in all of his province," and that Tanixtetl "did this [turned into animals] in the same manner." Next the cleric interrogated the children, whose names never appeared in the proceedings. He required the assistance of two interpreters, one who could translate from Otomi to Nahuatl and other from Nahuatl to Otomi. When asked "if they saw the said Tacatetl and Tanixtetl transform into *tigre* [jaguar]," they responded that "they had seen the accused [as] tigers, jackals, and pigs and dogs," and described the process by which they transformed themselves."[64] The coercive context that produced this testimony, and the language and cultural barriers shaping it, make it impossible to know what the boys actually believed. It is almost certain, however, that Spanish colonizers—and perhaps also their former students like Xiutl—were predisposed to find diabolically inspired animal transformations.

Allegations of shape shifting surfaced again a few months later in the case that Zumárraga brought against a man aptly named Martín Ocelotl (Jaguar), hispanized as "Ucelo."[65] The document begins with Zumárraga's declaration that it had "come to [his] attention" that "Martín Ucelo had made many enchantments and spells and had turned himself into a tiger, lion, and dog," and had encouraged other "natives of this New Spain" to do "things against our faith." Nevertheless, an examination of this testimony reveals that the witnesses first deposed were elite Indigenous men who offered many details about the accused's activities, but none involving animal transformation.[66] According to the testimony, Ocelotl had already achieved some prominence during Moctezuma's time and adeptly navigated the early colonial period. He initially impressed Franciscans with his ability to explain Christian dogma, until he made too many enemies among powerful Indigenous leaders and Spaniards alike. Nonetheless, he clearly had many supporters, for another charismatic leader assumed Ocelotl's identity after the latter's deportation to the Inquisition jails of Sevilla.[67] He was a renowned soothsayer, cloud conjurer, and fire master. An extremely successful farmer, amassing substantial wealth from cultivating traditional Mesoamerican crops such as cotton, magueys, cacti, and maize, he also became an accomplished cultivator of European fruit trees.[68] His healing abilities and traditional remedies containing greenstone, pulverized bones, and herbs attracted Indigenous and European clients alike. These curative talents extended to nonhuman beings: in his own testimony, Ocelotl declared that the royal official Cristóbal de Cisneros, who had been *corregidor* of Texcoco, had summoned him "in order that he cure a mare," suggesting that Ocelotl may have been practiced in arts of familiarization now applied to European vassal animals.[69] Ocelotl came to own at least five different properties and many prestige goods, including fine cotton cloaks, and, notably, animal skins and feathered artifacts, all of which figured among the belongings seized after his arrest.[70] The traditional Indigenous elite of Texcoco and other communities where he resided seemingly envied these riches, and their hostility, along with his turn toward anticlericalism, may have precipitated his downfall. Ocelotl does appear to be a quintessential *nahualli*, as the figure was described in the "Primeros Memoriales."

Ocelotl was first denounced by a European, Antonio de Ciudad Rodrigo, one of the twelve Franciscan "apostles" accompanying Hernán Cortés and the former guardian of the Franciscan convent in Texcoco. He testified that Ocelotl "was a sorcerer and said things about the future and made himself into a cat and tiger, and that he went inciting the Indians." This assertion was echoed by the official Cisneros, who testified that Ocelotl "was said" to be "a great sorcerer" who "made himself into a lion and tiger."[71] However, Nahua witnesses discussed animal transformation only when asked leading questions, as was the case with the testimony of the Indigenous rulers of Huaxtepec, who responded in the affirmative when asked whether Ocelotl had "turned into a tiger, and a lion, and a dog."[72] However, some Nahua witnesses decline to affirm this allegation, even when prompted.[73]

Zumárraga, experienced in investigating witches in the Basque country and inculcated with discourses about diabolical witchcraft, was on the lookout for sorcerers who turned into animals. When he and his fellow Franciscans found themselves immersed in an Indigenous milieu that celebrated the transformative power of skins—particularly jaguar and coyote pelts among elite men—their convictions were confirmed. For the most part, the testimony that supported animal transformation came from Europeans who were conversant with demonological witchcraft beliefs, particularly Franciscans and those in their orbit. Indigenous witness testimony supporting such views came from people such as Xiutl, likely exposed to Franciscan demonological ideas through his friendship with Tacatetl's son, or through a relationship with a patron like Suárez. Sometimes the testimony emerged from aggressive leading questions posed by an interpreter, and was informed by enormous power imbalances, as was the case with the terrified child witnesses compelled to testify against Tacatetl and Tanixtetl.

The trial records of Tacatetl, Tanixtetl, and Ocelotl are not so much the traces of the shape-shifting powers attributed to *nanahualtin* as they are traces of the generative power of trials. Much in the same way priests disseminated ideas about witchcraft in late medieval and early modern Europe through their witch hunts, the trials themselves disseminated new colonial forms of knowledge that entangled European and Indigenous concepts. The sentences imposed on Tacatetl, Tanixtetl, and Ocelotl included public shaming. They were mounted on a donkey and paraded through the Indigenous marketplace and Mexico City's other significant public spaces. All the while "the voice of the town crier (*pregonero*) proclaim[ed] their crimes" in both Spanish and Nahuatl so that "others [would] see and hear their example."[74] The listeners—of all ethnicities—were not only learning that idolatrous practices would not go unpunished but also learning about shape-shifting, the animal-transforming capacities of certain, powerful Indigenous people.

Neither the term *nahualli* nor cognate terminology appears in the trials' testimony. However, by the mid-sixteenth century, the wide semantic gap between the European *bruja/o* and the Nahuatl *nahualli* began to narrow. Although scholars have long recognized that the concept of the *nahualli* became mixed with European ideas of witchcraft in the colonial era, it is useful to look closely at a particular inflection point: Olmos, renowned for his abilities in Nahuatl, penned a loose translation of "Tratado de las supersticiones y hechicerías y vanos conjuros y abusiones y otras cosas" (Treatise on superstitions and spells and vain conjurations and abuses and other things), the 1529 witchcraft treatise penned by de Olmos's fellow Basque witch-hunter Martín de Castañega.[75] The surviving manuscript is addressed to the "Indiano letor" (Indian reader), seemingly aimed at elite Nahuas as part of the campaign to encourage them to remain steadfast in the renunciation of "sorcery" (*hechicerías*).[76] In translating Castañega's treatise into Nahuatl, Olmos was populating the concept of the *nahualli* with European beliefs about the propensity of the devil and witches to transform into animals. The translation included a chapter entitled "On the various shapes the ministers of the Devil can take" which recounted how "a long time ago," Circe transformed Odysseus's companions into pigs.[77] Olmos used the term *nahualli* to translate "witch" or "sorcerer."[78] The missionary explained, for instance, how the "Devil" (using the Spanish word *diablo*) could give a *nahualli* the appearance "of a bird (*tototl*) or maybe a cat (*mizton*) or maybe even a *coyotl* or a jaguar (*ocelotl*)."[79] Olmos not only made *nahualli* synonymous with *brujo* but perhaps made it inadvertently alluring by associating the animal doubles with prestige and potent Mesoamerican animals. In so doing, Olmos helped construct the colonial-era *nahual* by reinterpreting the Indigenous *nahualli* with the concept of the European witch or sorcerer. Olmos sometimes deviated from the 1529 text to refer to events that had taken place in New Spain during the preceding twenty years. Tellingly, however, none of the American incidents involved nonhuman animals, with the exception of a brief anecdote about a "man named Don Juan, the lord of Amecameca, who told me in earlier years that the Devil appeared to his father in the form of a monkey."[80] This elliptical reference—obscured by problems of both linguistic and conceptual translation—tells us more about what Olmos expected to understand than what "Don Juan" actually believed. The shape-shifting attributes of the *nahualli* were, at least in part, the result of the missionaries' conflation of the European witch and sorcerer with the Nahua *nahualli*. This was further corroborated and authorized by Alonso de Molina's 1555 and 1571 Spanish-Nahuatl dictionaries, which indicate that *nahualli* ought to be translated as *bruja*.[81]

By 1577, one can discern the emergence of a colonial *nahual* that merged the *brujería* of early modern Europe with the Nahua *nahualli*. When revising the calendrical prognostications in Book 4 of the Florentine Codex, Sahagún, his Nahua collaborators, or both, made a revealing and influential addition. Now they identified the *nahualli* with animal shape-shifting: if elite, he transformed into a predator like a jaguar, whereas for a commoner, "it was his work to turn himself into perhaps a turkey, or a weasel or a dog."[82] In the revised text of Book 10 the Tlatelolco humanists defined the *nahualli* as someone "who transforms himself, who assumes the guise of an animal . . . who turns himself into a dog, a bird, a screech owl, a horned owl." In the accompanying Spanish translation, the semantic transformation is complete, as the *nahualli* becomes "the man who has a pact with the devil and turns into various animals and for hatred desires the deaths of others and uses spells and much malefice against them."[83] It is impossible to know, of course, whether the Nahua scholars were in complete agreement with Sahagún (or each other) in the diabolization of the *nahualli*, but there is every reason to assume that they were as invested as Sahagún in finding ways to reconcile Nahua and European concepts as we have seen previously.

This colonial redefinition of *nahualli* was further disseminated by missionaries and elite Indigenous Christians in the later sixteenth century through texts such as Olmos's, liturgical texts and confessional manuals and, certainly, countless sermons and private confessional conversations of which we have only the faintest traces. In his 1583 *Psalmodia christiana* (Christian Psalms), Sahagún redeployed the terminology used for ritual practitioners in the "Historia universal" to describe how the Devil's minions cast darkness: "At night they go about shape-changers ("nanaoalti"), the witches who spit fire, those who have the coyote as their animal form, those who frighten things, the diviners."[84] Sahagún's consolidation of other friars' renderings of the *nahualli*, in turn, filtered its way into subsequent missionary texts. In his confessional manual, Juan Bautista explained that he was drawing from "what the Father Friar Bernardino de Sahagún wrote" about the beliefs that "Natives had in their heathendom," noting that it was imperative for confessors to "understand them well." The manual instructed confessors to be watchful for "necromancers who transform . . . their appearance into a Tiger [i.e., jaguar], or into a Dog, or Weasel, who are called *Nanahualtin*," and others who "appear as a hen or as an Owl."[85] Paradoxically, while such manuals and confessional practices were meant to help priests root out superstitious and idolatrous beliefs and practices, they also instructed Indigenous confessants about the reality of animal-transforming *nanahualtin*, thus becoming a vector for European demonological beliefs. Thus, in addition to teaching Indigenous people about the Trinity and the Virgin Mary, priests instructed them about Christian devils and witches—and clerical interpretations of *nanahualtin*. However, such teachings may have had unintended consequences. While the intention of proselytizing friars and confessing priests was to uproot what they viewed as idolatrous practices and beliefs, they may have instead helped create a very appealing personage for Nahuas and other Mesoamericans: they enhanced and extended the power of *nanahualtin*.

In the seventeenth century there was an important shift in the missionary discourse about the *nahualli*. Hernando Ruiz de Alarcón, Thomas Gage, and Francisco Burgoa applied the term *nahual* to the animal rather than human double.[86] Common to their accounts was the idea that when a *nahualli* was wounded or killed, s/he manifested injuries identical to those of their animal "doubles." Ruiz de Alarcón devoted an entire chapter to *nahuallis* in his "Treatise" and summarized stories that he heard from other colonists. Not insignificantly, the first story was told to him by a Dominican friar named Andrés Ximénez. The Dominican told Ruiz de Alarcón that one evening, around dusk, two of his fellow friars were in a cell in their monastery when a bat "much larger than the ordinary ones, entered by a window." The men chased away the bat, "throwing their hats and other things at it until it got away from them and left." The following day "an old Indian woman came to the gate of the convent" and asked one of the priests "why he had mistreated her so, for he had almost killed her." And then when the priest "asked her if she was crazy" she responded by "asking if it was true, that the night before, he and another religious had mistreated and knocked around a bat that had entered the cell by a window?" Ximénez then told Gage that the woman told him, "Well that bat was I and I have been left very tired."[87] The priests tried to detain her but she slipped away before they could do so. Ruiz de Alarcón then recounted various incidents reported to him by others "worthy of credence"—that is, colonists—in which a Spaniard inflicted bodily harm or death to an animal (e.g., a bat, fox, or caiman), and then it appeared that an Indigenous man or woman was injured in the same manner, exhibiting "the same blows and wounds" as their animal double.[88]

It is no accident that these stories follow the same template as an account within a European demonological treatise, *Tractatus de strigibus et lamiis* (1523) by Bartolomeo Spina, a Venetian Dominican. The friar described how a man suspected that a witch, taking the form of a black cat, had enchanted his son and made him sick. The evidence supporting this suspicion was the feline's great desire for affection and propensity for "behaving in a playful fashion." Seeking to rid his family of the cat, the father stabbed her with a spear, delivering "a very heavy blow." When the elderly woman was found "confined to her bed for a good long time, since every bone in her body had been broken," this was deemed proof that she and the cat were indeed one and the same. Martín del Río included this episode in his influential treatise on magic and witchcraft, as an illustration of his broader view that an uncommonly tame and affectionate animal, or an uncommonly intelligent or personable animal might reflect a diabolical presence.[89] This view is also discernable in the beliefs about cats as witches' familiars and the idea that devils entered monkeys or dogs and use them "as their own instrument through whose tongue they speak and say what they want."[90] Río's influential work likely helped shape the way Ruiz de Alarcón, Gage, and Burgoa described *nahuals*. However, I am not suggesting that Ruiz de Alarcón's discussion only reveals a European demonological narrative of animal doubles projected onto Indigenous subjects mistreated or killed by Europeans. He also links these episodes to practices that were, in fact, deeply rooted in Mesoamerican tradition. Ruiz de Alarcón explained, for example, that "when a child is born, the Devil, by the express or tacit pact that its parents have with him, dedicates or subjects [the child] to the animal which the child is to have as a *nahual* . . . and by virtue of this pact the child remains subject to all the dangers and travails that the animal may suffer until its death."[91] In other words, he described Indigenous calendrical and animal attunement practices through a demonological lens. Alarcón here merged the long-standing Indigenous practice of teaching people to cultivate attunement with non-human animals with the European tradition of seeing close relationships with animals as evidence of sorcery. His account also reflects *nahualli* practices that were described in sixteenth-century sources, namely that the *nahualli* possesses mastery in the use of skins. Ruiz de Alarcón appears to be the first outsider to connect cloaking to the power of the *nahualli*, explaining that it came from the word meaning "to hide oneself" or "to wrap oneself in a cloak." Alarcón then defined the *nahualli* as "a person wrapped up or disguised the appearance of such or such an animal."[92]

In sum, the colonial *nahual* was a composite cocreated by colonists, Indigenous people, and their progeny in the entangled world of early colonial New Spain. From Europe came the notions of witches who could turn into animals and suspicions about animals who displayed too much intelligence and people who cultivated relationships with these animals outside of vassal or servant relationships. From Mesoamerica came attunement and calendar practices related to familiarization, and cloaking practices related to predation. These practices were related to but not synonymous with the precolonial *nahualli*. As the subtext of violence against Indigenous people pervading the stories collected by Ruiz de Alarcón reflects, settler-colonists played an important role in the emergence of the colonial *nahualli*. However, it is also evident that Indigenous people also participated in its making. The entanglement of the shape-shifting and animal-loving *bruja* and the predator-skin-cloaking and animal-taming *nahualli* reveal both the ontological divide generated by divergent European and Indigenous modes of interaction, and the narrowing of that gap in the early modern period.

The first missionaries did not have the intellectual resources to fully comprehend the Mesoamerican ontology—produced by predation and familiarization—in which transmutation was perceived as a constant rather than an aberration and the line between humans and other beings was not only more porous than in Europe but celebrated for being so. In some ways, the colonial *nahual* differed from the concepts generated by Indigenous modes of interaction. In Amazonia and Mesoamerica alike, people transformed themselves constantly, and, in the words of Lisa Sousa, recognized the "instability of the body."[93] They became like the animals they hunted, taking on their properties when wearing their skins. They nourished themselves with the animals' flesh and blood; and in turn, they became sources of skin, hair, bone, flesh, and blood to nourish others. The notion of a special kind of person in which all of these transformative powers reside is quite contrary to the concept that constant and ubiquitous transmutation was the natural order of things. In the prologue to his *Historia de los indios de la Nueva España* (History of the Indians of New Spain), Motolinia declared that "reason" makes "men capable and deserving of glory and distinguishes and sets him apart from brute animals."[94] It is no accident that this insistence on a rigid demarcation between humans and other animals appeared in a work clearly demonstrating that Indigenous peoples of Mesoamerica did not share the European perception of such boundaries. Motolinia found himself in a world where the species divide, from his perspective, was always being breached and trespassed.

9

Adopting Domesticates

*a*n Indigenous man had been living in a wild, largely de-populated area of Hispaniola for twelve years. Fluent in Spanish and familiar with Spanish ways, he fled the brutal oppression of enslavement or *encomienda*. The man survived in the wilderness through a special relationship with three feral pigs, two males and a female. They went hunting for "wild" pigs in the manner that Europeans hunted prey with dogs (one tracking, one seizing, one assisting), with the Indigenous man spearing the prey. Once the pig was killed, the man presided over the ritual distribution of its carcass, as was the custom in European hunting with dogs, "giving the interior parts to his companions," while he made a barbeque for himself and salted the flesh for several days' consumption. When prey was not readily available, the man foraged for roots and plants, again sharing the proceeds with his porcine company. In the nighttime, "the said Indian went to bed among that bestial company, petting for hours one and then the other, devoted to the swine (*la porcesa*)." One day in 1543, Spanish soldiers, searching for runaway slaves after a recent uprising, came across the man's pigs. Taking them for the wild ones who roamed the countryside, they thought nothing of slaughtering them. Then they encountered the pigs' human companion. Bereft, he told the soldiers, "These pigs have given me life and have maintained me as I have maintained them; they were my friends and good company; one I gave this name, and the other was called so-and-so, and the female pig was called so-and-so." The killing of "these three animals brought much pain and suffering to the Indian," making the soldiers feel "very bad for having slaughtered the companionable pigs."[1]

Gonzalo Fernández de Oviedo heard this tale from the soldiers involved. He marveled at "this great novelty" of "pigs being hunted . . . converted into being hunters." He further observed that "teaching those beasts in hunting, bringing a trainable friendship to that occupation," and convincing them "to kill others they came across, because their master did not have love for these others," demonstrated that the man was "a rational animal and human." However, Oviedo scorned the Indigenous man's decision to "fle[e] men and be content living with beasts and being bestial." Clearly, the conquistador was undecided: Was the man's relationship with the three pigs evidence of Indigenous people's human superiority over animals or of their bestial nature? For the Spanish conquistador, the human-animal and hunting-livestock binaries were organizing principles. Thus, he found any failure to recognize these boundaries or attempts to cross them troubling. The opposite held true for the Indigenous man accustomed to familiarization: the transformation of wild into tame was a desirable and necessary pursuit. For him, the fundamental boundary was that between wild and tame beings.

This episode reveals the chasm between European livestock husbandry and South American familiarization, but it also demonstrates how Indigenous people, when free to do so, incorporated colonizers' animals into their own modes of interaction. It also shows that aspects of European hunting practices—especially the use of vassal animals—could easily be incorporated into predation. While European-style hunting made sense within the framework of Indigenous modes of interaction, livestock husbandry did not. The process by which Indigenous communities adopted livestock husbandry was separate from, although related to, the process by which they incorporated European animals. The central features of European livestock husbandry—above all, the denial of subjectivity to livestock and the practices of killing animals who were fed—were fundamentally at odds with Indigenous predation and familiarization. The eventual Indigenous adoption of herd animals in their roles as laborers, consumers, and small-scale ranchers had profound transformative effects on Indigenous cultures. These cultures' enmeshment into institutions of European livestock husbandry was one of the most powerful drivers of cultural change in colonial America.

~

HORSES WERE OFTEN the first nonhuman, European-originating animals that Indigenous people experiencing the initial European-led assaults had ever seen. This is unsurprising given that animal's paramount and ubiquitous role in the military campaigns that preceded and accompanied colonization. (Indeed, like European-originating microbes, archaeological evidence shows that some Native peoples encountered horses before they encountered European humans.)[2] The unusually candid conquistador Galeotto Cei provides a few glimpses of early colonial period Indigenous reactions to horses in his account of participating in 1540s and 1550s campaigns of dispossession in present-day Venezuela. One such incident occurred in a place "not frequented by Christians" in New Granada. One day, an unaccompanied horse wandered into a settlement. Wanting to stay in good stead with the Europeans, the Indigenous people did their best to host the horse. Yet, as they didn't want the horse eating their crops, they built a house of wood and straw in which he could sleep and brought him "bread, cooked vegetables, and their drinks, pleading with him that he eat, thinking that he could maintain himself with as little [food] as one of themselves." When the horse refused the provisions and began to sicken from malnourishment, they sent one of the elders to the Spanish "to alert us of the situation, explaining that the horse had arrived on his own accord, not because they had robbed him." Cei and several others went to retrieve the horse and were surprised that the Indigenous people spoke to him "as if he were a rational animal."[3] In sharing this anecdote, Cei sought to show what he viewed as barbarian ignorance about horses, but his last comment revealed an even more profound divergence between European and Indigenous understandings of nonhuman animals. Europeans viewed horses as exemplary vassal animals, but Cei's Indigenous interlocutors attributed far greater subjectivity to the animals.

While noting that horses remained a novelty for some Indigenous people, the Italian conquistador also made it clear that many other Indigenous communities were already very familiar with them by the 1540s: "In many parts, such as near the coast around Santa Marta, they know well that horses are those who make war and they say it as such." Moreover, his offhand references to being accompanied by Indigenous men on horseback suggest that allied and even enslaved Native Americans had become equestrians. For example, Cei wrote of receiving permission from his commander to "hunt on horseback with an Indian of mine also on horseback." And in 1547, the same or another mounted "Indian of mine"—meaning an ally or a captive—saved the Italian's freedom, if not his life: that year, Cei was part of an expedition to conquer "certain Indians" who lived in a mountainous area twelve leagues from the conquistadores' settlement. During battle, an Indigenous combatant mortally wounded Cei's horse with an arrow, and "would have captured" him if not for the fact that "one of my Indians followed me on horseback," allowing Cei to leave the dying horse and mount the other one, thereby causing the hostile group to "flee precipitously."[4]

Indigenous South Americans' adoption of horses is best understood within the context of familiarization. Although the autonomous communities in the Orinoco region visited by Jesuit missionaries had not integrated horses into their lifeways to the extent that others had in South America, they were nonetheless familiar with horses and not infrequently tamed wild or stolen horses.[5] The Jesuit Felipe Gilij, who wrote extensively about the familiarizing practices of various groups living in the Orinoco region during the late eighteenth century, drew a connection between familiarization and Indigenous peoples' talent for taming and training horses. He concluded his musings about the "*rarissima* ability of the Indians to tame wild animals" by discussing their interactions with horses.[6] The missionary noted that horses in "free countries like the Orinoco" are "especially spirited and exceedingly impatient with the bit, like the *tigre* [jaguar]." However, Gilij continued, "if a horse of this type falls into the hands of an Indian, he immediately removes its fire." The Indigenous man would begin by mounting the horse, and despite the resistance of the equine "monster," the man—the "brave one, the patient one, the skillful Orinocon trainer"—would ride it on the savannah, staying on the horse despite his constant bucking and galloping. After then leaving the horse to "laze" for several days, the man returned "to take again the cord to lasso it and without bit or saddle with a miserable halter in hand, mounts anew and conducts [the horse] to new challenges." Gilij observed that they rode "Through the forest, to the hills to more dangerous places. And though there are no roads to ride, nothing distresses our Indian. . . . The man rides up and down, among harshest terrain and rocky summits, in such a way that the poor horse, so that it doesn't get worse, converts, as they say, into a sheep." The Jesuit emphasized that as with other familiarized animals, the horse was not confined in an enclosure and chose to stay within the relationship: the horse "walks calmly with his Indian and stops and waits when and where it pleases [the man]. His master gets drunk and he waits for him; he forgets the horse and returns alone home, and the horse, like a little dog, follows him and he puts himself in the stall without needing to think about it." Such accounts demonstrate that Indigenous Americans' facility in familiarizing wild animals well prepared them to become skillful trainers of horses.

Other groups in South America went even further: their systematic adoption of horses became one of the most central features of their cultures. The Guajiro of the Guajira Peninsula (Colombia and Venezuela) and Guaykurú-speaking peoples in the Gran Chaco and Matto Grosso (Paraguay, Brazil, and Argentina) became notable equestrians.[7] Although little is known about their initial experiments with horses, sources from later periods indicate that the creatures were assimilated in ways consistent with Indigenous modes of interaction. The Jesuits who lived in missions of the Gran Chaco in the mid-eighteenth century, for example, vividly portrayed the distinctive equestrian cultures that some of these Guaykurú communities had developed, often remarking that Indigenous equestrians' ability to tame, train, and ride horses surpassed that of Europeans.[8] By the time the Jesuits arrived in the area, a significant number of Guaykurú-speaking peoples had been equestrians for more than a century, either procuring horses from wild herds or trading with or raiding Spanish settlers.[9] Horses were also sometimes hunted. The Jesuit Florián Paucke (also known as Baucke) could not resist admiring the canopies and tables of tanned horse leather that Native Pampas dyed in multiple colors "that gave them a delightful aspect," whereas others were "all white, so stretched that they resembled a drum." Paucke found these products so beautiful that he experienced "more pleasure looking at" them "than the city of Constantinople."[10] He likewise valued and sought out the horse-leather reins and saddles found among the Mocoví.[11] However, "the stench of the horsemeat" that they ate caused him "horror and disgust."[12]

Other horses were tamed rather than killed. Paucke vividly evoked horses' integration into this mode of interaction, describing how a Mocoví family traveled on long expeditions: "The husband goes mounted in front with his lance in his hand with his lasso . . . and then follows the wife with smallest children, sometimes surrounded with two in front and two behind her, and follow her the children who can already ride on horseback." The woman was in charge of transporting the household goods in saddlebags, on top of which often sat tamed animals—baby wild felines, little parrots, and dogs and cats.[13] The Mocoví appear to have applied to feral horses the familiarization skills and technologies they had developed with all manner of wild animals. Much like Gilij, Paucke was awed by the taming skills of Indigenous men and women he witnessed while traveling with a group of Mocoví musicians of the San Xavier mission to their performance in Buenos Aires. On the return journey they rested at a Jesuit ranch where horses and mules were raised along with more than 12,000 cattle. Paucke and "his Indians" admired the horsemanship and cowboy skills of the Black men who operated the ranch. When rounding up horses, these men captured wild (feral) horses as well as the domestic ones. Because the *cimarrones* (feral horses) were "prejudicial to the tame ones when they mixed," the cowboys killed the former,

Figure 9.1   Florian Paucke, Cod. 420/1, Papier I, III, 236 Bl., 222 × 152. 160, Zwettl, 1770/1773–1780. Zisterzienserstift Zwettl, Stifsbibliothek.

excluding the "well formed foals," who they tamed and rode. Paucke wrote that "my musicians deplored the great loss of so many horses"—thereby revealing their discomfort with livestock husbandry that viewed culling as a normal process—"and pleaded with the Black [cowboys] to give them some of the young useful equines." Their request was granted, and they selected some, although "if they could have brought 100 horses they would have." The missionary waited a number of days while the Mocoví men captured wild horses, choosing twenty-four to bring back with them. Paucke described with great admiration their ability to tame them quickly: the men rode only the "surly horses" on the return trip, using the tame horses to teach the wild ones.[14]

Once assimilated and tamed into the community, the horses were ornamented in ways evocative of the development of personhood for people. For example, the archaeologist Peter Mitchell observes that during the eighteenth century, the Mbayá of the Gran Chaco treated "a newly broken colt" similarly to a "youth entering manhood: the colt's mane was shaved off, just as the latter's eyebrows, eyelashes and the front part of his hair was removed."[15] They also used red *achiote* dye to paint abstract designs on horses—subsequently adopting branding—just as they adorned captive humans brought into a community. These were all methods to endow a tamed being with personhood.[16] Origin stories documented by outsiders in the twentieth century attest to how thoroughly Wayúu and Guaykurú peoples had incorporated horses into cosmologies that insisted on the animals' personhood.[17]

Collaborations with familiarized horses during hunting expeditions both resembled and differed from Europeans' relationships with equine vassals. The Jesuit Sánchez Labrador concurred with Paucke that it was women's responsibility to ride horses in order to transport household goods, but he also recognized that women also participated in hunting and "could ride as well as the men." Labrador recalled women "sometimes capturing prey that had escaped their husbands" and noted that they "could ride at full gallop in terrain so bad that I did not expect them to return in any state other than dead or badly injured." As the missionary ate the prey caught by these women, they good-naturedly teased him for his inferior hunting and riding abilities, telling him that he didn't deserve to share in the food, and laughed while asking him what he had "learned at home."[18] Paucke's watercolor paintings show Mocoví men hunting jaguars on horseback, and his text describes the methods they used to prevent damage to the prized pelts they wore (fig. 9.1). The Mocoví used horses to hunt all manner of wild animals, which they cooked in ways that the Jesuit found delightful (and is the origin of the modern Argentine *parrilla* tradition), confessing that "after returning from the Indies I had more cravings for an Indian grilling than a piece of veal prepared in the best way."[19] Even if they were happy to eat "wild" horses and cows, they maintained an aversion to eating any animals that were fed. Paucke observed that "they don't eat sheep, pigs, or chickens: only what is wild."

~

IN MANY RESPECTS, Indigenous peoples of Central Mexico adopted horses through a process similar to that used in South America. Initial encounters elicited fascination and formed the perception that the Europeans' horses were their greatest military advantage. As a result, Indigenous groups combatting Europeans in the early sixteenth century made great efforts to kill the invaders' horses. The Spanish likewise wanted to maintain their equestrian advantage and at first attempted to prohibit Indigenous peoples from acquiring horses. Legislation in 1528 not only prohibited any "indio" from riding horses under saddle or carrying arms but also forbade them "tending horses or learning to ride them."

Despite such laws, horses were among the first European-originating species to be adopted by Native people in New Spain.[20] While apprehensive about how horses might enable Indigenous uprisings, colonial officials also made exemptions to their own laws forbidding Indigenous people to own horses because they relied on Native auxiliaries to wage expansionistic wars and defend regions that they already claimed. As early as the 1520s, Indigenous soldiers rode horses, and by the 1540s, licenses were routinely given to Indigenous soldiers assisting in Spanish-led *entradas* (campaigns) to quash uprisings. In the years 1550–1555, authorities granted a particularly large number of licenses because of the ongoing conflicts with Indigenous groups to the North that the Spanish labeled collectively as "Chichimeca."[21] Such exemptions worried many colonial elites. For example, the Franciscan Toribio de Benavente (Motolinia) warned Charles V that "if the Indians learn to deal with horses, many will become riders wanting to be equal for a time with the Spanish." Such fears prompted another edict forbidding Indigenous subjects from riding horses in 1568.[22] By the 1570s, according to Kathryn Renton's analysis of horse-riding licenses granted to Indigenous subjects, it became customary to grant exemptions to the Indigenous nobility, not because of military necessity but in order to acknowledge their high status. In that decade, Indigenous subjects in New Spain had become equestrians to the point that they were buying and selling horses among themselves, as is suggested by the *Relación geográfica* of Amatlan, which reported that members of the community "trade and train horses" to and for other Native communities.[23]

Explanations for Mesoamerican interest in horses have focused on their effectiveness as military technologies and status markers. In the words of Judith Zeitlin, "riding on horseback, like other forms of emulating the attire and material possessions of the conquerors, conferred a degree of added prestige."[24] However, as in South America, the particular way that Indigenous groups in New Spain adapted horses cannot be understood without also considering their traditional modes of interaction. For example, in his account of the wars of conquest in Central Mexico, the chronicler Francisco López de Gómara described several episodes in which Indigenous people responded to horses as if they were people. Also, an Indigenous man in

Tabasco, upon hearing horses neigh, asked Hernán Cortés what they were saying. When Cortés replied that the animals "were scolding him for not having punished" the Indigenous group for their resistance, the latter gave the horses "roses [i.e., flowers] and turkeys to eat and asked their forgiveness"— an episode recalling Cei's description of the Indigenous hospitality offered to a wayward horse in New Granada. In Texcoco, prior to allying with the Europeans, the Nahua ruler ritually killed Spanish horses alongside their soldiers in ways recalling the treatment of corpses of captive warriors in the *veintena* ceremonies: they flayed the horses, tanned their hides, and "with the hair and shoes still in place hung them up in the great temple" next to the clothes of the Spaniards. While one might be tempted to dismiss these details as efforts of the chronicler to portray "Indians" as alternatively gullible and grotesque, ample evidence of other types indicates that Indigenous inhabitants viewed horses as subjects who shared much in common with people. For example, pictorial conventions used by Indigenous artists indicate this equivalence with regard to horses. Colonial artists who illustrated manuscripts frequently gave equines speech scrolls such as those used for people and indicated the movement of horses with horseshoe prints in the same way they indicated that of humans with footprints.[25]

More precisely, as in South America, horses were viewed as good candidates for familiarization.

Linguistic evidence for this idea is the appearance of the word *mazatlatlacahuiloa* in the 1571 Nahuatl-Spanish dictionary.[26] Translated by Molina as "to tame colts" (*domar potros*), the term comprises the words *mazatl* (deer being a word Nahuas used to translate horse) and *tlacahuiloa* (to praise or to enchant). The neologism suggests familiarization since it contains the idea that a wild animal is best tamed by praise and seduction (and not forceful domination). Another source that illuminates how Nahuas may have regarded horses in terms of familiarization is the "Lienzo de Tlaxcala." Although it was painted over a decade after the first men in Tlaxcala had been given permission to ride horses, it nonetheless illuminates early Indigenous conceptions of horses.[27] Created by an Indigenous artist (or artists) in 1552, the work may have been intended to secure special privileges for Tlaxcalans by depicting their contributions to the downfall of the Mexica. Drawing from both Indigenous and European pictorial traditions, the artist painted scenes on panels arranged in a grid pattern to depict Indigenous and European allies' conquest of the Mexica, particularly highlighting the role of Tlaxcalans.[28] Although the *Lienzo* depicted events that took place several decades earlier—and before Indigenous peoples had begun to use horses—the animals' appearance in almost every scene conforms to the mid-sixteenth-century perception that horses were the Europeans' most important weapon. Horses appear as individuals—great pains were taken to include their brands and their particular regalia, and they were often given distinctive facial features. This presentation is similar to that of people whose individuality is depicted via patterns on their cloaks or their featherwork arrangements rather than facial details. Equine hoofprints, which indicate movement and travel, figure as prominently, if not more so, than do human footprints. Horses slain in battle are depicted similarly to their human counterparts. Perhaps most notable is the panel—one of the largest in the *Lienzo*—in which the Tlaxcalan ruler Xicotencatl I received Cortés and Doña Marina (fig. 9.2).

Demonstrating the support that the Tlaxcalans provided to the Spanish by their gifts of food (corn cobs, spit-roasted fowl, baskets of eggs, and a gaggle of turkeys), it is notable that there is nearly as much emphasis on the offerings made to horses as those made to the humans. A European commoner—not wearing the marks of nobility that identified the conquistadores, portrayed in hats and coats of arms—gives a horse both grass and corn feed. The caption (in gothic script) calls attention to the act of feeding: "Here they went out to meet the Lords, and they gave them all kinds of food." The Mestizo chronicler Diego Muñoz Camargo later evoked this scene (also described in López de Gómara's chronicle). Camargo noted that the Tlaxcalans "gave servings to the horses as if they were men, that of turkeys and things of meat and bread, but that the deception lasted a short time because then they understood that they were irrational animals that were sustained with grass and pasture, though for a long time they were of the belief that they were fierce animals who ate people." In *feeding* the horses, the Tlaxcalans were undertaking the most definitive activity of familiarization.

The influence of familiarization can also be seen among Zoque-Black communities on the Isthmus of Tehuantepec. The Dominican Friar Francisco de Burgoa described the region around Chimalalpa as a place of wide plains, rushing rivers full of succulent fish, and mountain lions that came at night to kill dogs and horses—a place "so remote so that the little church had only a straw roof." The friar explained that small hamlets (with 30–100 families) were "founded by mulattos and free blacks" who were "cowboys [who] once served as ranch hands" and had married into Indigenous Zoque families. Their descendants were now "free in everything" and "more inclined

Figure 9.2   Tlaxcalan dignitaries greeting Hernán Cortés, Malintzin, and their human and equine entourage with offerings of food, detail of Lienzo de Tlaxcala, ca. 1550, copied in Alfredo Chavero, *Antigüedades mexicanas: homenaje á Cristóbal Colón* (Mexico City, 1892), p. 28. Digital image courtesy of the Getty's Open Content Program.

to be *vaqueros* (cowboys) than farmers."[29] He noted that during the dry season, "rather than hunt birds in the monte" or fish in the dried-up rivers, the people ate "cow's meat . . . in excess." Burgoa found that the "style of *vaquear*," practiced by women as well as men, had "much to admire." The priest explained that the "cowboys and even the women saddle a mare and with *garrochas* (poles) in hand, [and] go to the countryside" at night. Hidden with their horses, they would wait for the *cimarron* (feral) cattle to come looking for pasture. Having identified a good candidate, they would run

Eonca̅ qnamicq3 mtlatoque
qmaca q̅yxq̇d̲ qualom.

behind a bull and then fell him, "putting him on the ground, tying up his feet," and leaving him there. The cowboy then "mounts his horse for which they have them very disciplined and goes to look for another bull and in that way passes all the night and the same is done by the others." At dawn, the men returned with a *cabestro* (the tame bell-ox). The docile bovine helped the cowboys guide the bulls "to very strong corrals that they make and there enclose them until they are hungry and thirsty, and so break them of their anger." Once the bulls became less fierce, the men took them out "to feed them a bit and return them to prison until they were subjugated and domesticated, and this exercise lasts 3 or 4 months." Burgoa enjoyed listening to the men recount their expeditions and noted the danger of the work, remarking that "cowboys are sometimes killed or hurt."

The Zoque-Black equestrian culture resembles those of autonomous Indigenous groups in South America and those of the "Chichimec" communities to the North—and later the Navajo, Apache, and Comanche groups—that also became equestrian. In their first decades resisting the efforts of Spaniards and their Indigenous allies to enslave them and conquer their territories, Chichimec groups tried to kill horses. But by 1550, some groups—particularly those with connections to Spanish communities, because some of their members had lived as captives among them for a period of time—adopted horses for themselves, stealing them from their enemies or capturing wild ones.[30] According to the priest who wrote the *Relaciones geográficas* for the towns of San Miguel (later San Miguel de Allende), San Felipe de los Chichimecas, and San Francisco Chamacuero (Guanajuato), "those who have taken our cows and mares live better because they kill many cows and even mares and mules for food. They steal livestock and carry them north where they guard them in corrals like ours and slaughter them when needed," adding that some "go about on horseback."[31] Their equestrian skills elicited both grudging admiration and fear from Spanish observers, as in the case of a concerned missionary who wrote in 1595 that "they are no longer content to attack the highways on foot, but they have taken to stealing horses and fast mares and learning to ride horseback, with the result that their warfare is very much more dangerous than formerly."[32]

~

THE HISTORICAL TRAJECTORY of Europeans' dogs among Indigenous groups was similar in many respects to that of horses. Despite—or rather because of—the deployment of militarized dogs as one of the most effective conquistador strategies, Indigenous people incorporated European dogs into their communities. Much remains mysterious and controversial about the status of dogs in the Caribbean and South America before European colonization. This is due, in part, to the difficulty of untangling colonial-era innovation from long-standing practice. It may be that in some parts of South America, particularly the Amazon basin, dogs were not endemic when Europeans arrived in the fifteenth and sixteenth centuries. Archaeologist Peter Stahl has concluded on the basis of faunal remains, colonial accounts, and analysis of canid behaviors that when Europeans arrived, Indigenous groups in Amazonia most likely did not have domesticated dogs, despite their presence in highland cultures and other parts of the Americas.[33] The canids that chroniclers such as Christopher Columbus and Oviedo described as "mute" dogs, Stahl argues, may well have been foxes or other wild canids who were tamed. Whether or not dogs were present when Europeans arrived in this region, it is clear that Indigenous groups in lowland South America assimilated not only European dogs but also many European canid practices. Cei observed, for instance, that dogs "brought from Spain" were in "great numbers among Christians and some among the Indians, who before had none similar to ours."[34] The missionary explorer Charles Waterton, who traveled in Guiana at the beginning of the nineteenth century, concluded similarly: The fact that the Warau, Arawak, Macusi, and Carib groups he encountered used the Spanish word *perro* for dog—just as they used Spanish "loan words" for other exogenous things, such as *sombrero* for hat and *bala* for gunshot— "argues strongly against the existence of dogs in Guiana before it was discovered by the Spaniards."[35]

The linguistic evidence in Raymond Breton's dictionaries instantiate the broader entanglement of European and American modes of interaction. The dictionaries' signifiers for dogs included French loan words and Carib or Arawak terms.[36] Breton included at least three words for dog; one was *anli*, an Indigenous term, but *choŭ-chou* was undoubtedly of French origin and, notably, a term of endearment. Dogs were also referred to as *caicouchi*, which derived from the Carib word for "jaguar." Breton himself explained that *caicouchi* was the word for "the big dogs of the Galibi," and annotated the entry with a phrase he translated as "this dog scares me." Perhaps Galibi had adopted larger mastiffs and used them in warfare.[37] In many other South American Indigenous languages, the term for dog was derived from the Indigenous signifier for jaguar, a vestige of early encounters with ferocious and lethal war dogs. Kalinago vocabulary also suggests that they drew from both Indigenous and European traditions when incorporating dogs.

Breton also provided fleeting glimpses of Kalinago interactions with their dogs that intimate the influence of European hunting practices. Dogs were used in agouti, iguana, and feral pig hunts (the pigs were traded to Europeans). Breton's canine-specific vocabulary included a phrase that means "my dog is good for the lizard [iguana] hunt."[38] Another entry translates one of the terms used to refer to dogs (*kachirógouti anli*) as "a dog that can track well, smell well."[39] The Kalinago expressions concerning dogs recorded by Breton also indicate complex relationships with companion species. Some phrases evoke the loving and intimate nature of these relationships. Breton translated the expression *couchou-couchou tiemtilanli* as "the dog caresses with his tail, he wags his tail."[40] He also recorded a phrase that means "to whistle, to call a dog," conveying the importance of interspecies communication.[41] Other phrases speak to the inevitable frustration of cohabitation, even with cherished kin: Breton included terms that he translated as "put that dog outside" or "that dog there makes me angry."[42] Like other *iegue,* dogs themselves were hunted. In the Carib-French dictionary, the word *chien-chien* (or dog-dog), wrote Breton, "is what they say when they hunt a dog." He also included a phrase that means "do not hunt that dog."[43] Other terminology, however, might refer to intentional breeding practices, as Breton recorded several words and phrases associated with dogs being in heat. Human-canine interactions among the Kalinago were informed by both Indigenous and settler traditions: the practice of catching wild dogs came from familiarization, while the intentional breeding of dogs belonged to European hunting and husbandry practices.

Human-canine relations in Dominica, discernable in Breton's dictionaries, bear a striking correspondence to those found in Indigenous communities both temporally and spatially distant.[44] For example, missionaries and other Europeans who visited Indigenous communities in the Orinoco and Amazon in the eighteenth and nineteenth centuries described similar practices. Seventeenth-century Kalinago vocabulary reveals how dogs had become fully integrated into their hunting practices, and likewise, European visitors indicated their importance to Indigenous communities in the Gran Chaco and Orinoco regions. The Mocoví's ability to raise and train hunting dogs impressed Paucke, who noted that some families included as many as fourteen dogs. Dogs specialized in hunting different game: small, black hairless dogs were used "only to hunt lizards and other little wild animals that burrow in the ground," which implies that Indigenous hairless dogs had been transformed into vassal animals. Paucke thought that others were descended from European dogs, such as English bulldogs and water dogs. He was most taken with the "big dogs who are not afraid to fight against jaguars, especially when a group of them trap [one]," mentioning that he acquired one of these dogs for himself. The dog's name was "Soldier," and he was "so well trained against jaguars" that all he needed to do "was exhale and present himself" to send the big cats away. José de Gumilla also wrote about the Indigenous inhabitants of the Orinoco region who hunted with dogs.[45] The Taruma inhabitants who Richard Schomburkg met at a settlement on the Cuyuwin River were "great dog-fanciers" and "considered very skillful in training them for the chase," leading him to procure one for himself.[46] He observed that their dogs "stand next to their children in their affections" and described how the dogs slept in special beds in people's homes.[47] South American groups, like the Kalinago of Dominica, apparently bred dogs in the European fashion and also tamed wild dogs in the Indigenous mode of familiarization. A sixteenth-century source discussed Indigenous groups in northern South America capturing wild dogs, but in nineteenth- and twentieth-century Guiana, certain groups became known for their breeding programs and traded puppies for other desirable goods.[48]

Europeans noted that Indigenous peoples' use of dogs in hunting were similar to (and derivative of) their own methods, but the kind of affection they showered on their canid companions struck the Europeans as unusual. Paucke wrote that the Mocoví "love their dogs enormously and would rather go hungry than have their dogs go wanting [for food]." He also recounted seeing a woman astride her horse nursing an infant at one breast and a puppy at the other.[49] In the same expedition, Mocoví musicians returning from Buenos Aires attempted to familiarize puppies of the wild dogs that terrorized the region north of the city. Though they ultimately failed to tame them, the Mocoví saw the dogs as akin to any other animal—eligible for taming through a process of love and nurturing.[50]

European and Indigenous canid practices also became entangled in New Spain.[51] The cultural patterns parallel those found by geneticists of an "admixture" of "immigrant" and "native population in early generations."[52] As discussed in Chapter 8, among certain groups in certain communities the ritual eating of dogs persisted well into the colonial period. However, Indigenous subjects adopted both Europeans' dogs and aspects of the colonizers' modes of interaction. The missionary Motolinia described how Nahuas had started to employ Spanish-descended dogs against the growing threat of jaguars and livestock. He observed, like many others, that jaguar and mountain lion attacks on people had become frequent, "a thing that did not happen before the Spaniards came." Some attributed this to depopulation because "when the land was thickly inhabited, the tigers did not dare to leave and come down from the high mountains." Others attributed it to "the permission of God" as a punishment for resisting conversion, although it is most likely that the Spaniards' livestock prompted the increasing numbers of attacks, as was true throughout the Americas.[53] Motolinia reported that in Amatlan, "the Indian lord . . . had two of those dogs from Spain, one of them was very good, with which he had killed 120 lions and tigers," adding that he had personally seen "many of the hides."[54] A number of the *Relaciones geográficas* mentioned that

Indigenous communities had started raising "dogs of Castile," usually along-side "those of the land." The respondent for Tepexpa noted that its primarily Nahua residents "raise a quantity of dogs of those that come from Spain and some of the land, although few [of the latter]."[55] In Tuxtla y Cotaxtla (Vera-cruz), inhabitants used "dogs of Castile to guard their *milpas*"; in Cuacu-auhtzintlan (Veracruz), they fed such dogs with human excrement.[56]

Early in the colonial period, some Indigenous elites adopted the colonists' view that dogs should be exempt from human consumption, while also adopting the European practice of using dogs for hunting and guarding. Dogs are absent from the 1545 Tlaxcalan price lists of foods, although the 1568 *cabildo* (town council) records include a mention of commoners who raise dogs.[57] Indigenous elites' assimilation of the European categorization of dogs is suggested by the *Relación* for Texcoco. Its author, Juan Bautista de Pomar (1535–1601), had strong links to both Indigenous and Spanish milieus; his mother was the daughter of the Nahua ruler of Texcoco, and his father was the son of a Spanish conquistador and an Indigenous noblewoman. Ad-dressing the issue of "domestic animals," Pomar argued that preconquest In-digenous peoples in the area "had no kind of animal for their service nor to eat, except for a kind of dogs of the size of bird dogs (*perdigueros*) that were fattened for the commoners to eat."[58] Wanting to distance himself from practices that seemed barbaric to the Spanish—and, increasingly, to mem-bers of the Indigenous elite—Pomar helped invent a tradition of commoners in Nahua societies eating dogs, while the ruling classes did not.[59]

The manner in which Indigenous groups incorporated European dogs and European dog practices set in relief the common ground of European hunting and Indigenous modes of interaction, as well as these practices' areas of divergence. European hunting, like predation and familiarization, was or-ganized around mutual recognition of subjectivity. However, it differed in that European vassal animals were most prized for their martial qualities, whereas *iegue* were valued above all for their affective qualities. European hunting and Indigenous predation also altered the relationship of humans to prey. Horses, falcons, and dogs, when introduced as third parties, attenuated the relationship between hunter and hunted.

~

INDIGENOUS INHABITANTS OF the Caribbean and South America could under-stand European hunting through the lens of predation and familiarization, but that was not an option with the other European mode of interaction: livestock husbandry. The essence of livestock husbandry—one eats the animals that one feeds—was anathema to those shaped by familiarization. The unnamed Indigenous man and the three pigs who worked together and cherished each other demonstrated that it was entirely possible to assimilate those animals that Europeans considered livestock into Indigenous modes of interaction. His case is at once both extraordinary and exemplary. It is extraordinary because there are, to my knowledge, no other references to companionate pigs being trained to hunt other swine; it is exemplary because Indigenous people throughout the Caribbean and South America routinely incorporated animals that Europeans classified as livestock into their lives as *iegue*. Breton glossed the term *iegue*, noting that the Kalinago "do not feed any animal except out of necessity or diversion." He explained, "If they have roosters, it's so they can sound the alarm, if they have birds, it's to pluck feathers to decorate themselves; they have other [feathers] to prepare them for hunting and fishing; if they have dogs it's to hunt pigs and agoutis, if they have chickens, they would die before eating them, not even an egg, though maybe they are less disgusted by this now."[60] The missionary left behind a tantalizing trace of Indigenous reactions to European domesticated animals and modes of interaction. In doing so, he articulated a central paradox. On the one hand, the Kalinago eagerly embraced chickens but on their own terms. They treated them like other *iegue*—they appreciated them as ideal candidates for familiarization, given their lovely feathers, companionability, and labor contributions (wake-up calls). On the other hand, although enthusiastic about chickens, Breton's Kalinago hosts rejected livestock husbandry as a mode of interaction; they were repulsed by its central tenet of eating what one feeds and so "would die before eating them" or even their eggs.

The example of the Kalinago was far from unique. Across time and space, South Americans reacted with amazing consistency to the poultry introduced by Europeans; chickens, it turned out, were perfect *iegue* candidates. A century before Breton lived among the Kalinago, Caquetio villages had already incorporated European poultry.[61] Several decades later, Jean de Léry offered a thicker description of Tupinamba interactions with their chickens. He noted, like Breton, their revulsion at the idea of eating chickens and even eggs:

> The Portuguese have introduced among them a breed of ordinary little hens that they did not have before, which they call *arignanmiri*. Although they set great store by the white ones for their feathers, which they dye red

and use to adorn their bodies, they seldom eat any of either breed. They even believe that eggs, which they call *arignanropia* are poisonous. When they saw us eating them instead of having the patience to let them hatch, they were astonished, and would say "You are too gluttonous; when you eat an egg, you are eating a hen." They keep no more reckoning of their hens than of wild birds, letting them lay wherever they please; the hens most often bring their chicks from the woods and thickets where they have brooded them, so the savage women do not take the trouble that we do over here, raising turkey chicks on egg-yolks.[62]

These Tupinamba put chickens in the same category as other desirable "wild" bird species. Women nurtured them, their feathers became incorporated into ritual adornments, and eggs were categorized as embryonic chickens.

Unlike Europeans, Indigenous South Americans eschewed controlling the birds' reproduction. Léry's comment that the women "keep no more reckoning of their hens than of wild birds" suggests that Tupinambas' treatment of "domesticated" animals was similar to their existing interactions with "wild" animals chosen for taming. Antoine Biet, the French missionary who lived in the Orinoco *llanos,* likewise observed that the "savages of these counties don't raise or feed any domestic animals whether they are four-legged animals or birds, unless they are chickens and of these still only a few. . . . They don't take the trouble to make [chickens] lay eggs, but they [the hens] hatch their eggs in some hole in the woods, they incubate them there and bring back their little ones to the house."[63] What Léry and Biet both ascribed to laziness—the women's lack of involvement in the chickens' reproductive lives—is more likely a product of their already developed habits and proclivities with "undomesticated" animals. As we have seen, these habits and proclivities put a premium on allowing *iegue* a degree of liberty at odds with European livestock practices.

Breton understood that, for his Kalinago hosts, eating an adopted animal was anathema, akin to devouring an adopted child. Such was also the understanding of Juan de Ulloa, the Spanish naturalist and explorer who visited South America in the first half of the eighteenth century. Referring to his time in the western Amazon in the region around Quito, he wrote:

> Though the Indian women breed fowl and other domestic animals in their cottage, they never eat them: and even conceive such a fondness for them, that they will not even sell them, much less kill them with their own hands; so that if a stranger, who is obliged to pass the night in one of their

cottages, offers ever so much money for a fowl, they refuse to part with it, and he finds himself under the necessity of killing the fowl himself: At this his landlady shrieks, dissolves into tears, and wrings her hands, as if it had been an only son, till seeing the mischief past mending, she wipes her eyes, and quietly takes what the traveler offers her.[64]

This passage echoes Breton's comment that the Kalinago "would die before eating" domesticated animals, including chickens and their eggs. Like the Taino man with his companion pigs and Breton's hosts, Ulloa's "landlady" treated "domestic" animals like another variety of adopted animals. If these customs were eroded by prolonged contact with Europeans and the disruptions caused by colonialism, as Breton suggested, they also exhibited remarkable longevity. Paucke observed that "although the Indians tend to eat a variety of wild game and fowl they don't eat any chickens," preferring to treat the latter as companions who had favored places to sleep in their huts.[65]

Although autonomous Indigenous groups in lowland South America maintained their aversion to European livestock husbandry even after embracing colonizers' animals, it is also the case that some groups did eventually begin to incorporate elements of animal husbandry. This transition is implied by Breton's aside that perhaps his Kalinago hosts "are less disgusted by" eating chickens and eggs "now." It might be tempting to see the integration of European domesticates as a bridge toward the *telos* of husbandry, but it is more likely the consequence of Indigenous communities' entanglement in colonial relationships with Europeans. It was paradoxically the case that many Indigenous communities engaged in trading relationships and military alliances with certain European settlers to maintain their autonomy. This was the case when the Kalinago made strategic alliances with the French to keep the Spanish at bay.[66] In the early seventeenth century, Antonio Vázquez de Espinosa observed in his "Compendium and Description of the Occidental Indies" a number of autonomous Indigenous groups, referring to them as "Indians at War," "barbarians," or "gentile," who provisioned Europeans with chickens in exchange for tools. He wrote, for instance, that even though at settlements around Cartagena "numerous hens and cocks are raised," they were insufficient to provision the "many people who are in the city," and so "ships go to the Uruaba Province which is of *Indios de Guerra* in order to trade for chickens" in exchange for "axes, machetes, knives and other things."[67]

~

IN COMPARISON TO the autonomous and semiautonomous communities of South America that resisted livestock husbandry, the Indigenous subjects of Central Mexico appear to have adapted this mode of interaction quickly and enthusiastically. Already by 1525, a Spanish official asserted that the Indigenous subjects of New Spain not only ate chickens but also "pigs and mutton and beef, and the other meats that they see the Christians eating."[68] As we have already seen, a midcentury survey of tribute given to *encomenderos* ("Suma de visitas de pueblos de la Nueva España"), among other sources, corroborate that Indigenous-owned chickens spread very quickly in the years after the Spanish arrived.[69]

Native ownership of European-introduced livestock—sheep in particular— became wide-spread by the second half of the sixteenth century. A bird's-eye view of Indigenous ownership is afforded by the licenses (*mercedes*) that individuals and communities (Indigenous and non-Indigenous alike) needed in order to own herds of animals according to colonial law. Although the records are notoriously incomplete, studies of the *mercedes* give a general picture of the advance of ranching among Indigenous communities. Using these and other sources, Chris Valesey, Elinor Melville, and María de los Angeles Romero Frizzi have shown that elite individuals and collectives in Bajío, the Valley of Oaxaca, Mixteca Alta, and Tlaxcala were first adopters in sheep raising, and that sheep in general was the most popular among the *ganado* species.[70] Indigenous acquisition of licenses spiked in the years 1560– 1561 and 1580–1581 across New Spain.[71] While the adoption of animal husbandry in New Spain was transformative for Indigenous communities, it is also important to keep in mind that Spanish colonists owned the vast preponderance of livestock and ranching land in New Spain. (Only in the Mixteca Alta did Indigenous ownership of herd animals rival that of Europeans.)[72] This bird's-eye view of the expansion of Indigenous livestock husbandry might suggest that it was a simple and straightforward process that grew naturally from Mesoamericans' existing traditions of raising domesticated animals and desire to emulate powerful colonizers. However, when considered on a granular level, the Indigenous adoption of livestock husbandry appears to be a more gradual, uneven, and variable process and resembles trajectories in South America, albeit on a much more compressed level.

Indigenous people in New Spain, as in South America, first sought to incorporate the animals that Europeans categorized as livestock into their own modes of interaction. We have seen already that chickens were sometimes understood to be homologous with quail (appropriate for offerings to deities associated with solar and geologic entities) and more often turkey (a quintessentially maize-eating animal).[73] Traces in the record suggest that other kinds of European livestock were approached in a similar fashion. Much like the Indigenous man on Hispaniola who adopted and trained three pigs, an act consistent with familiarization, so too did Nahuas initially accommodate pigs in ways that aligned with their traditional modes of interaction. Motolinia discussed how Christian converts made offerings of animals in Tlaxcala, speaking admiringly of the Nahuas' offerings of chickens during celebrations of Christmas in the 1530s.[74] He was more disconcerted by their treatment of pigs, noting, "That year they brought a lamb and two live, big pigs," and "everyone who offered a pig had it fastened to a pole in the way they carry other burdens, and, in this way, they entered the church." He continued, "To see them take the pigs in their arms and offer them . . . it seemed like the church was Noah's Ark." The friar recalled the laughter and shock of his fellow friars and other Spaniards at what was, for them, a very strange activity.[75] It made Motolinia and his compatriots uneasy that Tlaxcalans would treat pigs and sheep with such reverence and gentleness before they were killed. However, from the Mesoamericans' perspective, these pigs and sheep were understood as turkeys and dogs traditionally were: as full subjects who could be treated with great tenderness and who also became food and offerings.

Other sources left tantalizing traces of early Nahua responses to colonizers' livestock. The lords of Ocuituco, Cristóbal, and Catalina were persecuted for idolatry in August of 1539. Among their confiscated goods were "four feather headdresses of those that the Indians wear on their backs when they dance" and "sixteen heads of little goats and of pigs and other little things that the Indians bring when they perform *areitos* (the Spanish colonizers used the Taino word for ritual dances)."[76] In other words, the bones of domesticated animals were used in ceremonies, much as the bones of ritually killed animals were used in ceremonies and rites in the postclassic period. Another intriguing trace of the early adoption of pigs is found in a pictorial manuscript created in the mid-sixteenth century (perhaps a copy of an earlier one) in which an annotation notes that human and pig flesh taste similar.[77]

Other less evocative but nonetheless suggestive clues suggest that Nahuas initially categorized pigs similarly to turkeys and dogs. In Tlaxcala, the 1568 *cabildo* worried about the colonial policy of required resettlement known as *congregación*. They were concerned about commoners who "will leave behind their houses and all they take care of—their edible cactus fruit, their cochineal-bearing cactus, their American cherry trees, their maguey, and their fruits, sweet potatoes, sapotes, chayotes, and quinces, peaches . . . and then also the household fields which they clear and cultivate, and their dogs and turkeys that they raise—*some raise pigs*—and their maize, the grain bins."[78] The notion that pig raising was a natural extension of dog and turkey raising is also suggested by Muñoz Camargo's survey of Tlaxcalan political economy. He noted that "some of these peasants raise swine in pig sties, . . . side by side to this they raise poultry of the land (e.g., turkeys)."[79]

It is the case that Indigenous individuals and groups living in New Spain not only incorporated Old World domesticated animals within Indigenous modes of interaction but also became immersed into European livestock husbandry on multiple levels. They became shepherds and swineherds and drove pack mules. They toiled in slaughterhouses and textile mills. They ate pork, mutton, and beef. A few came to own herds of sheep and other livestock. The question of Indigenous "agency" is fraught when considering the reception of livestock husbandry. Across the hemisphere, European colonizers forced Indigenous Americans to participate in the practice. Whether enslaved or "entrusted" to an *encomienda*, thousands of Indigenous men, women, and children had no choice but to grow food for pigs, build corrals for horses and cows, and herd sheep. They had no choice but to eat the flesh of pigs, carry equipment made of the fat and skins of cows, and wear the wool of sheep.[80] Many were forcibly brought into livestock husbandry almost as soon as Spanish authorities consolidated control. They faced the onslaught of grazing animals who destroyed their agriculture. The absorption of Indigenous communities into livestock husbandry cannot be separated from the coercion that characterized colonial rule. For those Indigenous subjects living under Spanish rule in New Spain, it was not possible to fully opt out of the European mode of livestock husbandry.

The timeline of the Tlaxcalans' adoption of different elements of livestock husbandry reveals that the Indigenous acceptance of European-style husbandry cannot be divorced from the tribulations of colonial rule. As shown by Andrea Martínez Baracs and Carlos Sempat Assadourian, Tlaxcalans had both advantages and disadvantages in their struggle to maintain autonomy and protect their communities. On the one hand, they received special concessions as a reward for their military assistance in overthrowing the Mexica and their continuing collaboration in numerous other expeditions in the following decades.[81] They also benefited from the Crown's intermittent desire to rein in the *encomendero*-ranchers. As a result of all these factors, colonists were prohibited from establishing *estancias* near the city's limit. On the other hand, the Tlaxcalans' proximity to Puebla—a city founded in 1531 to support the creation of European-descended peasantry that instead became the locus of the powerful *encomendero*-turned-rancher class—meant that they had to struggle against the most powerful interest group in New Spain. As Charles Gibson explained, "On the one side were the king, the viceroy, and the disaffected Indians. On the other were the civilian cattle interests and the Audiencia."[82]

From the beginning of colonization, Spanish officials in Tlaxcala tried to engage Indigenous subjects in livestock husbandry. Cortés, who served as the Spanish official supervising early colonization, wrote to the king in 1524 that because all of the silver, gold, and jewels there "had been exhausted," the community would need to provide tribute in other ways. Part of his proposed plan was having "two or three guardians" to ensure they "plant maize for His Majesty as well as raise some livestock and construct a fort in this city [Tlaxcala]."[83] In addition to the tribute collected by Cortés for himself and the Crown, Franciscans also required poultry and assistance with livestock. Tlaxcala was free of the colonists' ranches that had already led to trampling and devouring cattle and sheep in the Valley of Mexico, but all the same, its residents' crops suffered damage from the herds being moved between Panuco, on the Gulf Coast, and the Central Plateau.[84] After Puebla was founded in 1533 and became a livestock center, roving herds caused problems.[85] Things got worse in 1538 when Charles V broke a promise, made only three years earlier, to "not make any grants [to Spaniards] within the said city or its boundaries," when he authorized an *estancia* to be established by Diego de Ordaz, the famous conquistador and a founder of the city of Puebla. Soon after, the viceroy Antonio de Mendoza granted to other Spaniards at least twelve *mercedes*—grants permitting livestock operations—for both cattle and sheep *estancias*.

Though there is no reason to doubt genuine interest among Tlaxcalans in adopting livestock husbandry, their enthusiasm also cannot be separated from disruptions caused by the arrival of Spaniards and their ranches, livestock, slaughterhouses, and diseases.[86] Indeed, the epidemic outbreak of 1544–1545, and the corresponding spike in deaths, likely interfered with crop cultivation and so perhaps made less labor intensive animal husbandry even more attractive. According to its minutes, the Tlaxcala *cabildo* began to take an active interest in sheep and wool in the late 1540s, although the enterprise initially seemed to be a failure. In 1547, council members were ready to abandon the herding enterprise and sell the sheep.[87] In August 1549, voicing concern about Tlaxcalans' lack of experience and expertise in sheep, the *cabildo* moved to approve a partnership with a Spanish expert who could instruct them on how to herd, manage breeding, and make cheese from sheep's milk and wool from their coats. They also received assistance from enslaved Indigenous and Black people who were forced to "watch sheep for the city." When reform laws led to the emancipation of Indigenous subjects from slavery in 1552 the former slaves continued to work as wage laborers.[88] Tlaxcala was not unique in seeking outside expertise for nascent sheep husbandry. In 1563 the community of Teposcolula (Mixteca Alta, Oaxaca) contracted with a Spaniard to oversee the ranching operation of almost nine thousand *ganado menor* to take charge of such work as castrating, shearing, and tanning and to instruct at least twelve Indigenous shepherds how to perform this work.[89]

The relationship with outsider shepherds was not always harmonious. In 1555, the *cabildo* expressed concern that the hired shepherd Juan López was not upholding the agreement to share proceeds from sheep husbandry. The council also worried about their community's vulnerability to shepherds who "take their children away from them; sometimes they snatch their daughters away, and they take their turkeys, mats, etc. from them."[90] Sheep became profitable for the Tlaxcala *cabildo* in the early 1550s, and in that decade, individual Indigenous nobles also became owners of their own *estancias* of *ganado menor* (mostly sheep and some goats).[91] But Muñoz Camargo reported in the late 1580s that Indigenous investment in sheep was still unstable, particularly in comparison with pig husbandry. He wrote that the *estancia* owned by the "community of Tlaxcala" was "at the present depopulated since the sheep [have] died and been lost."[92] He made clear that aside from pigs, livestock—sheep, goats, and mules—was much more the domain of Spaniards, and a few Mestizos like himself, than the Indigenous population of Tlaxcala.[93]

Colonial conditions also impacted Indigenous subjects who raised pigs for the market. Muñoz Camargo mentioned that "the Indians have as a business making candles of white wax and of pig tallow and to sell pig lard from the many that they kill."[94] Many Indigenous, as well as Spanish, residents of other towns in the greater Tlaxcala region also raised pigs, alongside turkeys and sometimes chickens, often selling them to Spaniards from Puebla or muleteers going on the road that connected Veracruz and Mexico

City. Muñoz Camargo noted that communities located near marshland (providing pigs with tasty vegetation and comforting mud) specialized in raising swine.[95] By the 1580s, Tlaxcalans were eating abundant amounts of pork, lighting homes with lard candles, and producing pig commodities for the market. The pig husbandry practiced by Tlaxcalans at that time appears to have been similar to that practiced by Europeans for centuries, if not millennia. Indigenous producers who engaged in pig husbandry were responding not only to market conditions but also to tribute requirements. Colonial officials who reported on tribute and commercial practices of Indigenous communities in 1548–1550 noted that the forty-person community of Calpan (Panuco) "gives no other tribute except to make a field and with the maize raise some pigs."[96]

Indigenous subjects in New Spain also became absorbed into livestock husbandry through their involvement with slaughterhouses as laborers and consumers. Even as settlers' livestock destroyed their crops, Indigenous subjects of New Spain, by all accounts, were developing a taste for the easy access to beef, mutton, and pork afforded by the exploding populations of livestock. Colonists were shocked by the ubiquity and low cost of meat. From the late 1530s through the 1550s, beef became astoundingly inexpensive due to the explosive proliferation of livestock. At the same time, maize prices had skyrocketed because of the extreme hardships that colonialism was causing Indigenous farmers.[97] Although Spanish ranchers were in control of the meat trade in New Spain, they hired so many Indigenous men to work in slaughterhouses and butchers, that the "*indio carnicero*" (Indian butcher) became a stock figure.[98] By 1547, the Tlaxcala *cabildo* records indicate that the provisioning of meat was systematized in the region.[99] In 1568, Tlaxcalans were affected by legislation that prohibited butchers from operating in Indigenous towns throughout New Spain. Partly due to the perception that Indigenous people were illegally slaughtering ranchers' cattle and sheep, colonial authorities forbade the selling of their meat in municipal slaughterhouses.[100] However, the viceroy Martín Enríquez issued an edict in 1570 exempting Tlaxcalans. It stated:

Natives of the city of Tlaxcala have made a petition that in [the city] they suffer because there are six convents of clerics and a quantity of Spanish who live and reside and many Indian nobles who have the necessity of eating and need to go to buy [meat] in the city of Los Angeles [Puebla] where they receive vexation and they have requested that because as is well known they have always served His Majesty in the conquest of this New Spain and were after loyal and legally good vassals mandate that the said city can have the said butcher or at least provide license that they can kill and sell a moderate quantity of *novillos* and mutton so that the city does not suffer from the said want.[101]

Emulation is often adduced as a reason that Indigenous individuals and communities began raising European livestock; for example, Charles Gibson wrote that "in native society caciques and *principales* adopted sheepherding in imitation of wealthy Spaniards."[102] Nevertheless, such an interpretation is inadequate in that it underestimates both the coercive and destructive colonial conditions that prompted such decisions *and* the agency of Indigenous subjects vis-à-vis traditional Mesoamerican practices and beliefs. The interval between the arrival of Spanish-owned livestock and the Indigenous adoption of sheep herds was a period of cataclysmic change. There were the co-constitutive and devastating effects and damage to the food supply wrought by colonists' livestock and epidemics that led to enormous numbers of fatalities, which in turn facilitated colonists' usurpation of land.[103] There was the involuntary inclusion of some commoners in husbandry labor, the expansion of poultry raising, and the routinization of livestock animal consumption. There was also the termination of public rituals designed to demonstrate the common cross-species condition of both being fed and being food.[104] Moreover, by the later sixteenth century, tribute payments were increasingly demanded in money rather than goods, which increased pressure on communities to raise marketable items, such as wool.[105] Indigenous communities and individuals exerted agency by choosing to become ranchers, but these were choices made in a drastically transformed world.

~

ALTHOUGH MODERN SCHOLARSHIP has generally not recognized the ways in which Indigenous people both transformed livestock husbandry and were themselves transformed by it, contemporaries did. Because the available sources don't lend themselves to revelations about how Indigenous people themselves reflected on these changes, it is all the more striking that consciousness of the transformative effects of livestock husbandry can be found at all. The Nahua healers interviewed by the Tlatelolco scholars were insistent that an everyday carnivorous diet was not all for the good. The healers admonished that when one was suffering from a "bloody flux," one would be advised to drink "a well toasted chili . . . mixed with cacao," but "not to eat the flesh of cattle, the flesh of swine baked [or] cooked in an olla," or even native meats if they were fried (a Spanish cooking technique).[106] The *Relaciones geográficas*, too show that people did not view the custom of eating flesh as an ordinary food as entirely salubrious and perhaps even implicated it in the high mortality rates of the sixteenth century. In Tamazola (Oaxaca), people traditionally ate "tortillas and vegetables and cactus and its leaf, and that now . . . they rather eat meat of mutton, cow, pig, and deer, and now they say they experienced more health than [they do] now because they worked more and didn't [have the] luxury [regalo] of now."[107]

These concerns about physical well-being were connected to broader social transformations. According to some responses to the *Relaciones geográficas*, these dietary changes destabilized the social order. The respondent in Teotitlan del Valle (Oaxaca) reported that in the pre-Hispanic era, commoners "didn't eat meat (*carne*) and if they killed some game they sold it to pay tribute, and after the Spanish came and they became Christians they now eat beef, mutton, and the game they kill."[108] The author in Teposcolula contrasted commoners' diets before and after the arrival of the Spanish colonizers: "Their ordinary food was tortillas and chilis and beans, and if they hunted some deer or rabbit or rat, they ate it, although for the most part, they gave it to the native lord for that they gave them some thing or indulged them in another thing of food or garment because only to the Lords was it permitted to eat poultry and quail and deer" and other game. In contrast, "at present" it was possible for them to consume "the meat of our livestock and that which they hunt."[109] In Ostuma (Guerrero), "commoner Indians could not eat meat or poultry nor drink wine [but] which now they do in great quantities."[110] The responses reflect a major transformation in the meaning of eating meat. In the postclassic period, carnivorousness was a defining act of nobility; in other words, by aligning themselves with flesh-eating *tecuani* (literally "those who eat people")—above all jaguars and raptors—carnivorous elites embodied their domination over mostly vegetarian commoners. In contrast, during the colonial period animal flesh became part of the diet for all classes of people, even for the enslaved, leading carnivorousness to lose much of its power as a signifier of elite status.

The conversion of Mesoamericans to the lifeways of European livestock husbandry was one of the most transformative effects of colonial rule. This is vividly illustrated by a nativist revolt organized around the twinned rejection of Christianity and livestock husbandry.[111] Juan Teton galvanized the frustration that many of his compatriots felt at the social and ecological incursions of Europeans and their livestock. Teton had spent most of his life in the Tepaneca region northwest of Mexico City. By 1558, the year that he was arrested by colonial authorities, this area had been hit by European epidemic diseases and the ravaging effects of proliferating sheep.[112] For Teton, the imposition of Christianity, colonial rule, and the proliferation of nonhuman interlopers were entangled and collectively responsible for the region's depopulation.

Teton told his followers that the Indigenous leaders who had accepted Christianity had themselves turned into animal herds: "Look at the people from Xallatlauhco, who converted first into Christianity, the sons of Don Alonso were transformed into his cape and his hat. As for those who led the people, they were all transformed, they all turned into ruminants. The town and its people is no more. They who remain are just [ambling about] in the valley and in the forests, everywhere there are only cows." Teton preached that the only way to keep this transformation from happening elsewhere was for Mesoamericans to renounce Christianity and the use of livestock, as both food and clothing. He was explicit that the mechanisms that led people to transform into bovine, porcine, and ovine animals, as well as chickens, were diet and sumptuary practice along with baptism and Christian beliefs:

> Those who were baptized and believed in the Christian God will be transformed. Those who eat the flesh of cows will be transformed into that. Those who eat the flesh of pork will be transformed into that. Those who eat the flesh of sheep will be transformed into that, [and] the same will happen to those who dress in shirts made of wool. Those who eat Castilian chickens will be transformed into that. All that which is the food of those who live around here [e.g., the Spanish], if eaten, will transform everyone, they will be destroyed, nobody will exist anymore, [for] the end of their lives and their reckoning is up.[113]

Teton's message was persuasive. He convinced some Indigenous rulers to undergo a ceremony whereby they washed their heads to reverse the effects of Christian baptism, renounced eating the flesh of European-originating livestock, and promised to protect their traditional turkey-raising practices. Others opposed Teton and denounced him to Catholic clergy, which resulted in his and his followers' arrests. Teton's fame among the Indigenous population was such that Bautista, a craftsman based in Mexico City, wrote about him and his arrest in a Nahuatl chronicle, despite the fact that Bautista was a Christian who disapproved of Teton's beliefs and activism.

Bautista's account is an invaluable if fragmentary indication of how some Indigenous peoples responded to European livestock and modes of interaction. Teton's response to the entangled phenomena of unthinkable numbers of human deaths and shocking numbers of bovine and ovine births implicated the behaviors of Indigenous people and the Spanish colonizers. He thought his compatriots' decisions to eat, wear, and raise exogenous livestock—in other words, to adopt a European mode of interaction—was a major part of the problem. Teton's injunction to his Indigenous compatriots to disavow the raising, eating, and wearing of chickens, sheep, cows, and pigs implies the widespread Indigenous adoption of these European livestock as food and clothing.

Teton believed that a new sun and a new age were imminent, and he preached that to avoid going the way of those who had become herd animals, they needed to store the staples of traditional Mesoamerican diet: maize, tomatoes, squash, pulque, mushrooms, and—the only animal on the list—turkey. His exhortation shows not only awareness of the enormous and devastating changes that had been wrought by colonial livestock but also of continuity. In the words of León García Garagarza, "the traditional eschatology— sacred stories of the cyclical creations of the world" were for Teton a way to understand "this catastrophe of human to animal transformation" as "the signal of the end of the Fifth Sun era."[114] Just as in previous eras, a causal relationship held between the diet of the people and the animals that they became—in the colonial period, the acceptance of a European diet led to Indigenous peoples becoming European animals. Likewise, the notion that those "who dress in shirts made of wool" will turn into sheep is suggestive of the power of animal skins. The midcentury, when Teton was active, was a liminal period in which livestock husbandry was becoming increasingly hegemonic but not so totalizing as to extinguish powerful connections to traditional Mesoamerican modes of interaction.

The process by which Indigenous peoples adopted livestock husbandry was similar to the way they became Christians: the early phases were marked as much by coercion as by choice while, over time, they "indigenized" the practices of livestock husbandry. Although assimilation of European animal husbandry was one of the largest drivers of cultural change, it was not totalizing. It, too, could be changed by the incorporation of Mesoamerican technologies and beliefs. The free and unfree men and women who labored together in colonists' ranching operations created a cowboy subculture that entangled Indigenous, European, and African diasporic traditions, as already seen with Burgoa's description of Zoque-Black cowboys.[115] The emergence of multi-cultural cowboy culture was such that Ruiz de Alarcón felt compelled to stray from his obsession with Nahua idolatry and worry about the practices of "a large number of mulattos, mestizos, Indians and base people who are always occupied" with the "many herds of cattle." He bemoaned:

> The Devil, who . . . does not miss a chance to introduce a heathen superstition [led] people such as these to believe that, by carrying a certain root, they will never fall from their mount, nor will they be wounded by bulls, though they expose themselves to great risk. And though the majority of those of this occupation of cattle herding are mestizos or mulattos, even so I do make mention here of this because Indians also take part, and thus I say that the Devil has made these cowhands believe that the said root— whose name I intentionally do not mention—has in itself such great virtue that it suffices to protect one from the great risks that are always suffered by those who have to make use indiscriminately of every kind of beast, and to enter among wild bulls and feel encouraged to wound them or anger them so that they attribute divine virtue to this root, and thus they venerate it like a holy thing, carrying it as if it were a relic, around the neck, in little pouches, decorated the best they can, that they call amulets.

"Fearful of being caught," these cowboys and herders took care to "hide it in the pads, in the little cushions, the protective saddles on which they usually ride."[116]

The archives of the Inquisition offer more examples of such practices.[117] There was an Indigenous man from Pátzcuaro (Michoacán) who advised a Black cowboy to consume the hallucinogen *ololiuqui* to discover the whereabouts of some of his cattle. There was the Spaniard who relied on Indigenous experts from his father's ranch to help find lost livestock, and a mestizo named Diego who helped with disappearing oxen, applying methods to relocate mares he learned from a Purépechan man. There was Francisco Ruiz de Castrejón, a Black man who had a book in alphabetized Purépechan that helped him handle horses and cows to the extent that he could do impressive rodeo tricks and thereby seduce lovers. There was a Mestizo cowboy named Juan Luis, who as a young boy had been tattooed by an Indigenous man named Clemente. The tattoos were of Jesus and a creature that was part-owl and part-man that he called Mantelillos. The cowboy solicited this "demon"—who sometimes took the form of a finely dressed man with horns mounted on a horse—when he needed help rounding up cattle or taming fillies (and, again, the related activity of seducing women). There was Antonio de Soto, a transman who escaped slavery, and became an accomplished *vaquero*, adept at bullfighting, taming horses, and murdering accomplices. De Soto learned from an Indigenous guide how to consume peyote in order to have visions and how to use herbs, flowers, and supplications to the "devil" to escape captors.[118] Reading these Inquisition records against the grain, one sees the imprint of familiarizing techniques passed from Indigenous to Black and Mestizo people whose livelihoods depended on getting equine and bovine animals to do their bidding. Even through these faint outlines, it becomes clear, once again, that livestock husbandry practices in the Americas were not identical to those in Europe. Deeply rooted Mesoamerican cultural traditions played an important role in *how* Indigenous peoples—and the Black and mixed-race peoples with whom they worked—became *vaqueros*.

~

IN SOUTH AMERICA and Mesoamerica, when they could, Indigenous men and women responded to European domesticated animals and European modes of interaction on their own terms. They incorporated the colonizers' animals into their existing modes of interaction, adopted elements of hunting, and, by and large, rejected livestock husbandry. Nevertheless, over time, livestock husbandry became unavoidable in regions like Tepaneca, where the Spanish had a strong presence. There, Juan Teton and the Indigenous men who contributed to the *Relaciones geográficas* understood something that has been lost on many scholars today: Indigenous adoption of European livestock husbandry—both voluntary and involuntary—was one of the most important vehicles of cultural change. The entrance of significant numbers of Indigenous individuals and communities into European-style livestock husbandry as shepherds, consumers, and ranchers had profound effects. Generally, the question of cultural change among Indigenous communities is construed as a question about religion, whereas the impact of European domesticated animals belongs to the realm of social and ecological change. What Teton—and the missionaries who persecuted him—fully apprehended is that European colonialism brought new modes of interaction that had profound cultural consequences, and that ecological and religious change were deeply and meaningfully enmeshed.

10

Becoming Pets

On October 12, 1492, when Christopher Columbus first made landfall in the Caribbean, he presented the inhabitants of a small island with "red caps, and strings of beads to wear upon the neck, and many other trifles of small value." According to Columbus, the islanders were "much delighted" by the gifts and became "wonderfully attached to us." In return, they offered the seafaring strangers "parrots, balls of cotton thread, javelins, and many other things." This initial encounter and the seemingly guileless, even naive, generosity of the islanders, along with their lack of metal weapons, contributed to Columbus's conviction that these and other Indigenous people he subsequently met in the Caribbean would make "good servants" and that "victory" in conquest was assured.[1]

The islanders likely understood the exchange differently. The actions of the behatted, hairy men suggested to the islanders that these visitors were tame or at least tamable. The visitors' willingness to give precious items—the necklaces with glass beads in particular—indicated that they were presenting themselves peacefully. So the islanders, attracted to the strangers' novel objects and, noting their weapons, hopeful of their potential as useful allies, proceeded with rituals of socialization that would have been legible to peoples throughout the Circum-Caribbean and lowland South America. An offering of a tamed animal (*iegue*) demonstrated that the hosts were adept at socializing strangers. Gifting parrots, like arranging marriages, expressed the desire to become embedded in networks of affiliation and affection.

This exchange, occurring on the very first day that Europeans visited the Americas, initiated a centuries-long entanglement of Indigenous and European modes of interaction. Columbus was primed to be interested in tame parrots due to the late medieval obsession with exotic animals, who were discussed in Renaissance editions of Pliny and collected in menageries of aristocratic courts. But the "pull" factor of medieval interest in wondrous exotica is only one part of the story. No less important was the "push" factor of Indigenous modes of interaction. Columbus—and the Europeans who followed him—were incorporated into ritual gift and trade exchange networks that long predated their arrival. Thereby, they were immersed in a world marked by familiarization. The emergence of the modern pet was, at least in part, a result of this entanglement of European and Indigenous modes of interaction.

~

THE CULTURAL MINDSET of Columbus and the conquistadores who followed him initially made them eager to acquire parrots and other exotic animals, creatures that Europeans located in the category of the "court animal." Court animals entertained medieval and early modern royalty and aristocrats and, no less significantly, displayed the power of their owners by demonstrating these rulers' influence in foreign lands and ability to procure items of the greatest rarity and costliness.[2] The category encompassed delicate lapdogs, parrots, and monkeys, as well as charismatic megafauna like the cheetahs, leopards, and rhinos who populated menageries. Some creatures originated from nearby, such as songbirds from the surrounding countryside who were kept in cages and the ferret who amused Alfonso X of Castile in the thirteenth century.[3] Others came from far-away courts, such as the splendid Ottoman menagerie in Istanbul, or from the Mamluk Sultan Qaytbay in Cairo who sent a giraffe to the Medici.[4] Medieval and Renaissance rulers also included within the category of the court animal certain kinds of people, such as those of very small stature ("dwarves"), those of very great height ("giants"), and those with unusual hair growth.[5] Court animals thus located at the intersection of vassal animals and collections of natural and artificial wonders. By definition, they were rare; only those with great wealth and extraordinary diplomatic connections could procure the animals from far-flung places.

The primary purpose of the court animal was to show the power of the prince or princess: as precious, rare, and marvelous animals, they gave luster to the humans who possessed them. Some rulers formed powerful emotional bonds to some of these animals. The correspondence of Isabella d'Este (1474–1539), Marchesa of Mantua in northern Italy, made extensive mention of her *animalinos*, one of whom, her beloved cat Martino, was given a funeral.[6] Such expressions of affection, however, were of secondary significance to the rulers' desire to exhibit their magnificence by filling their courts with rare creatures. In fact, Isabella explicitly stated her determination to have "the most beautiful and best" animals in her royal residence.[7] The relationship between ruler and court animal lacked the intimacy of that between a caretaker and an *iegue*, as the former was mediated by functionaries like the "keeper of the birds and little animals" and other menagerie attendants.[8] The idea of the court animal was articulated by Pliny and by the entries on parrots and monkeys in medieval encyclopedias. "India sends us this," Pliny wrote of the parrot, "which it calls by the name of 'sittaces'" (the derivation of the modern Linnaean order of Psittaciformes). Celebrated for their ability to imitate human voices, he noted that the parrot "will duly salute an emperor, and pronounce the words it has heard spoken." He explained that "when it is being taught to talk," the bird "is beaten with a rod of iron, for otherwise it is quite insensible to blows."[9] The offhand juxtaposition of admiration, violence, and winsomeness visible in the entries on parrots (and monkeys) exemplified the intersubjectivity of the ruler and the court animal. These animals' coercive treatment, designed to ensure their wondrous affect, was far removed from the nurturing care given by those engaged in the taming work of familiarizing *iegue*.

Parrots and monkeys were well represented among court animals.[10] Pope Pius II taught his parrot to orate Latin verses, and his predecessor Martin V's retinue included two men who attended "the parrot of His Holiness with its cage."[11] Parrots were acquired from India, although by the fifteenth century, Portuguese mariners trading in West Africa were bringing back parrots on a regular basis.[12] The relationship between humans and parrots in West Africa was no less complex than that in Greater Amazonia. Nevertheless, as Africans did not tame parrots in the manner of *iegue*: historian Nancy Jacobs "has found no direct accounts of individual parrots as intimate companions in any part of Africa before the mid-nineteenth century."[13] When Alvise Cadamosto visited the Guinean coast in the fifteenth century, he commented on how Africans traded and trained their horses, but viewed parrots primarily as pests. They "dislike them intensely," he wrote, "for they damage the millet and vegetables in their fields." Cadamosto "took many from their nests," and transported more than "one hundred and fifty" to Spain, "selling them for half a ducat each."[14]

As we have seen, in the Americas the initial impetus for the exchange of parrots came from Indigenous people in the Caribbean rather than the Europeans. After the initial gift on October 12, 1492, Columbus continued to eagerly accept parrots during this and the subsequent voyages he led over the next ten years. Soon, he began to demand them as well. While exploring Hispaniola in December of that year, Columbus induced some of the island's inhabitants to come to his ship, and when they "understood that the Admiral wanted to have some parrots . . . the Indian who went with the Christians told the natives . . . so they brought parrots to them and gave as many as they were asked for," reportedly numbering at least forty.[15] He also obtained parrots from Guadalupe, the Venezuelan littoral, and other places in the Caribbean.[16]

The demand for parrots emanated from the royal court itself. Beginning with Columbus, colonial officials and others seeking royal favor obliged the sovereigns' desire for exotic American animals. Alonso de Zuazo, a colonial official in Hispaniola, wrote in 1518 that he was sending the Emperor Charles V parrots, along with turkeys (who "have a voice like a dog barking who has been hit in the head"), hawks, and falcons.[17] In 1525 the conquistador and chronicler Gonzalo Fernández de Oviedo "presented to his Majesty thirty or more parrots representing ten or twelve different species," most of whom "could speak very well."[18] In the 1560s Philip II acquired a pauxi (currasow) from the Isla Margarita, who entertained visitors with his somersaults.[19]

While birds and monkeys were the most common imports, jaguars or other large cats were especially prized as court animals. Oviedo described a visit to see a "tiger"—or rather a jaguar—and his trainer on a farm near Toledo. The trainer was the Emperor Charles V's *leonero* (lionkeeper) and he had begged the emperor for an opportunity to train a jaguar after their captive lion died. When Oviedo visited, the trainer proudly demonstrated the jaguar's docility and tameness by letting him walk outside of his cage with nothing more than "a thin cord." Encouraged by his success with his first jaguar, the trainer hoped "to go to the Indies and bring five or six small ones" in order to train them as hunting vassals and give Charles V "an Emperor's hunt," hoping that such a feat would win him great rewards. Oviedo found the lionkeeper's grandiosity delusional and irritating, so was smugly pleased when he heard news that the jaguar almost killed his "teacher" and that before too long the jaguar died perhaps because the betrayed "teacher helped it die."[20] Philip II also expressed his personal interest in these animals. In 1580, for example, he inquired about the whereabouts of a jaguar that had been captured in Yucatan and sent to him in the care of a friar.[21] In important respects, the animals who populated royal menageries after 1492 played a role that was indistinguishable from that of animals who had come from the

Near East, India, and Africa in previous centuries. In her study of the animal collecting practices of sixteenth-century Portuguese royalty, Annemarie Jordan-Gschwend documents identical treatment of court animals, whether they came from Africa, India, or the Americas.[22]

The monarchs desired raptors suitable for falconry as well as exotic animals for display. Decrees attest to the royals' interest in obtaining raptors from the Americas.[23] Within a decade of Columbus's arrival, King Ferdinand established an office on Hispaniola called the "redero mayor" (chief net-catcher) whose occupant was responsible for provisioning the royal palace with raptors from that island. Notably, the *redero* commissioned others to do the bird-catching, quite likely Indigenous experts skilled in techniques of capturing wild animals alive. The royal edict of 1502, for instance, directed the chief net-catcher Álvaro Pérez de Meneses to find "other persons who bring [the birds of prey] before him so that he could choose the ones most suitable, paying for them what they are worth," and authorized him to pay for the hens necessary to feed them. In 1513, a similar office was established on the mainland in Castilla del Oro.[24] Some decrees specified the number of raptors to be sent to the palace annually: In 1512, for instance, the edict ordered Diego Colón to provision the royal palace with six peregrine falcons every year.[25]

~

WHEREAS THE INITIAL European demand for American birds and quadrupeds was fueled by the late medieval desire for court animals, the ready supply of these animals was inextricably connected to millennia-old Indigenous familiarization. As a result, from the moment Columbus accepted gifts of tame animals, the invaders became enmeshed in this Indigenous mode of interaction, thereby changing them and European culture more broadly. Initially, the foreigners rarely plucked birds, monkeys, or jaguars out of trees or dens themselves. In this vein, Peter Martyr (also known as Pietro Martire d'Anghiera) tellingly observed that "the Spaniards are indifferent bird-hunters and are neglectful in catching them."[26] Europeans instead acquired animals from Native Americans who deployed skills and traditions honed over centuries for the capture of live birds and other animals. For example, Oviedo revealed that he acquired a tame fox from colonists in Cartagena, who had previously acquired the fox from a group of Caribs in exchange for some fishhooks.[27]

The contribution of Indigenous labor and expertise went well beyond the capture of wild animals. Many, if not all, of the animals that Europeans stole, purchased, or received as gifts had been nurtured by people (most likely women) practiced in the art of familiarization. The nature of colonial sources somewhat obscures this labor and expertise, but casual asides often reveal the skill required for taming and sustaining wild animals. The Italian conquistador Galeotto Cei wrote of certain green parrots who had "come into the hands of Christians" and "who in a short amount of time spoke three languages and two Indian ones." These birds' language abilities displayed the labor of local people who were expert in the arts of familiarization.[28] Hernán Cortés was another European who revealed the influence of Indigenous familiarization. In a December 1528 letter, for example, he requested that his father deliver a jaguar to His Majesty that had been raised in Cortés's palace in Huexotzinco. Cortés noted that he put the feline on the ship, which was very secure, so that hopefully he "would escape [the fate] of the many that had died." He explained that the "tiger had been raised in my house from very little and turned into the most beautiful animal which has ever been seen," adding that the animal "is *very tame and moves freely about the house and eats at the table what he is given*." Cortés's use of the passive voice obscures the knowledge and labor of Indigenous Mesoamericans skilled in arts of animal capture and taming.[29]

Iegue transmitted the nurturing that they had received to their new human companions. This idea may seem far-fetched, but today some dog breeders are unwilling to put their puppies in new homes until twelve weeks to ensure that they have been properly socialized. One such breeder in Switzerland said, "I pour all the love I have into these pups, and then they in turn pour that love out onto all those whose lives they touch."[30] When people socialize dogs, the task is eased by twelve thousand or more years of human-canine coevolution.[31] When familiarizing wild animals, there is no such advantage, thus a comparably greater amount of labor is required. In asides, European settler colonists revealed that they had succumbed to the pleasures afforded by these companionate animals. Even the vicious conquistador Oviedo was affected by his experiences with familiarized *iegue*. He expressed appreciation for the tame foxes, remarking that they were "great jesters and mischievous," and for the *bivana* (kinkajou) he acquired in Paria (Venezuela), who liked to nestle in the folds of his clothing.[32] The missionary Matías Ruiz Blanco, who lived among the Cumangoto, fondly remembered a songbird "who [he] raised" and "followed after him, flying" when he went to visit the sick or undertook other duties.[33] The Jesuit Gilij marveled at the affectionate nature of deer he met during his time in a Tamanaco community and rhapsodized several times about the "little *danta*" (tapir) brought to him by some locals, who also taught him how to care for it. He also appreciated the *mico* (monkey) "who seem to even understand one's very thoughts."[34] Europeans who became enamored of tame animals were themselves also inadvertently being socialized into a mode of interaction previously unknown to them: familiarization.

Further insight into how Europeans learned to interact with and think about animals in new ways because of Indigenous familiarization is provided by Martin Dobrizhoffer, the Austrian Jesuit who lived in Guaraní and Abipón communities in the eighteenth century. The missionary fondly reminisced about his beloved parrot, Don Pedro, who "articulately pronounced many words, and even whole sentences in the Spanish, Guarani, and Guaicuruan languages and learned to sing a little Spanish song admirably," as well as "to imitate violent coughing, laughing, weeping, barking." Don Pedro accompanied the priest on foot and on horse, sitting on his shoulder, "always chatty, always playful," sometimes demanding that he stop the journey for a respite. The parrot could be possessive: when the Jesuit got tired of his weight and gave the bird to a porter to carry, Don Pedro "angrily bit the man's ear and flew back to me." The bird likewise became envious when Dobrizhoffer "caress[ed] a smaller parrot of another species." Yet when "softened by a little coaxing," Don Pedro allowed the other bird to sleep under his wing and "ever afterward" treated the little one "as a pupil or rather a son."[35]

It may seem unremarkable that this European man bonded so intensely with a parrot, given that they were quite common in Europe by Dobrizhoffer's time. However, the same cannot be said of his close relationship with a deer. While deer were common in European forests, they were not made into companions. One day, an Abipón man brought Dobrizhoffer "a little fawn, only a few days old," a buck likely orphaned during a hunting expedition. It may be that local people felt sorry for the cleric, as a solitary man, and felt that he needed the company of familiarized animals. The priest "nourished it . . . on cow's milk" and raised him in his private quarters. The fawn was free to roam as it got older, and so daily roamed into plains and pastured alongside the cows. At night, the deer "on its own accord" would return to the Jesuit's room, announcing his arrival by knocking at the door with his feet. The deer followed him, wrote the priest, "like a dog" whenever he went walking or riding. Dobrizhoffer affixed him with a collar and tinkling bell so as to deter any predatory dogs. He fed the deer a diet of meat, bread, roots, and grass, but he discovered that "paper was quite a treat to him and sweeter than honey to his taste." One day, the deer got angry at his human (a misunderstanding about his collar) and left for the local forests. Dobrizhoffer sought his forgiveness and won it by entreating him with sheets of paper. Their relationship came to an end when the deer was killed during play with a donkey that got out of hand. The missionary greatly grieved this loss.[36] Other missionaries and ethnographers in the nineteenth and twentieth centuries likewise observed the familiarization practices of their subjects and were also drawn into that mode of interaction.[37]

Europeans often failed to tame wild animals or even keep them alive—unless they had access to Indigenous expertise. In this vein, the conquistador Cei observed, "The tiny little monkeys called *micos* are beautiful," but "they die and are difficult to bring to Spain," despite Indigenous people's ability "to keep them in their homes."[38] The French missionary Jean-Baptiste Labat, who lived in the Caribbean (mostly in Martinique) between 1694 and 1706, detailed the sad results of his incompetence in such matters.[39] He purchased a parrot in Guadeloupe who, instead of talking, "would only screech and because he had an extremely loud voice, it broke my ears, and this obligated me to have him killed." Labat soon "repented" of this act after he learned that the deceased parrot had been "still young and that his cries are what we call *cancaner* in the language of the islands, that he would have learned to speak in short time, and would have surpassed the others." "As the bad deed was without remedy," he "cooked it in a stew; [finding] his flesh . . . very good, delicate and succulent."[40] When Labat purchased two more parrots (from Dominica), he decided to "pension" them with a local woman so they would learn to talk. Having "attended such a good school," the parrots returned able to speak "to perfection" despite their advanced age. They became so tame that they would fly at liberty in the woods but return at the sound of a whistle. The parrots lived four years in Labat's care until "the husband" was crushed by a window shutter; his death "having left him with a little bit of sadness (*un peu de chagrin*), I got rid of the female so as not to have [the sadness] a second time."[41] Labat's account reveals how, by the eighteenth century, the arts of familiarization belonged as much to Creole and Mestizo spaces as they did to Indigenous ones. Nevertheless, Indigenous expertise was acknowledged a century later: When Henry Walter Bates, the English naturalist who journeyed in the Amazon, could not get a green parrot who had fallen from a tree to become docile and affectionate, he was referred to "an old Indian woman . . . who was said to be a skillful bird-tamer." In two days, the woman returned his parrot "as tame as the familiar love-birds of our aviaries."[42]

European exposure to familiarization technologies impacted the development of natural history, as familiarization was essential for the production of knowledge about animals. Oviedo describes with the most detail those animals who were tamed. The animal receiving the most extensive entry in his 1526 natural history was a sloth—one of the animals Oviedo kept "in [his] home." He described the creature thusly:

> They are a little narrower than they are long. They are quadrupeds, and on each small foot they have four long claws webbed together like those of a bird, but neither the claws nor the feet will support the animal. The legs are so small and the body so heavy that the animal almost drags its belly along the ground. Its neck is tall and straight and equal like the handle of an engraver's tool, being the same size all along, and the head is no longer than the neck. At the end of the neck it has a face almost round, very much like that of an owl, and its hair makes sort of outline of its almost round face, although it is a little longer than it is wide. Its eyes are small and round; its nose like that of a monkey. Its mouth is very small and it moves its neck from one side to another like a stupid thing.[43]

Oviedo continued to describe the sloth's vocalizations in great detail: "throughout the night at regular intervals it can be heard singing six tones, one higher and louder than the next." Such detailed knowledge came not only from watching sloths in the wild but also because "sometimes the Christians take this animal and bring them home." In other words, they imitated Indigenous South Americans by adopting *iegue*.

~

THE ANIMALS WHO began their lives as *iegue* in Indigenous villages and ended them as creatures of the court were oftentimes also commodities. I have not seen many archival traces of the animals' commodified trajectories because parrots, monkeys, jaguars, and other American animals rarely appear in trade records.[44] This is likely because ship captains, sailors, and passengers were permitted to transport a limited volume of cargo (living or otherwise) without incurring various taxes.[45] However, descriptive sources attest to an early and robust trade in captive animals. One example is Oviedo's comment in 1526 that he would decline to describe parrots, "since so many species have been carried to Spain, it is hardly worthwhile to take time to describe them here." He likewise noted that because monkeys "are everyday brought to

Figure 10.1   Indigenous traders exchanging parrots and monkeys for metal tools and mirror, Vallard Atlas, c. 1547, HM 29, detail. fol. 12. Huntington Library, San Marino, California.

Spain, I won't occupy myself in saying more than a little bit about them."[46] Testimony produced by the lengthy, thousand-page lawsuit related to the late-1520s voyage of Sebastián Caboto (known in English as Cabot) along the coast of South America also featured references to the commonality of trading in parrots and monkeys. One of the fleet's earliest stops was in the Portuguese settlement of Pernambuco, where trade with Portuguese merchants yielded "parrots and monkeys and other things." On Santa Catalina Island, mariners traded directly with Indigenous people for "many things," including "chickens and turkeys and venison and parrots."[47] An image in the 1547 Vallard Atlas shows Norman (French) traders exchanging mirrors and cutlasses for green parrots and leashed monkeys, providing evidence that these animals were systematically procured from Indigenous groups in Brazil by the mid-sixteenth century (fig. 10.1).[48] In addition, Francisco Hernández recounted that the jaguar (which he assumed, like many in his era, were the same as tigers) was "an animal known by many because we see them every day in Spain, mostly brought from the West Indies."[49]

The Cabot litigation also reveals that the early trade in captive animals was inextricably tied to the trade in enslaved humans. Born to a Venetian sailing family, Cabot was known for his service to both the Spanish and English monarchies (including an expedition to the Northwest Passage in the Arctic). In 1526, he received command of a fleet with four ships and 250 men bound for the Asian Spice Islands by way of South America. Hearing rumors of great mineral wealth upon landing in Pernambuco (Brazil), he instead explored the interior via the Río de la Plata. He thereby led the first European expedition into the region of present-day Argentina—a decision that caused an attempted mutiny—and founded the settlement of Espiritu Santo at the confluence of the Paraná and Carcarañá Rivers in present-day Uruguay. The settlement was promptly ambushed by Indigenous people angered by Cabot's and others' violent behavior.

Most surviving records of this expedition concern charges made against Cabot—accusations that he marooned sailors whom he suspected to be mutineers, illegally enslaved Indigenous people, and committed other crimes. A lawsuit Cabot pursued against another member of the expedition, Juan Junco, the treasurer of a vessel in Cabot's armada, the "Santa María de Espinar," left a 129-page paper trail.[50] In early 1530, when docked in São Vicente, Cabot purchased a boy from a man named Juan de León, as well as three parrots. The boy, whose Spanish name was Andrés, was described as a thirteen-year-old "Indian" with "loro" (brown) coloring. Andrés was put in a locked room with two Indigenous girls Cabot had acquired more than a year earlier, Margarida and Juana. The parrots were entrusted to Junco, who kept them in a room with other parrots. At least two of these three parrots died on the journey. When the expedition returned to Seville, Cabot was imprisoned for disobeying orders. While Cabot was locked up, Junco overcame the objections of Cabot's page, and seized Andrés and a "very small parrot," taking them to the inn where he was staying.[51]

Issues surrounding property and ownership were of paramount concern in the lawsuit. A secondary concern was Junco's violent assault and rape of Margarida, the enslaved girl from Paraná. In a letter presented by his lawyer,

Cabot claimed, "Juan de Junco with little fear of God and of justice" took "my thing (*cosa mia*) an Indian . . . called Andrés that I bought, maintained and brought as mine" "and [Junco] used him and took him where he wanted," as well as stealing "a parrot that was and is mine." And, finally, he alleged that "Juan de Junco broke into the said room," described as a "locked room with my things and some Indian girls . . . and by force slept with one of the said girls who is called Margarida." A number of witnesses testified to this effect, including a fifty-year-old interpreter named Enrique Montes (who had learned Guarani from living in South America for fourteen years and marrying into an Indigenous family).[52] In his appeal, Cabot sought the restoration of Andrés and the parrot, although he would accept sixty ducats for the latter. He also asked that Junco receive a death sentence.[53]

Junco claimed that Cabot had no right to either the parrot or the boy as they belonged to him, declaring that he had "brought to this city [Seville] from the coast of Cananea an Indian slave and a parrot, which is mine." He called witnesses to attest to his good character based, above all, on his noble lineage. These compatriots declared he was a nobleman and "an honorable man of good life and reputation."[54] During the trial, Junco lost possession of both Andrés and the parrot. They were first placed in the custody of Junco's son-in-law and then put under the supervision of an official in the House of Trade. During the depositions in December, both the parrot and Andrés appeared before witnesses. Officials of the House of Trade rendered their decision on June 21, 1531: "We order that the slave Andrés, an Indian, and the parrot who are the objects of this lawsuit . . . be returned and restored to . . . Sebastian Caboto, pilot . . . and we absolve . . . Juan de Junco of the accusation . . . that he had corrupted Margarida, the slave of . . . Sebastián Caboto."

The lawsuit reveals much about the transformation of *iegue* into commodities. For one, it reveals that their import was ordinary and the birds' individuality unimportant to those involved in their trade: the witnesses could not remember anything particular about the birds. It also indicates their high value. Sixty ducats was a substantial sum—eighty to ninety ducats was the price of a slave at this time. And this parrot, at least in physical terms, was not extraordinary, neither as large nor as colorful as macaws. It is also telling that Cabot was willing to accept a monetary value for the parrot rather than the parrot himself. The lawsuit against Cabot also makes clear that, in many respects, the trades in people and in nonhuman animals were understood in similar terms. The same stock phrase was used to describe proof of ownership. In fact, every element of this ruling insisted on the children's and the birds' status as property.

As suggested by this case, Europeans' treatment of *iegue* was often extremely harsh. A royal edict from 1526 indicates the poor conditions that exotic animals endured on their trans-Atlantic voyages: "because it sometimes happens that the captains and masters of the boats [as well as] people and passengers who bring things from these parts do not put in the capital (*recaudo*) that is appropriate." Thus parrots and raptors are "lost and die for not being well tended and treated." Consequently, it was required of "whatever masters of ships or captains or people or passengers or whatever other persons are in them who come to our kingdoms" to provide "the necessary funds" for "whatever falcons, parrots from Tierra Firme and other migratory birds" are being transported.[55]

The fact that two of three parrots died on the ship under Cabot's command suggests that captive animals were more likely to die than to survive ocean crossings. Sometimes the culprits were their hungry human captors. On one perilous ocean crossing, Jean de Léry described a range of attitudes toward eating shipboard parrots and monkeys when hungry. There were those who, when faced with even a modest amount of hunger, ate their avian and simian charges. There were others "who still had monkeys and parrots . . . which they had kept so as to teach them to speak a language that they did not yet know," but as starvation increased, "now put them into the cabinet of their memory, and made them serve as food." And finally, there was Léry's own experience: he claimed that "in spite of this inexpressible suffering and famine . . . nevertheless up to that time kept one, as big as a goose, that uttered words freely like a man, and was of excellent plumage." But he too finally succumbed to hunger and consumed the bird, "discard[ing] nothing but the feathers, so that not only the body but also the tripes, feet, claws, and hooked beak served me and some of my friends to keep ourselves alive for three or four days." He very much "regretted" his decision and felt great "distress" when they "soon after saw land."[56] Léry's account reveals how the animal trade could be lethal to *iegue*. It also reveals the variety and flexibility of their captors' attitudes. Léry was somewhat scornful of those who were quick to kill and eat their captives and sorrowful about his own decision to do so when he thought he faced starvation, both attitudes indicating his appreciation for these tame animals as fellow subjects. However, it is also clear that he viewed them as commodities, highly valued for their "excellent plumage" and ability to speak.

Iegue also sometimes experienced gory deaths due to the actions of ship-board rats. A mariner's account of a 1623 trans-Atlantic crossing described the havoc wrought by these rodents. They depleted stocks of ham and bacon, muti-lated chickens in the henhouse, bit the cats, and "many times" "entered in the cages of parrots and fought with them," leaving "many of them [parrots] dead and eaten."[57] During one eighteenth-century crossing, five of seven parrots died, two succumbing to colds and another drowning after falling overboard.[58]

The sources rarely reveal much about the violence and other afflictions that these animals suffered by being sequestered in cages; surrounded by unaccustomed sounds, smells, movements; and deprived of the company of their familiars. However, the Enlightenment naturalist Alexander von Hum-boldt somewhat unwittingly evoked the sadness animals experienced by being wrenched away from familiar environs and beings. Reflecting on his time residing with local Jesuits in the Orinoco basin, von Humboldt wrote that it "is very difficult to convey" the spider monkeys (*titis*) "from the Mis-sions of the Orinoco to the coast of Caracas, or of Cumana," as they "be-come melancholy and dejected in proportion as they quit the region of the forests, and enter the Llanos."[59] He attributed "this change" to "a greater in-tensity of light, a less degree of humidity, and some chemical property of the air of the coast." Yet it seems more likely that the shock of dislocation caused these animals' melancholy and dejection.

European involvement in Indigenous animal exchange, parallel to that of human captive exchange, changed the former practice. Just as the integration of Indigenous and European forms of slavery led to the commodification of war captives, so too did Europeans' involvement in increasingly colonized trade networks lead to the increasing commodification of familiarized ani-mals. This commodification affected different groups and individuals at dif-ferent times, depending on the nature of their involvement with European and settler colonists. In the late twentieth century, ethnographers Ellen Basso and Catherine Howard detected a shift toward greater monetization among the Kalapalo and Waiwai communities that they visited, respectively. The tamed animals became less "metaphorical children" and more "detach-able commodities."[60]

~

SOME OF THE earliest evidence of the kinds of relationships occurring between *iegue* and European owners is found in portraits of European royalty, aristocracy, and wealthy commoners.[61] Although these images are clearly in keeping with traditions of depicting court animals, they also display traces of Indigenous America. Among the earliest portraits featuring an *iegue* is Jean Clouet's 1530 painting of a green parrot with their human companion, the French princess and future queen of Navarre, Marguerite of Angouleme (fig. 10.2). While the striking green parrot gazing at the viewer with a piercing eye is clearly intended to augment their human companion's grandeur by showing her ability to procure such a rare and exotic creature, there is more to the portrait. The image also displays the bond between parrot and woman. While Marguerite is clearly dominant, reciprocity is also apparent. The princess has fashioned her hand into a comfortable perch for the bird, and the expression on the parrot's face suggests calm confidence rather than submission.

American-born animals also frequently appear in Alonso Sánchez Coello's portraits featuring Princess Isabella Clara Eugenia. In 1569–1570 Sánchez Coello painted Isabella and her sister Catalina when they were young girls. The work displays a green parrot perched on Isabella's wrist, and a small lapdog sitting between the sisters.[62] As an adult, Isabella appeared in portraits with monkeys. In one three-quarter-length portrait, Isabella Clara Eugenia appears in an exquisite brocaded gown of white silk with a hand resting on the head of her kneeling, elderly servant.[63] The latter is holding two monkeys, one brown and one a cotton-top tamarin, who likely originated from Amazonian regions then under Spanish control.[64] The brown monkey appears partially held aloft by the thick structure of the princess's skirt. While the princess is clearly the painting's dominant primate, the monkeys seem at least the equals of her human servant. Furthermore, the tamarin's freedom to play on the princess's clothing suggests the pair's comfortable familiarity. A strikingly different painting shows the princess from the waist up in somber black garments, tenderly holding a marmoset (fig. 10.3). Her left hand cradles the animal, while she protectively caresses the monkey with her right hand. Such images, of course, trumpet the American provenance of these court animals. Yet they also depict their tameness and capacity for affectionate intimacy with humans, products of the emotional and physical labor of Indigenous people skilled in the art and technology of familiarization. The animals' ability to engage with human companions after surviving a traumatic trans-Atlantic voyage suggests the resilience imbued by the nurturing of Indigenous caregivers. Moreover, the *iegue* themselves became transmitters of Indigenous modes of interaction, sharing with European humans some of the care lavished on them by Native humans.

Figure 10.2 Jean Clouet, Princess Marguerite of Angouleme, ca. 1530, oil on panel, 61.2 × 52.6 cm, Walker Art Gallery, National Museums Liverpool. Photo © National Museums Liverpool/Bridgeman Images.

Figure 10.3   Alonso Sánchez Coello, Infanta Isabella Clara Eugenia, before **1588**. Rafael Valls Gallery, London, UK / Bridgeman Images.

~

SCHOLARS DISAGREE ABOUT what constitutes a "pet." Some opt to use the term broadly to describe a vast array of multispecies relationships. James Serpell defines pets as animals "kept for no obvious practical or utilitarian purpose," and Kathleen Walker-Meikle considers pets to be "animals kept by humans for companionship."[65] Other scholars, while recognizing that strong emotional bonds have characterized many types of human-animal relationships throughout history, think that the category of the "pet," like the word itself, signifies a more specific category of human-animal relationship.[66] Preferring this narrower usage, I define the modern pet as a nonhuman animal who belongs to a species that is not to be killed for food and whose *socially valorized* raison d'etre is to provide and receive affection in the manner of a family member. My definition excludes companionate human-animal relationships that were considered transgressive of social norms. It also excludes *iegue*, for this concept applies to human as well as nonhuman animals, while the term "pet," in modern parlance, encompasses only nonhumans, above all those belonging to domesticated species.

Using a more restricted definition of *pet* allows us to see important historical shifts that broader definitions otherwise obscure. A pet differs from a vassal animal, a servant animal, and a court animal, whose purposes are, respectively, to collaborate in hunting and warfare, to provide a service (often related to livestock husbandry), or to elicit wonder and convey power. The affectionate relationships that may emerge are secondary effects rather than the animal's purpose. Human-feline relationships that existed outside of cats' pest-control functions in medieval and early modern Europe illustrate the absence of pets in medieval Europe, for such relationships were not socially sanctioned. Although there were medieval people who valued cats for their companionship as much as, if not more than, for their ability to combat vermin, such relationships were often viewed with suspicion.[67] As described in Chapter 8, women who had affectionate relationships with cats were often seen as transgressive: a sixteenth-century treatise on witchcraft portrayed a woman's relationship with her very affectionate cat as a sign of sorcery, and considered the feline and the woman to be one and the same witch. The text's Dominican author wrote approvingly of the fatal beating inflicted on the woman by her suspicious neighbor.[68] And although it is the case that courtiers fawned over Isabella d'Este and the exotic cat she briefly owned, his very rarity and preciousness, like that of his owner, underpinned the celebration of their relationship.[69]

Some might think I am drawing too much of a distinction between pets and vassal animals, particularly the hunting dogs who elicited such praise and appeared in noble portraiture. Accordingly, it is useful to recall the casual remark of the seventeenth-century Spanish hunter who thought it reasonable to kill a hound who barked at inopportune times during hunts. Even more revealing are the reactions of Europeans to the way that Indigenous people valued the "love," "friendship," and "company" given by and to their dogs. José de Acosta, the Jesuit author of the 1590 *Historia natural y moral de las Indias* (Natural and Moral History of the Indies), wrote disparagingly of the way Indigenous people related to their dogs because "they use them for nothing, only good friendship and company." He further detailed, "The Indians are so fond of them that they will go hungry in order to feed them, and when they are walking along the roads they will carry them on their backs or in their bosoms." Furthermore, he found it odd that if a person fell ill, then "the dog must stay by them."[70] Another cleric who visited the Audiencia of Quito in the sixteenth century offered similar commentary when he wrote disdainfully of the dogs "who serve [Indigenous people] as companions." He continued: "They allow these to poke their snouts in the dishes, and they take their conversations and entertainment from the show that the dogs themselves provide, farting and otherwise acting like brute animals." Rather than being "offended or sick to their stomachs" from the dogs' behavior, as the cleric clearly thought they should be, the Native South Americans might scold them or temporarily shoo them away but "then at once go back to pampering them and treating them lovingly."[71]

So, if the pet is a concept distinct from servant, animal, and court animals, when and why did it arrive in Europe? Keith Thomas links the emergence of the modern pet to the advent of secular cosmology in England during the late seventeenth and eighteenth centuries. However, his examples often conflate pets with other animal categories.[72] Harriet Ritvo identifies the nineteenth century as the period in Britain when "petkeeping became respectable among ordinary citizens" and relates it in part to "increased public indulgence of the softer emotions" in the late eighteenth century.[73] Similarly Kathleen Kete sees the pet as an outgrowth of romanticism and bourgeois domesticity in nineteenth-century France, noting that Parisians championed them as essential to "domestic sentiment and warmth."[74] I do not dispute that these developments contributed to the emergence of the modern pet, but this history is incomplete if we fail to consider earlier shifts in human-animal relationships.

The modern pet emerged, in part, from relationships with vassal animals. Urbanization and shifting ideas of nobility celebrating courtliness rather than martial valor created space for the celebration of people's relationships with dogs outside the context of hunting. One such relationship was praised in a 1568 book entitled *Del can, y del cavallo, y de sus calidades* (Of the dog and of the horse and their qualities), and tellingly subtitled *Dos animales de gran instincto y sentido, fidelissimos amigos de los hombres* (Two animals of great instinct and sense, the most faithful friends of men).[75] The author, Luis Pérez, began the book by celebrating vassal animals with the familiar tropes of martial valor, invoking examples from the Greek, Roman, medieval, and contemporary periods. However, he also discussed a dog of a different sort who lived in Palencia a few decades earlier and whom he had personally met. Bruto was a medium-sized "greyhound with coarse brown hair" belonging to a clergyman named Castillo. Bruto was a perfect "servant" (*criado*) who "did everything that was commanded of him." The priest sometimes ordered the dog to summon the priest's mother, sister, or a member of the choir, and the dog correctly identified the person, "never mistaking or confusing one for the other." Bruto went to the butcher, carrying a basket containing money and returning with meat. When not on errands, the dog "never left his master's side" and could open and close all of the doors of the house. Bruto became a local celebrity, and Castillo was offered a huge sum (1,500 ducats) for his dog. Of course, the priest declined to sell his friend, although he was willing to allow his canine companion to enter service with Emperor Charles V. However, just before the emperor was due to meet him, Bruto died. Castillo was so bereft by the loss of his companion that he died soon after, reportedly of a broken heart. Bruto inhabited a space between the categories of vassal animal and modern pet. Like a vassal, he was celebrated for his intelligence, loyalty, and obedience. But unlike vassal dogs, Bruto did not hunt; rather, he served his master in an urban context and, more specifically, a familial context, connecting the priest to his mother and sister and to close colleagues. Although widely admired for his remarkable feats and abilities, Bruto, from Castillo's perspective, was extraordinary because of his capacity for friendship, as evidenced by Castillo's unwillingness to sell him and despair upon Bruto's passing.

The writings of the dog lover and famous humanist Justus Lipsius also indicate the nascent transformation of the vassal animal. A scholar who brought his dogs when lecturing at the University of Louvain, Lipsius cele-brated his three dogs (Mopsus, Mopsulus, and Saphyrus)—and their mutual love—in a number of Latin verses in the early seventeenth century.[76] He explicitly acknowledged that his dogs were not for hunting and posited that dogs were more suitable companions for scholars than for hunters or sol-diers.[77] In doing so, he, like Pérez and Castillo, celebrated noble dogs' transi-tion into new roles. After the death of Saphyrus (he fell into a boiling caul-dron) in 1601, Lipsius wrote, "Who in the future will fawn on his master with mouth agape, who will fawn with wagging tail? Who will wait there for me at the threshold or the door and grab my attention as I prepare to enter . . . who will entertain me with his play?"[78] However, although this kind of expression of love and grief is the norm for many pet owners today, some contemporaries found Lipsius's emotional investment in Saphyrus ex-cessive, even blasphemous, particularly when he built a tomb for the dog. Another scholar, François Ogier, came to Lipsius's defense by asserting it was normal for someone to have his "parrot painted" or have "his dog, his cat, his wife" memorialized with "an inscription or verses."[79] Lipsius's decision to make public his exceptional affection for his dogs—and the controversy it provoked—is indicative that the modern pet was emerging but still nascent in the seventeenth century. Also notable is one of Lispius's defenders placing parrots first on the list of nonhuman animals for whom mourning, and me-morialization were appropriate. It is a clue that the history of the modern pet remains incomplete if we look exclusively at "internal" European devel-opments while ignoring the impact of Europe's entanglement with Indige-nous America.

The arrival and integration of Indigenous *iegue* in Europe contributed to the emergence of the modern pet. In part, the diffusion of *iegue* changed human-animal relationships by the expansion of exotic animal ownership. Princely courts were no longer the only possible destination for captive American animals. If parrots and monkeys were among the rare court ani-mals of the Middle Ages, they became increasingly common in urban house-holds during the early modern period.[80] Parrot-keeping extended to mari-ners, wealthy merchants, nobles, and, by the eighteenth century, artisans. Dobrizhoffer made a casual aside about the "many kinds of parrots . . . for sale at the shops of Lisbon" and the ones "exhibited in the gardens of the chief people" of that city.[81] Louise Robbins found that "exotic animals were a major presence in eighteenth-century Paris." Particularly well represented were parrots and monkeys from the Americas.[82]

These quantitative changes in exotic animal ownership were related to qualitative changes—the marvel and objectified wonder of the court menagerie gave way to the familiarity of the family pet. In his entry on the parrot in *Histoire naturelle des oiseaux* (1778), the Enlightenment naturalist Georges-Louis Leclerc, Comte de Buffon, defines by way of example the concept of the pet. The parrot "entertains, it distracts, it amuses; in solitude it is company; in conversation it is an interlocutor, it responds, it calls, it welcomes, it emits peals of laughter, it expresses a tone of affection . . . [it] seems to be moved and touched by caresses, it gives affectionate kisses; in a house of mourning, it learns to moan, and accustomed to repeating the dear name of a deceased person, it reminds sensitive hearts of their pleasure and sorrows."[83] Buffon depicted the pet as the ideal family member, offering and receiving affection, amusement, and solace, and sensitive to the energies and vicissitudes of the household as a whole. That the animal who exemplified the role of the pet was a parrot—the paradigmatic species for *iegue*—is a trace of the Indigenous contribution to the formation of the modern pet.

11

Indigenizing Science

ing Philip II received a much-awaited shipment in spring 1576. The sender was Francisco Hernández, a physician who had spent more than five years researching and writing about the flora and fauna of New Spain. The cargo included sixteen large volumes with text and images describing and depicting more than three thousand plants, as well as live and dried specimens.[1] It also included "Historiae animalium et mineralium novae hispaniae" (History of animals and minerals of New Spain), a copiously illustrated Latin treatises on quadrupeds, birds, reptiles, insects, and aquatic beings, and pelts, feathers, and dissected animal bodies.[2] The king found the illustrations so pleasing that he displayed several in his quarters in the Escorial palace, where they dazzled visitors.[3] Reflecting the excitement spawned by the "Historiae animalium" in the late sixteenth and seventeenth centuries, one visitor marveled at "all of the animals and plants that can be seen in the Occidental Indies in their own native colors . . . the caiman, the spider, the snake, the serpent, the rabbit, the dog and the fish with its scales, the most beautiful feathers of so many different birds, the claws and the beak." He exclaimed at "the greatest delight" one felt in looking at them.[4]

The accompanying text generated almost as much delight and excitement as the beautiful paintings. Even though, much to his dismay, Hernández failed to publish his "Natural History," it circulated in manuscript and eventually made its way into print in the seventeenth century. The European scholars who viewed the images and read the texts responded so strongly because of their epistemological novelty—a novelty produced by the entanglement of Indigenous and European epistemologies. Scholars have long recognized that Hernández relied on Nahua labor and knowledge to write and illustrate his natural history. However, the full extent to which Indigenous expertise and labor contributed to the natural history has gone unnoticed, largely due to Hernández's disavowal of it. Yet, like the footprints that dotted their pictorial works, Nahua experts left their marks on every page of the "Historiae animalium." By finding, identifying, and connecting these marks, it is possible to offer a more complete account of the production of this seminal zoological text. By centering "Historiae animalium" in the history of the natural sciences, I am contributing to an on-going, collective effort to make visible the Iberian world's centrality to the momentous epistemological changes of the sixteenth and seventeenth centuries traditionally designated the "Scientific Revolution."[5] The reconstruction of the inception, production, and reception of the "Historiae animalium," however, reveals an even larger erasure in the history of early modern science—that of Indigenous knowledge, and, more precisely, its appropriation and disavowal by European colonizers.[6] It is no small paradox that what made this knowledge so attractive to colonizers such as Hernández was the radically different way Indigenous people interacted with nonhuman beings, and, therefore what they perceived and understood about them.

~

THE ORIGINS OF the "Historiae animalium" lie, in part, in a 1569 edict appointing Hernández *protomédico* of the Indies."[7] A subsequent 1570 royal decree instructed the physician to "go to the Indies and consult all the doctors, medicine men, herbalists, Indians, and other persons with knowledge in such matters . . . and thus you shall gather information generally about herbs, trees, and medicinal plants in whichever province you are."[8] Hernández was a logical choice for this position and assignment. He had studied at the prestigious University of Alcalá de Henares, and had embarked on ambitious translations of the works of Pliny and Aristotle. He also had practical experience overseeing botanical expeditions in Andalucía, and he had served as a royal chamber physician. After a short stay in the Caribbean, Hernández arrived in New Spain in February 1571. For the next three years, he was mostly itinerant, covering vast distances with a large retinue, reaching Querétaro to the north, Guerrero to the west, the Tehuantepec Isthmus to the south, and Gulf Coast regions to the east. During his travels, Hernández usually lodged at Franciscan monasteries or friar-run hospitals. Reflecting back on these travels in the years after he returned to Spain, he, like Gonzalo Fernández de Oviedo, cast himself as a heroic researcher. He boasted of tolerating strange foods that "took a long time to get used to," extreme weather ("the intense heat, and the great cold"), and challenging travel conditions like "impassable mountains, rivers, swamps, vast lakes, and expansive lagoons." He particularly emphasized the dangers and discomforts he faced because of nonhuman creatures, both large and small. Hernández reported encountering "monstrous creatures swimming in the lakes, which have stomachs vast enough that they can swallow men whole" and "thousands of nasty insects everywhere that lacerated my tender skin with their bloodsucking stings."[9] For the last phase of his stay in the Americas, beginning in March 1574, the physician lived in Mexico City. There he organized and revised his data, experimented with *materia medica,* and tended to patients in the Hospital Real de Indios and continued his research on animals and plants. Sharing his lodgings with numerous caged birds provided by trappers, Hernández observed their behavior and listened to their mellifluous songs and garrulous chattering,

By 1576, Hernández was past his deadline. The impatient king had responded to the request for (another) extension by writing "that this doctor has frequently promised to send these books, but he never does" and so instructed the viceroy of New Spain to order the naturalist to "pack them up and send them on the first ship for safe keeping."[10] And so, in late March, a ship left the port of Veracruz bearing Hernández's five animal treatises totaling 414 chapters, ranging from a few sentences to several pages in length. The treatises concerned quadrupeds (40 chapters), birds (229 chapters), reptiles (58 chapters), insects (31 chapters), and aquatic animals (56 chapters).[11] In an apologetic letter to King Philip, Hernández explained that the works were still in draft form, and thus "not as clean or as ordered," as he intended: "I am still now finishing writing what more there is to be discovered and am perfecting the books."[12] He kept working on the natural history during his remaining months in New Spain, bringing another twenty-two volumes of manuscripts when he returned to Spain at the end of 1577.[13]

From Hernández's perspective, his project ended in failure because he never saw it in print. Despite—or perhaps because of—his enthusiasm for the illustrations, Philip II did not give permission for the book's publication. The royal rationale for this decision remains obscure. Some scholars believe that it was prompted by pique over repeated delays, others because the elderly physician was in failing health, or perhaps because Hernández strayed from the medical objectives of his mandate by discussing other characteristics and uses of American plants and animals. The king commissioned another physician, the Neapolitan Antonio Nardo Recchi, to make a "useable" digest of the natural histories, titled "De materia medica Novae Hispaniae: libri quatuor" (*Materia medica* of New Spain in four books) completed between 1580 and 1582.[14]

~

THE TRUE NOVELTY of "Historiae animalium" becomes apparent only in comparison to most of its precursors, including Oviedo's natural histories. Like Oviedo before him, Hernández modeled his project on that of Pliny. In a letter to Philip II, Hernández referred to the entirety of this opus as "the natural things of New Spain (las cosas naturales de la Nueva España) that I am describing, experimenting, and drawing," and elsewhere as "the history of natural things of the Indies," thereby making explicit his ambition to pursue the Plinian project in the Americas.[15] Like Oviedo, Hernández emphasized that his work was based on firsthand, sensory experience. But Oviedo's natural histories included 61 animal entries, less than a fourth of the number that appear in Hernández's work.[16] Moreover, the animal entries consist almost exclusively of text: Oviedo's faunal illustrations were limited in the printed works to rudimentary woodcuts of a manatee and iguana, despite the fact that he had many more drawings in his manuscripts.[17]

For the illustrations, Hernández clearly took inspiration from the natural histories created by authors in northern Europe. His models were those found in the works on animals, birds, and fish by the renowned humanists Pierre Belon, Guillaume Rondolet, and, above all, Conrad Gesner's *Historiae animalium* (1551–1558),[18] notwithstanding the fact that works by Gesner, a Protestant, were among those prohibited by the Inquisition.[19] These scholars' influence can also be seen in the organization. Like Gesner, Hernández followed Aristotle for his subdivisions rather than those found in Pliny or medieval encyclopedias. But the "Historiae animalium" also diverged from these antecedents in important ways. The natural histories of Gesner, Belon, and Rondolet had different epistemological foundations than Hernández's work. The former were, above all, humanist philological projects, as Brian Ogilvie has demonstrated. These humanists saw their primary task sifting through and collating the work of prior "authorities," a process of "textual collection and comparison" rather than composing entries based on their own empirical observations.[20] The divergence of "Historiae animalium" from earlier European natural histories can be attributed, in large degree, to Hernández's reliance on Indigenous expertise.

~

BEGINNING WITH THE seminal work of Germán Somolinos d'Ardois, scholars have long emphasized the contribution of Indigenous labor and knowledge to the "Historiae animalium."[21] Indeed, the 1570 edict commanding Hernández to interview "old Indians" and Indigenous healers acknowledged that this expertise was imperative for the project.[22] It is well known that the Spaniard relied on Native people to translate for him, guide him, carry him in litters, capture live animals, and collect specimens.[23] However, the full degree of his debt to Indigenous labor and knowledge has not been fully appreciated, largely because Hernández himself was loath to credit it and sometimes actively concealed it.

The influence of Indigenous expertise on Hernández's natural history project likely began even before the *protomédico* set foot in the Americas due to the intersection of Hernández's work and that of the Tlatelolco scholars.[24] In 1569, the Tlatelolco scholars had completed a draft of the twelve Nahuatl books of the "Historia universal."[25] The lead author, Franciscan Bernardino de Sahagún, sent the manuscript to the leaders in his order, but the response was not what he had hoped. Some of the order's leaders thought the project was worthy of "much esteem" and merited additional funding to bring it to completion; others opposed continued support. Sahagún later wrote that they were hostile to the project because its associated costs violated the order's vow of poverty. Nevertheless, it seems even more likely that this opposition stemmed from anxieties that the project would memorialize idolatry rather than eradicate it, as Sahagún and his supporters claimed. After the "Historia universal" fell out of favor with the Franciscan leadership, Sahagún decided to seek patronage elsewhere. He sent a "Breve compendio" (Brief compendium) to the Pope, hoping that he might get papal sponsorship for his project. Hedging his bets, he wrote a "Sumario" (now lost), which he described as "a summary of all the Books and of all the chapters of each Book and the Prologues wherein all that is contained in the Books is briefly stated," and persuaded well-connected Franciscan allies to present it to the president of the Council of the Indies in Spain. In the short run, neither strategy panned out. In the words of the friar, "nothing happened to the texts for the next five years."[26] This is not entirely true. In fact, Sahagún was required to submit the manuscript to his order for review, and copies were dispersed among different Franciscan monasteries in New Spain. Furthermore, the "Sumario" arrived in Spain soon after the king had appointed Hernández to his bio-prospecting mission. It is likely that Hernández became aware of the "Historia universal" shortly before he left for the Americas, and the physician likely carried Sahagún's "Sumario" (or a copy of it) when he disembarked in summer 1570.

Hernández's decision to include animals in his natural history may be a result of his exposure to the Nahuatl "Earthly Things" (*Yn ixquich tlalticpacyotl*) and to the Indigenous experts he met during his travels. The instructions that accompanied the royal decree compelled Hernández to collect *botanical* information. However, the *protomédico*'s correspondence with Philip II makes clear that his own understanding of the project had exceeded its original medical-pharmacological scope. In September 1572, he wrote, "I have so far drawn and painted three books full of rare plants"—in fact the illustrations were made by Nahua artists as discussed below—"most of them of great importance and medicinal virtue, as your Majesty will see, and almost two more [books] of terrestrial animals and exotic birds, unknown in our world, and I have written a draft of whatever could be discovered and investigated about their nature and properties, a subject on which I could spend my entire life."[27] By March 1573, Hernández had completed a volume containing illustrations of "200 animals, all exotic and native to this region" as well as text describing "the nature, climate, of the places to which they are native, the sounds they make, and their characteristics." While his aspirations to be the Pliny for the "New World" might partly account for the creep in his project's scope, he also explicitly credited Indigenous knowledge in his private correspondence, though not in the manuscripts he hoped to publish. In private communication, however, he employed greater candor. For example, in a letter to Philip II, he acknowledged that this knowledge came from "Indians, whose experience stretches over hundreds of years here."[28] The published manuscripts and drafts of "Historiae animalium" offer clues to his itineraries while researching animals. The extensive discussion of waterfowl suggests Indigenous contacts in Tlatelolco-Tenochtitlan and Texcoco, as he often mentioned these sites in reference to water birds.[29] His reliance on Indigenous knowledge also appears in lexical traces; almost all of the entries for animals native to Mexico employ Nahuatl names (see figs. 11.1, 11.2, and 11.3). In most cases, the Nahuatl term was presented as the primary signifier, followed by a literal translation, often revealing the Nahua practice of naming animals after defining features related to a distinctive aspect of their appearance, vocalization, or behavior.

One of the most foundational contributions of Nahua scholars to the "Historiae animalium" can be found in Hernández's obvious though unacknowledged use of "Earthly Things."[30] He likely saw a draft of the "Historia universal" during one of those stays with the Franciscans, as copies of the manuscript were dispersed among different Franciscan houses.[31] A comparison of the "Historiae animalium" and "Earthly Things" reveals that some details for entries on the monkey and coyote concur to such an extent that coincidence is implausible.[32] Moreover, Hernández's chapter on the quetzal is mostly a Latin translation of the entry penned by the Tlatelolco authors in Nahuatl.[33] Hernández's use of this Nahuatl manuscript is significant as it displays the influence of the Nahua authors on his manuscript, *and* suggests that these authors worked directly with him. Because the Spaniard knew little Nahuatl, he depended on Indigenous interpreters and translators. In a letter dated March 20, 1575, among the many in which he asked for an extension of his due date, he asserted that he needed extra time so that "an Indian who is translating my books into Mexican (e.g., Nahuatl)" could finish them, and in another letter he referred to the task of "translating [drafts] into Spanish and Mexican."[34] From this, we can infer that his collaborators included one or more people capable of translating from Latin into Nahuatl. This suggests that the translations were made by one or more of the Tlatelolco seminarians, perhaps Antonio Valeriano, who was renowned for his mastery of Latin.[35]

I believe that in addition to their work as translators, editors, and perhaps even coauthors of "Historiae animalium," the Tlatelolco scholars also conducted research under the auspices of Hernández.[36] The evidence for this scenario comes from a comparison of the "Historiae animalium" with the final version of "Earthly Things"—book II of the *Florentine Codex.* The latter contains forty-three "new" entries (i.e., not present in the 1565 draft).[37] Two are quadrupeds: the *tlacaxolotl* (tapir) and the *tzoniztac* (perhaps a weasel-type animal).[38] These entries include details that suggest influence rather than coincidence—in other words, the overlap between the new entries in the *Florentine Codex* and those in the "Historiae animalium" seems too precise to be a function of independent reporting. Both texts relate, for example, a belief that a chance encounter with a yellow-headed *tzoniztac* augured impending death, whereas an encounter with a white-headed one foretold a long yet impoverished life.[39] The entries for the tapir offer the detail that the animals ate and then defecated cacao beans, which were then foraged for by commoners.[40] The remaining forty-one new entries in the *Florentine Codex* are about birds. Many were either waterfowl who lived near Lake Texcoco (27) or raptors (9).[41] These entries reflect, respectively, Hernández's focus on the marshland birds that were in proximity to his base in Mexico City, and attentiveness to his royal patron's interest in falconry.[42] Moreover, the new raptor entries embedded Spanish terms within the Nahuatl text, such as "alcón" (falcon) and "gavilán" (hawk).[43] Another clue that the new entries were added during or after the Nahua authors worked on Hernández's project is that they often introduced redundancy into the text. The *Florentine Codex* included, for instance, a short entry for a raptor known as "tlho-quauhtli" [*tlhocuauhtli*] that was in the early draft and then a new, longer entry for a bird of the same name. Likewise, the *Florentine Codex* had two entries for the pelican.[44]

If the new entries in book II resulted from research conducted under the *protomédico*, then they can shed light on the research methods developed by the Nahua scholars in *both* projects. A notable aspect of a number of the entries on marshland birds is frequent mention of *atlaca*, suggesting them as the source for the information about aquatic animals. The literal meaning of *atlaca* is "people of the water," although Alonso de Molina translated the term as *marinero* (sailor or boat people), "gente malvada" (tough people); other contemporary sources suggest that it could be synonymous with fishermen.[45] Thus, it appears to be an appellation for commoners who made their living from the water. For instance, the authors wrote in the new entry for the pelican (*atotolin*) that the bird "does not fly very high; sometimes the *atlaca* only chase it in boats; they spear it."[46] The *atlaca* also told the Tlatelolco scholars about the *acuitlachtli*, described as a creature with a head "like those of the forest-dwelling *tecuani* (people-eaters)" and the tail of a caiman who "lived there Santa Cruz Quauhacalco, where there is a spring." "The heart of the lagoon," he was held responsible for making the water overflow, the fish well up, and agitating the mud like an earthquake. In other words the *acuitlachtli*—seemingly out of place in the section on aquatic birds—personified the lagoon itself. The *atlaca* "can testify, for they saw [the animal] and they also capture it."[47] The scholars were able to use their local contacts in Tlatelolco to interview these knowledgeable locals, who were intimately familiar with the lake environment and the dangers lurking in its flood-prone waters.[48]

Given Hernández's reliance on Indigenous expertise at every stage of the project, it is not surprising that much of the knowledge about animals transmitted in "Historiae animalium" was related to predation and familiarization. The details about animals' appearances, sounds, tastes, and behaviors comprising the entries in the "Historiae animalium" are observations often

M A P A C H.

C.I.

CAPVT XLII.
De animali Mapach.

CAPVT XLII.
De animali Mapach.

ANtra & cauitates montium atque col-
lium Tzozocolci hoſpitatur animal
péregrinum, quod cunſta manibus præten-
tat.*Mapach* ab Indis dicitur,ſed non firmo

nomine; alij *illamaton* ſeu *vetulam* appellât,
alij *maxtle* ſeu *goſſypinum cingulum* , alij
cioatlamacazquu ieu *ſacerdotiſſam*. Exæquat
magnitudinem quauhpecotli,imò cane Me-
litenſi paulò eſt maius,humile,teres,pilis ve-
ſtitum,nigro alboque colore promiſcuè va-
riatis, magno capite, paruis auriculis,roſtro
P 4   canis

Figure 11.1   Raccoon in Juan Eusebio Nieremberg, *Historia naturae, maxime peregrinae*
(Antwerp, 1635), p. 175. Reproduction courtesy of John Carter Brown Library, Brown University.

derived, directly or indirectly, from these Indigenous modes of interaction. We have already seen how familiarization may have been a prerequisite for some of the most detailed descriptions of animals' appearances and behaviors in the "Historiae animalium."[49] As discussed in Chapter 7, familiarized animals appearing in the treatise on quadrupeds include the raccoon (fig. 11.1), peccary, possum, porcupines (fig. 11.2), coati, monkeys, and squirrels.[50] Among the birds were a woodpecker, *tepetototl* (Crax rubra), parrots, and songbirds who "delight with their song those who hear them."[51] Familiarized reptiles included the rattlesnake (fig. 11.3) and the *tapayaxin* (mountain horned lizard).[52] This mode of interaction facilitated Hernández and the Nahua researchers' access to *live* animals whose appearances—and behaviors—could be described in great detail.

Predation also underpinned many descriptions. Such entries featured specific information about the manner in which people hunted, snared, fished, or otherwise captured wild animals. In the chapter on the caiman ("*aquetz-palin* or crocodile that others call *Cayman*"), Hernández observed admiringly that despite the enormity and ferocity of the animal, Indigenous children would lasso them by the neck and tow them to the shore.[53] Hernández's descriptions of the properties of animals' flesh, bones, feathers, and fur were related to predation. He focused frequently on edibility and offered his opinions about flavor.[54] Various parts of the "hoactzin" bird, for example, were used in remedies—the bones were used for pains caused by cuts, a smoke made from its feathers restored "reason" to those sickened by rage, and ashes made from feathers "admirably" cured victims of the "French disease" (syphilis).[55] The feathers of the *cozcaquauhtli* (king vulture), were, according to Hernández, applied to ulcerous sores, and its flesh was cooked and fed to those suffering from them.[56] He also mentioned prey whose bodies had medical, aesthetic, and sartorial uses. He noted the rabbit fur woven into tunics and cape and the peccary skin lining the inside of cloaks. Armadillo (*ayotochtli*) "related as much to war as to peace" for its tail could make blow darts and the shell was decocted for medicinal preparations.[57] Moreover, Indigenous hunters provided Hernández (and his collaborators) with the specimens that often became the basis of his entries.

It is not only details about hunting practices and the appearances, behaviors, and habitats of prey animals that reveal predation's constituent role in the "Historiae animalium's" epistemology. This mode of interaction generated a mode of observation and description. The quetzal entry is exemplary in this regard. It is no coincidence that the description of the quetzal whose feathers were valued above all others for making ritual garments is the most detailed about coloring and shape. Nor is it a coincidence that it was the entry that Hernández chose to transcribe it in its entirety from "Earthly Things." The significance of the quetzal entry is twofold: it reveals the authorship of the Tlatelolco scholars and provides a descriptive model for other entries. In other words, *teixiptla* helped transform the practices of natural history.[58]

The quetzal entry also reveals elements of cosmogrammatic logic that were likely invisible to Hernández—but not to his Nahua collaborators. A revealing divergence exists between the two surviving versions of "Historiae animalium," the manuscript draft and the seventeenth-century print edition based on the Escorial manuscript that Hernández sent to the king. In the draft, the quetzal entry appears first among the birds, as it did in the 1565 draft of "Earthly Things."[59] However, the quetzal chapter appears second in the version that Hernández sent to Spain, following the chapter about the "hoacton foemina" (female heron).[60] In both versions, the quetzal's singular and supreme importance in Nahua sacred geography was conveyed by chapter placement, but the differences are telling. By putting the heron first, the Nahua scholars alluded to the Mexica's origin story, in which the heron was the bird of Aztlan, the beautiful land associated with the western quadrant where they first attempted permanent settlement. The placement of the quetzal after the heron in "Historiae animalium" alludes to a particular central Mexican understanding of history, one that pays homage to migrating ancestors. In book 9 of the "Historia universal," featherworking informants explained that during early Chichimec times, heron feathers were "precious" and "corresponded to those of the quetzal" as "they were used to make the forked heron feather device" with which "the winding dance was performed."[61] The juxtaposition of the heron and the quetzal is a way of signaling that the Mexica live in the center, at the crossroads of different biomes of Mesoamerica, for these are feathers of the birds of the East and the West. Given that Hernández, unlike the Tlatelolco authors, did not usually organize animals in accordance with Mexica priorities, this trace suggests the intentionality of the unnamed and barely acknowledged Nahua scholars rather than that of the *protomédico* employing them.

Importantly, Hernández's lack of acknowledgment—or, more precisely, his disavowal—of his Nahua collaborators was a consistent feature rather than an accidental product of his method.[62] Hernández's acknowledgment of his dependence on Indigenous expertise and knowledge most often took the form of complaints, as when he lamented Native people's unwillingness to comply with his requests for information or demands to share their arcane knowledge: "I will not speak of the perfidious confabulation of the Indians, the perverse lies with which they mocked me . . . nor the many times I confided in false interpreters . . . so that it is necessary to recognize the savage condition of the Indians, never sincere, reluctant to reveal their secrets."[63] Hernández disavowed their contributions partly because he was concerned about perpetuating and perhaps even reinforcing "superstitious" or even "idolatrous" beliefs, bodies of knowledge from which he sought to distance himself. In the chapter about the *acitl* (an aquatic bird—perhaps a western grebe[64]), Hernández discussed a belief "told by the Indians."[65] "They say," wrote Hernández, that the duck "can summon the winds when pursued by hunters, making waves that overturn canoes and drown the pursuers"— something they do if the hunters don't succeed in killing them after five arrows are shot. This belief is similar to others held by hunters that proscribe pursuing too aggressively those prey that elude capture or killing. The Spaniard scorned such "childish beliefs and lies," attributing them to "the credulity and shallowness of these people." For example, when discussing the *cocotzin*, which he identified as a kind of dove slightly larger than a sparrow, he scoffed at a local belief that, if it was cooked and fed to a woman without her knowing what she was eating, it would cure her of jealousy. Tellingly, he added, "The theologians can investigate whether this can be so."[66] In addition, he related a belief of the "Indians" that sighting the *hoactzin* augured misfortune, and that hearing the song of the *cuapachtototl* (one that resembled laughter) was a bad omen held "by the Indians before they were illuminated by the splendid light of the Gospel."[67] Hernández's effort to remove information related to what he considered "childish beliefs" and "lies" reveals his anxiety about potential contamination by superstition or idolatry. The result was that most entries describe only appearance and behavior, leaving aside details related to cosmology. In this respect, the "Historiae animalium" lacks the magical and mythological references found in Pliny's "Natural History" that he was simultaneously editing.[68] Part of what would become known as "disenchantment" had its origins in Europeans' efforts to appropriate Indigenous knowledge without assimilating their alleged superstitions.

~

IN 1671 THE paintings and drawings of animals and plants that Philip II displayed to distinguished visitors, along with the sixteen volumes of text, were destroyed by a fire at the Escorial palace. Three Indigenous men, Pedro Vázquez, Anton [?] and Baltasar Elías, made these bedazzling images while in Hernández's employ. The *protomédico* expressed more appreciation for the artists who he trained to paint plants and animals than he did for the many other Indigenous experts who worked for him. The physician uncharacteristically articulated his high regard for them,[69] going so far as to request that the king command some of his "Indian painters" to accompany him to Peru on a proposed but unrealized research trip.[70] And though his letters reveal a reluctance to pay the Indigenous workers in his service adequately, he made provisions in his will to ensure that three of his painters received what he thought was proper compensation: "I desire that in the event that His Majesty does not recompense the Mexican painters in the amount that I requested, that to each of the three, namely Pedro Vázquez, and Anton and

Baltasar Elías, to each or to his heirs be given thirty ducats from my estate."[71] Nevertheless, per his customary practice, Hernández also complained about these Indigenous artists, thereby revealing that he regarded their contributions as crucial. He wrote, "I cannot begin to count the mistakes of the artists, who were to illustrate my work, and yet were the greatest part of my care, so that nothing, from the point of view of a fat thumb, would be different from what was being copied, but rather all would be as it was in reality."[72] In the text of the "Historiae animalium" itself, Hernández alluded to the labor of these Indigenous artists, as in the entry for the *hoactzin* bird, "who lives in warm regions, such as *Yauhtépec*, (Oaxaca) and that rests almost always in trees that are next to rivers, *where we saw it and made sure to hunt it and paint it.*"[73] Here and elsewhere, the fourth person both reveals and buries the contributions of his collaborators.

Despite the enormous loss wrought by the Escorial fire, we do know something about the images made by Vázquez, Anton, and Elías. Two of the seventeenth-century publications based on Hernández's works—Nieremberg's *Historia naturae, maxime peregrinae* (1635) and the Lincei Academy's *Rerum medicarum Novae Hispaniae thesaurus* (1648–51)—feature woodcuts made from the original paintings (figs. 11.1, 11.2, 11.3).[74] The illustrations made for the "Historiae animalium," like those in Gesner's and other humanist zoological texts, privilege the ocular and, more specifically, the one-way gaze.[75] It might seem obvious that an image emphasizes what can be known through the sense of sight, but it is possible for images to emphasize other forms of sensory apprehension. Images in a *tonalamatl* emphasize sound, with scrolls emitting from the mouths of people and other animals; smell, through the representation of flowers; and movement, through footsteps. The images in the "Historiae animalium" also exhibit what art historian Janice Neri called "specimen logic," in which "objects" are removed "from their contexts and plac[ed] . . . against the blank space of a page for the viewer's inspection."[76] It seems likely that Hernández showed the Nahua illustrators examples from Gesner, or the other humanist zoological books, so that they could depict animals in this pictorial mode. These images show the animal alone with minimal or no background elements.[77] Sometimes they include a few elements to suggest a landscape, but they are generic and do not suggest interaction with other beings, as is the case with the raccoon (fig. 11.1). In the case of the porcupine (fig. 11.2) and rattlesnake (fig. 11.3), background elements are entirely absent. The images, even more than the text, are worlds apart from the animals (and other

CAPVT II.

De animalibus spinosis.

ADmirandum genus bruti sagittatoris nouus orbis alit. Animal spinosum, mediocris canis exæquans magnitudinem. Ab Indis hoitztlaquatzin dicitur, siue spinosus tlacuatzin. Nomen forma metuit. Simile est illi, quod tlacuatzin vocant, de quo suo loco sermo erit. Vestitur cauis & acuminatis spinis, tres vncias productis pilis quoque nonnullis (si caput excipias) mollibus insertis, siue atrâ lanugine; & circa exortum candenti: venter tamen, crura, & brachia aculeis omnino carent. Spicula tenuia sunt, candentia, & lutea: vbi desinunt nigricant; mucrones peracuti. Cauda breuior est quàm tlacuatzin, crassitie tamen maiori compensatur. Inops aculeorum est à mediâ parte vsque ad extremitatem. Pedes similes habet quauhpecotli; sed latiores (misceo sæpe verba & sententias Francisci Hernandi, nec meo cerebro & stilo loquor semper) rostrum pænè caninum, nisi quòd resimum. Dentes suprà infraĝ; bini, quemadmodum ruccæ. Iaculatur spinas suas in canes insectantes, nullâ excutiendas industriâ, nullo conatu: sensim magis magisĝue vi quadam arcanâ subeunt, & iactatione plus figuntur,

donec viscera perfodiant. Alliciunt & ebibunt innatum humorem, donec transfixum & perforatum canem tabefaciant. Quærunt Indi aculeos illos dolori capitis placando. Admoti verò fronti & temporibus, sponte adhærent, nec priùs delabuntur, quàm hirudinum more hauserint noxium sanguinem, quo suam farciunt cauitatem. Causâ languoris remotâ, ægrotans valet. Cuicumque rei cuspis eius admisceatur, etiam postquam ab animantis cute est diuulsa, occultâ virtute, etiam cùm à nemine vrgeatur, sponte penetrat carnem. Feminis eius vsus perforandis auriculis ad inaurium suspensionem. Perforatio prorsus fit nemine impellente, quasi exuat setas. Experimento compertum, vnius noctis interuallo crassissimo corio admotam, sponte coriú totum, perinde atque acus hominis impulsa manu transmittitur, penetrasse. Eorumdem aculeorum puluis dragmæ vnius penderes sumptus, dysenterijs médetur, vrinam euocat. Gaudet hoc animal montosis & calidis locis Xonoltz & Yzotzocolci. Fortasse ad Bæticam nostram deportatus, non iniquum sibi cælum toleraret. Vescitur fructibus: cicurari potest. Aliqui putarunt hystricem aut mantychoræ speciem, cùm multis differat, & in nonnullis admirabilior fortasse sit, vt ex collatione

Figure 11.2 Porcupine in Juan Eusebio Nieremberg, *Historia naturae, maxime peregrinae*, (Antwerp, 1635), p. 154. Reproduction courtesy of John Carter Brown Library, Brown University.

beings) painted in the *tonalamatl* and other postclassic artifacts. For example, the cosmograms depict animals within relational networks, showing connections among different forms of life (animals, plants, soil, water, sun). In contrast, the images in the natural history portray decontextualized, self-contained organisms.

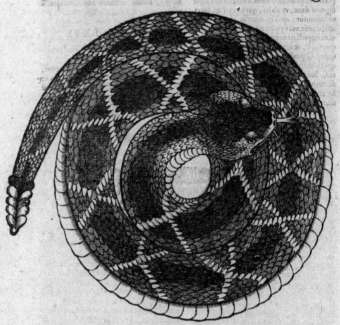

268

IOANNIS EVSEBII NIEREMBERGII
EX SOCIETATE IESV
HISTORIÆ NATVRÆ
LIBER DVODECIMVS.

DOMINA SERPENTVM, siue TEVHTLACOCAVHQVI.

CAPVT PRIMVM.

De dominá serpentum.

ON fine naturæ vsu reptilia sunt : nec minùs maiestatê Creatoris humilitate suâ exaggerant, non minùs bonitatem peste suâ. Scit peffimis Deus iuuare , scit veneno mederi: liberalem medicina opem è noxijs istis vsurpat. Exordium occupet atrox genus serpentum, Teuhtlacocauhqui, seu dominam serpentum Barbari vocant, viperam Hispani, siue ob similitudinem capitis , siue pestis. Anguis hic quaternos pedes aut ampliùs longus, & humanum, vbi mediocriter crassus est, latus : dorso eminenti , viperino capite, ventre ex albo pallescente, lateribus opertis, candentibus squamis, fascijs tamen pullis per interualla intermixtis; dorsum fuscum est, luteis tamen lineis sese in ipsâ spinâ secantibus insigne. Multæ sunt eius serpentis differétiæ, non plurimùm inter se distan-

tes,

Figure 11.3   Rattlesnake in Juan Eusebio Nieremberg, *Historia naturae, maxime peregrinae* (Antwerp, 1635), p. 368. Reproduction courtesy of John Carter Brown Library, Brown University.

Even so, some traces of Indigenous pictorial modes survive in these images. The coiled posture of the rattlesnake is more reminiscent of late postclassic sculpture than the European tradition that tended to depict snakes while undulating rather than coiled.[78] But perhaps the images' biggest debt to Indigenous practices and beliefs about nonhuman animals is that of familiarization. It is no accident that the most naturalistic engravings with the most precise detail disproportionately depict animals that were also discussed as objects of familiarization, for example, the raccoon, porcupine, rattlesnake, possum, and peccary.[79] It makes sense that the artists would render most vibrantly those animals whom they could draw from life. Although these naturalistic representations are stylistically European, they were made possible because the artists had close access to living animals. Paradoxically, the "specimen" images, even though they were deeply rooted in European aesthetic tradition and antithetical to postclassic Indigenous pictorial and epistemological conventions, were entangled with Indigenous people and modes of interaction. The drawings would have been impossible without the Indigenous artists whom Hernández trained and admired, or the practices that resulted from predation and familiarization that provided ample access to live and dead specimens. Thus the "Historiae animalium" was the result of the commingling of European and Indigenous epistemologies and the modes of interaction that underpinned them.

~

IT IS HARD to overstate the excitement generated by Hernández's coproduced "Natural History of New Spain." Although never printed, it became a sensation among literati in the late sixteenth and early seventeenth centuries.[80] Well-known figures in natural history across Europe, including José de Acosta, Ulisses Aldrovandi, Carlos Clusius, and Johannes Laet, expressed, in both published remarks and private correspondence, their desire to see the works.[81] Aldrovandi, the Italian polymath, for instance, was desperate to see the manuscripts and wrote to a contact whom he hoped could help get access to "the court of king Philip," where there was "a truly regal book with paintings of various plants and animals and other new things from the Indies."[82] Before long, portions of the natural history began to circulate in print. In 1615, Francisco Ximénez, a physician and Dominican friar based in Huaxtepec (one of the places Hernández stayed during his travels), published a translation of Recchi's digest in Mexico City.[83] In 1628, the Lincei

Academy in Rome (also a patron of Galileo) published a very limited print run of the Recchi digest in Latin, along with a lengthy commentary entitled "Animalia Mexicana."[84] Juan Eusebio Nieremberg, a Jesuit scholar at Imperial College in Madrid who had access to the volumes housed in the Escorial and the "drafts" that Hernández had retained for himself, extensively transcribed material from the "Historiae animalium" in *Historia naturae, maxime peregrinae* (Antwerp, 1635).[85] And in 1649, the Lincei Academy published the entirety of the text of the "Historiae animalium" as an appendix in its massive *Rerum medicarum Novae Hispaniae thesaurus, seu, Plantarum animalium mineralium Mexicanorum historia*.[86] As already mentioned, both the Rome and Madrid publications featured woodcuts based on the original illustrations. Many more works published in the seventeenth and eighteenth centuries transcribed or translated entries that first appeared in the "Historiae animalium."

Another impact of the "Historiae animalium" was its emulation by other authors. Particularly important in this respect is the Dutch imperial *Historia naturalis brasiliae* (1648).[87] Among its authors and sponsors was Johannes de Laet, who expressed admiration and envy for the project led by Hernández.[88] Its primary researchers, Georg Marcgrave and Willem Piso, who were based in Mauritstaad (Recife), relied heavily on Indigenous (primarily Tupinamba) knowledge and labor.[89] They also depended on familiarization and predation to generate knowledge about Brazilian animals. In the entry for the parakeet, "called by the Brasilians Tui," they explained that "these become very tame, so that they will take meat out of one's mouth and permit one to stroke and handle them." In the entry for the *cabure,* they note that the bird "plays with men like an Ape, making mowes and antic mimical faces, and snapping with its Bill."[90]

The "Historiae animalium" also found emulators in members of the Royal Society of London, including John Ray, Francis Willughby, and Hans Sloane.[91] The works on fish, birds, and mammals that Ray and Willughby published in the 1670s have long been seen as pivotal in the history of zoology, an epistemological break far removed from the sixteenth-century humanist scholarship about animals.[92] In the preface to *The Ornithology* (1678), written after Willughby's death, Ray asserted such novelty.[93] He explicitly and implicitly contrasted his and Willughby's methods with those of earlier humanists like Gesner and Aldrovandi and, in doing so, articulated the "epistemic virtues" of the ideal naturalist, a term only recently coined.[94] Ray wrote that he and Willughby "did not as some before us have done, only transcribe other mens' descriptions, but we our selves did carefully describe each Bird from the view and inspection of it lying before us." He insisted that authority came, above all, not from bookish "Authors" (he claimed that he and Ray "rectified many mistakes in the Writings of *Gesner* and *Aldrovandus*") but from people whose occupations gave them direct experience working with animals, such as falconers, "fowlers," and "a fisherman of Strasbourg." He considered that textual description was necessary but insufficient and that images drawn by skilled artists from life were key: "elegant and accurate Figures do much illustrate and facilitate the understanding of Descriptions," if these "Pictures" are "drawn in colours by the life" and "drawn by good Artists." Ray thought the naturalist ought to reject enchanted "fables, presages or ought else pertaining to Divinity, Ethics, Grammar, or any sort of Humane Learning." Instead, he was to "present" the reader "only with what properly relates to their Natural History." Although Ray implied that he and his collaborators were the inventors of these new methods, the "Historiae animalium" had laid the groundwork for them.[95]

In fact, the "epistemic virtues" named by Ray were first advanced in the "Historiae animalium." This earlier and much emulated work coproduced by Hernández and Indigenous experts modeled the epistemic virtues of observation, vocational mastery, life-drawn images, disenchantment, and disavowal. Some of these virtues are inseparable from the history of Indigenous ways of knowing: Hernández depended on Nahua scholars who were able to translate "Earthly Things" and interview the *atlaca* ("water folk") and numerous other unnamed Indigenous hunters, fishers, and tamers to understand how animals sounded, looked, and behaved. Hernández relied on the Nahua artists Vazquez, Anton, and Elías to describe, draw, and paint animals from "life." And Hernández not only depended on this multitude of Indigenous experts; he also learned about new modes of observation and description that had their basis in Indigenous ideals of *teixiptla* and other elements of predation and familiarization.

Other emergent epistemic virtues in the "Historiae animalium" emerged from Hernández's desire to maintain colonial hierarchies and guard against idolatrous contamination. Hernández's rejection of "fables" and "presages"— what he qualified as "childish beliefs and lies that originate in the credulity and shallowness of these people"—is inseparable from broader colonial anxieties about cultural contamination. In other words, the "disenchantment" that is often thought to characterize modern science cannot be understood without colonists' desire to appropriate Indigenous knowledge while maintaining a sense of cultural superiority. This epistemic virtue, in turn, is related to acts of disavowal—efforts to repackage Indigenous knowledge as European: in the case of Willughby and Ray, to claim Ibero-American innovations as English. Just as Hernández was discomfited by the heterodox beliefs of his Indigenous interlocutors, Protestants Willughby and Ray were uneasy about Catholicism, the "bad Religion" of their Spanish sources.[96]

One of the most significant legacies of the "Historiae animalium" was its contribution to constructing the naturalist and the specimen. This natural history was the progenitor of the later modern scientific framework that simultaneously insists on humans' fundamental commonalities with other animals and humans' entitlement to dominate them. In other words, it laid the groundwork for epistemologies that emphasized the common ancestry shared by humans and other animals *and* distinguished humans from other animals by segregating the knowing subject (a European man) from the passive object (an animal).

~

LATER GENERATIONS OF European and settler-colonial naturalists were not the only ones affected by their contact with the "Historiae animalium." So, too, were the Tlatelolco scholars who returned to the "Historia universal," the project directed by Sahagún in the wake of the scholars' experiences working under Hernández. Resumption of work on what became the *Florentine Codex* was made possible by a change in the Franciscan order's leadership in New Spain. Sahagún reacquired the manuscripts, and from fall 1575 through 1577, the Nahua scholars returned to the workshop in the Colegio de Santa Cruz in Tlatelolco.[97] The team of "grammarians" and scribes was now joined by a number of illustrators.[98] They also faced a new set of challenges. In the late summer of 1576, the severe outbreak of epidemic disease raging through New Spain reached Mexico City. In November 1576, Sahagún wrote that "many people have died, die and every day more are dying . . . the number of dead has always gone increasing: from ten [to] twenty, from thirty to forty, from fifty to sixty and to eighty die every day."[99] Members of the Tlatelolco team were among the epidemic's victims.

Book 11 of the *Florentine Codex* differed in several respects from the draft composed by the Tlatelolco scholars more than a decade before. As discussed previously, the text included forty-three new animal entries. It reorganized some sections, and, as in the rest of the books of "Historia universal," the right column featured the Nahuatl text, while Spanish translations and co-pious colorful images shared space in the left column (see figs. 8.1, 11.4). For the images, the illustrators drew upon both Indigenous and European pictorial traditions.[100] They depicted some of the animals in the specimen style, while they placed others in narrative sequences, often in vertically arranged panels. The Spanish "translation," as Kevin Terraciano has pointed out, should be considered as an independent text as it often diverged from Nahuatl in significant ways.[101] It was previously assumed that Sahagún was responsible for the translation, but Victoria Ríos Castaño has argued that some or all of it was likely the work of the Nahua scholars.[102]

In some respects, book 11 displays closer alignment with European antecedents than the earlier draft. This is evident in the book's new organization. The chapters were reordered in a schema that was closer to that of Pliny than that of the encyclopedias, with the animal chapters preceding those on plants.[103] Within the animal chapters, the organization no longer accorded to the cosmogramic logic affording primacy to animals of the arboreal canopy. Instead, by featuring land-based quadrupeds before birds, it followed the European tradition found in Pliny and the encyclopedias alike, perhaps reflecting Hernández's influence on the project. The Spanish title, "Book 11 is a Forest, Garden and Orchard of the Mexican Language," echoed that of the *Hortus Sanitatis* ("Garden of Health") and emphasized the text's linguistic uses, perhaps to assuage concerns about potentially heretical content.[104]

Although book 11 was "more" European than the earlier drafts of "Earthly Things" in some ways, the Tlatelolco scholars also managed to assert their voices and perspectives more strongly in this work. Or, in the words of Iris Montero Sobrevilla, the Nahua collaborators turned the natural history into a "powerful" form of "indigenous memory-keeping."[105] This is the case despite—or perhaps because—the authors appear to have composed these entries during or after working on Hernández's natural history research project. A close analysis of the new entries reveals that the Nahua contributors expressed their views of nonhuman animals in ways that were strikingly divergent from Hernández and, it would seem, Sahagún. Small but notable differences suggest that the authors were, in a sense, talking back to Hernández by offering divergent opinions about the taste of certain animals' flesh. In some instances where Hernández declared the flavor of particular birds unappetizing, the authors of book 11 praised it. Both sources agreed, for example, that the *xalcuani* was a migratory bird who sometimes inhabited marshlands (Hernández identified it as a type of duck) and whose Nahuatl name derives from "it always eats sand." Hernández concluded that its "fishy aftertaste" rendered it "not pleasing as a food," whereas the Tlatelolco seminarians insisted that the birds were "edible, savory."[106] Hernández considered the flesh of the *tzonyayauhqui* greasy and fatty. The seminarians, while conceding that "it is fat, like *tocino*" (inserting the Spanish word for bacon in the middle of the Nahuatl text, asserted that the bird's flesh was "good-tasting.")[107] Somewhat more provocative is the scholars' presentation of the tapir's flavor profile. The "Historiae animalium" entry simply states that it "contains both the flavor of animals and birds." The Tlatelolco authors described it more evocatively: "Not of only one flavor is its flesh; all the various meats are in it: human flesh, wild beast flesh—deer, bird, dog."[108] We can read in these small but telling divergences an expression of the Nahua scholars' disagreement with disrespectful and exploitative colonizers like their demanding and unappreciative employer Hernández. We can also see the scholars' insistence that the game found distasteful by the Spaniard was, in fact, quite delicious. The scholars' observation that the flesh of nonhuman animals could be comparable with that of human animals might express a desire to commemorate practices that had become forbidden. Perhaps this provocative act was prompted by the apocalyptic atmosphere produced by the devastating epidemic outbreak.

The Nahua authors' desire to refute Hernández's perspective on their culture and traditions went beyond disagreements about flavor and mouthfeel of game. A number of the entries offer more details about omens, origin stories, and traditional ritual practice than the entries written in the 1560s. Perhaps this shift indicates Sahagún's looser grip during this final phase of production, when he was racing the clock against the killing spree of epidemic disease and the project patrons' increasing unease. A new entry that offers a particularly potent example of this shift in tone and approach is that for the "quauhtlotli," a bird of prey.[109] It was also, according to the entry, known as a "tlhoquautli." The authors inserted the Spanish word falcon ("alcon") in the Nahuatl description. The "Historiae animalium" includes an entry for "quauhtlotli" which Hernández (or one of the Nahua scholars) translated as "Arborum Accipitrum" (forest falcon) and identified as a "sacrum falconem," that is "almost the same as that of our lands," although "more beautiful and fierce than those of the Old World."[110] Although contemporary scholars disagree about the species or even genus of this bird,[111] the aplomado falcon (*falco femoralis*) seems a likely candidate.[112]

Although Hernández provided no descriptive details of this bird's beauty or fierceness, his Nahua collaborators did. The entry for the *cuauhtlohtli* in the *Florentine Codex* is much more precise about the falcon's appearance, behaviors, and the methods employed to take it captive. The authors noted that the "bird has dark gray feathers, and a yellow bill and legs," while the "hen is somewhat large, and the cock somewhat small," the latter a characteristic of the aplomado. Regarding the raptor's manner of hunting, they observed that "When it goes flying over birds . . . it does not strike them with its wings; it only tries to seize them with its talons" until the prey "can no longer fly," a practice common to eagles who generally use talons to hunt. If the *cuauhtlohtli* "succeeds in catching one, it at once clutches [the prey] by the breast then it pierces its throat; it drinks its blood, consumes it all. It does not spill a drop of the blood." (Like falcons, their method of killing is to use their beak.) When ready to consume its catch, the bird "plucks out the bird's feathers." In this manner, the bird eats three times daily, "first before the sun has risen; second, at midday third when the sun has set." Regarding their parenting style, the birds, who bear "only two young," rear them "in inaccessible places," nesting in the "openings of the crags." Regarding their capture, the hunters find their nesting places and there "place a duck" and "in its breast cage," they "conceal a snare, though some only wrap the snare around it."[113]

Embedded near the end of the entry is a different sort of detail. The authors wrote, "And this falcon gives life to Uitzilopochtli because, they said, these falcons, when they eat three times day, as it were give drink to the sun (*tonatiuh*); because when they drink blood, they consume it all." Although brief, this text is dense with imagery and associations. With the reference to the deity Huitzilopochtli and the sun, it evokes the migration story of the Mexica and the sun's role as an apex predator, who like the eagles with whom it is identified, feeds on blood (see fig. 7.3). It also suggests the ritual practice of feeding the sun with quail multiple times throughout the day. Although the authors distance themselves slightly from the content by including what Paul Haemig has characterized as the warning phrase "they said," they refrain from condemning ritual practices, unlike several entries in the 1565 draft.[114]

In the left column, an abbreviated Spanish "translation" precedes the images. This translation describes the bird's manner of piercing the throat and plucking the feathers of prey and notes that "the males and females go separately and the female is larger and the better hunter," omitting information about the sun and Huitzilopochtli entirely. The Spanish-language silence is not surprising.[115] Perhaps Sahagún made the translation, or perhaps the Nahua scholars produced the abbreviated and anodyne Spanish to distract from the inflammatory and heterodox content of the Nahuatl text.

If the Spanish "translation" removes the potentially incendiary information in the Nahuatl text, the pictorial version intensifies and exceeds these provocations. No pictorial equivalent of a "warning phrase" appears. Instead, the images even more potently connect the behavior of these falcons to practices and beliefs underlying predation and familiarization. The images appearing on the second page of the entry are arranged in a vertical column of three panels (fig. 11.4). The intentionality of the illustrator is demonstrated by the fact that the image includes a whited-out portion. In the upper panel, a raptor seizes a smaller bird, the latter surrounded by falling feathers of green and red hues. In the middle panel a mother bird nests with her two young ones in a remote crag. In the bottom panel, a figure with a man's body and a hummingbird head offers a human heart to the *cuauhtlohtli* in the sky above him. Like the *tonalamatl* cosmogramic tradition that likely inspired them, these images can be read in multiple ways. The upper and middle panels correspond closely to the naturalistic description in the text: The top panel depicts *cuauhtlohtli*'s mode of catching prey with talons and plucking them of their feathers, and the middle one shows the female tending to her young.

Other interpretations are possible. The three panels also allude to the foundation story of Tenochtitlan. The middle panel recalls Mexica origins in the cave of Chicomoztoc amid the rocky, austere landscape associated with these northern biomes. The bottom panel suggests the casting of Copil's heart that will give rise to the nopal cactus, and Huitzilopochtli's promise to the Mexica's ancestors that they will know where to settle when the eagle bird alights on the cactus.[116] The upper panel depicts the moment when Mexica knew they had found the place to found Tenochtitlan: Although the nopal cactus is absent, the image, like other colonial-era Mexica cosmograms, shows a bird of the North and the West eviscerating colorfully plumed birds of the East and the South, some painted the blue-green of the quetzal, and others red, suggestive of macaws or roseate spoonbill.

The image also conveys the universality of familiarization: everything that provides food must also be fed. The identities of the figures in the bottom panel are, perhaps purposefully, ambiguous.[117] The *cuauhtlohtli* can be read as a solar entity (*tonatiuh*)—as the text itself suggests as well as the pictorial imagery of the *tonalamatl* and other postclassic artifacts that depict the sun as an eagle. The hummingbird-man might represent a *tlamacazqui*, one of the "priests" who wore the garb of the deities they served, as seen in the Borgia cosmogram (figs. 6.1, 6.2, 6.3, 6.4). If this is the case, this panel depicts a priest feeding a human heart to Huitzilopochtli, in his solar incarnation

aue que a caçado primero la
pela por aquel lugar donde
la ade comer.

macivi imimpan mocacanaoa,
amo ic qujnviteguj inj amatla
pal: çan iztitica qujn motzo
loznegui. Auh in iehoantin toto
me: aocmo vel patlanj, mpatla
njzneguj: aocmo vel vi, ca cha
chapanti vetzi. Auh in tlacen
totl velcaci: çan njman iclpa,
quj motzol tzitzqujia: njmâ guj
quechcotonja, catli injezço, vel
guj tlamja; amo tle cana itla
guj chipinja, in oztli. Auh inj
quac veltlaqua: achtopa guj
vi vitla, inhivio tutotl: in cen
huytl expan tlaqua. Injcceppa
iguac in aiamo valqujça, ona
tiuh. Injc vppa: nepantla to
tiuh. Injc expa: iguac in onca
lac tonatiuh, mopilhoatia:
ovican, texcalcamac in moch
pa: çan vnteme nj pilhoan
oan michoatl tleatli: guj
iollotlaia in vitzilobuchtli, ip
pa caguj tvaia: in iehoantin
tlo tlhotin, injc espa tlaqua
in cemjlhujtl: iuh qujn ma

Figure 11.4 *Cuauhtlotli* (raptor) in Florentine Codex, bk. 11, fol. 48r, ca. 1575–1577, Biblioteca Medicea Laurenziana, Florence, Med. Palat. 220, c. 199v. Reproduction used by permission of the Ministry for Heritage and Cultural Archives. All rights reserved.

and as the deity who encouraged the Mexica to wage war against other communities, thereby ensuring the sun a constant supply of food. It resembles, in content if not style, the Codex Borgia image depicting the coyote-skeletal *tlamacazqui* feeding a blood offering to the sun and the earth (fig. I.2). Like those in the Borgia *tonalamatl*, the image in book II conveys the essence of familiarization: the sun, the most apex of predators, must be fed blood and hearts, sustenance that enables it to feed the crops on which people subsist.

~

FOR THE INDIGENOUS peoples of Mesoamerica, hunting, taming and spiritual practice were commingled. Precise understanding of animal behavior and exquisitely detailed apprehension of bodily appearance were highly valued by the inhabitants of Mesoamerica before and after the European invasions. These faculties linked hunting and taming practices to the ritual use of feathers, skins, and pelts. Europeans would learn from these practices of observation and description in ways that would transform their own natural history traditions. This fact should not blind us to their origins in Indigenous America. European scholars and researchers—most notably Hernández and the northern European naturalists conventionally associated with "modern" zoology who followed him—stripped away anything they considered "fabulous." But the Tlatelolco scholars saw no reason to do so. Their story is as integral to modern natural history as those of Hernández and his successors.

One of the most significant legacies of the "Historiae animalium" was its construction of the modern naturalist. It modeled the tasks of the naturalist: identifying animal species, closely observing and describing appearances and behaviors, collecting specimens, and drawing from life. The labor and knowledge that made this zoological compendium possible was primarily Indigenous: the knowledge of hunters, tamers, *atlaca* and *amanteca* (featherworkers)— whose practices were conditioned by predation and familiarization—fills the pages. It was the Nahua Tlatelolco scholars and artists who creatively entangled the European genre of natural history and specimen drawing with the knowledge produced by those who worked directly with other species. The "Historiae animalium" was, of course, also the work of Francisco Hernández. His anxieties about Native idolatry and his commitment to colonial social hierarchies also left their mark on his opus. The Spanish *proto-médico* ensured that entries were disenchanted: they were, mostly, purified of "superstitious" and "childish" beliefs, resulting in text that not only had less ritual content than the *Florentine Codex* but also lacked the fantastical creatures that had characterized classical and medieval European works. Hernández disavowed Indigenous contributions: despite his enormous—and occasionally acknowledged—dependence on this expertise, he equated the exemplary naturalist with himself, an elite European man. Perhaps by realizing the entangled Indigenous and colonial origins of the modern biological sciences, we can appreciate their roots in ontologies that have long recognized the multiplicity and capacities of the inhabitants with whom people share the earth.

Epilogue

The history unveiled in this book lives with us in the present.

It is in the world's approximately 33 billion chickens (518 million in the United States in 2020) and 785 million pigs (75 million in the United States in 2021) raised to become food, the vast majority of whom live their short, torturously confined, antibiotic-pumped lives in factory farms.[1] It is in the hundreds of thousands of pigs and more than 2 million chickens who did not become food but were killed by "mass extermination methods" (gassing or other forms of asphyxiation) because of "supply chain blockages" and avian flu outbreaks in the United States in 2020 and 2021.[2] It is in the 4,700 US slaughterhouses that, in 2019, discharged polluted water into waterways, including the Chesapeake Bay, and the 6,000 diseased pig carcasses found in tributaries of the Huangpu River in China in 2013.[3] It is the staggering loss of biodiversity—1 million or so species threatened with extinction because of "human actions."[4] It is in the militarized dogs deployed against protesters at the Standing Rock Indian Reservation and the mounted Border Patrol agents menacing Haitian asylum seekers on the US-Mexican border.[5] It is in the laborers, overwhelmingly BIPOC (Black, Indigenous, and people of color), who toil in meat packing plants and industrial chicken farms and whose immigration status is used by industrial meat companies to put profits above basic safety, as reflected most recently in their disproportionately high death toll during the COVID-19 pandemic.[6] It is in the deforestation of the Amazon fueled by people the world over who desire to eat the flesh and fat of cows—a desire inflamed by multinational agribusiness, whose ability to manage international supply chains and flout local restrictions on land use ensures cheap "meat."[7]

For many readers, the "industrial animals" of today's enormous feedlots, meat packing companies, and global supply chains might seem like a radical departure from the livestock operations described in this book. In explaining the emergence of industrial animality, scholars—and concerned consumers and activists—tend to focus on developments in the past two hundred years, such as the emergence of industrial slaughterhouses in nineteenth-century America, or in the past sixty years, such as corporate restructuring in the chicken industry in the 1950s and 1960s that was emulated by meatpackers. These policies enabled corporate welfare schemes, environmental and labor deregulation, and even the decimation of working-class communities as a result of the 2008 recession.[8] Nevertheless, when I read the evocative and disturbing ethnographies of contemporary industrial animal farming in Timothy Pachirat's *Every Twelve Seconds* and Alex Blanchette's *Porkopolis,* it was the critical continuities that most struck me. When I read about the "ongoing conflict between the messiness of mass killing and a society's—our society's—demand for a cheap, steady supply of physically and morally sterile meat fabricated under socially invisible conditions,"[9] I heard the citizens of Castilian cities petitioning the Crown in the fifteenth century to separate and remove slaughtering operations outside of residential neighborhoods because they do not want to hear the cries of animals facing death or slog through mud coursing with blood. When I read of the "increasingly fine-grained division of labor across the porcine life and death cycle," I think of the proliferating number of occupations that emerged in the early modern slaughterhouse.[10] When I read of "postdeath ventures that derive value from the slaughterhouse's biological matter beyond meat in the form of bones, feces, fat, livers, lungs" and the impossibility of being alive today and not "touching dead traces of industrial pigs," I think of the way that the components of cow and pig carcasses became not only meat but medicine, wheel grease, animal feed, shoes, and more.[11] Putting industrial livestock farming in a longer time frame helps us stop seeing preindustrial husbandry through a romantic haze about the "grass-fed," "pastured" cows and sheep of old, the pig and chicken raised at home. It overturns false assumptions about the past ubiquity of the "small farmer" who "nurtures an animal across its entire life-and death course."[12] When I read about the supply chains that link US consumers to deforestation in the Amazon and the seizure of Indigenous lands and the conditions for workers in meat processing plants (American consumers bought 320 million pounds of cow flesh in 2021 linked to the deforestation of an area the size of Connecticut that year),[13] I think of early modern global trade in hides and the ranching conquistadores who enslaved Indigenous and Black people to feed and slaughter pigs and cows.

The present-day industrial animal is as much the logical culmination of processes that date to much earlier periods in European and Atlantic history, as they are in capitalist expansion of the past two hundred years. The conditions that made it possible for people to systemically feed animals in order to eat and wear them included the denial of subjectivity to the majority of nonhuman animals living in their midst, those known as *ganado*, cattle, and livestock. The anomalous understanding of human singularity and exceptionalism found in Genesis and other ancient texts reflected as much as caused livestock husbandry. The history of livestock expansion in the Americas is also inextricably bound with the most extreme forms of dispossession— enslavement, land expropriation, ecological destruction, and massacre—that anticipated and originated the forms of dispossession that continue into the present. The history of extractivism—a root cause of climate change—cannot be disentangled from livestock husbandry as it was *reinvented* in colonial America.

~

THIS HISTORY IS cause for hope as well as grief.

This history is also present in the struggle of Indigenous environmental activists and their allies against agribusiness and other extractivist endeavors. I read of Liz Chicaje Churay, a leader of the Indigenous Bora community of Loreto, Peru, who, since age 16, has worked to defend ancestral territory from illegal logging and mining; of the Guajajara "Guardians of the Forests," who persist in a lethal struggle to keep their reserve Araribóia in Brazil safe from illegal logging and animal poachers; and of Anabela Carlón Flores, a Yaqui lawyer who has fought against a gas pipeline that a transnational company is attempting to build through her community's territory in Sonora, Mexico, without their consent.[14] These examples make me think of the Indigenous people who sought to protect plants and animals, as well as traditions and communities, from livestock extractivism in the early modern period. I'm reminded of those who burned down ranches, hunted cattle, litigated in court against *conquistador* ranchers, moved their communities into mountainous or forested terrain that deterred horse-riding invaders, or incorporated European domesticated animals into traditional processes. Like resisters in the past, activists today frequently pay with their lives, as was the case with Lenca activist Berta Cáceres in Honduras and forty-two members of Guajajara who were killed between 2000 and 2018—a microcosm of the violence faced by Indigenous environmentalist activists throughout Latin America, whose killers often have links to US agribusiness.[15] The preservation—and repossession—of Indigenous lands not only benefits the people who live there: in the Amazon, Indigenous lands are "effective buffers against tropical deforestation," and "indigenous peoples and local communities have impeded deforestation and associated greenhouse gas emissions."[16] In the words of Dakota scholar Kim Tallbear, when Indigenous activists seek to rescue forests and rivers from extractive projects, they "call the settler state to account for its failures at kin-making here, with both humans and non-humans."[17] Similarly, Brazilian Indigenous leader and environmentalist Ailton Krenak makes explicit the connection between recognizing the subjectivities of myriad elements—birds, rivers, mountains, trees, earth itself—with struggle to stop degradation of the planet.[18] Human survival requires recognizing other-than-human kin.

This history is also present in the ever-growing body of scientific scholarship that details and explains the awesome sensory, cognitive, and emotional capacities of nonhuman animals.[19] It is in the studies, for instance, of marine biologists who have begun to decode the high-pitched vocalizations that manatees make to talk to each other,[20] of entomologists that show how forms of social organization can be transmitted among different ant species,[21] of evolutionary biologists who have demonstrated the importance birds place on scent,[22] and of Dog Genome project researchers who have proposed that dogs' ability to comprehend human pointing—essential to their "social intelligence"—is a genetic trait.[23] When I read about this research, I think of the Castilian hunter, lying on his stomach in Extremadura, watching a sow cooling herself in a mud bath or feasting on stork's nest grass, or the Kalinago man, perched on a boulder in careful silence, listening for fish. I recall the Nahua observer who watched a jaguar yawn, stir, shake; lick his paw; and then crouch, spring, and fly through the air. I think of the Amazonian women who deeply understood psittacid needs and behavior and so knew how to care for and raise chicks, or the ocelot who performed alongside "Eve" and "Adam" in an Easter performance in colonial Tlaxcala.

This history is also in the singular relationships I have experienced with my canine companions. My sweet Lilly (2003–2019), a gorgeous wolfy black and tan shepherd with piercing ice-blue eyes, gave me so much, including the idea for this book. She joined and protected me on countless hikes and runs; she accompanied me for even more hours, sitting next to me as I wrote on café patios or my living room couch. Her calm, accepting presence soothed when I was sad, and her ability to find pleasure inspired, even when she suffered with intense bodily pain. She still visits me in dreams. Iggy, a gravity-defying border-colliesh pup with a slightly upturned snout and the softest brindle coat, came into my life in April 2021. His labor-intensive transformation from a tiny, antic furball into an attentive, constant, and snuggly companion has taken place alongside—and made tolerable—the labor-intensive transformation of a feral manuscript into this book. The joy, healing, and contentment I have found in these attachments make me think of the brave, self-emancipated man on Hispaniola and his three affectionate and fierce companion pigs (who also inspired this book); the Salamanca clergyman and his astoundingly intelligent and devoted dog Bruto; and the Tupinamba woman and her beloved, talkative macaw, among so many others who have found profound meaning in the reciprocal care they experienced with animals. While each of these relationships is singular and unreplicable, they all came about because the human and nonhuman animals knew to recognize, respect, and cherish each other's personhood.

~

THE CONTEMPORARY INDUSTRIAL and related forms of extractivist violence toward animals has much deeper roots than many have realized, which may seem cause for even greater despair than what is already present for many who reckon with apocalyptic environmental degradation. But I think otherwise. One of the most powerful potentialities of knowing history is its capacity to liberate our imaginations from the false idea that what we are used to is what is natural. In the words of Krenak, "Our adherence to a fixed idea that the globe has always been this way and humanity has always related to it the way it does now is the deepest mark the Anthropocene has left." Although five hundred years is a long time in relationship to a human lifetime, it is still a blink in relationship to our species' history. This frame of five centuries allows us to see that colonial extractivism is a relatively recent development that has coexisted with other modes of interaction. Our current ideas and practices around objectifying nonhuman beings are a historical and, therefore, contingent development; we can see that it is our choice to end that practice. Nothing is natural or inevitable about seeing our planet, its soils, its waterways, and its atmosphere as a "resource" to be pillaged and exhausted to depletion and then used as a dumping ground.

It is easy to underestimate the powerful, critical, essential work of loving nonhuman kin. In fact, the underestimation is itself symptomatic of the problem. Valuing our caring, reciprocal relationships with other kinds of beings is reason to rejoice, and they present a reserve of possibility for finding new ways to be in harmony in the world. Being in the presence of wild animals and caring for those animal companions who live in our houses are pleasures. As such, they may be the strongest antidotes to extractivism. The contagious joy of birdsong, the thrill of seeing a coyote traipse across urban turf or a heron standing with stillness in a city creek, the comfort of nestling with a furry body, the harmony of synchronous walking with a happy dog—these experiences all teach us about our world, if we allow them. They reveal the falsity of the notion that humans can flourish if they look out only for their own interests. They can help us reject the ubiquitous—although not hegemonic—logic of alienation, the destructive magical thinking that there is no cost to approaching subjects, "nature," as things. If we take in the teachings of these experiences, we can expand the circle of subjects worthy of our care.

ABBREVIATIONS

NOTES

ACKNOWLEDGMENTS

INDEX

Abbreviations

Archives and Libraries

AGI	Archivo General de Indias, Seville
AGS	Archivo General de Simancas, Simancas
AHN	Archivo Histórico Nacional, Madrid and Toledo
AMS	Archivo Municipal de Sevilla, Seville
ARCHV	Archivo de la Real Chancillería de Valladolid, Valladolid
BML	Biblioteca Medicea Laurenziana, Florence
BNE	Biblioteca Nacional de España, Madrid
JCB	John Carter Brown Library, Providence, R.I.
LC	Library of Congress, Washington, D.C.
RAH	Real Academia de la Historia, Madrid
RGS	Registro del Sello de Corte

Notes

Introduction

1   Genesis 1:26, King James Version.

2   Gerónimo de Mendieta, *Historia eclesiástica indiana* (Mexico City: Cien de México, 1997), 186.

3   Ramón Pané, *An Account of the Antiquities of the Indians,* ed. José Juan Arrom and trans. Susan Griswold (Durham, NC: Duke University Press, 1999), 6–8.

4   A preliminary conceptualization of modes of interaction appears in Marcy Norton, "Going to the Birds: Animals as Things and Beings in Early Modernity," in *Early Modern Things: Objects and Their Histories, 1500–1800,* ed. Paula Findlen, 53–83 (London: Routledge, 2012); Marcy Norton, "The Chicken or the *Iegue:* Human-Animal Relationships and the Columbian Exchange," *American Historical Review* 120, no. 1 (2015): 28–60.

5   For predation, see, Eduardo Viveiros de Castro, *From the Enemy's Point of View: Humanity and Divinity in an Amazonian Society,* trans. Catherine V. Howard (Chicago: University of Chicago Press, 1992); Philippe Descola, *In the Society of Nature: A Native Ecology in Amazonia,* trans. Nora Scott (Cambridge: Cambridge University Press, 1994); Carlos Fausto, "Of Enemies and Pets: Warfare and Shamanism in Amazonia," trans. David Rodgers, *American Ethnologist* 26, no. 4 (1999): 933–956. For taming and familiarization, see, Ellen B. Basso, *The Kalapalo Indians of Central Brazil* (New York: Holt, Rinehart, & Winston, 1973), 18–23; Philippe Erikson, "De l'apprivoisement à l'approvisionnement: Chasse, alliance et familiarisation en Amazonie amériendienne," *Techniques & Culture* 9 (1987): 105–140; Aparecida Vilaça, "Making Kin Out of Others in Amazonia," *Journal of the Royal Anthropological Institute* 8, no. 2 (2002): 347–365.

6   Viveiros de Castro, *From the Enemy's Point of View.*

7   Guilhem Olivier, *Cacería, sacrificio y poder en Mesoamérica* (Mexico City: Fondo de Cultura Económica, 2015).

8   On dogs' arrival into the Americas and possible role in assisting Paleoindians during hunts, see Angela Perri et al., "New Evidence of the Earliest Domestic

Dogs in the Americas," *American Antiquity* 84, no. 1 (January 2019): 68–87. On the absence of dogs in certain regions at the time of contact, see Peter W. Stahl, "Early Dogs and Endemic South American Canids of the Spanish Main," *Journal of Anthropological Research* 69, no. 4 (December 1, 2013): 515–533.

9   Raymond Breton, *Dictionaire caraibe-françois* (Auxerre: Gilles Bouquet, 1665), 290; Raymond Breton, *Dictionaire françois-caraibe* (Auxerre: Gilles Bouquet, 1666), 2:19, 20.

10   Leonardo López Luján and Guilhem Olivier, *El sacrificio humano en la tradición religiosa Mesoamericana* (Mexico City: Instituto Nacional de Antropología e Historia, 2010); Eduardo Matos Moctezuma, *Life and Death in the Templo Mayor*, trans. B. R. Ortíz de Montellano and T. Ortíz de Montellano (Niwot: University Press of Colorado, 1995).

11   On the origins and development of this myth, see Kay Anderson, "A Walk on the Wild Side: A Critical Geography of Domestication," *Progress in Human Geography* 21, no. 4 (1997): 463–485; Tim Ingold, "From Trust to Domination: An Alternative History of Human-Animal Relations," in *Animals and Human Society*, ed. Aubrey Manning and James A. Serpell, 1–22 (London: Routledge, 1994).

12   Juan López de Palacios Rubios, *De las islas del Mar Océano*, trans. Agustín Millares Carlo (Mexico City: Fondo de Cultura Económica, 1954), 9.

13   Juan Ginés de Sepúlveda, *Democrates segundo*, trans. Angel Losada (Madrid: Consejo Superior de Investigaciones Científicas, 1951), 75–78, 81–84. See also Anthony Pagden, "Dispossessing the Barbarian: Rights and Property in Spanish America," in *Spanish Imperialism and the Political Imagination: Studies in European and Spanish-American Social and Political Theory 1513–1830* (New Haven, CT: Yale University Press, 1990), 13–36.

14   Nathaniel Shaler, *Domesticated Animals* (London: Smith, Elder, 1896) quoted in Anderson, "Walk on the Wild Side," 467.

15   Alfred W. Crosby, *The Columbian Exchange: Biological and Cultural Consequences of 1492*, 30th anniversary ed. (Westport, CT: Praeger, 2003), 21, 30, 74; Alfred W. Crosby, *Ecological Imperialism: The Biological Expansion of Europe, 900–1900* (Cambridge: Cambridge University Press, 1986), 74–82.

16   Jared Diamond, *Guns, Germs, and Steel: The Fates of Human Societies* (New York: W. W. Norton, 1997), 161–167, 163.

17   On relativizing Western concepts and "ontologies," see Descola, *In the Society of Nature* and Dipesh Chakrabarty, *Provincializing Europe: Postcolonial Thought and Historical Difference* (Princeton, NJ: Princeton University Press, 2000).

18   As an approach, entangled history attends "to the permeability of borders," "negotiations of power in colonial relations," "intercultural processes," and "the inextricability of material and symbolic factors," Ralph Bauer and Marcy Norton, "Entangled Trajectories: Indigenous and European Histories," *Colonial Latin American Review* 26, no. 1 (2017): 1–17, 3. See also Marcy Norton, *Sacred Gifts, Profane*

Pleasures: A History of Tobacco and Chocolate in the Atlantic World (Ithaca: Cornell University Press, 2008); Marcy Norton, "Subaltern Technologies and Early Modernity in the Atlantic World," *Colonial Latin American Review* 26, no. 1 (2017): 18–38.

19   Norton, "Subaltern Technologies," 22–25.

20   Although a comprehensive study of animals and the Black Atlantic is beyond the scope of this book, numerous Black people, some enslaved and some free, appear in these pages. For scholarship on different facets of African diaspora and human-animal interactions in the Atlantic world, see Zakiyyah Iman Jackson, *Becoming Human: Matter and Meaning in an Antiblack World* (New York: New York University Press, 2020); Andrew Sluyter, *Black Ranching Frontiers: African Cattle Herders of the Atlantic World, 1500–1900* (New Haven, CT: Yale University Press, 2012); Christopher Michael Blakley, *Enslaved People and Animals in the British Atlantic World* (Baton Rouge: Louisiana State University Press, 2023); Lauren (Robin) Derby, *Bêtes Noires: Sorcery as History in the Haitian-Dominican Borderlands* (Durham, NC: Duke University Press, forthcoming).

21   On the concept of dispossession as applied to Latin America, see María Josefina Saldaña-Portillo, *Indian Given: Racial Geographies across Mexico and the United States* (Durham: Duke University Press, 2016).

22   My understanding of extractivism in colonial Latin America has been particularly influenced by Vera S. Candiani, *Dreaming of Dry Land: Environmental Transformation in Colonial Mexico City* (Stanford, CA: Stanford University Press, 2014); Molly A. Warsh, *American Baroque: Pearls and the Nature of Empire, 1492–1700* (Chapel Hill: University of North Carolina Press, 2018); Maristella Svampa, *Neo-Extractivism in Latin America: Socio-Environmental Conflicts, the Territorial Turn, and New Political Narratives* (Cambridge: Cambridge University Press, 2019), 8; Gabriel de Avilez Rocha, "The Pinzones and the Coup of the *Acedares*: Fishing and Colonization in the Fifteenth-Century Atlantic," *Colonial Latin American Review* 28, no. 4 (2019): 427–449. On the relationship between livestock husbandry and colonialism, see François Chevalier, *Land and Society in Colonial Mexico: The Great Hacienda* (Berkeley: University of California Press, 1963); Elinor G. K. Melville, *A Plague of Sheep: Environmental Consequences of the Conquest of Mexico* (Cambridge: Cambridge University Press, 1994); Maria de los Angeles Romero Frizzi, *Economía y vida de los españoles en la Mixteca Alta, 1519–1720* (Mexico City: Instituto Nacional de Antropología e Historia, 1990); Virginia DeJohn Anderson, *Creatures of Empire: How Domestic Animals Transformed Early America* (Oxford: Oxford University Press, 2004); Justo Lucas del Río Moreno, *Ganadería, plantaciones y comercio azucarero antillano* (Santo Domingo, Dominican Republic: Academia Dominicana de la Historia, 2012).

23   Carol J. Adams, *The Sexual Politics of Meat: A Feminist-Vegetarian Critical Theory*, Bloomsbury Revelations ed. (New York: Bloomsbury Academic, 2015 [1990]); William Cronon, *Nature's Metropolis: Chicago and the Great West* (New York: W. W. Norton, 1991); Richard W. Bulliet, *Hunters, Herders, and Hamburgers: The Past and Future of Human-Animal Relationships* (New York: Columbia University Press,

2005); Robert W. Wilcox and Shawn Van Ausdal, "Hoofprints: Cattle Ranching and Land Transformation," in *A Living Past: Environmental Histories of Modern Latin America,* ed. John Soluri, Claudia Leal, and José Augusto Pádua (New York: Berghahn Books, 2018); Josh Berson, *The Meat Question: Animals, Humans, and the Deep History of Food* (Cambridge, MA: MIT Press, 2019).

24   Zoe Todd, "Indigenizing the Anthropocene," in *Art in the Anthropocene: Encounters among Aesthetics, Politics, Environment and Epistemology,* ed. Heather Davis and Etienne Turpin (London: Open Humanities Press, 2015), 241–254; Simon L. Lewis and Mark A. Maslin, "Defining the Anthropocene," *Nature* 519, no. 7542 (2015): 171–180.

25   For Book 11 as a repository of Indigenous knowledge, see, among others, Alfredo López Austin, Molly Bassett, Iris Montero Sobrevilla, Kelly McDonough, cited in Chaps. 6 and 11. For conceptualizing Indigenous knowledge in relation to Western science, see Maya Lorena Pérez Ruiz y Arturo Argueta Villamar, "Saberes indígenas y dialogo intercultural," *Cultura y representaciones sociales* 5, no. 10 (2011): 31–56; Robin Wall Kimmerer, *Braiding Sweetgrass: Indigenous Wisdom, Scientific Knowledge and the Teachings of Plants* (Minneapolis: Milkweed Editions, 2013); Melissa K. Nelson and Daniel Shilling, ed. *Traditional Ecological Knowledge: Learning from Indigenous Practices for Environmental Sustainability* (Cambridge: Cambridge University Press, 2018).

26   On Indigenous knowledge and Western science as it relates to Hernández' project, see José María López Piñero and José Pardo Tomás, *La influencia de Francisco Hernández (1512–1587) en la constitución de la botánica y la* materia médica *modernas* (Valencia: Universitat de València, 1996); chapters by Jaime Marroquín and Marcy Norton in *Translating Nature: Cross-Cultural Histories of Early Modern Science,* ed. Ralph Bauer and Jaime Marroquín Arredondo (Philadelphia: University of Pennsylvania Press, 2019); Juan Pimentel, *Fantasmas de la ciencia española* (Madrid: Marcial Pons Historia, 2020). See also Chap. 11.

27   See, for instance, Marc Bekoff, *Minding Animals: Awareness, Emotions, and Heart* (New York: Oxford University Press, 2002).

28   Cary Wolfe, "Flesh and Finitude: Thinking Animals in (Post)Humanist Philosophy," *SubStance* 37, no. 3 (2008): 8–36, 8.

29   Donna J. Haraway, *When Species Meet* (Minneapolis: University of Minnesota Press, 2007), 250.

30   Erica Fudge, *Renaissance Beasts: Of Animals, Humans, and Other Wonderful Creatures* (Urbana: University of Illinois Press, 2004), 3.

31   Martha Few and Zeb Tortorici, eds., *Centering Animals in Latin American History* (Durham, NC: Duke University Press, 2013); Abel A. Alves, *The Animals of Spain: An Introduction to Imperial Perceptions and Human Interaction with Other Animals, 1492–1826* (Boston: Brill, 2011).

32   Jacques Derrida, "The Animal That Therefore I Am (More to Follow)," *Critical Inquiry* 28, no. 2 (2002): 369–418.

33   See, for instance, Davi Kopenawa, *The Falling Sky: Words of a Yanomami Shaman*, ed. Bruce Albert and trans. Nicholas Elliott and Alison Dundy (Cambridge, MA: Harvard University Press, 2013); Kimmerer, *Braiding Sweetgrass*; Todd, "Indigenizing the Anthropocene."

34   Michel Foucault, "The Technology of the Self," in *Speaking the Truth about Oneself*, trans. Daniel Louis Wyche and ed. Henri-Paul Fruchaud and Daniele Lorenzini, 1–14 (Chicago: University of Chicago Press, 2021), 14; Lorraine Daston and Peter Galison, *Objectivity* (New York: Zone Books, 2007).

35   Cora Diamond, "Eating Meat and Eating People," *Philosophy* 53, no. 206 (1978): 465–479, 470.

36   Haraway, *When Species Meet*, 16, 23.

37   Maurice Merleau-Ponty is a key theorist of embodied subjectivity. See Merleau-Ponty, *Phenomenology of Perception*, trans. Colin Smith (London: Routledge, 1995).

38   Johannes Fabian, *Time and Other: How Anthropology Makes Its Object* (New York: Columbia University Press, 1983).

39   Vilaça, "Making Kin," 348; Joanna Overing and Alan Passes, *The Anthropology of Love and Anger: The Aesthetics of Conviviality in Native Amazonia* (London: Routledge, 2002).

40   Anna Roosevelt, ed., *Amazonian Indians from Prehistory to the Present: Anthropological Perspectives* (Tucson: University of Arizona Press, 1994); Carlos Fausto and Michael Heckenberger, eds., *Time and Memory in Indigenous Amazonia: Anthropological Perspectives* (Gainesville: University Press of Florida, 2007).

41   John M. Monteiro, "Indigenous Histories in Colonial Brazil," in *The Oxford Handbook of Borderlands of the Iberian World*, ed. Danna A. Levin Rojo and Cynthia Radding (New York: Oxford University Press, 2019).

42   David J. Weber, *Bárbaros: Spaniards and Their Savages in the Age of Enlightenment* (New Haven, CT: Yale University Press, 2008); Heather F. Roller, *Contact Strategies: Histories of Native Autonomy in Brazil* (Stanford, CA: Stanford University Press, 2021); Tessa Murphy, *The Creole Archipelago: Race and Borders in the Colonial Caribbean* (Philadelphia: University of Pennsylvania Press, 2021).

43   "Relation de l'île de Guadeloupe," in *Les Caraïbes. La Guadeloupe, 1635–1656*, ed. Joseph Rennard, 23–90 (Paris: G. Ficker, 1929), 48.

44   Several generations of scholars have contributed to this shift away from the conquest paradigm. Their work on New Spain is based on intensive archival research, Native-language documents, and/or pictorial sources made by Indigenous people. It includes the foundational work of Ángel M. Garibay, Miguel León Portilla, Alfredo López Austin, Luis Reyes, Charles Gibson, Nancy Farriss, James Lockhart, and Maarten Jansen and research from a more recent cohort that includes Mexico-based María Castañeda de la Paz, Michel R. Oudijk, Ethelia Ruiz Medrano, and Sebastián van Doesburg, and outside of Mexico, Laura Matthew, Barbara Mundy, Matthew Restall, Justyna Olko, Pete Sigal, Lisa Sousa, Kevin

Terraciano, Camilla Townsend, and Yanna Yannakakis. Citations to their work can be found in Chaps. 5, 6, 7, and 11.

1. Hunting Subjects

1   Suzanne Jablonski, "Acts of Violence: Rubens and the Hunt" (PhD diss., University of California, Berkeley, 2004).

2   Thomas T. Allsen, *The Royal Hunt in Eurasian History* (Philadelphia: University of Pennsylvania Press, 2006); José Manuel Fradejas Rueda, "Introduction," in *Textos clásicos de cetrería, montería y caza,* ed. José Manuel Fradejas Rueda, CD-ROM (Madrid: Fundación Histórica Tavera, 1999); José Ignacio Ortega Cervigón, "La funcionalidad política de la nobleza castellana: el oficio de Montero Mayor durante el siglo XV," *Historia, instituciones, documentos* 30 (2003): 399–428; J. B. Owens, "Diana at the Bar: Hunting, Aristocrats, and the Law in Renaissance Castile," *Sixteenth Century Journal* 8, no. 1 (1977): 17–35; Marcy Norton, "Going to the Birds: Animals as Things and Beings in Early Modernity," in *Early Modern Things: Objects and Their Histories, 1500–1800,* ed. Paula Findlen, 53–83 (London: Routledge, 2012), 54–58; Susan Crane, *Animal Encounters: Contacts and Concepts in Medieval Britain* (University of Pennsylvania Press, 2013), 101–199; Philippe Salvadori, *La Chasse sous L'ancien Régime* (Paris: Fayard, 1996); Emma Griffin, *Blood Sport: Hunting in Britain since 1066* (New Haven, CT: Yale University Press, 2007); Roger B. Manning, *Hunters and Poachers: A Social and Cultural History of Unlawful Hunting in England, 1485–1640* (Oxford: Clarendon, 1993); John Cummins, *The Hound and the Hawk: The Art of Medieval Hunting* (New York: St. Martin's, 1988).

3   Clifford Geertz, "Deep Play: Notes on the Balinese Cock Fight," in *The Interpretation of Cultures* (New York: Basic Books, 1973), 412–453. Susan Crane has written that the "cultural performance, game, and ritual overlap and co-inform hunting: no single category perfectly fits and accounts for it," 102.

4   Crane, *Animal Encounters,* 103; Norton, "Going to the Birds," 55.

5   Keith Thomas, *Man and the Natural World: Changing Attitudes in England, 1500–1800* (London: Allen Lane, 1983), 243, 41.

6   I first conceptualized hunting as a mode of interaction that facilitated Europeans' recognition of other animals' subjectivity in Norton, "Going to the Birds," 54–58 and "Animal (Spain)" in *Lexikon of the Hispanic Baroque: Transatlantic Exchange and Transformation,* eds. Evonne Levy and Kenneth Mills, 17–19 (Austin: University of Texas Press, 2014).

7   Karen Raber, *Animal Bodies, Renaissance Culture,* Haney Foundation Series (Philadelphia: University of Pennsylvania Press, 2013), 10–11; Erica Fudge, *Brutal Reasoning: Animals, Rationality, and Humanity in Early Modern England* (Ithaca, NY: Cornell University Press, 2006). Among the other important studies that investigate these issues are Bruce Thomas Boehrer, *Animal Characters: Nonhuman Beings in Early Modern Literature* (Philadelphia: University of Pennsylvania Press, 2010); Abel A. Alves, *The Animals of Spain: An Introduction to Imperial Perceptions and*

Human Interaction with Other Animals, 1492–1826 (Boston: Brill, 2011); John Beusterien, *Canines in Cervantes and Velázquez: An Animal Studies Reading of Early Modern Spain* (Farnham, Surrey: Ashgate, 2013); Steven Wagschal, *Minding Animals in the Old and New Worlds: A Cognitive Historical Analysis* (Toronto: University of Toronto Press, 2018).

8   The following account is based on Juan Mateos, *Origen y dignidad de la caça* (Madrid: Fran[cis]co Martinez, 1634), fols. 7v–9v, 61r–64v.

9   On the *concierto,* see Mateos, *Origen,* fols. 28r, 35r; Cummins, *Hound and Hawk.*

10   Alonso Martínez de Espinar, *Arte de ballestería y montería* (Madrid: Imprenta Real, 1644), fol. 56v.

11   Martínez de Espinar, *Arte.*

12   On different kinds of hunting dogs, Beusterien, *Canines,* 60–65, 87–99.

13   Mateos, *Origen,* fol. 8r.

14   Martínez de Espinar, fol. 57v.

15   Jablonski, "Acts of Violence."

16   Allsen, *Royal Hunt;* Griffin, *Blood Sport,* 8; Owens, "Diana at the Bar," 18, 5.

17   James Edmund Harting, *Bibliotheca Accipitraria: A Catalogue of Books Ancient and Modern Relating to Falconry* (London: B. Quaritch, 1891).

18   Mateos, *Origen,* fols. 16r–v; Martínez de Espinar discusses differences in hounds employed in Castile and France.

19   Allsen, *Royal Hunt.*

20   *Libro de la Montería de Alfonso XI* (Seville: Andrea Pescioni, 1582), fol. 2r.

21   Quoted in Ortega Cervignón, "La funcionalidad," 407n39, 408.

22   Pedro Núñez de Avendaño, *Auiso de caçadores y de caça* (Alcala: Ioan de Brocar, 1543), fols. 28r–v.

23   Núñez de Avendaño, chaps. 13–17; Gonzalo Argote de Molina, "Discurso sobre el libro de la montería," in *Libro de la montería que mando escreuir el muy alto y muy poederos rey don Alfonso de Castilla y de Leon* (Seville: Andrea Pescioni, 1582).

24   Robert Bartlett, *The Making of Europe: Conquest, Colonization and Cultural Change 950–1350* (Princeton, NJ: Princeton University Press, 1993), 45.

25   On breeding, see, Mackenzie Cooley, *The Perfection of Nature: Animals, Breeding, and Race in the Renaissance* (Chicago: University of Chicago Press, 2022), 31–47, 86–87; Kathryn Elizabeth Renton, "The Horse in the Spanish Atlantic World, 1492–1600" (PhD diss., University of California, Los Angeles, 2018), esp. 262–292; on raptors, see, Francisco Carcano, "Tres libros de las aves de rapiña," in *Textos clásicos de cetrería, montería y caza,* ed. José Manuel Fradejas Rueda, CD-ROM (Madrid: Fundación Histórica Tavera, 1999), fols. 3r–14r.

26   Michel de Montaigne, "Apology," in *The Complete Essays of Montaigne,* trans. Donald Murdoch Frame (Stanford, CA: Stanford University Press, 1976), 338.

27   Jacques du Fouilloux, *The Noble Arte of Venerie or Hunting,* trans. George Gascoigne (London: Henry Bynneman, for Christopher Barker, 1575), 26–28, 15–16.

28   Fadrique de Zúñiga y Sotomayor, *Libro de cetrería de caça de açor* (Salamanca: Juan de Canoua, 1565), fol. 21v.

29   Dennis P. Seniff, "Introduction" in *Libro de la Montería: Based on Escorial MS Y.II.19,* trans. and ed. Dennis P. Seniff (Madison, WI: Hispanic Seminary of Medieval Studies, 1983), v, vii.

30   *Libro de la Montería* (ed. Seniff), 29, 30. On expensive medicines: Pedro López de Ayala, *Libro de la caça de las aves,* ed. John G. Cummins (London: Tamesis, 1986), fols. 56v–57v; Allsen, *Royal Hunt,* 61.

31   Martínez de Espinar, *Arte,* fol. 116r; see also 76r.

32   Gervase Markham, *Country Contentments: or, the Husbandmans Recreations,* 5th ed. (London: John Harison, 1633), 4.

33   For France, see Salvadori, *La chasse,* 194–195.

34   Argote de Molina, "Discurso," fols. 4r–v.

35   AHN, Nobleza, Frías leg. 590, docs. 19, 27, 29.

36   Martínez de Espinar, *Arte,* fol. 62r.

37   Martínez de Espinar, fol. 60r.

38   Martínez de Espinar, fol. 65v.

39   Mateos, *Origen,* fol. 17r.

40   Michael Baret, *An Hipponomie or the Vineyard of Horsemanship: Deuided into Three Bookes* (London: printed by George Eld, 1618), bk. 3: 62.

41   Nicholas Cox, *The Gentleman's Recreation* (London: printed by [James] Cottrell, 1677), 30.

42   Argote de Molina, "Discurso," fols. 4v–5r.

43   Mateos, *Origen,* fols. 11r, 12r; Fouilloux, *Noble Arte,* 5, 8.

44   López de Ayala, *Libro de la caça de las aves,* fols. 13r, 18v; Simon Latham, *New and Second Booke of Falconrie* (London: Roger Jackson, 1618), 27, 74–75; see also Norton, "Going to the Birds," 54–58.

45   Martínez de Espinar, *Arte,* fol. 64r–v.

46   Cox, *Gentleman's Recreation,* 75; Fouilloux, *The Noble Arte,* 115.

47   John Astley, *The Art of Riding* (London: Henrie Denham, 1584), 50; Claudio Corte, *The Art of Riding, Conteining Diuerse Necessarie Instructions, Demonstrations, Helps, and Corrections Apperteining to Horssemanship* (London: H. Denham, 1584), 110.

48   On portraiture, John Beusterien, *Canines*, 87–99; on mourning, Luis Pérez, *Del can, y del cavallo, y de sus calidades* (Valladolid: Impresso por Adrian Ghemart, 1568).

49   Markham, *Country Contentments,* 37; López de Ayala, *Libro de la caça de las aves,* fols. 32v–33r.

50   Mateos, *Origen,* fols. 50r–v; 38r–v.

51   Cox, *Gentleman's Recreation,* 3; Crane, *Animal Encounters,* 112–113.

52   Latham, *New and Second Booke,* 27, 41, 42

53   Norton, "Going to the Birds," 57–58.

54   Sandra Blakeslee and Matthew Blakeslee, *The Body Has a Mind of Its Own: How Body Maps in Your Brain Help You Do (Almost) Everything Better* (New York: Random House, 2007), 4, 133–137.

55   Astley, *Art of Riding,* 5, 57.

56   Baret, *An Hipponomie,* bk. 3: 97, 99.

57   Edmund Bert, *An Approved Treatise of Hawkes and Hawking* (London: printed by Thomas Snodham for Richard Moore, 1619), 13, 21–22; Latham, *New and Second Booke,* 12.

58   Cox, *Gentleman's Recreation,* 80; Fouilloux, *Noble Arte,* 127; Cummins, *Hound and Hawk.*

59   Argote de Molina, "Discurso," fol. 19v.

60   For barefoot, see Mateos, *Origen,* fol. 25v.

61   Mateos, fols. 26r, 32r, 33r, 34v.

62   Mateos, fols. 27v, 53v, 29v.

63   Martínez de Espinar, *Arte,* fol. 83r.

64   For example, Mateos, *Origen,* fols. 23r, 25r, 35v.

65   Vittorio Gallese, Morris N. Eagle, and Paolo Migone, "Intentional Attunement: Mirror Neurons and the Neural Underpinnings of Interpersonal Relations," *Journal of the American Psychoanalytic Association* 55, no. 1 (2007): 131–177, at 144.

66   Gallese et al., "Intentional Attunement," 144.

67   Cox, *Gentleman's Recreation,* 16–18, 67–69.

68   Cox, 80, 31.

69   Argote de Molina, "Discurso," fol. 6r.

70   Mateos, *Origen,* fol. 49v.

71   Mateos, fols. 30v, 45r, 99v.

72   Mateos, fols. 10v, 22v.

73   Gesner quoted in Cox, *Gentleman's Recreation*, 60.

74   Cox, 60–66.

75   Cox, 60–61, see also 75, 76; Fouilloux, *Noble Arte*, 121.

76   Mateos, *Origen*, fols. 23v, 24r–v.

77   Mateos, fols. 30r–31v.

78   Mateos, fol. 65v.

79   Argote de Molina, "Discurso," fols. 10r, 6r, 20r.

80   Mateos, *Origen*, fols. 37r–38r.

81   Quoted in Matt Cartmill, *A View to a Death in the Morning: Hunting and Nature through History* (Cambridge, MA: Harvard University Press, 1996), 78.

82   Cartmill, *View to a Death*, 76.

83   On Gómez Pereira's views of animals, see Alves, *The Animals of Spain*, 43; Beusterien, *Canines*, 6–7.

2. Objectifying Livestock

1   See Julius Klein, *The Mesta: A Study in Spanish Economic History, 1273–1836* (Cambridge, MA: Harvard University Press, 1920), 5; Reyna Pastor de Togneri, "La lana en Castilla y León antes de la organización de la Mesta," *Moneda y Crédito*, no. 112 (1970): 363–390; Jean Paul Le Flem, "Las cuentas de la Mesta (1510–1709)," *Moneda y Crédito*, no. 121 (1972): 23–104; Carmen Argente del Castillo Ocaña, *La ganadería medieval andaluza, siglos XIII–XVI: reinos de Jaén y Córdoba*, 2 vols. (Jaén: Diputación Provincial de Jaén, 1991); Carla Rahn Phillips and William D. Phillips, *Spain's Golden Fleece: Wool Production and the Wool Trade from the Middle Ages to the Nineteenth Century* (Baltimore: Johns Hopkins University Press, 1997); José Ubaldo Bernardos Sanz, "No sólo de pan: ganadería, abastecimiento y consumo de carne en Madrid, 1450–1805" (PhD diss., Universidad Autonóma, Madrid, 1997); Antonio Luis López Martínez, *La ganadería en la Baja Andalucía, siglos XV–XX* (Seville: Universidad de Sevilla, 2001); Karl Butzer, "Cattle and Sheep from Old to New Spain: Historical Antecedents," *Annals of the Association of American Geographers* 78, no. 1 (2005): 35–42; David Vassberg, *Land and Society in Golden Age Castile* (Cambridge: Cambridge University Press, 1984). Archaeologists are able to add more and different kinds of details about its role in different periods; see, Idoia Grau-Sologestoa, "Livestock Management in Spain from Roman to Post-Medieval Times: A Biometrical Analysis of Cattle, Sheep/Goat and Pig," *Journal of Archaeological Science*, no. 54 (2015): 123–134.

2   Gabriel Alonso de Herrera, *Libro de agricultura* (Pamplona: Mathias Mares, 1605), fol. 156r.

3   Herrera, *Libro de agricultura*, fol. 168r. For edition history, Real Sociedad Económica Matritense, Prologue, *Agricultura general de Gabriel Alonso de Herrera*, 4 vols. (Madrid: Imprenta Real, 1818), 1: xi–xxv.

4   Leonard Mascall, *The Countreyman's Jewel: or, the Government of Cattel* (London: printed for William Thackery, 1680), 248.

5   Jamie Kreiner, *Legions of Pigs in the Early Medieval West* (New Haven, CT: Yale University Press, 2020); Fernand Braudel, *The Mediterranean and the Mediterranean World in the Age of Philip II*, trans. Sian Reynolds (London: Collins, 1972).

6   Lydia Zapata, Leonor Peña-Chocarro, Guillem Pérez-Jordá, and Hans-Peter Stika, "Early Neolithic Agriculture in the Iberian Peninsula," *Journal of World Prehistory* 18, no. 4 (2004): 283–325; Juliet Clutton-Brock, *The Walking Larder: Patterns of Domestication, Pastoralism, and Predation* (London: Unwin Hyman, 1989); Umberto Albarella, *Pigs and Humans: 10,000 Years of Interaction* (Oxford: Oxford University Press, 2007).

7   Antonio Palau y Dulcet, *Manual del librero hispano-americano*, 7 vols. (Barcelona: Librería Anticuaria, 1923), 6:574–575.

8   Butzer, "Cattle and Sheep," 35–42; Phillips and Phillips, *Spain's Golden Fleece*, 24–41.

9   Melinda A. Zeder, "Domestication and Early Agriculture in the Mediterranean Basin: Origins, Diffusion, and Impact," *Proceedings of the National Academy of Sciences* 105, no. 33 (2008): 11597–11604, 11600; João Zilhão, "Radiocarbon Evidence for Maritime Pioneer Colonization at the Origins of Farming in West Mediterranean Europe," *Proceedings of the National Academy of Sciences* 98, no. 24 (2001): 14180–14185.

10 Butzer, "Cattle and Sheep," 37–38. Archaeological evidence, however, allows us to see changes in animal size and differences in breeding strategies during the Roman period and Middle Ages, Grau-Sologestoa, "Livestock Management," 125–132.

11 Klein, *The Mesta*, 5.

12 Phillips and Phillips, *Spain's Golden Fleece*, 36–37; Klein, *The Mesta*.

13 Le Flem, "Las cuentas," 23–104; Butzer, "Cattle and Sheep," 41.

14 Argente del Castillo Ocaña, *La ganadería medieval*, 1:157–158.

15 Butzer, "Cattle and Sheep," 33, 38, 45.

16 López Martínez, *La ganadería en la Baja Andalucía*, 2.

17 Argente del Castillo Ocaña, *La ganadería medieval*, 1:164.

18 Argente del Castillo Ocaña, *La ganadería medieval*, 1:168.

19 "Privilegio de Don Alfonso X," in *Documentos del Archivo General de la villa de Madrid*, ed. Timoteo Domingo Palacio and Carlos Cambronero y Martínez (Madrid: Impr. y Lit. Municipal, 1888), 87.

20 For social background on shepherds, see Argente del Castillo Ocaña, *La ganadería medieval*, 1:176–195; AHN, Nobleza, Frías leg. 1096, leg. 1173, doc. 2, leg. 1169; AHN, Nobleza, Ovando leg. 4.

21 Argente del Castillo Ocaña, *La ganadería medieval*, 1:166–170.

22   "Privilegio de Don Alfonso X," 87.

23   Argente del Castillo Ocaña, *La ganadería medieval,* 1:169. For herd sizes between thirty and one hundred, see AHN, Nobleza, Frías leg. 1096, leg. 1173, doc. 2; Ovando, leg. 4.

24   Argente del Castillo Ocaña, *La ganadería medieval,* 1:171–173.

25   "Cuentas del condado de Oropesa," AHN, Nobleza, Frías, 1173 doc. 2, fols. 131r–152v; Manuel del Río, *Vida pastoril* (Madrid: Imp. de Repullés, 1828).

26   Antonio Ponz, *Viage de España* (Madrid: por la viuda de Ibarra, 1787), 212–214; Phillips and Phillips, *Spain's Golden Fleece,* 103.

27   Butzer, "Cattle and Sheep," 43.

28   "Cuentas del condado de Oropesa," fols. 131r–135r.

29   Del Río, *Vida pastoril.*

30   Mascall, *Countreyman's Jewel,* 329; see also Herrera, *Libro de agricultura,* fol. 165r.

31   Argente del Castillo Ocaña, *La ganadería medieval,* 1:195–197; Klein, *The Mesta,* 12–13, 54, 364.

32   Argente del Castillo Ocaña, *La ganadería medieval,* 1:29.

33   Ponz, *Viage,* 189–226.

34   Del Río, *Vida pastoril,* n.p., 119–120, 167–178.

35   Ponz, *Viage,* 203–206; Del Río, *Vida pastoril,* 134.

36   Del Río, *Vida pastoril,* 137–138; see also Ponz, *Viage,* 204–205.

37   Del Río, *Vida pastoril,* 69.

38   Del Río, *Vida pastoril,* 66–68.

39   Phillips and Phillips, *Spain's Golden Fleece,* 116, 121–122.

40   Phillips and Phillips, *Spain's Golden Fleece,* 117–118.

41   Del Río, *Vida pastoril,* 71–92; Ponz, *Viage,* 212–214; Phillips and Phillips, *Spain's Golden Fleece,* 117–118.

42   Del Río, *Vida pastoril,* 75–77.

43   Ponz, *Viage,* 213.

44   Del Río, *Vida pastoril,* 92.

45   Del Río, *Vida pastoril,* 159–163; Ponz, *Viage,* 189–191; Phillips and Phillips, *Spain's Golden Fleece,* 128–133.

46   AGS, RGS, leg. 149304, no. 44 (1493); ARCHV, Registro de ejecutorías, caja1124, no. 27 (1567).

47   ARCHV, Registro de ejecutorías, caja 269, no. 21; Bernardos Sanz, "No sólo de pan," 111–127.

48   AGS, RGS, leg. 150002, no. 349 (1500), ARCHV, Registro de ejecutorías, caja 1124, no. 27.

49   AGS, RGS, leg. 149912, no. 109 (1499).

50   AGS, RGS, leg. 149204, no. 258 (1492).

51   Quoted in Bernardos Sanz, "No sólo de pan," 59.

52   ARCHV, Registro de ejecutorías, caja 1124, no. 27.

53   "Cédula . . . que aya matadero," fol. 5r; Jodi Campbell, *At the First Table: Food and Social Identity in Early Modern Spain* (Lincoln: University of Nebraska Press, 2017).

54   AGS, RGS, leg. 150104, no. 22 (1501); Bernardos Sanz, "No sólo de pan," 56.

55   Idoia Grau-Sologestoa, "Food Taboos in Medieval Iberia: The Zooarchaeology of Socio-Cultural Differences," *Anthropozoologica* 58, no. 3 (March 2023): 23–33.

56   AGS, RGS, leg. 150101, no. 26 (1501).

57   AGS, RGS, leg. 150110, no. 246 (1501), leg. 148811, no. 177 (1488); ARCHV, Registro de ejecutorías, caja 342, no. 35 (1520).

58   AGS, RGS, leg. 148010, no. 108 (1480).

59   AGS, RGS, leg. 149508, no. 125 (1495); see also leg. 149606, no. 124 (1496); leg. 149708, no. 325 (1497); leg. 149908, no. 84 (1499).

60   AGS, RGS, leg. 149507, no. 94; leg. 149706, no. 41; for similar edicts in Cuenca and Medina, see leg. 149304, no. 44 (1493).

61   AGS, RGS, leg. 149606, no. 124.

62   Antonio J. Albardonedo Freire, "La génesis de la tauromaquia moderna: la presidencia de la autoridad y la construcción de tribunas," *Laboratorio de arte* 18 (2005): 397–416, 401; Bernardos Sanz, "No sólo de pan," 53; AGS, RGS, leg. 149908, no. 84.

63   Bernardos Sanz, "No sólo de pan," 168–169.

64   Bernardos Sanz, "No sólo de pan," 55.

65   José Luis de los Reyes Leoz, "Evolución de la población, 1561–1857," in *Madrid: Atlas histórico de la ciudad,* ed. Virgilio Pinto Crespo and Santos Madrazo Madrazo, 140–149 ([Madrid]: Fundación Caja de Madrid, 1995).

66   *Ordenanzas del matadero de la muy noble y muy leal ciudad de Sevilla* (Seville: Juan Francisco de Blas, 1686), fol. 2v, AMS, Sec. 4, 22–36; see also *Cédula, y provisión de su magestad, para que aya matadero, y carnicería, para los señores desta Real Audiencia de Granada* (Granada: en la imprenta de la Real Chancillería, Francisco Heylan, 1588).

67   Compare *Ordenanzas* to AHN, Órdenes Militares, legs. 6111, 7046, 6108, AHN, Nobleza, leg. 45034 AHN, transcribed in "Propiedades y establecimientos concejiles: La carnicería y el matadero," *La provincia de Zorita en el siglo XVI*, published by Departamento de Historia Moderna, Instituto de Historia, Consejo Superior de Investigaciones Científicas, http://www.moderna1.ih.csic.es/zorita.

68   Antonio Luis López Martínez, "Una élite rural: los grandes ganaderos andaluces, siglos XIV–XX, *Hispania* 65, no. 221 (2005): 1023–1042.

69   *Ordenanzas*, fols. 3v, 4r; Albardonedo Freire, "La génesis," 402.

70   *Ordenanzas*, nos. 1, 5, 17, 18, 19.

71   *Ordenanzas*, nos. 17; Albardonedo Freire, "La génesis," 402.

72   Quoted in Albardonedo Freire, "La génesis," 400n6.

73   *Ordenanzas*, nos. 14, 15, 23, 24, 2, 20, 21.

74   "Propiedades y establecimientos concejiles: La carnicería y el matadero," n.p.

75   *Ordenanzas,*, no. 16.

76   Bernardos Sanz, "No sólo de pan," 55, 215.

77   *Ordenanzas*, no. 20.

78   Bernardos Sanz, "No sólo de pan," 55.

79   Miguel de Cervantes, "The Dogs Colloquy," in *Exemplary Stories*, trans. C. A. Jones (London: Penguin Books, 2006).

80   *Ordenanzas*, nos. 5, 6.

81   Bernardos Sanz, "No sólo de pan," 216.

82   *Ordenanzas*, no. 13.

83   Karl Marx, "Economic and Philosophical Manuscripts of 1844," *The Marx-Engels Reader*, ed. Robert C. Tucker, 2nd ed., 53–65 (New York: W. W. Norton, 1978).

84   William Cronon, *Nature's Metropolis: Chicago and the Great West* (New York: W. W. Norton, 1991), 212–213.

85   Marcy Norton, "Going to the Birds: Animals as Things and Beings in Early Modernity," in *Early Modern Things: Objects and Their Histories, 1500–1800*, ed. Paula Findlen, 53–83 (London: Routledge, 2012), 58–60; Jean Liébault, *L'agriculture et maison rustique* (Lyon: Jaques du Puys, 1583), fol. 39v.

86   Herrera, *Libro de agricultura*, fols. 149r–155v; Liebault, *L'agriculture*, fols. 39v–51r.

87   Herrera, *Libro de agricultura*, fols. 150v–151r; Liebault, *L'agriculture*, fols. 41r–44r, 46r.

88   On herds, López Martínez, *La ganadería en la Baja Andalucía*, 24, 26; AHN, Consejos, leg. 25700, exp. 12 (1653); Miguel Agustí, *Libro de los secretos de agricvltvra casa de campo, y pastoril* (Luys Roure, 1626), 474–478; Herrera, *Libro de agricultura*, fol. 165r; James J. Parsons, "The Acorn-Hog Economy of the Oak Woodlands of Southwestern Spain," *Geographical Review* 52, no. 2 (1962): 211–235; on slaughterhouses, *Ordenanzas*, n. 6, 10.

89   Herrera, *Libro de agricultura*, fol. 149r.

90   Agustí, *Libro de los secretos*, 25.

91   Agustí, *Libro de los secretos,* 60.

92   Herrera, *Libro de agricultura,* fol. 164r; Agustí, *Libro de los secretos,* 476.

93   Herrera, *Libro de agricultura,* fols. 163–165v.

94   AGS, RGS, leg. 149207, no. 94.

95   ARCHV, Registro de ejecutorías, caja 1723, no. 7.

96   De los Reyes Leoz, "Evolución de la población," 140–149.

97   Consejo, Sala de Alcaldes, *Catálogo por materias,* "Cerdos," lib. 1233. fol. 75–76, AHN.

98   Norton, "Going to the Birds," 58–59.

99   Del Río, *Vida pastoril,* 3; Herrera, *Libro de agricultura,* fols. 164v, 144r–146v, 158r, 165r.

100   "Cuentas del condado de Oropesa," fols. 155v, 157r.

101   Marcy Norton, "Animals (Spain)," in *Lexikon of the Hispanic Baroque: Transatlantic Exchange and Transformation,* ed. Ken Mills and Evonne Levy, 17–19 (Austin: University of Texas Press, 2014), 18.

102   On the high estimation Spaniards had for many of these animals, see Abel A. Alves, *The Animals of Spain: An Introduction to Imperial Perceptions and Human Interaction with Other Animals, 1492–1826* (Boston: Brill, 2011). For dairy cows, see Erica Fudge, "Milking Other Men's Beasts," *History and Theory* 52, no. 4 (2013): 13–28.

103   Herrera, *Libro de agricultura,* fols. 144v, 145v, 168r; see also Agustí, *Libro de los secretos,* 380–390.

104   *Ordenanzas,* no. 17; Bernardos Sanz, "No sólo de pan," 213, 465.

105   On the role of slaughterhouse dogs, John Beusterien, *Canines in Cervantes and Velázquez* (Farnham, Surrey: Ashgate, 2013), 44.

106   Cervantes, "Dogs Colloquy"; Beusterien, *Canines,* 36.

107   Herrera, *Agricultura general,* fol. 144v.

108   Del Río, *Vida pastoril,* 3–4.

109   AHN, Nobleza, Frías, c. 1071, doc. 6.

110   Quoted in Beusterien, *Canines,* 87.

111   Charles-Philibert Comte de Lasteyrie du Saillant, *Traité sur les bêtes à laine d'Espagne* (Chez A.-J. Marchant, imprimeur du Muséum d'Histoire naturelle, 1799), 34–35; Del Río, *Vida pastoril,* 6, 10, 40, 139–140.

112   Lasteyrie du Saillant, *Traité sur les bêtes à laine,* 34.

113   Javier Irigoyen-García, *The Spanish Arcadia: Sheep Herding, Pastoral Discourse, and Ethnicity in Early Modern Spain* (Toronto: University of Toronto Press, 2013).

114   Norton, "Animals in Spain," 18.

115   Norton, "Animals in Spain," 18–19.

116   María Tausiet and James Amelang, eds., *El diablo en la edad moderna* (Madrid: Marcial Pons Historia, 2004); María Tausiet, "Avatares del mal: el diablo en las brujas," in Tausiet and Amelang, *El diablo en la edad moderna*, 45–66; Felipe Pereda and María Cruz de Carlos, "Deslmaldos: imágnes del demonio en la cultura visual de Castilla," in Tausiet and Amelang, 233–252.

117   Quoted in Pereda and Cruz de Carlos, "Deslmaldos," 246.

118   Julio Caro Baroja, *The World of the Witches* (London: Phoenix, 2001).

119   María Tausiet, *Ponzoña en los ojos: Brujería y superstición en Aragón en el siglo XVI* (Madrid: Turner, 2004); María Tausiet, *Urban Magic in Early Modern Spain* (Basingstoke: Palgrave Macmillan, 2014); James S. Amelang, "Sleeping with the Enemy: The Devil in Dreams in Early Modern Spain," *American Imago* 69, no. 3 (2012): 319–352.

120   See also Maerten de Vos, *Last Judgment* (1570), Museo de Bellas Artes de Sevilla.

121   Julio Caro Baroja, "Witchcraft and Catholic Theology," in *Early Modern European Witchcraft: Centres and Peripheries*, ed. Bengt Ankarloo and Gustav Henningsen, 20–43 (Oxford: Clarendon Press, 1990); Caro Baroja, *World of the Witches;* Stuart Clark, *Thinking with Demons: The Idea of Witchcraft in Early Modern Europe* (Oxford: Oxford University Press, 1997).

122   Caro Baroja, *World of the Witches;* Clark, *Thinking with Demons.*

123   Quoted in Caro Baroja, *World of the Witches,* 91; Carlo Ginzburg, *Ecstasies: Deciphering the Witches' Sabbath* (Chicago: University of Chicago Press, 2004), 73.

124   *The Hammer of Witches: A Complete Translation of the Malleus Maleficarum,* trans. Christopher S. Mackay (Cambridge: Cambridge University Press, 2009), 201–210, 330–334.

125   *Hammer of Witches,* 332.

126   Caro Baroja, *World of the Witches;* 143–155; Florencio Idoate, *La brujería en Navarra y sus documentos* (Pamplona: Diputación Foral de Navarra, 1978); William E. Monter, *Frontiers of Heresy: The Spanish Inquisition from the Basque Lands to Sicily* (Cambridge: Cambridge University Press, 2003), 258–262.

127   Ginzburg, *Ecstasies,* 10.

128   Martín de Castañega, *Tratado de las supersticiones y hechizerias y vanos conjuros y abusiones y otras cosas* (Logroño: Miguel de Equía, 1529), ch. 24; Martín de Arles y Andosilla, *De superstitionibus,* trans. Félix-Tomás López Gurpegui (Madrid: Cultiva Libros, 2011), chap. 8.

129   "Carta del Inquisidor de Navarra al Condestable de Castilla" (c. 1525) transcribed in Julio Caro Baroja, *Cuatro relaciones sobre la hechicería vasca* (Donostia–San Sebastián: Anuario de la Sociedad de Eusko-Folklore, 1993), 92–102, 94.

130   Arles y Andosilla, *De Superstitionibus*, chaps. 7, 8.

131   "Carta del Inquisidor de Navarra," 95–96; Caro Baroja, *World of the Witches*, 143.

132   Castañega, *Tratado de las supersticiones*, chaps. 5, 21.

133   Castañega, chaps. 4, 22; Caro Baroja, *World of the Witches*, 150.

134   Castañega, *Tratado de las supersticiones*, chaps. 23, 16.

135   Castañega, chaps. 16, 18, 15.

136   "Carta del Inquisidor de Navarra," 94, 96, 98–100.

137   Castañega, *Tratado de las supersticiones*.

138   Caro Baroja, "Witchcraft and Catholic Theology," 20–43.

139   Castañega, *Tratado de las supersticiones*, chap. 4.

140   Georges Baudot, "La brujería española importada a México por Fray Andrés de Olmos," *Arqueología mexicana* 6, no. 34 (1998): 54–57.

141   Castañega, chaps. 2, 3.

142   Castañega, chap. 3.

143   Castañega, chap. 21.

144   Castañega, chaps. 6–8.

145   Castañega, chaps. 9, 10.

146   Martín del Rio, *Investigations into Magic*, trans. P. G. Maxwell-Stuart (Manchester: Manchester University Press, 2000), 102, 103.

147   For more on the discourse around human-animal transformation in Spain, see Alves, *Animals of Spain*, 114–130.

3. Conquering Animals

1   Christopher Columbus, *The Diario of Christopher Columbus's First Voyage to America, 1492–1493*, transcribed and trans. Oliver Dunn and James E. Kelly, Jr. (Norman: University of Oklahoma Press, 1989), 63, 90–91.

2   Columbus, *Diario*, 233, 235.

3   Cristóbal Colón, "Relación del segundo viaje," in *Textos y documentos completos*, ed. Consuelo Varela and Juan Gil, 2nd ed. (Madrid: Alianza Editorial, 1992), 235; Bartolomé de Las Casas, *Historia de las Indias*, 3 vols. (Madrid: Impr. de M. Ginesta, 1875), 1:246.

4   Alfred W. Crosby, *The Columbian Exchange: Biological and Cultural Consequences of 1492*, 30th anniversary ed. (Westport, CT: Praeger, 2003 [1972]); Alfred W. Crosby, *Ecological Imperialism: The Biological Expansion of Europe, 900–1900* (Cambridge: Cambridge University Press, 1986), 74–82.

5   Crosby, *Columbian Exchange*, 21. See Introduction.

6   Rob Nixon, *Slow Violence and the Environmentalism of the Poor* (Cambridge, MA: Harvard University Press, 2011).

7   Increasingly scholars prefer to emphasize warfare rather than "conquest," since the latter word suggests Indigenous erasure that does not align with actual history. See, among others, Matthew Restall, *When Montezuma Met Cortés: The True Story of the Meeting That Changed History* (New York: Ecco, 2018), xxix.

8   Vera S. Candiani, *Dreaming of Dry Land: Environmental Transformation in Colonial Mexico City* (Stanford, CA: Stanford University Press, 2014); Maristella Svampa, *Neo-Extractivism in Latin America: Socio-Environmental Conflicts, the Territorial Turn, and New Political Narratives* (Cambridge: Cambridge University Press, 2019), 8; Gabriel de Avilez Rocha, "The Pinzones and the Coup of the Acedares: Fishing and Colonization in the Fifteenth-Century Atlantic," *Colonial Latin American Review* 28, no. 4 (2019): 427–449; Daviken Studnicki-Gizbert, *The Three Deaths of Cerro de San Pedro: Four Centuries of Extractivism in a Small Mexican Mining Town* (Chapel Hill: University of North Carolina Press, 2022), 3; Anne Berg, *Empire of Rags and Bones: Waste and War in Nazi Germany* (New York: Oxford University Press, forthcoming). See also Leonardo Marques and Gabriel de Avilez Rocha, eds., "The Environmental History of Capitalism in the Colonial World, 15th–19th Centuries (A história ambiental do capitalismo no mundo colonial, séc. XV ao XIX)" *Tempo* 28, no. 1 (2022): 145–160.

     Though they do not use the framework of extractivism, these works have deeply informed my approach: Andrew Sluyter, "The Ecological Origins and Consequences of Cattle Ranching in Sixteenth-Century New Spain," *Geographical Review* 86, no. 2 (1996): 161–177; Elinor G. K. Melville, *A Plague of Sheep: Environmental Consequences of the Conquest of Mexico* (Cambridge: Cambridge University Press, 1994); Virginia DeJohn Anderson, *Creatures of Empire: How Domestic Animals Transformed Early America* (Oxford: Oxford University Press, 2004); Justo Lucas del Río Moreno, *Ganadería, plantaciones y comercio azucarero antillano: siglow XVI y XVII* (Santo Domingo, Dominican Republic: Academia Dominicana de la Historia, 2012); Molly A. Warsh, *American Baroque: Pearls and the Nature of Empire, 1492–1700* (Chapel Hill: University of North Carolina Press, 2018).

9   On horses and warfare in the Americas, see, Francisco Morales Padrón, "Los caballos en la conquista," in *Libro de homenaje a Aurelio Miró Quesada Sosa*, 633–646 (Lima: [n.p.], 1987), 637–642; Kathryn Elizabeth Renton, "The Horse in the Spanish Atlantic World, 1492–1600" (PhD diss., University of California, Los Angeles, 2018). On dogs, see, John Grier Varner and Jeannette Johnson Varner, *Dogs of the Conquest* (Norman: University of Oklahoma Press, 1983); John Ensminger, "From Hunters to Hell Hounds: The Dogs of Columbus and Transformations of the Human-Canine Relationship in the Early Spanish Caribbean," *Colonial Latin American Review* 31 (2022): 354–380.

10   Las Casas, *Historia de las Indias*, 1:98; Carl Ortwin Sauer, *The Early Spanish Main* (Berkeley: University of California Press, 1992), 89; Varner and Varner, *Dogs of the Conquest*, 7–8.

11 On Indigenous slavery, see Nancy E. Van Deusen, *Global Indios: The Indigenous Struggle for Justice in Sixteenth-Century Spain* (Durham, NC: Duke University Press, 2015); Andrés Reséndez, *The Other Slavery: The Uncovered Story of Indian Enslavement in America* (Boston: Houghton Mifflin Harcourt, 2016).

12 Las Casas, *Historia de las Indias*, 2:1.

13 Las Casas, *Historia de las Indias*, 1:100.

14 Bernardo de Vargas Machuca, *Milicia y descripcion de las Indias* (Madrid: P. Madrigal, 1599). On the expansion of these methods, see Sara E. Johnson, "'You Should Give Them Blacks to Eat': Waging Inter-American Wars of Torture and Terror," *American Quarterly* 61, no.1 (2009): 65–92; and Tyler D. Parry and Charlton W. Yingling, "Slave Hounds and Abolition in the Americas," *Past & Present*, 246, no. 1 (2020): 69–108.

15 Las Casas, *Historia de las Indias*, 2:96.

16 Las Casas, *Historia de las Indias*, 2:74.

17 Galeotto Cei, *Viaje y descripción de las Indias, 1539–1553,* trans. Marisa Vannini de Gerulewicz (Caracas: Fundación Banco Venezolano de Crédito, 1995), 114, 83; Vargas Machuca, *Milicia*.

18 Colón, "Relación del segundo viaje," 97.

19 Bernal Díaz del Castillo, *The Conquest of New Spain,* trans. J. M. Cohen (Harmondsworth: Penguin Books, 1963), 78.

20 Díaz del Castillo, *Conquest of New Spain*, 80, see also 116.

21 Morales Padrón, "Los caballos en la conquista," 637–642.

22 Las Casas, *Historia de las Indias*, 2:74.

23 Díaz del Castillo, *Conquest of New Spain*, 48, 55; John J. Johnson, "The Introduction of the Horse into the Western Hemisphere," *Hispanic American Historical Review* 23, no. 4 (1943): 587–610, 606.

24 Hernán Cortés, "The Third Letter" to Charles V, *Letters from Mexico*, ed. and trans. Anthony Pagden (New York: Grossman, 1971), 160–281, 252; see also "Letter of Hernando Pizarro to the Royal Audience of Santo Domingo," in *Reports on the Discovery of Peru*, ed. Clements R. Markham (New York, 1963), 116.

25 On chronology of deaths and conquest, see Reséndez, *The Other Slavery*.

26 Díaz del Castillo, *Conquest of New Spain*, 138.

27 Morales Padrón, "Los caballos en la conquista," 642; D. K. Abbass, "Horses and Heroes: The Myth of the Importance of the Horse to the Conquest of the Indies," *Terrae Incognitae* 18, no. 1 (1986): 21–41; Johnson, "Introduction of the Horse."

28 Las Casas, *Historia de las Indias*, 2:28, 34.

29 Las Casas, *Historia de las Indias*, 2:97.

30 Cei, *Viaje*, 114.

31   Cei, *Viaje,* 77, 67–68.

32   For example, Díaz del Castillo, *Conquest of New Spain,* 74.

33   Discussed in Chap. 9.

34   Abbass, "Horses and Heroes," 21–41.

35   Ensminger, "From Hunters to Hell," 357.

36   Pietro Martire d'Anghiera, *De orbe novo: The Eight Decades of Peter Martyr d'Anghera,* trans. and ed. Francis Augustus MacNutt, 2 vols. (New York: G. P. Putnam's Sons, 1912), 1:117.

37   Gonzalo Fernández de Oviedo y Valdés, *Historia general y natural de las Indias,* ed. Juan Pérez de Tudela Bueso, 2nd ed. (Madrid: Ediciones Atlas, 1992), 2:29, 30. This is based on the unpublished manuscript that includes material not in the published editions.

38   Oviedo, *Historia general,* 2:29, 50.

39   Varner and Varner, *Dogs of the Conquest,* 6.

40   Sauer, *Early Spanish Main,* 89; Varner and Varner, *Dogs of the Conquest,* 5–8; Las Casas, *Historia de las Indias,* 1:289; Ensminger, "From Hunters to Hell," 363–364.

41   Las Casas, *Historia de las Indias,* 3:41.

42   Oviedo, *Historia general,* 3:211–212.

43   Martire d'Anghiera, *De orbe novo,* 1:301.

44   Ensminger, "From Hunters to Hell," 360.

45   Martire d'Anghiera, *De orbe novo,* 1:285.

46   "Carta del licenciado Alonso de Zuazo," Jan. 22, 1518, in *Colección de documentos inéditos relativos al descubrimiento, conquista y colonización de las posesiones españolas en América y Oceanía . . .:: [1ª Serie],* 42 vols. (Madrid: Imprenta de M. B. de Quirós [etc.], 1864), 1:304–332, 315–317, 319.

47   AGI Lima 566, L. 4, fol. 242v (1541).

48   AGI Santa Fé 987, L. 2, fols. 248v–249r (Cartagena, 1549); Quito 215, L.1, fol. 45r–v (Santa Fé and Popayán 1565).

49   *Florentine Codex: General History of the Things of New Spain,* 12 bks. in 13 vols., trans. Arthur J. O. Anderson and Charles Dibble (Santa Fe, NM: School of American Research and Salt Lake City: University of Utah Press, 1950–1987), bk. 12:17, 19, 20.

50   Lori Boornazian Diel, "Manuscrito del aperreamiento (Manuscript of the Dogging): A 'Dogging' and Its Implications for Early Colonial Cholula," *Ethnohistory* 58, no. 4 (October 1, 2011): 585–611.

51   Oviedo, *Historia general,* 2:30.

52   Oviedo, *Historia general,* 3:211–212.

53   Pedro Núñez de Avendaño, *Auiso de caçadores y de caça* (Alcalá de Henares: Joan de Brocar, 1543), fol. 11.

54   Anderson, *Creatures of Empire.*

55   Martire d'Anghiera, *De orbe novo,* 1:355, 364.

56   "Capitulos de carta del licenciado Alonso de Zuazo," January 22, 1518, in *Colección de documentos inéditos,* 1:292–298, 293–294.

57   Sauer, *Early Spanish Main,* 157; Oviedo, *Historia general,* 2:38–39.

58   Oviedo, *Historia general,* 2:38, 71. These numbers, while somewhat exaggerated, are not that different from those found in archival records from the period; Lorenzo E. López y Sebastián and Justo L. del Río Moreno, "La ganadería vacuna en la isla Española (1508–1587)," *Revista complutense de historia de América* 25 (1999): 11–49.

59   Judith Francis Zeitlin, "Ranchers and Indians on the Southern Isthmus of Tehuantepec: Economic Change and Indigenous Survival in Colonial Mexico," *Hispanic American Historical Review* 69, no. 1 (1989): 23–60, 36, 49; Lolita Gutiérrez Brockington, *The Leverage of Labor: Managing the Cortés Haciendas in Tehuantepec, 1588–1688* (Durham, NC: Duke University Press, 1989).

60   Melville, *Plague of Sheep,* 51.

61   François Chevalier, *Land and Society in Colonial Mexico: The Great Hacienda* (Berkeley: University of California Press, 1963), 93–94, Samuel Champlain quoted 94. See also Charles Gibson, *Aztecs under Spanish Rule: A History of the Indians of the Valley of Mexico, 1519–1810* (Stanford, CA: Stanford University Press, 1964), 280; Carlos Sempat Assadourian, "The Colonial Economy: The Transfer of the European System of Production to New Spain and Peru," *Journal of Latin American Studies* 24 (1992): 55–68, 63.

62   Warren Dean, *With Broadax and Firebrand: The Destruction of the Brazilian Atlantic Forest* (Berkeley: University of California Press, 1995), chap. 4.

63   Oviedo, *Historia general,* 2:29.

64   Oviedo, *Historia general,* 2:51.

65   "Relación y descripción de la provincia de Caracas," *Relaciones geográficas de Indias,* ed. Germán Latorre, 3 vols. (Seville: Tip. Zarzuela, 1919), 3:86.

66   See Chap. 7.

67   López y Sebastián and Río Moreno, "La ganadería vacuna," 64.

68   For a characterization of the views of Karl Butzer and his collaborators, see Andrew Sluyter, "From Archive to Map to Pastoral Landscape: A Spatial Perspective on the Livestock Ecology of Sixteenth-Century New Spain," *Environmental History* 3, no. 4 (1998): 508–528, 508–509.

69   Río Moreno, *Ganadería,* 112.

70   Quoted in Río Moreno, *Ganadería,* 47.

71   Río Moreno, *Ganadería*, 47.

72   Río Moreno, *Ganadería*, 49, 52, 63.

73   Río Moreno, *Ganadería*, 48.

74   Río Moreno, *Ganadería*, 128.

75   Río Moreno, *Ganadería*, 63.

76   David E. Vassberg, "Concerning Pigs, the Pizarros, and the Agro-Pastoral Background of the Conquerors of Peru," *Latin American Research Review* 13, no. 3 (1978): 47–61, 58n5.

77   Río Moreno, *Ganadería*, 104–105, 135.

78   Río Moreno, *Ganadería*, 119, 123, 135–138, 141.

79   López y Sebastián and Río Moreno, "La ganadería vacuna," 32.

80   Río Moreno, *Ganadería*, 63, 145.

81   Río Moreno, *Ganadería*, 53–54, 62, 144–145.

82   Río Moreno, *Ganadería*, 118–120; Jane M. Rausch, *A Tropical Plains Frontier: The Llanos of Colombia, 1531–1831* (Albuquerque: University of New Mexico Press, 1984).

83   Justo Lucas del Río Moreno, "El cerdo. Historia de un elemento esencial de la cultura castellana en la conquista y colonización de América (siglo XVI)," *Anuario de estudios americanos* 53, no. 1 (1996): 13–35, 14–17.

84   Cei, *Viaje*, 56–57, 62, 70, 72–74, 79–81.

85   Cei, *Viaje*, 58, 67, 85–86, 98.

86   Río Moreno, *Ganadería*, 68.

87   Río Moreno, *Ganadería*, 68.

88   Dean, *With Broadax and Firebrand*, chap. 4.

89   José Miranda, "Notas sobre la introducción de la Mesta en la Nueva España," *Revista de historia de América* 17 (1944): 1–26, 6. See also Lesley Byrd Simpson, *The Encomienda in New Spain: The Beginning of Spanish Mexico* (Berkeley: University of California Press, 1982); Chevalier, *Land and Society;* Gibson, *Aztecs under Spanish Rule,* 276–281; José Matesanz, "Introducción de la ganadería en Nueva España 1521–1535," *Historia mexicana* 14, no. 4 (1965): 533–566; Melville, *Plague of Sheep,* 120–139; María de los Angeles Romero Frizzi, *Economía y vida de los españoles en la Mixteca Alta, 1519–1720* (Mexico City: Instituto Nacional de Antropología e Historia, Gobierno del Estado de Oaxaca, 1990); Río Moreno, *Ganadería*.

90   Sluyter, "From Archive to Map," 511.

91   Chevalier, *Land and Society,* 93–94.

92   Lesley Byrd Simpson, *Exploitation of Land in Central Mexico in the Sixteenth Century* (Berkeley: University of California Press, 1952), 5–7.

93   Sauer, *Early Spanish Main,* 90–91, 150; López y Sebastián and Río Moreno, "La ganadería vacuna."

94   López y Sebastián and Río Moreno, "La ganadería vacuna," 32–34; Chevalier, *Land and Society,* 112, 306.

95   On the linkages between systems of slavery and livestock, see also Christopher Michael Blakley, "Inhuman Empire: Slavery and Nonhuman Animals in the British Atlantic World" (PhD diss., Rutgers University, 2019). For a philosophical approach to the "animalization of blackness" in the context of Atlantic slave trade, see Zakiyyah Iman Jackson, *Becoming Human: Matter and Meaning in an Antiblack World* (New York: New York University Press, 2020).

96   Silvio Arturo Zavala, *El servicio personal de los Indios en la Nueva España* (Mexico City: Colegio de México, Centro de Estudios Históricos, 1984).

97   Diego de Ysla, "Venta," December 21, 1541, https://cpagncmxvi.historicas.unam.mx /ficha.jsp?idFicha=1-YSD-185-66, Catálogo de Protocolos del Archivo General de Notarías de la Ciudad de México, Fondo Siglo XVI. Online. Ivonne Mijares (coord.). Seminario de Documentación e Historia Novohispana, (Mexico City: Universidad Nacional Autónoma de México-Instituto de Investigaciones Históricas, 2014.

98   Chevalier, *Land and Society,* 282.

99   Río Moreno, *Ganadería,* 62–63, 128–129.

100 Zavala, *El servicio personal.*

101 Zeitlin, "Ranchers and Indians," 36, 49; Gutiérrez Brockington, *Leverage of Labor,* 126–142.

102 René García Castro, *Suma de visitas de pueblos de la Nueva España, 1548–1550* (Mexico City: Universidad Autónoma del Estado de México, 2013), 1–447.

103 García Castro, *Suma de visitas,* 342.

104 "Huexotzinco Codex," transcribed and trans. Warren J. Benedict, in *The Harkness Collection in the Library of Congress: Manuscripts Concerning Mexico: A Guide,* 49–211 (Washington DC: Library of Congress, 1974), 51, 54–57, 68.

105 "Huexotzinco Codex," 93–94, 102–203.

106 Gibson, *Aztecs under Spanish Rule,* 204–205, 280.

107 García Castro, *Suma de visitas,* 1–447; documents sometimes refer generically to *gallinas* (e.g., 213) and "aves" (e.g., 215) and other times specify *gallinas de la tierra* (e.g., 220), or *aves de la tierra* and *gallinas de Castilla* (e.g., 224). See also the Relaciones geográficas in *Papeles de Nueva España,* ed. Francisco del Paso y Troncoso (Mexico City: Estab. Tip. "Sucesores de Rivadeneyra," 1906), vols. 4–7.

108 Chevalier, *Land and Society,* 84–85.

109 García Castro, *Suma de visitas,* 118.

110 Chevalier, *Land and Society,* 66–67; Gutiérrez Brockington, *Leverage of Labor,* 101–108.

111   Chevalier, *Land and Society*, 281–282, quotation 281.

112   Zavala, *El servicio personal;* Chevalier, *Land and Society,* 283–284; Carmen Viqueira and José Ignacio Urquiola, *Los obrajes en la Nueva España, 1530–1630* (Mexico City: Consejo Nacional para la Cultura y las Artes, 1990); Richard J. Salvucci, *Textiles and Capitalism in Mexico: An Economic History of the Obrajes, 1539–1840* (Princeton, NJ: Princeton University Press, 1987).

113   Chevalier, *Land and Society,* 102–103, 107–108.

114   Chevalier, *Land and Society,* 283–284, quotation 283.

115   Zavala, *El servicio personal,* 114–123; Woodrow Borah, "Tithe Collection in the Bishopric of Oaxaca, 1601–1867," *Hispanic American Historical Review* 29, no. 4 (1949): 498–517; Chevalier, *Land and Society,* 230–258; Gibson, *Aztecs under Spanish Rule,* 123–124.

116   Alonso de Zorita, "Breve y sumaria relación," in *Varias relaciones antiguas,* ed. Joaquín García Icazbalceta, 73–227 (Mexico City: F. D. de León, 1891), 96.

117   Gibson, *Aztecs under Spanish Rule,* 280.

118   Gibson, *Aztecs under Spanish Rule,* 278; Melville, *Plague of Sheep,* 49–51, 145.

119   Andrea Martínez Baracs and Carlos Semperat Assadourian, *Tlaxcala: Una historia compartida,* vol. 9 (Tlaxcala: Gobierno del Estado de Tlaxcala, 1991), 115–128; Gibson, *Aztecs under Spanish Rule,* 80–85, 152.

120   Chevalier, *Land and Society,* 93–94.

121   Relación Geográfica of Gueytlalpa (Hueytlalpan, Puebla), 158, Benson Latin American Collection, LLILAS Benson Latin American Studies and Collections, University of Texas at Austin, https://fromthepage.lib.utexas.edu/llilasbenson/rel aciones-geograficas-of-mexico-and-guatemala/hueytlalpan-zacatlan-jojupango -matlatlan-chila-y-papantla-tlaxcala-1581/display/2777.

122   Chevalier, *Land and Society,* 93.

123   Hernando Ruiz de Alarcón, *Treatise on the Heathen Superstitions and Customs That Today Live among the Indians Native to This New Spain, 1629,* trans. and ed. Richard Andrews and Ross Hassig (Norman: University of Oklahoma Press, 1984), 107–111.

124   Martínez Baracs and Semperat Assadourian, *Tlaxcala,* 127.

125   "Anales de San Gregorio Acapulco 1520–1606," ed. and trans. Byron McAfee and Robert Barlow and trans. Fernando Horcasitas, *Tlalocan* 3, no. 2 (2016): 103–141, 136–139.

126   William Howard Dusenberry, *The Mexican Mesta: The Administration of Ranching in Colonial Mexico* (Urbana: University of Illinois Press, 1963).

127   Melville, *Plague of Sheep,* 120–121.

128   Gibson, *Aztecs under Spanish Rule,* 277, 274; Chevalier, *Land and Society.*

129   Massimo Livi-Bacci, "The Depopulation of Hispanic America after the Conquest," *Population and Development Review* 32, no. 2 (2006): 199–232, 226; David S. Jones, "Virgin Soils Revisited," *William and Mary Quarterly* 60, no. 4 (2003): 703–742.

4. Absorbing Prey

1   Ramón Pané, *An Account of the Antiquities of the Indians,* ed. José Juan Arrom and trans. Susan Griswold (Durham, NC: Duke University Press, 1999), 5–6, 47–48.

2   "Relation de l'île de la Guadeloupe," in *Les Caraïbes. La Guadeloupe, 1635–1656: Histoire des vingt premières années de la colonisation de la Guadeloupe d'après les relations du R.P. Breton,* ed. Joseph Rennard, 23–90 (Paris: G. Ficker, 1929), 46. Rennard convincingly attributes this anonymous manuscript to Raymond Breton, Introduction, *Les Caraïbes,* 19–21.

3   José Gumilla, *El Orinoco ilustrado y defendido,* 2 vols. (Madrid: Manuel Fernández, 1745), 1:235, 2:112–113.

4   I infer this based on later reports, such as those discussed below, including Richard Schomburgk, *Travels in British Guiana, 1840–1844,* ed. and trans. Walter Roth, 2 vols. (Georgetown, British Guiana: "Daily Chronicle" Office, 1922), 1:119; Theodor Koch-Grünberg, *Del Roraima al Orinoco,* trans. Federica de Ritter, 3 vols. (Caracas: Ediciones del Banco Central de Venezuela, 1979), 3:143.

5   Quoted in Carlos Fausto, "Of Enemies and Pets: Warfare and Shamanism in Amazonia," trans. David Rodgers, *American Ethnologist* 26, no. 4 (1999): 933–956, 937. For foundational work on predation, see Eduardo Batalha Viveiros de Castro, *From the Enemy's Point of View: Humanity and Divinity in an Amazonian Society,* trans. Catherine V. Howard (Chicago: University of Chicago Press, 1992); Philippe Descola, *Beyond Nature and Culture,* trans. Janet Lloyd (Chicago: University of Chicago Press, 1993); Fernando Santos-Granero, *Vital Enemies: Slavery, Predation, and the Amerindian Political Economy of Life* (Austin: University of Texas Press, 2009); Carlos Fausto, *Warfare and Shamanism,* trans. David Rodgers (Cambridge: Cambridge University Press, 2012).

6   Aparecida Vilaça, "Making Kin Out of Others in Amazonia," *Journal of the Royal Anthropological Institute* 8, no. 2 (2002): 347–365, 348. Also important is her observation that the body is, above all, "mutable," existing "only within relations," 362n.14.

7   Though my analysis is indebted to the work concerning recent and contemporary Indigenous Amazonian philosophies and practices, I do not "upstream"—e.g., assume that current-day thoughts and practices reflect those of the past. Rather, I build this chapter from sources produced in the early modern period, though I sometimes note where there are continuities with later periods. I avoid upstreaming because it is a practice that often assumes timeless ethnographic present for Indigenous people. While some beliefs and practices appear largely constant, others did

seem to change, though it also possible, of course, that absences in earlier records was a result of early modern observers' failure to notice or understand. A topic where there is considerable divergence between early modern sources and later outsider (and insider) accounts is shamanism, as discussed briefly below.

8   See, e.g., Jean-Baptiste du Tertre, *Histoire générale des isles de S. Christophe, de la Guadeloupe, de la Martinique et autres dans l'Amérique'* (Paris: J. Langlois, 1654), 425.

9   Jalil Sued Badillo, *Caribe taíno: Ensayos históricos sobre el siglo XVI* (San Juan, PR: Luscinia C.E., 2020); Neil L. Whitehead, "The Crises and Transformations of Invaded Societies: The Caribbean (1492–1580)," in *The Cambridge History of the Native Peoples of the Americas,* vol. 3, *South America,* ed. Frank Salomon and Stuart B. Schwartz, 2 pts. (Cambridge: Cambridge University Press, 1999), 882–888; Neil Whitehead, *Lords of the Tiger Spirit: A History of the Caribs in Colonial Venezuela and Guyana, 1498–1820* (Dordrecht: Foris Publications, 1988); John M. Monteiro, "Indigenous Histories in Colonial Brazil," in *The Oxford Handbook of Borderlands of the Iberian World,* ed. Danna A. Levin Rojo and Cynthia Radding (New York: Oxford University Press, 2019); Heather F. Roller, *Contact Strategies: Histories of Native Autonomy in Brazil* (Stanford, CA: Stanford University Press, 2021); Kay Scaramelli, "La negociación de la supervivencia en la frontera misional del Orinoco Medio," in *Arqueología del contacto en Latinoamérica,* ed. Lourdes S. Domínguez and Pedro Paulo A. Funari, 272–284 (São Luís: Jundiaí, SP: EDUFMA; Paco Editorial, 2019); Nelly Arvelo-Jiménez and Horacio Biord, "The Impact of Conquest on Contemporary Indigenous Peoples of the Guiana Shield," in *Amazonian Indians from Prehistory to the Present: Anthropological Perspectives,* ed. Anna Curtenius Roosevelt (Tucson: University of Arizona Press, 1994); José del Rey Fajardo, ed., *Misiones jesuíticas en la Orinoquía (1625–1767),* 2 vols. (Táchira, Venezuela: Universidad Católica del Táchira, 1992); Nancy K. C. Morey, "Ethnohistory of the Colombian and Venezuelan Llanos" (PhD diss., University of Utah, 1975); James Schofield Saeger, *The Chaco Mission Frontier: The Guaycuruan Experience* (Tucson: University of Arizona Press, 2000); Tessa Murphy, *The Creole Archipelago: Race and Borders in the Colonial Caribbean* (Philadelphia: University of Pennsylvania Press, 2021).

10   Raymond Breton, *Dictionaire caraibe-françois: Meslé de quantité de remarques historiques pour l'esclaircissement de la langue* (Auxerre: Gilles Bouquet, 1665), 265, 359.

11   Breton, *Dictionaire caraibe-françois,* 68–71, see also 31, 49, 51, 208; Raymond Breton, *Dictionaire françois-caraibe* (Auxerre: Gilles Bouquet, 1666), 70 (shellfish); *Dictionaire caraibe-françois,* 290 (birds), 29 (iguana), 430; *Dictionaire françois-caraibe,* 70, 307, 310 (agouti).

12   Filippo Salvadore Gilij, *Ensayo de historia americana,* trans. Antonio Tovar, 3 vols. (Caracas: Academia Nacional de la Historia, 1965), 2:263–264; Gumilla, *Orinoco ilustrado,* 1:190.

13   Gumilla, *Orinoco ilustrado,* 1:260–261.

14   See, e.g., Matías Ruiz Blanco, *Conversión de Píritu* (Madrid: Por Iuan Garcia Infançon, 1690), 15–18, 25–26, 36, 39; Jean de Léry, *History of a Voyage to the Land of*

15   *Brazil,* trans. Janet Whatley (Berkeley: University of California Press, 1990), 79–87; on caiman, see Gilij, *Ensayo,* 1:10.

15   Léry, *History of a Voyage,* 154.

16   Antoine Biet, *Voyage de la France Eqvinoxiale en L'isle de Cayenne* (Paris: F. Clovzier, 1664), 357–358.

17   Gilij, *Ensayo,* 2:223. See also, Gumilla, *Orinoco ilustrado,* 1:207, 197, 2:285, 90–91; Tertre, *Histoire générale des isles de S. Christophe,* 417; Breton, *Dictionaire caraibe-françois,* 225; Walter E. Roth, *An Inquiry into the Animism and Folk-lore of the Guiana Indians* (Washington, DC: Government Printing Office, 1915), 156.

18   *Histoire naturelle des Indes: The Drake Manuscript in the Pierpont Morgan Library,* trans. Ruth S. Kraemer (New York: W. W. Norton 1996), fols. 112v–114r, 107r–108v. See also "Relation de l'île," 47; Tertre, *Histoire générale des isles de S. Christophe,* 422.

19   Gumilla, *Orinoco ilustrado,* 1:207, 197.

20   Gumilla, *Orinoco ilustrado,* 1:285; Breton, *Dictionaire caraibe-françois,* 359–360, Gilij, *Ensayo,* 2:265.

21   Gonzalo Fernández de Oviedo y Valdés, *De la natural hystoria de las Indias* (Toledo: Remo[n] de Petras, 1526), fol. 9r–v; Pietro Martire d'Anghiera, *De orbe novo: The Eight Decades of Peter Martyr d'Anghera,* trans. Francis Augustus MacNutt, 2 vols. (New York: G. P. Putnam's Sons, 1912), 1:410–411.

22   Ruiz Blanco, *Conversión,* 36–37; on Ruiz Blanco, see Fernando Arellano, *Una introducción a la Venezuela prehispánica: Culturas de las naciones indígenas venezolanas* (Caracas: Universidad Católica Andrés, 1987), 238–240; William Henry Brett, *The Indian Tribes of Guiana* (New York: R. Carter & Brothers, 1852), 274–275; Gumilla, *Orinoco ilustrado,* 2:261.

23   Gilij, *Ensayo,* 2:142–143; Ruiz Blanco, *Conversión,* 36–37; Rafael Karsten, *The Head-Hunters of Western Amazonas: The Life and Culture of the Jibaro Indians of Eastern Ecuador and Peru* (Helsingfors: Societas Scientiarum Fennica, 1935), 175.

24   Tertre, *Histoire générale des isles de S. Christophe,* 399.

25   Jean-Baptiste du Tertre, *Histoire générale des Antilles habitées par les François* (Paris: T. Jolly, 1667), 200–201.

26   Tertre, *Histoire générale des isles de S. Christophe,* 446.

27   Karsten, *Head-Hunters,* 167, 179.

28   Ruiz Blanco, *Conversión,* 40–41.

29   Gilij, *Ensayo,* 2:123–124.

30   Roth, *Inquiry into the Animism,* 281; Koch-Grünberg, *Del Roraima al Orinoco,* vol. 2.

31   Ruiz Blanco, *Conversión,* 36–37; Brett, *Indian Tribes of Guiana,* 274–275; Gumilla, *Orinoco ilustrado,* 2:261.

32   Gumilla, *Orinoco ilustrado,* 1:264–265.

33   Gumilla, *Orinoco ilustrado*, 2:261.

34   Francisco de Figueroa, *Relación de las misiones de la Compañía de Jesús en el país de los Maynas* (Madrid: V. Suarez, 1904), 214; see also, Schomburgk, *Travels*; Karsten, *Head-Hunters*, 168; Koch-Grünberg, *Del Roraima al Orinoco*, 3:138.

35   Breton, *Dictionaire caraibe-françois*, 206.

36   Ruiz Blanco, *Conversión*, 15; Karsten, *Head-Hunters*, 168, 176.

37   Gumilla, *Orinoco ilustrado*, 2:99; Biet, *Voyage*, 151; Figueroa, *Relación de las misiones*, 258; Karsten, *Head-Hunters*, 261–263.

38   Tertre, *Histoire générale des isles de S. Christophe*, 446–447.

39   Figueroa, *Relación de las misiones*, 233; Karsten, *Head-Hunters*, 154–157.

40   Oviedo, *De la natural hystoria*, fol. 11r; Breton, *Dictionaire caraibe-françois*, 141; William Henry Brett, *Legends and Myths of the Aboriginal Indians of British Guiana*, 2nd ed. (London: W. W. Gardner, 1880), 161, 169.

41   Gumilla, *Orinoco ilustrado*, 1:284, 285; Gilij, *Ensayo*, 1:153, 2:263–264; Figueroa, *Relación de las misiones*, 73, 208; Karsten, *Head-Hunters*, 177–179.

42   Gumilla, *Orinoco ilustrado*, 2:124–136; *Histoire naturelle des Indes*, fols. 86v–87r.

43   Gumilla, *Orinoco ilustrado*, 2:125.

44   Brett, *Legends and Myths*, 172; Koch-Grünberg, *Del Roraima al Orinoco*, 2:66–72; Claude Lévi-Strauss, *The Raw and the Cooked: Introduction to a Science of Mythology*, trans. John Weightman and Doreen Weightman (New York: Harper & Row, 1969; Chicago: University of Chicago Press, 1983), 59–60, 181, 256, 262.

45   For example, Gumilla, *Orinoco ilustrado*, 2:90–91.

46   Alexander von Humboldt, *Personal Narrative of Travels to the Equinoctial Regions of America, during the Years 1799–1804*, 3 vols. (London: Henry G. Bohn, 1852), 2:439–440.

47   Breton, *Dictionaire caraibe-françois*, 83, 167, 216–218, 283, 300; Ruiz Blanco, *Conversión*, 34; Gumilla, *Orinoco ilustrado*, 2:174–176, 237; Pierre Barrère, *Essai sur l'histoire naturelle de la France Equinoxiale* (Paris: chez Piget, 1741), 163–166; Roth, *Inquiry into the Animism*, 328–339.

48   Pané, *Account of the Antiquities*, 25.

49   Pané, *Account of the Antiquities*, 25–26, 24.

50   Although later outsiders asserted that shamans were credited with the ability to transform into predators—jaguars, above all—this kind of shape-shifting is notably absent in the earlier sources. I suspect the later accounts reflect influence of European witchcraft beliefs that became central to descriptions of ritual activity in Central Mexico, as argued in Chap. 8.

51   Breton, *Dictionaire caraibe-françois*, 234.

52 Carlos Fausto, "Feasting on People: Eating Animals and Humans in Amazonia," *Current Anthropology* 48, no. 4 (2007): 497–530, 503, 504; Luiz Costa, "Making Animals into Food among the Kanamari of Western Amazonia," in *Animism in Rainforest and Tundra: Personhood, Animals, Plants and Things in Contemporary Amazonia and Siberia,* ed. Marc Brightman, Vanessa Elisa Grotti, and Olga Ulturgasheva (New York: Berghahn Books, 2012).

53 André Thevet, *Les singvlaritez de la France Antarctiqve* (Paris: Heritiers de Maurice de la Porte, 1558), fol. 56r.

54 Biet, *Voyage,* 361.

55 Vilaça, "Making Kin," 351.

56 Tertre, *Histoire générale des isles de S. Christophe,* 415; Breton, *Dictionaire caraibe-françois,* 275; see also Ruiz Blanco, *Conversión,* 39.

57 Gilij, *Ensayo,* 2:126–127; see also Vilaça, "Making Kin," 355–358.

58 Viveiros de Castro, *From the Enemy's Point of View*; Vilaça, "Making Kin," Fausto, "Feasting," 504.

59 Breton identified the "mansfenix," as a *milan,* or a kite, *Dictionaire caraibe-françois,* 37; see also 21, 37, 132, 231, 254–255, 290. This ceremony, or similar ones, are also described in "Relation de l'île"; Tertre, *Histoire générale des isles de S. Christophe,* 418; Tertre, *Histoire générale des Antilles,* 2:252.

60 "Relation de l'île," 69. Breton considered Baron and another man, Hamichon (or Oukalé), who were the Kalinago military leaders on Dominica, to be "brave captains" (69–70).

61 Charles de Rochefort, *Histoire naturelle et morale des îles Antilles de l'Amérique* (Rotterdam: chez Arnould Leers, 1658), 21; on Kalinago "dominion" in the eastern Caribbean through the early eighteenth century, Murphy, *Creole Archipelago,* 19–47.

62 Breton, *Dictionaire caraibe-françois,* 21, 132, 327. Tertre, *Histoire générale des Antilles* 2:377. On using agouti teeth in rituals generally, see Breton, *Dictionaire françois-caraibe,* 297, 365, 373–375.

63 Breton, *Dictionaire caraibe-françois,* 327.

64 Breton, *Dictionaire caraibe-françois,* 202.

65 See, e.g., Biet, *Voyage,* 353, 435; Ruiz Blanco, *Conversión,* 14; Pierre Pelleprat, *Relation des missions des Pp. de la Compagnie de Jesvs dans les Isles, & dans la Terre Ferme* (Paris: Chez S. Cramoisy & G. Cramoisy, 1655), 2:67; Peter G. Roe, "Paragon or Peril? The Jaguar in Amazonian Indian Society," in *Icons of Power: Feline Symbolism in the Americas,* ed. Nicholas J. Saunders (London: Routledge, 1998), 177–178.

66 Breton, *Dictionaire caraibe-françois,* 192, see also 21; "Relation de l'île," 55, 66–67; Tertre, *Histoire générale des isles de S. Christophe,* 435.

67 "Relation de l'île," 55.

68   Ruiz Blanco, *Conversión,* 14–15; Barrère, *Essai sur l'histoire naturelle;* Brett, *Indian Tribes of Guiana,* 57; Schomburgk, *Travels,* 1:158.

69   Gumilla, *Orinoco ilustrado,* 1:126; Gilij, *Ensayo,* 1:101.

70   See also, Biet, *Voyage,* 353, 435; Ruiz Blanco, *Conversión,* 14; Pelleprat, *Relation des missions,* 2:67; Figueroa, *Relación de las misiones,* 257; Karsten, *Head-Hunters,* 91; Koch-Grünberg, *Del Roraima al Orinoco,* 3:45–49; Roe, "Paragon or Peril?" 177–178; Fausto "Feasting," 507.

71   "Relation de l'île," 52.

72   Gumilla, *Orinoco ilustrado,* 1:199; Santos-Granero, *Vital Enemies,* 216.

73   Santos-Granero, *Vital Enemies,* 210, 213–215; Roe, "Paragon or Peril?" 177–178; Fausto "Feasting," 507.

74   Gumilla, *Orinoco ilustrado,* 1:139–140.

75   "Relation de l'île," 55; Tertre, *Histoire générale des isles de S. Christophe,* 435.

76   Figueroa, *Relación de las misiones,* 257.

77   Figueroa, *Relación de las misiones,* 257–258, 252; Karsten, *Head-Hunters.*

78   Santos-Granero, *Vital Enemies,* 212, 209–213.

79   For example, Thevet, *Les singvlaritez,* fols. 92v–93v; Léry, *History of a Voyage,* 88; Ruiz Blanco, *Conversión;* Gumilla, *Orinoco ilustrado,* 1:125, 159, 161; Gilij, *Ensayo,* 1:172; Figueroa, *Relación de las misiones,* 257; Barrère, *Essai sur l'histoire naturelle.*

80   Christopher Columbus, *The Diario of Christopher Columbus's First Voyage to America, 1492–1493,* transcribed and trans. Oliver Dunn and James E. Kelly, Jr. (Norman: University of Oklahoma Press, 1989), 333, 329.

81   "Relation de l'île," 54–55; Breton, *Dictionaire caraibe-françois,* 80, 88, 93, 329, 90–91; Breton, *Dictionaire francois-caraibe,* 219.

82   Breton, *Dictionaire caraibe-françois,* 310, 410; Breton, *Dictionaire francois-caraibe,* 68. See also Pelleprat, *Relation des missions,* 2:69; Figueroa, *Relación de las misiones,* 233.

83   Ruiz Blanco, *Conversión,* 26; Gumilla, *Orinoco ilustrado,* 1:263; Biet, *Voyage,* 344, 354; Gilij, *Ensayo,* 1:172; Koch-Grünberg, *Del Roraima al Orinoco,* 2:104; Ruben E. Reina and Kenneth M. Kensinger, eds., *The Gift of Birds: Featherwork of Native South American Peoples* (Philadelphia: University of Pennsylvania Museum of Archaeology, 1991).

84   Léry, *History of a Voyage,* 145.

85   Activist and scholar Glicéria Jesus da Silva's investigation of some of these mantles inform her creation of new art, Daniela Fernandes Alarcon and Glicéria Jesus da Silva, "Bringing the Feathered Mantle Back: Cultural Revitalization among the Tupinambá, Brazil" paper delivered at the Second International Conference "Dispossessions in the Americas," at the University of Pennsylvania, in Philadelphia, November 17–18, 2022.

86 Fernandes Alarcon and Glicéria Jesus da Silva, "Bringing the Feathered Mantle Back," 12; Glicéria Jesus da Silva, "These Objects Are Our Ancestors: It Is Time to Listen to Them," paper delivered at the Second International Conference "Dispossessions in the Americas"; Glicéria Jesus, "O Manto Tupinamb," in *Odù: Contracolonialidade e Oralitura* 1 (2021): 8–15.

87 Breton, *Dictionaire caraibe-françois*, 184, 326 [226 sic], 377; Breton, *Dictionaire françois-caraibe*, 271.

88 Gilij, *Ensayo*, 1:210, 2:124–125.

89 Figueroa, *Relación de las misiones*, 240. See also, Breton, *Dictionaire caraibe-françois*, 184, 326 [226 sic]; *Dictionaire françois-caraibe*, 271.

90 Breton, *Dictionaire caraibe-françois*, 293.

91 See, e.g., Lévi-Strauss, *Raw and the Cooked*, 303–304.

92 Gumilla, *Orinoco ilustrado*, 1:125.

93 Léry, *History of a Voyage*, 141–142; Breton, *Dictionaire françois-caraibe*, 38, 203. Ruiz Blanco, *Conversión*, 37–40; Gilij, *Ensayo*, 2:230–235.

94 Breton, *Dictionaire françois-caraibe*, 38.

95 Gumilla, *Orinoco ilustrado*, 1:218–219.

96 Ruiz Blanco, *Conversión*, 40.

97 Ruiz Blanco, *Conversión*, 37.

98 Ruiz Blanco, *Conversión*, 40, 37.

99 Gilij, *Ensayo*, 2:235.

100 Schomburgk, *Travels*, 1:119.

101 Koch-Grünberg, *Del Roraima al Orinoco*, 3:143.

102 Koch-Grünberg, *Del Roraima al Orinoco*, 2:108–110.

103 Karsten, *Head-Hunters*, 527–532, 527.

104 My reading is informed by Viveiros de Castro's and Descola's (among others) analyses of these "myths," but I think their understanding of Indigenous conception is distorted by not considering the way that European understanding of the "soul" mediates some of the sources on which their readings depend.

105 Ralph Bauer and Jaime Marroquín Arredondo, *Translating Nature: Cross-Cultural Histories of Early Modern Science* (Philadelphia: University of Pennsylvania Press, 2019).

106 On the impact of Oviedo on early modern natural history, see Ralph Bauer, *The Alchemy of Conquest: Science, Religion, and the Secrets of the New World* (Charlottesville, VA: University of Virginia Press, 2019), 343, 371–376. Clusius transcribes many of Oviedo's fauna entries in *Exoticorum libri decem* ([Antwerp?]: Plantinianâ

Raphelengij, 1605), e.g., 10, 11, 95–96, 106, 111, 114, 118, 135, 232. On Oviedo's methods see Bauer, *ibid*, 344–346; Antonio Barrera-Osorio, *Experiencing Nature: The Spanish American Empire and the Early Scientific Revolution* (Austin, TX: University of Texas Press, 2006), 103–116; Miguel de Asúa and Roger French, *A New World of Animals: Early Modern Europeans on the Creatures of Iberian America* (Alershot, Hants, England: Ashgate, 2005).

107   Marcy Norton, *Sacred Gifts, Profane Pleasures: A History of Tobacco and Chocolate in the Atlantic World* (Ithaca, NY: Cornell University Press, 2008), 86–92; Marcy Norton, "Subaltern Technologies and Early Modernity in the Atlantic World," *Colonial Latin American Review* 26, no. 1 (2017): 18–38.

108   Gonzalo Fernández de Oviedo y Valdés, *La historia general de las Indias* (Seville: en la empre[n]ta de Juan Cromberger, 1535), proemio, n.p.

109   Gonzalo Fernández de Oviedo y Valdés, *Historia general y natural de las Indias,* ed. and intro. Juan Pérez de Tudela Bueso, 2nd ed., 5 vols. (Madrid: Ediciones Atlas, 1992), 2: 29, 32, 53, 84; see also, 39, 42–43, 52–55.

5. Taming Strangers

1   Gonzalo Fernández de Oviedo y Valdés, *Historia general y natural de las Indias,* ed. and intro. Juan Pérez de Tudela Bueso, 2nd ed. (Madrid: Ediciones Atlas, 1992), 3:211–212.

2   Oviedo, *Historia general,* 3:211.

3   Philippe Erikson, "De l'apprivoisement à l'approvisionnement: Chasse, alliance et familiarisation en Amazonie amériendienne," *Techniques & Culture* 9 (1987): 105–140; Philippe Descola, *In the Society of Nature: A Native Ecology in Amazonia,* trans. Nora Scott (Cambridge: Cambridge University Press, 1994), 379–385; Carlos Fausto, "Of Enemies and Pets: Warfare and Shamanism in Amazonia," trans. David Rodgers, *American Ethnologist* 26, no. 4 (1999): 933–956; Anne Christine Taylor, "Wives, Pets, and Affines: Marriage among the Jivaro," in *Beyond the Visible and the Material: The Amerindianization of Society in the Work of Peter Rivière,* ed. Peter Rivière, Laura M. Rival, and Neil L. Whitehead (Oxford: Oxford University Press, 2001), 45–56.

4   Raymond Breton, *Dictionaire caraibe-françois* (Auxerre: Gilles Bouquet, 1665), 290.

5   Raymond Breton, *Dictionaire françois-caraibe* (Auxerre: Gilles Bouquet, 1666), 2:19, 20.

6   On the interdependent nature of familiarization and predation, see Erikson, "De l'apprivoisement à l'approvisionnement," 105–140; Fausto, "Of Enemies and Pets," 933–956.

7   On the related terms "itologu" and "egu" used by Kalapalo and Txicáo Carib speakers, see Ellen B. Basso, *The Kalapalo Indians of Central Brazil* (New York: Holt, Rinehart, & Winston, 1973), 21; Patrick Menget, "Note sur l'adoption chez les Txicáo du Brésil central," *Anthropologie et sociétés* 12, no. 2 (1988), 63–72, 102; Marcy Norton, "The Chicken or the *Iegue:* Human-Animal Relationships and the Columbian Exchange," *American Historical Review* 120, no. 1 (2015): 28–60, 40–41.

In common with "pets," *iegue* are valued chiefly as kin. However, *iegue* emerge from relationships with (formerly) wild rather than domesticated animals, and they historically precede pets, so I do not refer to *iegue* as pets. See also Chap. 10.

8   Everard Ferdinand Im Thurn, "Tame Animals among the Red Man," *Timehri: Royal Agricultural and Commercial Society of British Guiana* 1 (1882): 25–43; Basso, *The Kalapalo Indians*; Nancy Kathleen Creswick Morey, "Ethnohistory of the Colombian and Venezuelan Llanos" (PhD diss., University of Utah, 1975). Other significant contributions include the works cited above and Menget, "Note sur l'adoption"; Eduardo Batalha Viveiros de Castro, *From the Enemy's Point of View: Humanity and Divinity in an Amazonian Society*, trans. Catherine V. Howard (Chicago: University of Chicago Press, 1992); Philippe Erikson, "The Social Significance of Pet-Keeping among Amazonian Indians," in *Companion Animals and Us: Exploring the Relationships between People and Pets*, ed. Anthony L. Podberscek, Elizabeth S. Paul, and James A. Serpell, 7–26 (Cambridge: Cambridge University Press, 2005); Catherine Vaughan Howard, "Wrought Identities: The Waiwai Expeditions in Search of the 'Unseen Tribes' of Northern Amazonia" (PhD diss., University of Chicago, 2001); Aparecida Vilaça, "Making Kin Out of Others in Amazonia," *Journal of the Royal Anthropological Institute* 8, no. 2 (2002): 347–365; Loretta A. Cormier, *Kinship with Monkeys: The Guajá Foragers of Eastern Amazonia* (New York: Columbia University Press, 2003); Felipe Vander Velden, *Inquietas Companhias: sobre os animais de estimação entre os Karitiana* (São Paulo: Alameda, 2010); Luiz Costa, "Alimentação e comensalidade entre os Kanamari da Amazônia Occidental," *Mana* 19, no. 3 (2013): 473–504. For other ethnographies, see Norton, "The Chicken or the *Iegue*," 28–60.

9   For scholarship on deep history of Indigenous animal taming, see Morey, "Ethnohistory of the Colombian and Venezuelan Llanos"; James Serpell, *In the Company of Animals: A Study of Human-Animal Relationships*, rev. ed. (Cambridge: Cambridge University Press, 1996 [1986]), 61–64; R. A. Donkin, *The Peccary: With Observations on the Introduction of Pigs to the New World* (Philadelphia: American Philosophical Society, 1985); Felipe Ferreira Vander Velden, "As galinhas incontáveis: Tupis, europeus e aves domésticas na conquista no Brasil," *Journal de la société des américanistes* 98, no. 2 (2012): 97–140; Marcy Norton, "Going to the Birds: Animals as Things and Beings in Early Modernity," in *Early Modern Things: Objects and Their Histories, 1500–1800*, ed. Paula Findlen, 53–83 (London: Routledge, 2012), 66–69; Norton, "The Chicken or the *Iegue*. A collaboration between archaeologist Eduardo Neves and anthropologist Carlos Fausto offers an innovative model for exploring familiarization in deep time and extending the concept to plants, Carlos Fausto and Eduardo G. Neves, "Was There Ever a Neolithic in the Neotropics? Plant Familiarisation and Biodiversity in the Amazon," *Antiquity* 92, no. 366 (2018): 1604–1618.

10 The data for this map is from this chapter and Marcy Norton, "The Chicken or the *Iegue*," esp. 58–60. I am grateful to William Keegan, Juan Arboleda, and Girmay Misgna for their work in making this map come to fruition.

11 This teleological view characterizes the work of Donkin, *The Peccary* as well as Jared Diamond, *Guns, Germs, and Steel: The Fates of Human Societies* (New York: W. W. Norton, 1997), 161–167. For more about the problem of this teleology, see Introduction and Norton, "The Chicken or the *Iegue*," 30–32.

12 Galeotto Cei, *Viaje y descripción de las Indias, 1539–1553*, ed. José Rafael Lovera and trans. Marisa Vannini de Gerulewicz (Caracas: Fundación Banco Venezolano de Crédito, 1995), 147.

13 Filippo Salvadore Gilij, *Ensayo de historia americana*, trans. Antonio Tovar, 3 vols. (Caracas: Academia Nacional de la Historia, 1965), 1:252.

14 Fernando Santos-Granero, *Vital Enemies: Slavery, Predation, and the Amerindian Political Economy of Life* (Austin: University of Texas Press, 2009), 179, 180; Cormier, *Kinship with Monkeys*, 93; Descola, *In the Society of Nature*, 90; Costa, "Alimentação e comensalidade."

15 Viveiros de Castro, *From the Enemy's Point of View*, 73.

16 Pietro Martire d'Anghiera, *De orbe novo: The Eight Decades of Peter Martyr d'Anghera*, trans. Francis Augustus MacNutt, 2 vols. (New York: G. P. Putnam's Sons, 1912), 1:344.

17 Christopher Columbus, *The Diario of Christopher Columbus's First Voyage to America, 1492–1493*, transcribed and translated Oliver Dunn and James E. Kelley, Jr. (Norman: University of Oklahoma Press, 1989), 65, 71, 223, 259; Bruce Thomas Boehrer, *Parrot Culture: Our 2,500-Year-Long Fascination with the World's Most Talkative Bird* (Philadelphia: University of Pennsylvania Press, 2004), 50–55.

18 André Thevet, *Les singvlaritez de la France Antarctiqve* (Paris: Heritiers de Maurice de la Porte, 1558), fols. 92v–93r.

19 Jean de Léry, *History of a Voyage to the Land of Brazil, Otherwise Called America*, trans. Janet Whatley (Berkeley: University of California Press, 1990), 88–89, 170–171.

20 Martire d'Anghiera, *De orbe novo*, 1:373–374.

21 Oviedo, *Historia general*, 2:64–66.

22 Martire d'Anghiera, *De orbe novo*, 1:373–374.

23 Martire d'Anghiera, *De orbe novo*, 1:97; Gonzalo Fernández de Oviedo y Valdés, *De la natural hystoria de las Indias* (Toledo: Remo[n] de Petras, 1526), fols, 8v–9r; Oviedo, *Historia general*, 2:65–66.

24 Oviedo, *Historia general*, 2:65–66.

25 Oviedo, *Historia general*, 2:66. For similar techniques used in contemporary West Indies and Madagascar, see Donna J. Haraway, *When Species Meet* (Minneapolis: University of Minnesota Press, 2007), 377n5.

26 Martire d'Anghiera, *De orbe novo*, 1:97.

27 Breton, *Dictionaire caraibe-françois*, 341.

28 Hans Sloane, *A Voyage to the Islands Madera, Barbados, Nieves, St Christophers and Jamaica*, 2 vols. (London: printed for the author, 1725), 2:346.

29 Antoine Biet, *Voyage de la France Eqvinoxiale en L'isle de Cayenne* (Paris: F. Clovzier, 1664), 342; Paul Boyer, *Veritable Relation de tovt ce qvi s'est fait et passé au*

Voyage que monsieur de Bretigny fit a l'Amerique Occidentale (Paris: P. Rocolet, 1654), 300.

30   José Gumilla, *El Orinoco ilustrado y defendido*, 2 vols. (Madrid: Manuel Fernández, 1745) 1:291.

31   Gilij, *Ensayo*, 1:252.

32   Gilij, *Ensayo*, 1:209, 229, 252, 227.

33   Gilij, *Ensayo*, 1:252.

34   Gilij, *Ensayo*, 1:252–253.

35   "Relación de la entrada que hizo el gobernador D. Diego Vaca de Vega al descubrimiento y pacificación de las provincias de los Indios Maynas, Cocamas y Gíbaros," in *Relaciones geográficas de Indias*, ed. Marcos Jiménez de la Espada (Madrid: Tip. de M. G. Hernández, 1897), cxxxix–cli, cxlvii–cxlviii. Francisco de Figueroa, *Relación de las misiones de la compañía de Jesús en el país de los Maynas* (Madrid: V. Suárez, 1904), 73, 137.

36   Manuel María Albis, *Curiosità della foresta d'Amazzonia e arte di curar senza medico*, ed. and trans. Alberto Guaraldo (Turin: Segnalibro, 1991), 205.

37   Francis Galton, *Inquiries into Human Faculty and Its Development* (London: Macmillan, 1883), 248.

38   Martin Dobrizhoffer, *An Account of the Abipones, an Equestrian People of Paraguay*, trans. Sara Coleridge (London: John Murray, Albemarle Street, 1822 [1784]), 220, 311–314 see also 263, 266, 279–280, 283–287, 295, 320–323, 329.

39   José Sánchez Labrador, *El Paraguay católico*, 2 vols. (Buenos Aires: Imprenta de Coni hermanos, 1910), 1:205, 209, 191, 2:258; see also, Florián Baucke, *Hacia allá y para acá: Una estada entre los Indios Mocobíes, 1749–1767*, trans. Edmundo Wernicke, 2 vols. (Córdoba, Argentina: Editorial Nuevo Siglo, 1999); Jan-Åke Alvarsson, *The Mataco of the Gran Chaco* (Uppsala: Academiae Upsaliensis, 1988).

40   Ruth S. Kraemer, trans., *Histoire naturelle des Indes: The Drake Manuscript in the Pierpont Morgan Library* (New York: W. W. Norton, 1996), fol. 88; see also Jean-Baptiste du Tertre, *Histoire générale des isles de S. Christophe, de la Guadeloupe, de la Martinique et autres dans l'Amérique* (Paris: J. Langlois, 1654), 83, 88; Antonio de Herrera y Tordesillas, *Historia general de los hechos de los castellanos en las Islas i Tierra Firme del Mar Oceano*, 4 vols. (Madrid: En la Emplenta Real, 1601), 1:295; William Curtis Farabee, *The Central Caribs* (Philadelphia: University Museum, 1924), 47.

41   Figueroa, *Relación de las Misiones*, 137; see also, Im Thurn, "Tame Animals," 39.

42   Gilij, *Ensayo*, 1:252. See also, Biet, *Voyage*, 342; Cormier, *Kinship with Monkeys*, 114.

43   Gilij, *Ensayo*, 2:265.

44   Léry, *History of a Voyage*, 88. Thevet, *Les singvlaritez*, fol. 92r; Catherine V. Howard, "Feathers as Ornaments among the Waiwai," in *The Gift of Birds: Featherwork of Native South American Peoples*, ed. Ruben E. Reina and Kenneth M. Kensinger

(Philadelphia: University of Pennsylvania Museum of Archaeology, 1991), 56, 60–61, 50; and Howard, "Wrought Identities," 247; Viveiros de Castro, *From the Enemy's Point of View,* 42, 131, 281; Cormier, *Kinship with Monkeys,* 114–116; Vander Velden, *Inquietas Companhias,* 164–166, 178.

45   Matías Ruiz Blanco, *Conversión de Píritu* (Madrid: Por Iuan Garcia Infançon, 1690), 33.

46   Albis, *Curiosità della foresta d'Amazzonia,* 205.

47   Howard, "Wrought Identities," 247–252.

48   Carlos Fausto and Luiz Costa, "Feeding (and Eating): Reflections on Strathern's 'Eating (and Feeding),'" *Cambridge Anthropology* 31, no. 1 (2013): 156–162, 157; see also Costa, "Alimentação e comensalidade."

49   Léry, *History of a Voyage,* 88; Vander Velden, *Inquietas Companhias.*

50   Ruiz Blanco, *Conversión,* 33.

51   William Henry Brett, *The Indian Tribes of Guiana* (New York: R. Carter & Brothers, 1852), 185; Im Thurn, "Tame Animals," 40; Richard Schomburgk, *Travels in British Guiana, 1840–1844,* ed. and trans. Walter Roth, 2 vols. (Georgetown, British Guiana: "Daily Chronicle" Office, 1922) 1:128–129; Pablo J. Anduze, *Shailili-Ko: Relato de un naturalista que también llegó a las fuentes del Río Orinoco* (Caracas: Talleres Graficos Ilustraciones, 1960), 255; Howard, "Wrought Identities," 242; Cormier, *Kinship with Monkeys,* 114.

52   Im Thurn, "Tame Animals," 40; Henry Walter Bates, *The Naturalist on the River Amazons,* 2nd ed. (London: J. Murray, 1864), 256–257; Viveiros de Castro, *From the Enemy's Point of View,* 131.

53   Howard, "Wrought Identities," 245–246.

54   Gumilla, *Orinoco ilustrado,* 1:146–147.

55   Breton, *Dictionaire caraibe-françois,* 79. See also Tertre, *Histoire générale des isles de S. Christophe;* Oviedo, *Historia general,* 3:230; Charles Rochefort, *The History of the Caribby-Islands,* trans. John Davies (London: T. Dring and J. Starkey, 1666), 254–255; Ruiz Blanco, *Conversión,* 32.

56   Breton, *Dictionaire caraibe-françois,* 327.

57   Juan Rivero, *Historia de las misiones de los llanos de Casanare y los ríos Orinoco y Meta [1783]* (Bogotá: Impr. de Silvestre y compañía, 1883), 9; Amy J. Buono, "Feathered Identities and Plumed Performances: Tupinambá Interculture in Early Modern Brazil and Europe" (PhD diss., University of California, Santa Barbara, 2008), 113–118; Im Thurn, "Tame Animals," 28.

58   Im Thurn, "Tame Animals," 39–40.

59   Cei, *Viaje,* 144.

60   Biet, *Voyage,* 339.

61   Lionel Wafer, *A New Voyage and Description of the Isthmus of America* (Cleveland, OH: Burrows, 1903), 120.

62   Gilij, *Ensayo*, 1:252.

63   Martire d'Anghiera, *De orbe novo*, 1:344, 254.

64   Léry, *History of a Voyage*, 88.

65   Rochefort, *History of the Caribby-Islands*.

66   University of Pennsylvania Museum of Anthropology, South America Expedition, John Ogilvie, box 9, folder 2; Howard, "Feathers as Ornaments," 50.

67   Im Thurn, "Tame Animals," 30–31.

68   Thevet, *Les singvlaritez*, fols. 85v, 88v.

69   Antonio Caulín, *Historia coro-graphica natural y evangelica de la Nueva Andalucia, provincias de Cumaná, Guayana y Vertientes del Rio Orinoco* (Madrid: por Juan de San Martín, 1779), 46.

70   Gumilla, *Orinoco ilustrado*, 1:299.

71   Basso, *Kalapalo Indians*, 21; see also, Patrick Menget, "Note sur l'adoption," 67.

72   Wafer, *New Voyage and Description*, 120; see also, Thevet, *Les singvlaritez*, fols. 92r–93v.

73   Gilij, *Ensayo*, 1:252.

74   Bates, *Naturalist on the River Amazons*, 256–257.

75   Im Thurn, "Tame Animals," 33–36. See also, Brett, *Indian Tribes of Guiana*, 185; Descola, *In the Society of Nature*, 90.

76   See also Rivero, *Historia de las misiones*, 9; Biet, *Voyage*, 343; Caulín, *Historia Corographica*, 50.

77   Gilij, *Ensayo*, 1:252.

78   See Chap. 10. On preexisting indigenous networks of trade, see Franz Scaramelli and Kay Tarble de Scaramelli, "The Roles of Material Culture in the Colonization of the Orinoco, Venezuela," *Journal of Social Archaeology* 5, no. 1 (2005): 135–168, 153.

79   António Carlos da Fonseca Coutinho to João Pereira Caldas, Borba, June 13, 1786, Arquivo Histórico Ultramarino, Rio Negro Avulsos, Cx. 11, Doc. 435. I am grateful to Heather Roller for sharing this document.

80   Heather F. Roller, *Contact Strategies: Histories of Native Autonomy in Brazil* (Stanford: Stanford University Press, 2021), 81.

81   Howard, "Wrought Identities," 247–252.

82   Neil L. Whitehead, "Indigenous Slavery in South America, 1492–1820," in *The Cambridge World History of Slavery*, vol. 1, *The Ancient Mediterranean World*, ed. Keith Bradley and Paul Cartledge, vol. 3, 248–274 (Cambridge: Cambridge University Press, 2011), 249.

83   Howard, "Wrought Identities," 249, 252.

84   Whitehead, "Indigenous Slavery."

85   Breton, *Dictionaire caraibe-françois,* 1:216; Martire d'Anghiera, *De orbe novo,* 1:63, 71; Rochefort, *History of the Caribby-Islands,* 326, 266, 271, 323, 325, 327–331; Pierre Pelleprat, *Relation des missions des Pp. de la Compagnie de Jesus dans les Isles, and dans la Terre Ferme* (Paris: Chez S. Cramoisy & G. Cramoisy, 1655), 2:57–63; Neil L. Whitehead, "The Crises and Transformations of Invaded Societies: The Caribbean (1492–1580)," in *The Cambridge History of the Native Peoples of the Americas,* vol. 3, *South America,* pt. 1, ed. Frank Salomon and Stuart B. Schwartz (Cambridge: Cambridge University Press, 1999), 877–888.

86   Menget, "Note sur l'adoption," 67; see also, Basso, *Kalapalo Indians,* 19–24.

87   Santos-Granero, *Vital Enemies,* 217; Whitehead, "Crises and Transformations," 882–888.

88   Quoted in Whitehead, "Crises and Transformations," 864–903, 877–888.

89   Breton, *Dictionaire caraibe-françois,* 1:290.

90   See Chap. 9.

6. Hunting Ecologies

1   *Codex Chimalpopoca,* ed. and trans. John Bierhorst (Tucson: University of Arizona Press, 1992), 151–152. I also used Molly H. Bassett's translations in "Wrapped in Cloth, Clothed in Skins: Aztec Tlaquimilolli (Sacred Bundles) and Deity Embodiment," *History of Religions* 53, no. 4 (2014): 369–400, 384–387.

2   Joaquín García Icazbalceta, ed., "Historia de los mexicanos por sus pinturas," *Anales del Instituto Nacional de Antropología e Historia* 1, no. 2 (1882): 85–106, 90–91; Michel Graulich, *Myths of Ancient Mexico* (Norman: University of Oklahoma Press, 1997), 169–170.

3   Camilla Townsend, *Annals of Native America: How the Nahuas of Colonial Mexico Kept Their History Alive* (New York, NY: Oxford University Press, 2017).

4   My analysis is informed by Bassett, "Wrapped in Cloth," 369–400, 384–387 and Guilhem Olivier, *Cacería, sacrificio y poder en Mesoamérica* (Mexico City: Fondo de Cultura Económica, 2015), 38–42, 244–246.

5   On the importance of oppositional but complementary forces more generally, see Miguel León Portilla, *Aztec Thought and Culture: A Study of the Ancient Nahuatl Mind* (Norman: University of Oklahoma Press, 1963); Alfredo López Austin, *Tamoanchan, Tlalocan: Places of Mist* (Niwot: University Press of Colorado, 1997); James Maffie, *Aztec Philosophy: Understanding a World in Motion* (Boulder: University Press of Colorado, 2013).

6   Guilhem Olivier uses archaeological, pictorial, and textual sources to show how ruling elite used hunting practice and discourse to legitimize their authority,

Cacería; see also Daniele Dehouve, "El venado, el maíz y el sacrificado," *Diario de campo, cuadernos de etnología* 4 (2008): 1–39. For archaeological evidence, see Robbie L. Brewington and Mary G. Hodge, *Place of Jade: Society and Economy in Ancient Chalco* (Pittsburgh, PA: University of Pittsburgh, 2008); Christopher M. Götz and Kitty F. Emery, *The Archaeology of Mesoamerican Animals* (Atlanta: Lockwood Press, 2013).

7   Toribio de Benavente (Motolinia), *Memoriales de Fray Toribio de Motolinía,* ed. Francisco del Paso y Troncoso (Mexico City: En casa del editor, 1903), 344.

8   Olivier, *Cacería,* 374–376.

9   My analysis draws from seminal studies by Johanna Broda, "The Sacred Landscape of Aztec Calendar Festivals," in *To Change Place: Aztec Ceremonial Landscapes,* ed. David Carrasco (Niwot: University Press of Colorado, 1991); Olivier, *Cacería,* 354–460.

10   For translations of the Nahuatl text, I used *Florentine Codex: General History of the Things of New Spain,* trans. Arthur J. O. Anderson and Charles Dibble, 12 books in 13 vols. (Santa Fe: School of American Research and the University of Utah Press, 1981), bk. 2:25, 137–139 (hereafter *Florentine Codex*). For transcriptions of the Spanish text, I used Bernardino de Sahagún, *Historia general de las cosas de Nueva España,* 2 vols. (Barcelona: Linkgua, 2011), hereafter *Historia general.* I also consulted and sometimes cite the digitized original, Florentine Codex, 3 vols., Med. Palat. 218–220, BML, available through the Library of Congress, https://hdl.loc.gov/loc.wdl/wdl.10096.

11   On its creation, Sahagún, *Historia general,* 2:27–32, 77–81; Lluís Nicolau d'Olwer, *Fray Bernardino de Sahagún, 1499–1590,* trans. Mauricio J. Mixco (Salt Lake City: University of Utah Press, 1987 [1952]), 13–20; Alfredo López Austin, "Estudio acerca del método de investigación de fray Bernardino de Sahagún," *Estudios de cultura náhuatl* 42 (2011): 353–400; Jesús Bustamante, *Fray Bernardino de Sahagún: una revisión crítica de los manuscritos y de su proceso de composición* (Mexico City: Universidad Nacional Autónoma de México, 1990); Charles E. Dibble, "Los manuscritos de Tlatelolco y México y el Códice Florentino," *Estudios de cultura náhuatl* 29 (1999): 27–64; Kevin Terraciano and Jeanette Favrot Peterson, eds., *The Florentine Codex: An Encyclopedia of the Nahua World in Sixteenth-Century Mexico* (Austin: University of Texas Press, 2019).

12   Sahagún, *Historia general,* 2:27.

13   Gerónimo de Mendieta, quoted in D'Olwer, *Fray Bernardino de Sahagún,* 15.

14   Sahagún, *Historia general,* 2:77–79.

15   López Austin, "Estudio acerca del método," 353–400; Kevin Terraciano, "Introduction," in Terraciano and Peterson, *The Florentine Codex: An Encyclopedia,* 1–20.

16   Sahagún, *Historia general,* 2:78.

17   Diego Durán, "Historia de las Indias de Nueva España e Islas de la Tierra Firme," Ms. Vitr / 26 / 11, BNE, fols. 256r–260v, 340r–v; Diego Durán, *Book of the Gods and Rites and the Ancient Calendar,* trans. and ed. Fernando Horcasitas and Doris

Heyden (Norman: University of Oklahoma Press, 1971), 142–153, 455–456. See also Toribio de Benavente (Motolinia), *Historia de los indios de la Nueva España*, ed. Claudio Esteva Fabregat (Madrid: Dastin, 2001), 102.

18   Fernando Horcasitas and Doris Heyden, "Fray Diego Durán: His Life and Works," in Durán, *Book of the Gods*, 38–39.

19   *Florentine Codex*, bk. 2: 134–136.

20   Durán, *Book of the Gods*, 146, 456.

21   Durán, *Book of the Gods*, 456.

22   Bernardino de Sahagún, *Primeros Memoriales*, trans. Thelma D. Sullivan and H. B. Nicholson (Norman: University of Oklahoma Press, 1997), 141–142, see also 135–136, 138–139, 151–152.

23   Jane Bennett, *Vibrant Matter: A Political Ecology of Things* (Durham, NC: Duke University Press, 2009), 21.

24   Broda, "Sacred Landscape," 83, 104.

25   *Florentine Codex*, bk. 2:137.

26   Durán, *Book of the Gods*, 146–147.

27   *Florentine Codex*, bk. 2:137.

28   *Florentine Codex*, bk. 2: 134.

29   *Florentine Codex*, bk. 2:139.

30   Durán, *Book of the Gods*, 455; see also, Gerónimo de Mendieta, *Historia eclesiástica indiana* (Mexico City: Cien de México, 1997), 202.

31   *Codex Chimalpopoca*, 149–152; "Histoyre du Mechique, manuscrit français inédit du XVIe Siècle," ed. Edouard de Jonghe, *Journal de la société des Américanistes* 2, no. 1 (1905): 1–41, 18.

32   Hernán Cortés, "The Second Letter," in Cortés, *Letters from Mexico*, ed. and trans. Anthony Pagden, 47–159 (New York: Grossman Publishers, 1971), 101, 103–104; Hernán Cortés, *Carta de relacion embiada a Su. S. Majestad* (Seville: Jacobo Cro[m]berger, 1522), n. f.

33   Olivier, *Cacería*, 436–437, 442–443, 454; Charles Gibson, *The Aztecs under Spanish Rule; a History of the Indians of the Valley of Mexico, 1519–1810* (Stanford, CA: Stanford University Press, 1964), 341–343.

34   René García Castro, ed., *Suma de visitas de pueblos de la Nueva España, 1548–1550* (Mexico City: Universidad Autónoma del Estado de México, 2013), 312, see also 396, 420. For game sold in markets, see Gibson, *Aztecs*, 341–343.

35   "Relación de Chichicapa y su partido," 115–143, *Papeles de Nueva España*, 4:141.

36   "Relación de Guatulco y su partido," 232–251, *Papeles de Nueva España*, 4:244.

37   "Relación de Xalapa y su partido," 252–266. *Papeles de Nueva España*, 258–261. See also "Relación de Texupa," 53–57, 56; "Relación de Chichicapa y su partido," 115–143,

136; "Relación de Macuilsúchil y su partido," 100–108, 106; "Relación de Guaxilotitlan," 96–205, 200; "Relación de Ahuatlan y su partido," *Papeles de Nueva España*, 5: 81–98, 82, 85 in *ibid.*

38   "Relación de Papaloticpac y su partido," 4: 88–99, 96; 4:96; "Relación de Tilantongo y su partido," 69–87, 84; "Relación de Zaluya [Sayula]," 6:178–182, 180, in *Papeles de Nueva España*. See also Chap. 7.

39   See also Gonzalo de Balsalobre, *Relación auténtica de las idolatrías* (Spain: Linkgua, 2011), 22–23, 45–46.

40   Durán, "Historia de las Indias," fol. 260r–v; Durán, *Book of the Gods*, 152.

41   See Chap. 9.

42   David Tavárez, *Las guerras invisibles: devociones indígenas, disciplina y disidencia en el México colonial* (Oaxaca: Universidad Autónoma Benito Juárez, 2012), 139–144.

43   Hernando Ruiz de Alarcón, *Tratado de las idolatrías, supersticiones, dioses, ritos, hechicerías y otras costumbres gentílicas de las razas aborígenes de Mexico*, ed., notes, and intro. Francisco del Paso y Troncoso (Mexico City: Ediciones Fuente Cultural, 1953); Hernando Ruiz de Alarcón, *Treatise on the Heathen Superstitions and Customs That Today Live among the Indians Native to This New Spain, 1629*, trans. and ed. Richard Andrews and Ross Hassig (Norman: University of Oklahoma Press, 1984).

44   Ruiz de Alarcón, *Treatise on the Heathen Superstitions*, 94–95.

45   Ruiz de Alarcón, *Treatise on the Heathen Superstitions*, 94–104. For different translation of the deer conjuration see Tavárez, *Las guerras invisibles*, 86; and Olivier, *Cacería*, 210–224.

46   Ruiz de Alarcón, *Treatise on the Heathen Superstitions*, 96–97.

47   Ruiz de Alarcón, *Treatise on the Heathen Superstitions*, 99.

48   Ruiz de Alarcón, *Treatise on the Heathen Superstitions*, 100.

49   All appear in the second treatise of Ruiz de Alarcón, *Treatise on the Heathen Superstitions*, 73–120.

50   Ruiz de Alarcón, *Treatise on the Heathen Superstitions*, 124, 90, 113, 116, 119, 92, 107, 112, 115.

51   See the discussions in Elizabeth Hill Boone, *Cycles of Time and Meaning in the Mexican Books of Fate* (Austin: University of Texas Press, 2007), 19–20; Ana Díaz Álvarez, *El maíz se sienta para platicar: Códices y formas de conocimiento nahua, más allá del mundo de los libros* (Mexico City: Universidad Iberoamericana, 2016), 30–33.

52   García Icazbalceta, "Historia de los mexicanos," 85.

53   Díaz, *El maíz*, 45–48.

54   Quoted in León Portilla, *Aztec Thought*, 18–19.

55   Davide Domenici, David Buti, Chiara Grazia, Élodie Dupey García, Aldo Romani, Laura Cartechini, Antonio Sgamellotti, and Costanza Miliani, "Non-invasive

Chemical Characterization of Painting Materials of Mesoamerican Codices Borgia (Borg. Mess. 1) and Vaticanus B (Vat. Lat. 3773) of the Biblioteca Apostolica Vaticana," *Miscellanea Bibliothecae Apostolicae Vaticanae* 25 (2019): 1–28.

56   Boone, *Cycles* 5–6, 11; Domenici, et al, "Non-invasive Chemical Characterization," 8.

57   Domenici, et al, "Non-invasive Chemical Characterization," 202, 208–212.

58   Boone, *Cycles,* 32–65.

59   My characterization of this scholarship is indebted to Sebastián van Doesburg and Michel R. Oudijk, "La hemerología mántica del Grupo Borgia," *Revista española de antropología americana* 52, no. 2 (September 16, 2022): 261–280.

60   E.g., Eduard Seler, *Comentarios al Códice Borgia* (Mexico City: Fondo de Cultura Económica, 1963 [1944]); Eduard Seler, *Codex Fejérváry-Mayer: An Old Mexican Picture Manuscript in the Liverpool Free Public Museums (12014/M),* trans. A. H. Keane ([Edinburgh]: printed by T. and A. Constable . . . at the Edinburgh University Press, 1901).

61   Karl Anton Nowotny, *Tlacuilolli: Style and Contents of the Mexican Pictorial Manuscripts with a Catalog of the Borgia Group,* trans. and ed. George A. Everett, Jr. and Edward B. Sisson (Norman: University of Oklahoma, 2005).

62   E.g., Ferdinand Anders, Maarten E. R. G. N. Jansen, and Luis Reyes García, *Los templos del ielo y de la oscuridad: libro explicativo del llamado Códice Borgia* (Madrid: Sociedad Estatal Quinto Centenario, 1993); Doesburg and Oudijk, "La hemerología mántica, 261–268.

63   Boone, *Cycles,* 171–210.

64   Robin Wall Kimmerer, *Braiding Sweetgrass: Indigenous Wisdom, Scientific Knowledge and the Teachings of Plants* (Minneapolis: Milkweed Editions, 2013).

65   While for some my reading may seem a return to the Selerian over-reach, I think it is important to recognize that the modern scholarly interpretive apparatus is inextricably tied to the early modern Christian missionary framework and its ontological limitations. More precisely I believe that the colonial-era texts privilege mythological and political readings over the ecological meanings that are also present in the pre-Hispanic cosmograms. On the way that both Nahuatl and Spanish texts from colonial period project Christian concepts that do not reflect pre-Hispanic Indigenous ontological categories have distorted influential modern scholarship; see Michel Oudijk, "The Making of an Academic Myth" in *Indigenous Graphic Communication Systems: A Theoretical Approach,* eds. Jerome A. Offner and Katarzyna Mikulska (Louisville: University Press of Colorado, 2019), 340–375 and Ana Díaz, ed. *Reshaping the World: Debates on Mesoamerican Cosmologies* (Louisville: University Press of Colorado, 2020).

66   My analysis is based on the facsimile, *Codex Borgia: Biblioteca apostolica vaticana (Cod. Borg. Messicano 1),* ed. Karl Anton Nowotny (Graz, Austria: Akadem.

Druck-u. Verlagsanstalt, 1976), the digitized version at https://digi.vatlib.it/view
/MSS_Borg.mess.1, and an in-person consultation of the codex (Cod. Borg. Messicano 1) at Biblioteca Apostolica Vaticana (Rome) in October 2021.

67   Codex Borgia, pl. 22; a similar image is in *Códice Vaticano B.3773* (Madrid: Sociedad
Estatal Quinto Centenario, 1993), pl. 77.

68   Boone, *Cycles*, 121.

69   Codex Borgia, pl. 47–53.

70   Alfredo López Austin, "Ligas entre el mito y el ícono en el pensamiento cos-
mológico mesoamericano," *Anales de Antropología* 43 (2010): 9–50, 27–29; López
Austin, *Tamoanchan*, 19–21, 93–94.

71   E.g., *Códice Vaticano B*, pl. 17–18, 23–28; Boone, *Cycles*, 113–134. Colonial-era copies
with a cosmogram include *Códice Vaticano A. 3738*, eds. Ferdinand Anders, Maarten
E. R. G. N. Jansen, and Luis Reyes García (Austria: Akademische Druck- und
Verlagsanstalt, 1996), fols, 6r–9r.

72   *Códice Fejérváry-Mayer*, facsimile ed. (Austria: Akademische Druck- und Verlagsanstalt, 1994), pl. 1.

73   There is no existing consensus on how to understand this section of the Codex
Borgia.: Anders, Jansen, and Reyes García suggest that the "principal theme" of the
panels is "the foundation and establishment of a kingdom, a dynasty or a human
vivencia," *Los templos del cielo*, 261–269; Boone focuses on its divinatory functions,
Cycles, 83–84, 113–116, 121–132; Susan Milbrath argues that it draws connections between planetary phases, historical events, and ritual activity, "Thresholds of Time
and Space Year-Bearer Imagery in Postclassic Codices," *Latin American and Latinx
Visual Culture* 2, no. 3 (2020): 8–28; see also Nowotny, *Tlacuilolli*, 34–47, 112–120;
Eduard Seler, *Comentarios*, 2: 85–103.

74   Brian D. Fath, "Ecosystems" in *Encyclopedia of Ecology*, Vol. 2, ed. Sven Erik Jor-
gensen and Brian D. Fath, 473–488, (Amsterdam: Elsevier, 2019), 473.

75   Codex Borgia, pl. 50; *Códice Vaticano B.3773*, pl. 24–27; *Códice Fejérváry-Mayer*, pl.
41–42.

76   See Introduction to this book and Mendieta, *Historia eclesiástica indiana*, 204.

77   *Codex Chimalpopoca*, 149; see also, "Historia de los mexicanos," 89; Sahagún, *Primeros Memoriales*, 88.

78   Scholars have identified the male figure in the cells as a Macuiltonaleque, deified
men who died in battle, and the female figures as Cihuateteo, deified women who
died in childbirth, Boone, *Cycles*, 122. The linkage between warfare and childbirth as
processes that are generative—producing captives and babies—as well as destructive further underscores the interconnectedness of predation and familiarization.

79   In the northern and central directional panels, the association between these figures and the aquatic element is made explicit (figs. 6.3 and 6.4).

80   Boone, *Cycles,* 128–129.

81   On fire drilling, see César A. Sáenz Vargas, *El fuego nuevo* (Mexico City: Instituto Nacional de Antropología e Historia, 1967); Guilhem Olivier, "Sacred Bundles, Arrows, and the New Fire,'" in *Cave, City and Eagle's Nest,* ed. David Carrasco and Scott Sessions, 281–313 (Albuquerque: University of New Mexico Press, 2007).

82   "Historia de los mexicanos," 88.

83   See also, *Códice Vaticano B.3773,* pl. 17–18.

84   López Austin, *Tamoanchan,* 93–94.

85   For imagery related to eagles feeding trees, see "Historia Tolteca-Chichimeca," in Dana Leibsohn, *Script and Glyph: Pre-Hispanic History, Colonial Bookmaking, and the Historia Tolteca-Chichimeca* (Washington, DC: Dumbarton Oaks Research Library and Collection, 2009), fol. 20r.

86   Fath, "Ecosystems," 474.

87   Fath, "Ecosystems," 474.

88   Other scholars, beginning with Seler, interpret these animals as "animated day signs"; my reasons for thinking they are (also/instead) humans transformed into other kinds of animals are explained more fully below.

89   Seler, *Codex Fejérváry-Mayer,* 10.

90   Seler, *Comentarios al Códice Borgia,* 87.

91   *Florentine Codex,* bk. 11: 18; *Códice Vaticano B,* pl.18.

92   Boone, *Cycles,* 123.

93   On *picietl* and *tonalli,* see López Austin, *Cuerpo humano e ideología: Las concepciones de los antiguos nahuas* 2 vols. (Mexico City: Universidad Nacional Autónoma de México, 1980), 1: 292–293, 310–311.

94   Fath, "Ecosystems," e.g., 473, 481, 476, 474.

95   Domenici, et al, "Non-Invasive," 202.

96   E.g., *Códice Vaticano A. 3738.*

97   "Historia de los mexicanos," 85.

98   "Histoyre du Mechique," 23–24; Graulich, *Myths of Ancient Mexico,* 66, 69, 71. On its composition, see, Angel María Garibay K., *Teogonía e historia de los mexicanos* (Mexico City: Porrúa, 1979), 11–14.

99   de Jonghe, "Histoyre du Mechique," n. 8.

100   "Histoyre du Mechique," 26.

101   "Histoyre du Mechique," 27.

102   *Codex Chimalpopoca,* 146; Mendieta, *Historia eclesiástica indiana,* 182.

103   Graulich, *Myths of Ancient Mexico*, 72–74.

104   A similar image is found in *Códice Vaticano A*. 3738, fol, 7r.

105   On this pictorial tradition, see, Doris Heyden, *The Eagle, the Cactus, the Rock: The Roots of Mexico-Tenochtitlan's Foundation Myth and Symbol* (Oxford: B.A.R., 1989), esp. p. 60.

106   Barbara E. Mundy, *The Death of Aztec Tenochtitlan, the Life of Mexico City* (Austin: University of Texas Press, 2015), 1, 32; Heyden, *The Eagle*.

107   Juan de Tovar, "Historia de la benida de los yndios," c. 1585, Codex Ind 2, JCB. "Crónica Mexicáyotl" in *Tres crónicas mexicanas: textos recopilados por Domingo Chimalpáhin*, trans. Rafael Tena's (Mexico City: Dirección General de Publicaciones del Consejo Nacional para la Cultura y las Artes, 2012), 25–156. On the debates over the relationship between these texts and the role of Alvarado Tezozómoc, see, most recently, Sylvie Peperstraete and Gabriel Kenrick Kruell, "Determining the Authorship of the Crónica Mexicayotl: Two Hypotheses," *The Americas* 71, no. 2 (2014): 315–338.

108   It appears in the preface to the "rites" section (which appears in the manuscript as the second part but was completed first), Durán "Historia de las Indias," fol. 227v.

109   "Crónica Mexicáyotl," 27; see also Mundy, *Death of Aztec Tenochtitlan*, 28, and, *Codex Chimalpahin: Society and Politics in Mexico*, trans. Arthur J. O. Anderson and Susan Schroeder, 2 vols. (Norman: University of Oklahoma Press, 1997), 1: 27, 129.

110   Durán, *History*, 42–43; "Crónica Mexicáyotl," 73.

111   Durán, *History*, 44.

112   "Crónica Mexicáyotl," 75.

113   Federico Navarrete Linares, *Los orígenes de los pueblos indígenas del Valle de México: los altépetl y sus historias* (Mexico City: Universidad Nacional Autónoma de México, 2011).

114   "Crónica Mexicáyotl," 36–37; see also Diego Durán, *The History of the Indies of New Spain*, trans. Doris Heyden (Norman: University of Oklahoma Press, 1994), 11–12.

115   "Crónica Mexicáyotl," 73; Durán, *History of the Indies*, 40.

116   The bird is commonly identified as a hummingbird (e.g., Boone, *Cycles*, 116) but I think it is likely a heron.

117   "Crónica Mexicáyotl," 75; Durán, *History of the Indies*, 41. For this meaning of Anahuac, see Allison Caplan, "The Living Feather: Tonalli in Nahua Featherwork Production," *Ethnohistory* 67, no. 3 (2020): 383–406, 388–389.

118   "Crónica Mexicáyotl," 41–43; *Codex Chimalpahin*, 75, 79.

119   Olivier, *Cacería*, 18–19; Navarrete Linares, *Los orígenes de los pueblos*.

120   "Crónica Mexicáyotl," 73; Durán, *History*, 32.

121   "Yn ixquich tlalticpacyotl," in Ms. 9/5524[1] (also known as the "Códice matritense"), Real Academia de la Historia, Madrid, fols. 200r–342.

122   Bustamante, *Fray Bernardino de Sahagún: Una revisión crítica*, 300–305.

123   I counted as separate entries those that the Nahua authors clearly distinguished with a marginal mark in "Yn ixquich tlalticpacyotl," fols. 248r–308v. I used the translations by Charles E. Dibble and Arthur J. O. Anderson in *Florentine Codex*, bk. 11:1–103. Dibble and Anderson note the divergences between the Códice Matritense and the Florentine Codex in their edition. In arriving at 327 animal entries, I excluded those that describe different parts of avian anatomy (fols. 262r–264r). I also excluded entries that were cross-references. The entries loosely but not entirely accord to modern-day ideas about species: for instance, since sometimes a seemingly single species will get multiple entries because of their sex, color, or age, and sometimes an entry will describe a general category of animal (akin to a genus) that seemingly encompasses more than one species.

124   López Austin, "Estudio acerca del método," 385–386.

125   "Yn ixquich tlalticpacyotl," fol. 254v.

126   Bustamante, *Fray Bernardino de Sahagún: Una revisión crítica*, 300–305.

127   "Yn ixquich tlalticpacyotl," fols. 251r, 260r; see also, for instance, 251v, 252v, 255v, 256v, 258r.

128   "Yn ixquich tlalticpacyotl," fol. 266r.

129   Andrew Laird, "Universal History and New Spain's Indian Past: Classical Knowledge in Nahua Chronicles," *Bulletin of Latin American Research* 37, no. S1 (2018): 86–103.

130   Pablo Escalante Gonzalbo, "Los animales del Códice Florentino en el espejo de la tradición occidental," *Arqueología Mexicana* 6, no. 36 (1999): 52–59; Ilaria Palmieri Capesciotti, "La fauna del libro XI del Códice Florentino de fray Bernardino de Sahagún," *Estudios de cultura náhuatl* 32 (2001): 189–221.

131   Med. Palat. 220, fol. 152r; Escalante Gonzalbo, "Los animales del Códice Florentino"; Kevin Terraciano, "Introduction," in Terraciano and Peterson, *The Florentine Codex: An Encyclopedia*, 9–10.

132   Pliny, *Caii Plynii Secundi naturalis hystoriae liber primus* (Parma: Andreas Portilia, 1481); *Ortus sanitatis* (Mainz: Jacob Meydenbach, 1491), fols. 249r, 299r, 335r.

133   Scholarship that focuses on Indigenous epistemological contribution to Book 11 of the Florentine Codex includes López Austin, "Estudio acerca del método"; Molly H. Bassett, "Bundling Natural History: Tlaquimilolli, Folk Biology, and Book 11" in Terraciano and Peterson, *The Florentine Codex: An Encyclopedia*, 139–151; Marcy Norton, "The Quetzal Takes Flight: Microhistory, Mesoamerican Knowledge, and Early Modern Natural History," in *Translating Nature*, ed. Ralph Bauer and Jaime Marroquín Arredondo, 119–147 (Philadelphia: University of Pennsylvania Press, 2019); Iris Montero Sobrevilla, "The Disguise of the Hummingbird: On the Natural History of Huitzilopochtli in the Florentine Codex," *Ethnohistory* 67, no. 3 (2020): 429–453; Kelly McDonough, *Indigenous Science and Technology: Nahuas and the World around Them* (Tucson: University of Arizona Press, forthcoming 2024).

134   See also *Florentine Codex*, bk. 11:31, 33, 52, 44, 49; for familiarization, see Chap. 7.

135   *Florentine Codex*, bk. 11:13, 15.

136   *Florentine Codex*, bk. 11:12.

137   *Florentine Codex*, bk. 11:1–2, 75, 82. Dibble and Anderson follow Martín del Campo in identifying this snake as a *Crotalus durissus*.

138   *Florentine Codex*, bk. 11:11–12.

139   *Florentine Codex*, bk. 11:2–3; Bassett, "Bundling Natural History," 147–151.

140   "Yn ixquich tlalticpacyotl": "de los aves," fols. 248r–264r; "de los animales," 264r–275v; "de los animales del agua," fols. 275v–285v; "de las serpientes y otros animales de tierra de diferentes maneras," fols. 285v–308v.

141   "Yn ixquich tlalticpacyotl," fol. 248v.

142   "Yn ixquich tlalticpacyotl," fols. 249v–252r.

143   "Yn ixquich tlalticpacyotl," fols. 252r–254v.

144   "Yn ixquich tlalticpacyotl," fols. 254v–256v.

145   See, e.g., "Yn ixquich tlalticpacyotl," fols. 283r–v, 285v, 286r.

7. Nourishing Bodies

1   Hernán Cortés, "The Second Letter," in *Letters from Mexico*, ed. and trans. Anthony Pagden, 47–159 (New York: Grossman Publishers, 1971), 110–111; Hernán Cortés, *Carta de relacion embiada a Su. S. Majestad* (Seville: Jacobo Cro[m]berger, 1522), n.f.; H. B. Nicholson, "Montezuma's Zoo," *Pacific Discovery* 8 (1955): 3–17; Leonardo López Luján, Ximena Chávez Balderas, Belem Zúñiga-Arellano, Alejandra Aguirre Molina, and Norma Valentín Maldonado, "Entering the Underworld: Animal Offerings at the Foot of the Great Temple of Tenochtitlan," in *Animals and Inequality in the Ancient World*, ed. Benjamin S. Arbuckle and Sue Ann McCarty, 33–62 (Boulder: University Press of Colorado, 2014); Ximena María Chavez Balderas, "The Offering of Life: Human and Animal Sacrifice at the West Plaza of the Sacred Precinct" (PhD diss., Tulane University, 2019).

2   Cortés, "Second Letter," 107.

3   Alonso de Molina, *Aqui comiença vn vocabulario enla lengua castellana y mexicana* (Mexico City: En casa de Juan Pablos, 1555), fols. 16v, 140r; Alonso de Molina, *Vocabulario en lengua castellana y mexicana* (Mexico City: En casa de Antonio de Spinosa, 1571), fols. 9r, 47r, 81v, 114v–115r, 136r. For these and other Nahuatl terms I also consulted Gran Diccionario Náhuatl (online), (Mexico City: Universidad Nacional Autónoma de México, 2012), http://www.gdn.unam.mx; Online Nahuatl Dictionary, ed. Stephanie Wood (Eugene, OR: Wired Humanities Projects, College of Education, University of Oregon, 2000–present), https://nahuatl.wired-humanities.org. Frances E. Karttunen, *An Analytical Dictionary of Nahuatl* (Norman: University of Oklahoma Press, 1992). I am grateful to Michael Swanton,

Kelly McDonough, and Barbara Mundy for helping me think about this terminology.

4   Antonio Rincón, *Arte mexicana*, ed. Antonio Peñafiel (Mexico City: Oficina Tip. de la Secretaría de Fomento, 1885), 42–43.

5   Juan de Córdova, *Vocabulario en lengua çapoteca* (Mexico: Pedro Charte [*sic*], y Antonio Ricardo, 1578), fols. 25r, 293; Francisco de Alvarado, *Vocabulario en lengua Mixteca*, ed. Wigberto Jiménez Moreno (Mexico City: Instituto Nacional Indigenista, 1962), fols. 18r, 83, 124v.

6   I am grateful for the email communication with Michel Oudijk, October 18, 2021.

7   *Florentine Codex: General History of the Things of New Spain,* trans. Charles E. Dibble and Arthur J. O. Anderson, 12 books in 13 vols. (Santa Fe: School of American Research and the University of Utah Press, 1950–1987), bk. 11:22, 23. I slightly altered this and other translations by Anderson and Dibble by using "tamed" rather than domesticated for *tlacaciuhqui* and its variants.

8   *Florentine Codex,* 11:51.

9   *Florentine Codex*, bk. 11:23.

10   *Florentine Codex,* bk. 11:48.

11   *Florentine Codex,* bk. 11:76, 79.

12   *Florentine Codex,* bk. 11:14.

13   See Chap. 6.

14   *Ortus sanitatis* (Mainz: Jacob Meydenbach, 1491), fol. 291v; Johannes von Cuba, "Traicte des bestes," in *Le Jardin de sante translaté de latin en françoys* (Paris: Lenoir, 1539), chap. 35; Noel Hudson, ed., *An Early English Version of Hortus Sanitatis* (London: B. Quaritch, 1954), 77.

15   *Florentine Codex,* bk. 11:14.

16   *Florentine Codex,* bk. 11:14.

17   See Chap. 11.

18   Francisco Hernández, "Historiae animalium et mineralium novae hispaniae," in *Rerum medicarum Novae Hispaniae thesaurus, seu Plantarum animalium mineralium Mexicanorum historia* (Rome: Vitalis Mascardi, 1651), 1–99. The translations are based on Francisco Hernández, "Historia de los Animales de Nueva España," trans. José Rojo Navarro in *Obras Completas,* vol. 3, ed. Germán Somolinos d'Ardois (Mexico City: Universidad Nacional de México, 1959). Because the translation cut duplicate entries, the chapter numbers do not always accord; where the chapter numbers diverge from the original and translation, I put the chapter number of the translation in parentheses.

19   Hernández, "Historiae animalium," tr. 1, chaps. 1, 5, 6, 17, 19, 25, 26, 27.

20   Hernández, "Historiae animalium," tr. 1, chap. 1.

21 Hernández, "Historiae animalium," tr. 1, chap. 17.

22 See, for instance, Hernández, "Historiae animalium," tr. 2, chaps. 4, 17, 20, 28, 29, 30, 35, 38, 39, 57, 58, 59, 61, 65, 114, 120, 123. See also chaps. 202 (201), c. 206 (205), c. 209 (208).

23 Hernández, "Historiae animalium," tr. 2, chap. 111.

24 Hernández, "Historiae animalium," tr. 2, chap. 120.

25 Hernández, "Historiae animalium," tr. 2, chap. 101.

26 Hernández, "Historiae animalium," tr. 2, chap. 165.

27 Hernández, "Historiae animalium," tr. 5, chap. 1.

28 Hernández, "Historiae animalium," tr. 3, chap. 24.

29 Hernández, "Historiae animalium," tr. 3, chap. 44.

30 Hernández, "Historiae animalium," tr. 3, chap. 45.

31 Maarten Jansen and Gabina Aurora Pérez Jiménez, *The Mixtec Pictorial Manuscripts: Time, Agency, and Memory in Ancient Mexico* (Leiden: Brill, 2011), 9, 14; Nancy Farriss, *Tongues of Fire: Language and Evangelization in Colonial Mexico* (New York: Oxford University Press, 2018).

32 Francisco de Burgoa, *Geográfica descripción de la parte septentrional* (Mexico City: Juan Ruyz, 1674), fol. 356r–v.

33 For calendar readers in colonial Oaxaca, see Lisa Sousa, *The Woman Who Turned into a Jaguar, and Other Narratives of Native Women in Archives of Colonial Mexico* (Stanford, California: Stanford University Press, 2017), 29–30.

34 See also Hernando Ruiz de Alarcón, *Treatise on the Heathen Superstitions and Customs That Today Live among the Indians Native to This New Spain, 1629* trans. and ed. Richard Andrews and Ross Hassig (Norman: University of Oklahoma Press, 1984), 47.

35 See Chap. 8 for a discussion of the *nahual*.

36 Francisco de Burgoa, *Palestra historial de virtudes, y exemplares apostólicos* (Mexico City: Juan Ruyz, 1670), fols. 85v, 96r.

37 Burgoa, *Palestra historial,* fols. 89v–91v.

38 Burgoa, *Palestra historial,* fol. 90v.

39 Jansen and Pérez Jiménez, *The Mixtec Pictorial Manuscripts,* 12, 56, 65.

40 Ferdinand Anders, Maarten E. R. G. N. Jansen, Luis Reyes García, and Gabina Aurora Pérez Jiménez, *Libro explicativo del llamado Códice Zouche-Nuttall* (Graz, Austria: Akademische Druck- und Verlagsanstalt, 1992); Jansen and Pérez Jiménez, *The Mixtec Pictorial Manuscripts.*

41 Codex Zouche-Nuttall (Tonindeye Codex), pl. 54–66, 70, 71. It can be found on the website of its current owner, the British Museum, https://www.britishmuseum.org/collection/object/E_Am1902-0308-1. Animal identifications follow Anders

et al., *Libro explicativo*, 53–76. I identify them as juveniles based on comparisons within the manuscript.

42   M. Jansen and G. A. Pérez Jiménez, *Codex Bodley: A Painted Chronicle from the Mixtec Highlands, Mexico* (Oxford: Bodleian Library, 2005), 16.

43   Amos Megged, "Nahua Patterns of Colonization in Maya Towns of Guatemala, 1524 to 1582," *Colonial Latin American Review* 22, no. 2 (2013): 209–234.

44   Thomas Gage, *The English-American His Travail by Sea and Land: Or, A New Survey of the West-Indias* (London: R. Cotes, 1648), 167–168.

45   Gage, *New Survey*, 167, 168, 169.

46   Codex Zouche-Nuttall, pl. 47.

47   Fernando de Alva Ixtlilxóchitl, *Historia de la nación chichimeca* (Barcelona: Linkgua Ediciones, 2008), 93, 179–180.

48   Hernández, "Historiae animalium," tr. 2, chaps. 197–215.

49   Diego Durán, *The History of the Indies of New Spain*, trans. Doris Heyden (Norman: University of Oklahoma Press, 1994), 203.

50   "Libro de matrícula," Mexico City, c. 1522–1530, available through the Library of Congress, https://www.wdl.org/en/item/3248/view/1/10/.

51   *The Codex Mendoza*, trans. and ed. Frances Berdan and Patricia Rieff Anawalt (Berkeley: University of California Press, 1992), 3: fols. 3:31r, 55r; 4: 67, 115.

52   "Relación de Acatlan y su partido," in *Papeles de Nueva España*, ed. Francisco del Paso y Troncoso (Mexico City: Estab. Tip. "Sucesores de Rivadeneyra," 1906), 5: 55–80, 75; and "Relación de Tlacotalpan y su partido," in *ibid.*, 5:1–11, 1.

53   Nawa Sugiyama, William L. Fash, and Christine A. M. France, "Jaguar and Puma Captivity and Trade among the Maya: Stable Isotope Data from Copan, Honduras," *PLoS One* 13, no. 9 (2018): e0202958; Andrew D. Somerville, Ben A. Nelson, and Kelly J. Knudson, "Isotopic Investigation of Pre-Hispanic Macaw Breeding in Northwest Mexico," *Journal of Anthropological Archaeology* 29, no. 1 (2010): 125–135; Nawa Sugiyama, Gilberto Pérez, Bernardo Rodríguez, Fabiola Torres, and Raúl Valadez, "Animals and the State: The Role of Animals in State-Level Rituals in Mesoamerica," in *Animals and Inequality*.

54   Sugiyama et al., "Animals and the State."

55   Leonardo López Luján et al., "Entering the Underworld," 50; Chávez Balderas, "The Offering of Life."

56   López Luján et al., "Entering the Underworld," 50–51.

57   Matthew Restall, *When Montezuma Met Cortés: The True Story of the Meeting That Changed History* (New York: Ecco 2018), 77–85; Camilla Townsend, *Fifth Sun: A New History of the Aztecs* (New York: Oxford University Press, 2019), 3–4.

58   Leonardo López Luján and G. Olivier, *El sacrificio humano en la tradición religiosa Mesoamericana* (Mexico City: Instituto Nacional de Antropología e Historia/ Universidad Nacional Autónoma de México, 2010); Eduardo Matos Moctezuma,

Life and Death in the Templo Mayor, trans. B. R. Ortíz de Montellano and T. Ortíz de Montellano (Niwot: University Press of Colorado, 1995).

59 The theorists on sacrifice who have shaped writings about Mesoamerica are preeminently Henri Hubert and Marcel Mauss, *Sacrifice: Its Nature and Function,* trans. W. D. Halls ([Chicago]: University of Chicago Press, 1964).

60 Molina, *Vocabulario,* fol. 125r; Olivier, 38.

61 Molina, *Vocabulario,* fol. 125r; Graulich 229, 379 n. 191.

62 Bernardino de Sahagún, *Primeros Memoriales,* trans. Thelma D. Sullivan and H. B. Nicholson (Norman: University of Oklahoma Press, 1997), 72.

63 Sahagún, *Primeros Memoriales,* 74.

64 Slight modification of Anderson and Dibble translation in *Florentine Codex,* bk. 6:58, see also, 11, 12, 13, 72.

65 Sahagún, *Primeros Memoriales,* 56–57; *Florentine Codex,* bk. 2:3–4, 47–56; Diego Durán, *Book of the Gods and Rites and the Ancient Calendar,* trans. and ed. Fernando Horcasitas and Doris Heyden (Norman: University of Oklahoma Press, 1971), 172–185.

66 Johanna Broda, "Tlacaxipehualiztli: A Reconstruction of an Aztec Calendar Festival from 16th Century Sources," *Revista española de antropología americana* 5 (1970): 197–274; David Carrasco, *City of Sacrifice: The Aztec Empire and the Role of Violence in Civilization* (Boston: Beacon Press, 1999), 140–147.

67 *Florentine Codex,* bk. 2:349.

68 Durán, *Book of the Gods,* 179, 180; *Florentine Codex,* 2:47, 50, 54.

69 Diana K. Moreiras Reynaga, Jean-François Millaire, Ximena Chávez Balderas, Juan A. Román Berrelleza, Leonardo López Luján, and Fred J. Longstaffe, "Residential Patterns of Mexica Human Sacrifices at Mexico-Tenochtitlan and Mexico-Tlatelolco: Evidence from Phosphate Oxygen Isotopes," *Journal of Anthropological Archaeology* 62 (2021): 101296.

70 *Florentine Codex,* bk. 2:48.

71 *Florentine Codex,* bk. 2:55.

72 *Florentine Codex,* bk. 2:51, 52, 53; Durán, *Book of the Gods,* 179.

73 *Florentine Codex,* bk. 2:52–53.

74 *Florentine Codex,* bk. 2:48, 53, 54.

75 *Florentine Codex,* bk. 2:48, 55.

76 *Florentine Codex,* bk. 2:54.

77 *Florentine Codex,* bk. 2:54; Durán, *Book of the Gods,* 176.

78 Ashley E. Sharpe, "A Reexamination of the Birds in the Central Mexican Codices," *Ancient Mesoamerica* 25, no. 2 (2014): 317–336; Eduard Seler, *Comentarios al Códice Borgia* (Mexico City: Fondo de Cultura Económica, 1963 [1944]).

79   E.g., Codex Zouche-Nuttall, pl. 1, 2, 5, 14, 16, 17, 18, 19, 20, 22, 45, 50, 59, 70, 81, 82, 84.

80   Durán, *History of the Indies*, 42, 274, 302, 309, 376, 380, 400, 486; Sahagún, *Primeros Memoriales*, 69, 74; *Florentine Codex*, bk. 2:35, 37, 39.

81   *Florentine Codex*, bk. 2:216.

82   Durán, *History of the Indies*, 218.

83   López Luján et al., "Entering the Underworld," 51.

84   Sahagún, *Primeros Memoriales*, 74.

85   See also, Codex Borgia, pl. 75–76.

86   See, e.g., Codex Borgia, pl. 11, 12, 13.

87   Toribio de Benavente (Motolinía), *Historia de los indios de la Nueva España*. ed. Claudio Esteva Fabregat (Madrid: Dastin, 2001), 98.

88   *Florentine Codex*, bk. 4:6, 33; Sahagún, *Primeros Memoriales*, 74; see also Chap. 8.

89   For other explanations, see Sharpe, "Reexamination of the Birds," 332–333.

90   *Florentine Codex*, bk. 11:49.

91   See Chap. 6.

92   Alessandra Russo, Gerhard Wolf, and Diana Fane, *El vuelo de las imágenes: arte plumario en México y Europa* (Mexico City: Instituto Nacional de Bellas Artes, 2011); Sabine Haag, Alfonso de María y Campos, Lilia Rivero Weber, and Christian Feest, eds., *El penacho de Moctezuma. Plumaria del México antiguo* (Altenstadt: ZKF Publishers, 2012); Frances Berdan, "Circulation of Feathers in Mesoamerica," *Nuevo Mundo, Mundos Nuevos*, January 2006, https://doi.org/10.4000/nuevo mundo.1387; Allison Caplan, "The Living Feather: Tonalli in Nahua Featherwork Production," *Ethnohistory* 67, no. 3 (2020): 383–406.

93   Durán, *History of the Indies*, 203.

94   Arild Hvidtfeldt, *Teotl and *Ixiptlatli: Some Central Conceptions in Ancient Mexican Religion* (Copenhagen: Munksgaard, 1958), 98–99.

95   Molly H. Bassett, "Bundling Natural History," 139–151; *The Florentine Codex: An Encyclopedia of the Nahua World in Sixteenth-Century Mexico*, eds. Kevin Terraciano and Jeanette Favrot Peterson (Austin: University of Texas Press, 2019), 141; Molly H. Bassett, *The Fate of Earthly Things: Aztec Gods and God-Bodies* (Austin: University of Texas Press, 2015), 130–136; Elizabeth H. Boone, *Incarnations of the Aztec Supernatural: The Image of Huitzilopochtli in Mexico and Europe* (Philadelphia: American Philosophical Society, 1989), 4.

96   For an in-depth and linguistically informed discussion, see Allison Caplan "*Tlazohtli, Mahuiztic*: Aesthetic Value in Nahua Luxury," paper delivered at "Tenochtitlan: Imperial Ideologies on Display," Dumbarton Pre-Columbian Studies Symposium, 8–9 April 2022; slated for publication in 2024.

97   *Florentine Codex*, bk. 2:91.

98 *Florentine Codex*, bk. 2:161; Bassett, "Bundling Natural History," 149.

99 Justyna Olko, *Insignia of Rank in the Nahua World: From the Fifteenth to the Seventeenth Century* (Boulder: University Press of Colorado, 2014).

100 *Florentine Codex*, bk. 8:23–25, 29, 25.

101 *Florentine Codex*, bk. 9:89–93; Berdan, "Circulation of Feathers in Mesoamerica."

102 *Florentine Codex*, bk. 11:19–20; Marcy Norton, "The Quetzal Takes Flight: Microhistory, Mesoamerican Knowledge, and Early Modern Natural History," in *Translating Nature: Cross-Cultural Histories of Early Modern Science*, ed. Ralph Bauer and Jaime Marroquín Arredondo, 119–147 (Philadelphia: University of Pennsylvania Press, 2019).

103 *Florentine Codex*, bk. 11:19–20; Norton, "Quetzal Takes Flight," 130–134.

104 Aurelie Manin, Eduardo Corona-M, Michelle Alexander, Abigail Craig, Erin Kennedy Thornton, Dongya Y. Yang, Michael Richards, and Camilla F. Speller, "Diversity of Management Strategies in Mesoamerican Turkeys: Archaeological, Isotopic and Genetic Evidence," *Royal Society Open Science* 5, no. 1 (2018): 171613; Elizabeth M. Brumfiel, "Introduction: Production and Power at Postclassic Xaltocan," in *Production and Power at Postclassic Xaltocan*, ed. Elizabeth M. Brumfiel (Mexico City: Instituto Nacional de Antropología e Historia; and Pittsburgh: University of Pittsburgh Press, 2005); Robbie L. Brewington and Mary G. Hodge, *Place of Jade: Society and Economy in Ancient Chalco* (Pittsburgh, PA: University of Pittsburgh, 2008); Christopher M. Götz and Kitty F. Emery, *The Archaeology of Mesoamerican Animals* (Atlanta: Lockwood Press, 2013); Marion Schwartz, *A History of Dogs in the Early Americas* (New Haven, CT: Yale University Press, 1997).

105 Mackenzie Cooley, *The Perfection of Nature: Animals, Breeding, and Race in the Renaissance* (Chicago: University of Chicago Press, 2022), 136.

106 For differences in European and Mesoamerican ideas about breeding, see Cooley, *The Perfection of Nature*, esp. 134–147.

107 Codex Borgia, pl. 10, 64; Guilhem Olivier, *Mockeries and Metamorphoses of an Aztec God* (Boulder: University Press of Colorado, 2003), 34.

108 See Chap. 6.

109 *Florentine Codex*, bk. 11, 16 (dogs), 53 (turkeys).

110 Toribio de Benavente (Motolinía), *Memoriales de Fray Toribio de Motolinía*, ed. Francisco del Paso y Troncoso (Mexico City: En casa del editor, 1903), 319–325; Durán, *Book of the Gods*, 279–286; *Florentine Codex*, Bk. 1:44, 4:2, 5; Sahagún, *Primeros Memoriales*, 161, 163; Jacques Soustelle, *The Daily Life of the Aztecs*, trans. Patrick O'Brian (New York: Macmillan, 1961), 73–78.

111 "Historia de los Mexicanos por sus pinturas," ed. Joaquín García Icazbalceta, *Anales del Instituto Nacional de Antropología e Historia* 1, no. 2 (1882): 85–106, 103–105; Motolinía, *Memoriales*, 320–321; Durán, *Book of the Gods*, 282.

112 Motolinía, *Memoriales*, 322–323; Durán, *Book of the Gods*, 282.

113   Moreiras Reynaga et al., "Residential Patterns," 6.

114   Motolinía, *Memoriales*, 244–245.

115   *Florentine Codex*, bk. 7:27.

116   Sahagún, *Primeros Memoriales*, 202.

117   *Florentine Codex*, bk. 8:37.

118   *Florentine Codex*, bk. 9, 48; Cooley, *The Perfection of Nature*, 137.

119   *Florentine Codex*, bk. 11:54, 56.

120   Sahagún, *Primeros Memoriales*, 202.

121   Ashley E. Sharpe, William A. Saturno, and Kitty F. Emery, "Shifting Patterns of Maya Social Complexity through Time: Preliminary Zooarchaeological Results from San Bartolo, Guatemala," in *Animals and Inequality in the Ancient World*, ed. Benjamin S. Arbuckle and Sue Ann McCarty, 85–106 (Boulder: University Press of Colorado, 2014).

122   Alonso de Zorita, *The Lords of New Spain: The Brief and Summary Relation of the Lords of New Spain* (London: Phoenix, 1965). Durán, *History of the Indies*, 165, 166; Charles Gibson, *Aztecs under Spanish Rule: A History of the Indians of the Valley of Mexico, 1519–1810* (Stanford, CA: Stanford University Press, 1964), 344. See also Cooley, *The Perfection of Nature*, 134–136 and references below to the *Relaciones geográficas*.

123   "Relación de Ichcateopan y su partido," in *Papeles de Nueva España*, 6: 87–152, 91.

124   "Relación de Texupa," in *Papeles de Nueva España*, 4: 53–57, 55.

125   "Relación de Guaxilotitlan," in *Papeles de Nueva España*, 4: 96–205, 200.

126   "Relación de Iztepexi," in *Papeles de Nueva España*, 4: 9–23, 19.

8. Transforming Animals

1   Louise M. Burkhart, "Flowery Heaven: The Aesthetic of Paradise in Nahuatl Devotional Literature," *RES: Anthropology and Aesthetics* 21 (1992): 88–109; Alessandra Russo, "Plumes of Sacrifice: Transformations in Sixteenth-Century Mexican Feather Art," *RES: Anthropology and Aesthetics* 42 (2002): 226–250.

2   Translated and quoted in Louise Burkhart, "The Cult of the Virgin of Guadalupe," in *South and Meso-American Native Spirituality: From the Cult of the Feathered Serpent to the Theology of Liberation*, ed. Gary H. Gossen and Miguel León Portilla (New York: Crossroad, 1993), 210.

3   Russo, "Plumes of Sacrifice"; Justyna Olko, *Insignia of Rank in the Nahua World: From the Fifteenth to the Seventeenth Century* (Boulder, CO: University Press of Colorado, 2014).

4   Motolinía, *Historia de los indios*, 131.

5   Olko, *Insignia,* 351–353.

6   Olko, *Insignia,* 342–345, 352.

7   Motolinía, *Historia de los indios,* 131.

8   Motolinía, *Historia de los indios,* 132–133.

9   For analysis of the cosmogram, see Chap. 6.

10   Motolinía, *Historia de los indios,* 147–148.

11   Bernardino de Sahagún, *Primeros Memoriales,* trans. Thelma D. Sullivan and H. B. Nicholson (Norman: University of Oklahoma Press, 1997), 79, 59.

12   Burkhart, *The Slippery Earth*; David Tavárez, ed., *Words & Worlds Turned Around: Indigenous Christianities in Colonial Latin America* (Boulder, CO: University Press of Colorado, 2017).

13   Motolinía, *Historia de los indios,* 136–138.

14   Arthur J. O. Anderson and Charles Dibble, trans., *Florentine Codex: General History of the Things of New Spain,* 12 books in 13 vols. (Santa Fe: School of American Research and the University of Utah Press, 1950–1987), bk. 2:23, 122.

15   Gonzalo Aguirre Beltrán, *Medicina y magia: el proceso de aculturación en el estructura colonial* (Mexico City: Instituto Nacional Indigenista, 1963).

16   "Carta del Fray Toribio de Motolinía al emperador Carlos V," January 2, 1555, in *Historia de los indios,* 302.

17   Fernando Cervantes, *The Devil in the New World: The Impact of Diabolism in New Spain* (New Haven, CT: Yale University Press, 1997).

18   Patricia Lopes Don, *Bonfires of Culture: Franciscans, Indigenous Leaders, and the Inquisition in Early Mexico, 1524–1540* (Norman: University of Oklahoma Press, 2012), 7–9.

19   See, for instance, *Procesos de indios idolatras y hechiceros* (Mexico City: Guerrero Hermanos, 1912), 142–143, 202, 211, 119.

20   María Teresa Sepúlveda y Herrera, "Introduction," in *Procesos por idolatría al cacique, gobernadores y sacerdotes de Yanhuitlán, 1544–46,* ed. María Teresa Sepúlveda y Herrera, 43–112 (Mexico City: Colección Científica, Instituto Nacional de Antropología e Historia, 1999); María Teresa Sepúlveda y Herrera, *Procesos por idolatría al cacique, gobernadores y sacerdotes de Yanhuitlán, 1544–46* (Mexico City: Colección Científica, Instituto Nacional de Antropología e Historia, 1999), the trial testimony is transcribed on 113–229.

21   Sepúlveda y Herrera, *Procesos por idolatría,* 120.

22   Sepúlveda y Herrera, *Procesos por idolatría,* 134, 140.

23   Sepúlveda y Herrera, *Procesos por idolatría,* 114–115, 116, 125–126, 128, 137, 137–138, 142, 143, 148, 170, 201.

24   Sepúlveda y Herrera, *Procesos por idolatría,* for tribute, 86, 121.

25   Sepúlveda y Herrera, *Procesos por idolatría*, 143.

26   Sepúlveda y Herrera, *Procesos por idolatría*, 114, 119–122, 125, 128, 140, 143, 149 163.

27   "Proceso e información que se tomó contra [Cristó]bal y su mujer," in *Procesos de indios idolatras y hechiceros* (Mexico City: Guerrero Hermanos, 1912), 141–175. Peter Gerhard, *A Guide to the Historical Geography of New Spain*, rev. ed. (Norman: University of Oklahoma Press, 1993), 92–93.

28   "Proceso contra [Cristó]bal," 142–145, 148, 153–154.

29   "Proceso contra [Cristó]bal," 142–143.

30   "Proceso contra [Cristó]bal," 148.

31   "Proceso contra [Cristó]bal," 161–162, 168.

32   See Chap. 6.

33   "Fragmento de un proceso contra Diego Díaz," in *Procesos de indios idolatras y hechiceros*, 221–236 (Mexico City: Guerrero Hermanos, 1912), 222.

34   Motolinía, *Historia de los indios*, 127, 136.

35   On similar practices in recent times, see, for instance, Johanna Broda and Catharine Good Eshelman, eds., *Historia y vida veremonial en las comunidades mesoamericanas: los ritos agrícolas* (Mexico City: Instituto Nacional de Antropología e Historia, 2004).

36   Pedro Ponce, "Breve relación de los dioses y ritos de in gentilidad," in *Teogonía e historia de los mexicanos*, ed. Angel María Garibay K. (Mexico City: Porrúa, 1979), 212–213, 214–215, 216. See also Aguirre Beltrán, *Medicina y magia*, 74, 290n3, 289n2.

37   Ponce, "Breve relación," 122.

38   Diego Jaime Ricardo Villavicencio, *Luz, methodo, de confesar idolatras* (Puebla: Diego Fernandez de Leon, 1692), pt. 1:54, 125–129, pt. 2:31.

39   Juan Bautista, *Advertencias: para los confessores de los naturales* (Mexico: Convento de Santiago Tlatelolco: Por M. Ocharte, 1600), fols, 110v–111r.

40   Diego Durán, *Book of the Gods and Rites and the Ancient Calendar*, trans. and ed. Fernando Horcasitas and Doris Heyden (Norman: University of Oklahoma Press, 1971), 278.

41   Gonzalo de Balsalobre, *Relación auténtica de las idolatrías* (Spain: Linkgua, 2011), 22–25, 44–45.

42   Inquisition case quoted and cited in Aguirre Beltrán, *Medicina y magia*, 74, 290n3, see also 289n2.

43   On "sacrifice" and feeding the earth in contemporary Mixtec communities, John Monaghan, *The Covenants with Earth and Rain: Exchange, Sacrifice, and Revelation in Mixtec Sociality* (Norman: University of Oklahoma Press, 1995).

44   On cultural translation more generally, Burkhart, *The Slippery Earth;* Nancy Farriss, *Tongues of Fire: Language and Evangelization in Colonial Mexico* (Oxford: Oxford University Press, 2018).

45   Foundational scholarship on the *nahualli* and *nahuallismo* includes Alfredo López Austin, *The Human Body and Ideology: Concepts of the Ancient Nahuas,* 2 vols. (Salt Lake City: University of Utah Press, 1988) 1:369–370; Aguirre Beltrán, *Medicina y magia,* 98–104; Alfredo López Austin, "Cuarenta clases de magos del mundo náhuatl," *Estudios de cultura náhuatl* 7 (1967): 87–117, 89–95; Marie L. Musgrave-Portilla, "The Nahualli or Transforming Wizard in Pre- and Postconquest Mesoamerica," *Journal of Latin American Lore* 8 no. 1 (1982): 3–62; Roberto Martínez González, *El nahuallismo* (Mexico City: Universidad Nacional Autónoma de México, 2011). For attention to gender, Lisa Sousa, *The Woman Who Turned into a Jaguar, and Other Narratives of Native Women in Archives of Colonial Mexico* (Stanford, CA: Stanford University Press, 2017), 21–25. Most scholars recognize that the colonial-era *nahualli* was affected by clerical discourse about witches, but they disagree on the nature and importance of the changes.

46   Musgrave-Portilla, "The Nahualli," 56.

47   Maarten Jansen and Gabina Aurora Pérez Jiménez, in accounting for the overlap between sorcery texts of late medieval period and missionary accounts in the colonial period, have explained it as attributable to shared "shamanic roots," Maarten Jansen and Gabina Aurora Pérez Jiménez, *The Mixtec Pictorial Manuscripts: Time, Agency, and Memory in Ancient Mexico* (Leiden: Brill, 2011), 251. The classic account of a "shamanic substratum" is Carlo Ginzburg, *Ecstasies: Deciphering the Witches' Sabbath* (Chicago: University of Chicago Press, 2004), 170. I think when one takes seriously the ontological divergences produced by divergent modes of interaction, the temporality of colonial-era entanglement looks more persuasive than that of millennia-old shamanic substratum.

48   Sahagún, *Primeros Memoriales,* 210–219; López Austin, "Cuarenta clases de magos," 98.

49   Sahagún, *Primeros Memoriales,* 210–219.

50   Alonso de Molina, *Vocabulario en lengua castellana y mexicana* (Mexico City: Antonio de Spinosa, 1571), pt. 2, Nahuatl to Spanish, fol. 118r.

51   Sahagún, *Primeros Memoriales,* 213–215.

52   *Florentine Codex,* 10:31–32.

53   Sousa, *The Woman,* 25

54   Sahagún, *Primeros Memoriales,* 214.

55   *Florentine Codex,* Bk. 11:1, 3.

56   Katarzyna Mikulska Dabrowska, "'Secret Language' in Oral and Graphic Form: Religious-Magic Discourse in Aztec Speeches and Manuscripts," *Oral Tradition* 25, no. 3 (2010), 325–363, 327.

57   Jansen and Pérez Jiménez write that "several names of individuals in the codices express the strength of animals or beings that may have been the nahual or alter ego of those persons," *The Mixtec Pictorial Manuscripts*, 36–37.

58   Georges Baudot, "Apariciones diabólicas en un texto náhuatl de fray Andrés de Olmos," *Estudios de Cultura Náhuatl* 10 (1972): 349–357; Victoria Ríos Castaño, "El tratado de hechicerías y sortilegios (1553) que 'avisa y no emponzoña' de fray Andrés de Olmos," *Revista de historia de la traducción* 8 (2014): 1–9. Georges Baudot, ed. and trans., *Tratado de hechicerías y sortilegios* (Mexico City: Universidad Nacional Autónoma de México, 1990), ix–x.

59   "Proceso del Santo Oficio contra Tacatetl y Tanixtetl," in *Procesos de indios idolatras y hechiceros* (Mexico City: Guerrero Hermanos, 1912), 1–16.

60   On Suárez, see Gerhard, *Guide to the Historical Geography*, 295–297.

61   "Proceso contra Tacatetl y Tanixtetl," 2.

62   "Proceso contra Tacatetl y Tanixtetl," 6–7.

63   "Proceso contra Tacatetl y Tanixtetl," 2.

64   "Proceso contra Tacatetl y Tanixtetl," 6–7.

65   "Proceso del Santo Oficio contra Martín Ucelo," in *Procesos de indios idolatras y hechiceros* (Mexico City: Guerrero Hermanos, 1912), 17–52; Lopes Don, *Bonfires of Culture,* 52–82.

66   "Proceso contra Martín Ucelo," 17–18.

67   Serge Gruzinski, *Man-Gods in the Mexican Highlands: Indian Power and Colonial Society, 1520–1800* (Stanford, CA: Stanford University Press, 1989), 39.

68   "Proceso contra Martín Ucelo," 18–28.

69   "Proceso contra Martín Ucelo," 18, 26; about the mare, 32.

70   "Proceso contra Martín Ucelo," 18, 21, 36–37, 41, 48.

71   "Proceso contra Martín Ucelo," 25, 28–29.

72   "Proceso contra Martín Ucelo," 27.

73   "Proceso contra Martín Ucelo," 28.

74   "Proceso contra Tacatetl y Tanixtetl," 15; "Proceso contra Martín Ucelo," 36.

75   Martín de Castañega, *Tratado de las supersticiones y hechizerías y vanos conjuros y abusiones y otras cosas* (Logroño: Miguel de Eguia, 1529); Ríos Castaño, "El tratado de hechicerías," 1–9.

76   Andrés de Olmos, *Tratado de hechicerías y sortilegios,* ed. and trans. Georges Baudot (Mexico City: Universidad Nacional Autónoma de México, 1990), 3.

77   Olmos, *Tratado de hechicerías,* 56–57.

78   Olmos, *Tratado de hechicerías,* e.g., 46, 48, 50, 52, 56, 58, 60, 70.

79   Olmos, *Tratado de hechicerías,* 58–59.

80   Olmos, *Tratado de hechicerías,* 43, 44.

81   Alonso de Molina, *Aqui comiença vn vocabulario en la lengua castellana y mexicana* (Mexico City: En casa de Juan Pablos, 1555), fol. 36v; Alonso de Molina, *Vocabulario,* fol. 63v.

82   *Florentine Codex,* 4:11, 42.

83   *Florentine Codex,* 10:31–32.

84   Quoted and translated in Burkhart, *Slippery Earth,* 84–85.

85   Bautista, *Advertencias,* fols. 105r, 112r.

86   Thomas Gage, *The English-American His Travail by Sea and Land: Or, A New Survey of the West-Indias* (London: R. Cotes, 1648), 169–171; Francisco de Burgoa, *Geografica descripcion de la parte septentrional, del poloartico de la America* (Mexico City: Juan Ruyz, 1674), fols. 355v–356v. See also Villavicencio, *Luz,* 134.

87   Hernando Ruiz de Alarcón, *Treatise on the Heathen Superstitions and Customs That Today Live among the Indians Native to This New Spain, 1629,* trans. and ed. Richard Andrews and Ross Hassig (Norman: University of Oklahoma Press, 1984), 45–46.

88   Ruiz de Alarcón, *Treatise on the Heathen Superstitions,* 46–47.

89   Martín Antoine del Río, *Investigations into Magic,* trans. P. G. Maxwell-Stuart (Manchester: Manchester University Press, 2000), 99–101.

90   Antonio de Torquemada quoted in John Beusterien, *Canines in Cervantes and Velázquez* (Farnham, Surrey: Ashgate, 2013), 51. See also Chap. 2. On cats and witches' familiars, James A. Serpell, "Guardian Spirits or Demonic Pets: The Concept of the Witch's Familiar in Early Modern England, 1530–1712," in *The Human/Animal Boundary,* ed. Angela Creager and William C. Jordan, 157–190 (Rochester: University of Rochester Press, 2002).

91   Ruiz de Alarcón, *Treatise on the Heathen Superstitions,* 47.

92   Ruiz de Alarcón, *Treatise on the Heathen Superstitions,* 48.

93   Sousa, *The Woman,* 19–21, 30.

94   Motolinía, *Historia de los indios,* 55.

9. Adopting Domesticates

1   Gonzalo Fernández de Oviedo y Valdés, *Historia general y natural de las Indias,* ed. and intro. Juan Pérez de Tudela Bueso, 2nd ed. (Madrid: Ediciones Atlas, 1992), 1:221–222. This source is based on the unpublished manuscript that includes material not in the published editions.

2   William Timothy Treal Taylor, Pablo Librado, Mila Hunska Tašunke Icu, Carlton Shield Chief Gover, et al., "Early Dispersal of Domestic Horses into the Great Plains and Northern Rockies," *Science* 379, no. 6639 (2023): 1316–1323.

3   Galeotto Cei, *Viaje y descripción de las Indias, 1539–1553*, ed. José Rafael Lovera and trans. Marisa Vannini de Gerulewicz (Caracas: Fundación Banco Venezolano de Crédito, 1995), 114–115.

4   Cei, *Viaje*, 83, 69.

5   Nancy Kathleen Creswick Morey, "Ethnohistory of the Colombian and Venezuelan Llanos" (PhD diss., University of Utah, 1975), 56.

6   Filippo Salvadore Gilij, *Ensayo de historia americana,* trans. Antonio Tovar, 3 vols. (Caracas: Academia Nacional de la Historia, 1965), 1:253

7   Peter Mitchell, *Horse Nations: The Worldwide Impact of the Horse on Indigenous Societies Post-1492* (Oxford: Oxford University Press, 2015), 219–252; François-René Picon, *Pasteurs du Nouveau Monde: Adoption de l'élevage chez les Indiens Guajiros* (Paris: Éditions de la Maison des sciences de l'homme, 2017); François-René Picon, "Le cheval dans le Nouveau Monde," *Études rurales* 151, no. 1 (1999): 51–75.

8   Florián Baucke, *Hacia allá y para acá: una estada entre los indios mocobíes, 1749–1767,* trans. Edmundo Wernicke, 2 vols. (Cordoba: Editorial Nuevo Siglo, 1999); José Sánchez Labrador, *El Paraguay católico,* 2 vols. (Buenos Aires: Imprenta de Coni hermanos, 1910–1917); Martin Dobrizhoffer, *An Account of the Abipones, an Equestrian People of Paraguay,* trans. Sara Coleridge (1784; London: John Murray, Albemarle Street, 1822).

9   Picon, "Le cheval," 68–69; Sánchez Labrador, *El Paraguay,* 2:68–77.

10 Baucke, *Hacia allá y para acá,* 2:167, 179, 1:164–165.

11 Baucke, *Hacia allá y para acá,* 2:233.

12 Baucke, *Hacia allá y para acá,* 2:167, 179, 1:164–165.

13 Baucke, *Hacia allá y para acá,* 2:233.

14 Baucke, *Hacia allá y para acá,* 2:264–265.

15 Mitchell, *Horse Nations,* 240; Sánchez Labrador, *El Paraguay,* 2:28. See also Baucke, *Hacia allá y para acá;* 2:169; Picon, "Le cheval," 70.

16 Mitchell, *Horse Nations,* 240.

17 Mitchell, *Horse Nations,* 226–227; Picon, "Le cheval."

18 Sánchez Labrador, *El Paraguay,* 2: 28.

19 Baucke, *Hacia allá y para acá,* 2:167, 179, 181.

20 Kathryn Elizabeth Renton, "The Horse in the Spanish Atlantic World, 1492–1600" (PhD diss., University of California, Los Angeles, 2018), 91–98; Chris Valesey, "Managing the Herd: Nahuas, Animals, and Colonialism in Sixteenth-Century New Spain" (PhD., diss. Pennsylvania State University, 2019), esp. 104–107, 120–123.

21 Renton, "The Horse," 91–98; Philip Wayne Powell, *Soldiers, Indians, and Silver; the Northward Advance of New Spain, 1550–1600* (Berkeley: University of California Press, 1952), 159–164.

22   Quoted in Renton, "'The Horse,'" 106.

23   "Relación de Chichicapa y su partido," in *Papeles de Nueva España*, ed. Francisco del Paso y Troncoso (Mexico City: Estab. Tip. "Sucesores de Rivadeneyra," 1906), 4: 115–143, 122.

24   Judith Francis Zeitlin, *Cultural Politics in Colonial Tehuantepec: Community and State among the Isthmus Zapotec, 1500–1750* (Stanford, CA: Stanford University Press, 2005), 147.

25   On hoofprints in colonial maps, see Alex Hidalgo, *Trail of Footprints: A History of Indigenous Maps from Viceregal Mexico* (Austin: University of Texas Press, 2019) 25, 52, 97.

26   Alonso de Molina, *Vocabulario en lengua castellana y mexicana* (Mexico City: Antonio de Spinosa, 1571), pt. 2, Nahuatl to Spanish, fol. 50 r; *Gran Diccionario Náhuatl* (online), (Mexico City: Universidad Nacional Autónoma de México, 2012), http://www.gdn.unam.mx.

27   *The Tlaxcalan Actas: A Compendium of the Records of the Cabildo of Tlaxcala, 1545–1627*, trans. and ed. James Lockhart, Frances Berdan, and Arthur J. O. Anderson (Salt Lake City: University of Utah Press, 1986), 50, 58; Renton, "The Horse," 91–92.

28   On the circumstances of its production, see Byron Ellsworth Hamann, "Object, Image, Cleverness: The Lienzo de Tlaxcala," *Art History* 36, no. 3 (2013): 518–545. *Lienzo de Tlaxcala: publicado por Alfredo Chavero, México, 1892* (Mexico City: Artes de México, 1964). The *Lienzo* disappeared in the nineteenth century, so the source survives as a copy that was made into a set of lithographs in 1892. Hamann's annotated reconstruction of "Lienzo de Tlaxcala" is available at http://www.mesolore.org/viewer/view/2/The-Lienzo-de-Tlaxcala.

29   Francisco de Burgoa, *Geográfica descripción de la parte septentrional* (Mexico City: En la Imprenta de Iuan Ruyz, 1674), 2:402–403.

30   Powell, *Soldiers, Indians, and Silver.*

31   Quoted in John Tutino, *Making a New World: Founding Capitalism in the Bajío and Spanish North America* (Durham, NC: Duke University Press, 2011), 88.

32   Quoted in Powell, *Soldiers, Indians, and Silver,* 50.

33   Peter W. Stahl, "Early Dogs and Endemic South American Canids of the Spanish Main," *Journal of Anthropological Research* 69, no. 4 (2013): 515–533; Richard Schomburgk, *Travels in British Guiana, 1840–1844*, ed. and trans. Walter Roth, 2 vols. (Georgetown, British Guiana: "Daily Chronicle" Office, 1922), 1:154.

34   Cei, *Viaje*, 148.

35   Charles Waterton, *Wanderings in South America* (London: Macmillan, 1879), 79.

36   Raymond Breton, *Dictionaire francois-caraibe* (Auxerre: Gilles Bouquet, 1666), 81; Raymond Breton, *Dictionaire caraibe-françois: Meslé de quantité de remarques historiques pour l'esclaircissement de la langue* (Auxerre: Gilles Bouquet, 1665), 41.

37   Breton, *Dictionaire françois-caraibe*, 131.

38   Breton, *Dictionaire caraibe-françois*, 29.

39   Breton, *Dictionaire caraibe-françois*, 188 [*sic* 288].

40   Breton, *Dictionaire caraibe-françois*, 182.

41   Breton, *Dictionaire françois-caraibe*, 363; Breton, *Dictionaire caraibe-françois*, 478.

42   Breton, *Dictionaire françois-caraibe*, 246, 428.

43   Breton, *Dictionaire caraibe-françois*, 154; Breton, *Dictionaire françois-caraibe*, 74.

44   Ruth S. Kraemer, trans., *Histoire naturelle des Indes: The Drake Manuscript in the Pierpont Morgan Library* (New York: W. W. Norton, 1996), fols. 106v–107r; Manuel María Albis, *Curiosità della foresta d'Amazzonia e arte di curar senza medico*, ed. Alberto Guaraldo (Turin: Segnalibro, 1991), 205.

45   José Gumilla, *El Orinoco ilustrado y defendido*, 2 vols. (Madrid: Manuel Fernández 1745), 2:229–230; Baucke, *Hacia allá y para acá*, 2:233.

46   Schomburgk, *Travels*, 1:344.

47   Schomburgk, *Travels*, 1:154, 316.

48   Schomburgk, *Travels*, 1:154, 316, 344.

49   Baucke, *Hacia allá y para acá*, 2:20, 264.

50   See also, *Histoire naturelle des Indes*, fols. 65v–66r; Baucke, *Hacia allá y para acá*, 2:233.

51   See also Mackenzie Cooley's examination of "canine mestizaje" in New Spain, *The Perfection of Nature: Animals, Breeding, and Race in the Renaissance* (Chicago: University of Chicago Press, 2022), 140–142.

52   Heidi G. Parker et al., "Genomic Analyses Reveal the Influence of Geographic Origin, Migration, and Hybridization on Modern Dog Breed Development," *Cell Reports* 19, no. 4 (April 1, 2017): 697–708, 706.

53   Toribio de Benavente (Motolinía), *Historia de los indios de la Nueva España.*, ed. Claudio Esteva Fabregat (Madrid: Dastin, 2001), 250.

54   Motolinia, *Historia de los indios*, 250–251.

55   "Relación de Teciutla y su partido," *Papeles de Nueva España*, 6:209–236, 236. See also, among others, "Relación de Hueypustla y su partido," 6:12–18, 18; "Relación de la Villa de Tepoztlán, 6: 237–250, 249 in the same volume.

56   "Relación de Tlacotalpan y su partido," in *Papeles de Nueva España*, 5:1–11, 10; "Relación de Jalapa de la Veracruz," 99–123, 110 in the same volume.

57   Lockhart et al., *Tlaxcalan Actas*, 105.

58   Juan de Pomar, "Relación de Texcoco," in *Varias relaciones antiguas*, ed. Joaquín García Icazbalceta, 1–69 (Mexico City: F. D. de León, 1891), 67.

59   Compare also the divergent attitudes in different parts of Arthur J. O. Anderson and Charles Dibble, trans., *Florentine Codex: General History of the Things of New Spain*, 12 books in 13 vols. (Santa Fe: School of American Research and the University of Utah Press, 1950–1987), bk. 4:19–22; bk.11: 15–16.

60   Breton, *Dictionaire caraibe-françois*, 290; see also, Jean-Baptiste du Tertre, *Histoire générale des isles de S. Christophe, de la Guadeloupe, de la Martinique et autres dans l'Amérique* (Paris: J. Langlois, 1654), 2:389.

61   Morey, "Ethnohistory," 56.

62   Jean de Léry, *History of a Voyage to the Land of Brazil, Otherwise Called America*, trans. Janet Whatley (Berkeley: University of California Press, 1990), 86. See also, Felipe Ferreira Vander Velden, "As galinhas incontáveis: Tupis, europeus e aves domésticas na conquista no Brasil," *Journal de la Société des Américanistes* 98, no. 2 (2012): 97–140.

63   Antoine Biet, *Voyage de la France Eqvinoxiale en l'isle de Cayenne* (Paris: F. Clovzier, 1664), 339.

64   Jorge Juan and Antonio de Ulloa, *A Voyage to South America*, trans. John Adams, 5th ed. (London: Stockdale, 1807), 1:409.

65   Baucke, *Hacia allá y para acá*, 2; for examples from later periods, see Marcy Norton, "The Chicken or the *Iegue*: Human-Animal Relationships and the Columbian Exchange," *American Historical Review* 120, no. 1 (2015): 28–60, 53–54.

66   See Chap. 4.

67   Antonio Vázquez de Espinosa, *Compendio y descripción de las Indias Occidentales*, ed. Charles Upson Clark (Washington, DC: Smithsonian Institution, 1948), 294; Eiver Miguel Durango Loaiza, "Contagiando la insurreción: los indios guajiros y los revolucionarios franceses, 1769–1804" (master's thesis, Departamento de Historia, Universidad de los Andes, 2013), 23, 49.

68   Rodrigo de Albornoz to Charles V, December 15, 1525, in *Colección de documentos inéditos relativos al descubrimiento, conquista y colonización de las posesiones españolas en América y Oceanía . . . [1ª Serie]*, 42 vols. (Madrid: Imprenta de M. B. de Quirós [etc.], 1864), 2: 484–489, 488.

69   See Chap. 3.

70   Lesley Byrd Simpson, *Exploitation of Land in Central Mexico in the Sixteenth Century* (Berkeley: University of California Press, 1952), 11; William B. Taylor, *Landlord and Peasant in Colonial Oaxaca* (Stanford, CA: Stanford University Press, 1972), 95–106; Elinor G. K. Melville, *A Plague of Sheep: Environmental Consequences of the Conquest of Mexico* (Cambridge: Cambridge University Press, 1994), 134–143; María de los Angeles Romero Frizzi, *Economía y vida de los españoles en la Mixteca Alta, 1519–1720* (Mexico City: Instituto Nacional de Antropología e Historia, 1990), 48–63, 544; María de los Angeles Romero Frizzi, *El sol y la cruz: los pueblos indios de Oaxaca colonial* (Mexico City: CIESAS, 1996); Romero Frizzi, *Economía*, 52; Zeitlin, *Cultural Politics*, 149–155; Karine Lefebvre, "Los procesos de colonización agropecuaria

de la región de Acámbaro-Maravatío durante el siglo XVI," *Estudios de historia novohispana* 58, no. 1 (2018): 31–71; Kevin Terraciano, *The Mixtecs of Colonial Oaxaca* (Stanford, CA: Stanford University Press, 2004), 234, 452n225; Valesey, "Managing the Herd, 104–122, 223–242; Charles Gibson, *Aztecs under Spanish Rule: A History of the Indians of the Valley of Mexico, 1519–1810* (Stanford, CA: Stanford University Press, 1964), 345–346.

71   Simpson, *Exploitation of Land,* 11; Karine Lefebvre, "Los procesos de colonización"; Zeitlin, *Cultural Politics,* 146–148; Gibson, *Aztecs under Spanish Rule,* 156, 345–346.

72   Gibson, *Aztecs under Spanish Rule,* 264–299; Melville, *Plague of Sheep,* 127–144; Simpson, *Exploitation of Land.*

73   See Chap. 8.

74   Motolinía, *Historia de los indios,* 127, 136

75   Motolinía, *Historia de los indios,* 127, see also 136.

76   "Proceso e información que se tomó contra [Cristó]bal y su mujer," in *Procesos de indios idólatras y hechiceros* (Mexico City: Guerrero Hermanos, 1912), 141–175, 152.

77   Codex Magliabechiano, quoted in Gibson, *Aztecs under Spanish Rule,* 567n87.

78   Lockhart et al., *Tlaxcalan Actas,* 105; emphasis added.

79   Diego Muñoz Camargo, *Suma y epíloga de toda la descripción de Tlaxcala,* ed. Andrea Martínez Baracs and Carlos Sempat Assadourian (Tlaxcala: Universidad Autónoma de Tlaxcala, 1994), 143, 145.

80   See Chap. 4.

81   Andrea Martínez Baracs and Carlos Sempat Assadourian, *Tlaxcala: una historia compartida,* vol. 9 (Tlaxcala: Gobierno del Estado de Tlaxcala, 1991); Charles Gibson, *Tlaxcala in the Sixteenth Century* (New Haven, CT: Yale University Press, 1952).

82   Gibson, *Tlaxcala in the Sixteenth Century,* 83.

83   Hernán Cortés, "Carta inédita," in *Cartas y documentos [de] Hernán Cortés,* ed. Mario Hernández Sánchez-Barba, 2 vols. (Mexico City: Editorial Porrúa, 1963), 1:476.

84   Andrew Sluyter, "The Ecological Origins and Consequences of Cattle Ranching in Sixteenth-Century New Spain," *Geographical Review* 86, no. 2 (1996): 161–177.

85   Hanns J. Prem, "Spanish Colonization and Indian Property in Central Mexico, 1521–1620," *Annals of the Association of American Geographers* 82, no. 3 (1992): 444–459.

86   See Chap. 3.

87   Gibson, *Tlaxcala in the Sixteenth Century,* 151–152.

88   Lockhart et al., *Tlaxcalan Actas,* 42, 56, 78, 96.

89   Romero Frizzi, *El sol,* 154–159.

90   Lockhart et al., *Tlaxcalan Actas,* 105.

91   Martínez Baracs and Sempat Assadourian, *Tlaxcala.*

92   Muñoz Camargo, *Suma y epíloga,* 184.

93   Muñoz Camargo, *Suma y epíloga,* 187–191.

94   Muñoz Camargo, *Suma y epíloga,* 143, 145.

95   Muñoz Camargo, *Suma y epíloga,* 150, 154, 156 (Indigenous pig husbandry); 168, 179, 186, 187 (Spanish pig husbandry).

96   René García Castro, ed., *Suma de visitas de pueblos de la Nueva España, 1548–1550* (Mexico City: Universidad Autónoma del Estado de México, 2013), 118.

97   François Chevalier, *Land and Society in Colonial Mexico: The Great Hacienda* (Berkeley: University of California Press, 1963), 92–93.

98   María Xóchitl Galindo Villavicencio, "Los 'señores de la tierra' y los mecanismos del abasto de carne en Tlaxcala en el siglo XVI," *Revista complutense de historia de América* 40 (2014): 155–177.

99   Galindo Villavicencio, "Los 'señores de la tierra,'" 155–161.

100   Gibson, *Tlaxcala in the Sixteenth Century,* 153; Martínez Baracs and Sempat Assadourian, *Tlaxcala,* 127.

101   Quoted in Galindo Villavicencio, "Los 'señores de la tierra,'" 163.

102   Gibson, *Aztecs under Spanish Rule,* 345; Terraciano, *Mixtecs of Colonial Oaxaca,* 234.

103   See Chap. 3.

104   See Chap. 8.

105   Terraciano, *Mixtecs of Colonial Oaxaca,* 234.

106   Anderson and Dibble, *Florentine Codex,* 10:28, 155.

107   "Relación de Tilantongo y su partido" in *Papeles de Nueva España,* 4:69–87, 84; see also "Relación de Huexolotitlan," 4:196–205, 200.

108   "Relación de Macuilsúchil y su partido," in *Papeles de Nueva España,* 4:100–108, 106.

109   "Relación de Papaloticpac y su partido," in *Papeles de Nueva España,* 4:88–98, 96.

110   "Relación de Ichcateopan y su partido," in *Papeles de Nueva España,* 6:87–152, 111.

111   Luis Reyes García, trans. and ed., *Anales de Juan Bautista* (Mexico City: Centro de Investigaciones y Estudios, Superiores en Antropología Social, 2001), 157–158; León García Garagarza, "The Year the People Turned into Cattle: The End of the World in New Spain, 1558," in *Centering Animals in Latin American History,* ed. Martha Few and Zeb Tortorici, 31–61 (Durham, NC: Duke University Press, 2013).

112   García Garagarza, "Year the People Turned," 38–39.

113   Reyes García, *Anales de Juan Bautista,* 157–158.

114   García Garagarza, "Year the People Turned," 53. See also, J. Jorge Klor de Alva, "Nahua Colonial Discourse and the Appropriation of the (European) Other," *Archives de sciences sociales des religions* 37, no. 77 (1992): 15–35, 21–22.

115   On the role of Black cowboys generally, see Andrew Sluyter, *Black Ranching Frontiers: African Cattle Herders of the Atlantic World, 1500-1900* (New Haven: Yale University Press, 2012).

116   Hernando Ruiz de Alarcón, *Treatise on the Heathen Superstitions and Customs That Today Live among the Indians Native to This New Spain, 1629,* trans. and ed. Richard Andrews and Ross Hassig (Norman: University of Oklahoma Press, 1984), 67–68.

117   Gonzalo Aguirre Beltrán, *Medicina y magia: el proceso de aculturación en el estructura colonial* (Mexico City: Instituto Nacional Indigenista, 1963), 113, 160, 298, 315–316; Fernando Cervantes, *The Devil in the New World* (New Haven, CT: Yale University Press, 1994), 88, 90–91; Laura A. Lewis, *Hall of Mirrors: Power, Witchcraft, and Caste in Colonial Mexico* (Durham, NC: Duke University Press, 2003); Juan Ricardo Jiménez Gómez, *Creencias y prácticas religiosas en Querétaro, siglos XVI–XIX* (Mexico City: Universidad Autónoma de Querétaro, 2004), 188, 204–206.

118   Lewis, *Hall of Mirrors,* 142–143, 138–141, 167–169.

10. Becoming Pets

1   Christopher Columbus, *The Diario of Christopher Columbus's First Voyage to America, 1492–1493,* transcribed and trans. Oliver Dunn and James E. Kelly, Jr. (Norman: University of Oklahoma Press, 1989), 63–69.

2   Silvio A. Bedini, *The Pope's Elephant* (Manchester: Carcanet Press, 1997); Almudena Pérez de Tudela and Annemarie Jordan-Gschwend, "Renaissance Menageries: Exotic Animals and Pets at the Habsburg Courts in Iberia and Central Europe," in *Early Modern Zoology: The Construction of Animals in Science, Literature and the Visual Arts,* ed. Karel A. E. Enenkel and Paulus Johannes Smith, 427–455 (Leiden: Brill, 2007); Annemarie Jordan-Gschwend, *The Story of Süleyman: Celebrity Elephants and Other Exotica in Renaissance Portugal* (Zurich: Pachyderm Production, 2010); Carlos Gómez-Centurión Jiménez, *Alhajas para soberanos: los animales reales en el siglo XVIII* (Valladolid: Junta de Castilla y León, 2011); Kathleen Walker-Meikle, *Medieval Pets* (Rochester: Boydell Press, 2012); Gustave Loisel, *Histoire des ménageries de l'antiquité à nos jours,* 3 vols. (Paris: O. Doin et fils, 1912), vol. 1; Sarah Cockram, "Sleeve Cat and Lap Dog: Affection, Aesthetics and Proximity to Companion Animals in Renaissance Mantua," in *Interspecies Interactions: Animals and Humans between the Middle Ages and Modernity,* ed. Sarah D. P. Cockram and Andrew Wells, 34–65 (London: Routledge, Taylor & Francis Group, 2018); Mark Hengerer and Nadir Weber, ed. *Animals and Courts: Europe, c. 1200–1800* (Berlin: De Gruyter Oldenbourg, 2020).

3   Walker-Meikle, *Medieval Pets,* 51.

4   Alan Mikhail, *The Animal in Ottoman Egypt* (New York: Oxford University Press, 2014), 110–175; Sarah Cockram, "Interspecies Understanding: Exotic Animals and

Their Handlers at the Italian Renaissance Court," *Renaissance Studies* 31, no. 2 (2017): 277–296, 281–282.

5   Touba Ghadessi, *Portraits of Human Monsters in the Renaissance: Dwarves, Hirsutes, and Castrati as Idealized Anatomical Anomalies* (Kalamazoo: Medieval Institute Publications, 2018); Mackenzie Cooley, *The Perfection of Nature: Animals, Breeding, and Race in the Renaissance* (Chicago: University of Chicago Press, 2022), 83–85.

6   On Isabella's affection, see Cockram, "Sleeve Cat and Lap Dog," 38–34; Walker-Meikle, *Medieval Pets*.

7   Quoted in Cooley, *The Perfection of Nature*, 91, and, generally, 81–89.

8   Carlos Gómez Centurion, "Chamber Animals at the Spanish Court during the Eighteenth Century," *The Court Historian* 16, no. 1 (2011): 43–65; Sarah Cockram, "Interspecies Understanding: Exotic Animals and Their Handlers at the Italian Renaissance Court," *Renaissance Studies* 31, no. 2 (2017): 277–296. For *iegue*, see Chap. 5.

9   Pliny, "Historia Natural de Cayo Plinio," bk. 10, chap. 42, trans. Francisco Hernández in *Obras completes de Francisco Hernández*, Vol. 5 (Mexico City: Universidad Nacional Autónoma de México, n.d.), published online at http://www.franciscoher nandez.unam.mx/tomos/05_TOMO/tomo005a_010/tomo005a_010_042.html.

10   Bedini, *Pope's Elephant*, 19, 28; Jordan-Gschwend, *Story of Süleyman*, 7; Walker-Meikle, *Medieval Pets*, 5–6, 15–16, 24–25, 54–56.

11   Bruce Boehrer, "The Cardinal's Parrot: A Natural History of Reformation Polemic," *Genre* 41, no. 1–2 (2008): 1–37, 5; Loisel, *Histoire des ménageries*, 1:202.

12   Boehrer, "Cardinal's Parrot," 4; Jordan-Gschwend, *Story of Süleyman*, 7; Donald F. Lach, *Asia in the Making of Europe* (Chicago: University of Chicago Press, 1970), 179–180.

13   Nancy J. Jacobs, "Reflection: Conviviality and Companionship: Parrots and People in the African Forests," *Environmental History* 26, no. 4 (2021): 647–670.

14   Alvise Cà da Mosto, *The Voyages of Cadamosto and Other Documents on Western Africa in the Second Half of the Fifteenth Century*, trans. G. R. Crone (London: Printed for the Hakluyt Society, 1937), 47–49. See also Pieter van den Broecke, *Pieter Van Den Broecke's Journal of Voyages to Cape Verde, Guinea and Angola, 1605–1612*, ed. and trans. J. D. La Fleur (London: Hakluyt Society, 2000), 102.

15   Columbus, *Diario*, 223.

16   Pietro Martire d'Anghiera, *De orbe novo: The Eight Decades of Peter Martyr d'Anghera*, trans. Francis Augustus MacNutt, 2 vols. (New York: G. P. Putnam's Sons, 1912), 1:64, 72, 154, 254.

17   "Capítulos de carta del licenciado Alonso de Zuazo," January 22, 1518, in *Colección de documentos inéditos relativos al descubrimiento, conquista y colonización de las posesiones españolas en América y Oceanía . . . [1ª Serie]*, 42 vols. (Madrid: Imprenta de M.B. de Quirós [etc.], 1864), 1:292–298, 298.

18   Gonzalo Fernández de Oviedo y Valdés, *Natural History of the West Indies*, trans. Sterling A. Stoudemire (Chapel Hill: University of North Carolina Press, 1959),

60; Gonzalo Fernández de Oviedo y Valdés, *De la natural hystoria de las Indias* (Toledo: Remo[n] de Petras, 1526), fols. 24v–25r.

19   Francisco Hernández, "Historia de los Animales de Nueva España," trans. José Rojo Navarro in *Obras Completas*, vol. 3, ed. Germán Somolinos d'Ardois (Mexico City: Universidad Nacional de México, 1959), tr. 2, chp. 221.

20   Gonzalo Fernández de Oviedo y Valdés, *Historia general y natural de las Indias*, ed. and intro. Juan Pérez de Tudela Bueso, 2nd ed. (Madrid: Ediciones Atlas, 1992), 2:41–42.

21   AGI Indiferente 1956, lib. 3, fol. 96r–v, see also lib. 1, fols. 16r–17v; AGI Indiferente 426, lib. 25, fol. 24v-2.

22   Jordan-Gschwend, *Story of Süleyman;* Bedini, *Pope's Elephant*, 19, 28, 41.

23   AGI Indiferente, 418, lib. 3, fol. 319r–319v (1510), fols. 318r–319v (1512), fol. 320r (1512); AGI Indiferente, 420, lib. 10, fol. 175r–176r (1525), fols. 313v-2 (1526); AGI Indiferente, 421, lib. 11, fols. 186v–187v (1526).

24   AGI Panamá, 233, lib.1, fol. 111r–v.

25   AGI Indiferente, 418, lib. 3, fol. 320r.

26   Martire d'Anghiera, *De orbe novo,* 265.

27   Oviedo, *Historia general,* 2:48.

28   Galeotto Cei, *Viaje y descripción de las Indias, 1539–1553,* ed. José Rafael Lovera and trans. Marisa Vannini de Gerulewicz (Caracas: Fundación Banco Venezolano de Crédito, 1995), 154, 155.

29   Hernán Cortés, *Cartas y documentos [de] Hernán Cortés,* ed. Mario Hernández Sánchez-Barba, 2 vols. (Mexico City: Editorial Porrúa, 1963), 407–408; emphasis added.

30   Breeder, quoted in Monks of New Skete, *The Art of Raising a Puppy,* rev. ed. (New York: Little, Brown, 2011), 290–291.

31   Pat Shipman, *Our Oldest Companions: The Story of the First Dogs* (Cambridge, MA: Harvard University Press, 2021).

32   Oviedo, *Historia general,* 2:49, 52, 430–431.

33   Matías Ruiz Blanco, *Conversion de Píritu* (Madrid: Por Iuan Garcia Infançon, 1690), 25.

34   Filippo Salvadore Gilij, *Ensayo de historia americana,* trans. Antonio Tovar, 3 vols. (Caracas: Academia Nacional de la Historia, 1965), 1:209, 252, also 227–229.

35   Martin Dobrizhoffer, *An Account of the Abipones, an Equestrian People of Paraguay,* trans. Sara Coleridge (London: John Murray, 1822 [1748]), 320–323.

36   Dobrizhoffer, *Account of the Abipones,* 279–280.

37   See, e.g., Everard Ferdinand Im Thurn, "Tame Animals among the Red Man," *Timehri: Royal Agricultural and Commercial Society of British Guiana* 1 (1882): 25–43,

36; Ellen B. Basso, *The Kalapalo Indians of Central Brazil* (New York: Holt, Rinehart and Winston, 1973).

38   Cei, *Viaje*, 119.

39   Jean Baptiste Labat, *Nouveau voyage aux isles de l'Amerique* (The Hague: P. Husson, 1724), 2:155–159; for more on his experiences, see Marcy Norton, "Going to the Birds: Animals as Things and Beings in Early Modernity," in *Early Modern Things: Objects and Their Histories, 1500–1800*, ed. Paula Findlen, 3–83 (London: Routledge, 2012), 74–75.

40   Labat, *Nouveau voyage*, 2:157–158.

41   Labat, *Nouveau voyage*, 2:158–159.

42   Henry Walter Bates, *The Naturalist on the River Amazons*, 2nd ed. (London: J. Murray, 1864), 256–257.

43   Oviedo, *Natural History*, 54–55; Oviedo, *De la natural hystoria*, fol. 22v.

44   This is based on research at the Archivo General de Indias in Seville.

45   Marcy Norton, *Sacred Gifts, Profane Pleasures: A History of Tobacco and Chocolate* (Ithaca: Cornell University Press, 2008), 142.

46   Oviedo, *De la natural hystoria*, fol. 23v; Oviedo, *Historia general*, 2:50. On the early trade, see Bernardo Urbani, "Further Information on Neotropical Monkeys in the XVI Century," *Neotropical Primates* 18, no. 2 (2011): 62–64.

47   José Toribio Medina, ed., *El veneciano Sebastián Caboto*, vol. 2, *Documentos* (Santiago de Chile: Impr. y encuadernación universitaria, 1908), 526, 324, 391.

48   Jean de Léry, *History of a Voyage to the Land of Brazil*, trans. Janet Whatley (Berkeley: University of California Press, 1990), 72, 88, 197, 201, 208; Neil L. Whitehead and Michael Harbsmeier, ed., *Hans Staden's True History: An Account of Cannibal Captivity in Brazil* (Durham, NC: Duke University Press, 2008), 82, 96.

49   Francisco Hernández, "Historia natural" (commentary on Pliny), in *Obras Completas*, 4 vols. (Universidad Nacional de México: Mexico, 1960), 4:96.

50   "Juan de Junco, vecino de Sevilla, apela al Consejo la sentencia dictada por los jueces de la Contratación en el pleito que Sebastián Caboto, capitán, vecino de Sevilla, le puso reclamándole un indio y un papagayo que trajeron de India" (1530), AGI Justicia 713, n. 3; AGI Indiferente, 422, lib. 16.

51   "Juan de Junco, vecino de Sevilla," fols. 30r, 10r, 12r.

52   Toribio Medina, *El veneciano Sebastián Caboto*, 2:161.

53   "Juan de Junco, vecino de Sevilla," fols. 3r–3v, 6r, 6v.

54   "Juan de Junco, vecino de Sevilla," fols. 9v, 11v, 12r–v.

55   AGI Contratación 5787, n.1, lib. 1, fols. 33r–34v.

56   Léry, *History of a Voyage*, 208, 213, also 210.

57   Antonio Vázquez de Espinosa, *Tratado verdadero del viage y nauegacion deste año de seiscientos y veinte y dos* (Malaga: Juan Regnè, 1623), fol. 38v.

58   Louise E. Robbins, *Elephant Slaves and Pampered Parrots: Exotic Animals in Eighteenth-Century Paris* (Baltimore: Johns Hopkins University Press, 2002), 9.

59   Alexander von Humboldt, *Personal Narrative of Travels to the Equinoctial Regions of America during the Years 1799–1804,* trans. and ed. Thomasina Ross, 3 vols. (London: Henry G. Bohn, 1852), 2:212.

60   Catherine Vaughan Howard, "Wrought Identities: The Waiwai Expeditions in Search of the 'Unseen Tribes' of Northern Amazonia" (PhD diss., University of Chicago, 2001), 248, 250.

61   See, e.g., Barthel Beham, *Portrait of a Woman with a Parrot,* painting, 1529, Kunsthistorisches Museum, Vienna (reproduced in Norton, "Going to the Birds," 73); Hans Holbein the Younger, *Edward Prince of Wales with Monkey,* chalk, pen, ink, and watercolor, 1541, Kunstmuseum, Basel; Antonis Mor, *Portrait of Lady with a Parrot,* oil on panel, 1556, Hunterian Art Gallery, Glasgow; Hermann tom Ring, *Porträt der Familie Rietberg,* oil on panel, 1564, Landesmuseum für Kunst und Kulturgeschichte, Münster.

62   Attributed to Alonso Sánchez Coello, *Isabella Clara Eugenia and Catharina,* oil on canvas, ca. 1569–1570, Royal Collection Trust, London, https://www.rct.uk/collection /404331/isabella-clara-eugenia-and-catharina-daughters-of-philip-ii-king-of-spain.

63   Alonso Sánchez Coello, *Infanta Isabel Clara Eugenia y Magdalena Ruiz,* oil on canvas, 1585–1588, Museo del Prado, Madrid, https://www.museodelprado.es/en /the-collection/art-work/infanta-isabel-clara-eugenia-and-magdalena-ruiz/f5ba d972-2c95-4b8d-8f73-6ed6151ccob8.

64   I am grateful to Dr. James Serpell for the monkey identifications.

65   James Serpell, *In the Company of Animals: A Study of Human-Animal Relationships,* rev. ed. (Cambridge: Cambridge University Press, 1996), 10; Walker-Meikle, *Medieval Pets,* 1.

66   Marc Shell, "Family Pet," *Representations* 15 (1986): 121–153; Keith Thomas, *Man and the Natural World: Changing Attitudes in England, 1500–1800* (London: Allen Lane, 1983); Kathleen Kete, *The Beast in the Boudoir: Petkeeping in Nineteenth-Century Paris* (Berkeley: University of California Press, 1994).

67   Walker-Meikle, *Medieval Pets,* 12–13.

68   James A. Serpell, "Guardian Spirits or Demonic Pets: The Concept of the Witch's Familiar in Early Modern England, 1530–1712," in *The Human/Animal Boundary,* ed. Angela Creager and William C. Jordan, 157–190 (Rochester: University of Rochester Press, 2002); Walker-Meikle, *Medieval Pets,* 12–13.

69   Cockram, "Sleeve Cat and Lap Dog," 42, 48.

70   José de Acosta, *Natural and Moral History of the Indies,* ed. Jane E. Mangan and trans. Frances M. López-Morillas (Durham, NC: Duke University Press, 2002), 231–232.

71 John Beusterien quoting Frank Salomon in *Canines in Cervantes and Velázquez: An Animal Studies Reading of Early Modern Spain* (Farnham, Surrey: Ashgate, 2013), 60.

72 Thomas, *Man and the Natural World*, 117; Shell, "Family Pet."

73 Harriet Ritvo, *The Animal Estate: The English and Other Creatures in the Victorian Age* (Cambridge, MA: Harvard University Press, 1987), 85.

74 Kete, *Beast in the Boudoir*, 40.

75 Luis Pérez, *Del can, y del cavallo, y de sus calidades* (Valladolid: Impresso por Adrian Ghemart, 1568), fols. 22v–26v.

76 Jan Papy, "Lipsius and His Dogs: Humanist Tradition, Iconography and Rubens's Four Philosophers," *Journal of the Warburg and Courtauld Institutes* 62 (1999): 167–198.

77 Papy, "Lipsius and His Dogs," 169, 181.

78 Quoted in Papy, "Lipsius and His Dogs," 168.

79 Quoted in Papy, "Lipsius and His Dogs," 170.

80 Bruce Thomas Boehrer, *Parrot Culture: Our 2,500-Year-Long Fascination with the World's Most Talkative Bird* (Philadelphia: University of Pennsylvania Press, 2010), 50, 55–73.

81 Dobrizhoffer, *Account of the Abipones*, 326.

82 Robbins, *Elephant Slaves*, 3, 10, 101, 103, 110, 117, 119–120, 126–132; Boehrer, *Parrot Culture*, 56.

83 Quoted in Robbins, *Elephant Slaves*, 129.

11. Indigenizing Science

1 José María López Piñero and José Pardo Tomás, *La influencia de Francisco Hernández (1512–1587) en la constitución de la botánica y la* materia médica *modernas* (Valencia: Universitat de València, 1996), 44–45. See also José María López Piñero and José Pardo Tomás, *Nuevos materiales y noticias sobre la historia de las plantas de Nueva España de Francisco Hernández* (Valencia: Instituto de Estudios Documentales, 1994). Important scholarship, mostly focusing on botanical works in the Hernández corpus, includes Germán Somolinos d'Ardois, *Obras completas de Francisco Hernández*, Vol. 1 (Mexico City: Universidad Nacional de México, 1960); Simon Varey and Rafael Chabrán, eds., *Searching for the Secrets of Nature: The Life and Works of Dr. Francisco Hernández* (Stanford, CA: Stanford University Press, 2000); 353–358; Marcy Norton, *Sacred Gifts, Profane Pleasures: A History of Tobacco and Chocolate* (Ithaca, NY: Cornell University Press, 2008), 121–136; José Ramón Marcaida López, *Arte y ciencia en el barroco español: historia natural, coleccionismo y cultura visual* (Seville; Madrid: Fundación Focus-Abengoa; Marcial Pons Historia, 2014), 136–147; Jaime Marroquín Arredondo, *Diálogos con Quetzalcóatl: humanismo, etnografía y ciencia (1492–1577)* (Madrid: Iberoamericana, 2014); Jaime Marroquín

Arredondo, "The Method of Francisco Hernández," in *Translating Nature,* ed. Ralph Bauer and Jaime Marroquín Arredondo, 45–69 (Philadelphia: University of Pennsylvania Press, 2019). For animals see, Eduardo Corona Martínez, *Las aves en la historia natural Novohispana* (Mexico City: Instituto Nacional de Antropología e Historia, 2002); Miguel de Asúa and Roger French, *A New World of Animals: Early Modern Europeans on the Creatures of Iberian America* (Alershot, Hants: Ashgate, 2005); Marcy Norton, "The Quetzal Takes Flight," in *Translating Nature,* 119–147; Mackenzie Cooley, *The Perfection of Nature: Animals, Breeding, and Race in the Renaissance* (Chicago: University of Chicago Press, 2022), 144–151, 199–213.

2   Francisco Hernández, "Historiae animalium et mineralium novae hispaniae," in *Rerum medicarum Novae Hispaniae thesaurus, seu Plantarum animalium mineralium Mexicanorum historia* (Rome: Vitalis Mascardi, 1651), 1–90. I also consulted the surviving draft, Francisco Hernández, "De historia plantarum, animalium et mineralium Novae Hispanae," mss. 22436–22438, BNE. The translations are based on Francisco Hernández, "Historia de los animales de Nueva España," trans. José Rojo Navarro in *Obras Completas,* vol. 3, ed. Germán Somolinos d'Ardois (Mexico City: Universidad Nacional de México, 1959). I am grateful to Edward Chappell for answering my questions about vocabulary in the original Latin.

3   Marcaida López, *Arte y ciencia,* 136–147.

4   José de Sigüenza, quoted in Marcaida López, *Arte y ciencia,* 146.

5   Among the scholars who have contributed to the Iberian "turn" in the history of early modern science are José Pardo-Tomás, Juan Pimentel, Maríaluz López-Terrada, Jorge Cañizares-Esguerra, William Eamon, Ralph Bauer, Antonio Barrera-Osorio, Neil Safier, Paula de Vos, Daniela Bleichmar, John Slater, Angélica Morales Sarabia, José Ramón Marcaida López , Peter Mason, Maria Portuondo, Mauricio Nieto, Pablo Goméz, Jaime Marroquín Arredondo, and Hugh Cagle. For overviews of many of their contributions to this "turn," see Rosa Angélica Morales Sarabia, José Pardo Tomás, y Mauricio Sánchez Menchero, ed., *De la circulación del conocimiento a la inducción de la ignorancia: culturas médicas trasatlánticas, siglos XVI y XVII* (Mexico City: Universidad Nacional Autónoma de México 2017); Special issue "Iberian Science: Reflections and Studies" *History of Science,* 55, Isis. no. 2 (2017), 133–147 and Antonio Sánchez, "The "empirical turn" in the historiography of the Iberian and Atlantic science in the early modern world, *Tapuya: Latin American Science, Technology and Society,* 2 no. 1 (2019), 317–334.

6   On appropriation and disavowal, see also Norton, *Sacred Gifts,* 10, 126–128; Norton, "The Quetzal Takes Flight," 119–147; Marcy Norton, "Subaltern Technologies and Early Modernity in the Atlantic World," *Colonial Latin American Review* 26, no. 1 (2017): 18–38. For complementary approaches to early modern Indigenous science, technology and knowledge production, see, in addition to the above-cited work on Hernández, Alejandro de Ávila Blomberg, "The Codex Cruz-Badianus: Directions for Future Research," in *Flora: The Aztec Herbal,* ed. Martin Clayton, Liugi Guerrini, and Alejandro de Ávila Blomberg, 45–50 (London: Royal Collection, 2009); Barbara E. Mundy, *The Death of Aztec Tenochtitlan, the Life of Mexico City* (Austin: University of Texas Press, 2015); Neil Safier, "Global Knowledge on the Move:

Itineraries, Amerindian Narratives, and Deep Histories of Science," *Isis* 101, no. 1 (2010): 133–145; Miruna Achim, "From Rustics to Savants: Indigenous *Materia Medica* in Eighteenth-Century Mexico," *Studies in History and Philosophy of Science Part C*, 42, no. 3 (2011): 275–284; Angélica Morales Sarabia, "The Culture of Peyote: Between Divination and Disease in Early Modern New Spain," in *Medical Cultures of the Early Modern Spanish Empire*, ed. John Slater, José Pardo-Tomás, Maríaluz López-Terrada, 21–39 (London: Routledge, 2014); Gabriela Ramos and Yanna Yannakakis, ed., *Indigenous Intellectuals: Knowledge, Power, and Colonial Culture in Mexico and the Andes* (Durham: Duke University Press, 2014); Iris Montero Sobrevilla, "The Disguise of the Hummingbird: On the Natural History of Huitzilopochtli in the Florentine Codex," *Ethnohistory* 67, no. 3 (2020): 429–453; Kelly McDonough, *Indigenous Science and Technology: Nahuas and the World around Them* (Tucson: University of Arizona Press, forthcoming 2024); Allison Margaret Bigelow, *Mining Language: Racial Thinking, Indigenous Knowledge, and Colonial Metallurgy in the Early Modern Iberian World* (Chapel Hill: University of North Carolina Press, 2020); Bauer and Marroquín Arredondo, ed. *Translating Nature*; Aline da Cruz and Walkíria Neiva Praç, "Reconnecting Knowledges: *Historia Naturalis Brasiliae* back to Indigenous Societies" in *Toward an Intercultural Natural History of Brazil: The Historia Naturalis Brasiliae Reconsidered*, ed. Mariana de Campos Françozo, 142–165 (New York, NY: Routledge, 2023). See also Maya Lorena Pérez Ruiz y Arturo Argueta Villamar, "Saberes indígenas y dialogo intercultural," *Cultura y representaciones sociales* 5, no. 10 (2011): 31–56; Melissa K. Nelson and Daniel Shilling, ed. *Traditional Ecological Knowledge: Learning from Indigenous Practices for Environmental Sustainability* (Cambridge: Cambridge University Press, 2018).

7   This paragraph follows Somolinos d'Ardois, *Obras completas*, 1:194–195.

8   "Instructions of Philip II to Dr. Francisco Hernández," January 11, 1570, in *The Mexican Treasury: The Writings of Dr. Francisco Hernández*, trans. Rafael Chabrán, Cynthia L. Chamberlin, Simon Varey and ed. Simon Varey (Stanford, CA: Stanford University Press, 2000), 45–47, 46.

9   Francisco Hernández, "An Epistle to Arias Montano," trans. Rafael Chabrán and Simon Varey, *Huntington Library Quarterly* 55, no. 4 (1992): 628–634, 630, 631.

10   Hernández to Philip II, March 20, 1575, in *Mexican Treasury*, 55–56, 56.

11   Hernández, "Historiae animalium et mineralium novae hispaniae," in *Rerum medicarum*, 1–88.

12   Hernández to Philip II, March 24, 1576, in *Biblioteca hispanoamericana, 1493–1810*, ed. José Toribio Medina, 7 vols. (Santiago de Chile: Fondo Histórico y Bibliográfico José Toribio Medina, 1968 [1900]), 2:273, 274, 285–286; López Piñero and Pardo Tomás, *La influencia*, 45.

13   López Piñero and Pardo Tomás, *La influencia*, 40–51.

14   A critical edition of the manuscript is Francisco Hernández, *De materia medica Novae Hispaniae: libri quatuor: el manuscrito de Recchi* (Madrid: Doce Calles, 1998), 727–763; for its composition, see López Piñero and Pardo Tomás, *Nuevos materiales*, 20–29.

15   Hernández to Philip II, April 15, 1572, and December 12, 1572, in *Biblioteca hispano-americana*, 2:273, 274.

16   Gonzalo Fernández de Oviedo y Valdés, *Historia general y natural de las Indias*, ed. and intro. Juan Pérez de Tudela Bueso, 2nd ed. (Madrid: Ediciones Atlas, 1992), 2:27–85.

17   Daymond Turner, "Forgotten Treasure from the Indies: The Illustrations and Drawings of Fernández de Oviedo," *Huntington Library Quarterly* 48, no. 1 (1985): 1–46.

18   The influence of Belon and Gesner can be seen not only in the organization of Hernández's "Natural History" itself but also in the references he makes to them in his critical edition of Pliny, e.g., Hernández, "Historia natural de Cayo Plinio Segundo" in *Obras completas*, 4: 368, 391, 398, 399, 400, 401, 405, 409, 422.

19   Sachiko Kusukawa, *Picturing the Book of Nature: Image, Text, and Argument in Sixteenth-Century Human Anatomy and Medical Botany* (Chicago: University of Chicago Press, 2012).

20   Brian W. Ogilvie, *The Science of Describing: Natural History in Renaissance Europe* (Chicago: University of Chicago Press, 2006), 262–263.

21   Somolinos d'Ardois, *Obras completas*, 1:174–178. See also, López Piñero and Pardo Tomás, *La influencia*, 15; Norton, *Sacred Gifts*, 123–128; Marroquín Arredondo, *Diálogos*, 180–185.

22   "Instructions of Philip II," 46–47.

23   Somolinos d'Ardois, *Obras completas*, 1:164–175, 191–195.

24   Norton, "The Quetzal Takes Flight," 134–138; Marcy Norton, "The Production and Reception of the 'Historiae animalium' of New Spain," paper presented at the Max Planck Institute for the History of Science, Berlin, November 4, 2021.

25   This paragraph follows Jesús Bustamante, *Fray Bernardino de Sahagún: una revisión crítica de los manuscritos y de su proceso de composición* (Mexico City: Universidad Nacional Autónoma de México, 1990), 350–358; Lluís Nicolau d'Olwer, *Fray Bernardino de Sahagún, 1499–1590*, trans. Mauricio J. Mixco (Salt Lake City: University of Utah Press, 1987 [1952]); Charles E. Dibble, "Los manuscritos de Tlatelolco y México y el Códice Florentino," *Estudios de cultura náhuatl* 29 (1999): 27–64.

26   Bernardino de Sahagún, "Introduction and Indices" (prologue to bk. 2, pt. 1), in *Florentine Codex: General History of the Things of New Spain*, 12 books in 13 vols., trans. Arthur J. O. Anderson and Charles Dibble (Santa Fe: School of American Research and the University of Utah Press, 1950–1987).

27   Hernández to Philip II, September 22, 1572, in *Mexican Treasury*, 50.

28   Hernández to Philip II, March 31, 1573, in *Mexican Treasury*, 52.

29   See, e.g., Hernández, "Historiae animalium," tr. 2, chaps. 139, 140, 197–200, 205, 207–211, 215.

30   Norton, "Quetzal Takes Flight," 134–138.

31   Bustamante, *Fray Bernardino de Sahagún,* 357–362. On intersections between Hernández and the Tlatelolco team directed by Sahagún, see also Jeanette Favrot Peterson, *The Paradise Garden Murals of Malinalco* (Austin: University of Texas Press, 1993), 52–54.

32   Compare *Florentine Codex,* bk. 11:6–7, 14; Hernández, "Historiae animalium," tr. 1, chaps. 13, 19.

33   Compare *Florentine Codex,* bk. 11: 18; Hernández, "Historiae animalium," tr. 2, chap. 1; Norton, "Quetzal Takes Flight," 134, 304n55.

34   Hernández to Philip II, March 20, 1575, in *Mexican Treasury,* 55–56; Hernández to Philip II, March 24, 1576, in *Biblioteca hispanoamericana,* 286, see also 291.

35   On Valeriano and his Latin abilities, see Andrew Laird, "Humanismo nahua y etnohistoria: Antonio Valeriano y una carta de los regidores de Azcapotzalco a Felipe II, 1561," *Estudios de cultura náhuatl* 52 (2016): 23–75. See also María Castañeda de la Paz, "Historia de una casa real," *Nuevo mundo, mundos nuevos* 2011, https://doi.org/10.4000/nuevomundo.60624; Mundy, *The Death of Aztec Tenochtitlan,* 24, 190–191, 205–208.

36   Norton, "Production and Reception," 18–21.

37   Compare Med. Palat. 220, BML, fols. 182r–195r, 199r–200v, available through the Library of Congress, https://hdl.loc.gov/loc.wdl/wdl.10096 to "Yn ixquich tlalticpacyotl," in Ms. 9/5524[1] (also known as the "Códice matritense"), RAH, fols. 200r–342r. Dibble and Anderson note which of the entries are new in *Florentine Codex,* bk. 11, 33–34, 293–339, 413–442, 433–444. Paul Haemig has also analyzed the differences between the two manuscripts as they relate to birds, though he does not consider the possibility that Hernández's project may have been a factor in the additions, "A Comparison of Contributions from the Aztec Cities of Tlatelolco and Tenochtitlan to the Bird Chapter of the Florentine Codex," *Huitzil* 19, no. 1 (2017): 40–68, 44–50, 53–54.

38   Med. Palat. 220, fols. 158r–159v; *Florentine Codex,* 11:3–4; Martín del Campo suggests it might be a *tayra barbara senex, Florentine Codex,* bk. 11:4n10.

39   *Florentine Codex,* bk. 11:3–4; Hernández, "Historiae animalium," tr. 1, chap. 7.

40   *Florentine Codex,* bk. 11:4; Hernández, "Historiae animalium," tr. 1, chap. 8.

41   Med. Palat. 220, bk. 11, fols. 182r–195r, 199r–200v; *Florentine Codex,* bk. 11:29–39, 44–45; Haemig, "A Comparison," 44–50, 53–54.

42   Entries mentioning "Lake of Mexico" include Hernández, "Historiae animalium," tr. 2, chaps. 5, 6, 26, 31, 44, 53, 63, 69, 72, 78, 79.

43   Med. Palat. 220, bk. 11, fols. 199r, 200r–v; *Florentine Codex,* bk. 11:44.

44   Med. Palat. 220, bk. 11, fols. 181r, 182v–184v.

45   Alonso de Molina, *Vocabulario en lengua castellana y mexicana* (Mexico City: En casa de Antonio de Spinosa, 1571), fol. 8r; "Atlaca" in *Online Nahuatl Dictionary,* Stephanie Wood, ed. (Eugene, OR: University of Oregon, 2000–present), https://nahuatl.wired-humanities.org.

46 *Florentine Codex*, bk. 11:30, 31.

47 *Florentine Codex*, bk. 11:33–34.

48 On Nahua ecological knowledge about aquatic environment, see Mundy, *Death of Tenochtitlan*.

49 See Chap. 8.

50 Hernández, "Historiae animalium," tr. 1, chaps. 1, 5, 6, 17, 19, 25, 26, 27.

51 Hernández, "Historiae animalium," tr. 2, chaps. 165, 101, 145; for songbirds, see tr. 2, chaps. 4, 17, 20, 28, 29, 30, 35, 38, 39, 57, 58, 59, 61, 65, 114, 120, 123, 202 (201), c. 206 (205), c. 209 (208), etc. Numbers in parentheses refer to chapter numbers used in the translation.

52 Hernández, "Historiae animalium," tr. 3, chap. 44.

53 Hernández, "Historiae animalium," tr. 3, chap. 5.

54 See, e.g., "Historiae animalium," tr. 1, chaps. 2. 4, 16, 24, 25, 30; 2: 3, 8, 12, 16, 17, 22, 23, 24, 25, 29, 34, 37, 38, 39, 40, 41, 42, 44, 45, 47, 48, 57, 58.

55 Hernández, "Historiae animalium," tr. 2, chap. 50.

56 Hernández, "Historiae animalium," tr. 2, chap. 27.

57 Hernández, "Historiae animalium," tr. 1, chap. 2.

58 This and the following paragraph follow Norton, "Quetzal Takes Flight," 130–132, 137–138.

59 "Yn ixquich tlalticpacyotl," fol. 264r; "De historia plantarum, animalium et mineralium," ms. 22438, fol. 21r–v.

60 Hernández, "Historiae animalium," tr. 2, chaps. 1, 2.

61 *Florentine Codex*, bk. 9:89–90; Diana Magaloni Kerpel, "Real and Illusory Feathers: Pigments, Painting Techniques, and the Use of Color in Ancient Mesoamerica," *Nuevo mundo, mundos nuevos*, January 25, 2006, http://nuevomundo.revues.org/1462.

62 Norton, *Sacred Gifts*, 10, 126–128; Norton, "Quetzal Takes Flight."

63 Quoted in Somolinos d'Ardois, *Obras completas*, 195; Hernández, "Epistle to Arias Montano," 630–631; Norton, *Sacred Gifts*, 126.

64 For this identification, of *acitli* as *Aechmophorus occidentalis*, see *Florentine Codex*, 31, n.20.

65 Hernández, "Historiae animalium," tr. 2, chap. 130.

66 Hernández, "Historiae animalium," tr. 2, chap. 44.

67 Hernández, "Historiae animalium," tr. 2, chaps. 50, 179 (178).

68 See, for instance, discussion of unicorns in Hernández, "Historia natural de Cayo Plinio," 378.

69 Hernández to Philip II, March 31, 1573; Hernández to Philip II, March 20, 1575; Hernández to Philip II, March 24, 1576, in *Mexican Treasury,* 52–53, 56, 59; "The Will of Francisco Hernández," May 8, 1578, in same volume, 61–64.

70 Hernández to Philip II, March 31, 1573, in *Mexican Treasury,* 52.

71 "The Will of Francisco Hernández," 62.

72 Hernández, "Epistle to Arias Montano," 631.

73 Hernández, "Historiae animalium," tr. 2, chap. 50; emphasis added.

74 The animals can be found in Nieremberg, *Historia naturae,* 153, 154, 156, 160–164, 170, 172, 175–177, 181–183, 185, 189; Hernández, *Rerum medicarum,* 315, 316 320–322, 327, 329–333, 479–498, 412. The engraver for the *Historiae* was Christoffel Jegher, known for his collaborations with Peter Paul Rubens, José Ramón Marcaida, "Retratos de la naturaleza peregrina," *Investigación y ciencia,* no. 549 (2022): 40–44.

75 On Gesner's images, see Kusukawa, *Picturing the Book;* Florike Egmond, *Eye for Detail: Images of Plants and Animals in Art and Science, 1500–1630* (London: Reaktion Books, 2017).

76 Janice Neri, *The Insect and the Image: Visualizing Nature in Early Modern Europe, 1500–1700* (Minneapolis: University of Minnesota Press, 2011), xxii.

77 Because the two separate sets of copies of the original images treat the background in similar ways, I infer that this was a feature of the original paintings and drawings, rather than an addition made by the engravers.

78 Compare to Conrad Gesner, *Historiae animalium. Lib. V de serpe* (Zurich: Apud Christ. Froschouerum, 1557), 163, see also, 28, 42, 59, 70.

79 The fact that Nieremberg, the Lincei authors, or their collaborators chose these rather than other images for their books might support this argument. In other words, the "selection bias" that characterizes the extant corpus is likely related to the fact that the original paintings had particular vitality, a result of their being drawn from life.

80 López Piñero and Pardo Tomás, *La influencia;* Varey and Chabrán, *Searching for the Secrets;* Marcaida López, *Arte y ciencia.*

81 López Piñero and Pardo Tomás, *La influencia,* 139–150; Varey and Chabrán, *Searching for the Secrets;* Marcaida López, *Arte y ciencia;* Matthijs Jonker, "The Accademia dei Lincei's Network and Practices in the Publication of the 'Tesoro Messicano,'" *Incontri. Rivista europea di studi italiani* 34, no. 1 (2019): 119–147.

82 Varey and Chabrán, *Searching for the Secrets,* 127.

83 Francisco Ximénez, *Quatro libros: de la naturaleza, y virtudes de las plantas y animales* (Mexico City: En casa de la viuda de Diego Lopez Daualos, 1615), fols. 177v–197r.

84 Jonker, "Accademia dei Lincei's Network."

85 Juan Eusebio Nieremberg, *Historia naturae, maxime peregrinae* (Antwerp: Ex Officina Plantiniana Balthasaris Moreti, 1635).

86   Hernández *Rerum Medicarum Novae Hispaniae thesaurus, seu plantarum animalium mineralium Mexicanorum historia* (Rome: Vitalis Mascardi, 1651), 1–99. On the Linceian project, see David Freedberg, *The Eye of the Lynx Galileo, His Friends, and the Beginnings of Modern Natural History* (Chicago: University of Chicago Press, 2002), Cooley, *Perfection*, 199–213; Jonker, "The Accademia dei Lincei's Network."

87   Willem Piso and Georg Marggraf, *Historia naturalis brasiliae* (Leiden: Apud Franciscum Hackium, et Amstelodami, apud Lud. Elzevirium, 1648).

88   López Piñero and Pardo Tomás, *La influencia,* 191–192; Jonker, "Accademia dei Lincei's Network."

89   da Cruz and Neiva Praç, "Reconnecting Knowledges," 142–165; Peter J. P. Whitehead, "Georg Markgraf and Brazilian Zoology," in *Johan Maurits Van Nassau-Siegen, 1604–1679,* ed. E. van den Boogaart (The Hague: Johan Maurits van Nassau Stichting, 1979).

90   Translated by Ray in *The Ornithology,* 107; Marggraf, *Historia naturalis brasiliae,* 212–213.

91   James Delbourgo, *Collecting the World: Hans Sloane and the Origins of the British Museum* (Cambridge, MA: Harvard University Press, 2017), 114–116, 154, 156, 182.

92   Charles E. Raven, *John Ray, Naturalist, His Life and Works* (Cambridge: University Press, 1950), 322–325; Tim R. Birkhead, ed., *Virtuoso by Nature: The Scientific Worlds of Francis Willughby FRS (1635–1672)* (Boston: Brill, 2016); Asúa and French, *A New World of Animals,* 213–219.

93   John Ray, Preface in *The Ornithology of Francis Willughby* (London: John Martyn, 1678). n.p.

94   For the concept of "epistemic virtue," I am drawing from analysis in Lorraine Daston and Peter Galison, *Objectivity* (New York: Zone Books, 2007), esp. 39–42.

95   John Ray, Preface in *The Ornithology of Francis Willughby* (London: John Martyn, 1678). n.p.

96   Quoted in Mark Greengrass, Daisy Hildyard, Christopher D. Preston, and Paul J. Smith, "Science on the Move: Francis Willughby's Expeditions," in *Virtuoso by Nature,* 142–226 (Boston: Brill, 2016), 178; Norton, "Quetzal Takes Flight," 143.

97   Kevin Terraciano, Introduction, *The Florentine Codex: An Encyclopedia of the Nahua World in Sixteenth-Century Mexico,* ed. Kevin Terraciano and Jeanette Favrot Peterson, 1–18 (Austin: University of Texas Press, 2019), 3–4, 7–8.

98   Jeanette Favrot Peterson, "Images in Translation: A Codex 'Muy Historiado,'" in *The Florentine Codex: An Encyclopedia,* 21–36 (Austin: University of Texas Press, 2019); Diana Magaloni Kerpel, *The Colors of the New World: Artists, Materials, and the Creation of the Florentine Codex* (Los Angeles: Getty Research Institute, 2014).

99   Sahagún, "Introduction and Indices," 1:94.

100   Magaloni Kerpel, *Colors of the New World.*

101 Kevin Terraciano, "Three Texts in One: Book XII of the Florentine Codex," *Ethnohistory* 57, no. 1 (2010): 51–72.

102 Victoria Ríos Castaño, "From the 'Memoriales Con Escolios' to the Florentine Codex: Sahagún and His Nahua Assistants' Co-Authorship of the Spanish Translation," *Journal of Iberian and Latin American Research* 20, no. 2 (2014): 214–228.

103 Med. Palat. 220, bk. 11, fols. 155v–261r.

104 Med. Palat. 220, bk. 11, fol. 151r.

105 Montero Sobrevilla, "The Disguise of the Hummingbird," 448.

106 Hernández, "Historiae animalium," tr. 2, chap. 121; *Florentine Codex*, bk. 11:2, 36–37.

107 Hernández, "Historiae animalium," tr. 2, chaps. 108, 109; *Florentine Codex*, bk. 11:2, 37.

108 Hernández, "Historiae animalium," tr. 1, chap. 8; *Florentine Codex*, bk. 11:4.

109 Med. Palat. 220, bk. 11, fols. 199r–200r; *Florentine Codex*, bk. 11:43–44.

110 Hernández, "Historiae animalium," tr. 2, chap. 92.

111 Corona Martínez, *Las aves en la historia natural*, 156.

112 D. P. Keddy-Hector, P. Pyle, and M. A. Patten, "Aplomado Falcon (*Falco femoralis*)," version 1.0, *Birds of the World*, ed. P. G. Rodewald (Ithaca, NY: Cornell Lab of Ornithology, 2020).

113 *Florentine Codex*, bk. 11:43–44.

114 Haemig, "Comparison of Contributions"; for an example of such comment, see the entry on *nahualli*'s use of jaguar skins, *Florentine Codex*, bk. 11:1.

115 Terraciano, "Three Texts in One," 51–72.

116 See Chap. 6.

117 Iris Montero Sobrevilla interprets the figure with the hummingbird head as the deity Huitzilopochtli, whereas I am suggesting that he is a *tlamacazqui* feeding the sun. I think that the image could allow for both of these interpretations, "The Disguise of the Hummingbird," 442.

Epilogue

1 M. Shahbandeh, "Poultry: Number of Chickens Worldwide, 2020," Statista, January 21, 2022, https://www.statista.com/statistics/263962/number-of-chickens-worldwide-since-1990/; M. Shahbandeh, "US Chicken Inventory: Total Number 2020," Statista, January 8, 2022, https://www.statista.com/statistics/196028/total-number-of-all-chickens-in-the-us-since-2000/. M. Shahbandeh, "Total Number of Hogs and Pigs in the US, 2021," Statista, April 20, 2021, https://www.statista.com/statistics/194365/total-number-of-hogs-and-pigs-in-the-us-since-2000/.

2 Michael Corkery and David Yaffe-Bellany, "Meat Plant Closures Mean Pigs Are Gassed or Shot Instead," Business Section, *New York Times*, May 14, 2020; Sophie

Kevany, "Millions of US Farm Animals to Be Culled by Suffocation, Drowning, and Shooting," *The Guardian*, May 19, 2020.

3   Alex Blanchette, *Porkopolis: American Animality, Standardized Life, and the Factory Farm* (Durham, NC: Duke University Press, 2020), 3, 27; Nina Lakhani, "EPA Sued for Allowing Slaughterhouses to Pollute Waterways," *The Guardian*, December 18, 2019; Nicola Davison, "Rivers of Blood: The Dead Pigs Rotting in China's Water Supply," *The Guardian*, March 29, 2013.

4   Brad Plumer, "Humans Are Speeding Extinction and Altering the Natural World at an 'Unprecedented' Pace," *New York Times*, May 6, 2019.

5   "Dakota Access Pipeline Co. Attacks Native Americans with Dogs and Pepper Spray," *Democracy Now!* September 6, 2016, http://www.democracynow.org/2016/9 /6/full_exclusive_report_dakota_access_pipeline; Moustafa Bayoumi, "Men on Horses Chasing Black Asylum Seekers? Sadly, America Has Seen It Before," *The Guardian*, September 23, 2021.

6   Eric Schlosser, "America's Slaughterhouses Aren't Just Killing Animals," *The Atlantic*, May 12, 2020.

7   Dom Phillips, Daniel Camargos. Andrew Wasley, and Alexandra Heal, "Revealed: Rampant Deforestation of Amazon Driven by Global Greed for Meat," *The Guardian*, July 2, 2019.

8   William Cronon, *Nature's Metropolis: Chicago and the Great West* (New York: W. W. Norton, 1991); Joshua Specht, *Red Meat Republic: A Hoof-to-Table History of How Beef Changed America* (Princeton, NJ: Princeton University Press, 2019); Blanchette, *Porkopolis*, 5, 14–16, 24.

9   Timothy Pachirat, *Every Twelve Seconds: Industrialized Slaughter and the Politics of Sight* (New Haven: Yale University Press, 2011), 3.

10   Blanchette, *Porkopolis*, 19; Pachirat, *Every Twelve Seconds*.

11   Blanchette, *Porkopolis*, 19, 13.

12   See the critique in Blanchette, *Porkopolis*, 27.

13   Terrence McCoy and Júlia Ledur, "How Americans' Love of Beef Is Helping Destroy the Amazon Rainforest," *Washington Post*, April 30, 2022.

14   Rodrigo Soberanes, "México: gasoducto de Sonora divide a comunidades yaqui y desata ola de violencia," *Noticias ambientales*, May 22, 2018, sec. Environmental news, https://es.mongabay.com/2018/05/mexico-gasoducto-de-sonora-comunidades -yaqui-violencia/; see also Jonathan Watts, "'A Hitman Could Come and Kill Me': The Fight for Indigenous Land Rights in Mexico," *The Guardian*, July 21, 2018; Ariel Zambelich and Cassi Alexandra, "In Their Own Words: The 'Water Protectors' of Standing Rock," *NPR*, December 11, 2016, https://www.npr.org/2016/12/11 /505147166/in-their-own-words-the-water-protectors-of-standing-rock; Nick Estes, *Our History Is the Future: Standing Rock versus the Dakota Access Pipeline, and the Long Tradition of Indigenous Resistance* (London: Verso Books, 2019), 56.

15   Salomé Gómez-Upegui, "The Amazon Rainforest's Most Dogged Defenders Are in Peril," *Vox,* September 1, 2021, https://www.vox.com/down-to-earth/22641038/indigenous-forest-guardians-brazil-guajajaral; Sam Eaton, "Indigenous Tribes Are the Last Best Hope for the Amazon," *Public Radio International,* October 4, 2018, https://interactive.pri.org/2018/10/amazon-carbon/guardians.html; Nina Lakhani, "Second Winner of Environmental Prize Killed Months after Berta Cáceres Death," *The Guardian,* January 18, 2017; Dom Phillips, "World's Biggest Meat Company Linked to 'Brutal Massacre' in Amazon," *The Guardian,* March 3, 2020. Phillips himself was murdered for his investigations into extractivist activities in the Amazon and efforts of Indigenous groups to resist them, "Dom Phillips and Bruno Pereira's Last Journey," NACLA, accessed May 10, 2023, https://nacla.org/dom-bruno-last-journey.

16   Jeff Tollefson, "Illegal Mining in the Amazon Hits Record High amid Indigenous Protests," *Nature* 598, no. 7879 (2021): 15–16; Wayne S. Walker, Seth R. Gorelik, Alessandro Baccini, +15, and Stephan Schwartzman, José Luis Aragón-Osejo, Carmen Josse, Chris Meyer, Marcia N. Macedo, et al., "The Role of Forest Conversion, Degradation, and Disturbance in the Carbon Dynamics of Amazon Indigenous Territories and Protected Areas," *Proceedings of the National Academy of Sciences* 117, no. 6 (2020): 3015–3025.

17   Quoted in Heather Davis and Zoe Todd, "On the Importance of a Date, or, Decolonizing the Anthropocene," *ACME: An International Journal for Critical Geographies* 16, no. 4 (2017): 761–780, 771.

18   Ailton Krenak, *Ideas to Postpone the End of the World,* trans. Anthony Doyle (Toronto: Anansi International, 2020).

19   See, for instance, Alexandra Horowitz, *Inside of a Dog: What Dogs See, Smell, and Know* (New York: Scribner, 2009); Marc Bekoff, *The Emotional Lives of Animals: A Leading Scientist Explores Animal Joy, Sorrow, and Empathy—and Why They Matter* (Novato, CA: New World Library, 2010); Ed Yong, *An Immense World: How Animal Senses Reveal the Hidden Realms Around Us* (New York: Random House, 2022).

20   Beth Brady, Jon Moore, and Kim Love, "Behavior Related Vocalizations of the Florida Manatee (*Trichechus manatus latirostris*)," *Marine Mammal Science* 38, no. 3 (2022): 975–989.

21   Eckart Stolle, Rodrigo Pracana, Federico López-Osorio, Marian K. Priebe, Gabriel Luis Hernández, Claudia Castillo-Carrillo, María Cristina Arias, et al., "Recurring Adaptive Introgression of a Supergene Variant That Determines Social Organisation," *Nature Communications* 13, no. 1 (2022), 1180.

22   Danielle Whittaker, *The Secret Perfume of Birds: Uncovering the Science of Avian Scent* (Baltimore: Johns Hopkins University Press, 2022).

23   David Grimm, "These Adorable Puppies May Help Explain Why Dogs Understand Our Body Language," *Science News,* March 17, 2021, https://www.science.org/content/article/these-adorable-puppies-may-help-explain-why-dogs-understand-our-body-language.

Acknowledgments

I am filled with gratitude for the help and care I have received from so many. I could not have written this book without numerous large and small acts of generosity.

Essential enthusiasm, mentoring, and letter writing came at the inception of this project from James Amelang, William Eamon, Alison Games, Lynn Hunt, Pamela Smith, and Nancy Farriss. I am profoundly indebted to the colleagues, friends, and family who read and commented on all or large portions of the manuscript: Claudia Verhoeven, Barbara Mundy, Dana Leibsohn, Michael Swanton, Nancy Farriss, Pete Sigal, James Delbourgo, John Kuhn, David Díaz, Rita Norton, and Kent Norton and an anonymous reader.

Many other colleagues read individual chapters, discussed conceptual issues, helped me gain access to archives, or shared their research; some did many of these things. I thank Daniela Alarcón, Alejandro de Ávila Blomberg, Gabriel de Avilez Rocha, Antonio Barrera Osorio, Ralph Bauer, Anne Berg, Allison Caplan, Paul Crispo, Surekha Davies, Davide Domenici, Ann Farnsworth-Alvear, Carlos Fausto, Martha Few, Jamie Forde, Karen Graubart, Holger Hoock, Nancy Jacobs, Ada Kuskowski, Kittya Lee, Kristina Lyons, James Maffie, Jaime Marroquín Arredondo, Kelly McDonough, Ken Mills, Jeremy Mumford, Amy Offner, Guilhem Olivier, José Pardo Tomás, Juan Pimentel, Ethan Pollock, Ethelia Ruiz Medrano Heather Roller, David Sartorius, Stephanie Smallwood, Vikram Tamboli, and Molly Warsh. I learned much from informal exchanges with colleagues and students who think a lot about animals, among them, Zeb Tortorici, Martha Few, Nancy Jacobs, Kathryn Renton, Chris Valesey, Mackenzie Cooley, Miguel Durango Loaiza, and KC O'Hara.

This book was nurtured by several intellectual—and social—communities. The friends and colleagues who supported me in Washington DC, many of them my former colleagues at George Washington University, are too numerous to name. They include Mona Atia, Tyler Anbinder, Ralph Bauer, Johanna Bockman, Nemata Blyden, Erin Chapman, Ben Cowan, Paul Crispo, Ilana Feldman, Kevin Martin, Greg Childs , Jaime Marroquín Arredondo, Susannah Vance Gopalan, Katharine Norris, David Sartorius, Norma Rosso, Shira Robinson, Michael Weeks, Angela Zimmerman, and the much-missed, late Colin McEwan.

In Los Angeles, while at the Huntington Library (2010–2011), I made friends with people who have become important interlocutors, among them Andrew Apter, Lauren (Robin) Derby, Mary Fuller, Margaret Garber, Lynn Hunt, Tara Nummedal, Seth Rockman, and Susannah Shaw Romney. Likewise, at the John Carter Brown Library (2011 and 2016–2017), friendships were started or rekindled with Kittya Lee, Iris Montero Sobrevilla, Neil Safier, Ethan Pollack, Zeb Tortorici, Bathsheba Demuth, Justyna Olko, Nancy Jacobs, Linda Heuman, and Amy Remensnyder. I am grateful to the former directors Roy Ritchie (Huntington) and JCBL (Norman Fiering and Neil Safier) as well as the staff at both institutions, who supported this project in so many ways. During research trips to Mexico City and Oaxaca, I enjoyed tremendous hospitality and learned much from Haydée García Bravo, Angélica Morales Padrón, Michael Swanton, Alejandro de Ávila Blomberg, and Sebastián van Doesburg. In Madrid, Guillermina Achleitner and Pablo Urrutia Jordana opened their homes to me, as they have done for more than thirty years.

I so appreciate my friends and colleagues, as well as wonderful students, in and beyond the history department at the University of Pennsylvania, my intellectual home for the final stages of research and writing. Among the many who welcomed and helped me are Kathy Brown, Etienne Benson, Yvie Fabella, Jared Farmer, Antonio Feros, Sally Gordon, Projit Mukharji, Joan Plonski, John Pollack, Eve Troutt Powell, James Serpell, Dan Richter, Sophie Rosenfeld, and Beth Wenger. For memorable meals and Covid-era walks in Philadelphia, as well as intellectual stimulation, I thank Anne Berg, Ada Kuskowski, Kristina Lyons, Amy Offner, Oscar Aguirre Mandujano, Mia Bay, Ann Farnsworth-Alvear, Nancy Farriss, Gabriel de Avilez Rocha, Miranda Featherstone, Roquinaldo Ferreira, and Melissa Teixeira. My sojourn at the Max Planck Institute for the History of Science in Berlin (2021) was an exhilarating post-Covid return to in-person community, and I extend my appreciation to Dagmar Schäfer, Tamar Novick, Marta Hanson, and Maria Pirogovskaya.

I acknowledge, with great appreciation, support from Columbian College and the History Department at George Washington University and the School of Arts and Sciences, History Department, and Price Laboratory at the University of Pennsylvania. I am also grateful for National Endowment for the Humanities (NEH) fellowships from the Huntington Library and the John Carter Brown Library, as well as the NEH-funded "Pictorial Histories and Myth-Histories" course in Mexico in 2014. I am also very fortunate to have received fellowships from the Guggenheim Foundation and the Max Planck Institute for the History of Science.

I want to acknowledge my debt to the scholars who have translated Nahuatl texts into English and Spanish, and contributed to online Nahuatl dictionaries, among them Luis Reyes García, Arthur Anderson, Charles Dibble, Frances Kartunnen, Eduardo de la Cruz Cruz, John Sullivan, and Stephanie Wood, and to those who helped me with questions about Indigenous language vocabulary, including Michael Swanton, Michel Oudijk, Barbara Mundy, Kelly McDonough, Allison Caplan. I benefited from the extraordinary research assistance of Asma Bouhrauss in Spain, and Juan Ignacio Arboleda, Edward Chappell, Andrés De los Ríos, and Plum Xu in this hemisphere. Ardeth Anderson made the wonderful drawings. Gina Broze did incredible work helping me obtain copyright permissions. William Keegan created the excellent maps, and Girmaye Misgna helped me think about how to spatialize data. At Harvard University Press, I worked with two wonderful editors, Andrew Kinney and Joyce Seltzer. I also greatly appreciate the additional editorial help provided by Kevin Martin, Jamie Armstrong, and Pamela Haag.

Lilly was both muse and constant companion from before the project's inception until her death in 2019, and, beginning in 2021, mirthful Iggy taught me new lessons about canine subjectivity. The conversations (and fun times!) with Claudia, Robin, and Iris that moved seamlessly between the personal and the historical were so important for integrating life and scholarship. For listening, reassuring, and laughing, thank you Danny Norton, Sharon Naimon, Jules Norton, Louise Lurkis, Elizabeth Gessel, Marcy Freedman, Gay White, and Sarah Moseley. My loving parents, Rita and Kent, as always, have helped me beyond measure; they also remain an inspiration for their creativity, curiosity, and adventurousness. For the last part of the journey, I am immensely grateful for the love, support, and companionship of David Díaz, whose eagle-eyed perceptiveness, dry wit, and kindness have helped me more than I can express.

Index

Page numbers that appear in italics indicate an illustration or map.